BMW F650
Service and Repair Manual

by Matthew Coombs

Models covered
F650 Funduro 1994 to 2000
F650 ST Strada 1997 to 2000
F650 GS 2000 to 2007
F650 GS Dakar 2001 to 2007
F650 CS 2002 to 2005

(4761 - 304 - 6AS2)

© J H Haynes & Co Ltd 2020

ABCDE
FGHIJ
KL

A book in the Haynes Service and Repair Manual Series

ISBN 978 0 85733 866 2

British Library Cataloguing in Publication Data
A catalogue record for this book is available from the British Library.

Library of Congress Control Number 2008931450

Printed in Malaysia

J H Haynes & Co Ltd
Sparkford, Yeovil, Somerset BA22 7JJ, England

Haynes North America, Inc
859 Lawrence Drive, Newbury Park, California 91320, USA

Printed using NORBRITE BOOK 48.8gsm (CODE: 40N6533) from NORPAC; procurement system certified under Sustainable Forestry Initiative standard. Paper produced is certified to the SFI Certified Fiber Sourcing Standard (CERT - 0094271)

Contents

Contents

REPAIRS AND OVERHAUL

Engine, transmission and associated systems

Chassis components

Electrical system

Wiring diagrams

REFERENCE

Index

BMW – They did it their way

by Julian Ryder

BMW - Bayerische Motoren Werke

If you were looking for a theme tune for BMW's engineering philosophy you'd have to look no further than Francis Albert Sinatra's best known ditty: 'I did it my way.' The Bayerische Motoren Werke, like their countrymen at Porsche, takes precious little notice of the way anyone else does it, point this out to a factory representative and you will get a reply starting: 'We at BMW... '. The implication is clear.

It was always like that. The first BMW motorcycle, the R32, was, according to motoring sage L J K Setright: 'the first really outstanding post-War design, argued from first principles and uncorrupted by established practice. It founded a new German school of design, it established a BMW tradition destined to survive unbroken from 1923 to the present day.' That tradition was, of course, the boxer twin. The nickname 'boxer' for an opposed twin is thought to derive from the fact that the pistons travel horizontally towards and away from each other like the fists of boxers.

Before this first complete motorcycle, BMW had built a horizontally-opposed fore-and-aft boxer engine for the Victoria company of Nuremburg. It was a close copy of the British Douglas motor which the company's chief engineer Max Friz admired, a fact the company's official history confirms despite what some current devotees of the marque will claim. In fact BMW didn't really want to make motorcycles at all, originally it was an aero-engine company - a fact celebrated in the blue-and-white tank badge that is symbolic of a propeller. But in Germany after the Treaty of Versailles such potentially warlike work was forbidden to domestic companies and BMW had to diversify, albeit reluctantly.

Friz was known to have a very low opinion of motorcycles and chose the Douglas to copy simply because he saw it as fundamentally a good solution to the engineering problem of powering a two-wheeler. In the R32 the engine was arranged with the crankshaft in-line with the axis of the bike and the cylinders sticking out into the cooling airflow, giving a very low centre-of-gravity and perfect vibration-free primary balance. It wasn't just the motor's layout that departed from normal practice, the clutch was a single-plate type as used in cars, final drive was by shaft and the rear wheel could be removed quickly. The frame and suspension were equally sophisticated, but the bike was quite heavy. Most of that description could be equally well applied to any of the boxer-engined bikes BMW made in the next 70-plus years.

Development within the surprisingly flexible confines of the boxer concept was quick. The second BMW, the R37 of 1925, retained the 68 x 68 mm Douglas bore and stroke but had overhead valves in place of the side valves. In 1928 two major milestones were passed. First, BMW acquired the car manufacturer Dixi and started manufacturing a left-hand-drive version of the Austin 7 under license. Secondly, the larger engined R62 and R63 appeared, the latter being an OHV sportster that would be the basis of BMW's sporting and record-breaking exploits before the Second World War.

The 1930s was the era of speed records on land, on sea and in the air, and the name of Ernst Henne is in the record books no fewer than ten times: eight for two-wheeled exploits, twice for wheel-on-a-stick 'sidecar' world records. At first he was on the R63 with supercharging, but in 1936 he switched to the 500 cc R5, high-pushrod design reminiscent of the latest generation of BMW twins. Chain-driven camshafts operated short pushrods which opened valves with hairpin - not coil - springs. A pure racing version of this motor also appeared, this time with shaft and bevel-gear driven overhead camshafts, but with short rockers operating the valves so the engine can't be called a true DOHC design. Again with the aid of a blower, this was the motor that powered the GP 500s of the late '30s to many wins including the 1939 Senior TT. After the War, this layout would re-emerge in the immortal Rennsport.

From 1939 to 1945 BMW were fully occupied making military machinery, notably the R75 sidecar for the army. The factory didn't restart production until 1948, and then only with a lightweight single. There was a false start in 1950 and a slump in sales in 1953 that endangered the whole company, before the situation was rescued by one of the truly classic boxers. Their first post-War twin had been the R51/2, and naturally it was very close to the pre-War model although simplified to a single-camshaft layout. Nevertheless, it was still a relatively advanced OHV design not a sidevalve sidecar tug which enabled a face-lift for the 1955 models to do the marketing trick.

The 1955 models got a swinging arm - at

F650 Funduro

both ends. The old plunger rear suspension was replaced by a swinging arm while leading-link Earles forks adorned the front. Thus were born the R50, the R60 and the R69. The European market found these new bikes far too expensive compared to British twins but America saved the day, buying most of the company's output. The car side of the company also found a product the market wanted, a small sports-car powered by a modified bike engine, thus BMW's last crisis was averted

In 1960 the Earles fork models were updated and the R69S was launched with more power, closer transmission ratios and those funny little indicators on the ends of the handlebars. Very little changed during the '60s, apart from US export models getting telescopic forks, but in 1970 everything changed...

The move to Spandau and a new line of Boxers

BMW's bike side had outgrown its site in Munich at the company's head-quarters, so, taking advantage of government subsidies for enterprises that located to what was then West Berlin, surrounded by the still Communist DDR, BMW built a new motorcycle assembly plant at Spandau in Berlin. It opened in 1969, producing a completely new range of boxers, the 5-series, which begat the 6-series, which begat the 7-series.

In 1976, at the same time as the launch of the 7-series the first RS boxer appeared. It's hard to believe now, but it was the only fully faired motorcycle, and it set the pattern for all BMWs, not just boxers, to come. The RS suffix came to mean a wonderfully efficient fairing that didn't spoil a sporty riding position. More sedate types could buy the RT version with a massive but no less efficient fairing that protected a more upright rider. Both bikes could carry luggage in a civilised fashion, too,

thanks to purpose-built Krauser panniers. Both the RT and RS were uncommonly civilised motorcycles for their time.

When the boxer got its next major makeover in late 1980 BMW did something no-one thought possible, they made a boxer trail bike, the R80G/S. This wasn't without precedent as various supermen had wrestled 750 cc boxers to honours in the ISDT and in '81 Hubert Auriol won the Paris-Dakar on a factory boxer. Some heretics even dared to suggest the roadgoing G/S was the best boxer ever.

The K-series

By the end of the '70s the boxer was looking more and more dated alongside the opposition, and when the motorcycle division's management was shaken up at the beginning of 1979 the team working on the boxer replacement was doubled in size. The first new bike wasn't launched until late '83, but when it was it was clear that BMW had got as far away from the boxer concept as possible.

The powerplant was an in-line water-cooled DOHC four just like all the Japanese opposition, but typically BMW did it their way by aligning the motor so its crank was parallel to the axis of the bike and lying the motor on it side. In line with their normal practice, there was a car-type clutch, shaft drive and a single-sided swinging arm. It was totally novel yet oddly familiar. And when RT and RS version were introduced to supplement the basic naked bike, the new K-series 'flying bricks' felt even more familiar.

It was clear that BMW wanted the new four, and the three-cylinder 750 that followed it, to be the mainstay of the company's production - but in a further analogy with Porsche the customers simply wouldn't let go of the old boxer. Just as Porsche were forced to keep the 911 in production so BMW had to keep the old air-cooled boxer going by pressure

from their customers. It kept going until 1995, during which time the K-bikes had debuted four-valve heads and ABS. And when the latest generation of BMWs appeared in 1993 what were they? Boxers. Granted they were four-valve, air/oil-cooled and equipped with non-telescopic fork front ends, but they were still boxers. And that high camshaft, short pushrod layout looked remarkably similar to something that had gone before...

The New 4-valve Boxers

Even by BMW's standards, the new-generation Boxers were a shock. Maybe we shouldn't have been surprised after the lateral thinking that gave us the K-series, but the way in which the men from Munich took the old opposed-twin Boxer concept that launched the company and projected it into the 21st-Century was nothing short of breath-taking in its audacity. About the only design features the old and new Boxers had in common was that they both had two wheels and two cylinders. The 4-valve engine was produced in 850 and 1100 cc version, with the later eventually being upgraded to 1150 cc for GS, R, RS and RT versions, and stretched further to 1200 cc for the C model made famous in the 007 film Golden Eye.

The new bikes mixed old and new technology in a very clever way. Fuel injection and four-valve heads were very cutting edge, high camshafts operating pushrods (for ground clearance) and air cooling (albeit with some substantial help from oil) was not. The really revolutionary stuff was in the chassis department: Telelever at the front and Paralever at the rear bolted to the motor via tubular steel sub-frames and nothing in the way of a conventional frame in the middle. The Telelever front fork is carried on a couple of wishbones with anti-dive built into the linkage. Rear Paralever suspension uses a single-sided swingingarm with a shaft drive running inside it which forms not quite a

F650ST

F650CS 2003

F650CS 2005

with the unfortunate Funduro name, used an Austrian motor and was assembled in Italy.

The last BMW to use a single was made in 1966, nearly thirty years before the first F650. Most of BMW's singles were the 250cc R24 with which the factory got back into production after the War. The R24 and its derivatives were really a Boxer twin minus one cylinder and turned through 90 degrees to get the cylinder vertical. The F650 could not be more different in design or concept, it was consciously meant to be different and appeal to a new type of customer. Previously, BMW customers were always seen as very loyal to the brand, once the company had sold them a bike they had them for life. The only problem was that there weren't enough of them, so the idea of the F650 was to attract new, younger customers who, once they'd sampled the high-quality of BMW's products and dealer network, would be likely to buy another BeeEm.

The other revolutionary aspect of the first F650 was that it was produced in close co-operation with another manufacturer, the Italian Aprilia concern (this was well before Aprilia became part of the Piaggio group). Like Aprilia's own Pegaso, the F650 used the Austrian-made Rotax (part of the Bombardier group) single and final assembly took place in the Italian company's Noale factory in the Veneto region near Venice. Despite the outward similarity of the Pegaso and the BMW, the two machines have almost no components in common; wheels, tyre and switchgear, that's it. Perhaps the most revolutionary aspect of the F650 was its final drive: for the first time a BMW motorcycle did not have shaft drive. Heresy of heresies! It had a nasty, messy, inefficient chain. It didn't matter, BMW sold over 30,000 F650s in the first three model years before introducing the more touring orientated ST, seen as a pure roadster where the original bike purported to have some off-road capability.

parallelogram shaped system with a tie-arm running from just below to the swinging arm pivot to the rear hub. It ensures the rear axle moves in an (almost) straight line and suppresses the old BMW habit of the rear end rising when the throttle is opened. The styling was also anything but safe; the old cliché of the boring BMW was blown out of the water.

Single Minded

BMW have never been a factory that follows fashion, nor have they taken any notice at all of what anyone else does. Much like their fellow individualists at Porsche they have stuck with a hallmark design (albeit with a bit of pressure from their loyal customers) that none of their competitors have, or would dare, to emulate. What car maker has produced a rear-engined flat four in recent years? And has any other bike maker even considered for a moment producing a horizontally-opposed flat twin?

Yes, BMW have tried to persuade their buyers that there are other engine configurations but the average Boxer buyer doesn't seem interested in four-cylinder power. So why did they think a single was a good idea? And one that contained a high percentage of non-Bavarian input at that. Against all of their previous practice, the F650, the first models of which were saddled

F650GS 2003

F650GS 2005

Mind you, you wouldn't have thought the Boxer twins had any off-road capability yet they won the Paris-Dakar Rally four times in the 1980s. So to prove the F650 could win the world's toughest race BMW developed a 'double-R' F650 and with French rider Richard Sainct won the Dakar in 1999 and 2000. Not surprisingly given the popularity of the Paris-Dakar in Europe, the new-generation, fuel-injected, Berlin-built F650 that appeared for the 2000 model year wore full-on trailbike styling and called itself a GS, two years later the GS Dakar appeared. The GS also became the first single to be offered with ABS as an option.

Perhaps the most radical F650 was the street version of the fuel-injected GS, the CS. This is an unashamed street bike, and as such is the first F650 with cast wheels. Radical styling, attention to luggage carrying and a range of accessories show the CS is trying to sell to the scooter rider who is moving up and the urban professional market the Philippe Starck-designed Aprilia Six-Fifty tried to corner. It also marks another first for BMW – the first bike with single-sided swinging arm and belt drive. And to think that BMWs used to be thought of as staid transport for rather boring old blokes. Does anyone make a range as radical as BMW's GS and HP twins or the F650 singles and 800cc twins? Thought not.

F650GS Dakar

Acknowledgements

Our thanks are due to CW Motorcycles of Dorchester, Bridge Motorcycles of Exeter and Motorcycle Mania of Frome who supplied the machines featured in the illustrations throughout this manual. We would also like to thank NGK Spark Plugs (UK) Ltd for supplying the colour spark plug condition photographs, the Avon Rubber Company for supplying information on tyre fitting and Draper Tools Ltd for some of the workshop tools shown.

Thanks are also due to Julian Ryder who wrote the introduction.

About this Manual

The aim of this manual is to help you get the best value from your motorcycle. It can do so in several ways. It can help you decide what work must be done, even if you choose to have it done by a dealer; it provides information and procedures for routine maintenance and servicing; and it offers diagnostic and repair procedures to follow when trouble occurs.

We hope you use the manual to tackle the work yourself. For many simpler jobs, doing it yourself may be quicker than arranging an appointment to get the motorcycle into a dealer and making the trips to leave it and pick it up. More importantly, a lot of money can be saved by avoiding the expense the shop must pass on to you to cover its labour and overhead costs. An added benefit is the sense of satisfaction and accomplishment that you feel after doing the job yourself.

References to the left or right side of the motorcycle assume you are sitting on the seat, facing forward.

We take great pride in the accuracy of information given in this manual, but motorcycle manufacturers make alterations and design changes during the production run of a particular motorcycle of which they do not inform us. No liability can be accepted by the authors or publishers for loss, damage or injury caused by any errors in, or omissions from, the information given.

Illegal Copying

Coolant level

> ⚠️ **Warning: DO NOT remove the radiator pressure cap to add coolant. Topping up is done via the coolant reservoir tank filler. DO NOT leave open containers of coolant about, as it is poisonous.**

Before you start:

✔ Make sure you have a supply of coolant available (a mixture of 50% distilled or soft water and 50% corrosion inhibited ethylene glycol nitrite-free anti-freeze is needed).
✔ Always check the coolant level when the engine is cold.
✔ Support the motorcycle upright on level ground.

✔ On Funduro and ST models the coolant reservoir is under the seat, and the level lines are visible via the cut-out in the rear mudguard. If topping-up is necessary remove the seat and the right-hand side cover (see Chapter 8).

✔ On GS and Dakar models the coolant reservoir is behind the left-hand front side cover, and the level lines are visible via a cut-out in the cover. If topping-up is necessary remove the left-hand front side cover (see Chapter 8).

✔ On CS models the coolant reservoir is behind the left-hand front side cover, and the level is visible after removing the access panel.

Bike care:

● Use only the specified coolant mixture. It is important that anti-freeze is used in the system all year round, and not just in the winter. Do not top the system up using only water, as the system will become too diluted.

● Do not overfill the reservoir. If the coolant is significantly above the MAX or FULL level line at any time, the surplus should be siphoned or drained off to prevent the possibility of it being expelled out of the overflow hose.

● If the coolant level falls steadily, check the system for leaks (see Chapter 1). If no leaks are found and the level continues to fall, it is recommended that the machine is taken to a BMW dealer for a pressure test.

Funduro and ST

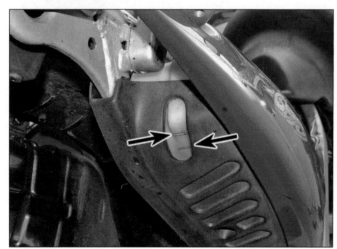

1 With the motorcycle vertical and level, the coolant level should lie between the FULL and LOW level lines (arrowed) that are marked on the reservoir.

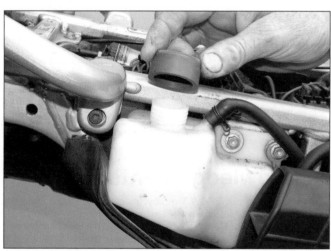

2 If the coolant level is on or below the LOW line, remove the seat and the right-hand side cover (see Chapter 8), then unscrew the reservoir filler cap.

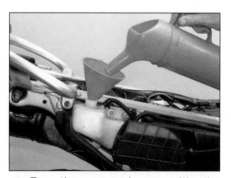

3 Top the reservoir up with the recommended coolant mixture almost to the FULL level line, using a suitable funnel if required. Fit and tighten the cap, then install the side panel and seat.

GS and Dakar

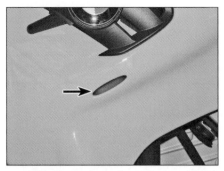

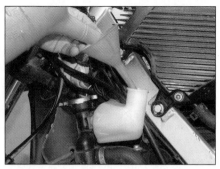

1 With the motorcycle vertical and level, the coolant level should lie above the MIN level line (arrowed) that is marked on the reservoir (the MAX level line is only visible with the side cover removed).

2 If the coolant level is on or below the MIN line, remove the left-hand front side cover (see Chapter 8), then remove the reservoir filler cap.

3 Top the reservoir up with the recommended coolant mixture almost to the MAX level line, using a suitable funnel if required. Fit the cap and the fairing side panel.

CS

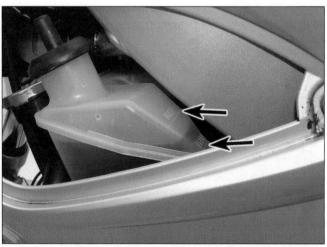

1 Carefully pull the rear of the access panel to release the peg from the grommet in the side cover, then remove the panel, noting how the tabs at the front locate.

2 With the motorcycle vertical and level, the coolant level should lie between the MAX and MIN level lines (arrowed) that are marked on the reservoir.

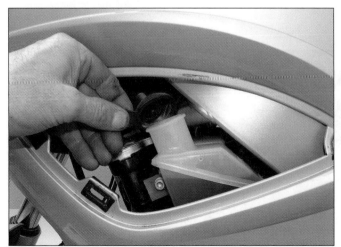

3 If the coolant level is on or below the MIN line, remove the reservoir filler cap.

4 Top the reservoir up with the recommended coolant mixture almost to the MAX level line, using a suitable funnel if required. Fit the cap and the access panel.

Engine oil level

Before you start:

✔ Support the motorcycle upright on level ground. Make sure the engine is at normal working temperature then allow it to idle for one minute before checking the oil level. If you check the oil level when the engine is cold or only warm you will get a false reading.

✔ On Funduro, ST and CS models the oil is stored in a tank within the top frame tube and the level is measured using a dipstick that screws into the frame.

✔ On GS and Dakar models the oil is stored in a tank located behind the left-hand front side cover. On 2000 to 2003 models the level is visible through the inspection window in the front of the tank. If necessary remove the left-hand front side cover and/or wipe the window so that it is clean. On 2004-on models the level is measured using a dipstick that screws into the tank.

The correct oil:

● Modern, high-revving engines place great demands on their oil. It is very important that the correct oil for your bike is used.

● Always top up with a good quality motorcycle oil – do not use motor oils designed for car engines. Do not overfill the tank – the difference between the MAX and MIN level lines on the dipstick or the top and bottom of the inspection window (according to model) is approximately 0.3 litre on Funduro and ST models and 0.4 litre on GS, Dakar and CS models.

Oil type	SAE 10W/40 mineral or semi-synthetic motorcycle oil.

Bike care:

● If you have to add oil frequently, check whether you have any oil leaks from the engine joints, oil seals and gaskets, or from the oil hoses between the engine and the frame or tank (according to model). If not, the engine could be burning oil, in which case there will be white smoke coming out of the exhaust (see *Fault Finding*).

Funduro and ST

1 Unscrew the dipstick and wipe it clean.

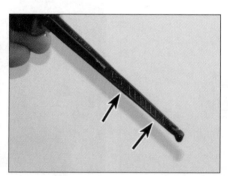

2 Insert the dipstick in its hole as far as the threads, but do not screw it in, then withdraw it – with the motorcycle level and vertical the oil level should lie between the MAX and MIN level lines (arrowed) on the dipstick.

3 If the level is near, on or below the MIN line, top up the tank with the recommended grade and type of oil so the level lies mid-way between the MAX and MIN lines. Do not overfill. On completion, thread the dipstick back into the tank. Repeat the warm-up procedure and re-check the level.

GS and Dakar (2000 to 2003)

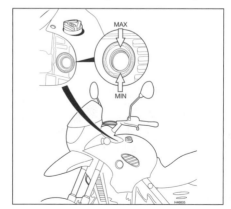

1 With the motorcycle vertical, the oil level should lie mid-way between the top and bottom of the inspection window.

2 If the level is near, on or below the bottom of the window, unscrew the filler cap from the tank, using the spark plug wrench provided in the toolkit if necessary.

3 Top up the engine with the recommended grade and type of oil so the level is mid-way up the inspection window. Do not overfill. On completion, make sure the filler cap is secure in the tank. Repeat the warm-up procedure and re-check the level.

GS and Dakar (2004-on)

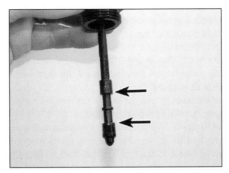

1 On 2004-on models unscrew the dipstick and wipe it clean – use the spark plug wrench provided in the toolkit to unscrew it if necessary.

2 Insert the dipstick in its hole as far as the threads, but do not screw it in, then withdraw it – with the motorcycle level and vertical the oil level should lie between the MAX and MIN level lines (arrowed) on the dipstick.

3 If the level is near, on or below the MIN line, top up the tank with the recommended grade and type of oil so the level lies mid-way between the MAX and MIN lines. Do not overfill. On completion, thread the dipstick back into the tank. Repeat the warm-up procedure and re-check the level.

CS

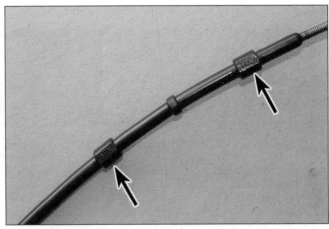

1 Unscrew the dipstick and wipe it clean – use the spark plug wrench provided in the toolkit to unscrew it if necessary.

2 Insert the dipstick in its hole as far as the threads, but do not screw it in, then withdraw it – with the motorcycle level and vertical the oil level should lie between the MAX and MIN level lines (arrowed) on the dipstick.

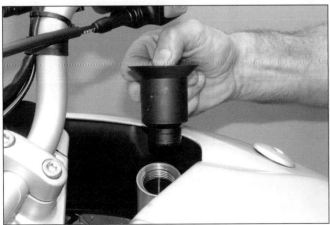

3 If the level is near, on or below the MIN line, remove the seat (see Chapter 8), locate the funnel provided, and fit it into the filler orifice.

4 Top up the tank with the recommended grade and type of oil so the level lies mid-way between the MAX and MIN lines. Do not overfill. On completion, thread the dipstick back into the tank. Repeat the warm-up procedure and re-check the level.

Brake fluid levels

> ⚠️ *Warning: Brake hydraulic fluid can harm your eyes and damage painted surfaces, so use extreme caution when handling and pouring it and cover surrounding surfaces with rag. Do not use fluid that has been standing open for some time, as it is hygroscopic (absorbs moisture from the air) which can cause a dangerous loss of braking effectiveness.*

Before you start:

✔ The front brake fluid reservoir is on the right-hand handlebar. When checking the fluid level turn the handlebars so the reservoir is level.

✔ On Funduro and ST models the rear brake fluid reservoir is located behind the right-hand side cover and the level is visible via a cut-out in the panel.

✔ On GS, Dakar and CS models the rear brake fluid reservoir is located below the right-hand rear side cover.

✔ Make sure you have the correct hydraulic fluid. DOT 4 is recommended.

✔ Wrap a rag around the reservoir being worked on to ensure that any spillage does not come into contact with painted surfaces.

Bike care:

● The fluid in the front and rear brake fluid reservoirs will drop as the brake pads wear down. If the fluid level is low check the brake pads for wear (see Chapter 1), and replace them with new ones if necessary (see Chapter 7). Do not top the reservoir up until the new pads have been fitted, and then check to see if topping up is still necessary – when the caliper pistons are pushed back to accommodate the extra thickness of the pads some fluid will be displaced back into the reservoir. The difference between the MAX and MIN levels in the reservoir should equate to the amount of fluid that will be displaced during the lifetime of a brake pad.

● If either fluid reservoir requires repeated topping-up there could be a leak somewhere in the system, which must be investigated immediately.

● Check for signs of fluid leakage from the hydraulic hoses and/or brake system components – if found, rectify immediately (see Chapter 7).

● Check the operation of both brakes before taking the machine on the road; if there is evidence of air in the system (spongy feel to lever or pedal), it must be bled (see Chapter 7).

Front

1 The front brake fluid level is visible through the window in the reservoir body – it must be between the MIN level line (arrowed) and the top of the window on Funduro and ST models . . .

2 . . . and between the top and bottom of the window (arrowed) on GS, Dakar and CS models.

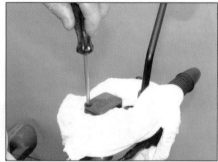

3 If the level is near, on or below the MIN line or the bottom of the window, and the brake pads are not worn, undo the reservoir cover screws then remove the cover and diaphragm.

4 Top up with new clean DOT 4 hydraulic fluid, until the level is above the MIN line or the bottom of the window and proportional to the extent of wear in the pads – i.e. if the pads are half worn, set the fluid level mid-way up the window. Do not overfill (or you will have to siphon some out when new pads are fitted), and take care to avoid spills (see *Warning* above).

5 Wipe any moisture off the diaphragm with a clean paper towel.

6 Ensure that the diaphragm is correctly seated before installing the cover. Secure the cover with the screws.

Rear

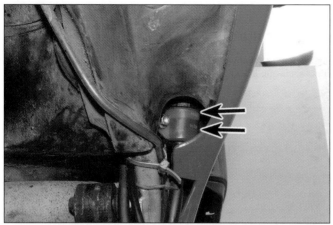

1 On Funduro and ST models the rear brake fluid level is visible through the aperture in the right-hand side panel – it must be between the MAX and MIN level lines (arrowed).

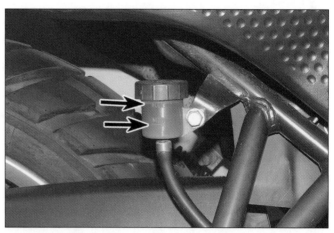

2 On GS, Dakar and CS models the rear brake fluid level is visible through the reservoir body – it must be between the MAX and MIN level lines (arrowed).

3 If the level is near, on or below the MIN line, and the brake pads are not worn, unscrew the cap and remove the diaphragm – on Funduro and ST models remove the side cover to access the reservoir (see Chapter 8).

4 Top up with new clean DOT 4 hydraulic fluid, until the level is above the MIN line and proportional to the extent of wear in the pads – i.e. if the pads are half worn, set the fluid level mid-way between the MIN and MAX lines. Do not overfill (or you will have to siphon some out when new pads are fitted), and take care to avoid spills (see *Warning* on page 0•12).

5 Wipe any moisture off the diaphragm with a clean paper towel.

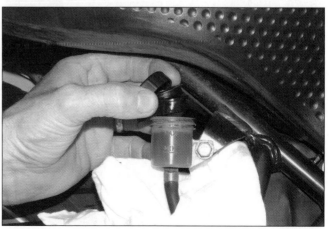

6 Ensure that the diaphragm is correctly seated before installing the cap. On Funduro and ST models refit the side panel.

Tyres

The correct pressures:

● The tyres must be checked when **cold**, not immediately after riding. Note that incorrect tyre pressures will cause abnormal tread wear and unsafe handling. Low tyre pressures may cause the tyre to slip on the rim or come off.

● Use an accurate pressure gauge. Many forecourt gauges are wildly inaccurate. If you buy your own, spend as much as you can justify on a quality gauge.

● Proper air pressure will increase tyre life and provide maximum stability and ride comfort.

Funduro

Loading	Front	Rear
Rider only	27.5 psi (1.9 Bar)	29 psi (2.0 Bar)
Rider, passenger and luggage	32 psi (2.2 Bar)	36 psi (2.5 Bar)

GS and Dakar

Loading	Front	Rear
Rider only	27.5 psi (1.9 Bar)	30.5 psi (2.1 Bar)
Rider, passenger and luggage	30.5 psi (2.1 Bar)	33.5 psi (2.3 Bar)

ST

Loading	Front	Rear
Rider only	27.5 psi (1.9 Bar)	32 psi (2.2 Bar)
Rider, passenger and luggage	32 psi (2.2 Bar)	36 psi (2.5 Bar)

CS

Loading	Front	Rear
Rider only	32 psi (2.2 Bar)	36 psi (2.5 Bar)
Rider, passenger and luggage	32 psi (2.2 Bar)	36 psi (2.5 Bar)

Tyre care:

● Check the tyres carefully for cuts, tears, embedded nails or other sharp objects and excessive wear. Operation of the motorcycle with excessively worn tyres is extremely hazardous, as traction and handling are directly affected.

● Check the condition of the tyre valve and ensure the dust cap is in place and tight.

● Pick out any stones or nails which may have become embedded in the tyre tread. If left, they will eventually penetrate through the casing and cause a puncture.

● If tyre damage is apparent, or unexplained loss of pressure is experienced, seek the advice of a tyre fitting specialist without delay.

● Check the wheel rims and spokes for damage. The spoke tension on wire-spoked wheels can change; refer to Chapter 1 if you suspect spoke tension is incorrect.

Tyre tread depth:

● At the time of writing UK law requires that tread depth must be at least 1 mm over 3/4 of the tread breadth all the way around the tyre, with no bald patches. Many riders, however, consider 2 mm tread depth minimum to be a safer limit. BMW recommend a minimum of 2 mm on the front and 3 mm on the rear for normal speeds, but note that German law requires a minimum of 1.6 mm for each tyre.

● Many tyres now incorporate wear indicators in the tread. Identify the location marking on the tyre sidewall (either an arrow, triangle, the letters TWI, or the manufacturer's logo) to locate the indicator bar and replace the tyre if the tread has worn down to the bar.

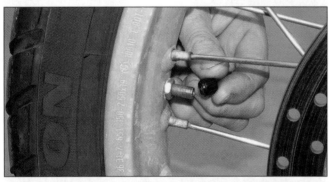

1 Remove the dust cap from the valve, and do not forget to fit the cap after checking the pressure.

2 Use an accurate gauge and make sure the tyres are cold.

3 Measure tread depth at the centre of the tyre using a depth gauge.

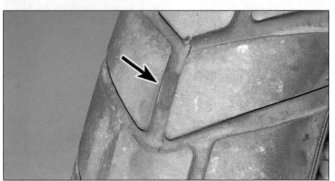

4 Tyre tread wear indicator (arrowed).

Suspension, steering and drive chain or belt

Suspension and Steering:

● Check that the front and rear suspension operates smoothly without binding (see Chapter 1).
● Check that the rear shock absorber is adjusted as required (see Chapter 6).
● Check that the steering moves smoothly from lock-to-lock.

Drive chain – Funduro, ST, GS and Dakar models:

● Check that the chain isn't too loose or too tight, and adjust it if necessary (see Chapter 1).
● If the chain looks dry, lubricate it (see Chapter 1).

Drive belt – CS models:

● Check the belt for broken teeth, splits, cracks and any exposed wires.

Legal and safety

Lighting and signalling:

● Take a minute to check that the headlight, sidelight, tail light, brake light, licence plate light, instrument lights and turn signals all work correctly.

● Check that the horn sounds when the button is pressed.

● A working speedometer, graduated in mph, is a statutory requirement in the UK.

Safety:

● Check that the throttle grip rotates smoothly when opened and snaps shut when released, in all steering positions. Also check for the correct amount of freeplay (see Chapter 1).
● Check that the brake lever and pedal, clutch lever and gearchange lever operate smoothly. Lubricate them at the specified intervals or when necessary (see Chapter 1).
● Check that there is good pressure in both front and rear brake systems when lever or pedal is applied.

● Check that the engine shuts off when the kill switch is operated.
● Check that sidestand return springs hold the stand up securely when retracted.

Fuel:

● This may seem obvious, but check that you have enough fuel to complete your journey. If you notice signs of fuel leakage – rectify the cause immediately.
● Ensure you use the correct grade fuel – see Chapter 4A or 4B Specifications.

Model development

F650 Funduro

The original F650 was launched in 1994 in Europe, and assembled by Aprilia.

Its 652 cc Rotax engine was a single cylinder liquid-cooled unit. Drive to the double overhead camshafts which actuate the four valves per cylinder was by chain from the left-hand end of the crankshaft. A balancer shaft ironed out vibration for smooth running. It had a dry sump lubrication system with the oil stored in the frame.

The clutch was a conventional wet multi-plate unit and the gearbox was 5-speed. Drive to the rear wheel was by chain and sprockets.

Twin 33 mm Mikuni CV carburettors supplied fuel and air to the engine. Twin spark plugs ignited the mixture.

The engine sat in a tubular steel cradle frame which used the engine as a stressed member. Front suspension was by conventional non-adjustable 41 mm oil-damped forks. Rear suspension was by a single shock absorber with adjustable spring pre-load and rebound damping, via a three-way rising rate linkage. The wheels were wire spoked.

The front brake system had a single dual-piston sliding caliper acting on a conventional fixed disc. The rear brake system had a single piston sliding caliper acting on a conventional fixed disc.

Revised in 1997, and launched for the first time in America – changes included a new fairing and screen, lower seat and different instruments.

F650 ST (Strada)

Launched in 1997.

A slightly more road-biased version of the Funduro, with smaller front wheel, narrower handlebars, and less travel in the rear suspension.

A special edition was launched in 2000, with different handlebars and heated grips, a taller windshield and fitted top box and pannier rails.

F650 GS

Launched in 2000, and now built by BMW using a single spark version of the Rotax engine.

Styled more as a trail bike, but at home on the road, the GS comes with BMS-C fuel injection and has ABS that can be switched on and off as an optional extra.

It still has a dry sump lubrication system but the oil is now stored in a tank rather than in the frame.

Many styling and detail changes were made to the bodywork and luggage, the fuel tank was relocated under seat, a different radiator and exhaust were fitted, modifications were made to the front and rear suspension and to the frame, and different headlights and instruments were fitted.

Revised in 2004 – changes included a return to dual spark ignition with a modified management system (BMS-C11), different headlights, instruments, windshield and mudguard.

F650 GS Dakar

Launched in 2001, with extra off-road bias than the standard GS. The Dakar differed in having a larger front wheel and modified suspension, different mudguard arrangement, taller screen, hand guards, and a Dakar graphic on the side.

Revised in 2004 – changes include a return to dual spark ignition with a modified management system (BMS-C11).

F650 CS

Launched in 2002 as a street version of the GS, using the single spark version of the Rotax engine with BMS-C fuel injection. It still had a dry sump lubrication system but the oil was stored in the frame as on the original F650 model. Final drive was by belt rather than chain, and it featured a single-sided swingarm. ABS was available as an option.

Many styling and detail changes include bodywork, exhaust, different headlights and instruments, cast alloy wheels. An optional adjustable rear shock absorber for touring use became available in 2003.

Dual spark ignition with a modified management system (BMS-C11) was fitted from 2004.

Dimensions and weights

F650 Funduro – 1994 to 1996

Overall length	2180 mm
Overall width	880 mm
Overall height	1220 mm
Wheelbase	1480 mm
Seat height	810 mm
Weight (wet)	189 kg
Max. load	182 kg
Max gross weight	371 kg

F650 Funduro – 1997 to 2000

Overall length	2180 mm
Overall width	880 mm
Overall height	1345 mm
Wheelbase	1480 mm
Seat height	800 mm
Weight (wet)	191 kg
Max. load	180 kg
Max gross weight	371 kg

F650 ST

Overall length	2160 mm
Overall width	880 mm
Overall height	1190 mm
Wheelbase	1470 mm
Seat height	785 mm
Weight (wet)	191 kg
Max. load	180 kg
Max gross weight	371 kg

F650 GS – 2000 to 2003

Overall length	2101 mm
Overall width	890 mm
Overall height	1265 mm
Wheelbase	1479 mm
Seat height	780 mm
Weight (wet, unladen)	193 kg
Max. load	187 kg
Max gross weight	380 kg

F650 GS – 2004 to 2007

Overall length	2175 mm
Overall width	910 mm
Overall height	1265 mm
Wheelbase	1479 mm
Seat height	780/750 mm
Weight (wet, unladen)	193 kg
Max. load	187 kg
Max gross weight	380 kg

F650 GS Dakar

Overall length	
2001 to 2003 models	2101 mm
2004-on models	2189 mm
Overall width	
2001 to 2003 models	890 mm
2004-on models	910 mm
Overall height	1412 mm
Wheelbase	1489 mm
Seat height	870 mm
Weight (wet, unladen)	192 kg
Max. load	188 kg
Max gross weight	380 kg

F650 CS

Overall length	2143 mm
Overall width	893 mm
Overall height	1342 mm
Wheelbase	1479 mm
Seat height	780/750 mm
Weight (wet, unladen)	187 kg
Max. load	183 kg
Max gross weight	370 kg

Engine

Type	Four-stroke 4V single
Capacity	652 cc
Bore	100 mm
Stroke	83 mm
Compression ratio	
Funduro and ST	9.7 to 1
GS, Dakar and CS	11.5 to 1
Cooling system	Liquid cooled
Clutch	Wet multi-plate
Transmission	Five-speed constant mesh
Final drive	
Funduro, ST, GS and Dakar	Chain and sprockets
CS	Belt and pulleys
Camshafts	DOHC, chain-driven
Fuel system	
Funduro and ST	Carburettor
GS, Dakar and CS	Fuel injection
Ignition system	Computer-controlled digital transistorised with electronic advance

Chassis

Frame type	Tubular steel
Rake and Trail	
Funduro	28.6', 112 mm
ST	28.6', 100 mm
GS	29.2', 113 mm
Dakar	29.2', 123 mm
CS	27.9', 86 mm
Fuel tank capacity (including reserve)	
Funduro and ST	17.5 litres (res. 2 litres)
GS and Dakar	17.3 litres (res. 4 litres)
CS	15.0 litres (res. 4 litres)
Front suspension	
Type	41 mm oil-damped telescopic forks
Travel	
Funduro, ST and GS	170 mm
Dakar	210 mm
CS	125 mm
Rear suspension	
Type	Single shock absorber, rising rate linkage, aluminium swingarm (single-sided on CS)
Travel (at rear wheel axle)	
Funduro and GS	165 mm
ST	120 mm
Dakar	210 mm
CS	140 mm or 120 mm (according to model)
Adjustment	Spring pre-load and rebound damping (optional on CS models)

Wheels	Front	Rear
Funduro	2.15 x 19 MT	3.00 x 17 MT
ST	2.15 x 18 MT	3.00 x 17 MT
GS	2.50 x 19 MT	3.00 x 17 MT
Dakar	1.60 x 21 MT	3.00 x 17 MT
CS	3.00 x 17 MT	4.50 x 17 MT

Tyres		
Funduro	100/90-19 57S tubed	130/80-17 65S tubed
ST	100/90-18 57S tubed	130/80-17 65S tubed
GS	100/90-19 57S tubed	130/80-17 65S tubed
Dakar	90/90-21 54S tubed	130/80-17 65S tubed
CS	110/70-ZR17 tubeless	160/60-ZR17 tubeless

Front brake	Single 300 mm fixed disc with twin piston sliding caliper
Rear brake	Single 240 mm fixed disc with single piston sliding caliper

Frame and engine numbers

The frame number is stamped into the right-hand side of the steering head. The engine number is stamped into the left-hand crankcase half just below the clutch cover. Both of these numbers should be recorded and kept in a safe place so they can be given to law enforcement officials in the event of a theft. The VIN plate is under the seat on the sub-frame cross-member on Funduro and ST models, and on the outside of the right-hand frame beam on GS, Dakar and CS models.

The frame and engine numbers should also be kept in a handy place (such as with your driver's licence) so they are always available when purchasing or ordering parts for your machine.

The procedures in this manual identify models by name (e.g. Funduro, ST, GS, Dakar and CS) and by year of manufacture when there are model year differences (e.g. 2000 to 2003 GS models).

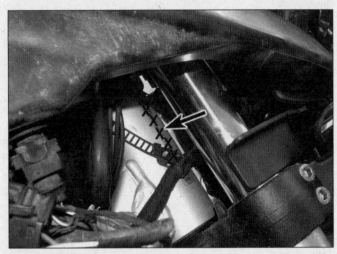

1 The frame number is stamped into the right-hand side of the steering head

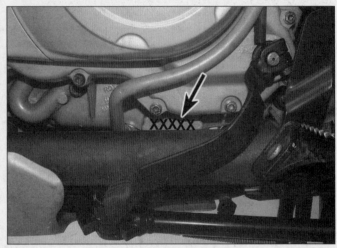

2 The engine number is stamped into the left crankcase half just below the clutch cover

3 On Funduro and ST models the VIN plate is under the seat on the sub-frame cross-member (arrowed)

4 On GS, Dakar and CS the VIN plate is on the frame behind the steering head (arrowed)

Buying spare parts

Once you have found all the identification numbers, record them for reference when buying parts. Since the manufacturers change specifications, parts and vendors (companies that manufacture various components on the machine), providing the ID numbers is the only way to be reasonably sure that you are buying the correct parts.

Whenever possible, take the worn part to the dealer so direct comparison with the new component can be made. Along the trail from the manufacturer to the parts shelf, there are numerous places that the part can end up with the wrong number or be listed incorrectly.

The two places to purchase new parts for your motorcycle – the franchised or main dealer and the parts/accessories store – differ in the type of parts they carry. While dealers can obtain every single genuine part for your motorcycle, the accessory store is usually limited to normal high wear items such as chains and sprockets, brake pads, spark plugs and cables, and to tune-up parts and various engine gaskets, etc. Rarely will an accessory outlet have major suspension components, camshafts, transmission gears, or engine cases.

Used parts can be obtained from breakers yards for roughly half the price of new ones, but you can't always be sure of what you're getting. Once again, take your worn part to the breaker for direct comparison, or when ordering by mail order make sure that you can return it if you are not happy.

Whether buying new, used or rebuilt parts, the best course is to deal directly with someone who specialises in your particular make.

Professional mechanics are trained in safe working procedures. However enthusiastic you may be about getting on with the job at hand, take the time to ensure that your safety is not put at risk. A moment's lack of attention can result in an accident, as can failure to observe simple precautions.

There will always be new ways of having accidents, and the following is not a comprehensive list of all dangers; it is intended rather to make you aware of the risks and to encourage a safe approach to all work you carry out on your bike.

Asbestos

● Certain friction, insulating, sealing and other products - such as brake pads, clutch linings, gaskets, etc. - contain asbestos. Extreme care must be taken to avoid inhalation of dust from such products since it is hazardous to health. If in doubt, assume that they do contain asbestos.

Fire

● Remember at all times that petrol is highly flammable. Never smoke or have any kind of naked flame around, when working on the vehicle. But the risk does not end there - a spark caused by an electrical short-circuit, by two metal surfaces contacting each other, by careless use of tools, or even by static electricity built up in your body under certain conditions, can ignite petrol vapour, which in a confined space is highly explosive. Never use petrol as a cleaning solvent. Use an approved safety solvent.

● Always disconnect the battery earth terminal before working on any part of the fuel or electrical system, and never risk spilling fuel on to a hot engine or exhaust.

● It is recommended that a fire extinguisher of a type suitable for fuel and electrical fires is kept handy in the garage or workplace at all times. Never try to extinguish a fuel or electrical fire with water.

Fumes

● Certain fumes are highly toxic and can quickly cause unconsciousness and even death if inhaled to any extent. Petrol vapour comes into this category, as do the vapours from certain solvents such as trichloro-ethylene. Any draining or pouring of such volatile fluids should be done in a well ventilated area.

● When using cleaning fluids and solvents, read the instructions carefully. Never use materials from unmarked containers - they may give off poisonous vapours.

● Never run the engine of a motor vehicle in an enclosed space such as a garage. Exhaust fumes contain carbon monoxide which is extremely poisonous; if you need to run the engine, always do so in the open air or at least have the rear of the vehicle outside the workplace.

The battery

● Never cause a spark, or allow a naked light near the vehicle's battery. It will normally be giving off a certain amount of hydrogen gas, which is highly explosive.

● Always disconnect the battery ground (earth) terminal before working on the fuel or electrical systems (except where noted).

Electricity

● When using an electric power tool, inspection light etc., always ensure that the appliance is correctly connected to its plug and that, where necessary, it is properly grounded (earthed). Do not use such appliances in damp conditions and, again, beware of creating a spark or applying excessive heat in the vicinity of fuel or fuel vapour. Also ensure that the appliances meet national safety standards.

● A severe electric shock can result from touching certain parts of the electrical system, such as the spark plug wires (HT leads), when the engine is running or being cranked, particularly if components are damp or the insulation is defective. Where an electronic ignition system is used, the secondary (HT) voltage is much higher and could prove fatal.

Remember...

✗ **Don't** start the engine without first ascertaining that the transmission is in neutral.

✗ **Don't** suddenly remove the pressure cap from a hot cooling system - cover it with a cloth and release the pressure gradually first, or you may get scalded by escaping coolant.

✗ **Don't** attempt to drain oil until you are sure it has cooled sufficiently to avoid scalding you.

✗ **Don't** grasp any part of the engine or exhaust system without first ascertaining that it is cool enough not to burn you.

✗ **Don't** allow brake fluid or antifreeze to contact the machine's paintwork or plastic components.

✗ **Don't** siphon toxic liquids such as fuel, hydraulic fluid or antifreeze by mouth, or allow them to remain on your skin.

✗ **Don't** inhale dust - it may be injurious to health (see Asbestos heading).

✗ **Don't** allow any spilled oil or grease to remain on the floor - wipe it up right away, before someone slips on it.

✗ **Don't** use ill-fitting spanners or other tools which may slip and cause injury.

✗ **Don't** lift a heavy component which may be beyond your capability - get assistance.

✗ **Don't** rush to finish a job or take unverified short cuts.

✗ **Don't** allow children or animals in or around an unattended vehicle.

✗ **Don't** inflate a tyre above the recommended pressure. Apart from overstressing the carcass, in extreme cases the tyre may blow off forcibly.

✔ **Do** ensure that the machine is supported securely at all times. This is especially important when the machine is blocked up to aid wheel or fork removal.

✔ **Do** take care when attempting to loosen a stubborn nut or bolt. It is generally better to pull on a spanner, rather than push, so that if you slip, you fall away from the machine rather than onto it.

✔ **Do** wear eye protection when using power tools such as drill, sander, bench grinder etc.

✔ **Do** use a barrier cream on your hands prior to undertaking dirty jobs - it will protect your skin from infection as well as making the dirt easier to remove afterwards; but make sure your hands aren't left slippery. Note that long-term contact with used engine oil can be a health hazard.

✔ **Do** keep loose clothing (cuffs, ties etc. and long hair) well out of the way of moving mechanical parts.

✔ **Do** remove rings, wristwatch etc., before working on the vehicle - especially the electrical system.

✔ **Do** keep your work area tidy - it is only too easy to fall over articles left lying around.

✔ **Do** exercise caution when compressing springs for removal or installation. Ensure that the tension is applied and released in a controlled manner, using suitable tools which preclude the possibility of the spring escaping violently.

✔ **Do** ensure that any lifting tackle used has a safe working load rating adequate for the job.

✔ **Do** get someone to check periodically that all is well, when working alone on the vehicle.

✔ **Do** carry out work in a logical sequence and check that everything is correctly assembled and tightened afterwards.

✔ **Do** remember that your vehicle's safety affects that of yourself and others. If in doubt on any point, get professional advice.

● If in spite of following these precautions, you are unfortunate enough to injure yourself, seek medical attention as soon as possible.

Chapter 1
Routine maintenance and servicing

Contents

Degrees of difficulty

Easy, suitable for novice with little experience		**Fairly easy,** suitable for beginner with some experience	⚒	**Fairly difficult,** suitable for competent DIY mechanic	⚒	**Difficult,** suitable for experienced DIY mechanic	⚒	**Very difficult,** suitable for expert DIY or professional	

Specifications

Engine

Spark plug type
  Funduro and ST .... NGK D8 EA
  GS and Dakar (2000 to 2003) .... NGK D8 EA
  GS and Dakar (2004-on) .... NGK DR8 EB
  CS .... NGK DR8 EB
Spark plug electrode gap .... 0.6 to 0.7 mm
Engine idle speed
  Funduro and ST .... 1300 to 1400 rpm
  GS and Dakar (2000 to 2003) .... 1350 to 1450 rpm
  CS, GS and Dakar (2004-on) .... 1480 rpm
  CS (2002 and 2003) .... 1400 rpm
Valve clearances (COLD engine)
  Funduro and ST
    Intake valves .... 0.10 to 0.15 mm
    Exhaust valves .... 0.10 to 0.15 mm
  GS and Dakar (2000 to 2003)
    Intake valves .... 0.10 to 0.15 mm
    Exhaust valves .... 0.25 to 0.30 mm
  GS and Dakar (2004-on), all CS
    Intake valves .... 0.03 to 0.11 mm
    Exhaust valves .... 0.25 to 0.33 mm

Chassis

Drive chain slack
    Funduro and ST .... 20 to 30 mm
    GS... 35 to 45 mm
    Dakar .... 40 to 50 mm
Clutch cable freeplay
    Funduro and ST .... 1.5 to 2.5 mm
    GS, Dakar and CS .... 1 to 2 mm
Throttle cable freeplay
    Funduro and ST .... 1 to 2 mm
    GS, Dakar and CS .... 1 mm
Choke cable freeplay (Funduro and ST)..................... 1 to 3 mm
Tyre pressures (cold)... see *Pre-ride checks*
Brake pad lining minimum thickness .... 1 mm

Lubricants and fluids

Engine oil .... see *Pre-ride checks*
Engine oil capacity
    Funduro and ST .... approx 2.1 litres
    GS and Dakar.. approx 2.3 litres
    CS... approx 2.5 litres
Coolant type... 50% distilled or soft water, 50% corrosion inhibited ethylene glycol anti-freeze, nitrite-free
Coolant capacity .... approx.1.3 litres
Brake fluid .... DOT 4
Drive chain .... Aerosol chain lubricant suitable for O-ring chains
Steering head bearings .... Multi-purpose grease with EP2 rating
Swingarm pivot bearings .... Multi-purpose grease with EP2 rating
Suspension linkage bearings .... Multi-purpose grease with EP2 rating
Bearing seal lips .... Multi-purpose grease
Gearchange lever/rear brake pedal/footrest pivots .... Multi-purpose grease
Clutch lever pivot .... Multi-purpose grease
Sidestand pivot .... Multi-purpose grease
Throttle twistgrip... Multi-purpose grease
Front brake lever pivot and piston tip .... Silicone grease
Cables .... Cable lubricant

Torque settings

Drive belt adjuster screw (CS models) .... 10 Nm
Drive belt eccentric adjuster clamp screws (CS models)
    Initial torque .... 10 Nm
    Final torque.. 21 Nm
Drive chain adjuster screws (Funduro, ST, GS and Dakar)........... 10 Nm
Engine oil drain plug.. 40 Nm
Engine oil filter cover screws .... 10 Nm
Engine oil tank drain plug
    Funduro and ST .... 10 Nm
    GS, Dakar and CS .... 21 Nm
Fork clamp bolts (top yoke)
    Funduro and ST .... 25 Nm
    GS and Dakar.. 23 Nm
    CS... 23 Nm
Rear axle nut (Funduro, ST, GS and Dakar) .... 100 Nm
Spark plug(s) .... 20 Nm
Steering head bearing adjuster
    GS and Dakar
        Initial setting .... 25 Nm
        Final setting .... 60° anti-clockwise
        Hex-headed threaded tube............................ 65 Nm
    CS
        Initial setting .... 25 Nm
        Final setting .... 60° anti-clockwise
Steering stem clamp bolt (CS models)......................... 23 Nm
Steering stem nut
    Funduro and ST .... 100 Nm
    GS and Dakar.. 65 Nm
Water pump drain bolt .... 10 Nm

Maintenance schedule – Funduro and ST models

Note: *The Pre-ride checks outlined in the owner's manual cover those items which should be inspected before every ride.*

Also perform the pre-ride inspection at every maintenance interval (in addition to the procedures listed). The intervals listed

below are the intervals recommended by the manufacturer for the models covered in this manual.

Pre-ride
☐ See '*Pre-ride checks*' at the beginning of this manual.

After the initial 600 miles (1000 km)
Note: *This check is usually performed by a BMW dealer after the first 600 miles (1000 km) from new. Thereafter, maintenance is carried out according to the following intervals of the schedule.*

Every 600 miles (1000 km)
☐ Check, adjust, clean and lubricate the drive chain (Section 1)

Every 6,000 miles (10,000 km)
☐ Change the engine oil and oil filter, clean tank strainer (Section 3).
☐ Fit new air filter element (Section 4)
☐ Check and adjust the valve clearances (Section 5) – see **Note** below
☐ Fit new spark plugs (Section 6)
☐ Check the fuel system and hoses (Section 7)
☐ Check and adjust the engine idle speed and check CO level (Section 8)
☐ Check and adjust the clutch cable freeplay (Section 9)
☐ Check the cooling system (Section 10)
☐ Check the brake pads for wear (Section 11)
☐ Check the brake system and brake light switch operation (Section 11)
☐ Check the condition of the wheels and tyres (Section 12)
☐ Check the drive chain and sprocket wear (Section 1)
☐ Check the front and rear suspension (Section 13)
☐ Check and adjust the steering head bearings (Section 14)
☐ Check and lubricate the clutch, gearchange and brake levers, brake pedal, sidestand and centrestand pivots, and the cables (Sections 15 and 16)
☐ Check the tightness of all nuts, bolts and fasteners (Section 16)

Note: *It has been found that the valve clearance check need only be carried out every 12,000 miles or 20,000 km. If in doubt seek the advice of your dealer.*

Every 12,000 miles (20,000 km)
Carry out all the items under the 6,000 mile (10,000 km) check, plus the following:
☐ Change the front fork oil (Section 13)
☐ Check the wheel bearings (Section 12)

Every year
Note: *The following service items should be carried out once a year irrespective of the mileage covered.*
☐ Change the engine oil and oil filter (Section 3).
☐ Change the coolant (Section 10)
☐ Change the brake fluid (Section 11)
☐ Check the battery (Section 17)

Non-scheduled maintenance
☐ Fit new brake hoses (Section 11)
☐ Re-grease the steering head bearings (Section 14)
☐ Re-grease the swingarm and suspension linkage bearings (Section 13)
☐ Fit new cooling system hoses (Section 10)
☐ Fit new fuel system hoses (Section 7)

Maintenance schedule – GS, Dakar and CS models

Note 1: *The Pre-ride checks outlined in the owner's manual cover those items which should be inspected before every ride. Also perform the pre-ride inspection at every maintenance interval (in addition to the procedures listed). The intervals listed below are the intervals recommended by the manufacturer for the models covered in this manual.*

Note 2: *If you use your bike off-road service intervals should be halved where specified in the procedure Section.*

Pre-ride
☐ See *'Pre-ride checks'* at the beginning of this manual.

After the initial 600 miles (1000 km)
Note: *This check is usually performed by a BMW dealer after the first 600 miles (1000 km) from new. Thereafter, maintenance is carried out according to the following intervals of the schedule.*

Every 600 miles (1000 km)
☐ Check, adjust, clean and lubricate the drive chain (GS and Dakar) (Section 1)

Every 6,000 miles (10,000 km)
☐ Check the drive chain and sprocket wear (Section 1)
☐ Check the drive belt and pulleys (CS models) (Section 2)
☐ Have fault code memory read by BMW dealer
☐ Change the engine oil and oil filter (Section 3).
☐ Clean air filter element (Section 4)
☐ Check and adjust the valve clearances (Section 5) – see Note below
☐ Check the fuel system and hoses (Section 7)
☐ Check and adjust the clutch cable freeplay (Section 9)
☐ Check the cooling system (Section 10)
☐ Check the brake pads for wear (Section 11)
☐ Check the brake system and brake light switch operation (Section 11)
☐ Check the condition of the wheels and tyres (Section 12)
☐ Check the front and rear suspension (Section 13)
☐ Check and adjust the steering head bearings (Section 14)
☐ Check and lubricate the clutch, gearchange and brake levers, brake pedal, sidestand and centrestand pivots, and the cables (Sections 15 and 16)
☐ Check the tightness of all nuts, bolts and fasteners (Section 16)
☐ Check the battery (Section 17)
Note: *It has been found that the valve clearance check need only be carried out every 12,000 miles or 20,000 km. If in doubt seek the advice of your dealer.*

Every 12,000 miles (20,000 km)
Carry out all the items under the 6,000 mile (10,000 km) check, plus the following:
☐ Fit new air filter element (Section 4)
☐ Fit new spark plugs (Section 6)
☐ Fit new fuel filter (GS and Dakar to 2003) (Section 7)
☐ Change the front fork oil (Dakar models only) (Section 13)
☐ Check the wheel bearings (Section 12)

Every 24,000 miles (40,000 km)
Carry out all the items under the 12,000 mile (20,000 km) check, plus the following:
☐ Fit a new brake master cylinder cup and seal (ABS models) (Section 11)
☐ Fit a new fuel filter (GS and Dakar 2004-on, CS) (Section 7)
☐ Fit a new drive belt (CS) (Section 2)

Every year
Note: *The following service items should be carried out once a year irrespective of the mileage covered.*
☐ Change the engine oil and oil filter (Section 3).
☐ Change the brake fluid (Section 11)

Every two years – 2000 to 2003 models
☐ Change the coolant (Section 10)

Every four years – 2004-on models
☐ Change the coolant (Section 10)

Non-scheduled maintenance
☐ Change the front fork oil (GS and CS models) (Section 13)
☐ Re-grease the steering head bearings (Section 14)
☐ Re-grease the swingarm and suspension linkage bearings (Section 13)
☐ Fit new brake hoses (Section 11)
☐ Fit new cooling system hoses (Section 10)
☐ Fit new fuel system hoses (Section 7)

Funduro and ST right side

1 Coolant reservoir
2 Rear brake fluid reservoir
3 Spark plugs
4 Throttle cable adjuster
5 Front brake fluid reservoir
6 Steering head bearing
   adjuster
7 Fork oil drain plug
8 Fork oil seal
9 Inspection plug in
   alternator cover
10 Engine oil filter
11 Drive chain adjuster

Funduro and ST left side

1 Clutch cable adjuster
2 Fuel tap filter
3 Engine oil level dipstick
4 Rear shock adjuster
5 Battery
6 Air filter
7 Drive chain adjuster
8 Engine oil drain plug
9 Idle speed adjuster
10 Coolant drain bolt
11 Engine oil tank strainer
12 Engine oil tank drain plug
13 Fork oil seal
14 Fork oil drain plug

GS and Dakar right side

1 Rear brake fluid reservoir
2 Fuel filter
3 Air filter
4 Spark plug(s)
5 Throttle cable adjuster
6 Front brake fluid reservoir
7 Fork oil drain plug
8 Fork oil seal
9 Steering head bearing adjuster
10 Rear shock adjuster
11 Inspection plug in alternator cover
12 Engine oil filter
13 Drive chain adjuster

GS and Dakar left side

1 Clutch cable adjuster
2 Engine oil dipstick/filler
3 Engine oil tank drain bolt
4 Battery
5 Drive chain adjuster
6 Engine oil drain bolt
7 Coolant drain bolt
8 Coolant reservoir window
9 Fork oil seal
10 Fork oil drain plug

CS right side

1 Rear brake fluid reservoir
2 Fuel filter
3 Spark plug(s)
4 Engine oil dipstick
5 Throttle cable adjuster
6 Front brake fluid reservoir
7 Fork oil seal
8 Inspection plug in alternator cover
9 Oil filter
10 Drive belt adjuster

CS left side

1 Clutch cable adjuster
2 Steering head bearing adjuster
3 Coolant reservoir
4 Air filter
5 Battery
6 Engine oil tank drain bolt
7 Engine oil drain bolt
8 Rear shock adjuster
9 Coolant drain bolt
10 Fork oil seal

Introduction

1 This Chapter is designed to help the home mechanic maintain his/her motorcycle for safety, economy, long life and peak performance.

2 Deciding where to start or plug into the routine maintenance schedule depends on several factors. If your motorcycle has been maintained according to the warranty standards and has just come out of warranty, start routine maintenance as it coincides with the next mileage or calendar interval. If you have owned the machine for some time but have never performed any maintenance on it, start at the nearest interval and include some additional procedures to ensure that nothing important is overlooked. If you have just had a major engine overhaul, then start the maintenance routine from the beginning. If you have a used machine and have no knowledge of its history or maintenance record, combine all the checks into one large service initially and then settle into the specified maintenance schedule. Note that each procedure is covered as a separate item but may include removal of parts for access (such as body panels) that may need to be removed for another procedure in the same service interval – to avoid more work than necessary read through all items you intend to carry out so you know what you need to do.

3 Before beginning any maintenance or repair, the machine should be cleaned thoroughly. Cleaning will help ensure that dirt does not get where it shouldn't when parts are removed or disassembled and will allow you to detect wear and damage that could otherwise easily go unnoticed.

4 Certain maintenance information is sometimes printed on labels attached to the motorcycle. If the information on the labels differs from that included here, use the information on the label.

1   Drive chain and sprockets (Funduro, ST, GS and Dakar)

Caution: If the machine is continually ridden in wet or dusty conditions, the drive chain should be checked, cleaned and lubricated more frequently.

Check chain slack

1 A neglected drive chain won't last long and will quickly damage the sprockets. Routine chain adjustment and lubrication isn't difficult and will ensure maximum chain and sprocket life.

2 On Funduro, ST and GS models, place the bike on its centrestand. On Dakar models, rest on the bike on its sidestand. Shift the transmission into neutral. Make sure the ignition switch is OFF.

3 Push up on the bottom run of the chain midway between the two sprockets and measure the slack, then compare your measurement to that listed in this Chapter's Specifications **(see illustration)**. Since the chain will rarely wear evenly, rotate the rear wheel so that another section of chain can be checked; do this several times to check the entire length of chain, and mark the tightest spot. As the chain stretches with wear, adjustment will periodically be necessary (see below).

Caution: Riding the bike with excess slack in the chain could lead to damage, or in extreme cases it could jump off the rear sprocket.

4 In some cases where lubrication has been neglected, corrosion and dirt may cause the links to bind and kink, which effectively shortens the chain's length and makes it tight **(see illustration)**. Thoroughly clean and work free any such links, then highlight them with a marker pen or paint. Take the bike for a ride.

5 After the bike has been ridden, repeat the measurement for slack in the highlighted area. If the chain has kinked again and is still tight, replace it with a new one (see Chapter 7). A rusty, kinked or worn chain will damage the sprockets and can damage transmission bearings. If in any doubt as to the condition of a chain, it is far better to install a new one than risk damage to other components and possibly yourself.

6 Check the entire length of the chain for damaged rollers, loose links and pins, and missing O-rings and replace it with a new one if necessary. **Note:** *Never install a new chain on old sprockets, and never use the old chain if you install new sprockets – replace the chain and sprockets as a set.*

7 Inspect the drive chain slider on the front of the swingarm for excessive wear and damage and replace it with a new one if necessary (see Chapter 7).

Adjust chain slack

8 Move the bike so that the chain is positioned with the tightest point at the centre of its bottom run, then put it on the stand.

9 Slacken the rear axle nut **(see illustration)**.

10 Turn each adjuster screw evenly and a little at a time until the amount of freeplay specified at the beginning of the Chapter is obtained at the centre of the bottom run of the chain **(see illustration)** – if the chain was slack turn the screws clockwise; if the chain was tight turn them anti-clockwise.

11 Following adjustment, check that the alignment of the numbered marks as seen in the cut-out in the swingarm is the same on each side **(see illustration)**. It is important the alignment is identical otherwise the rear wheel will be out of alignment with the front. If there is a difference in the positions, adjust one of them so that its position is exactly the same as the other. Check the chain freeplay again at its tightest point and readjust if necessary.

12 When adjustment is complete tighten

1.3 Push up on the chain and measure the slack

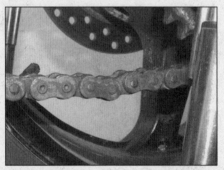

1.4 Neglect has caused the links in this chain to kink

1.9 Slacken the axle nut (arrowed)

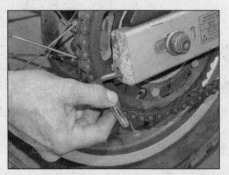

1.10 Turn the adjuster screw in the end of the swingarm on each side . . .

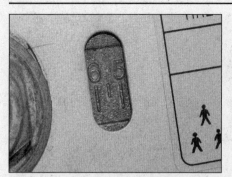

1.11 ... then check the alignment of the numbered marks on each side

1.15 Apply the lubricant to the overlapping sections of the sideplates

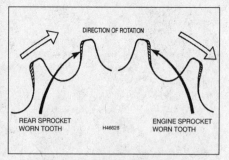

1.16 Check the sprockets in the areas indicated to see if they are worn excessively

the axle nut to the torque setting specified at the beginning of the Chapter. Recheck the adjustment as above, then spin the wheel to make sure it runs freely.

13 Now tighten the adjuster screws to the specified torque setting.

Clean and lubricate the chain

14 If required, wash the chain using a dedicated aerosol cleaner that will not damage the O-rings, or in paraffin (kerosene), using a soft brush to work any dirt out if necessary. Wipe the cleaner off the chain and allow it to dry, using compressed air if available. If the chain is excessively dirty remove it from the machine and allow it to soak in the paraffin or solvent (see Chapter 7).

Caution: Don't use petrol (gasoline), an unsuitable solvent or other cleaning fluids which might damage the internal sealing properties of the chain. Don't use high-pressure water to clean the chain. The entire process shouldn't take longer than ten minutes, otherwise the O-rings could be damaged.

15 The best time to lubricate the chain is after the motorcycle has been ridden. When the chain is warm, the lubricant will penetrate the joints between the side plates better than when cold. **Note:** *BMW specifies an aerosol chain lube that it is suitable for O-ring (sealed) chains; do not use any other chain lubricants – the solvents could damage the chain's sealing rings.* Apply the lubricant to the area where the sideplates overlap – not the middle of the rollers **(see illustration).**

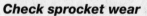

HAYNES HiNT *Apply the lubricant to the top of the lower chain run, so centrifugal force will work the oil into the chain when the bike is moving. After applying the lubricant, let it soak in a few minutes before wiping off any excess.*

⚠️ *Warning: Take care not to get any lubricant on the tyres or brake system components. If any of the lubricant inadvertently contacts them, clean it off thoroughly using a suitable solvent or dedicated brake cleaner before riding the machine.*

Check sprocket wear

16 Remove the front sprocket cover (see Chapter 7). Check the teeth on the front sprocket and the rear sprocket for wear **(see illustration).** If the sprocket teeth are worn excessively, replace the chain and both sprockets with a new set. **Note:** *Never fit a new chain onto old sprockets, and never use the old chain if you fit new sprockets – replace the chain and sprockets as a set.*

2 Drive belt and pulleys (CS models)

Check belt slack

1 To check the amount of slack in the belt a special measuring tool (BMW part No. 270501

or 271501) and a weight (BMW part No. 270502 or 271502) are required **(see illlustration).** This tool comprises a gauge and 7kg weight, which when fitted should show the belt deflected by 10 mm – coloured zones indicate the tension. Mechanics familiar with the CS belt system will most likely be able to assess correct belt tension without the tool, otherwise the tool is the only reliable means of ensuring the correct tension.

2 Place the bike on its centrestand or an auxiliary stand – make sure no load is on the rear suspension. Shift the transmission into neutral. Make sure the ignition switch is OFF. Turn the rear wheel until the coloured mark on the rear pulley is pointing to the rear **(see illustration).**

3 Fit the measuring tool (without the weight as this stage) onto the bottom run of the belt just below the angled section of the swingarm. Lock the rear wheel so it cannot turn – applying the brake is the easiest way, but you may need an assistant to help. Slacken the knurled screw on the tool and set the scale marker against the bottom of the guard so that the coloured scale isn't visible, then tighten the screw. Hook the weight onto the bottom of the tool.

Caution: No other method of assessing belt tension should be substituted for the service tool.

4 If belt tension is correct the bottom edge of the belt guard should be within the green section on the measuring tool **(see illustration).** If the belt guard aligns with the rod section the belt is too tight, and if aligned with the orange section, it is too loose.

2.1 BMW belt tension gauge and 7kg weight

2.2 Paint mark (arrowed) on rear pulley must face to the rear

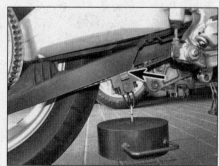

2.4 Tension gauge correctly shown in green zone (arrowed) with 7kg weight applied

2.6 Slacken the clamp screws (A) then the adjusting screw (wheel shown removed for clarity). Use a rod in the hole (B) to turn the eccentric adjuster so there is slack in the belt

3.3a Unscrew the oil filler cap to vent the tank – Funduro and ST models

Adjust belt slack

5 Set up the bike as described in Step 2.

6 Slacken the eccentric adjuster clamp screws by half to one turn **(see illustration)**. Slacken the adjusting screw several turns. Turn the eccentric adjuster using BMW tool part No. 111780, or a rod in the hole to use as a lever, until the belt is slack.

7 Fit the measuring tools as in Steps 1 and 3.

8 Turn the adjuster screw until the green section aligns with the bottom edge of the belt guard.

9 Remove the weight. Tighten the eccentric adjuster clamp screws evenly and a bit at a time first to the initial torque setting specified at the beginning of the Chapter, then tighten them to the final torque setting specified. Back off the adjusting screw slightly, then apply the final torque setting again to the clamp screws. Now tighten the adjusting screw to its specified torque setting.

Check belt and pulley wear

10 Remove the front pulley cover (see Chapter 7). Check the teeth on the belt and pulleys for wear and damage, and check the belt for any splits, cracks or exposed wires. If necessary, replace the belt and/or pulleys with new ones (see Chapter 7).

Fit a new drive belt

11 Replace the drive belt with a new one at the specified interval whatever the apparent condition of the old one (see Chapter 7).

3 Engine oil and filter

 Warning: Be careful when draining the oil, as the exhaust pipes, the engine, and the oil itself can cause severe burns.

1 Consistent routine oil and filter changes are the single most important maintenance procedure you can perform. The oil not only lubricates the internal parts of the engine, transmission and clutch, but it also acts as a coolant, a cleaner, a sealant, and a protector. Because of these demands, the oil takes a terrific amount of abuse and should be replaced often with new oil of the recommended grade and type. The oil filter should be changed with every oil change.

 HAYNES HiNT *Saving a little money in cost between a good oil and a cheap oil won't pay off if the engine is damaged.*

2 Before changing the oil, warm up the engine so the oil will drain easily. Make sure the bike is on level ground. On GS and Dakar models remove the left-hand front side cover and the sump guard (see Chapter 8). On all models remove the front sprocket cover or pulley cover according to model (see Chapter 7).

3 On Funduro and ST models position a clean drain tray below the radiator. Unscrew the oil filler cap **(see illustration)**. Unscrew the oil tank drain plug and allow the oil to drain into the tray **(see illustration)** – remove the section of trim on the bottom of the radiator to improve access to the drain plug if required (depending on the tools available). When the tank has drained refit the plug using a new sealing washer and tighten it to the torque setting specified at the beginning of the Chapter.

4 On GS and Dakar models position a clean drain tray on a stool or box so its is near the oil tank on the left-hand side of the bike. Unscrew the oil filler cap, using the spark plug wrench supplied in the bike's tool kit if required **(see illustration)**. Unscrew the oil tank drain plug and allow the oil to drain **(see illustrations)**. To ensure all oil is drained undo the oil tank screw and release the two clips, then draw the tank out and tilt it so the rest of the oil drains into the tray **(see illustrations)**. When the

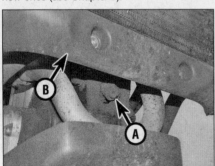

3.3b Oil drain plug (A) – remove the trim section (B) if required

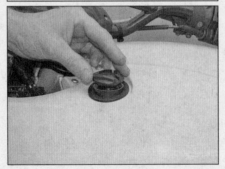

3.4a Unscrew the oil filler cap to vent the tank

3.4b Unscrew the oil drain plug (arrowed) . . .

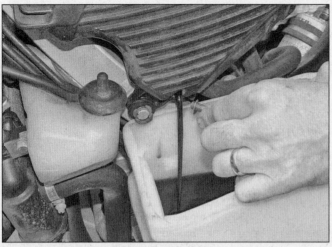

3.4c . . . and drain the oil – GS and Dakar

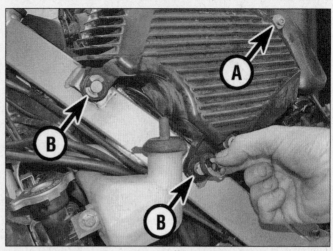

3.4d Undo the screw (A) and release the clips (B) . . .

3.4e . . . then displace and tilt the tank –
GS and Dakar

3.5a Unscrew the oil filler cap to vent the
tank – CS model

3.5b Unscrew the oil drain plug (arrowed)
and drain the oil – CS model

tank has drained refit it, then fit the drain plug using a new sealing washer and tighten it to the torque setting specified at the beginning of the Chapter.

5 On CS models put the bike on its sidestand and position a clean drain tray below the frame on the left-hand side. Unscrew the oil filler cap **(see illustration)**. Unscrew the oil tank drain plug and allow the oil to drain into the tray **(see illustration)**. When the tank has drained refit the plug using a new sealing washer and tighten it to the torque setting specified at the beginning of the Chapter.

6 Put the bike on its centrestand or on an auxiliary stand so it is level and upright.

Position the drain tray under the engine. Unscrew the oil drain plug and allow the oil to flow into the drain tray **(see illustrations)**. When the oil has completely drained, fit the plug using a new sealing washer and tighten it to the torque setting specified at the beginning of the Chapter **(see illustration)**.

7 Place the drain tray below the oil filter on the right-hand side of the engine. Make up a chute to fit under the oil filter housing to direct oil from the filter into the drain tray – for GS, Dakar and CS models BMW can supply a tool (part No. 117511) that fits onto the pins below the cover (around which the neutral switch wiring is routed), or alternatively (and

for Funduro and ST models) a piece of old plastic guttering or something similar suitably positioned should work. On GS, Dakar and CS models, if using the BMW chute, unscrew the bottom cover bolt and move the neutral switch wiring aside, then locate the tool onto the pins **(see illustration)**. On all models, if using a home-made chute, fit it under the cover and above the drain tray. Unscrew the (remaining) filter cover bolts then remove the cover and the filter **(see illustrations)**. Discard the filter. Allow the oil to drain then remove the chute and wipe out the housing with clean lint free rag.

8 Check the condition of the cover O-ring and

3.6a Unscrew the oil drain plug
(arrowed) . . .

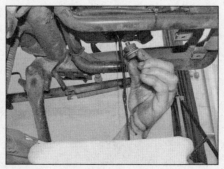

3.6b . . . and allow the oil to completely
drain

3.6c Use a new sealing washer and
tighten the bolt to the specified torque

3.7a Undo the screw (A) then locate the chute onto the pins (B)

3.7b Remove the filter cover . . .

replace it with a new one if necessary **(see illustration)**. Smear clean engine oil onto the O-ring and fit it into the groove in the cover. Fit the new filter into the housing, then fit the cover and tighten the bolts to the specified torque **(see illustrations)**. Reposition the neutral switch wiring.

9 On Funduro and ST models detach the oil hose from the tank strainer on the left-hand side **(see illustration)** – remove the engine trim panel and fairing for best access (see Chapter 8). Unscrew the strainer, clean it with solvent and blow it through with compressed air. Thread the filter back in and tighten it, then connect the oil hose.

10 On Funduro and ST models fill the oil tank up to the MAX level on the dipstick to the proper level using the recommended type and amount of oil (see *Pre-ride checks*). Fit the filler cap, then start the engine and let it run

for one minute (make sure that the oil pressure light extinguishes after a few seconds). Shut it off then recheck the oil level. If necessary, add more oil to bring the level mid-way between the MAX and MIN lines as described in Pre-ride checks.

11 On GS, Dakar and CS models fill the oil tank with 2 litres of the recommended type and amount of oil (see *Pre-ride checks*). Fit the filler cap, then start the engine and let it run for thirty seconds (make sure that the oil pressure light extinguishes after a few seconds). Shut it off then add another 0.3 litre on GS and Dakar models and 0.5 litre on CS models. Now run the engine up to normal temperature and follow the procedure in *Pre-ride checks* to make a final level check.

12 Check around the drain plugs and the oil filter cover. If there is a leak and a new washer or O-ring wasn't used, then repeat

the procedure using a new part. Otherwise make sure the drain plugs and cover bolts are tightened to the specified torque.

13 The old oil drained from the engine cannot be re-used and should be disposed of properly. Check with your local refuse disposal company, disposal facility or environmental agency to see whether they will accept the used oil for recycling. Don't pour used oil into drains or onto the ground.

OIL CARE *OIL BANK LINE* **0800 66 33 66** www.oilbankline.org.uk

Note: It is antisocial and illegal to dump oil down the drain. To find the location of your local oil recycling bank, call this number free.

3.7c . . . and withdraw the filter

3.8a Use a new O-ring if required

HAYNES HiNT *Check the old oil carefully – if it is very metallic coloured, then the engine is experiencing wear from break-in (new engine) or from insufficient lubrication. If there are flakes or chips of metal in the oil, then something is drastically wrong internally and the engine will have to be disassembled for inspection and repair. If there are pieces of fibre-like material in the oil, the clutch is experiencing excessive wear and should be checked.*

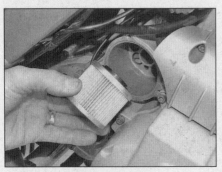

3.8b Fit the new filter . . .

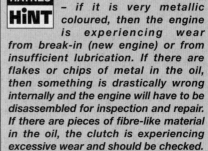

3.8c . . . then install the cover

3.9 Oil tank strainer (arrowed) – Funduro and ST

4.2a Displace the relay . . .

4.2b . . . then undo the screws (arrowed) and remove the cover

4.3 Draw the filter out of the housing

4 Air filter

Caution: If the machine is continually ridden in wet or dusty conditions, the filter should be cleaned and replaced more frequently.

Funduro and ST

1 Remove the left-hand side cover (see Chapter 8).

2 Displace the starter relay from the air filter cover **(see illustration)**. Remove the cover **(see illustration)**.

3 Withdraw the filter from the housing, noting how it fits **(see illustration)**.

4 To clean the filter, tap it on a hard surface to dislodge any dirt and use compressed air to clear the element, directing the air in the opposite way to normal flow, i.e. from the outside. Do not use any solvents or cleaning agents on the element. Check the filter element for damage.

5 If the filter is damaged or ingrained with dirt that cannot be removed, or has reached the end of its service life according to the schedule, replace it with a new one.

6 Remove the plug from the end of the air filter housing drain hose and allow any residue to drain out. Refit the plug.

7 Fit the filter into the housing, making sure it is properly seated **(see illustration 4.3)**. Fit the cover and tighten the screws **(see illustration)**. Fit the starter relay onto the cover **(see illustration 4.2a)**.

8 Fit the left-hand side cover (see Chapter 8).

GS and Dakar

9 Remove the right-hand front side cover (see Chapter 8).

10 Disconnect the intake air temperature (IAT) sensor wiring connector **(see illustration)**. Undo the air intake duct joint flange screws and remove the flange **(see illustration)**. Remove the air intake duct, noting how the peg at the front locates in the grommet **(see illustration)**.

11 Remove the filter from the housing, noting how it fits **(see illustration)**.

12 To clean the filter, tap it on a hard surface to dislodge any dirt and use compressed air to clear the element, directing the air in the opposite way to normal flow, i.e. from the outside **(see illustration)**. Do not use any solvents or cleaning agents on the element. Check the filter element for damage.

13 If the filter is damaged or ingrained with dirt that cannot be removed, or has reached the end of its service life according to the schedule, replace it with a new one.

14 Remove the plug from the end of the air

4.7 Slide the filter in then fit the cover

4.10a Disconnect the sensor wiring connector

4.10b Undo the screws and remove the flange . . .

4.10c . . . then remove the duct . . .

4.11 . . . and the filter

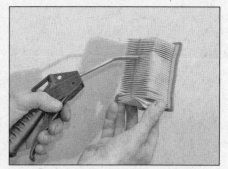

4.12 Blow through the element with compressed air

4.14 Remove the plug (arrowed) and drain any residue

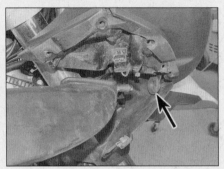

4.15a Make sure the peg at the front locates in the grommet (arrowed) . . .

4.15b . . . then slide the flange into place

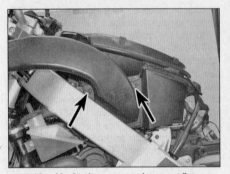

4.18a Undo the screws (arrowed) . . .

4.18b . . . and remove the duct . . .

4.19 . . . then remove the filter

filter housing drain hose and allow any residue to drain out **(see illustration)**. Refit the plug.

15 Fit the filter into the housing, making sure it is properly seated **(see illustration 4.11)**. Fit the air intake duct and joint flange and tighten the screws **(see illustrations)**. Connect the IAT sensor wiring connector **(see illustration 4.10a)**.

16 Fit the right-hand front side cover (see Chapter 8).

CS

17 Remove the left-hand front side cover (see Chapter 8).

18 Undo the air intake duct screws **(see illustration)**. Swing the duct out to the side and lift it up and out of the hook, then remove the duct, noting how the peg at the front locates in the grommet **(see illustration)**.

19 Remove the filter from the housing, noting how it fits – compressing the front part of

the element makes it easier to remove **(see illustration)**.

20 To clean the filter, tap it on a hard surface to dislodge any dirt and use compressed air to clear the element, directing the air in the opposite way to normal flow, i.e. from the outside **(see illustration 4.12)**. Do not use any solvents or cleaning agents on the element. Check the filter element for damage.

21 If the filter is damaged or ingrained with dirt that cannot be removed, or has reached the end of its service life according to the schedule, replace it with a new one.

22 Remove the plug from the end of the air filter housing drain hose and allow any residue to drain out. Refit the plug.

23 Fit the filter into the housing, compressing the front end to help it in **(see illustration 4.19)**. Fit the air intake duct and tighten the screws **(see illustrations 4.18b and a)**.

24 Fit the left-hand front side cover.

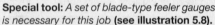

5 Valve clearances

Special tool: *A set of blade-type feeler gauges is necessary for this job* **(see illustration 5.8)**.

Check

1 The engine must be completely cool for this maintenance procedure.

2 Remove the spark plug – on twin spark models you only need to remove the outer plug (see Section 6).

3 Remove the valve cover (see Chapter 2).

4 Make a chart or sketch of the valve positions so that a note of each clearance can be made against the relevant valve. The intake valves are on the back of the cylinder head and the exhaust valves are on the front.

5 Unscrew the plug from the centre of the alternator cover **(see illustration)**. Discard the O-ring as a new one must be used.

6 To check the valve clearances the engine must be turned in a clockwise direction so it is at top dead centre (TDC) on its compression stroke, at which point all the valves are closed. The engine can be turned using an Allen key or hex bit fitted in the end of the crankshaft via the hole in the alternator cover.

7 Turn the engine clockwise until the index lines on the camshaft sprockets are parallel with the top of the cylinder head, and the small hole in each sprocket is at the top **(see illustrations)**. If the sprocket holes are at the bottom, rotate the engine clockwise one full turn (360°) until the index lines are again

5.5 Unscrew the plug (arrowed)

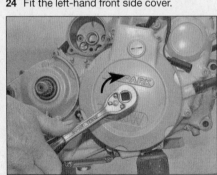

5.7a Turn the engine clockwise . . .

5.7b ... until the sprocket marks are as shown

5.8 Insert the feeler gauge between the base of the cam lobe and the top of the follower as shown

parallel with the head. The sprocket holes will now be at the top.

8 Insert a feeler gauge of the same thickness as the correct valve clearance (see Specifications) between the camshaft lobe and the follower of each valve and check that it is a firm sliding fit – you should feel a slight drag when the you pull the gauge out **(see illustration)**. If not, use the feeler gauges to obtain the exact clearance. Record the measured clearance on the chart.

9 When all four clearances have been measured and charted, identify whether the clearance on any valve falls outside the specified range. If any do, the shim must be replaced with one of a thickness which will restore the correct clearance.

Adjustment

10 Shim replacement requires removal of the camshafts (see Chapter 2). Place rags over the spark plug holes and the cam chain tunnel to prevent a shim from dropping into the engine on removal. Work on one valve at a time. If you want to remove more than one shim at a time, store them in a marked container or bag, denoting which valve the shim, and where applicable the follower, are from, so that they do not get mixed up.

11 On Funduro and ST models, and on GS, Dakar and CS models with a single spark plug, turn the follower so the shim removal notch is accessible, then ease the shim out of the follower using a small screwdriver or similar. Alternatively lift it out of the top of the follower using a magnet or valve lapping tool. Do not allow the shim to fall into the engine.

12 On GS, Dakar and CS models with twin spark plugs, lift out the cam follower using a magnet or the suction created by a valve lapping tool **(see illustration 5.16a)**. Retrieve the shim from the inside the follower or pick it out of the top of the valve spring retainer using either a magnet, a screwdriver with a dab of grease on it (the shim will stick to the grease), or a very small screwdriver and a pair of pliers

(see illustrations). Do not allow the shim to fall into the engine.

13 Calculate the required size of replacement shim – if the clearance measured was too big you need a shim that is thicker than the existing shim by the amount that the clearance was too great; if the clearance was too small you need a shim that is thinner than the existing shim by the amount that the clearance was too small. A size mark should be stamped on one face of the shim, but you should measure the shim to check whether it has worn **(see illustrations)**.

14 Shims are available from 2.00 mm to 3.00 mm thick on Funduro and ST models, and on GS, Dakar and CS models with a

single spark plug, and from 2.30 to 3.00 on GS, Dakar and CS models with twin spark plugs, all in increments of 0.05 mm. **Note:** *If the required replacement shim is greater than 3.00 mm (the largest available), the valve is probably not seating correctly due to a build-up of carbon deposits and should be checked and cleaned or resurfaced as required (see Chapter 2).* Obtain the replacement shim, then lubricate it with molybdenum disulphide oil (a 50/50 mixture of molybdenum disulphide grease and engine oil).

15 On Funduro and ST models, and on GS, Dakar and CS models with a single spark plug, fit the shim into the recess in the top of

5.12a Retrieve the shim (arrowed) from inside the follower ...

5.12b ... or from the top of the valve

5.13a The shim size is marked on one face ...

5.13b ... but check the thickness of the shim using a micrometer

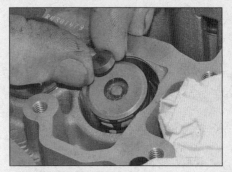

5.16a Fit the shim into its recess . . .

5.16b . . . then fit the follower onto the valve

5.20 Fit the plug with a new O-ring (arrowed)

the follower. Check that the shim is correctly seated.

16 On GS, Dakar and CS models with twin spark plugs, fit the shim into the recess in the valve spring retainer **(see illustration)**. Check that the shim is correctly seated, then lubricate the follower with molybdenum disulphide oil and fit it onto the valve, making sure it fits squarely in its bore **(see illustration)**.

17 Repeat the process for any other valves until the clearances are correct, then install the camshafts (see Chapter 2).

18 Rotate the crankshaft clockwise several turns to seat the new shim(s), then check the clearances again.

19 Install the valve cover (see Chapter 2).

20 Fit the plug into the alternator cover using a new O-ring **(see illustration)**.

21 Install the spark plug (Section 6). On Funduro and ST models check and adjust the idle speed (see Section 8).

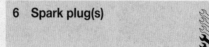

6 Spark plug(s)

Note: *GS and Dakar models with twin spark plugs and all CS models have direct ignition coils (stick coils) that fit directly onto the spark plugs (i.e. no HT lead and plug cap). Do not drop the coil. Do not get the coils mixed up as they are different.*

Special *tool: A wire or blade type feeler gauge is necessary for this job* **(see illustration 6.6a)**.

1 On Funduro and ST models, and on GS and Dakar with a single spark plug, pull the cap off the plug **(see illustration)**.

2 On GS and Dakar with twin spark plugs and all CS models remove the ignition stick coil(s) (Chapter 5).

3 Make sure your spark plug socket is the correct size before attempting to remove

6.1 Pull the cap(s) off the plug(s) – on twin plug models note which fits where

6.4 Unscrew and remove the plug

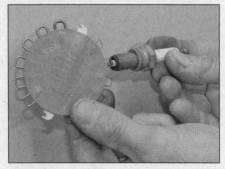

6.6a Using a wire type gauge to measure the spark plug electrode gap . . .

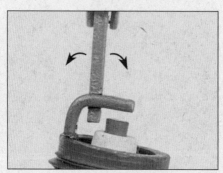

6.6b . . . and to adjust it if necessary

the plugs – a suitable one is supplied in the motorcycle's tool kit which is stored under the passenger seat.

4 Using either the plug removing tool and spanner supplied in the bike's toolkit or a deep spark plug socket, unscrew and remove the plug(s) from the cylinder head **(see illustration)**. Discard the plugs if they are to be replaced with new ones, but note that it is always worth having a spare (or two) around just in case.

5 If you are checking the plugs in between renewal intervals or because of a suspected problem, inspect the electrodes for wear. Both the centre and side electrodes should have square edges and the side electrode should be of uniform thickness. Look for excessive deposits and evidence of a cracked or chipped insulator around the centre electrode. Compare your spark plug(s) to the colour spark plug reading chart at the end of this manual. Check the threads, the washer and the ceramic insulator body for cracks and other damage. If the electrodes are not excessively worn, and if the deposits can be easily removed with a wire brush, and there are no cracks or chips visible in the insulator, the plugs can be re-used. If in doubt concerning the condition of the plugs, replace them with new ones, as the expense is minimal. Note that new spark plugs should be fitted at the prescribed service interval whatever the apparent condition of the old ones.

6 Before installing the plugs, make sure they are the correct type and heat range and check the gap between the electrodes **(see illustration)**. Compare the gap to that specified and adjust as necessary. If the gap must be adjusted, bend the side electrode and be very careful not to chip or crack the insulator nose **(see illustration)**. Make sure the sealing washer is in place on the plug before installing it.

7 Initially thread the plug(s) into the head by hand to avoid the possibility of cross-threading it/them and damaging the head **(see illustration)**. Once the plugs are finger-tight, the job can be finished with a spanner on the tool supplied or a socket drive **(see illustration 6.4)**. If new plugs are being used, tighten them by 1/2 a turn after the washer has seated. If the old plugs are being reused, tighten them by 1/8 to 1/4 turn after they have seated, or if a torque wrench can be applied, tighten the spark plugs to the torque setting specified at the beginning of the Chapter. Otherwise tighten them according the instructions on the box. Do not over-tighten them.

HAYNES HiNT *As the plugs are quite recessed, slip a short length of hose over the end of the plug to use as a tool to thread it into place. The hose will grip the plug well enough to turn it, but will start to slip if the plug begins to cross-thread in the hole – this will prevent damaged threads.*

8 On Funduro and ST models, and on GS and Dakar with a single spark plug, fit the cap onto the plug **(see illustration 6.1)**.

9 On GS and Dakar with twin spark plugs and all CS models install the ignition stick coils (Chapter 5).

HAYNES HiNT *Stripped plug threads in the cylinder head can be repaired with a Heli-Coil insert – see 'Tools and Workshop Tips' in the Reference section.*

7 Fuel system

Warning: Petrol (gasoline) is extremely flammable, so take extra precautions when you work on any part of the fuel system. Don't smoke or allow open flames or bare light bulbs near the work area, and don't work in a garage where a natural gas-type appliance is present. If you spill any fuel on your skin, rinse it off immediately with soap and water. When you perform any kind of work on the fuel system, wear safety glasses and have a fire extinguisher suitable for a Class B type fire (flammable liquids) on hand.
Note: *Three types of hose clamp are used*

6.7 Thread the plug in by hand to start with

on the various hoses across the range of models covered – the non-re-usable type, the re-usable clip type and the screw type. A small screwdriver is required to release the non-reusable type and clip type clamps. Special pliers are required to close them, and these are available from automotive tool suppliers, or from BMW (part No. 131500), along with the clamps where new ones are required.

General check

1 On Funduro and ST models remove the fuel tank (see Chapter 4A). On GS, Dakar and CS models remove the air filter housing (see Chapter 4B).

2 Check the entire fuel system and all hoses from the tank to the carburettors or from the fuel filter to the throttle body (according to model) for signs of leaks, deterioration or damage, and insecure connection. In particular check that there are no leaks from the fuel hoses or hose unions. Also check the engine breather hoses and all other hoses to the air filter housing, and the oil feed and return hoses and pipes between the frame or oil tank (according to model) and the engine. Replace any hose that is cracked or deteriorated with a new one **(see illustration)**.

3 On Funduro and ST models check the carburettors for signs of leakage, particularly around the float chamber. If there is leakage from the bottom tighten the drain screw. If there is leakage from the joint fit a new seal (see Chapter 4A).

4 On GS, Dakar and CS models inspect the joints between the fuel hose, the injector and

the throttle body. If there are any leaks, remove the injector and fit a new seal and O-ring (see Chapter 4B).

5 Models fitted with a catalytic converter should have the CO level checked by a dealer – special equipment is needed.

Fuel filter

6 On Funduro and ST models remove the tap from the tank and clean the strainers (see Chapter 4A).

7 On GS, Dakar and CS models the in-line fuel filter must be replaced with a new one at the prescribed interval or if fuel starvation is suspected (and the pump is fine). Note that there is also a strainer fitted on the fuel pump inside the tank – refer to Chapter 4B for details on removal and cleaning.

8 On GS and Dakar models remove the left-hand front side cover (see Chapter 8). Undo the oil tank screw and release the two clips, then draw the tank out and support it clear **(see illustration 3.4d)**. Remove the ECU (see Chapter 5).

9 On CS models remove the top and front side covers (see Chapter 8).

10 Undo the filter clamp screw **(see illustrations)**. Fit hose clamps onto the inlet and outlet hoses. Stuff some rag around the filter to catch residual fuel. Release the hose clamps and detach the hoses, noting which fits where. Remove the filter and replace it with a new one. Make sure the hoses are secure.

8 Idle speed (Funduro and ST models)

Idle speed

1 The idle speed should be checked and adjusted after checking the valve clearances, and when it is obviously too high or too low. Before adjusting the idle speed, make sure the air filter is clean (Section 4), the valve clearances are correct (Section 5), and the spark plugs are in good condition (Section 6). Also, turn the handlebars from side-to-side and check the idle speed does not change as you do. If it does, the throttle cables may not be adjusted or routed correctly, or may be

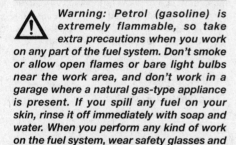

7.2 This hose needs renewing

7.10a Fuel filter clamp screw (arrowed) – GS and Dakar

7.10b Undoing the fuel filter clamp screw – CS

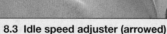

8.3 Idle speed adjuster (arrowed)

9.3 Measuring clutch cable freeplay

worn out. This is a dangerous condition that can cause loss of control of the bike. Be sure to correct this problem before proceeding.

2 The engine should be at normal operating temperature, which is usually reached after 10 to 15 minutes of stop-and-go riding. Make sure the transmission is in neutral.

3 The idle speed adjuster is a small knurled knob located on the left-hand side **(see illustration)**. With the engine running, turn the knob until the engine idles at the speed specified at the beginning of the Chapter. Turn the screw clockwise to increase idle speed, and anti-clockwise to decrease it.

4 Snap the throttle open and shut a few times,

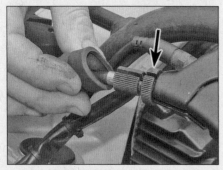

9.4a Pull the boot off and slacken the locknut (arrowed) . . .

9.4b . . . then turn the adjuster as required

then recheck the idle speed. If necessary, repeat the adjustment procedure.

5 If a smooth, steady idle can't be achieved, and the plug(s), air filter and valve clearances are all good, the problem may lie in the carburettors or the ignition system.

CO level

6 On models equpped with a catalytic converter, the exhaust gas CO content should be checked by a BMW dealer.

9 Clutch, throttle and choke cables

Clutch

1 Check that the clutch lever operates smoothly and easily.

2 If the clutch lever operation is heavy or stiff, remove the cable (see Chapter 2) and lubricate it (Step 11). Check that the inner cable slides freely and easily in the outer cable. If the cable is still stiff, replace it with a new one. Install the lubricated or new cable (see Chapter 2).

3 With the cable operating smoothly, check that it is correctly adjusted. Periodic adjustment is necessary to compensate for wear in the clutch plates and stretch of the cable. Pull lightly on the clutch lever until

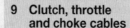

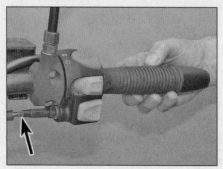

9.9 Measure throttle cable freeplay at this point (arrowed)

freeplay is taken, up then measure the gap between the inner front edge of the lever and the lever bracket **(see illustration)**. Check that the gap is as specified at the beginning of the Chapter.

4 If adjustment is required, pull the rubber boot off the adjuster and fully slacken the adjuster locknut **(see illustration)**. Turn the adjuster in or out until the specified amount of freeplay is obtained **(see illustration)**. To increase freeplay, thread the adjuster into the lever bracket. To reduce freeplay, thread the adjuster out of the bracket. Tighten the locknut on completion, then fit the rubber boot.

5 Make sure that the slots in the adjuster, locknut and lever bracket are not aligned – these slots are to allow removal of the cable, and if they are all aligned while the bike is in use the cable could jump out. Also make sure the adjuster is not threaded too far out of the bracket so that it is only held by a few threads – this will leave it unstable and the threads could be damaged.

Throttle and choke

6 Make sure the throttle and choke (Funduro and ST models) cables operate smoothly and freely with the front wheel turned at various angles. The throttle grip should return automatically from fully open to fully closed when released.

7 If action is sticky, this is probably due to a cable fault. Remove the cable (see Chapter 4A or 4B) and lubricate it (see Step 11). Check that the inner cable slides freely and easily in the outer cable. If not, replace the cable with a new one.

8 With the cable removed, make sure the throttle twistgrip or choke lever operates freely on the handlebar – dirt combined with a lack of lubrication can cause the action to be stiff. If necessary, remove, clean and lubricate the twistgrip or lever (see Chapter 6).

9 With the cable operating smoothly, check for a small amount of freeplay in twistgrip rotation or choke lever travel before the throttle or choke opens **(see illustration)**.

9.10a Pull the boot off to expose the locknut (A) and adjuster (B) –
Funduro and ST throttle cable

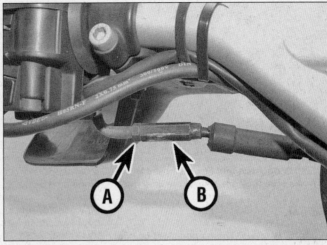

9.10b Pull the boot off to expose the locknut (A) and adjuster (B) –
Funduro and ST choke cable

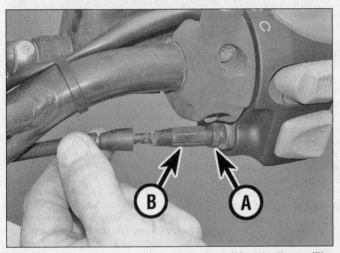

9.10c Pull the boot off to expose the locknut (A) and adjuster (B) –
GS, Dakar and CS

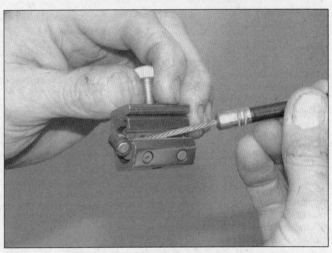

9.11a Fit the cable into the adapter . . .

10 If adjustment is required, pull the rubber boot off the adjuster and fully slacken the adjuster locknut (see illustrations). Turn the adjuster in or out until the specified amount of freeplay is obtained. To increase freeplay, thread the adjuster into the lever bracket. To reduce freeplay, thread the adjuster out of the bracket. Tighten the locknut on completion, then fit the rubber boot.

Lubrication

Special tool: *A cable lubricating adapter is necessary for this procedure.*

11 To lubricate the cables, disconnect the relevant cable at its upper end, then lubricate it with a pressure adapter and aerosol lubricant cable lube (see illustrations).

⚠️ *Warning: Turn the handlebars all the way through their travel with the engine idling. Idle speed should not change. If it does, the cables may be routed incorrectly. Correct this condition before riding the bike.*

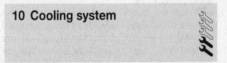

10 Cooling system

Note: *Three types of hose clamp are used on the various hoses across the range of models covered – the non-re-usable type,* the re-usable clip type and the screw type. A small screwdriver is required to release the non-reusable type and clip type clamps. Special pliers are required to close them, and these are available from automotive tool suppliers, or from BMW (part No. 131500), along with the clamps where new ones are required.

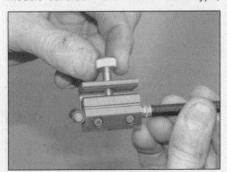

9.11b . . . and tighten the screw to seal it in . . .

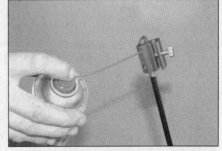

9.11c . . . then apply the lubricant using the nozzle provided, inserted in the hole in the adapter

10.2 Squeeze and flex the hoses to make sure they are neither cracked nor hardened

Check

⚠️ *Warning: The engine must be cool before beginning this procedure.*

1 On Funduro and ST models remove the fuel tank cover (see Chapter 8). On GS, Dakar and ST models remove the front side covers (see Chapter 8).

2 Check the entire cooling system for evidence of leaks. Examine each rubber coolant hose along its entire length. Look for cracks, abrasions and other damage. Squeeze each hose at various points to see whether they are dried out or hard **(see illustration)**. They should feel firm, yet pliable, and return to their original shape when released. If necessary, replace them with new ones (see Chapter 3).

3 Check each cooling system joint, the inlet and outlet unions on the engine, the thermostat housing, and around the pump on the left-hand side of the engine. Make sure all hose clips and joint screws are tight enough. If the pump is leaking around the cover or a detachable hose union is leaking around its flange, check that the bolts or screws are tight. If they are, remove the cover or union and replace the O-ring with a new one (see Chapter 3).

4 To prevent leakage of coolant from the cooling system to the lubrication system and vice versa, two seals are fitted on the pump shaft. On the bottom of the pump housing there is a drain hole **(see illustration)**. If either seal fails, the drain allows the coolant or oil to escape and prevents them mixing – tell-tale signs are a constantly dropping coolant

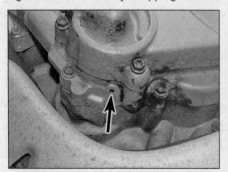

10.4 Check the drain hole (arrowed) for signs of leakage

level in the reservoir, and oil that has turned milky due to contamination by coolant. If on inspection the drain shows signs of leakage, remove the pump and replace the seals with new ones (see Chapter 3) – they come as a kit with a new shaft and impeller. If you find that the new seals do not last very long then you may need either a new clutch cover or at worst a new set of crankcases, as the bore in which the pump shaft runs could be worn oval or off-centre.

5 Check the radiator for leaks and other damage. Leaks in the radiator leave tell-tale scale deposits or coolant stains on the outside of the core below the leak. If leaks are noted, remove the radiator (see Chapter 3) and have it repaired or replace it with a new one – do not use a liquid leak stopping compound to try to repair leaks.

6 Check the radiator fins for mud, dirt and insects, which may impede the flow of air through the radiator. If the fins are dirty, remove the radiator (see Chapter 3) and clean it using water or low pressure compressed air directed through the fins from the inner side of the radiator. If the fins are bent or distorted, straighten them carefully with a screwdriver. If airflow is restricted by bent or damaged fins over more than 20% of the radiator's surface area, replace the radiator with a new one.

⚠️ *Warning: Do not remove the pressure cap when the engine is hot. It is good practice to cover the cap with a heavy cloth and turn the cap slowly anti-clockwise. If you hear a hissing sound (indicating that there is still pressure in the system), wait until it stops, then continue turning the cap until it can be removed.*

7 Remove the pressure cap from the radiator filler neck by turning it anti-clockwise until it reaches the stop. Now press down on the cap and continue turning it until it can be removed **(see illustration)**.

8 Check the condition of the coolant in the system. If it is rust-coloured or if accumulations of scale are visible, drain, flush and refill the system with new coolant (see below). Check the cap seal for cracks and other damage. If in doubt about the pressure cap's condition, have it tested by a BMW dealer or fit a new one.

10.7 Remove the pressure cap as described

9 Check the antifreeze content of the coolant with an antifreeze hydrometer. If the system has not been topped-up with the correct coolant mixture (see *Pre-ride checks*) the coolant will be too weak to offer adequate protection. If the hydrometer indicates a weak mixture, drain, flush and refill the system (see below).

10 Fit the cap by turning it clockwise until it reaches the first stop then push down on it and continue turning until it can turn no further. Start the engine and let it reach normal operating temperature, then check for leaks again. As the coolant temperature increases, the electric fan (mounted on the back of the radiator) should come on automatically and the temperature should begin to drop. If it does not, refer to Chapter 3 and check the fan and fan circuit carefully.

11 If the coolant level is consistently low, and no evidence of leaks can be found, have the entire system pressure checked by a BMW dealer.

Change the coolant

⚠️ *Warning: Allow the engine to cool completely before performing this maintenance operation. Also, don't allow anti-freeze to come into contact with your skin or the painted surfaces of the motorcycle. Rinse off spills immediately with plenty of water. Anti-freeze is highly toxic if ingested. Never leave anti-freeze lying around in an open container or in puddles on the floor; children and pets are attracted by its sweet smell and may drink it. Check with local authorities (councils) about disposing of anti-freeze. Many communities have collection centres which will see that anti-freeze is disposed of safely. Anti-freeze is also combustible, so don't store it near open flames.*

Draining

12 Support the motorcycle on its sidestand stand. On Funduro and ST models remove the fuel tank cover and the right-hand side cover (see Chapter 8). On GS, Dakar and CS models remove the left-hand front side cover (see Chapter 8).

13 Remove the pressure cap from the top of the filler neck by turning it anti-clockwise until it reaches a stop **(see illustration 10.7)**. If you hear a hissing sound (indicating there is still pressure in the system), wait until it stops. Now press down on the cap and continue turning until it can be removed. Also remove the coolant reservoir cap.

14 Position a suitable container beneath the water pump on the left-hand side of the engine. Unscrew the drain bolt and allow the coolant to completely drain from the system **(see illustrations)**. Retain the old sealing washer for use during flushing (if required). Move the bike off its stand and wiggle it about to release any more coolant. On GS, Dakar and CS models release the clamp and detach

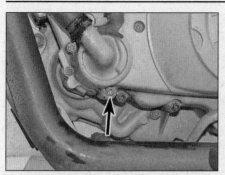

10.14a Unscrew the drain bolt (arrowed) . . .

10.14b . . . and allow the coolant to drain

10.14c Detach the hose from the frame for complete draining

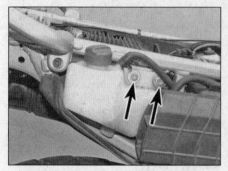

10.15a Reservoir screws (arrowed) – Funduro and ST

10.15b On GS, Dakar and CS draw the reservoir out . . .

10.15c . . . noting how the peg locates

the hose from the left-hand side of the frame to help drain the radiator **(see illustration)**. Refit the hose and secure it with the clamp, using a new one if necessary.

15 Undo the screw(s) securing the reservoir and displace it or draw it out (according to model, then remove the reservoir cap and drain the coolant into the container **(see illustrations)**. On GS, Dakar and CS note how the peg on the inner end of the reservoir locates in the grommet **(see illustration)**.

Flushing

Note: *Under normal circumstances, i.e. where the coolant has been regularly changed and the correct mixture used, flushing should not be necessary. However if the coolant has become contaminated with rust, dirt or oil, all of which will be evident when the system is drained, the system should be flushed.*

16 Flush the system with clean tap water by inserting a hose in the filler neck. Allow the water to run through the system until it is clear and flows out cleanly. If the radiator is extremely corroded, remove it (see Chapter 3) and have it cleaned by a specialist. Also flush the reservoir, then refit it.

17 Clean the drain hole in the water pump then install the drain bolt using the old sealing washer **(see illustration 10.14a)**.

18 Fill the cooling system with clean water mixed with a flushing compound **(see illustration 10.25)**. Make sure the flushing compound is compatible with aluminium components, and follow the manufacturer's instructions carefully. Fit the radiator cap.

19 Start the engine and allow it to reach normal operating temperature. Let it run for about ten minutes.

20 Stop the engine. Let it cool for a while, then cover the pressure cap with a heavy rag and turn it anti-clockwise to the first stop, releasing any pressure that may be present in the system. Once the hissing stops, push down on the cap and remove it completely.

21 Drain the system once again.

22 Fill the system with clean water and repeat Steps 19 to 21.

Refilling

23 Clean the drain bolt then fit it using a new sealing washer and tighten it to the torque setting specified at the beginning of the Chapter **(see illustration 10.14a)**.

24 Put the bike on its centrestand or on an auxiliary stand so it is upright. On GS, Dakar and CS slacken the bleed screw on the cylinder head and attach a hose to it, placing its end in a container **(see illustration)**.

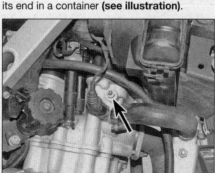

10.24 Slacken the bleed screw (arrowed)

25 Fill the system with the proper coolant mixture (see this Chapter's Specifications), on GS, Dakar and CS until it starts to come out of the bleed hole **(see illustration)**. **Note:** *Pour the coolant in slowly to minimise the amount of air entering the system.* Tap and squeeze the hoses to dislodge any trapped air. On GS, Dakar and CS when all air has been bled tighten the bleed screw and detach the hose. Top up the radiator if necessary to the top of the narrow section of the filler neck. Fill the reservoir to the FULL or MAX level line (see *Pre-ride checks*).

26 Cover the filler neck. Start the engine and allow it to idle for 2 to 3 minutes. Flick the throttle twistgrip part open 3 or 4 times, so that the engine speed rises to approximately 3000 to 4000 rpm, then stop the engine. Any air trapped in the system should bleed back to the filler neck.

27 If necessary, top up the coolant level to

10.25 Fill the system and bleed it as described

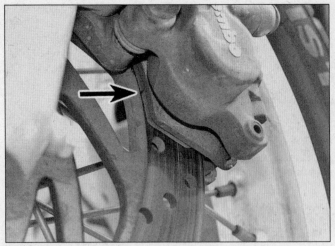
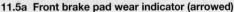

11.5a Front brake pad wear indicator (arrowed)

11.5b Rear brake pad wear indicator (arrowed)

the base of the filler neck, then fit the pressure cap. Also top up the coolant reservoir to the FULL or MAX level line, then fit the cap.

28 Start the engine and allow it to reach normal operating temperature, then shut it off. Let the engine cool then remove the pressure cap. Check that the coolant level is still up to the base of the radiator filler neck. If it's low, add the specified mixture until it reaches the base of the filler neck. Refit the cap.

29 Check the coolant level in the reservoir and top up if necessary.

30 Check the system for leaks. Install the fuel tank cover or left-hand front side cover (see Chapter 8).

31 Do not dispose of the old coolant by pouring it down the drain. Instead pour it into a heavy plastic container, cap it tightly and take it into an authorised disposal site or service station – see *Warning* above.

Hose renewal

32 The hoses will deteriorate with age and should be replaced with new ones at the specified interval regardless of their apparent condition (see Chapter 3).

11 Brake system

Brake system check

1 A routine general check of the brake system will ensure that any problems are discovered and remedied before the rider's safety is jeopardised.

2 Check the brake lever and pedal for loose fixings, improper or rough action, excessive play, bends, and other damage. Replace any damaged parts with new ones (see Chapter 6). Clean and lubricate the lever and pedal pivots if their action is stiff or rough (see Section 15).

3 Make sure all brake component fasteners are tight. Check the brake pads for wear (see below) and make sure the fluid level

in the reservoirs is correct (see *Pre-ride checks*). Look for leaks at the hose and pipe connections and check for cracks. On models with ABS remove the bodywork as required (see Chapter 8) and check the brake pipes, the pipe joints and the control unit for signs of fluid leakage and for any dents or cracks in the pipes. If the lever or pedal is spongy, bleed the brakes (see Chapter 7).

4 Make sure the brake light operates when the brake lever or pedal is applied. If it fails to operate properly, check the bulb and if necessary the switches (see Chapter 9).

Brake pad wear check

5 Each brake pad has wear indicators, in the form of cut-outs in the friction material on the front pads and a chamfered ledge on the rear pads. The wear indicators should be plainly visible by looking at the edges of the friction material from the best vantage point, but note that an accumulation of road dirt and brake dust could make them difficult to see **(see illustrations)**.

6 If the indicators aren't visible, then the amount of friction material remaining should be, and it will be obvious when the pads need replacing. BMW specify a minimum thickness of 1 mm for the friction material. **Note:** *Some after-market pads may use different indicators to those on the original equipment.*

7 If the pads are worn to the bottom of the cut-out on the front pads or to the beginning of the chamfered ledge on the rear pads, or there is little friction material remaining, they must be replaced with new ones, though it is advisable to fit new pads before they become this worn (see Chapter 7).

8 If the pads are dirty or if you are in doubt as to the amount of friction material remaining, remove them for inspection (see Chapter 7). If the pads are excessively worn, check the brake discs (see Chapter 7).

Brake fluid change

9 The brake fluid should be changed at the prescribed interval or whenever a master

cylinder or caliper overhaul is carried out. Refer to Chapter 7, Section 12 for details. Ensure that all the old fluid is pumped from the hydraulic system and that the level in the fluid reservoir is checked and the brakes tested before riding the motorcycle.

Brake hoses

10 The hoses deteriorate with age and should be replaced with new ones when necessary (see Chapter 7).

11 Always replace the banjo union sealing washers with new ones when fitting new hoses. Refill the system with new brake fluid and bleed the system as described in Chapter 7.

Brake caliper and master cylinder seals

12 Brake system seals will deteriorate with age and lose their effectiveness, leading to sticky operation of the brake master cylinders or the pistons in the brake calipers, or fluid loss. They should be replaced with new ones at the prescribed interval and particularly if fluid leakage or a sticking action is apparent – check with your dealer as to the availability of replacement seal kits or individual parts before disassembling the brakes (see Chapter 7).

12 Wheels, wheel bearings and tyres

Wire spoke wheels

1 Visually check the spokes for damage and corrosion. A broken or bent spoke must be replaced with a new one immediately because the load taken by it will be transferred to adjacent spokes which may in turn fail. Check the tension in each spoke by tapping each one lightly with a screwdriver and noting the sound produced – each should make the same sound of the correct pitch. Properly tensioned spokes will make a sharp pinging sound, loose ones will produce a lower pitch dull sound and tight ones will be higher pitched. If a spoke needs adjustment turn the adjuster at the rim using a spoke adjustment tool or an open-ended spanner (see illustration).

2 Unevenly tensioned spokes will promote rim misalignment – refer to information on wheel runout in Chapter 7 and seek the advice of a BMW dealer or wheel building specialist if the wheel needs realigning, which it may well do if many spokes are unevenly tensioned. Check front and rear wheel alignment as described in Chapter 7.

Cast wheels

3 Cast wheels as fitted to CS models are virtually maintenance free, but they should be kept clean and checked periodically for cracks and other damage. Also check the wheel runout and alignment (see Chapter 7). Never attempt to repair damaged cast wheels; they must be renewed if damaged. Check that the wheel balance weights are fixed firmly to the wheel rim. If you suspect that a weight has fallen off, have the wheel rebalanced by a motorcycle tyre specialist.

Tyres

4 Check the tyre condition and tread depth thoroughly – see *Pre-ride checks*.
5 Make sure the valve cap is in place and tight. Check the valve for signs of damage. If tyre deflation occurs and it is not due to a slow puncture the valve core may be loose or it could be leaking past the seal – remove the cap and make sure the core is tight; if it is, simply unscrew the core from the valve housing using a core removal tool and thread a new one in its place.

 HAYNES HiNT *A valve core tool can be made quite easily by cutting a slot into the threaded end of a bolt using a hacksaw – the bolt must fit inside the valve housing and the slot must be deep enough to locate around the flat sides of the core and grip it.*

Wheel bearings

6 Wheel bearings will wear over a considerable mileage and should be checked periodically to avoid handling problems.
7 Support the motorcycle upright using an auxiliary stand so that the wheel being examined is off the ground. When checking the front wheel bearings turn the handlebars to full lock on one side so you have something to push against. Check for any play in the bearings by pushing and pulling the wheel against the hub (see illustration). Also rotate the wheel and check that it turns smoothly and without any grating noises.
8 If any play is detected in the hub, or if the wheel does not rotate smoothly (and this is not due to brake or drive chain drag), the wheel should be removed and the bearings inspected for wear or damage (see Chapter 7). Note that

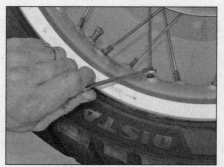

12.1 Turn the adjuster to increase or decrease tension

on CS models the rear wheel bearings are contained in the swingarm, not the wheel.

13 Suspension

1 The suspension components must be maintained in top operating condition to ensure rider safety. Loose, worn or damaged suspension parts decrease the motorcycle's stability and control.

Front suspension check

2 While standing alongside the motorcycle, apply the front brake and push on the handlebars to compress the forks several times (see illustration). See if they move up-and-down smoothly without binding. If binding is felt, the forks should be disassembled and inspected (see Chapter 6).
3 Inspect the fork inner tubes for scratches, corrosion and pitting which will cause premature seal failure – if the damage is excessive, new tubes should be installed (see Chapter 6). Minor rust spots can be treated and cleaned up using a whetstone.
4 Inspect the fork inner tube just above the dust seal for signs of oil leakage, then carefully lever the seal up using a flat-bladed screwdriver and inspect the area around the fork seal (see illustration). If leakage is evident, the seals must be replaced with new ones (see Chapter 6). If there is evidence of corrosion between the seal retaining ring and its groove in the fork outer tube spray the

13.2 Compress the forks as described

12.7 Checking for play in the front wheel bearings

ring and groove with a penetrative lubricant, otherwise the ring will be difficult to remove if needed, and fit a new dust seal – wipe any lubricant off the inner tube and from the top of the oil seal. Press the dust seal back into the fork outer tube on completion.
5 Check the tightness of all suspension nuts and bolts to be sure none have worked loose, referring to the torque settings specified at the beginning of Chapter 6.

Rear suspension check

6 Inspect the rear shock absorber for fluid leakage and tightness of its mountings. If leakage is found, the shock must be replaced with a new one (see Chapter 6).
7 With the aid of an assistant to support the bike, compress the rear suspension several times. It should move up and down freely without binding. If any binding is felt, the worn or faulty component must be identified and checked (see Chapter 6). The problem could be due to either the shock absorber, the suspension linkage components or the swingarm components.
8 Support the motorcycle on an auxiliary stand so that the rear wheel is off the ground. Grab the swingarm and rock it from side-to-side – there should be no discernible movement at the rear (see illustration). If there's a little movement or a slight clicking can be heard, inspect the tightness of all the swingarm and rear suspension mounting bolts and nuts, referring to the torque settings specified at the beginning of Chapter 6, and re-check for movement.

13.4 Check the inner tubes and seals for corrosion and signs of oil leakage

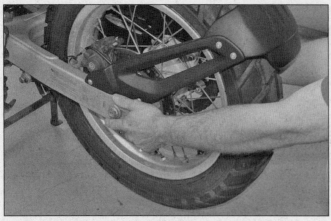

13.8 Checking for play in the swingarm bearings

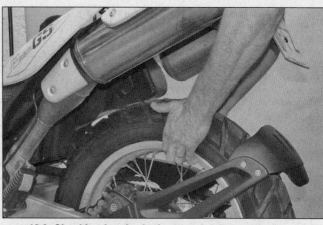

13.9 Checking for play in the rear shock mountings and suspension linkage bearings

9 Next, grasp the top of the rear wheel and pull it upwards – there should be no discernible freeplay before the shock absorber begins to compress **(see illustration)**. Any freeplay felt in either check indicates worn bearings in the suspension linkage or swingarm, or worn shock absorber mountings. The worn components must be identified and replaced with new ones (see Chapter 6).

10 To make an accurate assessment of the swingarm bearings, remove the rear wheel (see Chapter 7) and the bolts securing the suspension linkage rods to the swingarm (see Chapter 6). Grasp the rear of the swingarm with one hand and place your other hand at the junction of the swingarm and the frame. Try to move the rear of the swingarm from side-to-side. Any wear (play) in the bearings should be felt as movement between the swingarm and the frame at the front. If there is any play the swingarm will be felt to move forward and backward at the front (not from side-to-side). Next, move the swingarm up and down through its full travel. It should move freely, without any binding or rough spots. If there is any play in the swingarm or if it does not move freely, remove the bearings for inspection (see Chapter 6).

Front fork oil change

11 The fork oil will degrade over a period of time and lose its damping qualities. On Funduro, ST and Dakar models BMW specify

14.4 Checking for play in the steering head bearings

a fork oil change as a service item at a particular interval. On GS and CS models it is not specified as a service item, though is advisable after a high mileage and/or period of a few years. The forks on GS models are fitted with drain screws which makes the procedure easy (same as for the Dakar model). Drain screws are not fitted on CS models, so if an oil change is being done it is necessary to remove and partially strip the fork. Refer to Chapter 6, Section 7 for details.

Rear suspension bearing lubrication

12 Over time the grease in the bearings will be washed out or will harden allowing the ingress of dirt and water. The swingarm and linkage must be removed so the bearings can be cleaned and re-greased or replaced with new ones if necessary (see Chapter 6).

14 Steering head bearings

Freeplay check and adjustment

1 Steering head bearings can become dented, rough or loose during normal use of the machine. In extreme cases, worn or loose steering head bearings can cause steering wobble – a condition that is potentially

14.7 Slacken the fork clamp bolt (arrowed) on each side

dangerous. Bearings that are too tight will cause handling problems.

Check

2 Raise the front wheel off the ground using an auxiliary stand placed under the engine – make sure it is the engine that takes the weight, not the exhaust system or any other component. Always make sure that the bike is properly supported and secure.

3 Point the front wheel straight-ahead and slowly move the handlebars from lock to lock. Any notchiness or roughness will be felt, in which case new bearings should be fitted, assuming they are not too tight (see Chapter 6). If the bearings are too tight the bars will not move smoothly and freely, in which case they need to loosened. Again point the wheel straight-ahead, and tap the front of the wheel to one side. The wheel should 'fall' under its own weight to the limit of its lock, indicating that the bearings are not too tight (take into account the restriction that cables and wiring may have). Check for similar movement to the other side.

4 Next, grasp the bottom of the forks and gently pull and push them forward and backward **(see illustration)**. Any looseness or freeplay in the steering head bearings will be felt as front-to-rear movement of the forks. If play is felt, tighten the bearings as described below.

> **HAYNES HINT** *Make sure you are not mistaking any movement between the bike and stand, or between the stand and the ground, for freeplay in the bearings. Do not pull and push the forks too hard – a gentle movement is all that is needed. Freeplay between the fork tubes due to worn bushes can also be misinterpreted as steering head bearing play – do not confuse the two.*

Adjustment

Special tool: *On Funduro and ST models a suitably sized C-spanner is useful for this procedure. On GS and Dakar models a special socket (BMW part No. 316521) or a suitable*

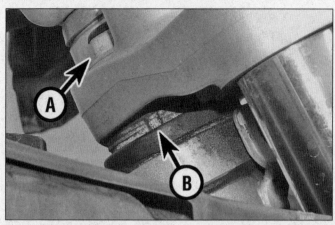

14.8 Slacken the stem nut (A) then use a C-spanner located in one of the notches (B) in the adjuster

14.9a Unscrew the stem nut . . .

home-made equivalent is required to tighten the adjuster to the specified torque setting.

5 As a precaution, on Funduro and ST models remove the fairing and the fuel tank cover, and on GS, Dakar and CS models remove the top cover and front side covers (see Chapter 8) – this prevents the possibility of damage to paintwork should a tool slip.

6 On Funduro, ST, GS and Dakar models displace the handlebars from the top yoke (see Chapter 6).

7 On all models slacken the fork clamp bolts in the top yoke (see illustration).

8 On Funduro and ST models slacken the steering stem nut (see illustration). Using a thin C-spanner or a drift located in one of the notches in the adjuster nut, either slacken or tighten the nut a little at a time until the bearings are correctly adjusted as described in Steps 2 to 4. Turn the steering from lock to lock a few times to settle the bearings, then recheck the adjustment. On completion tighten the steering stem nut to the torque setting specified at the beginning of the Chapter. Tighten the fork clamp bolts to the specified torque (see illustration 14.7). Check

14.9b . . . and displace the top yoke

14.9c Counter-hold the rim of the adjuster and unscrew the threaded tube in its centre

the bearing adjustment again as described above and re-adjust if necessary.

9 On GS and Dakar models unscrew the steering stem nut (see illustration). Gently ease the top yoke up off the forks and position it clear of the head bearings, using a rag to protect other components (see illustrations). Counter-hold the adjuster using a strap and unscrew the threaded tube (see

illustration). Slacken the adjuster using the special tool, then tighten it to the initial setting specified at the beginning of the Chapter (see illustrations). Turn the steering from lock-to-lock twice to settle the bearings, then position it at full left lock. Now slacken the adjuster by 60° (1/6th of a turn), using either a degree disc, or by marking a 40 mm arc using sticky tape or paint marks (see illustration).

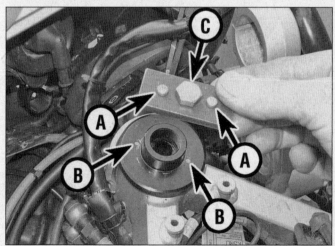

14.9d A tool can be made as shown – locate the lower ends of the small bolts (A) in the holes (B) in the adjuster and turn the tool using the large bolt head (C)

14.9e Paint marks (arrowed) can be used to mark the arc through which the adjuster must be slackened

14.9f Fit the threaded tube into the adjuster and tighten it as described

14.9g Fit the steering stem nut . . .

Check the mating surfaces of the top yoke and the adjuster and clean off any abrasion using a whetstone, then clean the surfaces. Fit the threaded tube (see illustration). Counter-hold the adjuster using a strap, and tighten the tube to the specified torque (see illustration 14.9c). Fit the top yoke onto the steering stem (see illustration 14.9b). Fit the steering stem nut and tighten it to the specified torque setting

14.9h . . . and tighten it to the specified torque

(see illustrations). Tighten the fork clamp bolts to the specified torque (see illustration 14.7). Check the bearing adjustment again as described above and re-adjust if necessary.
10 On CS models slacken the steering stem adjuster clamp bolt in the top yoke (see illustration). Remove the plug from the adjuster and slacken the adjuster, then tighten it to the initial setting specified at the beginning of the Chapter (see illustration). Turn the steering from lock-to-lock twice to settle the bearings, then position it at full left lock. Now slacken the adjuster by 60° (1/6th of a turn), using either a degree disc, or by making two marks, one on the adjuster and one 60° (1/6th of a turn) anti-clockwise from it on the top yoke, then bringing them into alignment. Tighten the steering stem clamp bolt and the fork clamp bolts in the top yoke to the specified torque (see illustrations 14.10a and 14.7). Check the bearing adjustment again as described above and re-adjust if necessary. Fit the plug into the adjuster (see illustration 14.10b).

11 The object is to set the adjuster so that the bearings are under a very light loading, just enough to remove any freeplay, but not so much that the steering does not move freely from side-to-side as described in the check procedure above. On GS, Dakar and CS models do not rely on the angle method alone and assume the loading to be correct – check the physical feel as described as well and make minor adjustments as required. Turn the adjuster only a little at a time, and after each adjustment repeat the checks outlined in Steps 2, 3 and 4.
Caution: Take great care not to apply excessive pressure because this will cause premature failure of the bearings.
12 If the bearings cannot be correctly adjusted, or after correct adjustment do still not feel free and smooth, disassemble the steering head and check the bearings and races, re-greasing them or replacing them with new ones as required (see Chapter 6).
13 On Funduro, ST, GS and Dakar models fit the handlebars (see Chapter 6).

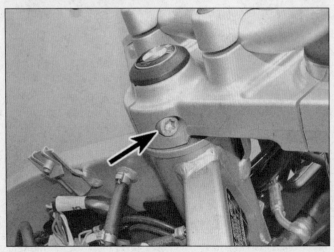

14.10a Slacken the adjuster clamp bolt (arrowed)

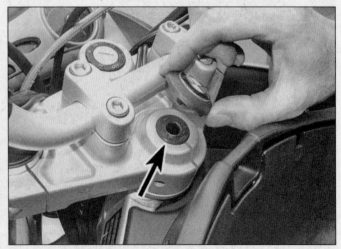

14.10b Remove the plug and turn the adjuster (arrowed) as described

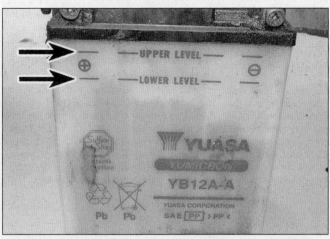

17.2 The levels should be between the UPPER and LOWER level lines (arrowed) – the battery shown has been severely neglected with only one cell anywhere near the correct level

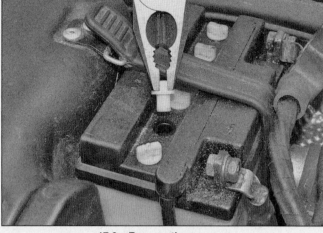

17.3a Remove the caps . . .

14 Check the bearing adjustment as described above and re-adjust if necessary.
15 Install the bodywork (see Chapter 8).

Lubrication

16 Over time the grease in the bearings will be dispersed or will harden allowing the ingress of dirt and water.
17 The steering head should be disassembled periodically and the bearings cleaned and re-greased (see Chapter 6).

15 General lubrication

1 Since the controls, stands, footrests and various other components of a motorcycle are exposed to the elements, they should be checked and lubricated periodically to ensure safe and trouble-free operation.
2 The footrest pivots, clutch and brake lever pivots, brake pedal and gearchange lever pivots and linkage and sidestand and centrestand pivot should be lubricated frequently.
3 In order for the lubricant to be applied where it will do the most good, the component should be disassembled (see Chapter 6). The lubricant recommended by BMW for each application is listed at the beginning of the Chapter. If an aerosol lubricant is used, it can be applied to the pivot joint gaps and will usually work its way into the areas where friction occurs, so less disassembly of the component is needed (however it is always better to do so and clean off all corrosion, dirt and old lubricant first). If motor oil or light grease is being used, apply it sparingly as it may attract dirt (which could cause the controls to bind or wear at an accelerated rate).
4 The stands are equipped with grease nipples to which a grease gun can be applied – squirt the grease in until it begins to ooze out the side of the pivot, then wipe the excess off.

16 Nuts and bolts

1 Since vibration of the machine tends to loosen fasteners, all nuts, bolts, screws, etc. should be periodically checked for proper tightness.
2 Pay particular attention to the following, referring to the relevant Chapter:
● Spark plug(s)
● Oil and coolant drain bolts
● Lever and pedal bolts
● Footrest and stand bolts
● Engine mounting bolts
● Shock absorber and suspension linkage bolts; swingarm pivot bolt and nut
● Handlebar clamp bolts
● Front fork clamp bolts (top and bottom yoke) and fork top bolts
● Steering stem nut (clamp bolt on CS model)
● Front axle and axle clamp bolts
● Rear axle nut
● Front and rear sprocket/pulley nuts
● Brake caliper and master cylinder mounting bolts
● Brake hose banjo bolts and caliper bleed valves

● Brake disc bolts
● Exhaust system bolts/nuts
3 If a torque wrench is available, use it along with the torque settings given at the beginning of this and other Chapters.

17 Battery

Note: *Standard type batteries are fitted to all models. It is possible however that the standard battery has been replaced with a maintenance free (MF) battery at some point, in which case see Step 10 only. The batteries are easy to distinguish – standard ones have removable caps across the top, while MF batteries do not, and are usually marked MF on the front.*

Conventional battery

1 Remove the battery (see Chapter 9).
2 The electrolyte level is visible through the translucent battery case – it should be between the UPPER and LOWER level marks **(see illustration)**.
3 If the electrolyte is low, remove the cell caps and fill each cell to the upper level mark with distilled water **(see illustrations)**. Do not use tap water (except in an emergency), and do

17.3b . . . and add distilled water as required to the necessary cells . . .

17.3c . . . until all are at the correct level

not overfill. The cell holes are quite small, so it may help to use a clean plastic squeeze bottle with a small spout to add the water. Fit the cell caps **(see illustration)**.

4 The battery case should be kept clean to prevent current leakage, which can discharge the battery over a period of time (especially when it sits unused). Wash the outside of the case with a solution of baking soda and water. Rinse the battery thoroughly, then dry it.

5 Look for cracks in the case and replace the battery if any are found. If acid has been spilled on the frame or battery box, neutralise it with a baking soda and water solution, dry it thoroughly, then touch up any damaged paint.

6 If the motorcycle sits unused for long periods of time, remove the battery and charge it once every month to six weeks (see Chapter 9).

7 The condition of the battery can be assessed by measuring its specific gravity and open-circuit voltage (see Chapter 9).

8 Check the battery terminals and leads for tightness and corrosion. If corrosion is evident, clean the terminals and lead ends with a wire brush or knife and emery paper. Apply a thin coat of petroleum jelly (Vaseline) or a dedicated battery terminal spray to the connections to slow further corrosion.

9 Install the battery (see Chapter 9).

Maintenance-free (MF) battery

10 If a sealed MF battery has been fitted all that should be done is to check that the terminals are clean and tight and that the casing is not damaged or leaking. See Chapter 9 for further details. **Note:** *Do not attempt to remove the battery caps to check the electrolyte level or battery specific gravity. Removal will damage the caps, resulting in electrolyte leakage and battery damage.*

Chapter 2
Engine, clutch and transmission

Contents

Degrees of difficulty

Easy, suitable for novice with little experience | **Fairly easy,** suitable for beginner with some experience 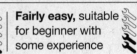 | **Fairly difficult,** suitable for competent DIY mechanic | **Difficult,** suitable for experienced DIY mechanic | **Very difficult,** suitable for expert DIY or professional

Specifications

General

Type . . . . Four-stroke single
Capacity . . . . 652 cc
Bore . . . . 100 mm
Stroke. . . . . 83 mm
Compression ratio
  Funduro and ST . . . . 9.7 to 1
  GS, Dakar and CS . . . . 11.5 to 1
Camshafts . . . . DOHC, chain-driven
Clutch. . . . . Wet multi-plate
Transmission. . . . . Five-speed constant mesh
Final drive
  Funduro, ST, GS and Dakar . . . . Chain
  CS. . . . . Belt
Cooling system. . . . . Liquid cooled
Lubrication . . . . Dry sump, 2 trochoid pumps

Camshafts and followers

	Standard	Service limit (min)
Camshaft lobe height		
Funduro and ST – intake and exhaust	39.838 to 39.938 mm	39.7 mm
GS, Dakar, and CS (2000 to 2003)		
Intake	39.35 to 39.45 mm	39.25 mm
Exhaust	39.15 to 39.25 mm	39.05 mm
GS, Dakar, and CS (2004-on) – intake and exhaust	40.37 to 40.47 mm	40.27 mm
Camshaft journal diameter	21.967 to 21.980 mm	21.95 mm
Camshaft holder bore diameter (max)	22.040 mm	
Oil clearance		
Standard	0.020 to 0.060 mm	
Service limit (max)	0.090 mm	
Follower diameter (min)	33.4 mm	
Follower bore diameter (max)	33.6 mm	

Valves, guides and springs

Valve clearances.	see Chapter 1	
Valve diameter		
Intake	36 mm	
Exhaust.	31 mm	
Valve 'wobble' in guide (see Section 11)	0.4 mm max.	

	Standard	Service limit
Stem diameter		
Funduro and ST		
Intake valve.	5.960 to 5.975 mm	5.950 mm(min)
Exhaust valve	5.945 to 5.960 mm	5.935 mm (min)
GS, Dakar and CS – intake and exhaust valves.	4.90 to 4.94 mm	4.89 mm (min)
Guide bore diameter		
Funduro and ST – intake and exhaust valves.	6.006 to 6.018 mm	6.080 mm (max)
GS, Dakar and CS – intake and exhaust valves.	5.006 to 5.018 mm	5.080 mm (max)
Stem-to-guide clearance		
Intake valve.	0.016 to 0.058 mm	0.130 mm
Exhaust valve	0.031 to 0.073 mm	0.145 mm
Valve guide projection above head		
Funduro and ST		
Intake valve.	max 15.4 mm	
Exhaust valve	max 17.9 mm	
GS, Dakar and CS	9.8 to 10.2 mm	

	Standard	Service limit
Seat width		
Funduro and ST		
Intake	1.05 to 1.35 mm	1.60 mm
Exhaust.	1.25 to 1.55 mm	1.80 mm
GS, Dakar and CS		
Intake	1.05 to 1.35 mm	1.60 mm
Exhaust.	1.25 to 1.55 mm	2.20 mm
Valve spring free length		
Funduro and ST	45.7 mm	44.5 mm (min)
GS, Dakar and CS (2000 to 2003)	40.5 mm	39.0 mm (min)
GS, Dakar and CS (2004-on)	46.37 mm	44.80 mm (min)
Stem runout	0.01 mm (max)	0.05 mm (max)

Cylinder bore

Bore (measured 60 mm below top edge, across three points)		
Tolerance group A		
Standard.	100.000 to 100.012 mm	
Service limit (max).	100.03 mm	
Tolerance group B		
Standard.	100.012 to 100.024 mm	
Service limit (max).	100.04 mm	

Piston

	Standard	Service limit
Piston diameter (measured 16 mm up from skirt, at 90° to piston pin axis)		
Tolerance group A.	99.975 to 99.985 mm	99.940 mm (min)
Tolerance group B	99.985 to 99.995 mm	99.950 mm (min)
Piston-to-bore clearance	0.015 to 0.040 mm	0.090 mm (max)
Piston ring groove width (max)		
Top ring		
Funduro and ST	1.35 mm	
GS, Dakar and CS	1.3 mm	
Second ring		
Funduro and ST	1.35 mm	
GS, Dakar and CS	1.6 mm	
Oil control ring		
Funduro and ST	2.6 mm	
GS, Dakar and CS	2.6 mm	
Piston pin diameter		
Standard.	21.996 to 22.000 mm	
Service limit (min)	21.98 mm	
Piston pin clearance		
In piston		
Standard.	0.012 to 0.021 mm	
Service limit (max).	0.05 mm	
In connecting rod small-end		
Standard.	0.015 to 0.029 mm	
Service limit (max).	0.05 mm	

Piston rings

	Standard	Service limit
Ring end gap (installed – all rings)	0.20 to 0.40 mm	1.0 mm (max)
Ring-to-groove clearance (all rings)	0.030 to 0.065 mm	0.150 mm (max)
Ring thickness		
Top ring	1.2 mm	1.15 mm (min)
Middle ring		
Funduro and ST	1.2 mm	1.15 mm (min)
GS, Dakar and CS	1.5 mm	1.45 mm (min)

Clutch

	Standard
Friction plate thickness	3.45 to 3.55 mm
Minimum thickness of all friction plates together	
Funduro and ST	24.0 mm
GS, Dakar and CS	27.5 mm
Plain plate warpage (max)	0.15 mm

Oil pump

	Standard
Oil pressure (oil @ 80°C)	
At idle speed	min 7.5 psi (0.5 Bar)
At 4500 rpm	65 psi (4.5 Bar)
Inner-to-outer rotor clearance (max)	0.25 mm
Outer rotor-to-housing clearance (max)	0.25 mm

Selector drum and forks

	Standard
Selector fork end thickness (min)	3.45 mm
Selector fork guide pin OD (min)	5.85 mm

Transmission

	Standard
Gear ratios (no. of teeth)	
Primary reduction	1.946 to 1 (72/37)
1st gear	2.750 to 1 (33/12)
2nd gear	1.750 to 1 (28/16)
3rd gear	1.313 to 1 (21/16)
4th gear	1.045 to 1 (23/22)
5th gear	0.875 to 1 (21/24)
Input shaft diameter at right-hand bearing seat (min)	24.98 mm
Input shaft diameter at left-hand bearing seat (min)	16.98 mm
Output shaft diameter at right-hand bearing seat (min)	16.98 mm
Output shaft diameter at left-hand bearing seat (min)	24.97 mm

Crankshaft and bearings

	Standard
End-float	0.1 to 0.3 mm
Main bearing oil clearance	
Standard	0.03 to 0.07 mm
Service limit (max)	0.10 mm
Main bearing journal diameter (min)	45.975 mm
Main bearing bore diameter (max)	46.08 mm
Runout (max)	0.05 mm

Balancer shaft

	Standard
End-float	0.1 to 0.3 mm
Journal diameter (min)	19.96 mm

Torque settings

Cam chain tensioner blade pivot bolt	10 Nm
Cam chain tensioner cap bolt	40 Nm
Camshaft holder bolts	10 Nm
Camshaft sprocket bolt	60 Nm
Clutch nut	140 Nm
Clutch spring bolts	10 Nm
Crankcase bolts	
Funduro and ST	10 Nm
GS, Dakar and CS – 2000 to 2003	10 Nm
GS, Dakar and CS – 2004-on	12 Nm
Cylinder block bolts	10 Nm
Cylinder head 10 mm nuts	
Initial setting	20 Nm
Final setting	
Funduro and ST	50 Nm
GS, Dakar and CS	60 Nm

Torque settings (continued)

Cylinder head 8 mm bolts	
Funduro and ST	28 Nm
GS, Dakar and CS (2000 to 2003)	33 Nm
GS, Dakar and CS (2004-on)	30 Nm
Cylinder head 6 mm bolts	10 Nm
Engine mountings – Funduro and ST	not available
Engine mountings	
GS and Dakar	
Adjuster	5 Nm max.
Adjuster locknut	100 Nm
Upper mounting bolts	41 Nm
Rear mounting bolt	41 Nm
Front mounting bolt	41 Nm
Front frame section-to-main frame	
2000 to 2003 models	21 Nm
2004-on models	24 Nm
Front frame section-to-bottom section	21 Nm
Bottom frame section-to-main frame	21 Nm
CS	
Adjuster	5 Nm max.
Adjuster locknut	100 Nm
Upper mounting bolts	41 Nm
Rear mounting bolt	50 Nm
Front mounting bolt	55 Nm
Front frame section-to-main frame	24 Nm
Front frame section-to-bottom section	55 Nm
Bottom frame section-to-main frame	55 Nm
Oil pump cover screws	6 Nm
Primary drive gear nut	180 Nm
Swingarm pivot bolt nut	100 Nm
Starter clutch bolts	
Funduro and ST	10 Nm
GS, Dakar and CS	35 Nm
Valve cover bolts	10 Nm

1 General information

The engine is a liquid-cooled single cylinder. The four valves are operated by double overhead camshafts which are chain driven off the left-hand end of the crankshaft. The engine/transmission is a unit assembly constructed from aluminium alloy. The crankcase divides vertically.

The crankcase incorporates a dry sump, pressure-fed lubrication system which uses two dual rotor trochoidal oil pumps that are gear-driven off the back of the clutch. The system has an oil strainer in the pick-up for the oil return (scavenge) pump, an oil filter, an oil pressure switch off the main gallery, and two sprung ball valves.

The alternator is on the right-hand end of the crankshaft and the rotor carries the starter clutch and the ignition timing triggers. The water pump is on the left-hand side of the engine, and is driven by the balancer shaft that sits at the front of the engine.

Power from the crankshaft is routed to the transmission via the clutch. The clutch is of the wet, multi-plate type and is gear-driven off the crankshaft. The clutch is operated by cable. The transmission is a five-speed constant-mesh unit. Final drive to the rear wheel is by chain and sprockets on Funduro, ST, GS and Dakar models, and by belt and pulleys on CS models.

2 Component access

Operations possible with the engine in the frame

The components and assemblies listed below can be removed without having to remove the engine from the frame. If however, a number of areas require attention at the same time, removal of the engine is recommended.

Valve cover
Cam chain tensioner and blades
Camshafts
Cam chain
Cylinder head
Cylinder block
Piston
Clutch
Alternator/starter clutch
Oil filter
Oil pumps
Primary drive gear
Starter motor
Water pump

Operations requiring engine removal

It is necessary to remove the engine from the frame to gain access to the following components.

Crankshaft and bearings
Balancer shaft and bearings
Gearchange mechanism
Selector drum and forks
Transmission shafts

3 Engine wear assessment

Cylinder compression check

Special tool: *A compression gauge is needed – they are available from good automotive tool suppliers. Get the type that threads into the spark plug hole (make sure it comes with an adapter with the same thread size and reach as the spark plug – it is very important the reach is not longer as the piston could contact it). Depending on the outcome of the initial test, a squirt-type oil can may also be needed.*
1 Poor engine performance may be caused by leaking valves, incorrect valve clearances, a leaking head gasket, or worn piston, piston rings or cylinder wall. A cylinder compression

3.4a Check the thread size and reach of the adapter – the adapter shown covers two thread sizes, but the total reach is the same as that of the plug

3.4b Thread the adapter into the plug hole and the gauge into the adapter

check will highlight these conditions and can also indicate the presence of excessive carbon deposits in the cylinder head, and a leakdown test (for which special equipment is needed – consult a BMW dealer) will pinpoint the actual cause(s) of the problem.

2 Start by making sure the valve clearances are correctly set (see Chapter 1) and that the cylinder head bolts are tightened to the correct torque setting (see Section 11).

3 Run the engine until it is at normal operating temperature. Disconnect the primary wiring connector from each ignition coil (see Chapter 5). Remove the spark plug (the outer one on dual spark models) (see Chapter 1).

4 Check that the gauge adapter thread size and reach is the same as the spark plug **(see illustration)**. Thread the adapter into the spark plug hole, then thread the gauge onto the adapter **(see illustration)**.

5 With the throttle held fully open, turn the engine over on the starter motor until the gauge reading has built up and stabilised **(see illustration)**.

6 Note the reading on the gauge. BMW do not specify a compression figure, but the Funduro model we tested showed 75 psi.

7 If the reading is lower, it could be due to a worn cylinder bore, piston or rings, failure of the head gasket, or worn valve seats. To determine which is the cause, pour a small quantity of engine oil into the spark plug hole to seal the rings, then repeat the compression test. If the figures are noticeably higher the cause is a worn cylinder, piston or rings. If there is no change the cause is a leaking head gasket or worn valve seats.

8 If the reading is much higher there could be a build-up of carbon deposits in the combustion chamber, or the cylinder head gasket is too thin. Remove the cylinder head and scrape all deposits off the piston and the cylinder head, and on installation fit a new gasket.

Engine oil pressure check

Special tool: *An oil pressure gauge and*

adapter (which screws into the main oil gallery) are needed – they are available from good automotive tool suppliers.

9 If there is any doubt about the performance of the engine lubrication system an oil pressure check must be carried out. The check provides useful information about the state of wear of the engine.

10 The oil pressure warning light should come on when the ignition switch is turned ON and extinguish a few seconds after the engine is started. If the oil pressure light comes on whilst the engine is running, low oil pressure is indicated – stop the engine immediately and check the oil level (see *Pre-ride checks*). If the oil level is good an oil pressure check must be carried out.

11 Warm the engine up to normal operating temperature then stop it.

12 Remove the oil pressure switch (see Chapter 9) and screw the gauge adapter in its place. Connect the oil pressure gauge to the adapter.

13 Start the engine and allow it idle, and note the reading on the gauge. Briefly increase the engine speed to 4500 rpm and again note the gauge reading. In each case the oil pressure should be similar to that given in the Specifications at the start of this Chapter.

14 If the pressure is significantly lower than

3.5 Allow the reading to build up and stabilise

the standard, either the pressure relief valve is stuck open, an oil pump or its drive mechanism is faulty, the oil strainer or filter is blocked, or there is other engine damage. Also make sure the correct grade oil is being used. Begin diagnosis by checking the oil filter, strainer and relief valve, then the oil pumps (see Section 18). If those items check out okay, chances are the bearing oil clearances are excessive and the engine needs to be overhauled.

15 If the pressure is too high, either an oil passage is clogged, the relief valve is stuck closed or the wrong grade of oil is being used.

16 Stop the engine. Unscrew the gauge and adapter from the crankcase and install the oil pressure switch (see Chapter 9).

 Warning: Be careful when removing the pressure gauge adapter as the engine will be hot.

4 Engine removal and installation

Caution: The engine is heavy. Engine removal and installation should be carried out with the aid of at least one assistant; personal injury or damage could occur if the engine falls or is dropped.

Removal

All models

Note: *Three types of hose clamp are used on the various hoses across the range of models covered – the non-re-usable type, the re-usable clip type and the screw type. A small screwdriver is required to release the non-reusable type and clip type clamps. Special pliers are required to close them, and these are available from automotive tool suppliers, or from BMW (part No. 131500), along with the clamps where new ones are required.*

4.6 Pull the caps off the plugs and secure them clear

1 Support the bike upright on level ground, on the centrestand if it has one, or using an auxiliary stand or stands that supports the bike through the frame – you cannot use the swingarm for support as it pivots through the back of the engine. Work can be made easier by raising the machine to a suitable working height on an hydraulic ramp or a suitable platform. Make sure the motorcycle is secure and will not topple over (also see *Tools and Workshop Tips* in the Reference section). Tie the front brake lever to the handlebar so the front wheel is locked.

2 On Funduro and ST models remove the fairing, side covers, fuel tank cover and sump guard (see Chapter 8). On GS and Dakar models remove the front side covers, top cover and sump guard (see Chapter 8). On CS models remove the front side covers and frame covers (see Chapter 8).

3 If the engine is dirty, particularly around its mountings, wash it thoroughly. This will make work much easier and rule out the possibility of caked on lumps of dirt falling into some vital component.

4 Drain the engine oil and coolant (see Chapter 1). If required remove the oil filter (see Chapter 1).

5 Before and during the removal procedure, make a careful note of the routing of all cables, wiring and hoses and of any ties, clips or clamps that secure or guide them, and the positions of all nuts, bolts and washers, so everything can be returned to its original location. Keep nuts, bolts and washers with the parts they secure. Use a digital camera if available to take as many pictures as you need to record things that you may otherwise forget in between removing and installing the engine.

Funduro and ST models

6 Disconnect the negative (–ve) lead from the battery (see Chapter 9). Pull the caps off the spark plugs, noting which fits where **(see illustration)**.

7 Remove the fuel tank (see Chapter 4A).

8 Remove the radiator along with its hoses, noting their routing (see Chapter 3).

9 Remove the exhaust downpipe (see Chapter 4A).

10 Detach the oil feed and return hoses from the frame and the oil tank breather hose from the valve cover **(see illustration)**. Detach the crankcase breather hose from the engine **(see illustration)**.

11 Remove the wiring cover from the top of the alternator cover on the right-hand side of the engine **(see illustration)**. Working round the engine disconnect the following wiring connectors: ignition timing sensor and alternator (trace the wiring from the alternator cover), oil pressure switch **(see illustration 4.29b)**, neutral switch **(see illustration 4.29c)**, coolant temperature sensor and fan switch **(see illustration)**, and sidestand switch where fitted. Detach the engine earth lead **(see illustration 4.29f)**. Free the loom side of all wiring from any clips or ties to the engine or the bottom section of the frame, and secure it clear, noting its routing.

12 Slacken the clamps securing the carburettors to the intake ducts **(see illustration)**.

13 Refer to Section 17, Step 2 and detach the clutch cable from the engine. Detach the tachometer cable from the engine. Position the cable clear.

14 Make an alignment mark where the slot

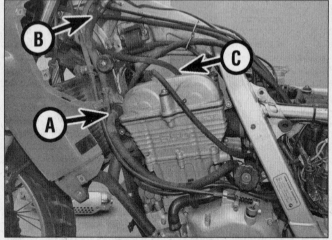

4.10a Detach the oil feed hose (A), return hose (B), tank breather hose (C) . . .

4.10b . . . and crankcase breather hose (D)

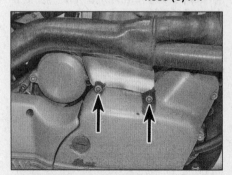

4.11a Unscrew the bolts (arrowed) and remove the cover

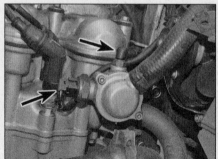

4.11b Temperature sensor and fan switch wiring connectors (arrowed)

4.12 Slacken the carburettor clamp screw (arrowed) on each side

4.17 Remove the lower section of the frame (arrowed)

4.20 Upper mounting bolt nut (arrowed)

4.25a Detach the feed and return hoses (arrowed) . . .

4.25b . . . and the tank breather hose

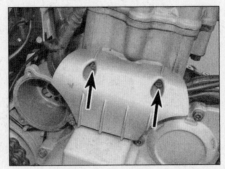

4.26a Unscrew the bolts (arrowed) and displace the cover . . .

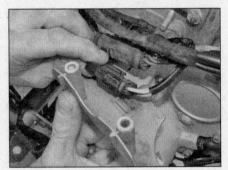

4.26b . . . then release the alternator wiring connector from its clip

in the gearchange lever aligns with the shaft **(see illustration 4.36)**. Unscrew the pinch bolt and slide the lever off the shaft.

15 Remove the front sprocket (see Chapter 6). Slip the drive chain off the end of the output shaft **(see illustration 4.28)**.

16 Detach the lead from the starter motor **(see illustration 4.30)**, and if required remove the starter motor (see Chapter 9).

17 Unscrew the nuts and remove the washers on the bolts securing the bottom section of the frame to the main section **(see illustration)**. Withdraw the bolts with their washers and remove the bottom section along with the sidestand.

18 Position an hydraulic or mechanical jack under the engine with a block of wood between them. Make sure the jack is centrally positioned so the engine will not topple in any direction when the last mounting bolt is removed. Raise the jack to take the weight of

the engine, but make sure it is not lifting the bike and taking the weight of that as well. The idea is to support the engine so that there is no pressure on the remaining mounting bolts so they can be easily withdrawn.

19 Place a support under the front of the swingarm. Where fitted remove the swingarm pivot caps from the frame. Unscrew the swingarm pivot bolt nut, then withdraw the bolt **(see illustrations 4.41a and b)**.

20 Unscrew the nut and remove the washer on the upper mounting bolt **(see illustration)**. Withdraw the bolt with its washer.

21 The engine can now be removed from the frame (see **Caution** above). Check around to make sure everything that needs to be has been detached or disconnected and is clear. Carefully lower the jack, detaching the carburettors from the intake duct, then with the aid of an assistant remove the jack from under the engine and remove the engine.

GS and Dakar models

22 Remove the battery (see Chapter 9).

23 Remove the air filter housing (see Chapter 4B).

24 Remove the exhaust downpipe (see Chapter 4B).

25 Detach the oil feed and return hoses from the tank **(see illustration)**. Detach the oil tank breather hose from the valve cover **(see illustration)**.

26 Remove the wiring cover from the right-hand side of the engine **(see illustrations)**.

27 On GS models remove the regulator/rectifier (see Chapter 9).

28 Remove the front sprocket (see Chapter 6). Slip the drive chain off the end of the output shaft **(see illustration)**.

29 Working round the engine disconnect the following wiring connectors: ignition timing sensor and alternator **(see illustration)**, oil pressure switch **(see illustration)**, neutral

4.28 Slip the chain off the shaft

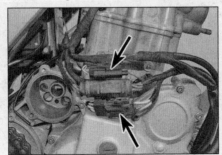

4.29a Disconnect the alternator and ignition timing sensor wiring connectors (arrowed) . . .

4.29b . . . the oil pressure switch wiring connector . . .

4.29c . . . the neutral switch wiring
connector (arrowed) . . .

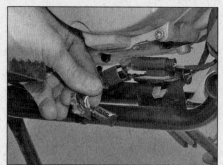

4.29d . . . the sidestand switch wiring
connector . . .

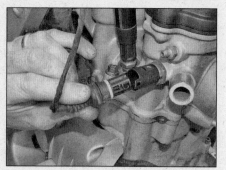

4.29e . . . and the temperature sensor
wiring connector

4.29f Unscrew the bolt and detach the
earth lead

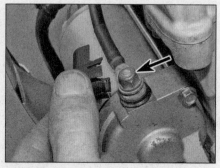

4.30 Remove the cover, unscrew the nut
(arrowed) and detach the lead

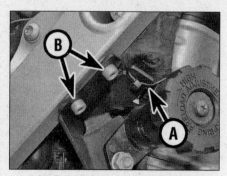

4.31 Release the cable-tie (A), then
unscrew the bolts (B)

switch **(see illustration)**, sidestand switch **(see illustration)**, coolant temperature sensor **(see illustration)**, regulator/rectifier (Dakar models). Detach the engine earth lead **(see illustration)**. Free the loom side of all wiring from any clips or ties to the engine or the bottom or front sections of the frame, and secure it clear, noting its routing.
30 Detach the lead from the starter motor **(see illustration)**, and if required remove the starter motor (see Chapter 9).
31 Release the cable-tie on the rear shock absorber pre-load adjuster, then unscrew the bolts and detach the adjuster **(see illustration)**.

32 Remove the throttle body (see Chapter 4B).
33 Remove the radiator along with its hoses, noting their routing (see Chapter 3).
34 Remove the ignition coil(s) (see Chapter 5).
35 Refer to Section 17, Step 2 and detach the clutch cable from the engine. Position the cable clear.
36 Make an alignment mark where the slot in the gearchange lever aligns with the shaft **(see illustration)**. Unscrew the pinch bolt and slide the lever or linkage arm off the shaft.
37 Remove the rear brake pedal and the footrest assemblies (see Chapter 6).
38 Unscrew the bolts securing the bottom

section of the frame to the front and main sections **(see illustration)**. Withdraw the bolts, noting the exact position and number of all washers (some of which act as shims to correctly space the bottom section of the frame from the main section on the right-hand side at the back), and remove the bottom section along with the sidestand **(see illustration)**.
39 Unscrew the nuts and remove the washers on the bolts securing the front section of the frame to the main section and the engine **(see illustration)**. On GS remove the regulator/rectifier bracket **(see illustration)**. Withdraw

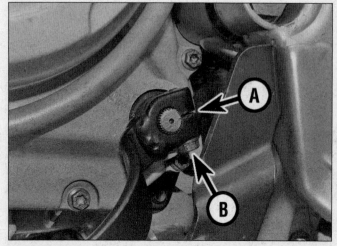

4.36 Make an alignment mark with the slit (A) then unscrew the
bolt (B)

4.38 Unscrew the bolts and remove the bottom section of the
frame

4.39a Unscrew the nuts . . .

4.39b . . . on GS remove the bracket . . .

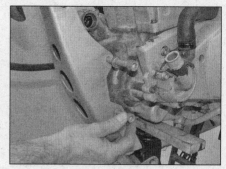

4.39c . . . then withdraw the bolts . . .

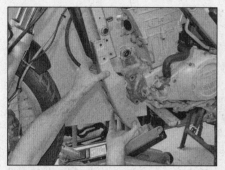

4.39d . . . and remove the front section of the frame

4.41a Unscrew the nut and remove the washer . . .

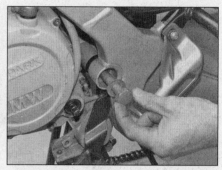

4.41b . . . then withdraw the bolt with its washer

the bolts with their washers and remove the front section **(see illustrations)**.

40 Position an hydraulic or mechanical jack under the engine with a block of wood between them. Make sure the jack is centrally positioned so the engine will not topple in any direction when the last mounting bolt is removed. Raise the jack to take the weight of the engine, but make sure it is not lifting the bike and taking the weight of that as well. The idea is to support the engine so that there is no pressure on the remaining mounting bolts so they can be easily withdrawn.

41 Place a support under the front of the swingarm. Unscrew the swingarm pivot bolt nut, then withdraw the bolt **(see illustrations)**.

42 Unscrew the lower rear mounting bolt, noting how it threads into a captive nut on the bracket for the rear brake pipe-to-hose joint **(see illustrations)**.

43 Unscrew the upper mounting bolt on each side and remove the washer **(see illustration)**. Unscrew the locknut on each adjuster using a peg spanner (BMW part No. 116661, or

4.42a Unscrew the lower rear bolt . . .

4.42b . . . noting how it threads into the bracket (arrowed)

equivalent either available from a motorcycle tool supplier or made by cutting castellations into an old socket of the correct size) **(see illustrations)**. Thread each adjuster away

4.43a Unscrew the upper mounting bolts

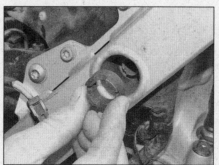

4.43b Unscrew the locknuts . . .

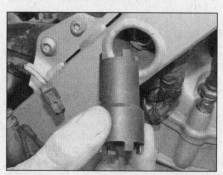

4.43c . . . using a peg spanner such as the one shown, which is commercially available

4.43d Thread the adjusters away from the engine . . .

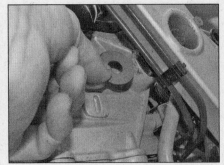

4.43e . . . and retrieve the washers

4.44 Lower the engine and manoeuvre it out

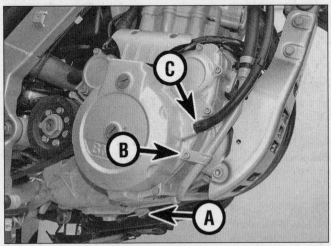

4.48 Unscrew the oil pipe banjo bolt (A) and holder bolt (B). Crankcase breather hose (C)

4.54 Unscrew the bolts (arrowed) and remove the bottom section of the frame

from the engine into the frame and retrieve the washer between the engine and the adjuster head **(see illustrations)**.

44 The engine can now be removed from the frame (see **Caution** above). Check around to make sure everything that needs to be has been detached or disconnected and is clear. Carefully lower the jack and manoeuvre the engine down, making sure it stays clear of the frame **(see illustration)**, then with the aid of an assistant remove the jack from under the engine and remove the engine.

CS model

45 Remove the exhaust system (see Chapter 4B).

46 Disconnect the negative (–ve) lead from the battery (see Chapter 9).

47 Refer to Section 17, Step 2 and detach the clutch cable from the engine. Position the cable clear.

48 Detach the oil feed hose from its union on the frame cross-member that runs above the back of the engine. Release the ABS sensor wire from the clip on the oil hose. Detach the oil return pipe from the underside of the engine and the alternator cover – the sealing washers on the banjo union must be replaced with new ones **(see illustration)**. Detach the crankcase breather hose from the engine. Detach the oil tank breather hose from the valve cover.

49 Remove the radiator along with its hoses, noting their routing (see Chapter 3).

50 Remove the wiring cover from the right-hand side of the engine **(see illustrations 4.26a and b)**.

51 Working round the engine disconnect the following wiring connectors: ignition timing sensor, alternator and regulator/rectifier **(see illustration 4.29a)**, oil pressure switch **(see illustration 4.29b)**, neutral switch **(see illustration 4.29c)**, sidestand switch and coolant temperature sensor **(see illustration 4.29e)**. Detach the engine earth lead **(see illustration 4.29f)**. Free the loom side of all wiring from any clips or ties to the engine or the

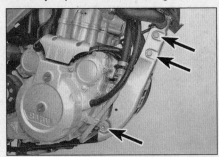

4.57 Unscrew the nuts, withdraw the bolts (arrowed) and remove the front section of the frame

bottom or front sections of the frame, and secure it clear, noting its routing.

52 Remove the front pulley (see Chapter 6). Slip the belt off the end of the output shaft.

53 Detach the lead from the starter motor **(see illustration 4.30)**, and if required remove the starter motor (see Chapter 9).

54 Unscrew the bolts securing the bottom section of the frame to the front and main sections **(see illustration)**. Withdraw the bolts and remove the bottom section along with the sidestand.

55 Remove the throttle body (see Chapter 4B).

56 Remove the ignition coil(s) (see Chapter 5).

57 Unscrew the nuts and remove the washers on the bolts securing the front section of the frame to the main section **(see illustration)**. Withdraw the bolts with their washers and remove the section.

58 Make an alignment mark where the slot in the gearchange linkage arm aligns with the shaft **(see illustration)**. Unscrew the pinch bolt and slide the linkage arm off the shaft.

59 Position an hydraulic or mechanical jack under the engine with a block of wood between them. Make sure the jack is centrally positioned so the engine will not topple in any direction when the last

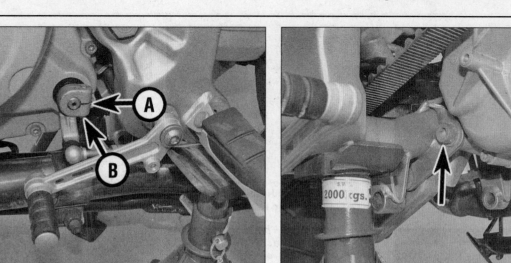

4.58 Make an alignment mark with the slit (A) then unscrew the bolt (B)

4.61 Unscrew the lower rear mounting bolt (arrowed)

mounting bolt is removed. Raise the jack to take the weight of the engine, but make sure it is not lifting the bike and taking the weight of that as well. The idea is to support the engine so that there is no pressure on the remaining mounting bolts so they can be easily withdrawn.

60 Place a support under the front of the swingarm. Unscrew the swingarm pivot bolt nut, then withdraw the bolt **(see illustrations 4.41a and b)**.

61 Remove the lower rear mounting bolt **(see illustration)**.

62 Unscrew the upper mounting bolt on each side and remove the washer **(see illustration 4.43a)**. Unscrew the locknut on each adjuster using a peg spanner (BMW part No. 116661, or equivalent either available from a motorcycle tool supplier or made by cutting castellations into an old socket of the correct size) **(see illustrations 4.43b and c)**. Thread each adjuster away from the engine into the frame and retrieve the washer between the engine and the adjuster head **(see illustrations 4.43d and e)**.

63 The engine can now be removed from the frame (see **Caution** above). Check around to make sure everything that needs to be has been detached or disconnected and is clear.

64 Carefully lower the jack and manoeuvre the engine down, making sure it stays clear of the frame **(see illustration 4.44)**, then with the aid of an assistant remove the jack from under the engine and remove the engine.

Installation

All models

65 The installation procedure is the reverse of removal, noting the following points:
● Manoeuvre the engine into position and onto the jack, then raise it so the mounting points are aligned and fit the mounting bolts and swingarm pivot with their washers where fitted, leaving them all loose until all are installed. Make sure the engine sits correctly in the frame – keep the jack adjusted so that

the weight of the engine is just taken by it, rather than being taken through the bolts, so they remain loose though the frame and are easy to tighten a certain amount by hand. On GS, Dakar and CS models when fitting the mounting bolt to the cylinder head on each side, do not forget the washer with the bolt, and also the washer that fits between the adjuster head and the engine **(see illustration 4.43e)**. Make sure no wires get trapped. Hook the drive chain or belt over the output shaft.

Funduro and ST models

● BMW give no specific order for tightening the engine mounting bolts and provide no torque settings, so tighten them evenly all round. Tighten the swingarm pivot bolt nut to the torque setting specified at the beginning of the Chapter.
● On models from frame No. WB 10161000S0335221-on make sure the support spring on the oil hose to the engine rests directly against the union.

GS, Dakar and CS models

● Thread each adjuster out of the frame until it contacts the cylinder head – make sure the engine is central in the frame and that each adjuster is exerting an equal but small amount of pressure on the head, no tighter than 5 Nm. Tighten each locknut using the peg spanner to the torque setting specified at the beginning of the Chapter. Now tighten each upper mounting bolt to the specified torque.
● On GS and Dakar models, when fitting the bottom section of the frame to the front and main sections, make sure the correct number of shims as noted on removal space the bottom section of the frame from the main section on the right-hand side at the back.
● Tighten the remaining engine and frame mounting bolts and the swingarm pivot bolt to the specified torque settings.

All models

● Make sure all wires, cables and hoses are correctly routed and connected, and secured by any clips or ties. Make sure there are no kinks in the oil hoses, and they are securely connected at each end.
● When fitting the gearchange linkage arm onto the gearchange shaft, align the slit in the arm with the mark on the shaft **(see illustration 4.36)**.
● Use new gaskets on the exhaust pipe connections.
● Refill the engine with oil and coolant to the correct levels (see Chapter 1 and *Pre-ride checks*).
● On Funduro, ST, GS and Dakar models adjust the drive chain (see Chapter 1). On CS models adjust the drive pulley tension (see Chapter 1).
● Check clutch cable freeplay (see Chapter 1).
● On Funduro and ST, GS and Dakar 2000 to 2003, and CS 2002 and 2003 models, if the engine has been disassembled, the oil circuit must be bled before it is run, and before completing the installation so you have access to the oil return hose connection at the oil tank. Remove the oil filter (see Chapter 1). Unscrew the pressure retaining valve **(see illustration)**. Remove the outer

4.65a Unscrew the pressure retaining valve (arrowed)

**4.65b Oil return hose (arrowed) –
Funduro and ST**

**4.65c Oil return hose (arrowed) –
GS and Dakar**

**4.65d Oil return pipe (arrowed) –
CS**

spark plug (see Chapter 1). Turn the engine over on the starter motor until oil emerges at the filter housing. Install the pressure retaining valve and the oil filter. Detach the oil return hose from the oil tank **(see illustrations)**. Turn the engine over on the starter motor until oil emerges at the hose. Connect the hose, then complete the installation procedure.

● Start the engine and run it for a few minutes. Check that there are no oil or coolant leaks. Adjust the idle speed (see Chapter 1). Switch the engine off and check oil and coolant levels.

5   Engine overhaul information

1 Before beginning the engine overhaul, read through the related procedures to familiarise yourself with the scope and requirements of the job. Overhauling an engine is not all that difficult, but it is time consuming. Check on the availability of parts and make sure that any necessary special tools are obtained in advance.

2 Most work can be done with a decent set of typical workshop hand tools, although a number of precision measuring tools are required for inspecting parts to determine if they are worn.

3 To ensure maximum life and minimum trouble from a rebuilt engine, everything must be assembled with care in a spotlessly clean environment.

Disassembly

4 Before disassembling the engine, thoroughly clean and degrease its external surfaces. This will prevent contamination of the engine internals, and will also make the job a lot easier and cleaner. A high flash-point solvent, such as paraffin (kerosene) can be used, or better still, a proprietary engine degreaser such as Gunk. Use old paintbrushes and toothbrushes to work the solvent into the various recesses of the casings. Take care to exclude solvent or water from the electrical components and intake and exhaust ports.

⚠ *Warning: The use of petrol (gasoline) as a cleaning agent should be avoided because of the risk of fire.*

5 When clean and dry, position the engine on the workbench, leaving suitable clear area for working. Gather a selection of small containers, plastic bags and some labels so that parts can be grouped together in an easily identifiable manner. Also get some paper and a pen so that notes can be taken. You will also need a supply of clean rag, which should be as absorbent as possible.

6 Before commencing work, read through the appropriate section so that some idea of the necessary procedure can be gained. When removing components note that great force is seldom required, unless specified (checking the specified torque setting of the particular bolt being removed will indicate how tight it is, and therefore how much force should be needed). In many cases, a component's reluctance to be removed is indicative of an incorrect approach or removal method – if in any doubt, re-check with the text.

7 A complete engine strip should be done in the following general order with reference to the appropriate Sections.

  Remove the valve cover
  Remove the camshafts
  Remove the cylinder head
  Remove the cam chain blades
  Remove the cylinder block and piston
  Remove the starter motor (see Chapter 9)
  Remove the alternator/starter clutch (see Chapter 9)
  Remove the water pump
  Remove the clutch
  Remove the primary drive gear and cam chain
  Remove the oil pumps
  Separate the crankcase halves
  Remove the crankshaft and connecting rod
  Remove the balancer shaft
  Remove the gearchange mechanism
  Remove the selector drum and forks
  Remove the transmission shafts

Reassembly

8 Reassembly is accomplished by reversing the general disassembly sequence.

6   Valve cover

Note: *The valve cover can be removed with the engine in the frame. If the engine has been removed, ignore the steps which do not apply.*

Removal

1 On Funduro and ST models remove the fuel tank (see Chapter 4A). Detach the oil tank breather hose from the valve cover **(see illustration 4.10a)**.

2 On GS and Dakar models remove the battery (see Chapter 9). Undo the oil tank screw and release the two clips **(see illustration)**. Draw the tank out to the side, detach the oil tank breather hose from the valve cover **(see illustration 4.25b)**, and support the tank. Remove the air filter housing (see Chapter 4B). Detach the throttle cable from the throttle body **(see illustration)**. Undo the clamp screw and displace the throttle body **(see illustration)**. Displace the starter relay **(see illustration)**. Remove the electrical tray cover **(see illustration)**. Remove the battery tray **(see illustration)**. Remove the heat shield, drawing the cable through **(see illustrations)**. Remove the ignition coil(s) (see Chapter 5). Displace the coolant reservoir **(see illustration)**.

3 On CS models remove the air filter housing (see Chapter 4B). Detach the throttle cable from the throttle body **(see illustration 6.2b)**. Undo the clamp screw and displace the throttle body **(see illustrations 6.2c and d)**. Remove the ignition coil(s) (see Chapter 5). Displace the coolant reservoir **(see illustrations 6.2j and k)**. Detach the oil tank breather hose from the valve cover.

4 On models with stick coils remove the coil holder **(see illustration)**. Unscrew the valve cover bolts and lift the cover off the cylinder head **(see illustration)**. If it is stuck, do not try to lever it off with a screwdriver. Tap it gently around the sides with a rubber hammer or block of wood to dislodge it. Note the rubber washers on the bolts and replace them with new ones if they are in poor condition **(see illustration)**.

5 Remove the rubber gasket noting how it

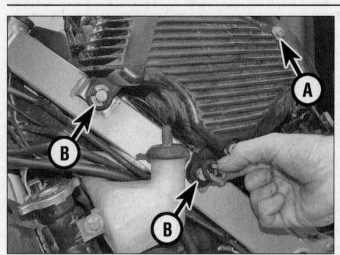

6.2a Undo the screw (A) and release the clips (B)

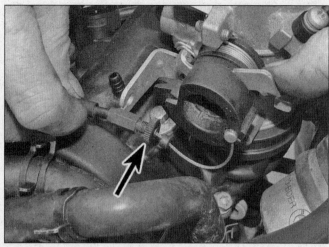

6.2b Unscrew the ring (arrowed), open the throttle cam by hand, free the cable from the bracket and the end from the pulley

6.2c Slacken the clamp screw (arrowed) . . .

6.2d . . . and displace the throttle body

6.2e Displace the starter relay, then undo the screw (arrowed) . . .

6.2f . . . and displace the cover

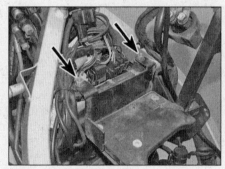

6.2g Unscrew the nuts (arrowed) and remove the tray

6.2h Release the clips (arrowed) . . .

6.2i . . . then displace the shield and draw the cable out

6.2j Unscrew the bolt and draw the reservoir out . . .

6.2k . . . noting how it locates in the grommet

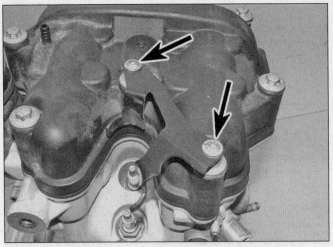

6.4a Undo the screws (arrowed) and remove the holder

6.4b Valve cover bolts (arrowed)

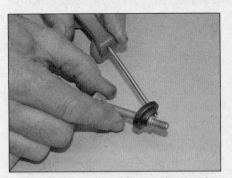

6.4c Remove the rubber washers and replace them with new ones if necessary

6.6 Fit the gasket into the groove in the cover . . .

6.7 . . . then fit the cover onto the head

locates (see illustration 6.6). If it is in any way damaged, deformed or deteriorated, replace it with a new one.

Installation

6 Clean the valve cover gasket if it is being reused. Clean the valve cover and cylinder head mating surfaces. Fit the valve cover gasket (see illustration).

7 Position the valve cover on the cylinder head, making sure the gasket stays in place (see illustration). If necessary fit new rubber washers onto the bolts (see illustration 6.4c). Install the cover bolts, on models with stick coils making sure the two with the threaded

heads for the coil holder are correctly positioned, and tighten them evenly and in a criss-cross sequence to the specified torque setting (see illustration 6.4b). Fit the coil holder (see illustration 6.4a).

8 Install the remaining components in the reverse order of removal.

7 Cam chain tensioner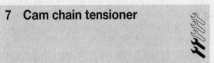

Note: *The cam chain tensioner can be removed with the engine in the frame.*

Removal

1 The tensioner is on the back of the cylinder head on the left-hand side; it is hydraulic in operation. Unscrew the tensioner cap bolt and remove the sealing washer (see illustration). Check the condition of the sealing washer and replace it with a new one if necessary.

2 Withdraw the tensioner from the engine (see illustration).

⚠️ *Warning: Do not turn the engine with the tensioner removed.*

Installation

3 Clean the tensioner cap bolt threads.

4 Install the tensioner (see illustration 7.2).

5 Fit a new sealing washer onto the cap bolt (see illustration 7.1). Tighten the bolt to the specified torque.

8 Camshafts and followers

Note: *The camshafts can be removed with the engine in the frame. Place clean rags over the spark plug holes and the cam chain tunnel to prevent any component from dropping into the engine.*

Special tool: *To ensure that the engine is precisely positioned at top dead centre (TDC)*

7.1 Unscrew the cap bolt . . .

7.2 . . . and withdraw the tensioner

on the compression stroke, a slot is cut into the crankshaft left-hand web into which the rounded end of the BMW special tool (part No. 116570) or an equivalent made from a strong M8 x 1.25 bolt, approx 5 cm long and with its end ground to a blunt taper, locates **(see illustrations 8.5a and b)**. Either obtain the special holding tool, or fabricate your own with the end rounded off as shown before commencing this procedure. If you make your own ensure the bolt is made from strengthened steel – this allows it to be used for other engine rebuild purposes, such as locking the engine when slackening and tightening the alternator rotor nut and primary drive gear nut, otherwise it could break under the strain. The good thing about using the BMW tool is that you know it is strong enough. If you are only using the tool to hold the engine at TDC, and are not going to use it to lock the engine against high torque, a standard bolt will do.

Removal

1 Remove the valve cover (see Section 6). Remove the spark plug – on twin spark models you only need to remove the outer plug (see Chapter 1).
2 Unscrew the plug from the centre of the alternator cover **(see illustration)**. Discard the O-ring as a new one must be used.

8.2 Unscrew the plug (arrowed)

8.4a Turn the engine clockwise . . .

3 The engine must be turned in a clockwise direction so it is at top dead centre (TDC) on its compression stroke. The engine can be turned using an Allen key or hex bit fitted in the end of the crankshaft via the hole in the alternator cover.
4 Turn the engine clockwise until the index lines on the camshaft sprockets are parallel with the top of the cylinder head, and the small hole in each sprocket is at the top **(see illustrations)**. If the sprocket holes are at the bottom, rotate the engine clockwise one full turn (360°) until the index lines are again parallel with the head. The sprocket holes will now be at the top.

5 Undo the blanking bolt on the left-hand side of the engine and replace it with the crankshaft locking tool (BMW part No. 116570) or a suitable and strong equivalent (see above) and locate it in the hole in the crankshaft web **(see illustrations)** – if the engine is in the frame and the oil hasn't been drained get a suitable container for oil or some rag and stuff it between the engine and the exhaust downpipe. You should be able to feel the point at which it locates by jiggling the crankshaft back and forth a very small amount either side of its current position as you thread the holding bolt in. When you can't turn the crankshaft any more the tool end has located in the hole.

0.4b . . . until the sprocket marks are as shown

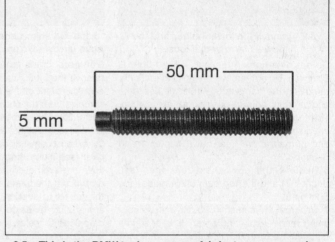

0.5a This is the BMW tool, or you can fabricate your own using the dimensions shown

50 mm

5 mm

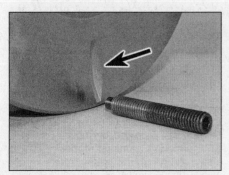

8.5b The tapered end of the tool locates in a slot in the crankshaft (arrowed)

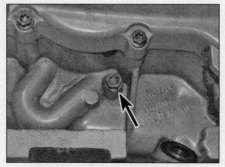

8.5c Unscrew the blanking bolt (arrowed) . . .

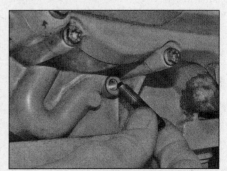

8.5d . . . and thread the tool in its place

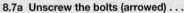

8.7a Unscrew the bolts (arrowed) . . .

8.7b . . . and remove the holder

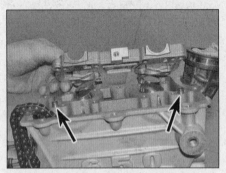

8.9 Remove the lower holder, and the dowels (arrowed) if loose

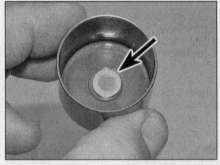

8.10a On shim-under models retrieve the shim (arrowed) from inside the follower . . .

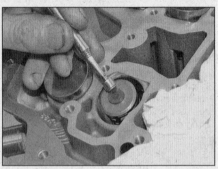

8.10b . . . or from the top of the valve

Do not over-tighten the bolt – hand-tight is sufficient. Do not remove the holding tool after removing the camshafts – this will keep the engine in its correct position for installation. The tool is also required to counter-hold the crankshaft for removal of the alternator nut and primary drive gear nut (Chapter 9 and Section 19).

6 Remove the cam chain tensioner (see Section 7) and the top cam chain guide (see Section 9).

7 Unscrew the camshaft holder bolts, slackening them evenly and a very little at a time **(see illustration)**. Remove the bolts with their washers and lift off the upper holder **(see illustrations)**.

8 If both camshafts are being removed, remove the intake camshaft first. Carefully lift each camshaft off the head and disengage the sprocket from the chain **(see illustrations 8.26 and 8.25)**. The camshafts are not marked for identification, but they are easily distinguished as the exhaust camshaft carries the decompression lever **(see illustration 8.21)**. If both camshafts have been removed do not allow the chain to drop down the tunnel – use some wire across the tunnel to support it. Place rags over the spark plug holes to prevent anything from dropping into the engine.

9 If required lift the lower holder off the head **(see illustration)**. Remove the dowels if they are loose.

10 If the followers and shims are being removed from the cylinder head, obtain a container which is divided into four compartments, and label each compartment with the location of a valve, i.e. intake or exhaust camshaft, left or right valve. If a container is not available, use labelled plastic bags (egg cartons also do very well!). Lift out each cam follower using a magnet or the suction created by a valve lapping tool **(see illustration 8.10b)**. Retrieve the shim from the top or inside of the follower (according to model), or on shim-under models pick it out of the top of the valve spring retainer using either a magnet, a screwdriver with a dab of grease on it (the shim will stick to the grease), or a very small screwdriver and a pair of pliers **(see illustrations)**. Do not allow the shim to fall into the engine.

Inspection

11 Inspect the bearing surfaces of the camshaft holders and the corresponding journals on the camshafts **(see illustration)**. Look for score marks, deep scratches and evidence of spalling (a pitted appearance). Check the oil passages for clogging.

12 Check the camshaft lobes for heat discoloration (blue appearance), score marks, chipped areas, flat spots and spalling. Measure the height of each lobe with a micrometer **(see illustration)** and compare

8.11 Check the bearing surfaces of the camshafts and holders for wear

8.12 Measure the height of the camshaft lobes with a micrometer

the results to the minimum height listed in this Chapter's Specifications. If damage is noted or wear is excessive, the camshaft must be replaced with a new one.

13 Next, check the camshaft journal oil clearances. Clean the camshafts and the bearing surfaces in the cylinder head and camshaft holder with a clean lint-free cloth. If removed fit the lower holder dowels, then fit the holder (see illustration 8.9). Lay each camshaft in its correct location in the cylinder head with the lobes pointing up, and on the exhaust camshaft so the decompression lever does not contact the follower (see illustration 8.25 and 26) – there is no need to fit the chain round the sprockets.

14 Cut four strips of Plastigauge and lay one piece on each journal, parallel with the camshaft centreline. Fit the upper holder and tighten the bolts evenly and a little at a time in a criss-cross sequence to the torque setting specified at the beginning of the Chapter (see illustration 8.27). While doing this, don't let the camshafts rotate, or the Plastigauge will be disturbed and you will have to start again.

15 Now unscrew the camshaft holder bolts and lift off the upper holder.

16 To determine the oil clearance, compare the crushed Plastigauge (at its widest point) on each journal to the scale printed on the Plastigauge container. Compare the results to this Chapter's Specifications. If the oil clearance is greater than specified, measure the diameter of each camshaft journal and compare the results to the minimum listed in this Chapter's Specifications (see illustration). If wear is excessive replace the camshaft with a new one. Also check the holder journal bore diameter with the holders bolted to the cylinder head but without the camshafts, and replace them with new ones if necessary (see illustration). Assemble the new components and recheck the clearance.

17 Except in cases of oil starvation, the cam chain should wear very little. To check, with the camshafts installed and the chain fitted round the sprockets, fit the tensioner into the cylinder head (do not fit the cap bolt) and push it in until it contacts the blade. Now measure the amount the outer end is recessed in its bore (see illustrations) – if it is greater than 9.0 mm replace the chain with a new one. If

8.16a Measure the diameter of the camshaft journal with a micrometer

8.16b Measure the diameter of the holder journal bore

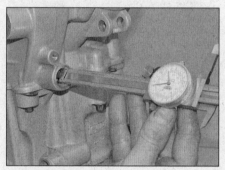
8.17a Checking for wear in the cam chain using a Vernier caliper . . .

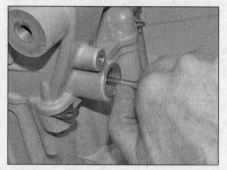
8.17b . . . if you don't have one insert a screwdriver, then measure its depth using a ruler

the chain is stiff or the links are binding or kinking, replace it with a new one. Refer to Section 9 for replacement.

18 Check the sprockets for wear, cracks and other damage, and replace them with new ones if necessary. Clamp the camshaft in a vice with soft jaws and some rag and unscrew the bolt, noting the washer where fitted (see illustration). On installation oil the threads of the bolt and tighten it to the torque setting specified at the beginning of the Chapter. If the sprockets are worn, the cam chain is also worn, and so probably is the sprocket on the crankshaft. If severe wear is apparent, the entire engine should be disassembled for inspection.

19 Inspect the cam chain guides and tensioner blade (see Section 9).

20 Inspect the outer surface of each cam follower for evidence of scoring or other

damage. If a follower is in poor condition, it is probable that the bore in the cylinder head in which it works is also damaged. Measure the outer diameter of the follower and the diameter of the bore and compare the results to the specifications (see illustrations). If any follower or bore is worn, out-of-round or tapered, replace the follower and/or cylinder head with a new one.

21 Do not remove the decompression lever unless either it or the camshaft is being replaced with a new one (see illustration). Check the tip of the decompression lever for wear. With the lever pointing down measure the amount the tip protrudes beyond the bottom of the base circle of the lobe – if it is less than 0.6 mm replace the lever and spring with new ones. Also check the spring tension. With the lever pointing up measure the amount the spring holds the lever weight away from the lobe – if

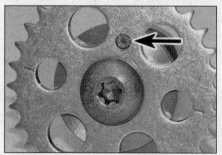
8.18 Each sprocket is secured by one bolt, and the small hole locates onto a pin (arrowed)

8.20a Measure the external diameter of the follower . . .

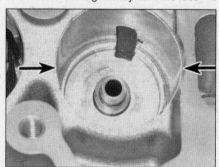
8.20b . . . and the internal diameter of its bore

8.21 The decompression lever (arrowed) is on the exhaust camshaft

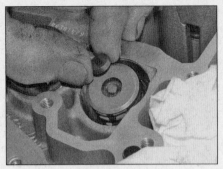

8.22a Fit the shim into its recess . . .

8.22b . . . then fit the follower onto the valve

it is less than 11.5 mm replace the spring with a new one. Note that if the lever is removed from the camshaft for any reason the spring should be replaced with a new one. To remove the lever drive the pivot pin out using a suitable punch, and note how the spring locates. Check the action of the lever after refitting it.

Installation

22 If removed, lubricate each shim and its follower with molybdenum disulphide oil (a 50/50 mixture of molybdenum disulphide grease and engine oil). Fit each shim into its recess in the top of the follower or valve spring retainer according to model, making sure it is correctly seated (see illustration). Note: *It is most important that the shims and followers are returned to their original valves otherwise the valve clearances will be inaccurate.* Install each follower, making sure it fits squarely in its bore (see illustration).

23 Make sure the contact surfaces of the cylinder head and the underside of the lower holder are clean and dry, and the bearing surfaces on the camshafts and in the lower holder are clean. Fit the lower holder dowels if removed, then fit the holder, making sure it seats squarely on the head (see illustration 8.9). Apply molybdenum disulphide oil (a 50/50 mixture of molybdenum disulphide grease and engine oil) to the lower holder journals, camshaft journals and lobes. Make sure that none gets on the mating surfaces between the holders, or in the bolt holes.

24 Check that the crankshaft is locked in position at TDC (see Step 5). If both camshafts have been removed, install the exhaust camshaft first, then the intake.

25 Lay the exhaust camshaft (the one with the decompression lever on its right-hand end) onto the head with the index lines on the camshaft sprockets parallel with the top of

the head, and the small hole in each sprocket at the top, fitting the cam chain around the sprocket as you install the camshaft, pulling up on the chain to remove all slack in the front run between the crankshaft and the camshaft (see illustration).

26 Lay the intake camshaft onto the head with the index lines on the camshaft sprockets parallel with the top of the head, and the small hole in each sprocket at the top, fitting the cam chain around the sprocket as you install the camshaft, pulling on it to remove all slack from between the two camshaft sprockets (see illustration). Any slack in the chain must lie in the rear run between the intake camshaft and the crankshaft so that it is later taken up by the tensioner. Check the alignment of the sprockets (see illustration 8.4b).

27 Make sure the bearing surfaces in the upper holder are clean, then apply molybdenum disulphide oil (a 50/50 mixture of molybdenum disulphide grease and engine oil) to each of them. Lay the holder on the head (see illustration 8.7b). Install the bolts with their washers, and tighten them finger-tight (see illustration). Now tighten the bolts evenly and a little at a time in a criss-cross sequence to the torque setting specified at the beginning of the Chapter.

28 Use a piece of wooden dowel to press on the back of the cam chain tensioner blade via the tensioner bore in the cylinder block to ensure that any slack in the cam chain is taken up and transferred to the rear run of the chain (where it will later be taken up by the tensioner). At this point check that the timing marks are still in **exact** alignment as described in Step 4. Note that it is easy to be slightly out (one tooth on the sprocket) without the marks appearing drastically out of alignment. If the marks are out, verify which camshaft is misaligned, then remove the wooden dowel. Displace the camshaft and disengage it from the chain, then move the camshaft round as required, refit the camshaft, and check the marks again.

Caution: If the marks are not aligned exactly as described, the valve timing will be incorrect and the valves may strike the pistons, causing extensive damage to the engine.

29 Install the top guide (see Section 9) and the cam chain tensioner (see Section 7).

30 Remove the crankshaft locking tool and

8.25 Fit the exhaust camshaft as described . . .

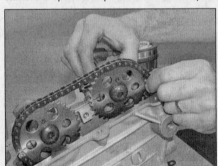

8.26 . . . then fit the intake camshaft

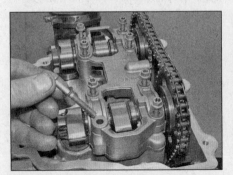

8.27 Fit the holder bolts and washers and tighten them as described

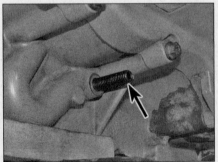

8.30a Remove the locking tool (arrowed) . . .

refit the blanking bolt using a new sealing washer **(see illustrations)**. If the engine is in the frame and the oil wasn't drained check the level and replenish if necessary (see *Pre-ride checks*).

31 Turn the engine clockwise through two full turns and check again that all the timing marks still align (see Steps 3 and 4). Check the valve clearances and adjust them if necessary (see Chapter 1).

32 Fit the plug into the alternator cover using a new O-ring **(see illustration)**.

33 Install the valve cover (see Section 6). Install the spark plug (see Chapter 1).

9 Cam chain and blades
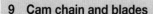

Note: *The cam chain and all blades can be removed with the engine in the frame.*

Removal

Front guide blade

1 Remove the valve cover (see Section 6).
2 Draw the blade out of the engine **(see illustration)**.

Top guide

3 Remove the valve cover (see Section 6).
4 Unscrew the bolts and lift the guide off **(see illustrations)**.

Tensioner blade

5 Remove the camshafts (see Section 8).
6 Remove the clutch (see Section 16).

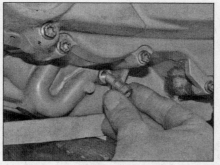

8.30b . . . and fit the blanking bolt with a new washer

7 Unscrew the pivot bolt and draw the blade out of the engine **(see illustration)**.

Cam chain

8 Remove the camshafts (see Section 8).
9 Remove the primary drive gear (see Section 19).
10 Remove the cam chain **(see illustration)**.

Inspection

Tensioner and guide blades

11 Check the sliding surface and edges of the blades for excessive wear, deep grooves, cracking and other obvious damage, and replace them with new ones if necessary.

Cam chain

12 Check the chain for binding, kinks and any obvious damage and replace it with a new one if necessary. Check the amount of wear (see Section 8, Step 17). Check the camshaft

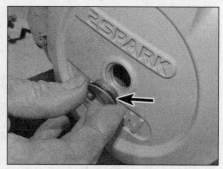

8.32 Fit the plug using a new O-ring (arrowed)

and crankshaft sprocket teeth for wear and chipped teeth. Damage is unlikely, but if found the camshaft sprockets must be renewed.

Installation

13 Installation of the chain and blades is the reverse of removal. Fit the tensioner blade using a new pivot bolt and tighten it to the torque setting specified at the beginning of the Chapter **(see illustration 9.7)**. Make sure the front guide blade locates correctly **(see illustration)**.

10 Cylinder head removal and installation

Note: *The cylinder head can be removed with the engine in the frame. If the engine has been removed, ignore the steps which do not apply.*

9.2 Draw the blade out of the engine

9.4a Unscrew the bolts (arrowed) . . .

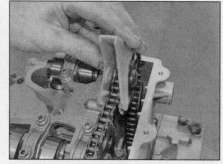

9.4b . . . and remove the guide

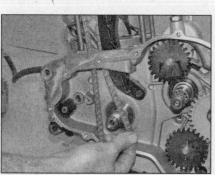

9.7 Unscrew the bolt and draw the blade out of the engine

9.10 Removing the cam chain

9.13 Locate the lugs in the cut-outs

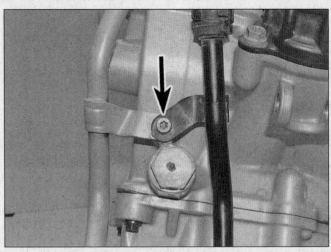

10.4a Undo the pipe holder bolt (arrowed)

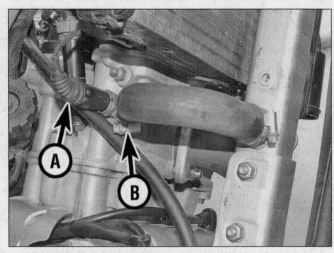

10.4b Disconnect the wiring connector (A) then slacken the clamp (B) and detach the hose

Removal

1 Remove the radiator, on Funduro and ST models disconnecting the right-hand hose at the thermostat housing (see Chapter 3).
2 Remove the starter motor (see Chapter 9).
3 On Funduro and ST models slacken the clamps securing the carburettors to the intake duct (see illustration 4.12). Disconnect the coolant temperature sensor and fan switch wiring connectors (see illustration 4.11b).
4 On GS and Dakar models undo the bolt securing the oil pipes just above the cam chain tensioner bore (see illustration). Disconnect the coolant temperature sensor

wiring connector and detach the coolant hose from the right-hand side of the cylinder head (see illustration).
5 Remove the exhaust downpipe (see Chapter 4A or B).
6 Refer to Section 4 and remove the upper engine mounting bolt(s).
7 Remove the camshafts, and if required the followers and shims (see Section 8).
8 Remove the cam chain front guide blade (see Section 9).
9 The cylinder head is secured by three 6 mm bolts, four 8 mm bolts on Funduro and ST models and five 8 mm bolts on GS, Dakar and CS models, and four 10 mm nuts. First unscrew

and remove the 6 mm bolts (see illustration). Now unscrew and remove the 8 mm bolts, slackening them evenly and a little at a time in a criss-cross pattern until they are all loose (see illustration). Finally unscrew the four 10 mm nuts, again slackening them evenly and a little at a time in a criss-cross pattern.
10 Pull the cylinder head up off the block, passing the chain down the tunnel and laying it over the front (see illustration). If the head is stuck, tap around the joint faces with a soft-faced mallet. Do not attempt to free the head by inserting a screwdriver between the head and block mating surfaces – you'll damage them.

10.9a Unscrew the 6 mm bolts (arrowed)

10.9b Unscrew the 8 mm bolt(s) (arrowed) at the front . . .

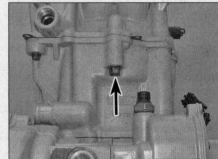

10.9c . . . and back . . .

10.9d . . . and sides as described

10.9e Unscrew the four 10 mm bolts (arrowed) as described

10.10 Carefully lift the head up off the block

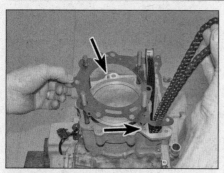

10.15 Locate the new gasket over the pins (arrowed)

11 Remove the cylinder head gasket and discard it as a new one must be used.

12 Check the cylinder head gasket and the mating surfaces on the cylinder head and block for signs of leakage, which could indicate warpage. Refer to Section 11 and check the cylinder head gasket surface for warpage.

13 Clean all traces of old gasket material from the cylinder head and block. If a scraper is used, take care not to scratch or gouge the soft aluminium. Be careful not to let any of the gasket material fall into the cylinder bore or the oil and coolant passages.

Installation

14 Lubricate the cylinder bore with engine oil.

15 Ensure both cylinder head and block mating surfaces are clean. Lay the new head gasket onto the block, locating it over the pins and making sure all the holes are correctly aligned **(see illustration)**. Never reuse the old gasket. Hook the cam chain out and hold it up.

16 Carefully fit the cylinder head over the studs and onto the block, passing the cam chain through the tunnel, making sure it locates correctly onto the pins **(see illustration 10.10)**.

17 Install all nuts and bolts and tighten them finger-tight **(see illustrations 10.9e to a)**.

18 On Funduro and ST models, first tighten the 8 mm bolts (1 and 2) lightly **(see illustration)**. Next tighten the 10 mm nuts following the numerical sequence (3 to 6), first to the initial torque setting specified at the beginning of the Chapter, then (7 to 10) to the final torque setting specified. Next tighten the 8 mm bolts (11 and 12) in sequence to the specified torque. Now tighten the 6 mm bolts (13) to the specified torque. Note that if there are signs of oil leakage from the cylinder head joint BMW advise to slacken bolts 13 to 16, then to tighten them to the specified torque settings.

19 On GS, Dakar and CS models, tighten the 10 mm nuts (1 to 4) following the numerical sequence, first to the initial torque setting specified at the beginning of the Chapter, then to the final torque setting specified **(see illustration)**. Next tighten the 8 mm bolts (5 to 9) in sequence to the specified torque. Now tighten the 6 mm bolts (10) to the specified torque.

20 If the cylinder block has been removed, fully tighten its bolts **(see illustration 12.4a)**.

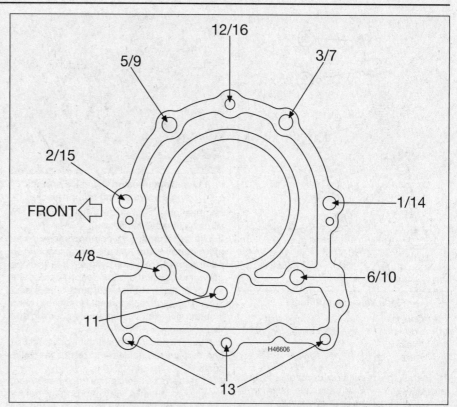

10.18 Cylinder head nut and bolt tightening sequence – Funduro and ST

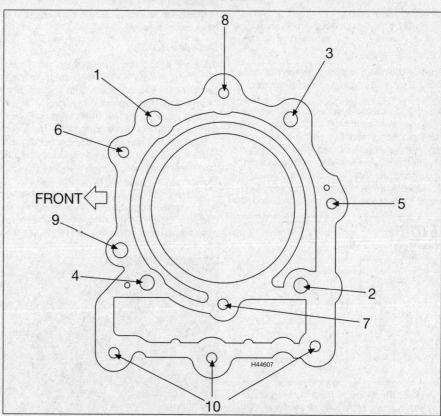

10.19 Cylinder head nut and bolt tightening sequence – GS, Dakar and CS

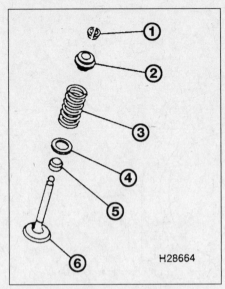

11.5 Valve components

1	Collets	4	Spring seat
2	Spring retainer	5	Valve stem oil seal
3	Valve spring	6	Valve

21 Install the remaining components in a reverse of the removal sequence, referring to the relevant Sections or Chapters (see Steps 8 to 1).

11 Cylinder head and valve overhaul

Special tool: *A valve spring compressor (small enough for motorcycle engines) is required.*
1 Because of the complex nature of this job and the special tools and equipment required, most owners leave servicing of the valves, valve seats and valve guides to a professional. However, you can make an initial assessment of whether the valves are seating correctly, and therefore sealing, by pouring a small amount of solvent into each of the valve ports. If the solvent leaks past any valve into the

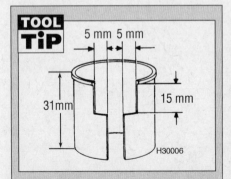

TOOL TiP

Protect the follower bore in the cylinder head from scratches by the valve spring compressor by fabricating a shield from a 35 mm film canister cut as required.

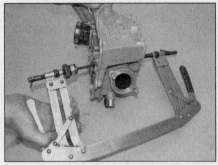

11.6a Compressing the valve springs using a valve spring compressor

combustion chamber area the valve is not seating correctly and sealing.
2 With a valve spring compressor you can also remove the valves and associated components from the cylinder head, clean them and check them for wear to assess the extent of the work needed, and, unless seat cutting or guide replacement is required, grind in the valves and reassemble them in the head.
3 A dealer service department or specialist can replace the guides and re-cut the valve seats.
4 After the valve service has been performed, be sure to clean it very thoroughly before installation on the engine to remove any metal particles or abrasive grit that may still be present from the valve service operations. Use compressed air, if available, to blow out all the holes and passages.

Disassembly

5 Before proceeding, arrange to label and store the valves along with their related components in such a way that they can be returned to their original locations without getting mixed up **(see illustration)**. Either use the same container as the cam followers and shims are stored in (see Section 8), or obtain a separate container and label each compartment accordingly. Alternatively, labelled plastic bags will do just as well.
6 Compress the valve spring on the first valve with a spring compressor, making sure it is correctly located onto each end of the valve assembly **(see illustration)**. On the top of the valve the adaptor needs to be about the same

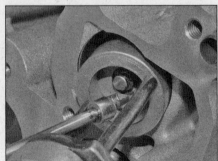

11.7a Remove the collets . . .

11.6b Make sure the compressor locates correctly both on the top of the spring retainer . . .

11.6c . . . and on the bottom of the valve

size as the spring retainer – if it is too big it will contact the follower bore and mark it, and if it is too small it will be difficult to remove and install the collets **(see illustration)**. On the underside of the head make sure the plate on the compressor only contacts the valve and not the soft aluminium of the head **(see illustration)** – if the plate is too big for the valve, use a spacer between them. Do not compress the spring any more than is absolutely necessary.
Caution: Take great care not to mark the cam follower bore with the spring compressor (see Tool Tip)
7 Remove the collets, using a magnet or a screwdriver with a dab of grease on it **(see illustration)**. Carefully release the valve spring compressor and remove the spring retainer, noting which way up it fits, the spring, again noting which way up it fits, and the valve **(see illustrations)**. If the valve binds in the guide

11.7b . . . the spring retainer and spring . . .

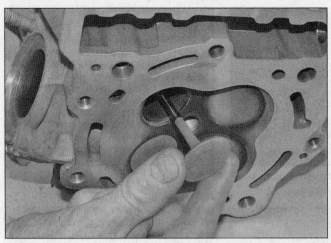

11.7c ... and the valve

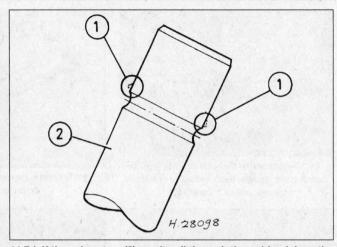

11.7d If the valve stem (2) won't pull through the guide, deburr the area above the collet groove (1)

and won't pull through, push it back into the head and deburr the area around the collet groove with a very fine file or whetstone **(see illustration)**.

8 Remove the spring seat noting which way up it fits – using a magnet is the easiest way to remove it **(see illustration)**. Pull the valve stem seal off the top of the valve guide with pliers and discard it (the old seals should never be reused) **(see illustration)**.

9 Repeat the procedure for the remaining valves. Remember to keep the parts for each valve together so they can be reinstalled in the same location.

10 Clean the cylinder head with solvent and dry it thoroughly. Compressed air will speed the drying process and ensure that all holes and recessed areas are clean. **Note:** *Do not use a wire brush mounted in a drill motor to clean the combustion chamber as the head material is soft and may be scratched or eroded away by the wire brush.*

11 Clean all of the valve springs, collets, retainers and spring seats with solvent and dry them thoroughly. Do the parts from one valve at a time so that no mixing of parts between valves occurs.

12 Remove any deposits that may have formed on the valve head using a scraper or a motorised wire brush. Again, make sure the valves do not get mixed up.

11.8a Remove the spring seat . . .

Inspection

13 Inspect the head very carefully for cracks and other damage. If cracks are found, a new head is required.

14 Using a precision straight-edge and a feeler gauge check the head gasket mating surface for warpage. Refer to *Tools and Workshop Tips* in the Reference section for details of how to use the straight-edge. If the head is warped, consult a BMW dealer or take it to a specialist repair shop for an opinion, though be prepared to have to buy a new one.

15 Examine the valve seats in the combustion chamber. If they are pitted, cracked or burned, the head will require work beyond the scope

11.8b ... then pull the seal off the valve stem

of the home mechanic. Measure the valve seat width and compare it to the Specifications **(see illustration)**. If either exceeds the service limit, or if it varies around its circumference, overhaul is required.

16 Working on one valve and guide at a time fit a valve into its guide until the stem end reaches the top of the guide, so that its head is above the seat **(see illustration)**. Mount a dial gauge against the side of the valve head and measure the amount of 'wobble' (side clearance) between the valve stem and its guide in two perpendicular directions. If wobble exceeds the limit specified, remove the valve and measure the valve stem diameter **(see illustration)**. Also measure

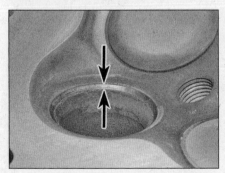

11.15 Measure the valve seat width

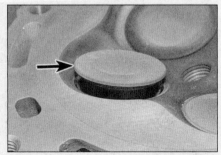

11.16a Mount the tip of the gauge against the valve and measure the amount of wobble

11.16b Measure the valve stem diameter with a micrometer

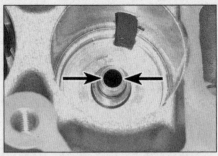

11.16c Measure the valve guide with a small bore gauge, then measure the bore gauge with a micrometer

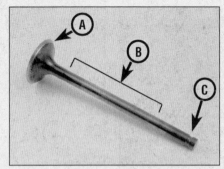

11.17 Check the face (A), stem (B) and collet groove (C)

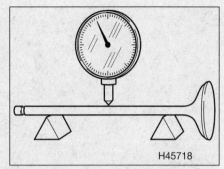

11.18 Check for any runout in the stem

11.19 Measure the free length of the valve springs and check them for bend

11.22 Fit a new valve stem seal and press it squarely into place

11.23 Fit the spring seat using a rod to guide it if necessary

the inside diameter of the guide with a small hole gauge and micrometer **(see illustration)**. Measure the guides at each end and at the centre to determine if they are worn unevenly. Replace any component that is worn beyond its specifications with a new one. If the valve guide is within specifications, but is worn unevenly, it should be replaced.

17 Carefully inspect each valve face, stem, stem end and collet groove for cracks, pitting and wear **(see illustration)**.

18 Rotate the valve and check for any obvious indication that it is bent, in which case it must be replaced with a new one. Using V-blocks and a dial gauge, check for valve stem runout and replace the valve with a new one if necessary **(see illustration)**.

19 Check the end of each valve spring for wear and pitting. Measure the spring free length and compare it to the specifications **(see illustration)**. If any spring is shorter than

specified it has sagged and must be replaced with a new one. Also place the spring upright on a flat surface and check it for bend by placing a ruler against it, or alternatively lay it against a set square. If the bend in any spring is excessive, it must be replaced with a new one.

20 Check the spring seats, retainers and collets for obvious wear and cracks. Any questionable parts should not be reused, as extensive damage will occur in the event of failure during engine operation.

21 If the inspection indicates that no overhaul work is required, the valve components can be reinstalled in the head.

Reassembly

22 Working on one valve at a time, fit a new valve stem seal onto the guide, using finger pressure, a stem seal fitting tool or an appropriate size deep socket, to push the seal

squarely onto the end of the guide until it is felt to clip into place **(see illustration)**.

23 Lay the spring seat in place with its shouldered side facing up **(see illustration)**.

24 Coat the valve stem with molybdenum disulphide oil (a 50/50 mixture of molybdenum disulphide grease and engine oil), then install it into its guide **(see illustration 11.7c)**. Check that the valve moves up-and-down freely in the guide.

25 Next fit the spring, with its paint marks at the top **(see illustration)**. Fit the spring retainer, with its coned side facing down so that it fits into the top of the spring **(see illustration)**.

26 Apply a small amount of grease to the collets to help hold them in place. Compress the valve spring with the spring compressor tool, making sure it is correctly located onto each end of the valve assembly (see Step 6) **(see illustrations 11.6a, b and c)**. Do not

11.25a Fit the spring with its paint marks at the top . . .

11.25b . . . and the retainer with its coned side facing down

11.26 Use grease to help stick the collets in the groove

compress the spring any more than is necessary to slip the collets into place. Locate each collet in turn into the groove in the valve stem using a screwdriver with a dab of grease on it (see illustration). Carefully release the compressor, making sure the collets seat and lock in the retaining groove.

27 Repeat the procedure for the remaining valves. Remember to keep the parts for each valve together and separate from the other valves so they can be reinstalled in the same location.

28 Support the cylinder head on blocks so the valves can't contact the work surface, then tap the end of each valve stem lightly to seat the collets in their grooves (see illustration).

HAYNES HiNT *Check for proper sealing of the valves by pouring a small amount of solvent into each of the valve ports. If the solvent leaks past any valve into the combustion chamber the valve grinding operation on that valve should be repeated.*

29 After the cylinder head and camshafts have been installed, check the valve clearances and adjust as required (see Chapter 1).

12 Cylinder block

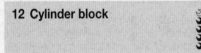

Note: *The cylinder block can be removed with the engine in the frame.*

Removal

Note: *Three types of hose clamp are used on the various hoses across the range of models covered – the non-re-usable type, the re-usable clip type and the screw type. A small screwdriver is required to release the non-reusable type and clip type clamps. Special pliers are required to close them, and these are available from automotive tool suppliers, or from BMW (part No. 131500), along with the clamps where new ones are required.*

1 Remove the cylinder head (see Section 10).
2 Remove the wiring cover from the right-hand side of the engine (see illustration 4.11a

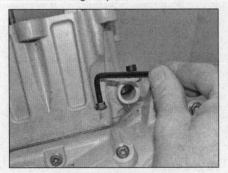

12.4b . . . using a Torx key

11.28 Seat the collets as described

or 4.26a and b). Unscrew the bolt securing the earth lead (see illustration 4.29f).

3 Release the clamp securing the coolant hose to the inlet union on the back of the block and detach it, being prepared with a rag to catch any residual coolant (see illustration).

4 Unscrew the bolts securing the block to the crankcase (see illustration) – due to their position and the shape of the block a Torx key is needed (see illustration).

5 Pull the cylinder block up off the crankcase, passing the cam chain through the tunnel and laying it over the front, and supporting the piston so the connecting rod does not knock against the crankcase (see illustration). If the block is stuck, tap around the joint faces with a soft-faced mallet. Do not attempt to free it by inserting a screwdriver between the block and crankcase mating surfaces – you'll damage them.

6 Remove the base gasket and discard it as a new one must be used.

12.3 Release the clamp (arrowed) and detach the hose

12.5 Lift the block up, making sure the connecting rod does not fall against the crankcase

7 Stuff some clean rag around the connecting rod to protect and support it and the piston and to prevent anything falling into the engine.

8 Clean all traces of old gasket material from the cylinder block and crankcase. If a scraper is used, take care not to scratch or gouge the soft aluminium. Be careful not to let any of the gasket material fall into the engine. Clean the block with solvent and blow through the oil passages for the cam chain tensioner.

Inspection

Note: *Do not attempt to separate the cylinder liner from the cylinder block. The liner is Nikasil coated and so must not be honed.*

9 Check the cylinder walls carefully for scratches and score marks.

10 Using a precision straight-edge and a feeler gauge check the block top surface for warpage. Refer to *Tools and Workshop Tips* in the Reference section for details of how to use the straight-edge. If the head is warped, consult a BMW dealer or take it to a specialist repair shop for an opinion, though be prepared to have to buy a new one.

11 Using a telescoping bore gauge and a micrometer, check the diameter of the cylinder to assess the amount of wear, taper and ovality – measure 60 mm from the top of the bore, and take three equally spaced measurements (see illustrations). Compare the results to the specifications at the beginning of the Chapter, noting the tolerance size must be matched to the cast A or B in the cylinder. If the cylinder is worn beyond the service limit or it is oval, replace the block with a new one.

12.4a Unscrew the bolts (arrowed) . . .

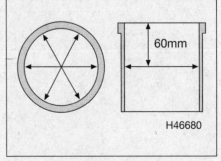

60mm

H46680

12.11a Measure the cylinder bore in the directions shown . . .

12.11b . . . using a telescoping gauge, then measure the gauge with a micrometer

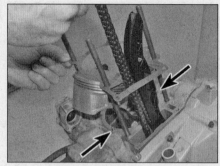

12.14 Locate the new gasket over the pins (arrowed)

12.18 Carefully feed the rings into the bore

12 If the precision measuring tools are not available, take the cylinder block to a BMW dealer or specialist motorcycle repair shop for assessment and advice.

Installation

13 Check that the mating surfaces of the cylinder block and crankcase are free from oil or pieces of old gasket.

14 Remove the rags from around the piston and the cam chain tunnel, taking care not to let the connecting rod fall against the crankcase. Lay the new base gasket onto the block, locating it over the pins and making sure all the holes are correctly aligned **(see illustration)**. Never re-use the old gasket.

15 Ensure the piston ring end gaps are staggered 120° apart. If required, fit a piston ring clamp onto the piston to ease its entry into the bore as the block is lowered. This is not essential as the cylinder has a good lead-in enabling the piston rings to be hand-fed into the bore. If possible, have an assistant to support the cylinder block while the piston rings are fed in, or place a wooden support under the piston to prevent the weight of the block pushing it down.

16 Lubricate the cylinder bore, piston and piston rings with clean engine oil.

17 Carefully lower the block over the studs and onto the piston until the crown fits into the bore, making sure it enters squarely and does not get cocked **(see illustration 12.5)**. Feed the cam chain up the tunnel and secure it over the front of the block.

18 Carefully compress and feed each ring into its bore as the block is lowered **(see**

illustration**).** If necessary, use a soft mallet to gently tap the block down, but do not use force if it appears to be stuck as the piston and/or rings will be damaged.

19 When the piston and rings are correctly located in the bore, carefully press the block down, making sure it locates on the pins.

20 Fit the bolts and tighten them lightly – tighten them fully after the cylinder head has been installed **(see illustration 12.4a)**. Turn the crankshaft to check that everything moves as it should.

21 Connect the coolant hose to its union and secure it with the clamp **(see illustration 12.3)**.

22 Fit the earth lead and tighten the bolt **(see illustration 4.29f)**. Fit the wiring cover **(see illustration 4.11a or 4.26b and a)**.

23 Install the cylinder head (see Section 11).

13 Piston

Removal

1 Remove the cylinder block (see Section 12). Make sure there is plenty of rag stuffed around the connecting rod to prevent anything falling into the engine.

2 Before removing the piston from the connecting rod, use a sharp scriber or felt marker pen to mark the front side of the piston so it is installed the same way round.

3 Carefully prise out the circlip on one side of the piston using needle-nose pliers or a small flat-bladed screwdriver inserted into the notch

(see illustration)**.** Push the piston pin out from the other side to free the piston from the connecting rod **(see illustration)**. Remove the other circlip and discard them as new ones must be used.

> **HAYNES HiNT** *If the piston pin is a tight fit in the piston bosses, use a heat gun to expand the alloy piston sufficiently to release its grip on the pin. If the piston pin is particularly stubborn, extract it using a drawbolt tool, but be careful to protect the piston's working surfaces.*

4 If required carefully remove the rings from the piston using your thumbs or a piston ring removal and installation tool **(see illustrations 14.8, 14.7, 14.4c, b and a)**. Do not nick or gouge the piston in the process. Carefully note which way up each ring fits and in which groove as they must be installed in their original positions if being reused. The upper surface of the top and middle rings should be marked **(see illustration 14.6b)**. The top and middle rings can also be identified by their different cross-section profiles **(see illustration 14.6a)**.

5 Scrape all traces of carbon from the tops of the piston. A hand-held wire brush or a piece of fine emery cloth can be used once most of the deposits have been scraped away. Do not, under any circumstances, use a wire brush mounted in a drill motor – the piston material is soft and will be eroded away.

6 Use a piston ring groove cleaning tool to remove any carbon deposits from the ring grooves. If a tool is not available, a piece broken off an old ring will do the job. Be very careful to remove only the carbon deposits. Do not remove any metal and do not nick or gouge the sides of the ring grooves.

7 Once the deposits have been removed, clean the piston with solvent and dry it thoroughly. If the orientation mark previously made on the piston is cleaned off, be sure to re-mark it. Make sure the oil return holes below the oil ring groove are clear.

Inspection

8 Carefully inspect the piston for cracks around the skirt, at the pin bosses and at the ring

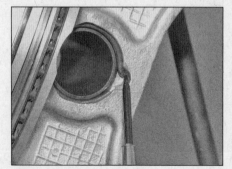

13.3a Prise out the circlip using a suitable tool in the notch . . .

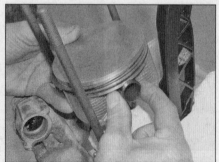

13.3b . . . then push out the pin and separate the piston from the rod

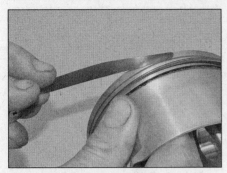

13.10 Measure the piston ring-to-groove clearance with a feeler gauge

13.11 Measure the piston diameter with a micrometer at the specified distance from the bottom of the skirt

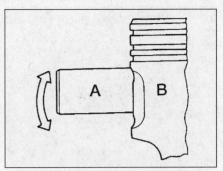

13.12a Check for any play between the pin (A) and its bore (B)

13.12b Measure the end of the pin and the bore in the piston and calculate the clearance

13.12c Measure the centre of the pin and the bore in the connecting rod and calculate the clearance

lands. Normal piston wear appears as even, vertical wear on the thrust surfaces. If the skirt is scored or scuffed, the engine may have been suffering from overheating and/or abnormal combustion, which causes excessively high operating temperatures. Also check that the circlip grooves are not damaged.

9 A hole in the top of the piston, in one extreme, or burned areas around the edge of the piston crown, indicate that pre-ignition or knocking under load have occurred. If you find evidence of any problems the cause must be corrected or the damage will occur again (see *Fault Finding* in the Reference section).

10 Measure the piston ring-to-groove clearance by laying each piston ring in its groove and slipping a feeler gauge in beside it **(see illustration)**. Make sure you have the correct ring for the groove (see Step 4). Check the clearance at three or four locations around the groove. If the clearance is greater than specified, measure the thickness of each ring and the width of each groove and replace the components worn beyond their limits with new ones, though if wear like this is evident it is advisable to replace the piston and rings as a complete new set.

11 Check the piston-to-bore clearance by measuring the bore (see Section 12), then measure the piston 16 mm up from the bottom of the skirt and at 90° to the piston pin axis **(see illustration)**. Note that the piston tolerance size must be matched to the A or B size code stamped on the piston. Refer to the Specifications at the beginning of the Chapter and subtract the piston diameter from the bore diameter to obtain the clearance. If it is greater than the specified figure, the piston must be replaced with a new one (assuming the bore itself is within limits).

12 Apply clean engine oil to the piston pin, insert it into the piston and check for any freeplay between the two **(see illustration)**. Measure the external diameter of the pin at each end and the internal diameter of the pin bore in each side of the piston, then subtract the pin diameter from the bore diameter to determine the clearance **(see illustration)**. Repeat the measurements between the centre of the pin and the small-end of the connecting rod **(see illustration)**. Replace component(s) that are worn beyond service limits with new ones to restore the clearance to specification.

Installation

13 Inspect and install the piston rings (see Section 14). Make sure there is plenty of rag stuffed around the connecting rod to prevent anything falling into the engine.

14 Lubricate the piston pin, the piston pin bore and the connecting rod small-end bore with molybdenum disulphide oil (a 50/50 mixture of molybdenum disulphide grease and clean engine oil).

15 When fitting the piston onto the connecting rod make sure the mark made on the piston crown faces the front of the engine.

16 Fit a *new* circlip into one side of the piston (do not reuse old circlips). Line up the piston on the connecting rod, and insert the piston pin from the other side **(see illustration)**. Secure the pin with the other *new* circlip **(see illustration)**. When fitting the circlips,

compress them only just enough to fit them in the piston, and make sure they are properly seated in their grooves with the open end away from the removal notch.

17 Install the cylinder block (see Section 12).

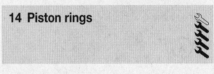

14 Piston rings

Inspection

1 It is good practice to replace the piston rings with new ones when an engine is being overhauled. Before installing the new rings, check the end gaps with the rings installed in the bore, as follows.

2 Fit the top ring into its bore, setting it 60 mm down from the top, and square it up with the

13.16a Line the piston up with the rod and insert the pin . . .

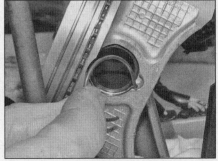

13.16b . . . then fit the circlip into its groove

14.2a Set the ring square in its bore using
the piston . . .

14.2b . . . and measure the end gap using
a feeler gauge

14.4a Fit the oil ring expander in its
groove . . .

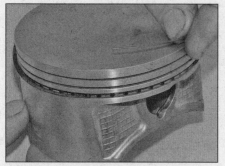

14.4b . . . then fit the lower side rail . . .

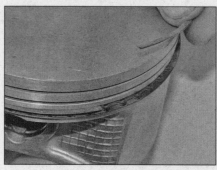

14.4c . . . and the upper side rail on each
side of it

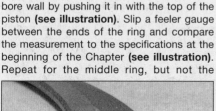

14.6a Note the different profiles of the top
ring (A) and second ring (B) . . .

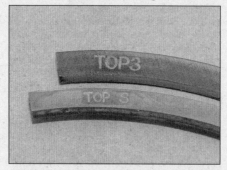

14.6b . . . and the markings denoting the
upper surface

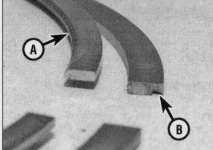

14.7 Install the middle ring . . .

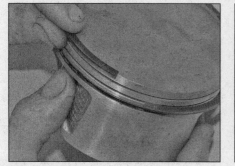

14.8 . . . and the top ring as described

bore wall by pushing it in with the top of the
piston **(see illustration)**. Slip a feeler gauge
between the ends of the ring and compare
the measurement to the specifications at the
beginning of the Chapter **(see illustration)**.
Repeat for the middle ring, but not the
three-piece oil control ring.

3 If the service limit is exceeded, check the
bore for wear (see Section 12). If the gap is
too small, the ring ends may come in contact
with each other during engine operation,
which can cause serious damage.

Installation

4 Install the oil control ring (lowest on the
piston) first. It is composed of three separate
components, namely the expander and the
upper and lower side-rails. Slip the expander
into the groove **(see illustrations)**. Next
fit the lower side-rail – do not use a piston
ring installation tool on the side-rails as they
may be damaged. Instead, place one end
of the side-rail into the groove between the
expander and the ring land. Hold it firmly in
place and slide a finger around the piston
while pushing the rail into the groove. Next, fit
the upper side-rail in the same manner **(see
illustration)**.

5 After the three oil ring components have
been installed, check to make sure that both
the upper and lower side-rails can be turned
smoothly in the ring groove.

6 The top and middle rings can be identified
by their different cross-section profiles **(see
illustration)**. The upper surface of each should
be marked **(see illustration)**.

7 Install the middle ring next. Make sure that
the mark near the end gap is facing up. Fit
the ring into the middle groove in the piston
(see illustration). Do not expand the ring any
more than is necessary to slide it into place.
To avoid breaking the ring, use a piston ring
installation tool.

8 Finally, install the top ring in the same
manner into the top groove in the piston **(see
illustration)**. Make sure the mark is facing up.

9 Once the rings are correctly installed, check
they move freely without snagging and stagger
their end gaps 120° apart.

15 Starter clutch and gears

Note: *The starter clutch can be removed with
the engine in the frame. If the engine has been
removed, ignore the steps which do not apply.*

Check

1 The operation of the starter clutch can be
checked while it is in situ. Remove the starter
motor (see Chapter 9). Check that the reduction
gear is able to rotate freely clockwise as you
look at it from the left-hand side via the starter

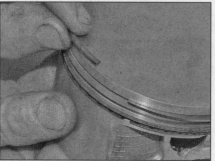

15.3 Remove the washer (A) and the spacer behind it, then remove the reduction gear (B) and the idle gear (C)

15.4 Check the operation of the clutch as described

motor aperture, but locks when rotated anti-clockwise. If not, the starter clutch is faulty and should be removed for inspection.

Removal

2 Remove the alternator rotor (see Chapter 9). Slide the starter driven gear off the end of the crankshaft if it didn't come off with the rotor.
3 Remove the washer and spacer from the idle gear **(see illustration)**. Draw the reduction gear off its shaft, on Funduro and ST models bringing the large washer on the idle gear with it. Draw the idle gear off its shaft.

Inspection

4 If separated fit the starter driven gear into the clutch, rotating it clockwise as you do to spread the sprags and allow the hub to enter. With the alternator rotor face down on a workbench, check that the starter driven gear rotates freely clockwise and locks against the rotor anti-clockwise **(see illustration)**. If it doesn't, the starter clutch should be dismantled for further investigation.

5 Withdraw the starter driven gear from the starter clutch, rotating it clockwise as you do to free it from the starter clutch.
6 Check the condition of the sprags in the starter clutch and the external surface of the driven gear hub – if the sprags are damaged, marked or flattened at any point, the sprag assembly must be replaced with a new one – see Steps 9 to 11 **(see illustration)**. If the hub is worn replace the driven gear with a new one.
7 Check the surface of the driven gear hub bush and the corresponding surface on the crankshaft **(see illustration)**.
8 Check the teeth of the reduction and idle gears and the corresponding teeth of the starter driven gear and starter motor drive shaft. Replace the gears and/or starter motor if worn or chipped teeth are discovered on related gears. Also check the idle and reduction gear shafts for damage, and check that the gears are not a loose fit on them.

Disassembly and reassembly

9 On Funduro and ST models, to separate the starter clutch from the alternator rotor, counter-hold the rotor and unscrew the clutch housing bolt nuts. Remove the cover, then release the sprag assembly from the housing and remove the housing, noting which way round everything fits. Check the housing for damage and wear.
10 On GS, Dakar and CS models, to separate the starter clutch from the alternator rotor, counter-hold the rotor and unscrew the clutch housing bolts **(see illustration)**. Detach the clutch from the back of the alternator, then release the sprag assembly from the housing, noting which way round everything fits. Check the housing for damage and wear.
11 On installation fit the sprag assembly with the arrow mark facing away from the rotor on Funduro and ST models, and towards it on GS, Dakar and CS models. Clean the starter clutch housing bolts and apply a drop of Loctite 648 to their threads. Tighten them to

15.6 Check the sprags (A) and the driven gear hub (B)

15.7 Check the bush (arrowed) and the crankshaft

15.10 Starter clutch bolts are on the inside of the rotor

15.12a Fit the idle gear . . .

15.12b . . . the reduction gear . . .

15.12c . . . then spacer . . .

15.12d . . . and the washer

15.13 Fit the starter driven gear into the clutch

the torque setting specified at the beginning of the Chapter.

Installation

12 Lubricate the idle and reduction gear shafts with oil. Slide the idle gear onto its shaft **(see illustration)**. Slide the reduction gear onto its shaft with its smaller pinion innermost, on Funduro and ST models fitting the large washer onto the idle gear with it **(see illustration)**. Slide the spacer onto the idle gear shaft, followed by the washer **(see illustrations)**.

13 Smear some molybdenum grease onto the inner flat section of the crankshaft (not the tapered section) and to the outer face of the gear where it seats on the clutch housing, and smear clean engine oil onto the outside of the starter driven gear hub where it contacts the sprags. Fit the starter driven gear into the clutch, rotating it clockwise as you do to

spread the sprags and allow the hub to enter **(see illustration)**.

14 Install the alternator rotor (see Chapter 9).

16 Clutch

Note 1: *The clutch can be removed with the engine in the frame. If the engine has been removed, ignore the steps which don't apply.*
Note 2: *The clutch nut must be discarded and a new one used on installation – it is best to obtain the new nut in advance.*
Special tool: *A clutch centre holding tool is required for this procedure (see Step 6).*

Removal

1 Drain the engine oil (see Chapter 1).
2 Remove the starter motor (see Chapter 9). Remove the water pump (see Chapter 3) –

there is no need to remove the pump cover or to remove the pump from the clutch cover, just follow the relevant steps to remove the clutch cover.

3 Working in a criss-cross pattern, gradually slacken the clutch spring bolts until pressure is released **(see illustration)**. To prevent the assembly from turning, cover it with a rag and hold it securely – the bolts are not very tight. If available, have an assistant to hold the clutch while you unscrew the bolts. Remove the bolts, spring seats and springs, then remove the pressure plate **(see illustration)**. Note that BMW specify that new springs should always be used whenever the clutch is disassembled.

4 Remove the clutch friction and plain plates as a pack, noting how they fit – in particular note whether the tabs on the outermost friction plate locate in the shallow slots offset from the main slots or not (some models do and some don't) – and keep them in order **(see illustration)**.

16.3a Unscrew the bolts (arrowed) and remove the springs . . .

16.3b . . . then remove the pressure plate

16.4 Remove the clutch plates, keeping them in order

5 Bend the lockwasher tab(s) down off the nut **(see illustration)**.

6 To remove the clutch nut, the input shaft must be locked. This can be done in several ways. If the engine is in the frame, engage 5th gear and have an assistant hold the rear brake on hard with the rear tyre in firm contact with the ground. Alternatively, the BMW service tool (Pt. No. 214600) or a similar commercially available tool can be used to stop the clutch centre from turning whilst the nut is slackened **(see illustration)**. Note that a threadlock is used on the nut threads and some heat may be required to release it. Unscrew the nut and remove the washer. Check the condition of the washer and replace it with a new one if necessary.

7 Remove the clutch centre and the outer thrust washer from the shaft **(see illustrations 16.19b and a)**.

8 Remove the clutch housing **(see illustration 16.18a)**. Remove the needle bearings and the inner thrust washer **(see illustrations 16.17c and b)**. Pick the O-ring out of its groove – check its condition and replace it with a new one if required **(see illustration 16.17a)**.

Inspection

9 After an extended period of service the clutch friction plates will wear and promote clutch slip. Assemble the complete set of friction plates and measure their combined thickness using a ruler or Vernier caliper **(see illustration)**. If the plate pack has worn to or beyond the service limit given in the Specifications at the beginning of the Chapter, or if any of the plates smell burnt or are glazed or warped, the friction plates must be replaced with a new set.

10 The plain plates should not show any signs of excess heating (bluing). Check for warpage using a flat surface and feeler gauges **(see illustration)**. If any plate exceeds the maximum permissible amount of warpage, or shows signs of bluing, all plain plates must be replaced with a new set.

11 Inspect the friction plates and the clutch housing for burrs and indentations on the edges of the protruding tabs on the plates and/or the slots in the housing **(see illustration)**. Similarly check for wear between the inner teeth of the plain plates and the slots in the clutch centre **(see illustration)**. Wear of this nature will cause clutch drag and slow disengagement during gear changes as the plates will snag when the pressure plate is lifted. With care a small amount of wear can be corrected by dressing with a fine file, but if this is excessive the worn components should be replaced with new ones.

12 Inspect the needle roller bearings and the bearing surfaces in the clutch housing and on the shaft. If there are any signs of wear, pitting or other damage the affected parts must be replaced with new ones.

13 Check the pressure plate and its bearing for signs of wear or damage and roughness **(see illustration)**. Check that the bearing outer

16.5 Bend the tab(s) away from the nut

16.6 Using a clutch holding tool while unscrewing the nut

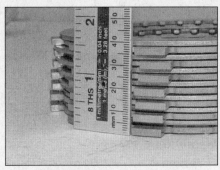

16.9 Measuring the assembled clutch plate pack thickness

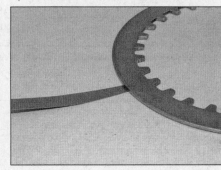

16.10 Check the plain plates for warpage

race is a good fit in the centre of the plate, and that the inner race rotates freely without any rough spots. Check the pull-rod teeth and the corresponding teeth on the release lever shaft for signs of wear or damage **(see illustration)**.

Replace any parts necessary with new ones – the pull-rod and bearing are held by a circlip, and some heat will be required to release the bearing.

14 Check the release mechanism in the clutch

16.11a Check the friction plate tabs and housing slots . . .

16.11b . . . and the plain plate teeth and centre slots as described

16.13a Check the pressure plate bearing and pull-rod teeth . . .

16.13b . . . and the teeth on the shaft

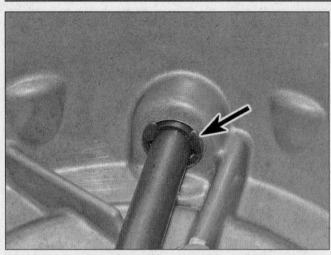

16.14 Remove the E-clip (arrowed) to release the shaft

16.15 Primary drive gear (A) and driven gear (B), oil pump drive gear (C)

cover for a smooth action. If the action is stiff or rough, remove the E-clip and withdraw the shaft (see illustration). Clean and check the oil seal and the two needle bearings in the cover. The seal can be replaced by levering the old one out with a seal hook or screwdriver and pressing the new one in. Refer to *Tools and Workshop Tips* in the Reference Section for details of removing and installing needle bearings. Lubricate the bearings with oil and the seal lips with grease before installing the shaft.

15 Check the teeth of the primary driven gear on the back of the clutch housing and the corresponding teeth of the primary drive gear on the crankshaft (see illustration). Replace

the clutch housing and/or primary drive gear with a new one if worn or chipped teeth are discovered. Similarly check the oil pump drive and driven gear teeth.

Installation

16 Remove all traces of old gasket from the crankcase and clutch cover surfaces.
17 Smear the inside of the clutch housing, the input shaft plain and splined surfaces, and the needle bearings with molybdenum disulphide oil (a 50/50 mixture of molybdenum disulphide grease and engine oil). Fit the O-ring into its groove, using a new one if necessary (see illustration). Slide the inner thrust washer and

the needle bearings onto the shaft, shorter one innermost (see illustrations).
18 Slide the clutch housing onto the bearings (see illustration). Make sure that the primary drive and driven gear teeth and the oil pump drive and driven gear teeth engage – turn the oil pump driven gears with your finger while pressing on the housing until the teeth are felt to engage and the housing moves in a bit further, then double-check by making sure the gear can't turn independently of the housing (see illustration).
19 Slide the outer thrust washer onto the shaft (see illustration). Slide the clutch centre onto the shaft (see illustration).

16.17a Fit the O-ring into the groove . . .

16.17b . . . then slide the thrust washer . . .

16.17c . . . and needle bearings onto the shaft

16.18a Slide the clutch housing onto the bearings

16.18b Check the teeth have meshed by turning the driven gear as described

16.19a Fit the outer thrust washer . . .

16.19b . . . and the clutch centre

16.20a Locate the washer onto the splines, with the raised tabs facing out

16.20b Fit the new clutch nut (recessed side inwards) . . .

16.20c . . . and tighten it to the specified torque

16.20d Bend the tabs up against the nut

16.21a Fit a plain plate . . .

20 Fit the lock washer with its tabs facing out, using a new one if required, and making sure it engages the splines as it can easily slip off the end **(see illustration)**. Apply Loctite 243 to the clutch nut and thread it onto the shaft with its recessed side facing in **(see illustration)**. Using the method employed on removal to lock the shaft (see Step 6), tighten the nut to the torque setting specified at the beginning of the Chapter **(see illustration)**. Bend the lockwasher tabs up against the nut **(see illustration)**.

21 If the original plates are being refitted return all to their original positions. If new plates are being fitted (or the old ones have become muddled up), install them as follows:
● On models with eight friction plates identify the single friction plate that is different to the rest – this is the outermost plate. Coat each clutch plate with engine oil prior to installation, then build up the plates as follows: first fit

a plain plate, then fit a friction plate, then alternate plain plates and friction plates until all are installed, making sure the outermost friction plate is the different one, and locating its tabs into the shallow slots in the housing so they are offset from the rest.
● On models with seven friction plates identify the single friction plate with an identity mark – this is the outermost plate (note that no mark was found on the model photographed). Coat each clutch plate with engine oil prior to installation, then build up the plates as follows: first fit a plain plate, then fit a friction plate, then alternate plain plates and friction plates until all are installed **(see illustrations)**.

22 Lubricate the pull-rod bearing with oil and each end of the pull-rod with molybdenum grease. Fit the pressure plate onto the clutch, engaging the castellations on its inner rim in the slots in the clutch centre **(see illustration)**.

Fit the new springs, spring seats and the bolts, making sure the recessed side of each seat faces in so it fits into the spring, and tighten the bolts evenly in a criss-cross sequence to the specified torque setting **(see illustration)**. Counter-hold the clutch housing to prevent it turning when tightening the spring bolts.

23 Install the water pump (see Chapter 3). Install the starter motor (see Chapter 9).

24 Fill the engine with oil and coolant to the correct levels (see Chapter 1 and *Pre-ride checks*). Adjust the clutch cable freeplay (see Chapter 1).

17 Clutch cable

1 Start at the handlebar end of the cable. Pull back the rubber boot and fully slacken

16.21b . . . then fit a friction plate, then alternate plain plates and friction plates

16.22a Make sure the castellations on the inner rim engage with those on the clutch centre

16.22b Fit the springs, seats and bolts

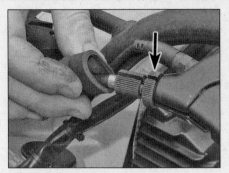

17.1a Pull the boot off and slacken the locknut (arrowed) . . .

17.1b . . . and turn the adjuster in

17.2a Turn the release lever forwards then slip the cable out of the bracket . . .

17.2b . . . and detach the end from the lever

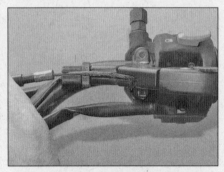

17.3a Align the slots and free the cable from the adjuster . . .

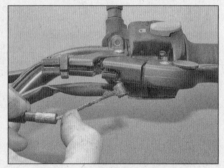

17.3b . . . and from the lever

the adjuster locknut (see illustration). Thread the adjuster fully in (see illustration). This provides freeplay in the cable and resets the adjuster to the beginning of its span.

2 Using a suitable pair of grips turn the release

lever to the front then draw the cable out of the holder and free the end from the release lever (see illustrations).

3 At the handlebar end of the cable align the slot in the adjuster and locknut with that in the lever bracket, then pull the outer cable end from the socket in the adjuster and release the inner cable from the lever (see illustrations). Remove the cable from the machine, noting its routing.

> **HAYNES HINT** *Before removing the cable from the bike, tape the lower end of the new cable to the upper end of the old cable. Slowly pull the lower end of the old cable out, guiding the new cable down into position. Using this method will ensure the cable is routed correctly.*

4 Installation is the reverse of removal. Apply grease to the cable ends. Make sure the cable is correctly routed. Adjust the amount of clutch lever freeplay (see Chapter 1). Tighten the locknut on completion.

18 Oil pumps

Note: *The oil pumps can be removed with the engine in the frame. If the engine has been removed, ignore the steps which don't apply.*

Removal

1 Drain the engine oil and the coolant (see Chapter 1). Remove the clutch (see Section 16).

2 There are two oil pumps, a feed pump at the top and a scavenge pump at the bottom – work on one pump at a time, and if both are being removed keep the parts from each pump separate. Remove the driven gear from the pump – on Funduro and ST models up to engine number 398297 pull or lever it up off the drive shaft to release it from the drive pin; on all other models remove the circlip, then pull or lever it up off the drive shaft to release it from the drive pin (see illustrations).

3 Turn the shaft to align the drive pin with the groove in the crankcase then withdraw the drive pin and remove the washer (see illustrations).

4 Undo the cover screws (see illustration).

5 Grasp the shaft and withdraw it along with the cover and inner rotor (see illustration). Remove the outer rotor from the pump housing

18.2a Remove the circlip . . .

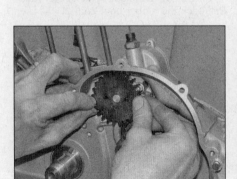

18.2b . . . then pull or lever the gear off the drive pin

18.3a Withdraw the drive pin . . .

18.3b . . . and remove the washer

18.4 Undo the screws (arrowed)

18.5a Withdraw the shaft, cover and inner rotor . . .

18.5b . . . and the outer rotor

18.6a Remove the circlip and washer . . .

18.6b . . . then slide the gear off the shaft

(see illustration). Slide the inner rotor up the pump shaft, then remove the drive pin and slide the inner rotor off (see illustrations 18.13b).

6 Remove the intermediate gear if required – on Funduro and ST models first disconnect the tachometer cable and remove the tachometer drive shaft, then slide the gear off its shaft. On all other models release the circlip and remove the spring washer, then draw the gear up off its shaft (see illustrations).

Inspection

7 Clean all the components in solvent.

8 Inspect the pump rotors and housings for scoring and wear.

9 Use a feeler gauge to measure the clearance between the inner rotor tip and the outer rotor, and between the outer rotor and the housing (see illustrations). Replace the rotors with new sets if the clearance in either of the checks exceeds the service limit specified.

10 Inspect the oil pump drive (on back of clutch housing) and driven gears and the intermediate gear for wear and damage to the teeth, and make sure the driven and intermediate gears are a good fit on the shafts.

Installation

11 Install the intermediate gear if removed, and on Funduro and ST models the tachometer drive shaft (see illustrations 18.6b and a).

12 Coat the outer rotor with clean oil and fit it into its housing with the punch mark facing out (see illustration 18.5b).

13 Slide the inner end of the shaft through the outer face of the cover (see illustration). Slide the inner rotor onto the shaft with the punch mark facing the cover (see illustration). Fit the drive pin into the its hole, then locate the

18.9a Measure inner-to-outer rotor clearance . . .

18.9b . . . and outer rotor-to-housing clearance

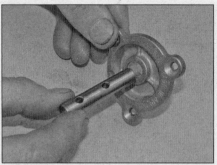

18.13a Fit the shaft into the cover . . .

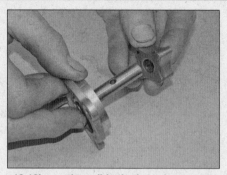

18.13b . . . then slide the inner rotor onto the shaft

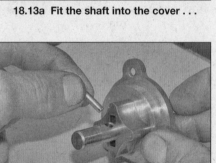

18.13c Fit the drive pin and locate the inner rotor over it

18.16 Align the slot with the drive pin then press the gear onto the pin

cut-outs in the inner face of the inner rotor onto the drive pin ends **(see illustration)**.
14 Coat the inner rotor with clean oil. Fit the shaft/inner rotor/cover assembly, engaging the inner rotor with the outer rotor and the locating shaft in its hole **(see illustration 18.5a)**. Apply

Loctite 243 to the threads of the screws and tighten them to the torque setting specified at the beginning of the Chapter.
15 Turn the shaft to align the drive pin hole with the groove in the crankcase. Fit the washer onto the shaft and the drive pin into

the hole **(see illustrations 18.3b and a)**.
16 Fit the driven gear over the shaft and press it onto the drive pin until it is felt to clip into place **(see illustration)**. On all except Funduro and ST models up to engine number 398297 fit the circlip into the groove **(see illustration 18.2a)**.
17 Install the clutch (Section 16). Replenish the engine oil and coolant (Chapter 1).

19 Primary drive gear

Note: *The primary drive gear can be removed with the engine in the frame. If the engine has been removed, ignore the steps which don't apply.*

Removal

1 Drain the engine oil and the coolant (see Chapter 1). Remove the camshafts (see Section 8). Remove the clutch (see Section 16).
2 Unscrew the primary drive gear nut and remove the washer **(see illustration)**.
3 Push the cam chain tensioner blade to the rear then draw the primary drive gear off the shaft, noting how the slot locates over the Woodruff key, and disengage the cam chain **(see illustration)**.
4 Remove the Woodruff key from the crankshaft if required **(see illustration)**.

Installation

5 If removed fit the Woodruff key into its slot in the crankshaft **(see illustration 19.4)**.
6 Make sure the cam chain is located in its tunnel and around the end of the crankshaft. Slide the primary drive gear onto the shaft with the chain sprocket innermost, aligning the slot in the gear with the Woodruff key, then slip the chain onto the sprocket and push the gear all the way on, holding the tensioner blade back out of the way **(see illustration)**.
7 Clean the crankshaft and nut threads and apply Loctite 243. Make sure the crankshaft is locked. Fit the nut with its washer and tighten it to the torque setting specified at the beginning of the Chapter **(see illustration)**.
8 Install the clutch (see Section 16). Install the camshafts (see Section 8). Replenish the engine oil and the coolant (see Chapter 1).

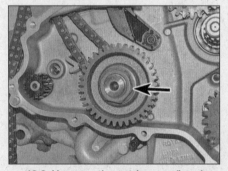

19.2 Unscrew the nut (arrowed) and remove the washer

19.3 Slide the gear off the shaft and disengage the chain

19.4 Remove the Woodruff key (arrowed)

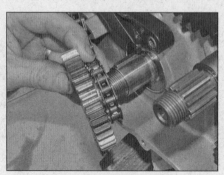

19.6 Fit the chain around the sprocket and slide the gear onto the shaft

19.7 Fit the washer and nut and tighten the nut

20.3a Lever the gear up off the shaft . . .

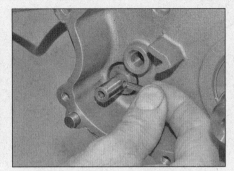

20.3b . . . and remove the drive pin

20.4 An example of a cardboard template to store crankcase bolts

20 Crankcases

Note: *To separate the crankcase halves, the engine must be removed from the frame.*

Separation

1 To access the crankshaft, balancer shaft, bearings, gearchange mechanism, selector drum and forks and transmission shafts, the crankcase must be split into its two halves.

2 Before the crankcases can be separated the following components must be removed:

Oil filter (Chapter 1)
Valve cover (Section 6)
Camshafts (Section 8)
Cylinder head (Section 10)
Cylinder block (Section 12)
Piston (Section 13)
Alternator (Chapter 9)
Water pump (Chapter 3)
Clutch (Section 16)
Oil pumps, if required (Section 18)
Cam chain tensioner blade (Section 9)
Primary drive gear (Section 19)
Cam chain
Neutral switch (Chapter 9)

3 Lever the water pump drive gear up off its drive pin in the end of the balancer shaft using a screwdriver **(see illustration)**. Remove the drive pin **(see illustration)**.

4 Make a cardboard template punched with holes to match all the bolts in the right-hand crankcase half – as each crankcase bolt is removed, store it in its relative position in the template **(see illustration)**. This will ensure all bolts and washers and any wiring clamps are installed in the correct location on reassembly. Note that new copper sealing washers should be used on assembly where fitted, though keep the old ones with the bolts for the time being as a guide for reassembly.

5 Unscrew the bolts in the right-hand side of the engine, evenly, a little at a time and in a criss-cross sequence until they are finger-tight, then remove them and fit them in the template **(see illustration)**.

6 Holding both halves of the crankcase set the engine on its right-hand side on some wooden blocks so the crankshaft and transmission output shaft are clear of the work surface. Remove the crankshaft locating tool **(see illustration 8.30a)**.

7 Carefully lift the left-hand crankcase half squarely off the right-hand half, using a soft-faced hammer to tap around the joint

to initially separate them if necessary, and to tap on the left-hand ends of the crankshaft, balancer shaft and transmission input shaft to ensure they remain in the right-hand crankcase **(see illustration)**. **Note:** *If the halves do not separate easily, make sure all fasteners have been removed. Do not try and separate the halves by levering against the crankcase mating surfaces as they are easily scored and will leak oil in the future if damaged. Note the shim(s) on the left-hand end of the crankshaft and the balancer shaft **(see illustration 26.2)** and the thrust washer on the end of the transmission output shaft **(see illustration 23.10)** – make sure they are on the shafts and have not got stuck to the crankcase.*

8 Remove the gasket and discard it – a new one must be used when joining the crankcases.

9 As required remove the crankshaft, balancer shaft, selector drum and forks, gearchange mechanism and the transmission shafts, and the oil pressure switch, referring to the relevant Sections of this Chapter, and to Chapter 9 for the oil pressure switch. Check all components and their bearings for wear as described in those Sections.

10 Unscrew the oil baffle plate bolts and remove the plate **(see illustration)**. Remove

20.5 Crankcase bolts (arrowed)

20.7 Carefully separate the crankcase halves

20.10a Unscrew the bolts (arrowed) and remove the plate . . .

20.10b . . . then lift out the strainer

20.19 Fit the strainer into its slot, thin end first

the internal oil strainer from the left-hand crankcase, noting how it fits **(see illustration)**. Clean the gauze and check it for damage.

11 Remove all traces of old gasket from the mating surfaces of the crankcases. Carefully clean up minor damage to the surfaces with a fine sharpening stone or grindstone.

12 Clean the crankcases thoroughly with new solvent and dry them with compressed air. Blow out all oil passages with compressed air.

Caution: Be very careful not to nick or gouge the crankcase mating surfaces or oil leaks will result. Check both crankcase halves very carefully for cracks and other damage.

Inspection

13 Small cracks or holes in aluminium castings can be repaired with an epoxy resin adhesive as a temporary measure. Permanent repairs can only be done by argon-arc welding, and only a specialist in this process is in a position to advise on the economy or practical aspect of such a repair, although some of the low temperature kits such as Lumiweld are suitable for small repairs. If any damage is found that can't be repaired, replace the crankcase halves as a set.

14 Damaged threads can be reclaimed using a diamond section wire insert, for example of the Heli-Coil type (though there are other makes), which are easily fitted after drilling and re-tapping the affected thread.

15 Sheared studs or screws can usually be removed with extractors, which consist of a tapered, left-hand thread screw of very hard

steel. These are inserted into a pre-drilled hole in the stud, and usually succeed in dislodging the most stubborn stud or screw. If a stud has sheared above its bore line, it can be removed using a conventional stud extractor which avoids the need for drilling.

16 Check that the cylinder studs are tight. If any are loose, remove them, then clean their threads and apply a suitable non-permanent thread locking compound and tighten them securely. Refer to Section 2 'Fasteners' of *Tools and Workshop Tips* in the Reference section at the end of this manual for details of how to slacken and tighten studs using two nuts locked together.

HAYNES HiNT *Refer to Tools and Workshop Tips for details of installing a thread insert and using screw extractors.*

Reassembly

17 If the transmission shafts have not been removed, check the condition of the oil seal on the right-hand end of the output shaft and replace it with a new one if it is damaged or deteriorated or shows signs of leakage **(see illustration 23.4)**. Install all components into the right-hand crankcase, with it on its side and supported on blocks as before so the shaft ends stay clear of the work surface.

18 Wipe over the mating surfaces of both crankcase halves using a rag soaked in high flash-point solvent to remove all traces of oil.

19 Fit the internal oil strainer into its slot in the left-hand crankcase half, with its thin end going

in first **(see illustration)**. Fit the oil baffle plate and tighten the bolts **(see illustration 20.10b)**.

20 Make sure the crankshaft is positioned at TDC as shown **(see illustration)**. Fit a new gasket onto the right-hand crankcase **(see illustration)**.

21 Check again that all components are in position **(see illustration 20.20a)**. Make sure the shim(s) are on the crankshaft and balancer shaft **(see illustration 26.2)** and the thrust washer is on the transmission output shaft **(see illustration 23.10)**. Carefully fit the left-hand crankcase half down onto the right-hand half, making sure the shafts all locate correctly **(see illustration 20.7)**.

22 Check that the left-hand crankcase half is correctly seated. Clean, fit and finger-tighten two of the crankcase bolts, inserting them from the underside in their original locations, one at the top and one at the bottom, to hold the cases together **(see illustration)**. Fit the crankshaft locating tool, making sure it locates in the groove in the crankshaft so it is held secure **(see illustration 8.5d)**. Turn the engine upright.

Caution: The crankcase halves should fit together without being forced. If the casings are not correctly seated, remove the left-hand crankcase half and investigate the problem. Do not attempt to pull them together using the crankcase bolts as the casing will crack and be ruined.

23 Clean the remaining crankshaft bolts, then insert them in their original locations **(see illustration 20.5)**. Secure all bolts finger-tight at first, then tighten them, working from

20.20a Position the crankshaft at TDC

20.20b Lay a new gasket onto the mating surface

20.22 Fit two of the bolts to hold the cases together

20.24 Cut away the gasket flush with the crankcase

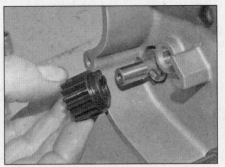

20.26a Slide the gear onto the shaft and over the drive pin . . .

20.26b . . . using a hammer and socket to seat it if necessary

the centre outwards, to the torque setting specified at the beginning of the Chapter.

24 Cut off the piece of gasket that bridges the cylinder bore **(see illustration)**.

25 With all crankcase fasteners tightened, check that the crankshaft, balancer shaft and transmission shafts rotate smoothly and easily. Check that the transmission shafts rotate freely and independently in neutral, then fit the gearchange lever and select each gear in turn whilst rotating the output shaft as fast as possible. Check that all gears can be selected and that the shafts rotate freely in every gear. If there are any signs of undue stiffness, tight or rough spots, or of any other problem, the fault must be rectified before proceeding further.

26 Fit the water pump drive gear drive pin into its hole in the end of the balancer shaft **(see illustration 20.3b)**. Press the gear down onto the pin so it locates in the cut-outs **(see illustration)** – use a hammer and socket to drive the gear on if necessary **(see illustration)**.

27 Install all other removed assemblies in a reverse of the sequence given in Step 2.

21 Gearchange mechanism

Removal

1 Remove the engine from the frame (see Section 4), and separate the crankcase halves (Section 20).

2 Note how the gearchange shaft centralising

spring ends fit on each side of the locating pin in the casing, and how the pawls on the selector arm locate onto the pins on the end of the selector drum cam. Pivot the selector arm away from the drum, then grasp the end of the shaft and withdraw the shaft/arm assembly **(see illustration)**.

3 Note how the stopper arm spring ends locate and how the roller on the arm locates in the neutral detent on the selector drum cam. Remove the arm and the spring, noting how they fit **(see illustrations 21.7b and a)**.

Inspection

4 Check the selector arm for cracks, distortion and wear of its pawls, and check for any corresponding wear on the pins on the selector drum cam **(see illustration)**. Also check the stopper arm roller and the detents in the cam for any wear or damage, and make sure the roller turns freely **(see illustration)**.

21.2 Pivot the arm away from the drum and withdraw the shaft/arm assembly, noting how it fits

Replace any components that are worn or damaged with new ones.

5 Inspect the shaft centralising spring, the selector arm spring and the stopper arm return spring for fatigue, wear or damage **(see illustration)**. If any is found, they must be replaced with new ones. To replace the shaft spring, slide the washer and spacer sleeve off the shaft, followed by the spring, noting how its ends locate **(see illustration)**. Fit the new spring, locating the ends on each side of the post, then fit the sleeve into the spring and the washer onto the sleeve. To replace the selector arm spring note how its ends locate before unhooking it **(see illustration)**.

6 Check the gearchange shaft is straight and look for damage to the splines. If the shaft is bent you can attempt to straighten it, but if the splines are damaged the shaft must be replaced with a new one. Also check the condition of the shaft oil seal in the clutch

21.4a Check the selector arm pawls and the pins on the cam . . .

21.4b . . . and the stopper arm roller and the detents on the cam

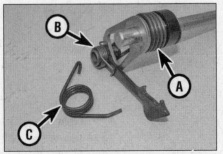

21.5a Check the centralising spring (A), the selector arm spring (B) and the stopper arm spring (C)

21.5b Slide the washer and spacer (arrowed) off the shaft, then remove the spring

21.5c Note how the spring ends (arrowed) locate

21.6a Lever out the seal

21.6b Press or drive the new seal into its housing

21.7a Locate the return spring on its post . . .

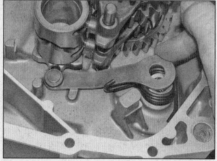

21.7b . . . then position the stopper arm and hold it aligned . . .

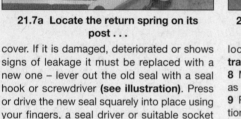

21.7c . . . while fitting the shaft

cover. If it is damaged, deteriorated or shows signs of leakage it must be replaced with a new one – lever out the old seal with a seal hook or screwdriver (see illustration). Press or drive the new seal squarely into place using your fingers, a seal driver or suitable socket (see illustration).

Installation

7 Check that the shaft centralising and stopper arm springs are properly positioned (see illustration 21.5a). Locate the stopper arm return spring and the stopper arm, with its roller against the neutral detent in the cam, making sure they are the correct way round, then hold the stopper arm so its hole is aligned with the shaft bore in the crankcase and fit the shaft through the arm and into the bore (see illustrations). Locate the selector arm pawls onto the pins on the selector drum and the centralising spring ends onto each side of the

locating pin in the crankcase (see illustration 21.2).
8 Make sure everything is correctly positioned as shown (see illustration).
9 Reassemble the crankcase halves (Section 20) and install the engine (see Section 4).

22 Selector drum and forks

Removal

1 Remove the engine from the frame (see Section 4), and separate the crankcase halves (Section 20).
2 Remove the gearchange mechanism (Section 21).
3 Before removing the selector forks, mark each one using a felt pen according to its location to aid identification on installation.

4 Support the selector forks and withdraw the shafts from the casing, then remove the forks, noting how the guide pins locate in the selector drum tracks (see illustrations 22.15e, d, c, b and a). Slide each fork back onto its shaft to keep them in the correct order.
5 Remove the selector drum (see illustration).

Inspection

6 Inspect the selector forks for any signs of wear or damage, especially around the fork ends where they engage with the groove in the pinion (see illustration). Check that each fork fits correctly in its pinion groove. If the forks are in any way damaged they must be replaced with new ones.
7 Measure the thickness of the fork ends and compare the readings to the specifications. Replace the forks with new ones if they are worn beyond their specifications.

21.8 Make sure everything is correctly positioned

22.5 Lift the drum out of the crankcase

22.6 Check the fork ends and pinion grooves

22.10 Check the fit of each fork on its shaft, and check the guide pins and their grooves in the drum

22.12a Check the switch contact (arrowed) and the insulating disc around it . . .

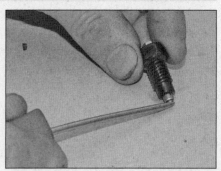

22.12b . . . and check the neutral switch plunger

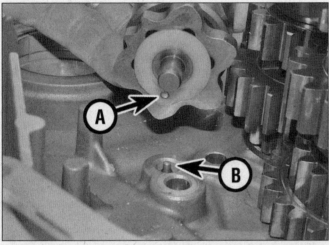

22.14 Position the drum so the neutral contact (A) will be against the neutral switch plunger (shown installed – B)

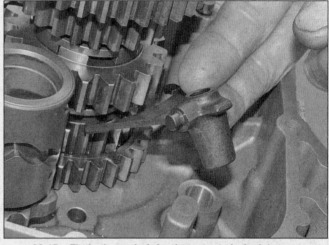

22.15a Fit the lower fork for the output shaft pinion . . .

8 Check closely to see if the forks are bent. Check that the forks fit correctly on their shaft. They should move freely with a light fit but no appreciable freeplay. Check that the fork shaft holes in the crankcases are neither worn nor damaged.

9 Check each fork shaft is straight by rolling it along a flat surface. A bent rod will cause difficulty in selecting gears and make the gearchange action heavy. Replace the shaft with a new one if it is bent.

10 Inspect the selector drum grooves and selector fork guide pins for signs of wear or damage (see illustration). Measure the diameter of the guide pins and compare the

readings to the specifications. Replace the forks with new ones if they are worn beyond their specifications.

11 Check that the selector drum rotates freely in each crankcase half with no sign of freeplay.

12 Check the neutral switch contact and the insulating disc on the end of the drum for wear and damage (see illustration). Check that the neutral switch plunger moves in and out freely (see illustration).

Installation

13 Prior to installation lubricate all moving and contacting surfaces (i.e. fork ends, pinion

grooves, guide pins, selector drum grooves, drum ends, fork shafts and bores) with molybdenum disulphide oil (a 50/50 mixture of molybdenum disulphide grease and engine oil).

14 Locate the selector drum in the crankcase with the neutral contact above the neutral switch housing (see illustration).

15 Fit the selector forks into the groove in their pinion according to the marks made on removal and locate the guide pins in the selector drum tracks (see illustrations). Slide each fork shaft through its fork(s) and into the crankcase (see illustrations). The installed assembly should be as shown (see illustration).

22.15b . . . and locate its guide pin in the drum track

22.15c Fit the upper fork . . .

22.15d . . . then slide the shaft through and into the crankcase

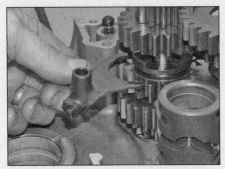

22.15e Fit the fork for the input shaft pinion . . .

22.15f . . . then slide the shaft through and into the crankcase

22.15g Make sure everything is correctly positioned

16 Install the gearchange mechanism (Section 21).

17 Reassemble the crankcase halves (Section 20) and install the engine (see Section 4).

23 Transmission shaft removal and installation

Removal

1 Remove the engine from the frame (see Section 4), and separate the crankcase halves (Section 20).

23.3 Lift the transmission shafts out together, holding the bottom gears as you do

2 Remove the gearchange mechanism (Section 21) and the selector drum and forks (Section 22). To give more working room if required also remove the crankshaft (Section 26).

3 Lift the output shaft and input shaft together out of the crankcase, noting their relative positions and how they fit together **(see illustration)**. If they are stuck, use a soft-faced hammer and gently tap on the ends of the shafts to free them. Hold the bottom three gears on the input shaft as you lift it out otherwise they will drop off. The top two gears on the output shaft are also loose, and note the thrust washer on the end **(see illustration 23.10)**.

4 Remove the oil seal from the right-hand

23.4 Lever out the oil seal and discard it

side of the crankcase and discard it as a new one must be used **(see illustration)**.

5 If necessary, the input shaft and output shaft can be overhauled (see Section 24).

6 Referring to *Tools and Workshop Tips* in the Reference Section, check the bearings **(see illustrations)**. Replace them with new ones if necessary – to do this the crankcases must be heated to 80 to 100°C. The bearings in housings that are open on each side (i.e. the input and output shaft bearings in the left-hand crankcase and the output shaft bearing in the right-hand crankcase) can be driven out using a suitable bearing driver or socket. The input shaft bearing in the right-hand crankcase is closed on the outer side and must be removed using an internal expanding puller, either with slide-hammer attachment or drawbolt and plate attachment. If using a slide-hammer you will need an assistant wearing oven gloves to hold the crankcase firmly down on a surface with protection to prevent marking the crankcase. If using a drawbolt you need to draw it through a plate laid across the crankcase with suitable protection for the mating surfaces. New bearings can be driven into place using a suitable driver or socket that bears only on the outer race – the case needs to be heated, and if available use a temperature reduction spray on the bearings or stick them in the fridge or freezer for a while.

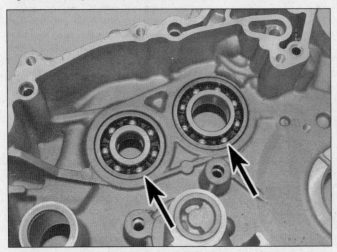

23.6a Check the transmission shaft bearings (arrowed) . . .

23.6b . . . in each crankcase half

23.7a Fit the new seal . . .

23.7b . . . and drive it in so it is flush

23.10 Make sure the thrust washer (arrowed) is on the shaft

Where applicable make sure the sealed side of the bearing faces the outside of the engine. Make sure the surfaces of the crankcase are suitably protected to prevent damage.

Installation

7 Apply some grease to the lips of the new oil seal. Fit the seal into the right-hand crankcase half, setting it flush with its housing **(see illustrations)**.

8 Lay the transmission shafts side by side so their related pinions are engaged. Smear the shaft journals where they locate in the bearings with molybdenum grease. Grasp the shafts, keeping a hold on the pinions on the right-hand end of the input shaft to prevent them dropping off, and hold them upright with the left-hand end uppermost **(see illustration 23.3)**.

9 Lower the shafts together into the right-hand crankcase half and tap them into the bearings using a soft-faced hammer until they seat.

10 Make sure both transmission shafts are correctly seated and their related pinions are correctly engaged. Make sure the thrust washer is on the left-hand end of the output shaft **(see illustration)**.

11 If removed install the crankshaft (Section 26). Install the selector drum and forks (Section 22) and the gearchange mechanism (Section 21).

12 Reassemble the crankcase halves (see Section 20) and install the engine (see Section 4).

24 Transmission shaft overhaul

1 Remove the transmission shafts from the crankcase (see Section 23). Always disassemble the transmission shafts separately to avoid mixing up the components **(see illustrations)**. When removing the needle bearings that sit between splined sections

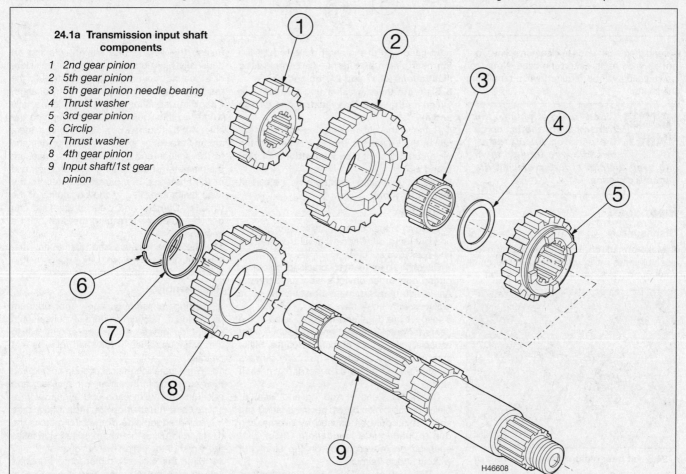

24.1a Transmission input shaft components

1 2nd gear pinion
2 5th gear pinion
3 5th gear pinion needle bearing
4 Thrust washer
5 3rd gear pinion
6 Circlip
7 Thrust washer
8 4th gear pinion
9 Input shaft/1st gear pinion

H46608

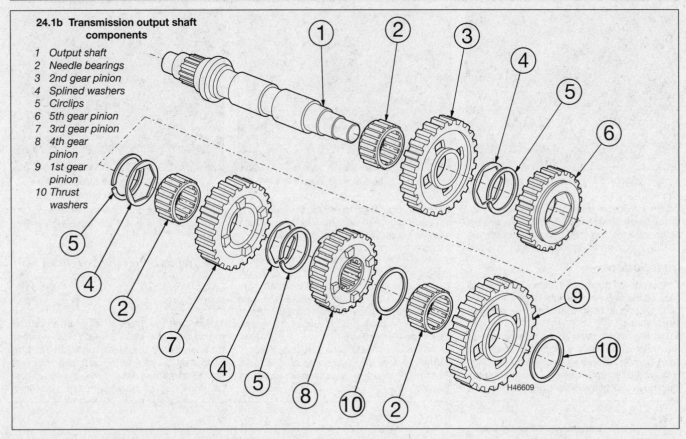

24.1b Transmission output shaft components

1 Output shaft
2 Needle bearings
3 2nd gear pinion
4 Splined washers
5 Circlips
6 5th gear pinion
7 3rd gear pinion
8 4th gear pinion
9 1st gear pinion
10 Thrust washers

spread their open ends to clear the splines, but not so wide as to distort the cage. Note that new circlips will be required when rebuilding the shafts.

> **HAYNES HINT** *When disassembling the transmission shafts, place the parts on a long rod or thread a wire through them to keep them in order and facing the proper direction.*

Input shaft

Disassembly

2 Make a mark on the outer face of the 2nd gear pinion so it can be installed the same way round. Slide the 2nd gear pinion off the

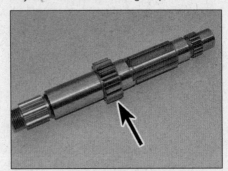

24.5 1st gear pinion (arrowed) is part of the shaft

right-hand end of the shaft, followed by the 5th gear pinion and its needle bearing **(see illustrations 24.17 and 24.16b and a)**.
3 Slide the thrust washer and the 3rd gear pinion off the shaft **(see illustrations 24.15b and a)**.
4 Remove the circlip securing the 4th gear pinion then slide the thrust washer and the pinion off the shaft **(see illustrations 24.14c, b and a)**.
5 The 1st gear pinion is integral with the shaft **(see illustration)**.

Inspection

6 Wash all of the components in clean solvent and dry them off. Check that all the oil holes and passages are clear.
7 Check the gear teeth for cracking, chipping, pitting and other obvious wear or damage. Any pinion that is damaged as such must be replaced with a new one.
8 Inspect the dogs and the dog holes in the gears for cracks, chips, and excessive wear especially in the form of rounded edges. Make sure mating gears engage properly. Always replace paired gears as a set (i.e. on each shaft).
9 Check for signs of scoring and wear or bluing on the pinion bores, needle bearing and shaft. This could be caused by overheating due to inadequate lubrication. Check that each pinion moves freely on the shaft but without undue freeplay.
10 The shaft is unlikely to sustain damage

unless the engine has seized, placing an unusually high loading on the transmission, or a bearing has broken up or seized, or the machine has covered a very high mileage. Check the surfaces of the shaft, especially where a pinion turns on it, and replace the shaft if it has scored or picked up, or if there are any cracks or excessive wear or damage to the splines and circlip grooves. Measure the diameter of the bearing seat on each end of the shaft and compare the results to the wear limits specified at the beginning of the Chapter. Damage and wear of any kind can only be cured by replacing the shaft with a new one.
11 Check the washers and replace any that are bent or appear worn. Use new ones if in any doubt. New circlips must be used.

Reassembly

12 During reassembly, apply molybdenum disulphide oil (a 50/50 mixture of molybdenum disulphide grease and clean engine oil) to the mating surfaces of the shaft, pinions and bearing.
13 When installing the circlips, do not expand their ends any further than is necessary and position them with each end aligned with a spline **(see illustration 24.14d)**. Make sure the round edged side of the circlip faces the direction thrust so the sharp edged side takes the thrust of the pinion it seats against.
14 Slide the 4th gear pinion onto the shaft with its dog holes facing away from the 1st

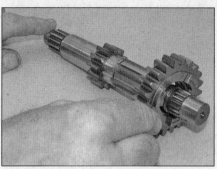

24.14a Slide the 4th gear pinion . . .

24.14b . . . and the thrust washer onto the shaft . . .

24.14c . . . and secure them with the circlip . . .

24.14d . . . making sure it locates properly in its groove

24.15a Slide the 3rd gear pinion . . .

24.15b . . . and the thrust washer onto the shaft . . .

gear pinion (see illustration). Slide the thrust washer onto the shaft, then fit the circlip, making sure that it locates correctly in the groove in the shaft (see illustrations).

15 Slide the 3rd gear pinion onto the shaft with the selector fork groove facing the 4th

gear pinion, and aligning the oil holes (see illustration). Slide the thrust washer onto the shaft (see illustration).

16 Slide the 5th gear pinion needle bearing onto the shaft (see illustration). Slide the 5th gear pinion onto the bearing, making

sure its dogs face the 3rd gear pinion (see illustration).

17 Slide the 2nd gear pinion onto the end of the shaft with the mark made on removal facing out so it is the same way round (see illustration).

18 Check that all components have been correctly installed (see illustration).

Output shaft

Disassembly

19 Remove the thrust washer from the end of the shaft, then slide the 1st gear pinion, its needle bearing, the thrust washer and the 4th gear pinion off the shaft (see illustrations 24.29c, b and a and 24.28b and a).

20 Slide the 5th gear pinion towards the 2nd gear pinion so the circlip is accessible, then release the circlip and slide it towards the 5th gear pinion (see illustrations). Now slide the splined washer, the 3rd gear pinion

24.16a . . . then fit the needle bearing . . .

24.16b . . . and slide the 5th gear pinion onto it

24.17 Slide the 2nd gear pinion onto the shaft

24.18 The complete input shaft should be as shown

24.20a Slide the 5th gear pinion along . . .

24.20b ... then release the circlip ...

24.20c ... and position it as shown

24.20d Slide the pinion and shaped washer back to expose the circlip (arrowed)

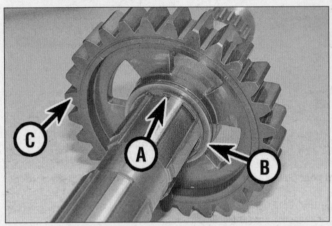

24.21 Remove the circlip (A) and slide the splined washer (B), 2nd gear pinion (C) and its needle bearing off

24.24 Make sure the circlip locates in the groove

and the angled splined washer towards the 5th gear pinion so the circlip is exposed (see illustration). Release the circlip and slide it off the shaft, followed by the angled splined washer, the 3rd gear pinion, its needle bearing, the splined washer, the circlip and the 5th gear pinion (see illustrations 24.27b and a, 24.26c, b and a).

21 Remove the circlip securing the 2nd gear pinion, then slide the splined washer, the pinion and its needle bearing off the shaft (see illustration).

Inspection

22 Refer to Steps 6 to 11 above.

Reassembly

23 During reassembly, apply molybdenum disulphide oil (a 50/50 mixture of molybdenum disulphide grease and clean engine oil) to the mating surfaces of the shaft, pinions and needle bearings. When installing the circlips, do not expand their ends any further than is necessary and position them with each end aligned with a spline (see illustration 24.24). Make sure the round edged side of the circlip faces the direction thrust so the sharp edged side takes the thrust of the pinion it seats against.

24 Slide the 2nd gear pinion needle bearing onto the shaft, then slide the 2nd gear pinion onto the bearing with its shouldered side facing the left-hand end, followed by the splined washer. Fit the circlip, making sure it is locates correctly in its groove in the shaft (see illustration).

25 Slide the 5th gear pinion onto the shaft with its selector fork groove facing away from the 2nd gear pinion, then fit the circlip, but slide it beyond its groove at this stage (see illustrations).

26 Slide the splined washer onto the shaft, then slide the needle bearing on (see illustrations). Slide the 3rd gear pinion onto the bearing, with its dogs facing away from the 5th gear pinion (see illustration).

27 Slide the shaped splined washer on with its recessed side facing away from the 3rd gear pinion (see illustration). Fit the circlip, making sure it is locates correctly in its groove in the shaft (see illustration). Slide the shaped splined washer against the circlip, then slide the 3rd gear pinion against

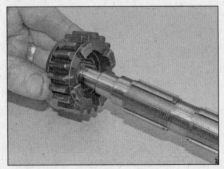

24.25a Slide the 5th gear pinion on to the shaft ...

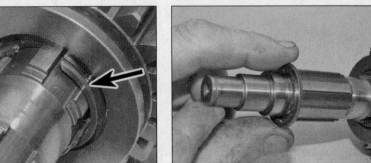

24.25b ... then fit the circlip (arrowed) in the position shown

24.26a Slide the splined washer on ...

24.26b ... then fit the needle bearing ...

24.26c ... and slide the 3rd gear pinion onto it

24.27a Slide the shaped splined washer on ...

24.27b ... then fit the circlip making sure it locates properly in its groove

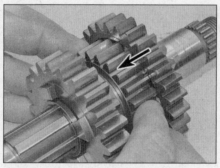

24.27c Slide the 5th gear pinion along so it pushes the circlip ...

24.27d ... into its groove

washer. Now locate the 5th gear pinion circlip in its groove by pulling the 5th gear pinion against it and sliding it along (see illustrations).

28 Slide the 4th gear pinion onto the shaft

with its selector fork groove facing the 3rd gear pinion, followed by the thrust washer (see illustrations).

29 Slide the needle bearing on, then slide the 1st gear pinion onto it with its deeper

recessed side facing the 4th gear pinion (see illustrations). Slide the thrust washer onto the end of the shaft (see illustration).

30 Check that all components have been correctly installed (see illustration).

24.28a Slide the 4th gear pinion onto the shaft ...

24.28b ... followed by the thrust washer ...

24.29a ... then fit the needle bearing ...

24.29b ... and slide the 1st gear pinion onto it ...

24.29c ... then fit the thrust washer

24.30 The assembled shaft should be as shown

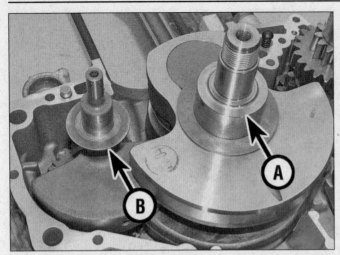

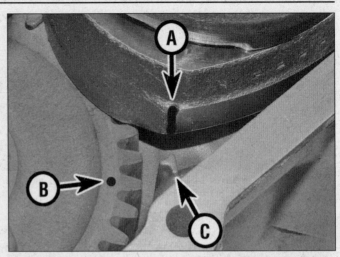

26.2 Crankshaft shim(s) – A; balancer shaft shim(s) – B

26.3 Align the mark on the crankshaft (A) and the punch mark on the balancer shaft (B) with the pointers on the index mark (C) on the crankcase – note that as the photo is not taken from above the punch mark appears offset to its pointer, but this is just the effect of the angle

25 Main bearing information

1 Bearing failure occurs mainly because of lack of lubrication, the presence of dirt or other foreign particles, overloading the engine and/or corrosion. Regardless of the cause of bearing failure, it must be corrected before the engine is reassembled to prevent it from happening again.

2 Dirt and other foreign particles get into the engine in a variety of ways. They may be left in the engine during assembly or they may pass through filters or breathers, then get into the oil and from there into the bearings. Metal chips from machining operations and normal engine wear are often present. Abrasives are sometimes left in engine components after reconditioning operations, especially when parts are not thoroughly cleaned using the proper cleaning methods. Whatever the source, foreign objects often end up imbedded in the soft bearing material and are easily recognised. Large particles will not embed in the bearing and will score or gouge the bearing and journal. The best prevention for this cause of bearing failure is to clean all parts thoroughly and keep everything spotlessly clean during engine reassembly. Regular oil and filter changes are also recommended.

3 Lack of lubrication or lubrication breakdown has a number of interrelated causes. Excessive heat (which thins the oil), overloading (which squeezes the oil from the bearing face) and oil leakage or throw off (from excessive bearing clearances, worn oil pump or high engine speeds) all contribute to lubrication breakdown. Blocked oil passages will starve a bearing of lubrication and destroy it. When lack of lubrication is the cause of bearing failure, the bearing material is wiped

or extruded from the steel backing of the bearing. Temperatures may increase to the point where the steel backing and the journal turn blue from overheating. Refer to *Tools and Workshop Tips* in the Reference section at the end of this manual for bearing fault finding.

4 Riding habits can have a definite effect on bearing life. Full throttle low, speed operation, or labouring the engine, puts very high loads on bearings, which tend to squeeze out the oil film. These loads cause the bearings to flex, which produces fine cracks in the bearing face (fatigue failure). Eventually the bearing material will loosen in pieces and tear away from the steel backing. Short trip riding leads to corrosion of bearings, as insufficient engine heat is produced to drive off the condensed water and corrosive gases produced. These products collect in the engine oil, forming acid and sludge. As the oil is carried to the engine bearings, the acid attacks and corrodes the bearing material.

5 Incorrect bearing installation during engine assembly will lead to bearing failure as well. Tight fitting bearings which leave insufficient bearing oil clearances result in oil starvation. Dirt or foreign particles trapped behind a bearing insert result in high spots on the bearing which lead to failure.

26.4 Lift the crankshaft out of the crankcase

6 To avoid bearing problems, clean all parts thoroughly before reassembly, double check all bearing clearance measurements and lubricate the new bearings on installation.

26 Crankshaft, connecting rod and main bearings

Removal

1 Remove the engine from the frame (see Section 4) and separate the crankcase halves (see Section 20).

2 Remove the shim(s) from the left-hand end of the crankshaft (see illustration).

3 Before removing the crankshaft turn it so the alignment marks between it, the balancer shaft and the crankcase are aligned as shown (see illustration). On models up to 2003 with a split sprung gear (as opposed to a helical cut gear on 2004-on models) now fit a locating pin (BMW part No. 116630 or suitable equivalent) into the hole in the balancer shaft gear to keep its sprung gear teeth in line with the main gear teeth after the crankshaft has been removed.

4 Lift the crankshaft out of the crankcase (see illustration). Note the connecting rod is part of the crankshaft assembly and is not available as a separate part.

Inspection

5 Clean the crankshaft with solvent, squirting it under pressure through all the oil passages. If available, blow it dry with compressed air, and also blow through the oil passages.

6 Check the balancer drive gear for wear or damage (see illustration). If any of the gear teeth are excessively worn, chipped or broken, the gear and its driven gear on the balancer shaft must be replaced with new ones – they come as a pair (see Section 27). To remove the gear first heat it to 140°C, then pull it off

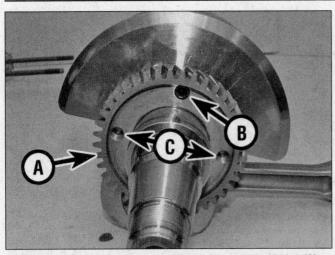

26.6a Balancer drive gear (A), roll pin (B), threaded holes (C)

26.6b Puller set ups for balancer drive and driven gear removal

using a suitable puller, noting how it locates on the roll-pin – there are two threaded holes in the gear into which the legs of a puller can be fitted (see illustration). The new gear must be heated to 140°C before being driven or pressed onto the shaft – make sure the roll-pin is fully seated in the web before fitting the gear as it must not protrude from the hole in the gear.

7 Refer to Section 25 and examine the main bearings (see illustrations). If they are scored, badly scuffed or appear to have been seized, new bearings must be installed. Always replace both main bearings together. If they are badly damaged, check the corresponding crankshaft journals. Evidence of extreme heat, such as discoloration, indicates that lubrication failure has occurred. Be sure to thoroughly check the oil pumps and pressure relief valve as well as all oil holes and passages before reassembling the engine.

8 Using V-blocks and a dial gauge check for run-out at each end of the crankshaft and replace it with a new one if it exceeds the maximum specified.

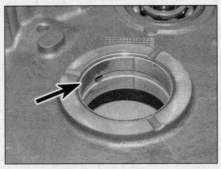

26.7a Right-hand main bearing (arrowed)

26.7b Left-hand main bearing (arrowed)

9 Refer to Section 13, Step 12 and check the connecting rod small-end and piston pin, if not already done.

Oil clearance check

10 Whether new bearing shells are being fitted or the original ones are being reused, the main bearing oil clearances should be checked before the engine is reassembled.

11 Measure the diameter of each crankshaft journal with a micrometer and compare your findings with this Chapter's Specifications (see illustration). Also, by measuring the diameter at a number of points around each journal's circumference, you'll be able to determine whether or not the journal is out-of-round.

12 Using a telescoping gauge and a micrometer, measure the diameter of each main bearing bore, then compare the measurements with the specifications (see illustration).

26.11 Measure the diameter of each main journal . . .

26.12 . . . and the diameter of its bearing

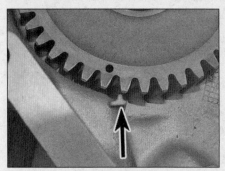

26.18 Make sure the balancer shaft gear punch mark is offset as shown

13 Subtract the journal diameter from the corresponding main bearing diameter to obtain the oil clearance.

14 If the oil clearance is greater than the maximum fit new main bearings then recheck the clearance. If the clearance is still too big, replace the crankshaft with a new one.

Main bearing removal and installation

Note: *BMW have specially made tools for this job, so if in doubt have a dealer remove and install the bearings.*

15 Make a note of the exact set depth of each bearing in its housing. Heat the crankcase to 100°C. Drive the bearing out using a suitable bearing driver or socket – make sure you do not mark the bearing housing.

16 Mark the position of the oil hole in the bearing housing on the crankcase – the oil hole in the bearing must align with it, and the end gap must face the balancer shaft **(see illustrations 26.7a and b)**. Heat the crankcase to 100°C. Drive the new bearing in using a suitable bearing driver or mandrel, aligning the holes. The bearing must not project beyond the oil pockets.

Installation

17 If removed install the balancer shaft (Section 27).

18 On models up to 2003 turn the balancer shaft so the punch mark on its gear aligns with that on the crankcase. On 2004-on models turn the balancer shaft so the punch mark on its gear is offset by about one tooth from that on the crankcase as shown **(see illustration)** – this is because when the helical cut gears mate the shaft will turn slightly, bringing itself into correct alignment.

19 Clean the bearings in both crankcase halves and the crankshaft journals. Lubricate them with molybdenum disulphide oil (a 50/50 mixture of molybdenum disulphide grease and clean engine oil).

20 Lower the tapered (alternator) end of the crankshaft into the right-hand crankcase **(see illustration 26.4)**. Align it so the mark on the web aligns with that on the crankcase, and engage its gear with that on the balancer shaft **(see illustration 26.3)**. Double check that the balancer shaft and crankshaft marks are correctly aligned.

21 On models up to 2003 remove the locating pin from the balancer shaft gear. Check that the crankshaft and balancer shaft rotate easily, then re-check the alignment marks.

22 If the crankshaft and/or crankcases were replaced with new ones, the crankshaft must be re-shimmed (Step 23). If all original components are being used lubricate the shim(s) and fit them onto the shaft **(see illustration 26.2)**.

23 To re-shim the crankshaft measure the height of the outside of the left-hand crankshaft web above the right-hand crankshaft mating surface – BMW have a tool for this (part No. 002550), or alternatively a depth gauge with suitably long levelling bar can be used. Now measure the depth of the shim contact surface in the left-hand crankcase below its mating surfaces. Subtract the first measurement from the second, then subtract 0.4 mm to allow for the thickness of the gasket. The result is the amount of crankshaft end-float without any shims. Select shims to bring the amount of end-float to within the 0.1 to 0.3 mm limit specified – shims are available in thicknesses

of 1.0 mm to 1.6 mm in 0.2 mm increments. Note that if the correct tools are not available to re-shim with the crankcases split, assemble them using the original shims and a new gasket (Section 20), then measure crankshaft end-float preferably using a dial gauge. If adjustment is necessary split the crankcases and adjust the shims as required.

24 Reassemble the crankcase halves (see Section 20).

27 Balancer shaft

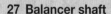

Removal

1 Remove the engine from the frame (see Section 4) and separate the crankcase halves (see Section 20).

2 Remove the crankshaft (Section 26).

3 Remove the shim(s) from the left-hand end of the balancer shaft **(see illustration 26.2)**.

4 Lift the balancer shaft out of the crankcase **(see illustration)**.

Inspection

5 Check the balancer driven gear for wear or damage. If any of the gear teeth are excessively worn, chipped or broken, the gear and its drive gear on the crankshaft must be replaced with new ones – they come as a pair (see Section 26). To remove the gear first heat it to 100°C, then pull it off using a suitable puller **(see illustration 26.6b)**, noting how it locates on the Woodruff key **(see illustration)**. The new gear must be heated to 100°C before being driven or pressed onto the shaft – make sure the key is correctly located in its cut-out and that the groove in the gear is correctly aligned with it.

6 Referring to *Tools and Workshop Tips* in the Reference Section, check the bearings. Replace them with new ones if necessary – to do this the crankcases must be heated to

27.4 Lift the balancer shaft out of the crankcase

27.5 Note how the slot in the gear locates over the Woodruff key (arrowed)

27.6 Balancer shaft bearing (arrowed) in right-hand crankcase

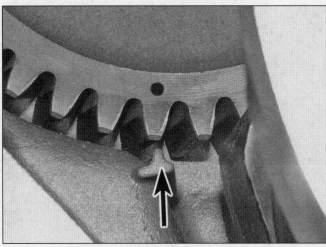

27.11 Punch mark must align with the index mark (arrowed) on the crankcase

80 to 100°C **(see illustration)**. The bearings must be removed using an internal expanding puller, either with slide-hammer attachment or drawbolt and plate attachment. If using a slide-hammer you will need an assistant wearing oven gloves to hold the crankcase firmly down on a surface with protection to prevent marking the crankcase. If using a drawbolt you need to draw it through a plate laid across the crankcase with suitable protection for the mating surfaces. Alternatively take the crankcases to a BMW dealer and let them do it. New bearings can both be driven into place using a suitable driver or socket that bears only on the outer race – the cases again need to be heated, and if available use a temperature reduction spray on the bearings or store them in the fridge or freezer overnight. Where applicable make sure the sealed side of the bearing faces the outside of the engine. Make sure the surfaces of the crankcase are suitably protected to prevent damage.

Installation

7 Clean the bearing journals. Lubricate them and the bearings with molybdenum disulphide oil (a 50/50 mixture of molybdenum disulphide grease and clean engine oil).
8 Lower the gear end of the balancer shaft into the right-hand crankcase **(see illustration 27.4)**. Align it as described in Section 26, step 18.
9 If the balancer shaft and/or crankcases were replaced with new ones, the balancer shaft must be re-shimmed (Step 10). If all original components are being used lubricate the shim(s) and fit them onto the shaft **(see illustration 26.2)**.
10 To re-shim the shaft measure the height of the outside of the shim seat surface above the right-hand crankcase mating surface – BMW

have a tool for this (part No. 002550), or alternatively a depth gauge with suitably long levelling bar can be used. Now measure the depth of the shim contact surface in the left-hand crankcase below its mating surfaces. Subtract the first measurement from the second, then subtract 0.4 mm to allow for the thickness of the gasket. The result is the amount of balancer shaft end-float without any shims. Select shims to bring the amount of end-float to within the 0.1 to 0.3 mm limit specified – shims are available in thicknesses of 0.8 mm to 1.4 mm in 0.2 mm increments. Note that if the correct tools are not available to re-shim with the crankcases split, assemble them using the original shims and a new gasket (Section 20), then measure balancer shaft end-float using a dial gauge. If adjustment is necessary split the crankcases and adjust the shims as required.
11 Install the crankshaft (Section 26). Check that the balancer shaft punch mark is correctly aligned **(see illustration)**.
12 Reassemble the crankcase halves (see Section 20).

28 Running-in procedure

1 Make sure the engine oil and coolant levels are correct (see *Pre-ride checks*). Note that on Funduro and ST, GS and Dakar 2000 to 2003, and CS 2002 and 2003 models it is important to bleed the oil circuit as described in Section 4.
2 Make sure there is fuel in the tank. Turn the engine kill switch to the ON position and shift the gearbox into neutral. Turn the ignition ON.
3 Start the engine and allow it to run at a

moderately fast idle until it reaches operating temperature.

 Warning: If the oil pressure warning light doesn't go off, or it comes on while the engine is running, stop the engine immediately.

4 If a lubrication failure is suspected, stop the engine immediately and try to find the cause. If an engine is run without oil, even for a short period of time, severe damage will occur.
5 Check carefully that there are no oil or coolant leaks and make sure the transmission and controls, especially the brakes, function properly before road testing the machine.
6 Treat the machine gently for the first few miles to make sure oil has circulated throughout the engine and any new parts installed have started to seat.
7 Upon completion of the road test, and after the engine has cooled down completely, recheck the valve clearances (see Chapter 1) and check the engine oil and coolant levels (see *Pre-ride checks*).
8 If a new piston and rings, a new cylinder block or a new crankshaft have been fitted, the bike will have to be run in as when new. This means greater use of the transmission and a restraining hand on the throttle, keeping engine speed below 5000 rpm and avoiding full throttle until at least 600 miles (1000 km) have been covered. There's no point in keeping to any set speed limit – the main idea is to keep from labouring (overloading) the engine. Between 600 and 1200 miles (1000 and 2000 km) gradually increase engine speeds, but again avoid labouring the engine, and do not use full throttle for prolonged periods. Experience is the best guide, since it's easy to tell when an engine is running freely.

Chapter 3
Cooling system

Contents

Degrees of difficulty

Easy, suitable for novice with little experience	Fairly easy, suitable for beginner with some experience	Fairly difficult, suitable for competent DIY mechanic	Difficult, suitable for experienced DIY mechanic	Very difficult, suitable for expert DIY or professional

Specifications

Coolant
Mixture type and capacity . . . .   see Chapter 1

Cooling fan switch/sensor
Switch closes (fan ON). . . . .   102°C

Temperature warning light sensor
Temperature warning light cut-in temperature. . . . .   118°C

Thermostat
Opening temperature
    Funduro and ST . . . .   75°C
    GS, Dakar and CS . . . .   85°C

Radiator
Cap valve opening pressure. . . . .   22 to 25 psi (1.5 to 1.7 Bar)
System test pressure
    Funduro and ST . . . .   14.5 psi (1 Bar) for 5 mins
    GS, Dakar and CS . . . .   22 psi (1.5 Bar) for 5 mins

Torque settings
Clutch cover bolts . . . .   11 Nm
Cooling fan thermo switch (Funduro and ST). . . . .   35 Nm
Oil pipe-to-engine (GS and Dakar). . . . .   35 Nm
Temperature sensor . . . .   15 Nm
Thermostat cover bolts (Funduro and ST) . . . .   6 Nm
Thermostat housing bolts (Funduro and ST) . . . .   6 Nm
Water pump cover bolts. . . . .   10 Nm

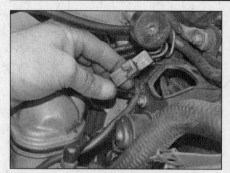

2.2a Fan wiring connector – Funduro and ST

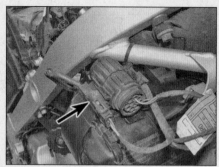

2.2b Fan wiring connector (arrowed) – GS, Dakar and CS

in overheating and severe engine damage. Distilled water must be used as opposed to tap water to avoid a build-up of scale which would also block the passages.

1 General information

The cooling system uses a water/anti-freeze coolant to carry away excess heat from the engine and maintain as constant a temperature as possible. The cylinder is surrounded by a water jacket from which the heated coolant is circulated by thermo-syphonic action in conjunction with a water pump, which is driven by the balancer shaft. The hot coolant passes via the thermostat and flows across the core of the radiator, then to the water pump and back to the engine where the cycle is repeated.

A thermostat is fitted in the system to prevent the coolant flowing through the radiator when the engine is cold, therefore accelerating the speed at which the engine reaches normal operating temperature. A temperature sensor controls the warning light on the instrument panel. A cooling fan fitted to the back of the radiator aids cooling in extreme conditions by drawing extra air through. The fan motor is controlled by a thermo switch on Funduro and ST models, and by the temperature sensor via the ECU on GS, Dakar and CS models.

The complete cooling system is partially sealed and pressurised, the pressure being controlled by a valve contained in the spring-loaded radiator cap. By pressurising the coolant the boiling point is raised, preventing premature boiling in adverse conditions. The overflow pipe from the system is connected to a reservoir into which excess coolant is

expelled under pressure. The discharged coolant automatically returns to the radiator by the vacuum created when the engine cools.

⚠️ *Warning: Do not remove the pressure cap from the radiator when the engine is hot. Scalding hot coolant and steam may be blown out under pressure, which could cause serious injury. When the engine has cooled, place a thick rag, such as a hand towel, over the pressure cap; slowly rotate the cap anti-clockwise to the first stop. This procedure allows any residual pressure to escape. When the steam has stopped escaping, press down on the cap while turning it anti-clockwise and remove it.*

Caution: Do not allow anti-freeze to come in contact with your skin or painted surfaces of the motorcycle. Rinse off any spills immediately with plenty of water. Anti-freeze is highly toxic if ingested. Never leave anti-freeze lying around in an open container or in puddles on the floor; children and pets are attracted by its sweet smell and may drink it. Check with the local authorities about disposing of used anti-freeze. Many communities will have collection centres which will see that anti-freeze is disposed of safely.

Caution: At all times use the specified type of anti-freeze, and always mix it with distilled water in the correct proportion. The anti-freeze contains corrosion inhibitors which are essential to avoid damage to the cooling system. A lack of these inhibitors could lead to a build-up of corrosion which would block the coolant passages, resulting

2 Cooling fan

Cooling fan

Check

1 If the engine is overheating and the cooling fan isn't coming on, first check the fan fuse (see Chapter 9).

2 To test the cooling fan motor, on Funduro and ST models remove the fairing, and on GS, Dakar and CS models remove the right-hand front side cover (see Chapter 8). Disconnect the fan wiring connector **(see illustrations)**. Using a 12 volt battery and two jumper wires with suitable connectors, connect the battery to the fan. Once connected the fan should operate.

3 If the fan works when connected to a battery, check the wiring and connectors in the circuit (refer to the wiring diagrams at the end of Chapter 9). If that is good, on Funduro and ST the fan switch could be faulty (see below). On GS, Dakar and CS the temperature sensor could be faulty (see Section 3).

Replacement

⚠️ *Warning: The engine must be completely cool before carrying out this procedure.*

4 On Funduro and ST models remove the fuel tank cover and for best access the fairing, and on GS, Dakar and CS remove the right-hand front side cover (see Chapter 8).

5 Disconnect the fan wiring connector **(see illustration 2.2a or b)**.

6 On Funduro and ST models unscrew the bolts and detach the fan and shroud from the radiator **(see illustration)**.

7 On GS, Dakar and CS models unclip the diagnostic plug from its holder **(see illustration)**. Release the temperature sensor wiring from its clip on the fan shroud **(see illustration)**. Release the top clip on the right-hand end then slide the fan assembly out

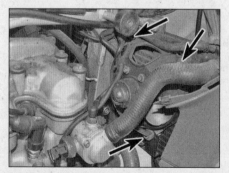

2.6 Cooling fan and shroud bolts (arrowed)

2.7a Release the diagnostic plug . . .

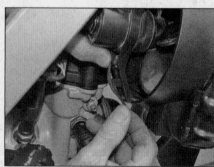

2.7b . . . and the sensor wiring

to release the tongues from the posts on the top and bottom inner ends **(see illustrations)**. Unscrew the bolts and detach the fan from the shroud **(see illustration)**.

8 Installation is the reverse of removal.

Cooling fan switch – Funduro and ST

Check

9 If the engine is overheating and the cooling fan isn't coming on, first check the fan circuit fuse (see Chapter 9). If the fuse is blown, check the fan circuit for a short to earth (see *Wiring diagrams* at the end of Chapter 9).

10 If the fuse is good, for best access remove the right-hand engine trim panel (see Chapter 8). Disconnect the wiring connector from the fan switch **(see illustration)**. Using a jumper wire connect between the terminals in the connector. The fan should come on. If it does, the fan switch is defective and must be replaced with a new one. If it does not come on, check the wiring and connectors for a fault or break.

11 If the fan is on the whole time, either the switch is defective and must be replaced with a new one, or there is a short in the switch wiring.

Replacement

 Warning: The engine must be completely cool before carrying out this procedure.

12 Drain the cooling system (see Chapter 1).

13 Disconnect the wiring connector from the switch **(see illustration 2.10)**. Unscrew the switch and withdraw it from the housing. Discard the sealing washer.

14 Install the switch using a new sealing washer and tighten it to the torque setting specified at the beginning of the Chapter. Take care not to overtighten it.

15 Reconnect the switch wiring and refill the cooling system (see Chapter 1).

3 Temperature sensor and warning light

Check

1 The circuit consists of the sensor mounted in the thermostat housing on Funduro and ST models and in the right-hand side of the cylinder head on GS, Dakar and CS models, and the warning light in the instrument cluster **(see illustration 3.3a or b)**. If the temperature goes above 118°C the warning light comes on.

2 If the warning light does not work first check the bulb (see Chapter 9). If that is good, check the wiring connectors in the circuit for loose wires or corroded or broken terminals, then check the wiring between the sensor and the instrument cluster for continuity (see Chapter 9). If all is good the sensor could be faulty – BMW provide no test details, so the best thing to do is to substitute it with one that is known to be good and see whether the fault clears.

2.7c Release the clip using a screwdriver . . .

2.7e Unscrew the bolts (arrowed) and separate the shroud from the fan

Replacement

 Warning: The engine must be completely cool before carrying out this procedure.

3 Drain the cooling system (see Chapter 1).

3.3a Temperature sensor (arrowed) – Funduro and ST

3.4a Disconnect the wiring connector – Funduro and ST

2.7d . . . then remove the fan as described to release the tongues from the posts

2.10 Fan switch wiring connector (arrowed)

The sensor is mounted in the thermostat housing on Funduro and ST models, and in the right-hand side of the cylinder head on GS, Dakar and CS models **(see illustrations)**. On GS, Dakar and CS models remove the right-hand front side cover (see Chapter 8).

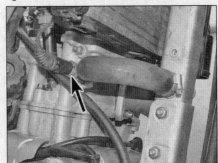

3.3b Temperature sensor (arrowed) – GS, Dakar and CS

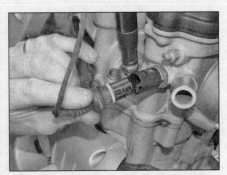

3.4b Disconnect the wiring connector – GS, Dakar and CS

4.3 Thermostat cover bolts (arrowed)

4 Disconnect the sensor wiring connector **(see illustrations)**. Unscrew and remove the sensor.
5 Install the sensor and tighten it to the torque setting specified at the beginning of the Chapter. Connect the wiring.
6 Refill the cooling system (see Chapter 1).

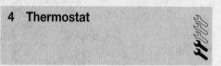

4   Thermostat

Note: *Three types of hose clamp are used on the various hoses across the range of models covered – the non-re-usable type, the re-usable clip type and the screw type. A small screwdriver is required to release the non-reusable type and clip type clamps. Special pliers are required to close them, and these are available from automotive tool*

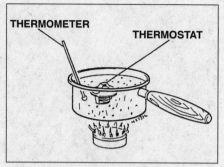

4.6 Thermostat testing set-up

suppliers, or from BMW (part No. 131500), along with the clamps where new ones are required.

1 The thermostat is automatic in operation and shouldn't require attention. In the event of a failure, the valve will probably jam open, in which case the engine will take much longer than normal to warm up. Conversely, if the valve jams shut, the coolant will be unable to circulate and the engine will overheat. Neither condition is acceptable, and the fault must be investigated promptly.

Funduro and ST

Removal

 Warning: The engine must be completely cool before carrying out this procedure.

2 Drain the coolant (see Chapter 1). Remove the fuel tank cover (see Chapter 8).
3 Unscrew the thermostat cover bolts and

detach the cover **(see illustration)**. Discard the O-ring as a new one must be used. Withdraw the thermostat, noting which way up it fits.
4 To remove the housing disconnect the temperature sensor and fan switch wiring connectors **(see illustration 3.3a and 2.10)**, then unscrew the bolts within the housing and detach it from the engine. Discard the gasket – a new one must be used. Clean the mating surfaces of the engine and housing.

Check

5 Examine the thermostat visually before carrying out the test. If it remains in the open position at room temperature, it should be replaced with a new one. Check the condition of the rubber seal around the thermostat and replace it with a new one if it is damaged, deformed or deteriorated.
6 Suspend the thermostat by a piece of wire in a container of cold water. Place a thermometer capable of reading temperatures up to 110°C in the water so that the bulb is close to the thermostat **(see illustration)**. Heat the water, noting the temperature when the thermostat opens, and compare the result with the specifications given at the beginning of the Chapter. Also check the valve opens fully (about 7 or 8 mm) after it has been heated for a few minutes. If the thermostat is faulty it must be replaced with a new one.
7 In the event of thermostat failure, as an emergency measure only, it can be removed and the machine used without it (this is better than leaving a permanently closed thermostat in, but if it is permanently open, you might as well leave it in). **Note:** *Take care when starting the engine from cold as it will take much longer than usual to warm up. Ensure that a new unit is installed as soon as possible.*

Installation

8 Installation is the reverse of removal.
9 Fit a new gasket between the housing and the engine (if removed). Fit a new O-ring between the cover and the housing. Tighten the housing bolts and the cover bolts to the torque setting specified at the beginning of the Chapter.
10 Refill the cooling system (see Chapter 1).

GS, Dakar and CS

Removal

 Warning: The engine must be completely cool before carrying out this procedure.

11 Drain the coolant (see Chapter 1). Release the clamp and detach the hose from the bottom of the thermostat holder **(see illustration)**.
12 Release the spring clip **(see illustrations)**. Withdraw the thermostat holder from the housing **(see illustration)**. Discard the O-ring as a new one must be used **(see illustration 4.17)**. Remove the thermostat from the holder **(see illustration)**.

Check

13 Examine the thermostat visually before carrying out the test. If it remains in the open

4.11 Release the clamp and detach the hose

4.12a Lever the spring clip out . . .

4.12b . . . then draw the thermostat holder out

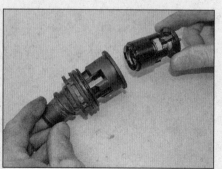

4.12c Remove the thermostat from the holder

position at room temperature, it should be replaced with a new one.

14 Suspend the thermostat by a piece of wire in a container of cold water. Place a thermometer capable of reading temperatures up to 110°C in the water so that the bulb is close to the thermostat **(see illustration 4.6)**. Heat the water, noting the temperature when the thermostat opens, and compare the result with the specifications given at the beginning of the Chapter. Also check the valve opens fully after it has been heated for a few minutes. If the thermostat is faulty it must be replaced with a new one.

15 In the event of thermostat failure, as an emergency measure only, it can be removed and the machine used without it (this is better than leaving a permanently closed thermostat in, but if it is permanently open, you might as well leave it in). **Note:** *Take care when starting the engine from cold as it will take much longer than usual to warm up. Ensure that a new unit is installed as soon as possible.*

Installation

16 Installation is the reverse of removal.
17 Fit a new O-ring onto the holder **(see illustration)**. Maker sure the spring clip locates correctly.
18 Refill the cooling system (see Chapter 1).

5 Radiator

Note 1: *If the radiator is being removed as part of the engine removal procedure, detach the hoses from their unions on the engine rather than on the radiator and remove the radiator with the hoses attached. Note the routing of the hoses.*

Note 2: *Three types of hose clamp are used on the various hoses across the range of models covered – the non-re-usable type, the re-usable clip type and the screw type. A small screwdriver is required to release the non-reusable type and clip type clamps. Special pliers are required to close them, and these are available from automotive tool suppliers, or*

from BMW (part No. 131500), along with the clamps where new ones are required.

Removal

⚠️ *Warning: The engine must be completely cool before carrying out this procedure.*

1 Drain the cooling system (see Chapter 1). On Funduro and ST models remove the fairing, and on GS, Dakar and CS models remove the front side covers (see Chapter 8).
2 Remove the cooling fan (see Section 2).
3 On GS, Dakar and CS models remove the reservoir, detaching the hose and draining it, and noting how it locates **(see illustrations)**.
4 Release the clamps securing the hoses to the radiator and detach them **(see illustrations)**.

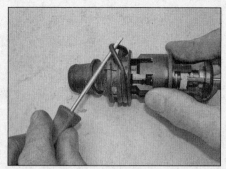

4.17 Use a new O-ring

5.3a Undo the screw and draw the reservoir out . . .

5.3b . . . noting how the peg locates in the grommet . . .

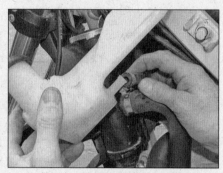

5.3c . . . and detach the hose

5.4a On Funduro and ST detach the hose (arrowed) from the right-hand side of the radiator . . .

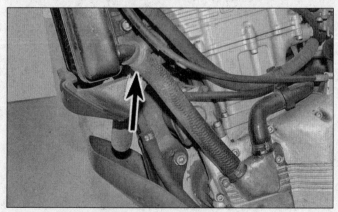

5.4b . . . and from the left-hand side (arrowed)

5.4c On GS, Dakar and CS detach the hoses (arrowed) from the left-hand side

5.5a Unscrew the bolt (arrowed) on each side . . .

5.5b . . . then lift the radiator to free the peg from the grommet . . .

5.5c . . . and draw it out to the left

5 Unscrew the radiator mounting bolts and remove the radiator from the left-hand side, noting how the peg on the bottom locates (see illustrations).

6 Note the arrangement of the collars and rubber grommets in the radiator mounts. Replace the grommets with new ones if they are damaged, deformed or deteriorated.

7 If necessary, on GS, Dakar and CS models remove the thermostat (see Section 4). Check the radiator for signs of damage and clear any dirt or debris that might obstruct airflow and inhibit cooling. If the radiator fins are badly damaged or broken the radiator must be replaced with a new one.

Installation

8 Installation is the reverse of removal, noting the following.
● Make sure the rubber grommets are in place and the collars are correctly fitted in the grommets.
● Ensure the coolant hoses are in good condition (see Chapter 1), and are securely retained by their clamps, using new ones if necessary.
● On completion refill the cooling system as described in Chapter 1.

Pressure checks

9 If problems such as overheating or loss of coolant occur, check the entire system as described in Chapter 1. The radiator cap opening pressure and the system pressure retention should be checked by a BMW dealer with the special testers required to do the job. If the cap is defective, replace it with a new one.

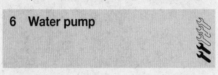

6 Water pump

Check

1 The water pump is located on the lower left-hand side of the engine. Visually check the area around the pump for signs of leakage.

2 To prevent leakage of coolant from the cooling system to the lubrication system and vice versa, two seals are fitted on the pump shaft. On the bottom of the pump housing there is a drain hole (see illustration). If either seal fails, the drain allows the coolant or oil to escape and prevents them mixing – tell-tale signs are a constantly dropping coolant level in the reservoir, and oil that has turned milky or chocolaty due to contamination by coolant.

3 If on inspection the drain shows signs of leakage, remove the pump and replace the seals with new ones – they come as a kit with a new shaft and impeller. If you find that the new seals do not last very long then you may need either a new clutch cover or at worst a new set of crankcases, as the bore in which the pump shaft runs could be worn oval or off-centre.

Removal

Note 1: *The top front bolt on the water pump cover and the top front, top and top rear bolts on the clutch cover all have open ends to their threaded bores, leaving them susceptible to corrosion. Despite a lot of careful work two of these bolts sheared of on the engine we stripped. Before attempting to unscrew these bolts apply some penetrating fluid to the open ends and to the heads of the bolts and hit the heads with a hammer and drift to break the corrosion. If necessary take care to work the bolts free, turning them a little in both directions to break up any corrosion, and using a heat gun if necessary to expand the bore around the bolt.*

Note 2: *Three types of hose clamp are used on the various hoses across the range of models covered – the non-re-usable type, the re-usable clip type and the screw type. A small screwdriver is required to release the non-reusable type and clip type clamps. Special pliers are required to close them, and these are available from automotive tool suppliers, or from BMW (part No. 131500), along with the clamps where new ones are required.*

4 Drain the engine oil and coolant (see Chapter 1).

5 Make an alignment mark where the slot in the gearchange lever or linkage arm (according to model) aligns with the shaft (see illustration). Unscrew the pinch bolt and slide the lever or linkage arm off the shaft.

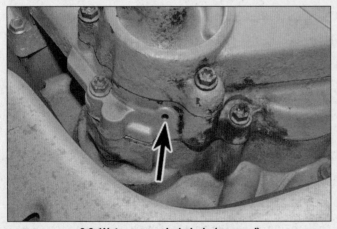

6.2 Water pump drain hole (arrowed)

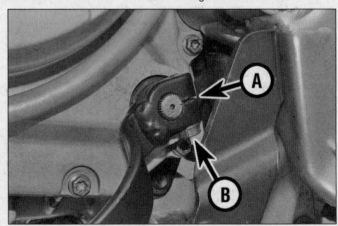

6.5 Make an alignment mark with the slit (A) then unscrew the bolt (B)

6.7a Unscrew the banjo bolt (arrowed) . . .

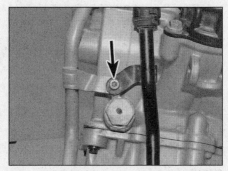

6.7b . . . and the pipe holder bolt (arrowed)

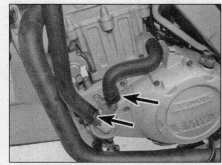

6.9 Release the clamps and detach the hoses (arrowed)

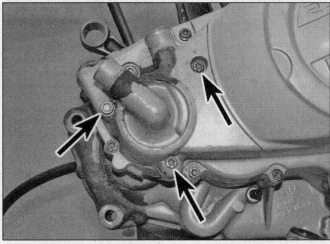

6.10 Unscrew the bolts (arrowed) and remove the pump cover

6.11 Unscrew the bolts (arrowed) and remove the clutch cover

6 Detach the clutch cable from the release lever on the engine (see Chapter 2).

7 On GS and Dakar models unscrew the left-hand footrest bracket bolts and remove the footrest assembly. Detach the oil return pipe from the bottom of the engine and the cylinder head **(see illustrations)** – have some rag ready to catch residual oil. Discard the banjo bolt sealing washers – new ones must be used.

8 Remove the starter motor (see Chapter 9).

9 Release the clamps securing the pump inlet and outlet hoses and pull the pipes off the pump **(see illustration)**.

10 Unscrew the pump cover bolts and remove the cover **(see illustration)**. Remove the O-ring and discard it as a new one must be used **(see illustration 6.19a)**.

11 Unscrew the clutch cover bolts and remove the cover **(see illustration)**. Remove the gasket and discard it as a new one must be used **(see illustration 6.18a)**.

12 Lever the driven gear off the drive pin on the inner end of the pump shaft then remove the drive pin and washer **(see illustrations)**. Grasp the impeller and withdraw the shaft from the cover **(see illustration)**. Check the shaft for wear grooves and fit the repair kit (incorporating seals, shaft and impeller) if any are found.

13 Check the shaft bore in the cover for wear

6.12a Lever the driven gear up off the drive pin – it is a clip fit

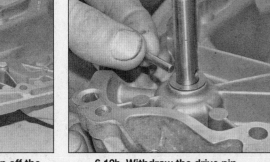

6.12b Withdraw the drive pin . . .

6.12c . . . and remove the washer . . .

6.12d . . . then draw the shaft out

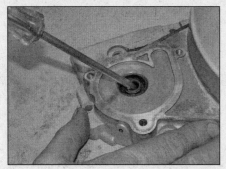

6.14 Hook the seals out

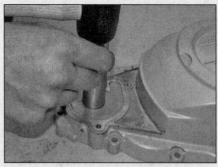

6.15 You can use a socket to drive the new seals in

6.17a Slide the gear on the shaft aligning the slot with the pin . . .

6.17b . . . then press or tap it onto the pin

6.18a Fit a new gasket

6.18b Align the pull rod . . .

(see Step 3) and replace the cover with a new one if necessary.

Seal replacement

14 Hook out the seal on each side of the clutch cover, noting on which side and which way round each one fits **(see illustration)**.

15 Apply a smear of EP2 (extreme pressure) grease to the inner lips of the new seals. Press or drive the inner seal into place with the marked side facing in until it seats. Pack the space between the seals with EP2 grease. Press or drive the outer seal in so it is flush with the surface of its housing **(see illustration)**.

Installation

16 Check for corrosion or a build-up of scale in the pump cover and clean it if necessary.

17 If not already done fit the drive pin and impeller onto the outer end of the shaft. Smear the shaft with EP2 grease the slide it through the seals **(see illustration 6.12d)**. Fit the washer and the drive pin **(see illustrations 6.12c and b)**. Push the driven gear onto the pin so it clicks into place **(see illustrations)**.

18 Fit a new gasket onto the engine **(see illustration)**. Make sure the clutch pull-rod is aligned as shown to engage with the shaft in the cover **(see illustration)**. Make sure the

shaft lever is aligned as shown so it finishes at the correct angle when the cover is fitted – it will rotate inwards when the teeth engage **(see illustrations)**. Fit the clutch cover, turning the pump impeller so the driven gear engages the drive gear. Fit the bolts and tighten them evenly in a criss-cross pattern to the torque setting specified at the beginning of the Chapter.

19 Smear the new pump cover O-ring with grease and fit it into its groove in the cover **(see illustration)**. Fit the cover onto the pump **(see illustration)**. Fit the bolts and tighten them to the specified torque setting **(see illustration 6.10)**.

6.18c . . . and the release shaft lever as shown . . .

6.18d . . . then fit the cover – the lever should end up pointing in

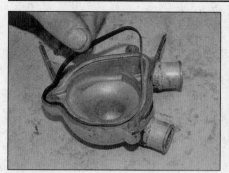

6.19a Fit a new O-ring into the groove . . .

6.19b . . . then fit the cover

6.21 Use new sealing washers

20 Fit the hoses and secure them with the clamps, using new ones if necessary **(see illustration 6.9)** – special pliers are needed to properly close the hoses fitted as original equipment, but they can be replaced with threaded ones if required so only a screwdriver is needed to tighten them.

21 Install all remaining components in a reverse of the removal procedure. On GS and Dakar models use new sealing washers on the oil pipe banjo union and tighten the bolt to the specified torque setting **(see illustration)**.

22 Refill the engine oil and coolant (see Chapter 1).

7   Coolant hoses and pipes

Note: *Three types of hose clamp are used on the various hoses across the range of models covered – the non-re-usable type, the re-usable clip type and the screw type. A small screwdriver is required to release the non-reusable type and clip type clamps. Special pliers are required to close them, and these are available from automotive tool suppliers, or from BMW (part No. 131500), along with the clamps where new ones are required.*

Removal

1 Before removing a hose or pipe, drain the coolant (see Chapter 1).

2 Release the clamps securing the hose, referring to the **Note** above. After releasing the clamps slide them back along the hose and clear of the union spigot.

Caution: The radiator unions are fragile. Do not use excessive force when attempting to remove the hoses.

3 If a hose proves stubborn, release it by rotating it on its union before working it off. If all else fails, cut the hose with a sharp knife. Obviously this means replacing the hose with a new one.

4 On early GS, Dakar and CS models the outlet pipe assembly on the cylinder head can be removed by unscrewing the bolts. The O-ring must be discarded and replaced with a new one.

Installation

5 Slide the clamps onto the hose and then work the hose on to its union as far as the spigot where present.

 HAYNES HiNT *If the hose is difficult to push on its union, soften it by soaking it in very hot water, or alternatively a little soapy water on the union can be used as a lubricant.*

6 On early GS, Dakar and CS models use a new O-ring when fitting the outlet pipe assembly to the cylinder head.

7 Rotate the hose on its unions to settle it in position before sliding the clamps into place and securing them.

8 Refill the cooling system with fresh coolant (see Chapter 1).

Chapter 4A
Fuel system and exhaust –
Funduro and ST models

Contents

Degrees of difficulty

Easy, suitable for novice with little experience	Fairly easy, suitable for beginner with some experience	Fairly difficult, suitable for competent DIY mechanic	Difficult, suitable for experienced DIY mechanic	Very difficult, suitable for expert DIY or professional

Specifications

Fuel
Grade . . . . Unleaded, 95 RON (Research Octane Number)
Fuel tank capacity
   Total (inc. reserve) . . . . 17.5 litres
   Reserve . . . . 2 litres

Carburettors
Type . . . . 2 x BST 33-B-316
Float height . . . . 14.6 mm
Idle speed . . . . see Chapter 1
Pilot screw base setting (no. of turns out) 3 1/2
Main jet
   Early (pre-80db noise restriction) models 140
   Late (post-80db noise restriction) models 132.5
Main air jet 0.6
Needle
   Type 5E 94-4
   Setting . . . . 4th groove from top
Needle jet 0-2
Idle jet 41.3
Idle air jet 1.5
Butterfly valve 105

Torque wrench settings
Downpipe flange nuts . . . . 10 Nm
Silencer mounting bolts . . . . 25 Nm

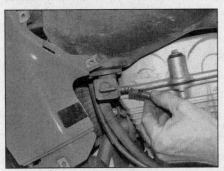

2.3 Release the clamp and detach the fuel hose

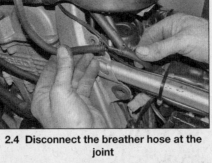

2.4 Disconnect the breather hose at the joint

2.5a Unscrew the bolt . . .

2.5b . . . and remove the tank

1 General information and precautions

General information

The fuel system consists of the fuel tank, the fuel tap with integral strainers, fuel hoses, carburettors and control cables.

The carburettors used are CV types. For cold starting, a choke lever is incorporated in the left-hand switch housing.

Air is drawn into the carburettors via an air filter, which is housed under the seat.

The exhaust is a two-into-one design.

Many of the fuel system service procedures are considered routine maintenance items and for that reason are included in Chapter 1.

Precautions

⚠ **Warning: Petrol (gasoline) is extremely flammable, so take extra precautions when you work on any part of the fuel system. Don't smoke or allow open flames or bare light bulbs near the work area, and don't work in a garage where a natural gas-type appliance is present. If you spill any fuel on your skin, rinse it off immediately with soap and water. When you perform any kind of work on the fuel system, wear safety glasses and have a fire extinguisher suitable for a class B type fire (flammable liquids) on hand.**

Always perform service procedures in a well-ventilated area to prevent a build-up of fumes.

Never work in a building containing a gas appliance with a pilot light, or any other form of naked flame. Ensure that there are no naked light bulbs or any sources of flame or sparks nearby.

Do not smoke (or allow anyone else to smoke) while in the vicinity of petrol (gasoline), or of components containing petrol. Remember the possible presence of vapour from these sources and move well clear before smoking.

Check all electrical equipment belonging to the house, garage or workshop where work is being undertaken (see the *Safety First!* section of this manual). Remember that certain electrical appliances such as drills, cutters etc. create sparks in the normal course of operation and must not be used near petrol (gasoline) or any component containing it. Again, remember the possible presence of fumes before using electrical equipment.

Always mop up any spilt fuel and safely dispose of the rag used.

2.11 Fuel tap screws (arrowed)

Any stored fuel that is drained off during servicing work must be kept in sealed containers that are suitable for holding petrol (gasoline), and clearly marked as such; the containers themselves should be kept in a safe place. Note that this last point applies equally to the fuel tank if it is removed from the machine; also remember to keep its filler cap closed at all times.

Read the *Safety first!* section of this manual carefully before starting work.

2 Fuel tank and fuel tap

⚠ *Warning: Refer to the precautions given in Section 1 before starting work.*

Fuel tank

Removal

1 Turn the fuel tap off.
2 Remove the fuel tank cover (see Chapter 8).
3 Have a rag ready to catch any residual fuel, then release the fuel hose clamp and detach the hose from the tap **(see illustration)**.
4 Disconnect the tank breather hose **(see illustration)**.
5 Unscrew the fuel tank bolt **(see illustration)**. Draw the tank back and remove it **(see illustration)**.
6 Inspect the tank mounting rubbers for signs of damage or deterioration and replace them with new ones if necessary.

Draining

7 If required remove the fuel tank as described above. Otherwise turn the fuel tap off, then have a rag ready to catch any residual fuel, release the fuel hose clamp and detach the hose from the tap **(see illustration 2.3)**.
8 Connect a drain hose to the fuel outlet union on the tap and insert its end in a container suitable and large enough for storing the fuel. Turn the fuel tap to the 'ON' position and allow the tank to drain. When the tank has drained, turn the tap to the 'OFF' position.

Installation

9 Installation is the reverse of removal, noting the following:
● Make sure the tank rubbers are correctly fitted and the collar is fitted with the rear mounting bolt.
● Make sure the hoses are fully pushed onto their unions, and are secured by their clamps.
● Turn the fuel tap ON and check that there is no sign of fuel leakage, then turn if off.

Fuel tap

Removal

10 Remove the fuel tank and drain it as described in Steps 1 to 8, then turn it over and rest it on some rag.
11 Undo the screws securing the tap to the tank and withdraw the tap **(see illustration)**.

3.2a Displace the relay from its mounts

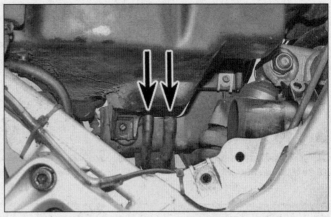

3.2b Detach the hoses (arrowed) from their unions

Note the wave washers. Remove the O-ring and discard it as a new one must be used.

Installation

12 Fit a new O-ring into the groove in the tap.
13 Install the tap, making sure the O-ring stays in place. Fit the screws with the wave washers and tighten them.
14 Install the fuel tank (see above).

Cleaning and repair

15 All repairs to the fuel tank should be carried out by a professional who has experience in this critical and potentially dangerous work. Even after cleaning and flushing of the fuel system, explosive fumes can remain and ignite during repair of the tank.
16 If the fuel tank is removed from the bike, it should not be placed in an area where sparks or open flames could ignite the fumes coming out of the tank. Be especially careful inside garages where a natural gas-type appliance is located, because the pilot light could cause an explosion.

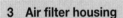

3   Air filter housing

  Warning: Refer to the precautions givven in Section 1 before starting work.

Removal

1 Remove the side covers (see Chapter 8).
2 Displace the starter relay from its bracket **(see illustration)**. Remove the battery (see Chapter 9). Detach the hoses from the underside of the air filter housing **(see illustration)**. Remove the battery holder **(see illustration)**.
3 Remove the silencer (Section 8).
4 Make sure the rear brake fluid reservoir cap is tight. Displace the reservoir, wrap it in rag and lay it aside, keeping it upright if possible **(see illustration)**.
5 Undo the bolt on the underside of the air filter housing **(see illustration)**.
6 Fully undo the clamp screws securing the air intakes to the carburettors and remove the

clamps to prevent them getting distorted **(see illustrations)**.

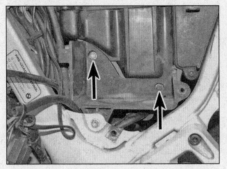

3.2c Unscrew the bolts (arrowed) and remove the holder

3.5 Unscrew the bolt (arrowed)

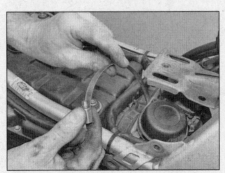

3.6b . . . and remove the clamps

7 Undo the bolts on the top of the air filter housing **(see illustration)**.

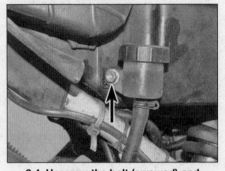

3.4 Unscrew the bolt (arrowed) and displace the reservoir

3.6a Fully slacken the clamp screw (arrowed) on each side . . .

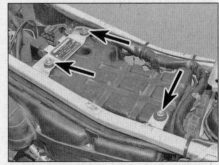

3.7 Unscrew the bolts (arrowed)

3.8a Release the overflow hose from its guide

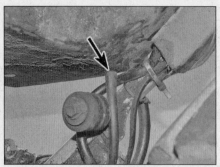

3.8b Detach the hose (arrowed) from its union . . .

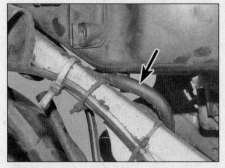

3.8c . . . and move the breather hose (arrowed) inside the post behind it

3.9 Draw the housing out to the right

8 Lift the radiator overflow hose out of its guides on the top of the air filter housing (see illustration). Detach the hose from the union on the underside of the housing on the right-hand side, then feed the reservoir breather hose inside the union to prevent it snagging (see illustrations).

9 Manoeuvre the air filter housing out to the right (see illustration).

Installation

10 Installation is the reverse of removal. Make sure the air intakes are fully engaged with the carburettors – they can be difficult to engage, so a squirt of WD40 or a smear of grease will ease entry. Make sure the clamps are positioned correctly (see illustration 3.6a).

4 Carburettor overhaul general information

1 Poor engine performance, hesitation, hard starting, stalling, flooding and backfiring are all signs that carburettor maintenance may be required.

2 Keep in mind that many so-called carburettor problems are really not carburettor problems at all, but mechanical problems within the engine, or ignition system malfunctions. Try to establish for certain that the carburettors are in need of maintenance before beginning a major overhaul.

3 Check the fuel tap, strainer, the fuel hose, the intake ducts on the cylinder head and their joint clamps, the air filter, the ignition system, the spark plugs, and valve clearances before assuming that a carburettor overhaul is required.

4 Most carburettor problems are caused by dirt particles, varnish and other deposits which build up in and block the fuel and air passages. Also, in time, gaskets and O-rings shrink or deteriorate and cause fuel and air leaks which lead to poor performance.

5 Before disassembling the carburettors, make sure you have some carburettor cleaner, a supply of clean rags, some means of blowing out the carburettor passages and a clean place to work. It is recommended that only one carburettor be overhauled at a time to avoid mixing up parts.

6 When overhauling the carburettors, disassemble them completely and clean the parts thoroughly with a carburettor cleaning solvent and dry them with filtered,

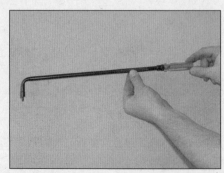

4.8 Mixture adjustment screwdriver

unlubricated compressed air. Blow through the fuel and air passages with compressed air to force out any dirt that may have been loosened but not removed by the solvent. Once the cleaning process is complete, reassemble the carburettor using new gaskets and O-rings.

Air/fuel mixture

7 If the engine runs extremely rough at idle or continually stalls, and an overhaul does not cure the problem (and it definitely is a carburation problem), the pilot screws may require adjustment. Note that in certain markets the CO content of the exhaust gases must be measured (a take-off point is provided in the silencer pipe) to ensure that emission regulations are not exceeded. This is particularly relevant where a catalytic converter is fitted. US models fitted with an evaporative emission control system will also require part of the system sealing off before testing. Machines will fall into this category must be tested by a BMW dealer.

8 Where adjustment is possible, note that due to the awkward locations of the pilot screws (see illustration 6.9) an angled mixture adjustment screwdriver will be required (see illustration).

9 Turn the pilot screw on each carburettor fully in so that it seats lightly, then unscrew it 3½ turns. This is the base position for adjustment.

10 Run the engine until it reaches normal operating temperature. Check the idle speed and if necessary adjust it to its specified value (see Chapter 1).

11 With the engine running, starting with the left carburettor turn the pilot screw by a small amount (¼ turn) either side of the base position to find the point at which the highest consistent idle speed is obtained. Lightly open the throttle two or three times, then readjust the idle speed. Now do the same with pilot screw on the right carburettor.

5 Carburettor removal and installation

⚠️ **Warning:** *Refer to the precautions given in Section 1 before starting work.*

Removal

1 Remove the fuel tank (see Section 2). Remove the air filter housing (see Section 3).

2 Remove the fuel tank bracket (see illustration).

3 Fully slacken the clamp screws securing the carburettors to the intake ducts – note the orientation of the clamps (see illustration).

4 Ease the carburettors back out of the intake ducts (see illustration). **Note:** *Keep the carburettors level to prevent fuel spillage from the float chambers.* Detach the throttle and choke cables (see Section 7).

Caution: Stuff clean rag into each cylinder head intake after removing the carburettors, to prevent anything from falling in.

5 Place a suitable container below the float chambers, then slacken the drain screw on each chamber in turn and drain all the fuel from the carburettors **(see illustration)**. Tighten the screws once all the fuel has been drained.

6 If required unscrew the bolts securing the intake adapters to the cylinder head and remove them.

Installation

7 Installation is the reverse of removal, noting the following.

● Check for cracks or splits in the air intake rubbers and the cylinder head intake ducts **(see illustration 5.3)**, and replace them with new ones if necessary.

● Refer to Section 7 for installation of the throttle and choke cables. Check the operation of the cables and adjust them as necessary (see Chapter 1).

● Make sure the carburettors are fully engaged with the cylinder head intake ducts – if they are difficult to engage a squirt of WD40 or a smear of grease will ease entry. Make sure the clamps are positioned correctly **(see illustration 5.3)**.

● Check idle speed and adjust as necessary (see Chapter 1).

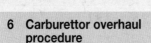

6 Carburettor overhaul procedure

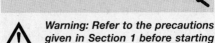

⚠ **Warning: Refer to the precautions given in Section 1 before starting work.**

Disassembly

1 Remove the carburettors (see Section 5). **Note:** *Do not separate the carburettors – individual bodies are not available, so if one needs replacing a new pair must be obtained. Each carburettor can be dismantled sufficiently for all normal cleaning and adjustments while joined together. Dismantle the carburettors separately to avoid interchanging parts.*

2 Undo the top cover screws and remove the cover **(see illustration)**. Remove the spring from inside the piston **(see illustration)**.

3 Carefully peel the diaphragm away from its sealing groove in the carburettor and withdraw the diaphragm/piston assembly **(see illustration)**. Carefully push the needle up from the bottom of the piston and remove it, noting the washer on the top of the circlip and the needle seat under it **(see illustration)**.

Caution: Do not use a sharp instrument to displace the diaphragm, as it is easily damaged.

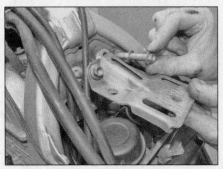

5.2 Unscrew the bolts and remove the bracket

5.4 . . . then draw the carburettors back and up and detach the cables

4 Undo the screws securing the float chamber to the base of the carburettor and remove it **(see illustration)**. Note the rubber seal.

5 Remove the float holder and float, noting

5.3 Slacken the clamp screw (arrowed) on each side . . .

5.5 Carburettor drain screws (arrowed)

how they fit **(see illustration)**. Unhook the needle valve from the tab on the float, noting how it fits **(see illustration)**. Remove the needle valve seat **(see illustration)**.

6.2a Undo the screws (arrowed) and remove the cover . . .

6.3a Lift the diaphragm/piston assembly out . . .

6.2b . . . and the spring

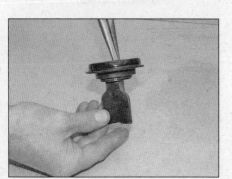

6.3b . . . then push the needle up and remove it

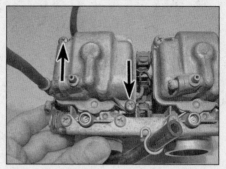

6.4 Undo the screws (arrowed) and remove the float chamber

6.5a Remove the float assembly

6.5b Remove the needle valve from the float . . .

6.5c . . . and the valve seat from the carburettor

6.6 Main jet (A) and idle jet (B)

6.7a Thread the screw into the needle jet and tap on its head . . .

6.7b . . . then remove the needle jet from the top, levering it up if necessary using a screwdriver

6 Unscrew and remove the main jet **(see illustration)**.

7 Thread one of the float chamber screws part-way into the needle jet in place of the main jet, then tap on its head to dislodge the needle jet. Lift the jet out of the piston guide via the venturi **(see illustration)**. Withdraw the piston guide and remove the O-ring from its base **(see illustration)**.

8 Unscrew and remove the idle jet **(see illustration 6.6)**.

9 The pilot screw can be removed from the carburettor, but note that its setting must be precisely noted first (see **Haynes Hint**). Where fitted remove the anti-tamper limiter plug. Unscrew and remove the pilot screw, along with its spring, washer and O-ring **(see illustration)**.

6.7c Lift the piston guide out

6.9 Pilot screw (arrowed)

> **HAYNES HiNT** *To record the pilot screw's current setting, turn the screw in until it seats lightly, counting the number of turns necessary to achieve this, then fully unscrew and remove it. On installation, the screw is simply backed out the number of turns you've recorded.*

Cleaning

Caution: Use only a dedicated carburettor

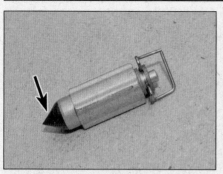

6.18 Check the tip of the needle valve for wear

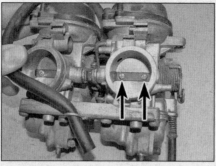

6.19 Check the butterfly screws (arrowed) are tight

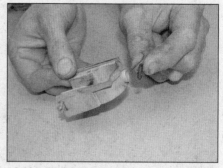

6.23a Fit the O-ring onto the base of the guide

cleaner or petroleum-based solvent for carburettor cleaning. Do not use caustic cleaners.

10 Clean the carburettor body and individual components according to the instructions on the cleaner container.

11 Loosen and remove the varnish and other deposits using a nylon-bristle brush. Rinse then dry with compressed air, blowing out all of the fuel and air passages.

Caution: Never clean the jets or passages with a piece of wire or a drill bit, as they will be enlarged, causing the fuel and air metering rates to be upset.

Inspection

12 Inspect the needle on the end of the choke plunger, the spring and the plunger. Replace any component that is worn, damaged or bent.

13 If removed from the carburettor, check the tapered portion of the pilot screw and the spring and O-ring for wear or damage. Replace any worn or damaged component with a new one if necessary.

14 Check the carburettor body, float chamber and top cover for cracks, distorted sealing surfaces and other damage. If any defects are found, replace the faulty component with a new one, although replacement of the entire carburettor may be necessary (check with a dealer on the availability of separate components).

15 Check the piston diaphragm for splits, holes, creases and general deterioration. Holding it up to a light will help to reveal problems of this nature. Replace the diaphragm/piston assembly with a new one if necessary. Make sure the spring is not stretched or distorted.

16 Insert the piston in the guide and check that it moves up and down smoothly. Check the surface of the piston for wear. If it is worn excessively or doesn't move smoothly in the guide, replace the components with new ones as necessary.

17 Check the needle is straight by rolling it on a flat surface such as a piece of glass. Replace it with a new one if it is bent, or if the tip is worn – remove the washer, circlip and needle seat first if not also replacing these, and fit them onto the new needle, locating the circlip in the 4th groove from the top **(see illustration 6.29a)**.

18 Check the tip of the float needle valve and the valve seat in the carburettor **(see illustration)**. Check the spring loaded rod in the valve operates correctly. If either is worn or damaged replace them with a new set.

19 Operate the throttle shaft to make sure the throttle butterfly valve opens and closes smoothly. If it doesn't, clean the throttle linkage, and also check the butterfly for distortion, or for any debris caught between its edge and the carburettor. Also check that the

butterfly is central on the shaft – if the screws securing it to the shaft have come loose it may be catching on the body **(see illustration)**.

20 Check the float for damage. This will usually be apparent by the presence of fuel inside the float. If it is damaged, replace it with a new one.

21 Check the condition of the float chamber seal and replace it with a new one if necessary **(see illustration 6.28a)**. Similarly check the O-ring for the piston guide **(see illustration 6.23a)**.

Reassembly

Note: *When reassembling the carburettors, be sure to use a new seal and O-rings if necessary. Do not overtighten the carburettor jets and screws, as they are easily damaged.*

22 Install the pilot screw (if removed) along with its spring, washer and O-ring, turning it in until it seats lightly **(see illustration 6.9)**. Now, turn the screw out the number of turns previously recorded on removal. Fit a new anti-tamper limiter plug where necessary.

23 Fit the O-ring onto the piston guide **(see illustration)**. Fit the guide into the carburettor – it can only fit one way **(see illustration 6.7c)**. Push the needle jet down through the piston guide, aligning the flat side of the jet against the pin in the carburettor **(see illustration)**.

24 Screw the main jet into the needle jet **(see illustration)**.

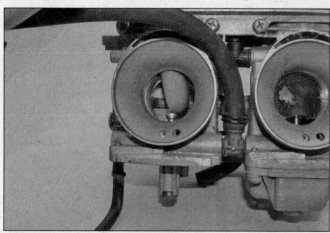

6.23b Make sure the jet is correctly aligned then push it in until it seats . . .

6.24 . . . then screw the main jet into it

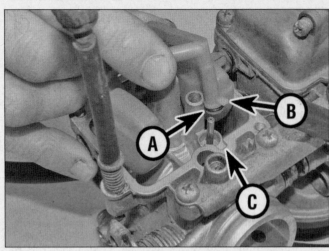

6.26 O-ring (A); locate tab (B) in the cut-out (C)

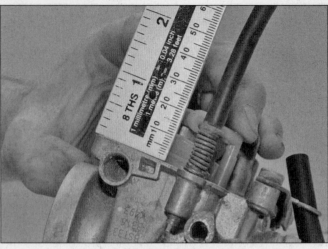

6.27 Checking float height

25 Screw the idle jet into the carburettor **(see illustration 6.6)**.

26 Hook the float needle valve onto the tab on the float **(see illustration 6.5b)**. Make sure the O-ring is fitted **(see illustration)**. Fit the float and float holder onto the carburettor, making sure the needle valve locates in the seat and the tab locates in its cut-out, and press it down so the O-ring seats.

27 To check the float height, hold the carburettor upside down, then lift the float so it is parallel with the float chamber mating surface, at the same time making sure the float holder is held against its seat – there must be no load on the needle valve. Measure the height of the float above the chamber mating surface with an accurate ruler **(see illustration)**. The height should be as specified at the beginning of the Chapter. If not, adjust the float height by carefully fitting small shims (ask your BMW dealer about obtaining them and where to put them) until the correct height is obtained.

28 Fit the rubber seal onto the float chamber, using a new one if necessary, making sure it is seated properly in its groove **(see illustration)**. Fit the chamber onto the carburettor and tighten the screws **(see illustrations)**.

29 Make sure the needle seat is fitted under the circlip, that the circlip is in the 4th groove from the top, and the washer is on top of the circlip, with its raised section uppermost **(see illustration)**. Fit the needle into the piston **(see illustration)**.

30 Fit the piston/diaphragm assembly into the guide (it only fits one way) and lightly push the piston down, making sure the needle is correctly aligned with the needle jet **(see illustration 6.3a)**. Press the rim of the diaphragm into its groove, making sure it is correctly seated. Fit the spring into the piston, making sure it locates correctly over the raised section of the washer on the top of the needle **(see illustration 6.2b)**.

31 Fit the top cover onto the carburettor,

6.28a Fit the O-ring into the groove . . .

6.28b . . . then fit the float chamber

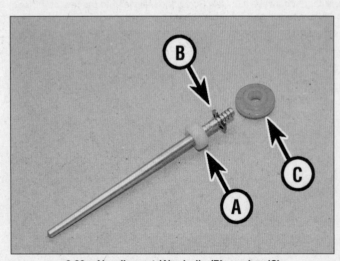

6.29a Needle seat (A), circlip (B), washer (C)

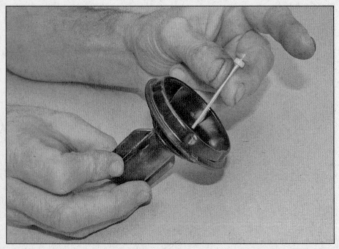

6.29b Fit the needle down into the hole in the bottom of the piston

locating the centre peg into the top of the spring, and tighten its screws **(see illustration)**. Check that the piston moves smoothly in the guide by pushing it up with your finger via the venturi. Note that the piston should descend slowly and smoothly as the diaphragm draws air into the chamber – it should not drop sharply under spring pressure.

32 Install the carburettors (see Section 5).

7 Throttle and choke cables

> *Warning: Refer to the precautions given in Section 1 before proceeding.*

Throttle cable

Removal

1 Remove the engine trim panels (see Chapter 8).

2 Remove the fuel tank (see Section 2). For easiest access displace the carburettors (see Section 5).

3 Hold the throttle pulley open and draw the cable out of the bracket then detach the cable end **(see illustrations)**.

4 Withdraw the cable from the machine, carefully noting its correct routing – you can tie string to the end which can be drawn through with the cable and used as a guide to draw the new cable in when installing it.

5 Pull the rubber boot off the cable at the switch housing end **(see illustration)**. Slacken the

6.31 Locate the peg in the spring and fit the cover

locknut. Undo the switch housing screws and separate the halves **(see illustration)**. Detach the cable end from the pulley in the housing, then thread the cable elbow out of the housing.

Installation

6 Thread the cable elbow into the switch housing, but not so it becomes tight – leaving it loose allows it to correctly align itself. Lubricate the cable nipple with multi-purpose grease and fit it into the throttle pulley – with the sockets facing up it goes into the front one. Join the housing halves and tighten the screws **(see illustration 7.5b)**.

7 Feed the cable through to the carburettors, making sure it is correctly routed – if used on removal tie the string to its end and pull it through. The cable must not interfere with any other component and should not be kinked or bent sharply. Now tighten the locknut against the switch housing and fit the rubber boot **(see illustration 7.5a)**.

8 Lubricate cable nipple with multi-purpose grease and fit it into the pulley **(see illustration 7.3b)**. Hold the throttle pulley open and locate the outer cable in its holder **(see illustration 7.3a)**.

9 Install the carburettors if displaced, and the fuel tank (see Sections 5 and 2). Adjust the cable freeplay (see Chapter 1). Operate the throttle to check that it opens and closes freely. Turn the handlebars back and forth to make sure the cable doesn't cause the steering to bind.

10 Start the engine and check that the idle speed does not rise as the handlebars are turned. If it does, the throttle cable is routed incorrectly. Correct the problem before riding the motorcycle. Install the engine trim panels (see Chapter 8).

Choke cable

Removal

11 Remove the engine trim panels (see Chapter 8).

12 Remove the fuel tank (see Section 2). For easiest access displace the carburettors (see Section 5).

13 Unscrew the choke plunger nut and withdraw the plunger from the carburettor body **(see illustrations)**. Pull the spring back and free the cable end from the plunger, then remove the spring.

14 Withdraw the cable from the machine, carefully noting its correct routing – you can tie string to the end which can be drawn through with the cable and used as a guide to draw the new cable in when installing it.

7.3a Draw the cable up out of the bracket . . .

7.3b . . . then detach the end from the pulley

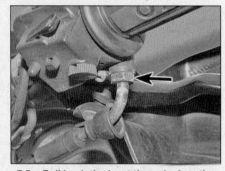

7.5a Pull back the boot then slacken the nut (arrowed)

7.5b Switch housing screws (arrowed)

7.13a Unscrew the nut (arrowed) . . .

7.13b . . . then withdraw the plunger

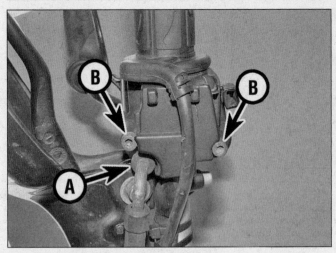

7.15 Slacken the locknut (A). Switch housing screws (B)

8.2 Slacken the clamp bolt (arrowed) . . .

15 Slacken the locknut at the switch housing end **(see illustration)**. Undo the switch housing screws and separate the halves. Detach the cable end from the lever in the housing, then thread the cable elbow out of the housing.

Installation

16 Thread the cable elbow into the switch housing, but not so it becomes tight – leaving it loose allows it to correctly align itself. Lubricate the cable nipple with multi-purpose grease and fit it into the choke lever. Join the housing halves and tighten the screws **(see illustration 7.15)**.

17 Feed the cable through to the carburettors, making sure it is correctly routed – if used on removal tie the string to its end and pull it through. The cable must not interfere with any other component and should not be kinked or bent sharply. Now tighten the locknut against the switch housing.

18 Fit the spring over the cable end and hold it back, then connect the cable to the choke plunger and release the spring. Fit the choke

plunger into the carburettor body and tighten the nut **(see illustrations 7.13b and a)**.

19 Install the carburettors if displaced, and the fuel tank (see Sections 5 and 2). Adjust the cable freeplay (see Chapter 1). Operate the choke to check that it opens and closes freely. Turn the handlebars back and forth to make sure the cable doesn't cause the steering to bind.

20 Start the engine and check that the idle speed does not rise as the handlebars are turned. If it does, the choke cable is routed incorrectly. Correct the problem before riding the motorcycle. Install the engine trim panels (see Chapter 8).

8 Exhaust system

> ⚠️ **Warning: If the engine has been running the exhaust system will be very hot. Allow the system to cool before carrying out any work.**

Note: *Before starting work on the exhaust system spray all the nuts, mounting bolts and clamp bolts with penetrating fluid – many of them are exposed and are prone to corrosion.*

Silencer

Removal

1 Remove the left-hand side cover (see Chapter 8).

2 Slacken the clamp bolt securing the silencer to the downpipe **(see illustration)**.

3 Unscrew the silencer mounting bolts **(see illustration)**.

4 Release the silencer from the downpipe assembly.

Installation

5 Check the condition of the sealing ring on the silencer-to-downpipe joint and replace it with a new one if necessary **(see illustration)**.

6 Fit the silencer onto the downpipe, making sure it is pushed fully home. Align the silencer mounts and tighten the bolts to the torque setting specified at the beginning of the

8.3 . . . then unscrew the mounting bolts (arrowed) and remove the silencer

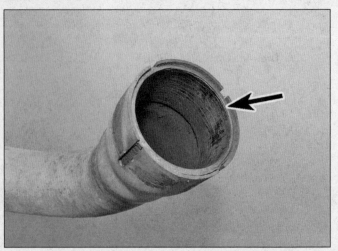

8.5 Use a new sealing ring (arrowed) if necessary

Chapter **(see illustration 8.3)**. Tighten the clamp bolt **(see illustration 8.2)**.

7 Run the engine and check the system for leaks.

8 Install the left-hand side cover (see Chapter 8).

Downpipe assembly

Removal

9 Remove the engine trim panels (see Chapter 8).

10 Unscrew the left downpipe flange nuts. Slacken the clamp bolt securing the left downpipe to the downpipe joint **(see illustration)**. Detach the left downpipe from the cylinder head and pull it off the downpipe joint.

11 Slacken the clamp bolt securing the downpipe assembly to the silencer **(see illustration 8.2)**. Unscrew the right downpipe flange nuts **(see illustration)**. Detach the right downpipe from the cylinder head and pull it off the silencer joint.

12 Remove the gasket from each port in the cylinder head and discard them – new ones must be fitted.

Installation

13 Check the condition of the sealing ring on the silencer-to-downpipe joint and replace it with a new one if necessary. Make sure the joint clamp is in place.

14 Fit a new gasket into each of the cylinder head ports. If necessary, apply a smear of grease to the gaskets to keep them in place whilst fitting the downpipe.

15 Manoeuvre the downpipe assembly into position and locate the head of the right downpipe in its port in the cylinder head and the end into the silencer joint.

16 Tighten the downpipe flange nuts evenly and a bit at a time to the torque setting specified at the beginning of the Chapter. Tighten the clamp bolt.

17 Fit the left downpipe into the downpipe joint and the cylinder head, then tighten the flange nuts as before and the clamp bolt.

18 Run the engine and check that there are no exhaust gas leaks.

19 Install the engine trim panels.

8.10 Slacken the clamp bolt (arrowed)

9 Catalytic converter

General information

1 A catalytic converter is incorporated in the exhaust system of 1997-on models sold in certain markets to minimise the level of exhaust pollutants released into the atmosphere. It is an open-loop system.

2 The catalytic converter consists of a canister containing a fine mesh impregnated with a catalyst material, over which the hot exhaust gases pass. The catalyst speeds up the oxidation of harmful carbon monoxide, unburned hydrocarbons and soot, effectively reducing the quantity of harmful products released into the atmosphere via the exhaust gases.

Precautions

3 The catalytic converter is a reliable and simple device which needs no maintenance in itself, but there are some facts of which an owner should be aware if the converter is to function properly for its full service life.

● DO NOT use leaded or lead replacement petrol (gasoline) – the additives will coat the precious metals, reducing their converting efficiency and will eventually destroy the catalytic converter.

● Always keep the ignition and fuel systems well-maintained in accordance with the manufacturer's schedule – if the fuel/air

8.11 Unscrew the downpipe flange nuts (arrowed)

mixture is suspected of being incorrect have it checked on an exhaust gas analyser.

● If the engine develops a misfire, do not ride the bike at all (or at least as little as possible) until the fault is cured.

● DO NOT use fuel or engine oil additives – these may contain substances harmful to the catalytic converter.

● DO NOT continue to use the bike if the engine burns oil to the extent of leaving a visible trail of blue smoke.

● Avoid bump-starting the bike unless absolutely necessary.

10 Evaporative emission control (EVAP) system

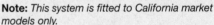

Note: This system is fitted to California market models only.

1 The evaporative emission control system (EVAP) is fitted to minimise the escape of fuel vapour into the atmosphere. The fuel tank is sealed and a charcoal canister collects the fuel vapours generated when the motorcycle is parked and stores them until they can be cleared from the canister to be burned by the engine during normal combustion.

2 The system is maintenance-free and is designed to operate throughout the life of the motorcycle. Periodically inspect the hose condition and renew any which are cracked, split or perished.

3 The charcoal canister is mounted on the right-hand side of the rear mudguard.

Chapter 4B
Fuel system and exhaust – GS, Dakar and CS models

Contents

Degrees of difficulty

Easy, suitable for novice with little experience	Fairly easy, suitable for beginner with some experience	Fairly difficult, suitable for competent DIY mechanic	Difficult, suitable for experienced DIY mechanic	Very difficult, suitable for expert DIY or professional

Specifications

Fuel
Grade
GS and Dakar – 2000 to 2003 . . . . Unleaded. Minimum 95 RON (Research Octane Number)
GS and Dakar – 2004-on . . . . Unleaded. Minimum 91 RON
CS . . . . Unleaded. Minimum 91 RON
Fuel tank capacity (including reserve)
GS and Dakar . . . . 17.3 litres (res. 4 litres)
CS . . . . 15.0 litres (res. 4 litres)

Fuel injection system
Idle speed . . . . see Chapter 1
Fuel pressure (at idle speed) . . . . 48 to 54 psi (3.3 to 3.7 Bars)

Torque settings
Exhaust system
GS and Dakar
Silencer mounting bolts . . . . 9 Nm
Silencer-to-downpipe clamp bolt . . . . 55 Nm
Downpipe flange nuts . . . . 20 Nm
CS
Silencer mounting bolt . . . . 41 Nm
Silencer-to-downpipe clamp bolt . . . . 55 Nm
Downpipe flange nuts . . . . 20 Nm
Fuel tank bolts . . . . 21 Nm
Oxygen sensor . . . . 45 Nm
Rear sub-frame bolts . . . . 24 Nm

1 General information and precautions

Fuel system

The fuel supply system consists of the fuel tank, an internal fuel pump and level sensor, external fuel filter, the fuel hoses, fuel injector, throttle body, and throttle cable. The injection system supplies fuel and air to the engine via a single throttle body. The injector is operated by the Electronic Control Unit (ECU) using the information obtained from the sensors it monitors (refer to Section 4 for more information on the operation of the fuel injection system). Cold start idle speed is controlled by the ECU via a throttle valve actuator.

All models have a low fuel warning light in the instrument cluster, actuated by a level sensor inside the fuel tank. When the light comes on there is approximately 4 litres of fuel left.

Precautions

⚠️ **Warning: Petrol (gasoline) is extremely flammable, so take extra precautions when you work on any part of the fuel system. Always remove the battery (see Chapter 9). Don't smoke or allow open flames or bare light bulbs near the work area, and don't work in a garage where a natural gas-type appliance is present. If you spill any fuel on your skin, rinse it off immediately with soap and water. When you perform any kind of work on the fuel system, wear safety glasses and have a fire extinguisher suitable for a class B type fire (flammable liquids) on hand.**

Residual pressure will remain in the fuel feed hose and fuel injector after the motorcycle has been used. Before disconnecting any fuel hose, ensure the ignition is switched OFF and have some rag handy to catch any fuel. It is vital that no dirt or debris is allowed to enter the fuel system. Any foreign matter could result in injector damage or malfunction. Ensure the ignition is switched OFF before disconnecting or

reconnecting any fuel injection system wiring connector. If a connector is disconnected or reconnected with the ignition switched ON, the electronic control unit (ECU) may be damaged.

Always perform service procedures in a well-ventilated area to prevent a build-up of fumes.

Never work in a building containing a gas appliance with a pilot light, or any other form of naked flame. Ensure that there are no naked light bulbs or any sources of flame or sparks nearby.

Do not smoke (or allow anyone else to smoke) while in the vicinity of petrol (gasoline) or of components containing it. Remember the possible presence of vapour from these sources and move well clear before smoking.

Check all electrical equipment belonging to the house, garage or workshop where work is being undertaken (see the Safety first! section of this manual). Remember that certain electrical appliances such as drills, cutters etc, create sparks in the normal course of operation and must not be used near petrol (gasoline) or any component containing it. Again, remember the possible presence of fumes before using electrical equipment.

Always mop up any spilt fuel and safely dispose of the rag used.

Any stored fuel that is drained off during servicing work must be kept in sealed containers that are suitable for holding petrol (gasoline), and clearly marked as such; the containers themselves should be kept in a safe place. Note that this last point applies equally to the fuel tank if it is removed from the machine; also remember to keep its filler cap closed at all times.

Read the Safety first! section of this manual carefully before starting work.

2 Fuel tank

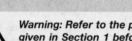
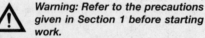

⚠️ **Warning: Refer to the precautions given in Section 1 before starting work.**

Note 1: Under normal circumstances the tank should never have to be removed. If you do, try to time the removal procedure with a near empty tank, which makes it much easier to lift.

Note 2: Three types of hose clamp are used on the various hoses across the range of models covered – the non-re-usable type, the re-usable clip type and the screw type. A small screwdriver is required to release the non-reusable type and clip type clamps. Special pliers are required to close them, and these are available from automotive tool suppliers, or from BMW (part No. 131500), along with the clamps where new ones are required.

Removal

1 Remove the seat, the toolkit, on CS models

the seat lock, and the rear side covers (see Chapter 8). Disconnect the battery (see Chapter 9).

2 On GS and Dakar models unscrew the nut on the chain take-up roller bolt and remove the washer – the roller is between the top run of the chain and the bottom of the tank on the right-hand side. Withdraw the bolt and remove the roller, noting the arrangement of the washers and spacer.

3 Remove the silencer(s) (Section 13).

4 Make sure the rear brake fluid reservoir cap is tight. Displace the reservoir from its bracket, wrap it in rag and lay it aside, keeping it upright if possible **(see illustration)**.

5 Remove the rubber cap from the pump and disconnect the fuel pump and level sensor wiring connectors **(see illustration 4.3)**. Release the fuel feed and return hose clamps and detach the hoses from the pump, noting which fits where **(see illustration 4.4)**. Catch any residual fuel in some rag or a suitable container, or alternatively block the hose ends or pinch the hoses using clamps.

6 Detach the hose from the roll-over valve **(see illustration 4.13a)**.

7 On GS and Dakar models displace the ECU, but do not disconnect it (see Chapter 5).

8 Disconnect all tail light and rear turn signal wiring connectors – on CS models make a note of which wire goes on which connector on the tail light. Release all rear sub-loom wiring and connectors from ties or holders so the rear sub-frame can be removed along with attached components and wiring to the tail light and turn signal assemblies.

9 On GS and Dakar models unscrew the nuts on the rear sub-frame bolts and on CS models slacken the rear sub-frame bolts. On all models remove the bolts, keeping the sub-frame supported as the last ones come out – note that the tank is secured to the sub-frame and is removed along with it. Carefully draw the sub-frame and tank assembly back, taking care not to snag the brake hose to the rear master cylinder.

10 Unscrew the fuel tank bolts and separate it from the sub-frame.

11 If required remove the fuel pump and the roll-over valve (Section 4).

Installation

12 Installation is the reverse of removal, noting the following:

● If removed install the fuel pump and roll-over valve (Section 4).

● Tighten the fuel tank bolts to the torque setting specified at the beginning of the Chapter.

● Make sure all wiring and hoses are on the top of the tank when installing the sub-frame/tank assembly, and take care not to snag the rear master cylinder brake hose.

● Tighten the sub-frame bolts to the torque settings specified at the beginning of the Chapter.

● Make sure all wiring and connectors and

2.4 Unscrew the bolt (arrowed) and displace the reservoir

correctly routed and secured. On CS models make sure the tail light connectors are in the correct place – the blue/black wire is for the right-hand terminal, the brown wire in the middle and the green/red on the left (terminals handed as though looking from the rear of the bike).

● Make sure the fuel feed and return hoses are secure on the pump unions – use new clamps if necessary. Note that BMW advise against using screw type clamps on the fuel feed hose as they could damage the hose.

● Start the engine and check that there is no sign of fuel leakage.

Repair

13 All repairs to the fuel tank should be carried out by a professional who has experience in this critical and potentially dangerous work. Even after cleaning and flushing of the fuel system, explosive fumes can remain and ignite during repair of the tank.

14 If the fuel tank is removed from the bike, it should not be placed in an area where sparks or open flames could ignite the fumes coming out of the tank. Be especially careful inside garages where a natural gas-type appliance is located, because the pilot light could cause an explosion.

3 Fuel pressure check

Special Tool: *A fuel pressure gauge is required for this procedure.*

Note: *Three types of hose clamp are used on the various hoses across the range of models covered – the non-re-usable type, the re-usable clip type and the screw type. A small screwdriver is required to release the non-reusable type and clip type clamps. Special pliers are required to close them,* and these are available from automotive tool suppliers, or from BMW (part No. 131500), along with the clamps where new ones are required.

1 To check the fuel pressure, a suitable gauge (BMW pt. No. 161500 or equivalent) is needed – if you use an aftermarket gauge you will also need suitable adapters and hoses with it to fit between the fuel feed hose and its union on the fuel pump.

2 Remove the seat (see Chapter 8).

3 Remove the rubber cap from the pump **(see illustration 4.3)**. Release the fuel feed hose clamp and detach the hose from the pump **(see illustration 4.4)**. Catch any residual fuel in some rag or a suitable container.

4 Connect the gauge between the hose and the pump.

5 Start the engine and check the pressure with the engine idling. It should be as specified at the beginning of this Chapter.

6 Turn the ignition OFF and remove the gauge. Use a rag to catch any residual fuel as before. Connect the fuel hose – use a new clamp if necessary. Note that BMW advise against using screw type clamps on the fuel feed hose as they could damage the hose.

7 If the pressure is too low, check for a leak in the fuel supply system, including the injector and its holder. If there is no leakage the pressure regulator could be faulty, the pick-up in the pump could be blocked, or the pump could be faulty. The pressure regulator is incorporated in the fuel filter which is a regular service item – replace it with a new one (see Chapter 1). Also check the pump (Section 4).

8 If the pressure is too high, either the pressure regulator or the fuel pump check valve is faulty or a fuel hose, the filter or the injector could be clogged. The pressure regulator is incorporated in the fuel filter which is a regular service item – replace it with a new one (see Chapter 1). Check the pump, fuel hose and injectors.

4 Fuel pump and roll-over valve

Fuel pump

Check

1 The fuel pump is located inside the fuel tank. When the ignition is switched ON, it should be possible to hear the pump run for a few seconds until the system is up to pressure. If you can't hear anything, check the fuse and relay (see Chapter 9). If they are good, check the wiring, connectors and terminals in the pump circuit for physical damage or loose or corroded connections and rectify as necessary (see Electrical system fault finding and the *Wiring Diagrams* in Chapter 9) – on the pump itself the black connector is for the pump and goes in the front socket, the white connector is for the level sensor and goes in the rear socket **(see illustration 4.3)**. If the pump still will not run, remove it (see below) and check that all its wiring and connectors are secure **(see illustration)**. If all is good refer to a BMW dealer – no test details are provided for the pump.

Removal

Note: *Three types of hose clamp are used on the various hoses across the range of models covered – the non-re-usable type, the re-usable clip type and the screw type. A small screwdriver is required to release the non-reusable type and clip type clamps. Special pliers are required to close them, and these are available from automotive tool suppliers, or from BMW (part No. 131500), along with the clamps where new ones are required.*

2 Remove the seat (see Chapter 8). Disconnect the battery (see Chapter 9).

3 Remove the rubber cap from the pump and disconnect the fuel pump and level sensor wiring connectors **(see illustration)**.

4 Release the fuel feed and return hose

4.1 Make sure all the pump wiring and connectors are secure

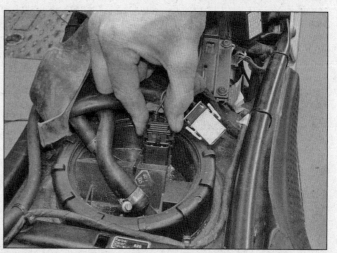

4.3 Remove the cap and disconnect the wiring connectors

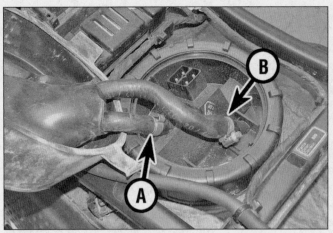

4.4 Fuel feed hose (A) and return hose (B)

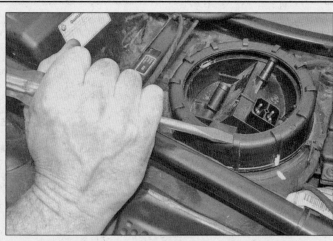

4.5 You can use a screwdriver to drive the ring round

4.6a Carefully withdraw the pump . . .

4.6b . . . and if required remove the sealing ring

4.7 Make sure the strainer (arrowed) is clean

clamps and detach the hoses from the pump, noting which fits where. Catch any residual fuel in some rag or a suitable container, or alternatively block the hose ends or pinch the hoses using clamps **(see illustration)**.

5 Unscrew the pump retaining ring – using a suitable wrench (BMW pt. No. 161021 or equivalent, such as the commercially available and not expensive clutch holding tool) **(see illustration 4.8b)** – you might manage it with your hands if you are strong! Alternatively you can drive it round using a screwdriver, but take care not to damage the ribs **(see illustration)**.

6 Note the orientation of the pump – there should be a couple of lines on it that align with a mark on the tank, or alternatively make you own. Carefully withdraw the pump assembly from the tank **(see illustration)**. Check the condition of the sealing ring and replace it with a new one if necessary – it is best to fit a new one whatever the condition **(see illustration)**. Do not disassemble the pump.

Installation

7 Ensure the pump and tank mating surfaces are clean and dry. Make sure the strainer is

clean – unclip it if necessary and clean it using solvent and compressed air **(see illustration)**. Note that the strainer is not listed as being available separately from the pump, but it is worth consulting a dealer if a new one is required before buying a whole new pump. Fit the sealing ring into the tank if removed, using a new one if necessary **(see illustration 4.6b)**.

8 Carefully manoeuvre the pump assembly into the tank with the wiring connector to the front, and align the marks **(see illustration 4.6a)**. Fit the retaining ring **(see illustrations)**.

9 Reconnect the wiring connectors **(see**

4.8a Fit the retaining ring

4.8b Using a clutch holding tool to tighten the retaining ring

illustration 4.3) – the black connector is for the pump and goes in the front socket, the white connector is for the level sensor and goes in the rear socket.

10 Connect the fuel feed and return hoses to the pump unions – use new clamps if necessary. Note that BMW advise against using screw type clamps on the fuel feed hose as they could damage the hose.

11 Connect the battery (see Chapter 9). Install the seat (see Chapter 8).

Roll-over valve

12 Remove the seat (see Chapter 8). Disconnect the battery (see Chapter 9).

13 Detach the hose from the roll-over valve (**see illustration**). Undo the valve screws and remove the valve (**see illustration**). Check the condition of the sealing ring and replace it with a new one if necessary – it is best to fit a new one whatever.

14 Install the roll-over valve, making sure the mating surfaces are clean and using a new sealing ring if necessary. Tighten the screws evenly in a criss-cross pattern, noting that they only need tightening lightly (2 Nm if a suitable torque wrench is available). Connect the hose.

4.13a Detach the hose (arrowed) . . .

4.13b . . . then undo the screws and remove the valve and its sealing ring

5 Air filter housing

Removal

GS and Dakar models

1 Remove the front side covers and the top cover (see Chapter 8).

2 Disconnect the intake air temperature (IAT) sensor wiring connector (**see illustration 7.8**).

3 Remove the air filter (see Chapter 1).

4 Release the battery strap from the housing (**see illustration**). Release the clamp and detach the hose (**see illustration**).

5 Unscrew the bolt securing the oil tank to the housing, noting the spacer (**see illustration**).

6 Unscrew the bolts securing the housing to the frame (**see illustration**). Ease the housing

5.4a Release the strap from the top of the housing . . .

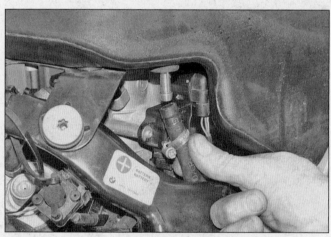

5.4b . . . and detach the hose from the right-hand side

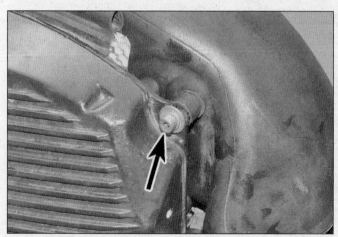

5.5 Unscrew the oil tank bolt (arrowed)

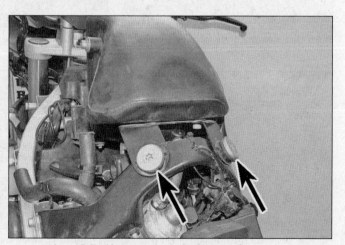

5.6a Unscrew the bolts (arrowed) . . .

5.6b . . . and remove the housing

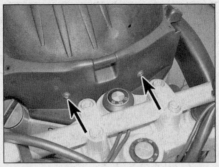

5.8a Undo the screws (arrowed) . . .

5.8b . . . and remove the panel

5.9a Release the fusebox from its bracket by twisting it anti-clockwise . . .

5.9b . . . and unscrew the bolt securing the fuel filter

up off the throttle body and disengage it from the battery holder **(see illustration)**.

7 Cover the throttle body with clean rag.

5.9c Unscrew the bolts (arrowed) on each side . . .

5.9d . . . and remove the frame

CS models

8 Remove the front side covers (see Chapter 8). Undo the screws and remove the front panel **(see illustrations)**.
9 Release the fuel filter and the fusebox from the storage compartment frame **(see illustrations)**. Unscrew the bolts and remove the frame **(see illustrations)**.
10 Ease the housing up off the throttle body, then release the clamp and detach the hose from the back of the housing and disconnect the intake air temperature (IAT) sensor wiring connector from the underside **(see illustrations)**. Remove the housing.
11 If required undo the air intake duct screws and remove the duct and the air filter.
12 Cover the throttle body with clean rag.

5.10a Displace the housing upwards . . .

5.10b . . . then detach the hose . . .

5.10c . . . and disconnect the wiring connector

Installation

13 Installation is the reverse of removal. Make sure the housing locates correctly onto the throttle body. On GS and Dakar models make sure it engages correctly with the battery holder **(see illustration)**. On CS models make sure the peg at the front of the air intake duct locates in its holder **(see illustration)**. Do not forget to connect the IAT sensor wiring connector.

6 Fuel injection system description

1 The Fuel injection system consists of the fuel circuit and the electronic control circuit.
2 The fuel circuit consists of the tank with internal integrated pump/strainer/level sensor, external integrated fuel filter/pressure regulator, the throttle body and injector. Fuel is pumped under pressure from the tank to the injector via the filter/pressure regulator. Operating pressure is maintained by the pump and pressure regulator. The injector sprays pressurised fuel into the throttle body where it mixes with air and vaporises, before entering the cylinder where it is compressed and ignited by the spark plugs.
3 The electronic control circuit consists of the electronic control unit (ECU), which operates and co-ordinates both the fuel injection and ignition systems, and the various sensors which provide the ECU with information on engine operating conditions.
4 The electronic control unit (ECU) monitors signals from the following sensors.
● Intake air temperature (IAT) sensor
● Throttle position (TP) sensor
● Ignition timing (crankshaft position or CKP) sensor
● Coolant temperature (ECT) sensor
● Oxygen (O^2) sensor (where fitted)
5 Based on the information it receives, the ECU calculates the appropriate ignition and fuel requirements of the engine. By varying the length of the electronic pulse it sends to each injector, the ECU controls the length of time the injectors are held open and thereby the amount of fuel that is supplied to the engine. Fuel supply varies according to the engine's

5.13a On GS models the flange rim (arrowed) engages the slot on the battery holder

needs for starting, warming-up, idling, cruising and acceleration.
6 BMW provide no information on fault diagnosis or on testing any of the individual components, and there is no warning light to let you know if there is a problem. In the event of a suspected fault the bike must be taken to a BMW dealer where it can be plugged into their diagnostic equipment.
7 However before going to the effort and expense of visiting a dealer first ensure that the relevant system wiring connectors are securely connected and free of corrosion – poor connections are the cause of the majority of problems (see the relevant Section of this Chapter, or to Chapter 3 for the coolant temperature sensor and Chapter 5 for the ignition timing sensor, for access). Also check the wiring itself for any obvious faults or breaks, and use a continuity tester to check the wiring between the component, its connector(s) and the ECU, referring to electrical fault finding and the Wiring Diagrams at the end of Chapter 9.

7 Fuel injection system sensors

Caution: Ensure the ignition is switched OFF before disconnecting/reconnecting any fuel injection system wiring connector. If a connector is disconnected/reconnected with the ignition switched ON the electronic control unit (ECU) could be damaged.

5.13b On CS models locate the peg in its holder (arrowed)

Throttle position (TP) sensor

1 Remove the air filter housing (see Section 5).
2 Disconnect the sensor wiring connector **(see illustration)**.
3 Undo the screws and detach the sensor from the throttle body, noting how it locates.
4 To install, slide the throttle valve tab into the slot in the sensor and locate the sensor on the throttle body. Fit the screws with their washers and tighten them.
5 Connect the wiring connector **(see illustration 7.2)**.
6 Install the air filter housing (see Section 5).

Intake air temperature (IAT) sensor

GS and Dakar models

7 Remove the right-hand front side cover (see Chapter 8).
8 Disconnect the intake air temperature (IAT) sensor wiring connector **(see illustration)**. Release the clip and draw the sensor out of the air filter housing.
9 Installation is the reverse of removal.

CS models

10 Remove the air filter housing (see Section 5).
11 Release the clip and draw the sensor out of the air filter housing.
12 Installation is the reverse of removal.

Oxygen sensor

13 The sensor is screwed into the exhaust downpipe **(see illustration)**. On GS and Dakar models remove the sump guard (see Chapter 8).

7.2 Throttle position sensor wiring connector and screws (arrowed)

7.8 Disconnect the wiring connector from the sensor

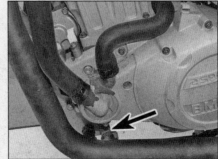

7.13 Oxygen sensor (arrowed)

7.14 Oxygen sensor wiring connector (arrowed) – GS shown

8.6a Slacken the clamp screw (arrowed) . . .

14 Trace the wiring from the sensor and disconnect it at the connector **(see illustration)**.

15 Unscrew and remove the sensor. Take care not to drop the sensor, and keep the sensing portion on the bottom and the filter holes on the top free of dirt and dust.

16 Installation is the reverse of removal. Lightly grease the threads with high temperature grease (Optimoly TA). If the correct tools are available tighten the sensor to the torque setting specified at the beginning of the Chapter.

8 Throttle body

⚠ **Warning: Refer to the precautions given in Section 1 before starting work.**

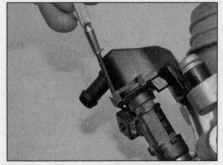

9.3a Release the clip . . .

8.3 Disconnect the injector wiring connector. Fuel feed hose clamp (arrowed)

8.6b . . . and remove the throttle body

Note: *Three types of hose clamp are used on the various hoses across the range of models covered – the non-re-usable type, the re-usable clip type and the screw type. A small screwdriver is required to release the non-reusable type and clip type clamps. Special pliers are required to close them, and these are available from automotive tool suppliers, or from BMW (part No. 131500), along with the clamps where new ones are required.*

Removal

1 Remove the air filter housing (Section 5).

2 Detach the throttle cable (Section 11).

3 Disconnect the fuel injector wiring connector **(see illustration)**. If required remove the injector (Section 9). If you don't, slacken the clamp securing the fuel feed hose and detach the hose from the injector holder – have some rag handy to catch residual fuel.

4 Disconnect the throttle position sensor

9.3b . . . then undo the screws (arrowed)

wiring connector **(see illustration 7.2)**. If required remove the sensor (Section 7).

5 Disconnect the throttle valve actuator wiring connector **(see illustration 10.2)**. If required remove the actuator (Section 10).

6 Loosen the clamp screw securing the throttle body in the intake adapter **(see illustration)**. Ease the throttle body out of the adapter and remove it **(see illustration)**.

Caution: Do not snap the throttle valve from fully open to fully closed once the cable has been disconnected because this can lead to engine idle speed problems.

Caution: Tape over or stuff clean rag into the cylinder head intake after removing the throttle body to prevent anything from falling in.

7 Check the intake adapter rubber for signs of cracking or deterioration and replace it with a new one if necessary. Make sure the mating surfaces are clean before refitting.

Installation

8 Installation is the reverse of removal, noting the following:

● Remove the tape/plug from the intake adapter.

● Make sure the throttle body is fully engaged with the intake adapter on the cylinder head before tightening the clamp.

● Make sure the fuel hose and wiring connectors are securely connected.

● Check the operation of the throttle and adjust the cable as necessary (see Chapter 1).

● Run the engine and check that the fuel system is working correctly before taking the machine out on the road.

9 Fuel injector

⚠ **Warning: Refer to the precautions given in Section 1 before starting work.**

Removal

1 Remove the air filter housing (Section 5).

2 Disconnect the fuel injector wiring connector **(see illustration 8.3)**. If required, slacken the clamp securing the fuel feed hose and detach the hose from the injector holder – have some rag handy to catch residual fuel.

3 Remove the spring clip from the injector **(see illustration)**. Undo the fuel injector holder screws **(see illustration)**.

4 Carefully lift off the holder then remove the injector **(see illustrations)**.

5 Remove the O-rings from the injector – new ones must be used **(see illustration)**.

Installation

6 Installation is the reverse of removal, noting the following:

● Fit new O-rings smeared lightly with clean engine oil **(see illustration 9.5)**.

● Make sure the injector locates correctly in the throttle body **(see illustration 9.4b)**.

● When fitting the injector into the holder align the lug on the injector with the cut-out in the holder (see illustration 9.4a).
● Push the clip fully in, making sure it locates correctly (see illustration).
● Make sure the fuel hose and wiring connector are securely connected (see illustration 8.3).
● Run the engine and check that the fuel system is working correctly before taking the machine out on the road.

10 Throttle valve actuator

 Warning: Refer to the precautions given in Section 1 before starting work.

Removal

1 Remove the air filter housing (see Section 5).
2 Disconnect the actuator wiring connector (see illustration).
3 Undo the screws and detach the actuator from the throttle body, noting how it locates (see illustration).
4 Check the condition of the O-ring and replace it with a new one if it is damaged, deformed or deteriorated (see illustration).

Installation

5 Fit the actuator onto the throttle body using a new O-ring if necessary (see illustrations 10.4 and 10.3b).
6 Clean the threads of the screws and apply Loctite 243 or equivalent, and tighten them.
7 Connect the wiring connector (see illustration 10.2).
8 Install the air filter housing (see Section 5).
9 Turn the ignition ON, wait for the temperature warning light to go out, then take the bike for a ride to initialise the actuator.

11 Throttle cable

 Warning: Refer to the precautions given in Section 1 before starting work.

Removal

1 Remove the left-hand front side cover (see Chapter 8).
2 Remove the E-clip or unscrew the nut (according to model), then draw the cable out of the bracket (see illustration). Hold the throttle pulley open and detach the cable end (see illustration).
3 Withdraw the cable from the machine, carefully noting its correct routing.

 HAYNES HiNT *Tie string to the cable end so that it's drawn through with the old cable and used as a guide to draw the new cable into place.*

9.4a Remove the holder . . .

9.4b . . . then remove the injector

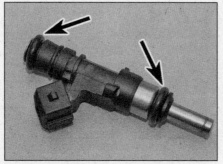

9.5 Remove the O-rings (arrowed) and fit new ones on installation

9.6 Make sure the clip locates correctly

4 Undo the switch housing screws and displace the switch face (see illustration). Release the cable pulley and detach the cable end (see illustrations) – note how the pulley and twistgrip align. Undo the cable retainer

10.2 Throttle valve actuator wiring connector (arrowed)

screw and draw the cable from the switch housing (see illustration).

Installation

5 Fit the cable into the housing and secure the retainer with its screw (see illustration 11.4d).

10.3a Undo the screws (arrowed) . . .

10.3b . . . and remove the actuator

10.4 Remove the O-ring and fit a new one on installation

11.2a Release the cable from the bracket . . .

11.2b . . . then turn the pulley and detach the cable end

11.4a Undo the screws (arrowed) and displace the face

11.4b Draw the pulley off its post . . .

11.4c . . . and detach the cable end

11.4d Cable retainer screw (arrowed)

Lubricate the cable nipple with multi-purpose grease and fit it into the throttle pulley, then fit the pulley, aligning and engaging it with the twistgrip **(see illustrations 11.4c and b)**. Fit the switch face and tighten the screws **(see illustration)**.

6 Feed the cable through to the throttle body, making sure it is correctly routed – if used on removal tie the string to its end and pull it through. The cable must not interfere with any other component and should not be kinked or bent sharply. Now tighten the locknut against the switch housing and fit the rubber boot.

7 Lubricate cable nipple with multi-purpose grease. Hold the throttle pulley open and fit the cable end **(see illustration 11.2b)**. Locate the outer cable in its bracket and fit the e-clip or tighten the nut.

8 Adjust the cable freeplay (see Chapter 1). Operate the throttle to check that it opens and closes freely. Turn the handlebars back and

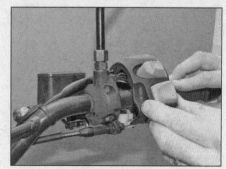

11.5 Fit the switch face onto the housing

forth to make sure the cable doesn't cause the steering to bind.

9 Start the engine and check that the idle speed does not rise as the handlebars are turned. If it does, the throttle cable is routed incorrectly. Correct the problem before riding the motorcycle.

10 Install the front side cover (see Chapter 8).

12 Fuel level sensor and warning light

⚠ *Warning: Refer to the precautions given in Section 1 before starting work.*

Check

1 The circuit consists of the sensor incorporated in the fuel pump, and the warning light in the instrument cluster. The warning light comes on when the amount of fuel drops to 4 litres.

2 If the warning light does not work, remove the seat (see Chapter 8). Remove the rubber cap from the pump and disconnect the sensor wiring connector (the white connector) **(see illustration 4.3)**. Short between the terminals in the loom side of the connector using an auxiliary piece of wire, with the ignition ON – the warning light should come on. If it doesn't first check the bulb (see Chapter 9). If that is good check the wiring connector for a loose wire or corroded or broken terminal, then check the wiring between the sensor and

the instrument cluster for continuity (see Chapter 9). If the light does come on the sensor is faulty.

Replacement

⚠ *Warning: The engine must be completely cool before carrying out this procedure.*

3 The sensor is part of the fuel pump assembly and is not available separately – refer to Section 4 for the fuel pump.

13 Exhaust system

⚠ *Warning: If the engine has been running the exhaust system will be very hot. Allow the system to cool before carrying out any work.*

Note: *Before starting work on the exhaust system spray all the nuts, mounting bolts and clamp bolts with penetrating fluid – many of them are exposed and are prone to corrosion.*

Silencer(s)

Removal – GS and Dakar

1 Remove the seat and the side covers (see Chapter 8).

2 Unscrew the right-hand silencer mounting bolt **(see illustration)**.

3 Draw the right-hand silencer off the left-hand silencer and out of the holder at the front and remove it **(see illustration)**.

4 Slacken the clamp securing the left-hand

13.2 Unscrew the bolt . . .

13.3 . . . and remove the right-hand silencer

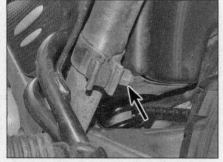

13.4 Slacken the clamp nut (arrowed)

silencer to the downpipe – note the orientation of the clamp **(see illustration)**.

5 Unscrew the left-hand silencer mounting bolt.

6 Release the left-hand silencer from the downpipe silencer and from the holder and remove it **(see illustration)**.

7 If required remove the heat shield from each silencer.

Removal – CS

8 Protect the rear wheel spoke and rim around the silencer to prevent the possibility of damage.

9 Slacken the clamp bolt securing the silencer to the downpipe.

10 Unscrew the silencer mounting bolt.

11 Release the silencer from the downpipe assembly.

Installation

12 Installation is the reverse of removal. Make sure the silencer joint clamp is in place and correctly positioned **(see illustration)**. Tighten the silencer mounting bolt(s) and clamp bolt to the torque settings specified at the beginning of the Chapter.

13 Run the engine and check the system for leaks.

Downpipe assembly

Removal

14 If required remove the silencer(s) (see above). If the centrestand or an auxiliary stand is being used also lower the sidestand.

15 On GS and Dakar models remove the sump guard (see Chapter 8), and the left-hand footrest bracket assembly (see Chapter 6).

16 Where fitted disconnect the oxygen sensor wiring connector **(see illustration 7.14)**. Feed the wiring to the sensor, noting its routing and freeing it from any ties.

17 Slacken the clamp securing the downpipe to the silencer **(see illustration 13.4)**.

18 Unscrew the downpipe flange nuts **(see illustration)**.

19 Detach the downpipe assembly from the cylinder head and pull it off the silencer if not removed **(see illustration)**.

20 Remove the gasket from the head of the pipe or from the port in the cylinder head and discard it – a new one must be fitted **(see illustration 13.22)**.

Installation

21 If the silence has not been removed make

sure the joint clamp is in place and correctly positioned **(see illustration 13.12)**.

22 Fit a new gasket onto the head of the downpipe, locating the tabs over the rim **(see illustration)**.

23 Manoeuvre the downpipe assembly into position and locate the head in the port in the cylinder head and the end into the silencer if not removed **(see illustration 13.19)**.

24 Tighten the downpipe flange nuts evenly and a bit at a time to the torque setting specified at the beginning of the Chapter **(see illustration 13.18)**. Tighten the silencer clamp bolt to the specified torque **(see illustration 13.12)**.

25 Run the engine and check that there are no exhaust gas leaks.

26 On GS and Dakar models fit the sump guard and the left-hand footrest bracket assembly.

13.6 Removing the left-hand silencer

13.12 Do not forget the clamp if removed

13.18 Unscrew the flange nuts (arrowed) . . .

13.19 . . . and remove the downpipe

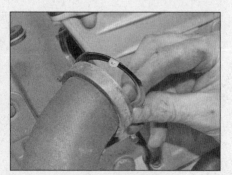

13.22 Fit a new gasket

14 Evaporative emission control (EVAP) system

Note: *This system is fitted to California market models only.*

1 The evaporative emission control system (EVAP) is fitted to minimise the escape of fuel vapour into the atmosphere. The fuel tank is sealed and a charcoal canister collects the fuel vapours generated when the motorcycle is parked and stores them until they can be cleared from the canister to be burned by the engine during normal combustion.

2 The system is maintenance-free and is designed to operate throughout the life of the motorcycle. Inspect the hoses periodically and replace any which are cracked, perished or split.

15 Catalytic converter

General information

1 A catalytic converter is incorporated in the exhaust system to minimise the level of exhaust pollutants released into the atmosphere. It is a closed-loop system with feedback to the ECU via an oxygen sensor.

2 The catalytic converter consists of a canister containing a fine mesh impregnated with a catalyst material, over which the hot exhaust gases pass. The catalyst speeds up the oxidation of harmful carbon monoxide, unburned hydrocarbons and soot, effectively reducing the quantity of harmful products released into the atmosphere via the exhaust gases.

Precautions

3 The catalytic converter is a reliable and simple device which needs no maintenance in itself, but there are some facts of which an owner should be aware if the converter is to function properly for its full service life.

● DO NOT use leaded or lead replacement petrol (gasoline) – the additives will coat the precious metals, reducing their converting efficiency and will eventually destroy the catalytic converter.

● Always keep the ignition and fuel systems well-maintained in accordance with the manufacturer's schedule – if the fuel/air mixture is suspected of being incorrect have it checked on an exhaust gas analyser.

● If the engine develops a misfire, do not ride the bike at all (or at least as little as possible) until the fault is cured.

● DO NOT use fuel or engine oil additives – these may contain substances harmful to the catalytic converter.

● DO NOT continue to use the bike if the engine burns oil to the extent of leaving a visible trail of blue smoke.

● Avoid bump-starting the bike unless absolutely necessary.

Chapter 5
Ignition system

Contents

Degrees of difficulty

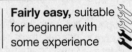

Easy, suitable for novice with little experience	**Fairly easy,** suitable for beginner with some experience	**Fairly difficult,** suitable for competent DIY mechanic	**Difficult,** suitable for experienced DIY mechanic	**Very difficult,** suitable for expert DIY or professional

Specifications

General information
Spark plugs . . . .   see Chapter 1

Ignition HT coil(s)
Funduro and ST
  Primary winding resistance . . . .   0.2 to 0.5 ohms
  Secondary winding resistance . . . .   6 to 14 K-ohms
  Spark plug cap resistance . . . .   approx. 5 K-ohms
GS and Dakar 2000 to 2003
  Primary winding resistance . . . .   0.45 to 0.55 ohms
  Secondary winding resistance . . . .   not available
GS and Dakar 2004-on
  Primary winding resistance . . . .   0.87 ohms
  Secondary winding resistance . . . .   not available
CS 2002 to 2003
  Primary winding resistance . . . .   0.50 to 0.53 ohms
  Secondary winding resistance . . . .   20 K-ohms
CS 2004-on
  Primary winding resistance . . . .   0.87 ohms
  Secondary winding resistance . . . .   not available

Ignition timing sensor
Air gap (Funduro and ST) . . . .   0.5 to 1.0 mm
Resistance
  Funduro and ST, GS and Dakar 2000 to 2003 . . . .   190 to 300 ohms
  GS and Dakar 2004-on, all CS . . . .   190 to 360 ohms

Torque settings
Ignition timing sensor screws
  Funduro and ST . . . .   6 Nm
  GS, Dakar and CS . . . .   8 Nm

1 General information

All models are fitted with a digital inductive ignition system, which due to its lack of mechanical parts is totally maintenance free. The system comprises a trigger on the alternator rotor, a timing sensor, electronic control unit and one or two ignition coils according to model (refer to the wiring diagrams at the end of Chapter 9 for details). Funduro and ST models have a twin spark head with two conventional coils. GS and Dakar models from 2000 to 2003 have a single spark head with a single conventional coil with HT lead and plug cap, and models from 2004-on have a twin spark head with two direct coils, which fit directly onto the spark plug. All CS models use the direct coils, with 2002 and 2003 models having a single spark head and all others a twin spark head.

The ignition trigger magnetically induces a signal in the timing sensor as the crankshaft rotates. The sensor sends a signal to the electronic control unit informing it of engine speed and crankshaft position. The control unit works out the optimum ignition timing and supplies the coil(s) with the power necessary to produce a spark. A rev limiter cuts in at 7500 rpm.

The system also incorporates a safety interlock circuit which will cut the ignition if the sidestand is extended whilst the engine is running and in gear, or if a gear is selected whilst the engine is running and the sidestand is extended. It also prevents the engine from being started if the engine is in gear while the sidestand is down. The engine can be started with the sidestand down as long as it is in neutral, or in gear as long as the sidestand is up and the clutch lever is pulled in.

Because of their nature, the individual ignition system components can be checked but not repaired. If ignition system troubles occur, and the faulty component can be isolated, the only cure for the problem is to replace the part with a new one. Keep in mind that most electrical parts, once purchased, cannot be returned. To avoid unnecessary expense, make very sure the faulty component has been positively identified before buying a replacement part.

Note that there is no provision for adjusting the ignition timing.

2 Ignition system check

⚠️ **Warning: The energy levels in electronic systems can be very high. On no account should the ignition be switched on whilst the plug(s) or plug cap(s) or coil(s) are being held. Shocks from the HT circuit can be most**

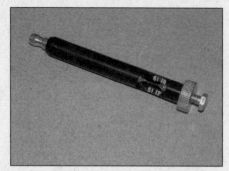

2.4 A typical spark gap testing tool

unpleasant. Secondly, it is vital that the engine is not turned over or run without the plug cap(s) or coil(s) connected, and that the plug(s) are soundly earthed (grounded) when the system is checked for sparking. The ignition system components can be seriously damaged if the HT circuit becomes isolated.

1 As no means of adjustment is available, any failure of the system can be traced to failure of a system component or a simple wiring fault. Of the two possibilities, the latter is by far the most likely. In the event of failure, check the system in a logical fashion, as described below.

2 Pull the cap or coil (according to model) off the spark plug (see Section 3). Fit a spare spark plug that is known to be good into the cap or coil and lay the plug against the cylinder head with the threads contacting it. If necessary, hold the spark plug with an insulated tool.

⚠️ *Warning: Do not remove the spark plug(s) from the engine to perform this check – atomised fuel being pumped out of the open spark plug hole could ignite, causing severe injury! Make sure the plug is securely held against the engine – if it is not earthed when the engine is turned over, the electronic control unit could be damaged.*

3 Check that the kill switch is in the 'RUN' position and the transmission is in neutral, then turn the ignition switch ON, and turn the engine over on the starter motor. If the system is in good condition a regular, fat blue spark should be evident at the plug electrodes.

3.3a Pull the cap off the spark plug

If the spark appears thin or yellowish, or is non-existent, further investigation will be necessary. Turn the ignition off. On twin spark models repeat the test for the other spark plug.

4 The ignition system must be able to produce a spark which is capable of jumping a particular size gap. A healthy system should produce a spark capable of jumping at least 8 mm. Simple ignition spark gap testing tools are commercially available **(see illustration)** – follow the manufacturer's instructions, and on twin spark models check each spark plug.

5 If the test results are good the entire ignition system can be considered good. If the spark appears thin or yellowish, or is non-existent, further investigation is necessary.

6 Ignition faults can be divided into two categories, namely those where the ignition system has failed completely, and those which are due to a partial failure. The likely faults are listed below, starting with the most probable source of failure. Work through the list systematically, referring to the subsequent sections for full details of the necessary checks and tests, and to the *Wiring Diagrams* at the end of Chapter 9. **Note:** *Before checking the following items ensure that the battery is fully charged and that all fuses are in good condition.*

● Loose, corroded or damaged wiring connections, broken or shorted wiring between any of the component parts of the ignition system (see Chapter 9).
● Faulty HT lead or spark plug cap (conventional coil models), faulty spark plug, dirty, worn or corroded plug electrodes, or incorrect gap between electrodes.
● Faulty ignition switch or engine kill switch (see Chapter 9).
● Faulty neutral, clutch or sidestand switch (see Chapter 9).
● Faulty timing sensor or damaged trigger.
● Faulty ignition coil(s).
● Faulty electronic control unit.

7 If the above checks don't reveal the cause of the problem, have the ignition system tested by a BMW dealer.

3 Ignition HT coils

Funduro and ST
Check

1 Make sure the ignition is switched OFF. Disconnect the battery (see Chapter 9).

2 Remove the fuel tank (see Chapter 4A). Check the coils visually for cracks, loose wiring connectors and HT leads or caps, and other damage.

3 The resistance of the coils can be tested in situ using an ohmmeter or multimeter. Pull the cap off the relevant spark plug **(see illustration)**. Disconnect the primary circuit wiring connector **(see illustration)**.

4 To measure the primary circuit resistance set the meter to the ohms x 1 scale. Connect one meter probe to the terminal on the coil and the other to one of the mounting bolts **(see illustration)**. If the reading obtained is not within the range shown in the Specifications, it is possible that the coil is defective.

5 To measure the secondary circuit resistance set the meter to the K-ohm scale. Connect one meter probe to the contact in the spark plug cap and the other to one of the mounting bolts **(see illustration)**. If the reading obtained is not within the range shown in the Specifications, it is possible that the coil is defective.

6 Before buying a new coil, unscrew the cap from the HT lead and measure the resistance of the cap **(see illustrations)**. If the reading obtained is not as specified, replace the spark plug cap with a new one. If the coil is still suspect, substitute it with one that is known to be good before condemning it. If the problem still exists, then the fault is probably in the primary wiring circuit – refer to Wiring Diagrams at the end of Chapter 9 and check the wiring and connectors in the circuit.

7 If the coil is confirmed to be faulty, it must be replaced with a new one – it is a sealed unit and cannot be repaired.

Removal

8 Make sure the ignition is switched OFF.

3.3b Disconnect the coil primary wiring connector

Disconnect the battery (see Chapter 9).

9 Remove the fuel tank (see Chapter 4A).

10 Pull the cap off the relevant spark plug **(see illustration 3.3a)**. Unscrew the cap from the lead **(see illustration 3.6a)**. Feed the lead through to the coil, noting its routing.

11 Disconnect the primary circuit wiring connector from the coil **(see illustration 3.3b)**. Unscrew the bolts securing the coil and remove it **(see illustration)** – note which fits on which side as they are not interchangeable.

Installation

12 Installation is the reverse of removal. Make sure the wiring connectors and HT lead are correctly routed and securely connected.

GS and Dakar (2000 to 2003)

Check

13 Make sure the ignition is switched OFF. Disconnect the battery (see Chapter 9).

14 Remove the air filter housing (see Chapter 4B). Check the coil visually for cracks, loose wiring connector and HT lead, and other damage.

15 The resistance of the coils can be tested in situ using an ohmmeter or multimeter. Pull the cap off the relevant spark plug. Disconnect the primary circuit wiring connectors.

16 To measure the primary circuit resistance set the meter to the ohms x 1 scale. Connect the meter probes to the terminals on the coil. If the reading obtained is not within the range shown in the Specifications, it is possible that the coil is defective.

17 BMW do not provide a value for the coil's secondary windings. You can, however, measure the secondary circuit resistance (set the meter to the K-ohm scale) by connecting one meter probe to the contact in the spark plug cap and the other to the positive primary wiring connector.

18 Before replacing what appears to be a faulty coil, check the HT lead and plug cap. Pull the HT lead out of its socket on the coil and measure the resistance of the lead and

3.4 To test the coil primary resistance connect the multimeter leads between the primary circuit terminal and a mounting bolt

3.5 To test the coil secondary resistance connect the multimeter leads between the contact in the cap and a mounting bolt

3.6a Unscrew the cap from the lead . . .

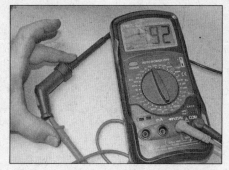

3.6b . . . and measure the resistance of the cap

3.11 Unscrew the bolts (arrowed) and remove the coil

3.30a Turn the outer coil clockwise and the inner coil anti-clockwise to release them from the tongues on the retainer

3.30b Lever the coil up using a spanner as shown if necessary

cap by connecting the meter probes between the HT lead end and the spark plug socket in the cap. No specific value is available, but the cap resistance should be around 5 K-ohms.

19 If the coil is confirmed to be faulty, it must be replaced with a new one – it is a sealed unit and cannot be repaired.

Removal

20 Make sure the ignition is switched OFF. Disconnect the battery (see Chapter 9).

21 Remove the air filter housing (see Chapter 4B).

22 Pull the cap off the spark plug. Feed the lead through to the coil, noting its routing.

23 Disconnect the primary circuit wiring connector from the coil. Unscrew the bolts securing the coil and remove it. Detach the HT lead if required.

Installation

24 Installation is the reverse of removal.

GS and Dakar (2004-on), all CS

Check

25 Remove the coil. To check the coil primary resistance set the meter to the ohms x 1 scale and connect its probes across terminals marked 1 and 3 located inside the connector socket of the coil. The terminal numbers are

very small and you may need a flashlight to see them. Compare the result with the specification at the beginning of this Chapter. BMW provide no test details for the coil's secondary windings. If a coil is confirmed to be faulty, it must be replaced with a new one – it is a sealed unit and cannot therefore be repaired.

Removal

26 Make sure the ignition is switched OFF. Disconnect the battery (see Chapter 9).

27 On CS models remove the right-hand front side cover (see Chapter 8).

28 On CS models with a single spark plug turn the ignition coil anti-clockwise, then pull it off the plug and disconnect the wiring connector.

29 On all twin spark plug models the coils are different and must not get mixed up – the outer coil is colour-coded with a tan retainer shroud and the inner coil is coded with a black one.

30 To remove the outer coil turn it as far as it will go clockwise to release the retainer tongue from the pocket in the shroud **(see illustration)**. Pull the coil off the plug, using a suitable lever under it if necessary **(see illustration)**. Disconnect the wiring connector, then mark it with sticky tape so you know it is for the outer coil.

31 To remove the inner coil first remove the outer coil. To remove the inner coil turn it as far as it will go anti-clockwise to release the retainer tongue from the pocket in the shroud **(see illustration 3.30a)**, then pull it off the plug, using a suitable lever under it if necessary. Disconnect the wiring connector.

Installation

32 Installation is the reverse of removal.

33 On all twin spark plug models the coils are different and must not get mixed up – the inner coil has a black retainer shroud and the outer coil has a tan one. Also make sure the wiring connectors do not get mixed up – the one you marked on disconnection is for the outer coil.

34 To install the inner coil connect the wiring connector, then fit the coil onto the plug and turn it as far as it will go clockwise, making sure the retainer tongue locates in the pocket in the shroud **(see illustration 3.35)**.

35 To install the outer coil connect the wiring connector, then fit the coil onto the plug and turn it as far as it will go anti-clockwise, making sure the retainer tongue locates in the pocket in the shroud **(see illustration)**.

---

4 Ignition timing sensor

Check

1 Disconnect the battery (see Chapter 9).

2 Remove the wiring connector cover **(see illustration)**.

3 If the timing sensor is thought to be faulty, first check that it is not due to a damaged or broken wire or terminal: pinched or broken wires can usually be repaired.

4 Disconnect the sensor wiring connector **(see illustration)**. Using a multimeter set to the ohms x 100 scale, check for a resistance between the terminals on the sensor side

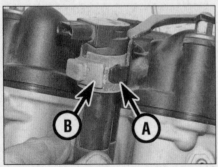

3.35 The tongue (A) locates in the pocket (B)

4.2 Unscrew the bolts (arrowed) and remove the cover

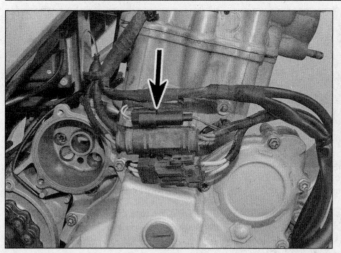

4.4 Disconnect the wiring connector (arrowed – GS shown) and measure the resistance of the sensor

4.9 Undo the screws (arrowed) and remove the sensor – GS shown

of the connector. If it is not within the range specified at the beginning of the Chapter (in which case it will most likely show infinite resistance) replace the sensor with a new one.

5 If the resistance is correct, the fault lies elsewhere in the ignition circuit.

Removal

6 Disconnect the battery (see Chapter 9).
7 Remove the wiring connector cover (see illustration 4.2). Disconnect the sensor wiring connector (see illustration 4.4).
8 Remove the alternator cover (see Chapter 9). On Funduro and ST models the sensor is mounted on the crankcase. On GS, Dakar and CS models the sensor is mounted in the alternator cover.
9 Undo the screws securing the sensor, then free its wiring grommet from the cut-out and remove the sensor (see illustration).

Installation

Note: *The screws securing the sensor are self-tapping – check the condition of the threads and use new ones if necessary. On GS, Dakar and CS models, if a new alternator cover is fitted the screw holes are not threaded. Use new self-tapping screws and do not apply threadlock – the screws will cut the thread as they are screwed in.*
10 Clean the screw threads to remove any old threadlock and the wiring grommet and cut-out to remove the old sealant.
11 Apply Loctite 243 or equivalent thread locking compound to the sensor screws. Fit the sensor and tighten the screws to the torque setting specified at the beginning of the chapter.
12 Smear some silicone sealant onto the wiring grommet and fit it into its cut-out (see illustration).
13 On Funduro and ST models align the trigger on the alternator rotor with the sensor pick-up tip and check the air gap between them is as specified at the beginning of the

Chapter using a feeler gauge. If necessary adjust the gap by bending the mounting plate.
14 Install the alternator cover (see Chapter 9).
15 Connect the wiring connector and fit the connector cover.
16 Reconnect the battery.

5   Electronic control unit

Check

1 If the tests shown in the preceding or following Sections have failed to isolate the cause of an ignition fault, it is possible that the electronic control unit itself is faulty. No test details are available with which the unit can be tested. Take the bike to your dealer.

Removal

Funduro and ST models

2 Remove the seat (see Chapter 8). Make sure the ignition is OFF. Disconnect the battery negative lead (see Chapter 9).
3 Unscrew the nuts on the underside of the

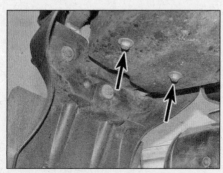

5.3a Unscrew the nuts (arrowed) . . .

4.12 Apply sealant to the wiring grommet

rear mudguard (see illustration). Displace the ECU and disconnect the wiring connector (see illustration).

GS and Dakar models

4 Remove the seat (see Chapter 8). Make sure the ignition is OFF. Disconnect the battery (see Chapter 9).
5 On 2000 to 2003 models unhook the retaining strap and lift the control unit up. Release the lock and disconnect the wiring connector.
6 On 2004 on models release the lock and disconnect the wiring connector (see

5.3b . . . then withdraw the bolts (arrowed), displace the ECU and disconnect the wiring

5.6a Release the lock . . .

5.6b . . . and disconnect the wiring connector

5.6c Undo the screws (arrowed) and remove the cover . . .

5.6d . . . then remove the ECU

5.8 Unhook the retaining strap (arrowed)

illustrations). Undo the screws and remove the cover, then lift the control unit off its holder **(see illustrations)**.

CS models

7 Make sure the ignition is OFF. Disconnect the battery (see Chapter 9). Remove the air filter housing (see Chapter 4B).

8 Unhook the retaining strap **(see illustration)**. Carefully lever the retaining bar up. Displace the control unit, carefully levering it up if necessary.

9 Release the lock and disconnect the wiring connector.

Installation

10 Installation is the reverse of removal. Make sure the wiring connector is correctly and securely connected.

6 Ignition timing

Since it is not possible to adjust the ignition timing and since no component is subject to mechanical wear, there is no provision for any checks. If the timing is suspected of being out or not advancing properly, first check the timing sensor and its wiring and connectors (see Section 4), then if that is fine substitute the electronic control unit with one that is known to be good to see if the problem is cured.

Chapter 6
Frame and suspension

Contents

Degrees of difficulty

Easy, suitable for novice with little experience 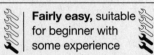	**Fairly easy,** suitable for beginner with some experience	**Fairly difficult,** suitable for competent DIY mechanic	**Difficult,** suitable for experienced DIY mechanic	**Very difficult,** suitable for expert DIY or professional

Specifications

Front forks

Type	41 mm oil-damped telescopic forks
Travel	
Funduro, ST and GS.	170 mm
Dakar	210 mm
CS.	125 mm
Fork oil type	BMW telescopic fork oil (10W)
Fork oil capacity (approx.)	
At oil change	
Funduro and ST	
Regular suspension	600 ml
Lowered suspension.	650 ml
GS	
Regular suspension	600 ml
Lowered suspension.	610 ml
Dakar	550 ml
CS.	470 ml
At overhaul	
Funduro and ST	
Regular suspension	610 ml
Lowered suspension.	660 ml
GS	
Regular suspension	610 ml
Lowered suspension.	620 ml
Dakar	560 ml
CS.	480 ml
Fork spring length	
Funduro and ST	527 mm
GS.	515 mm
Dakar	468 mm
CS.	365 mm
Inner tube runout (max)	0.1 mm

Rear suspension

Type	Single shock absorber, rising rate linkage, aluminium swingarm (single-sided on CS)
Travel (at rear wheel axle)	
Funduro and GS.	165 mm
ST	120 mm
Dakar	210 mm
CS.	140 mm or 120 mm (according to model)

Torque settings

Brake pedal pivot bolt
    Funduro and ST .... 25 Nm
    GS, Dakar and CS .... 21 Nm
Clutch lever bracket clamp bolts
    Funduro and ST .... 12 Nm
    GS, Dakar and CS .... 9 Nm
Footrest plate to frame
    Funduro and ST .... 50 Nm
    GS, Dakar and CS .... 30 Nm
Fork damper rod bolt .... 20 Nm
Fork top bolt – Funduro, ST and Dakar .... 25 Nm
Fork clamp bolts (top and bottom yokes)
    Funduro and ST .... 25 Nm
    GS, Dakar and CS .... 23 Nm
Front brake master cylinder clamp bolts
    Funduro and ST .... 12 Nm
    GS, Dakar and CS .... 9 Nm
Handlebars
    Funduro and ST
        Handlebar clamp bolts .... 25 Nm
        Handlebar holder lower nuts .... 40 Nm
        Handlebar holder upper nuts .... 10 Nm
    GS and Dakar (2000 to 2003)
        Handlebar clamp bolts .... 21 Nm
    GS and Dakar (2004-on) and all CS
        Handlebar clamp bolts .... 23 Nm
Rear sub-frame bolts
    GS and Dakar (2000 to 2003) .... 21 Nm
    GS and Dakar (2004-on) and all CS .... 24 Nm
Sidestand pivot
    Funduro and ST
        Pivot bolt .... 10 Nm
        Locknut .... 25 Nm
    GS, Dakar and CS .... 40 Nm
Steering head bearing adjuster
    GS and Dakar
        Initial setting .... 25 Nm
        Final setting .... 60° anti-clockwise
        Hex-headed threaded tube .... 65 Nm
    CS
        Initial setting .... 25 Nm
        Final setting .... 60° anti-clockwise
Steering stem clamp bolt (CS models) .... 23 Nm
Steering stem nut
    Funduro and ST .... 100 Nm
    GS and Dakar .... 65 Nm
Shock absorber
    Funduro and ST
        Top mounting bolt/nut .... 50 Nm
        Bottom mounting bolt .... 30 Nm
    GS and Dakar
        Top mounting bolt/nut .... 58 Nm + 45°
        Bottom mounting bolt .... 47 Nm
    CS
        Top mounting bolt/nut .... 58 Nm + 45°
        Bottom mounting bolt .... 41 Nm
Suspension linkage
    Funduro and ST
        Linkage arm-to-rods bolt/nut .... 80 Nm
        Linkage arm-to-frame bolt/nut .... 50 Nm
        Linkage rods-to-swingarm bolt/nut .... 50 Nm
    GS and Dakar
        Linkage arm-to-rods bolt/nut .... 71 Nm
        Linkage arm-to-frame bolt/nut .... 58 Nm + 45°
        Linkage rods-to-swingarm bolt/nut .... 41 Nm
    CS
        Linkage arm-to-rods bolt/nut .... 41 Nm
        Linkage arm-to-frame bolt/nut .... 58 Nm + 45°
        Linkage rods-to-swingarm bolt/nut .... 41 Nm
Swingarm pivot bolt nut .... 100 Nm

1 General information

All models have a tubular steel frame which uses the engine as a stressed member. On Funduro, ST and CS models the engine oil is stored in the frame.

Front suspension is by a pair of oil-damped telescopic forks that are non-adjustable.

At the rear, a box-section swingarm, conventional on Funduro, ST, GS and Dakar models and single-sided on CS models, acts on a single shock absorber via a three-way linkage. The swingarm pivots through the frame and engine. The shock absorber is adjustable for spring pre-load and rebound damping on all except standard CS models, but an optional adjustable shock is available for the CS.

2 Frame inspection and repair

1 The frame should not require attention unless accident damage has occurred. In most cases, fitting a new frame is the only satisfactory remedy for such damage. A few frame specialists have the jigs and other equipment necessary for straightening frames to the required standard of accuracy, but even then there is no simple way of assessing to what extent the frame may have been over stressed.

2 After a high mileage, examine the frame closely for signs of cracking or splitting at the welded joints. Loose engine mounting bolts can cause ovaling or fracturing of the mounting points. Minor damage can often be repaired by specialised welding, depending on the extent and nature of the damage. On Funduro, ST and CS models check that there is no sign of oil leakage from the integral engine oil tank in the frame's top section.

3 Remember that a frame that is out of alignment will cause handling problems. If, as the result of an accident, misalignment is suspected, it will be necessary to strip the machine completely so the frame can be

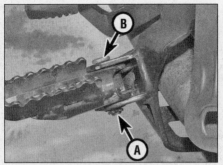

3.2 Remove the split pin (A) and washer, then withdraw the pivot pin (B) – GS and Dakar

thoroughly checked by a specialist using a frame alignment jig.

3 Footrests, brake pedal and gearchange lever

Footrests

Removal – rider's footrests

1 On Funduro and ST models, remove the split pin and washer from the bottom of the footrest pivot pin, then withdraw the pivot pin. Remove the footrest, noting the fitting of the return spring. If required undo the screw and separate the rubber and plate from the peg – all components are available separately.

2 On GS and Dakar models, remove the split pin and washer from the bottom of the footrest pivot pin, then withdraw the pivot pin **(see illustration)**. Remove the footrest, noting the fitting of the return spring and the spacer. If required and where fitted remove the rubber from the peg – all components are available separately.

3 On CS models, remove the split pin from the bottom of the footrest pivot pin, then withdraw the pivot pin. Remove the footrest, noting the fitting of the return spring. If required undo the screws and separate the rubber and plate from the peg – all components are available separately.

Removal – passenger's footrests

4 On Funduro, ST, GS and Dakar models

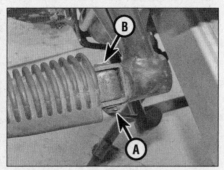

3.4 Remove the split pin (A) and washer, then withdraw the pivot pin (B) – CS

remove the split pin and washer from the bottom of the footrest pivot pin, then withdraw the pivot pin **(see illustration)**. Remove the footrest, noting the fitting. If required pull the rubber from the peg and remove the spacer – all components are available separately.

5 On CS models, remove the split pin from the bottom of the footrest pivot pin, then withdraw the pivot pin. Remove the footrest, noting the fitting of the detent plate, ball and spring – make sure the ball and spring do not ping away. If required undo the screws and separate the rubber and plate from the peg – all components are available separately.

Installation

6 Installation is the reverse of removal. Apply a small amount of grease to the pivot pin and the sliding surfaces of mated parts. Use new split pins.

Brake pedal

Removal

7 On Funduro and ST models release the breather hoses from the guide and move them clear **(see illustration)**. Unhook the pedal return spring from the frame. Remove the retaining ring from the master cylinder pushrod joint, then detach the joint from the pedal **(see illustration)**. Counter-hold the nut on the inner end of the pivot bolt then unscrew the bolt and remove the nut, washer, chain roller, spacer, pedal and O-rings **(see illustration)**.

8 On GS and Dakar models unscrew the right-hand footrest bracket bolts and remove

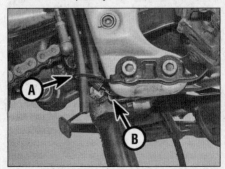

3.7a Draw the hoses out of the guide (A), then unhook the spring end (B)

3.7b Release the retaining ring (arrowed) and detach the pushrod

3.7c Unscrew the bolt (arrowed) and remove the pedal

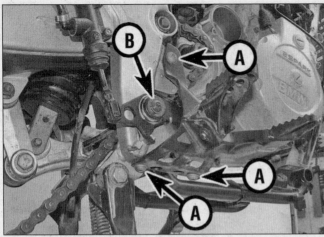

3.8a Footrest bracket bolts (A); pedal pivot bolt (B)

3.8b Release the clip . . .

3.8c . . . then withdraw the pin

3.9 Brake pedal pivot bolt (arrowed)

● Clean off any old grease and dirt. Apply grease to the pedal pivot components.
● Make sure the pedal locates correctly against the brake light switch.
● Tighten the pedal pivot bolt to the torque setting specified at the beginning of the Chapter
● On GS and Dakar models tighten the footrest bracket bolts to the specified torque setting.
● Make sure the return spring locates correctly.
● Check the operation of the rear brake light switch.

Gearchange lever

Removal

11 On Funduro, ST, GS and Dakar models make an alignment mark where the slot in the gearchange lever aligns with the shaft (see illustration). Unscrew the pinch bolt and slide the lever off the shaft.

12 On CS models make an alignment mark where the slot in the gearchange linkage arm aligns with the shaft (see illustration).

the footrest assembly (see illustration). Release and remove the clevis pin and detach the master cylinder pushrod from the pedal (see illustration). Unscrew the pedal pivot bolt and remove the pedal, noting the washers and how the return spring locates. Also note the bush in the pedal pivot and remove it for cleaning. Check for any wear in the bush and replace it with a new one if necessary.

9 On CS models release and remove the clevis pin (see illustrations 3.8b and c) and detach

the master cylinder pushrod from the pedal. Unscrew the pedal pivot bolt and remove the pedal, noting the washers and how the return spring locates (see illustration). Also note the bush in the pedal pivot and remove it for cleaning. Check for any wear in the bush and replace it with a new one if necessary.

Installation

10 Installation is the reverse of removal, noting the following:

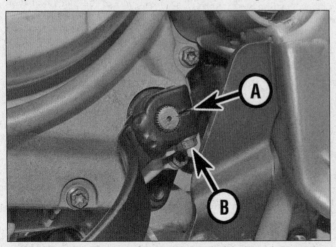

3.11 Make an alignment mark with the slit (A), then unscrew the bolt (B)

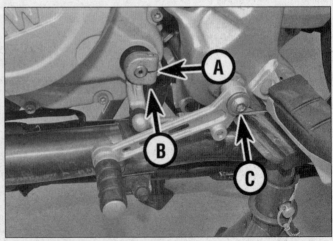

3.12 Make an alignment mark with the slit (A), then unscrew the linkage arm bolt (B), followed by the pivot bolt (C)

4.3a Unhook the springs (arrowed)

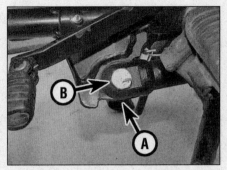

4.3b On Funduro and ST unscrew the nut (A) on the underside, then unscrew the bolt (B)

4.3c On GS, Dakar and CS models unscrew the bolt (arrowed)

4.6a Centrestand springs (arrowed) – Funduro and ST

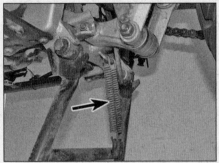

4.6b Centrestand springs (arrowed) – GS and Dakar

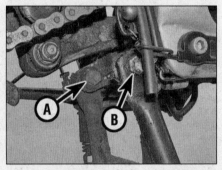

4.6c Unscrew the nut (A) on the inner end of each pivot bolt, then unscrew the bolts (B)

Unscrew the pinch bolt and slide the linkage arm off the shaft. Unscrew the lever pivot bolt and remove the lever and linkage assembly. If required release the retaining clips and detach the linkage rod from the lever and the linkage arm from the rod – all components are available separately.

Installation

13 Installation is the reverse of removal. On CS models clean off any old grease and dirt. Apply grease to the pivot and linkage joints. Adjust the gear lever height as required by slackening the locknut on the linkage rod and screwing the front section of the rod in or out of the rear section. Tighten the locknut on completion.

4 Sidestand and centrestand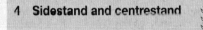

Sidestand

Removal

1 Support the bike on an auxiliary stand.
2 On all except early Funduro models displace the sidestand switch (see Chapter 9). There is no need to disconnect its wiring connector or remove it completely, just let it hang from its wiring.
3 Unhook the stand springs **(see illustration)**. On Funduro and ST models unscrew the nut from the pivot bolt **(see illustration)**. Unscrew the pivot bolt and remove the stand **(see illustration)**.

Installation

4 Installation is the reverse of removal, noting the following:
● Clean off any old grease and dirt. Apply grease to the stand pivot.
● Tighten the stand pivot bolt to the torque setting specified at the beginning of the Chapter. On Funduro and ST models then fit the nut and tighten that to the specified torque.
● Make sure the spring ends locate correctly.
● Do not forget to fit the sidestand switch.

Centrestand

Removal

5 Support the bike on the sidestand.
6 Unhook the stand springs **(see illustrations)**. Unscrew the nut and remove the washer from each pivot bolt **(see illustration)**. Unscrew the pivot bolts and remove the stand. Remove the spacer from each pivot.

5.3 Unscrew the bolts (arrowed) and displace the clutch lever bracket

Installation

7 Installation is the reverse of removal, noting the following:
● Clean off any old grease and dirt from the pivot spacers. Apply grease to the inside and outside of each spacer and fit them back into the pivots.
● Make sure the spring ends locate correctly.

5 Handlebars and levers

Note: *The handlebars can be displaced from the top yoke for access to the steering stem nut without displacing or removing the master cylinder, cables or switch housings, though it is best to remove the mirrors.*

Funduro and ST

Removal

1 To avoid the possibility of damaging anything, remove the fuel tank cover (see Chapter 8), or at least cover it in plenty of rag. Where fitted remove the hand guards. Cut the cable-ties on the handlebars.
2 Remove the mirrors (see Chapter 8).
3 Unscrew the clutch lever bracket clamp bolts and displace the lever/bracket/cable assembly, supporting it on some rag **(see illustration)**.
4 Undo the left-hand switch housing screws and separate the halves **(see illustration)**. Detach the choke cable from the lever.
5 Displace the front brake master cylinder and

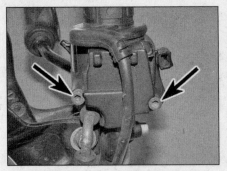

5.4 Undo the screws (arrowed) and displace the switch housing

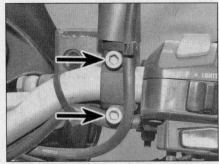

5.5 Unscrew the bolts (arrowed) and displace the master cylinder assembly

5.6 Undo the screws (arrowed) and displace the switch housing

support it clear of the handlebar, wrapping it in rag (see illustration). Ensure no strain is placed on the hydraulic hose and keep the reservoir upright.

6 Undo the right-hand switch housing screws and separate the halves (see illustration). Detach the throttle cable from the twistgrip.

7 Undo each handlebar end-weight screw and remove the weight (see illustration 5.18). Pull the throttle twistgrip and washer off the right-hand end and remove the grip from the left-hand end. Note: The grip will probably be stuck in place – try squirting some lubricant or compressed air under it, though it may be necessary to slit it with a sharp knife in order to remove it. Slide the choke lever off the left-hand end.

Caution: Wear eye protection if using aerosol lube or compressed air to dislodge the left-hand grip.

8 Look for an alignment punch mark on the handlebar at the clamp and holder mating surfaces – if none is visible make your own mark so the handlebars can be correctly aligned on installation. If you are removing the handlebar holders from the yoke, slacken the nuts on the underside slightly now.

9 Remove the blanking caps from the handlebar clamp bolts. Unscrew the bolts and remove the clamps, then displace or remove the handlebars – if they are only being displaced rest them either in front of or behind the top yoke, on plenty of rag.

10 If required unscrew the handlebar holder nuts on the underside of the top yoke, then remove the holders and rubber seats.

Installation

11 Installation is the reverse of removal, noting the following:

● Fit the rubber seats into the top yoke, then

fit the holders. Only finger-tighten the holder nuts at this stage to allow the handlebars to properly align the holders.

● Fit the clamps with the arrows pointing forwards. Align the bars so they are central and with the punch mark aligned with the holder/clamp mating surfaces. Fit the bolts, then tighten the front ones first, then the rear, to the torque setting specified at the beginning of the Chapter – note that there should be a gap between the clamp and each holder at the back. If necessary now tighten the handlebar holder nuts to the specified torque settings.

● Position the clutch lever and front brake master cylinder brackets and the switch housings by aligning the mating surfaces with the punch marks on the handlebar or by fitting the pegs into the holes as appropriate. Tighten the bracket clamp bolts to the torque setting specified at the beginning of the Chapter.

● Grease the cable ends.

● If new grips are being fitted, secure them using a suitable adhesive.

● Check the operation of the throttle and the choke, clutch and brake levers, and the front brake light switch and clutch switch, before riding the motorcycle.

GS, Dakar and CS

Removal

12 To avoid the possibility of damaging anything, remove the front side covers and the top cover (see Chapter 8), or at least cover them in plenty of rag. Where fitted remove the hand guards. Cut the cable-ties on the handlebars.

13 Remove the mirrors (see Chapter 8).

14 Undo the left-hand switch housing screws and displace the switch face and housing (see illustration).

15 Unscrew the clutch lever bracket clamp bolts and displace the lever/bracket/cable assembly, supporting it on some rag (see illustration).

16 Undo the right-hand switch housing screws and displace the switch face (see illustrations). Undo the throttle cable retaining screw (see illustration). Release the cable pulley and detach the cable end – note how the pulley and twistgrip align (see illustrations). Remove the switch housing.

5.14 Undo the screws (arrowed) and displace the switch face

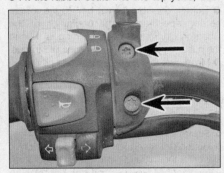

5.15 Unscrew the bolts (arrowed) and displace the clutch lever bracket

5.16a Undo the screws (arrowed) . . .

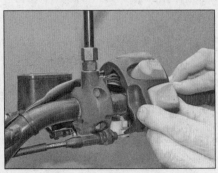

5.16b . . . and detach the face

5.16c Undo the screw (arrowed)

5.16d Draw the pulley off its post . . .

5.16e . . . and detach the cable end

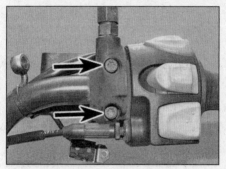

5.17 Unscrew the bolts (arrowed) and displace the master cylinder assembly

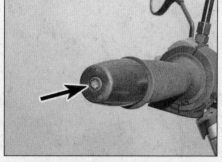

5.18 Handlebar end-weight screw (arrowed)

5.19 Undo the screws and remove the switch housing

17 Displace the front brake master cylinder and position it clear of the handlebar, wrapping it in rag **(see illustration)**. Ensure no strain is placed on the hydraulic hose and try to keep the reservoir upright to prevent air entering the system.

18 Undo each handlebar end-weight screw and remove the weight **(see illustration)**. Pull the throttle twistgrip and right-hand switch housing off the right-hand end and remove the grip and left-hand switch housing from the left-hand end. **Note:** *The grip will probably be stuck in place – try squirting some lubricant or compressed air under it, though it may be necessary to slit it with a sharp knife in order to remove it.*

Caution: Wear eye protection if using aerosol lube or compressed air to dislodge the left-hand grip.

19 Where fitted remove the auxiliary switch housing **(see illustration)**.

20 Look for an alignment punch mark on the handlebar at the clamp and holder mating surfaces **(see illustration)** – if none is visible make your own mark so the handlebars can be correctly aligned on installation.

21 Unscrew the bolts and remove the clamps, then displace or remove the handlebars **(see illustration)** – if they are only being displaced rest them either in front of or behind the top yoke, on plenty of rag **(see illustration)**.

Installation

22 Installation is the reverse of removal, noting the following:

● Fit the clamps with the hole spaced further from the handlebar bore at the front **(see**

illustration). Align the bars so they are central with the punch mark aligned with the holder/clamp mating surfaces **(see illustration 5.20)**. Fit the bolts, then tighten the front ones first, then the rear, to the torque setting specified at

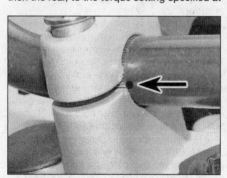

5.20 Make your own alignment mark (arrowed) if none is visible

5.21b . . . or displace them forwards or back and rest them on rag

the beginning of the Chapter – note that there should be a gap between the clamp and each holder at the back.

● Position the clutch lever and front brake master cylinder brackets and the switch

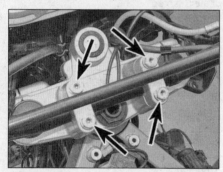

5.21a Unscrew the bolts (arrowed), remove the clamps and remove the handlebars . . .

5.22a Make sure the clamps are the correct way round

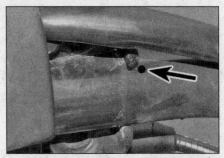

5.22b The front brake master cylinder clamp mating surfaces align with the punch mark (arrowed)

5.23a Unscrew the locknut . . .

5.23b . . . then unscrew the pivot bolt

5.24a Pull back the boot, and slacken the locknut (arrowed) . . .

5.24b . . . then turn the adjuster in

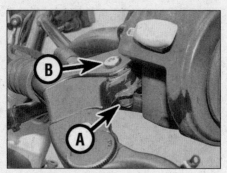

5.24c Unscrew the locknut (A) then unscrew the pivot bolt (B)

housings by aligning the mating surfaces with the punch marks on the handlebar or by fitting the pegs into the holes as appropriate **(see illustration)**. Tighten the bracket clamp bolts to the torque setting specified at the beginning of the Chapter.
● Grease the cable ends.
● If new grips are being fitted, secure them using a suitable adhesive.
● Check the operation of the throttle and the clutch and brake levers, and the front brake light switch and clutch switch, before riding the motorcycle.

Levers

23 To remove the front brake lever, undo the lever pivot screw locknut, then undo the pivot screw and remove the lever **(see illustrations)**.
24 To remove the clutch lever, slacken the cable freeplay adjuster locknut, then thread

the adjuster into the bracket to provide slack in the cable **(see illustrations)**. Undo the lever pivot screw locknut, then undo the pivot screw and remove the lever, detaching the cable nipple as you do **(see illustration)**.
25 Installation is the reverse of removal, noting the following:
● When fitting the brake lever apply silicone grease to the contact area between the master cylinder pushrod tip and the brake lever, to the pivot screw and the contact areas between the lever and its bracket. Tighten the pivot screw lightly, then counter-hold it and tighten the locknut **(see illustration)**.
● When fitting the clutch lever apply silicone grease to the pivot screw and the contact areas between the lever and its bracket, and to the cable end. Adjust clutch cable freeplay (see Chapter 1).
● Make sure the levers move smoothly.

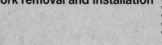

6 Fork removal and installation

Caution: Although not strictly necessary, before removing the forks it is recommended that the fairing and fairing panels are removed (see Chapter 8). This will prevent accidental damage to the paintwork.

Removal

1 Remove the fairing or front side covers as required according to model to give best

access to the fork clamp bolts in the top and bottom yokes, and to prevent the possibility of damaging paintwork should a tool slip (see Chapter 8).
2 Displace the front brake caliper and ABS sensor (where fitted) and secure out of the way.
3 Remove the front wheel (see Chapter 7). Remove the front mudguard (see Chapter 8). Note the routing of any cables, hoses and wiring around the forks.
4 Working on one fork at a time, slacken the fork clamp bolt in the top yoke **(see illustration)**. Measure and note the amount of protrusion (if any) of the fork above the top yoke.
5 On Funduro, ST and Dakar models, if the fork is to be disassembled, or if the fork oil is being changed, slacken the fork top bolt half a turn now **(see illustration)**.
6 Slacken the fork clamp bolts in the bottom

5.25 Counter-hold the pivot bolt when tightening the locknut

6.4 Slacken the top yoke fork clamp bolt (arrowed) – CS shown

6.5 Slacken the fork top bolt (arrowed) if the fork is to be disassembled

6.6 Slacken the fork clamp bolts (arrowed) in the bottom yoke then draw the fork down and out of the yokes

6.8 On GS and Dakar models use a ruler to set the top of the fork flush with the top of the yoke

yoke, and remove the fork by twisting it and pulling it downwards **(see illustration)**.

> **HAYNES HINT**
>
> *If the fork legs are seized in the yokes, spray the area with penetrating oil and allow time for it to soak in before trying again*

Installation

7 Remove all traces of corrosion from the fork tube and the yokes. Slide the fork up through the bottom yoke and into the top yoke, making sure all cables, hoses and wiring are routed on the correct side of the fork **(see illustration 6.6)**.
8 Set the amount of protrusion of the fork tube above the top yoke as noted on removal – as standard, on Funduro and ST models the top of the fork top bolt should be 3 mm above the

upper surface of the yoke **(see illustration 6.5)**. On GS and Dakar models the top of the fork tube without the cap (GS) or bolt (Dakar) should be flush with the upper surface of the top yoke **(see illustration)**. On CS models the top of the fork cap should be 12 mm above the upper surface of the yoke **(see illustration 6.4)**.
9 Tighten the fork clamp bolts in the bottom yoke evenly and a little at a time to the torque setting specified at the beginning of the Chapter for your model **(see illustration 6.6)**.
10 On Funduro, ST and Dakar models, if the fork has been dismantled or if the fork oil was changed, tighten the fork top bolt to the specified torque setting **(see illustration 6.5)**.
11 Tighten the fork clamp bolt in the top yoke to the specified torque **(see illustration 6.4)**.
12 Install the front mudguard (see Chapter 8), the front wheel (see Chapter 7), the front brake caliper and where fitted the ABS sensor (see

Chapter 7), and the bodywork as required (see Chapter 8).
13 Check the operation of the front forks and brake before taking the machine out on the road.

7 Fork oil change

1 After a high mileage the fork oil will deteriorate and its damping and lubrication qualities will be impaired. Always change the oil in both forks. Work on one fork at a time.

Funduro, ST, GS and Dakar models

2 Cover the area around the top of the fork in plenty of rag.
3 Place the bike on its centrestand or an auxiliary stand and raise the front using a jack under the engine so the fork is uncompressed (extended). When working on the left-hand fork, and where fitted, remove the air guide from the brake caliper **(see illustration)**.
4 Slacken the fork clamp bolt in the top yoke **(see illustration 6.4)**.
5 On Funduro, ST and Dakar models unscrew the fork top bolt from the top of the inner tube, noting that it is under pressure from the spring – it is best to use a ratchet tool and to keep constant downward pressure on the top bolt while unscrewing it **(see illustration 6.5)**. Remove the top bolt and allow the spring to relax.
6 On GS models remove the cap from the top of the fork **(see illustration)**. If any corrosion is evident, spray some penetrating fluid onto it, then tap the top plug with a hammer and drift to dislodge it. Press down on the fork top plug, which is under pressure from the fork spring, release the retaining ring from its groove, then slowly release pressure on the plug and allow the spring to relax **(see illustration)**.
7 Place a container suitable for catching the fork oil at the base of the fork. Undo the oil drain screw and allow the oil to drain for several minutes into the container **(see illustration)**. When it has completely drained fit the drain screw using a new sealing washer and tighten it.

7.3 Undo the screws (arrowed) and remove the air guide

7.6a Remove the cap . . .

7.6b . . . then press down on the top plug and release the retaining ring

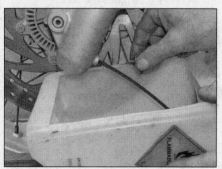

7.7 Undo the drain screw and drain the oil

7.12 Press the top plug down into the tube and fit the retaining ring into its groove

8 If the fork oil contains metal particles inspect the fork components for signs of wear (see Section 8).

9 Slowly pour in the correct quantity and type of fork oil as specified at the beginning of this Chapter.

10 Make sure the top bolt or plug O-ring is in good condition then smear some fork oil onto it and the threads.

11 On Funduro, ST and Dakar models fit the top bolt into the inner tube, compressing the spring as you do, and thread it in (making sure it does not cross-thread), keeping downward pressure on the spring, using a ratchet tool or by turning the tube while holding the bolt still as on removal. Tighten the bolt to the specified torque setting. Tighten the fork clamp bolt in the top yoke to the specified torque.

12 On GS models fit the top plug into the inner tube, compressing the spring as you do, then push down to expose the groove and fit the retaining ring into it **(see illustration)**. Fit the cap **(see illustration 7.6a)**. Tighten the

fork clamp bolt in the top yoke to the specified torque.

13 Remove the jack. Fit the caliper air guide if applicable **(see illustration 7.3)**.

CS models

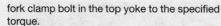

14 Remove the fork (see Section 6).

15 Support the fork leg in an upright position. Remove the cap from the top of the fork **(see illustration 8.4)**. If any corrosion is evident, spray some penetrating fluid onto it, then tap the top plug with a hammer and drift to dislodge it. Press down on the fork top plug, which is under pressure from the fork spring, release the retaining ring from its groove, then slowly release pressure on the plug and allow the spring to relax **(see illustration 8.29b)**.

16 Slide the inner tube down into the outer tube and remove the spacer and the spring as they become exposed **(see illustrations 8.5a and c)**. Wipe off any excess oil.

17 Invert the fork leg over a suitable container and pump the fork to expel as much oil as possible. Support the fork upside down in the container and allow it to drain for a few minutes. If the fork oil contains metal particles inspect the fork bush for wear (see Section 8).

18 Slowly pour in the specified quantity of the specified grade of fork oil, then pump the fork several times to distribute it evenly **(see illustration 8.27)**.

19 Fit the spring into the fork with its taper-wound coils at the bottom **(see illustration 8.5c)**. Lift the tube out of the slider then fit the spacer **(see illustration 8.5a)**.

20 Make sure the top plug O-ring is in good condition then smear some fork oil onto it. Fit the plug into the fork tube, compressing the

spring as you do, until the retaining ring groove is exposed, then fit the ring into the groove. Slowly release downward pressure and allow the plug to rest on the underside of the retaining ring. Fit the top cap **(see illustration 8.4)**.

21 Install the fork (see Section 6).

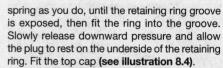

8 Fork overhaul

Disassembly

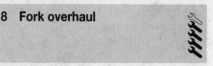

1 Remove the fork; on Funduro, ST and Dakar models ensure that the top bolt is loosened while the leg is still clamped in the bottom yoke (see Section 6). Always dismantle the fork legs separately to avoid interchanging parts. Store all components in separate, clearly marked containers.

2 Before dismantling the fork leg, slacken the damper rod bolt in the bottom of the outer tube, then lightly re-tighten it to prevent oil coming out **(see illustration)**. If the bolt does not loosen, turn the leg upside down and compress the fork so that the spring exerts maximum pressure on the damper rod to prevent it turning, then try to loosen the bolt. If you still have no luck, and an air wrench is not available, carry on and use a holding tool as described in Step 6.

3 On Funduro, ST and Dakar models unscrew the fork top bolt from the top of the inner tube, noting that it is under pressure from the spring – it is best to use a ratchet tool and to keep constant downward pressure on the top bolt while unscrewing it Remove the top bolt and allow the spring to relax.

4 On GS and CS models remove the cap from the top of the fork **(see illustration)**. If any corrosion is evident, spray some penetrating fluid onto it, then tap the top plug with a hammer and drift to dislodge it. Press down on the fork top plug, which is under pressure from the fork spring, release the retaining ring from its groove, then slowly release pressure on the plug and allow the spring to relax **(see illustration 8.29b)**.

5 Slide the inner tube down into the outer tube and remove the spacer, the spacer seat (not fitted on CS), and the spring as they become exposed **(see illustrations)**.

6 Remove the previously loosened damper rod bolt and its sealing washer from the bottom of

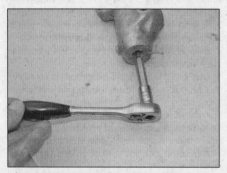

8.2 Slacken the damper rod bolt

8.4 Remove the cap

8.5a Remove the spacer . . .

8.5b . . . the seat . . .

8.5c . . . and the spring

the outer tube. Discard the washer as a new one must be fitted on reassembly. If the damper rod bolt was impossible to slacken as described in Step 2, get a suitable piece of wooden dowel, tapered at one end, or alternatively a broom handle, pass it down through the inner tube and press it into the top of the damper rod to prevent it turning, then unscrew the bolt.

7 Tip the damper rod and the rebound spring out of the fork (see illustration 8.20a).

8 Carefully prise the dust seal from the top of the outer tube to gain access to the oil seal retaining clip (see illustration). Discard the dust seal as a new one must be fitted on reassembly.

9 Carefully remove the retaining ring, taking care not to scratch the surface of the inner tube (see illustration).

10 Grasp the inner tube in one hand and the outer tube in the other, then quickly and repeatedly draw the inner tube out until the oil seal, washer and top bush are displaced from the top of the outer tube by the bottom bush on the bottom of the inner tube (see illustrations). Draw the oil seal, washer and top bush off the inner tube. Discard the oil seal as a new one must be fitted on reassembly.

11 Do not remove the bottom bush unless it is to be replaced with a new one. To remove it, spread its ends using a screwdriver to dislodge it from its seat and slide it off (see illustration).

12 Tip the oil lock piece out of the outer tube (see illustration).

Inspection

13 Clean all parts in a suitable solvent and blow them dry with compressed air, if available. Check the surface of the fork inner tube for score marks, scratches, pitting and flaking of the finish, and excessive or abnormal wear. Look for dents in the outer tube and replace the outer tubes in both forks with new ones if any are found.

14 Check the fork inner tube for runout using V-blocks and a dial gauge. If the amount of runout exceeds the specified limit, or if the condition of either inner tube is suspect, have it checked by a BMW dealer or suspension specialist.

 Warning: If the inner tube is bent or exceeds the runout limit, it should not be straightened, replace it with a new one.

15 Inspect the inside surface of the outer tube and the working surface of each bush for score marks, scratches and signs of excessive wear (in which case the grey Teflon outer surface will have worn away to reveal the copper inner surface). The bushes are available separately, and should be replaced with new ones if damaged or worn.

16 Check the fork oil seal seat for nicks, gouges and scratches. If damage is evident, leaks will occur. Also check the oil seal washer for damage or distortion and replace it with a new one if necessary.

17 Check the springs (both the main spring and the rebound spring on the damper rod) for cracks and other damage. Measure the main spring free length and compare the

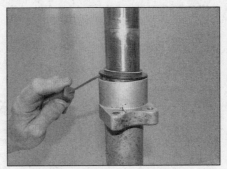

8.8 Prise out the dust seal using a flat-bladed screwdriver

8.9 Prise out the retaining clip using a flat-bladed screwdriver

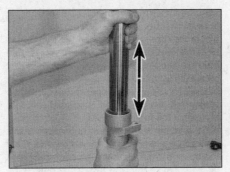

8.10a Repeatedly draw the tubes apart . . .

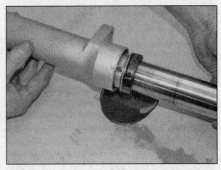

8.10b . . . to displace the oil seal, washer and top bush

measurement to the nominal specification for a new fork spring at the beginning of this Chapter (see illustration). If the spring is defective or has sagged, fit new springs in both forks. Never fit only one new spring.

18 Check the damper rod, and in particular the piston ring in its head, for damage and wear, and replace it with a new one if necessary (see illustration) – the ring is available separately.

8.11 Remove the bottom bush by levering its ends apart

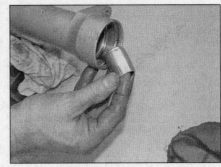

8.12 Tip the oil lock piece out

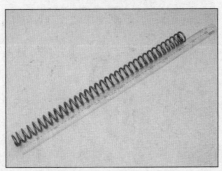

8.17 Measure the free length of the spring

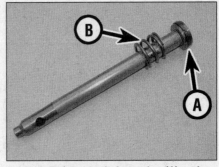

8.18 Damper rod piston ring (A) and rebound spring (B)

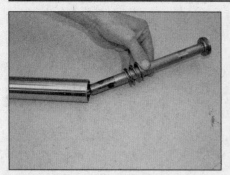

8.20a Insert the damper rod . . .

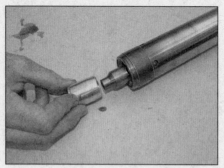

8.20b . . . then fit the oil lock piece onto its end

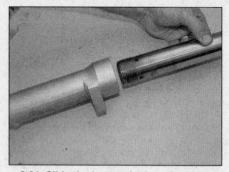

8.21 Slide the inner tube into the outer tube

Reassembly

19 Make sure the bottom bush is correctly located in its recess in the bottom of the inner tube **(see illustration 8.11)**.

20 Fit the piston ring into its groove in the top of he damper rod **(see illustration 8.18)**. Fit the rebound spring onto the damper rod. Insert the damper rod into the inner tube so its bottom end protrudes from the bottom of the tube **(see illustration)**. Fit the oil lock piece onto the bottom of the rod, then push them up into the bottom of the tube **(see illustration)**.

21 Lubricate the bottom bush and the inner surface of the outer tube with the specified fork oil. Slide the inner tube into the outer tube and seat it at the bottom **(see illustration)**.

22 Fit a new sealing washer onto the damper rod bolt. Fit the bolt into the bottom of the outer tube and thread it into the bottom of the damper rod and tighten it to the torque setting

specified at the beginning of this Chapter **(see illustration)**. If the damper rod rotates inside the tube as you tighten the bolt, either use the wooden dowel or broom handle method (Step 6), or wait until the fork is fully reassembled and tighten it then (the pressure of the spring on the damper rod head should prevent it from turning, especially if you compress the fork – Step 30).

23 Lubricate the inner and outer surfaces of the top bush with the specified fork oil. Slide the bush down the inner tube and press it as far as possible into the top of the outer tube by hand, making sure it fits squarely **(see illustration)**. Slide the washer onto the top of the bush, then carefully drive the bush into place until it seats using a suitable drift, a suitable piece of tubing, or the special service tool (Pt. No. 313650), using the washer as an interface to prevent damage to the upper rim

of the bush **(see illustrations)**. Take care not to mark the inner tube when driving the bush in. Remove the washer and make sure the bush has fully entered, then refit the washer **(see illustration)**.

24 Lubricate the inner and outer surfaces of the new oil seal with the specified fork oil. Slide the seal, with its marked side facing up, down the inner tube and press it as far as possible into the top of the outer tube by hand, making sure it fits squarely **(see illustration)**. Carefully drive the seal into place until it seats using a suitable drift or piece of tubing, or the service tool (Pt. No. 313650). Take care not to mark the inner tube when driving the bush in. Make sure the seal has fully entered, in which case the groove for the retaining ring will be fully exposed **(see illustration)**.

25 Fit the retaining ring, making sure it is correctly located in its groove **(see**

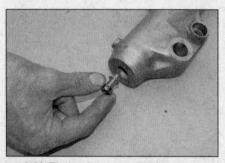

8.22 Fit the damper rod bolt using a new sealing washer and tighten it to the specified torque

8.23a Slide the top bush into the outer tube . . .

8.23b . . . then rest the washer on top . . .

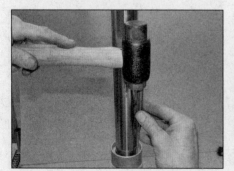

8.23c . . . to protect the bush as you drive it in

8.23d Make sure it has seated

8.24a Fit the oil seal . . .

8.24b . . . and drive it in until the groove (arrowed) is visible

8.25a Fit the retaining clip into the groove

8.25b Fill the groove with grease . . .

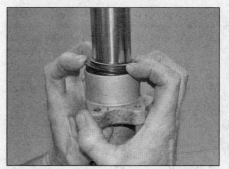

8.25c . . . then press the dust seal in

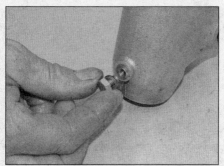

8.26 If removed fit the drain screw using a new sealing washer

8.27 Pour the oil in the top and pump the fork to distribute it

illustration). Fill the groove between the inner rims of the new dust seal with grease **(see illustration)**. Press the new dust seal into place **(see illustration)**.

26 On Funduro, ST, GS and Dakar models make sure the oil drain screw is fitted, with a new sealing washer if necessary, and is tight **(see illustration)**.

27 Slowly pour in the specified quantity of the specified grade of fork oil, then pump the fork several times to distribute it evenly **(see illustration)**. Fit the spring into the fork with its taper-wound coils at the bottom **(see illustration 8.5c)**. Lift the tube out of the slider then fit the spacer seat (except CS models) and the spacer **(see illustrations 8.5b and a)**.

28 On Funduro, ST and Dakar models make sure the top bolt O-ring is in good condition then smear some fork oil onto it and the threads. Fit the top bolt into the inner tube, compressing the spring as you do, and thread

it in (making sure it does not cross-thread), keeping downward pressure on the spring, using a ratchet tool or by turning the tube while holding the bolt still as on removal. Tighten the bolt to the specified torque setting now if you can hold the fork, or alternatively tighten it when the fork is being installed and is held in the bottom yoke.

29 On GS and CS models make sure the top plug O-ring is in good condition then smear some fork oil onto it **(see illustration)**. Fit the plug into the fork tube, compressing the spring as you do, until the retaining ring groove is exposed, then fit the ring into the groove **(see illustration)**. Slowly release downward pressure and allow the plug to rest on the underside of the retaining ring. Fit the top cap **(see illustration 8.4)**.

30 If the damper rod bolt requires tightening (see Step 22), place the fork upside down on the floor, using a rag to protect it, then have an

assistant compress the fork so that maximum spring pressure is placed on the damper rod head while tightening the bolt to the specified torque setting.

31 Install the fork (see Section 6).

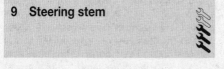

9   Steering stem

Removal

1 Remove the fairing and/or front side covers as required according to model to give best access and to prevent the possibility of damaging paintwork should a tool slip (see Chapter 8). Remove the front forks (see Section 6). Displace the handlebars and support them clear of the top yoke on some rag, or alternatively remove them completely (Section 5).

8.29a Fit a new O-ring if necessary

8.29b Fit the plug into the tube . . .

8.29c . . . then press it down and fit the retaining ring into its groove

9.3a Unscrew the steering stem nut . . .

9.3b . . . and lift the top yoke off

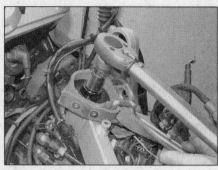

9.5a Counter-hold the rim of the adjuster and unscrew the threaded tube in its centre

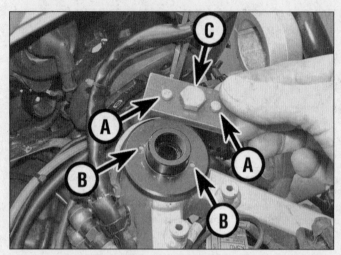

9.5b A tool can be made as shown – locate the lower ends of the small bolts (A) in the holes (B) in the adjuster and turn the tool using the large bolt head (C)

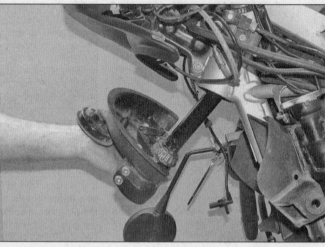

9.5c Lower the bottom yoke/steering stem out of the steering head

2 Remove the horn (see Chapter 9). Also detach the front brake hose holder and/or cable/wiring guide and/or trim panel from the bottom yoke as required for its removal, according to model.

3 On Funduro, ST, GS and Dakar models unscrew the steering stem nut (see illustration). Lift the top yoke up off the steering stem and position it clear, laying it on some rag (see illustration).

4 On Funduro and ST models support the bottom yoke and unscrew the adjuster nut using a C-spanner. Gently lower the bottom yoke and steering stem out of the frame.

Remove the bearing cover and bearing from the top of the steering head.

5 On GS and Dakar models counter-hold the adjuster using a holding strap and unscrew the threaded tube from its centre (see illustration). Support the bottom yoke and unscrew the adjuster using BMW tool part No. 316521 or a home-made equivalent as shown, with the bolts spaced so they fit into the holes in the adjuster and the centre bolt on which a socket can locate locked with a nut on the underside (see illustration). The bearing cover and bearing are fitted in the adjuster. Gently lower the bottom yoke and

steering stem out of the frame (see illustration).

6 On CS models slacken the steering stem clamp bolt in the top yoke (see illustration). Remove the plug from the adjuster (see illustration). Support the bottom yoke and unscrew the adjuster, then lift the top yoke up off the steering stem and position it clear, laying it on some rag. Gently lower the bottom yoke and steering stem out of the frame (see illustration 9.5c).

7 Remove the bearing from the base of the steering stem (see illustration).

8 Remove all traces of old grease from the

9.6a Slacken the adjuster clamp bolt (arrowed)

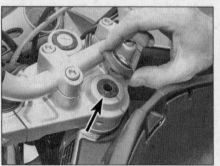

9.6b Remove the plug and turn the adjuster (arrowed) as described

9.7 Upper bearing (A – GS model shown); lower bearing (B)

bearings and the races in the steering head and check them for wear or damage as described in Section 10.

Installation

9 Smear a liberal quantity of multi-purpose grease onto the bearing races, and work some grease well into both the upper and lower bearings. Fit the lower bearing onto the steering stem **(see illustration 9.7)**.
10 On Funduro and ST models carefully lift the steering stem/bottom yoke up through the steering head and support it there **(see illustration 9.5c)**. Fit the upper bearing into the top of the steering head, then fit the bearing cover. Thread the adjuster nut onto the steering stem and tighten it so that there is no freeplay between the stem and the bearings. Fit the top yoke onto the steering stem then fit the nut but leave it loose.
11 On GS and Dakar models carefully lift the steering stem/bottom yoke up through the steering head and support it there **(see illustration 9.5c)**. Fit the adjuster, with the upper bearing and cover in place, onto the top of the steering head and tighten it using BMW tool part No. 316521 or a home-made equivalent to the initial setting specified at the beginning of the Chapter **(see illustration and 9.5b)**.
12 On CS models carefully lift the steering stem/bottom yoke up through the steering head and support it there **(see illustration 9.5c)**. Fit the upper bearing into the top of the steering head, then fit the bearing cover. Fit the top yoke onto the steering stem. Thread the adjuster in and tighten it to the initial setting specified at the beginning of the Chapter **(see illustration 9.6b)**.
13 Next temporarily install the forks and wheel as their leverage and inertia need to be taken into account. Now refer to the procedure in Chapter 1, Section 14, Step 8, 9 or 10 according to model, picking up at the relevant point in the Step, for final adjustment and installation details. With the bearings correctly adjusted remove the wheel.
14 Set the fork height correctly in the yokes (see Section 6), then fit the remaining components in a reverse of the removal procedure, referring to the relevant Sections or Chapters, applying torque settings where specified.
15 Carry out a final check of the steering head bearing freeplay as described in Chapter 1, and if necessary re-adjust.

10 Steering head bearings and races

Inspection

1 Remove the steering stem (see Section 9).
2 Remove all traces of old grease from the bearings and check them for wear or damage. Inspect the bearing rollers for signs of wear, damage or discoloration, and examine the retainer cage for signs of cracks or splits.

9.11 Fit the upper bearing/cover/adjuster assembly onto the stem and tighten as described

Replace them with new ones if necessary. On GS and Dakar models the upper bearing is pressed into the adjuster – BMW have special tools for the removal and installation of the bearing and its cover, or alternatively place the rim of the adjuster on a suitable socket as support, then drive the bearing out using a home-made tool as shown, with the bolt ends locating in the holes **(see illustration)** – this tool is the same as the one that can be used for slackening and tightening the adjuster on removal and installation, but with the centre nut and bolt removed.
3 Remove all traces of old grease from the bearing races in the steering head and check them for wear or damage. The races should be polished and free from indentations. If there are any signs of wear replace them with new ones. Only remove the outer races from the steering head if they need to be replaced with new ones – do not reuse them once they have been removed.

Replacement

4 The outer races are an interference fit in the steering head – tap them from position using a suitable drift located on the rim of the race, using the recesses provided where present **(see illustration)**. Tap firmly and evenly around each race to ensure that it is driven out squarely. Curve the end of the drift slightly to improve access if necessary.
5 Smear the new outer races with grease and press them into the head using a drawbolt arrangement **(see illustration)**, or alternatively

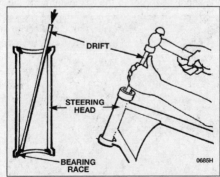

10.4 Drive the bearing races out with a brass drift locating it as shown

10.2 Fit the bearing/cover/adjuster assembly onto a suitable socket and use the tool inserted in the holes to drive the bearing out

(but less preferable) drive them in using a large diameter tubular drift. Ensure that the drawbolt washer or drift (as applicable) bears only on the outer edge of the race and does not contact the working surface. Alternatively, have the races installed by a BMW dealer equipped with the bearing race installation tools.

> **HAYNES HiNT**
> *Installation of new bearing outer races is made much easier if the races are left overnight in the freezer. This causes them to contract slightly making them a looser fit. Alternatively, use a freeze spray.*

6 Remove the dust seal from the bottom of the steering stem and replace it with a new one. Smear the new one with grease.
7 Install the steering stem (see Section 9).

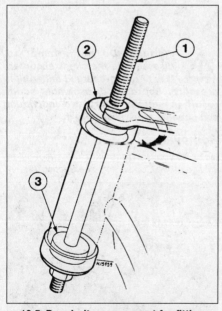

10.5 Drawbolt arrangement for fitting steering stem bearing races

1 Long bolt or threaded bar
2 Thick washer
3 Guide for lower race

11.3 Unscrew the bolt (arrowed)

11.6a Raise the rear wheel . . .

11.6b . . . unscrew the nut (arrowed) . . .

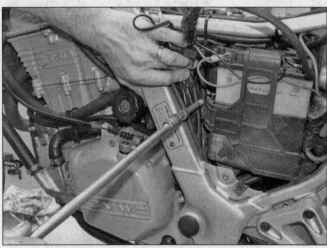

11.6c . . . withdraw the bolt . . .

11.6d . . . and remove the shock from the bottom

11 Rear shock absorber

⚠️ **Warning: Do not attempt to disassemble the shock absorber. It is nitrogen-charged under high pressure. Improper disassembly could result in serious injury. No individual components are available for it.**

Removal

Note: *If you are removing the suspension linkage as well, do so first (see Section 12).*

11.9 Release the fusebox from its holder

Funduro and ST models

1 Remove the seat and the side covers (see Chapter 8).
2 Support the motorcycle so that no weight is transmitted through any part of the rear suspension – tie the front brake lever to the handlebar to ensure the bike can't roll forward.
3 Unscrew the bolt securing the remote pre-load adjuster and displace it **(see illustration)**.
4 Unscrew the nut and withdraw the bolt securing the linkage rods to the linkage arm, noting the washers **(see illustration 12.3)**. Pivot the rods back off the arm.
5 Unscrew the bolt securing the bottom of the shock absorber to the linkage arm, noting

11.10 Unscrew the bolt (arrowed) and displace the reservoir

the washers **(see illustration 12.5)**. Pivot the linkage arm down.
6 Raise the rear wheel off the ground as high as it will go and support it using a block of wood or a jack **(see illustration)**. Unscrew the nut and remove the washer on the bolt securing the top of the shock absorber, then withdraw the bolt with its washer and manoeuvre the shock out, bringing the remote pre-load adjuster with it **(see illustrations)**.

GS, Dakar and CS models

7 Remove the seat and the rear side covers (see Chapter 8). On CS models also remove the silencer (see Chapter 4B).
8 Support the motorcycle so that no weight is transmitted through any part of the rear suspension – tie the front brake lever to the handlebar to ensure the bike can't roll forward. Position a support under the rear wheel or swingarm so that it does not drop when the shock absorber is removed, but also making sure that the weight of the machine is off the rear suspension so that the shock is not compressed.
9 On GS and Dakar models displace the ECU and lay it to one side, leaving the wiring connected (see Chapter 5). Unclip the fusebox **(see illustration)**.
10 Displace the rear brake fluid reservoir, then wrap it in rag and support it, keeping it upright **(see illustration)**.

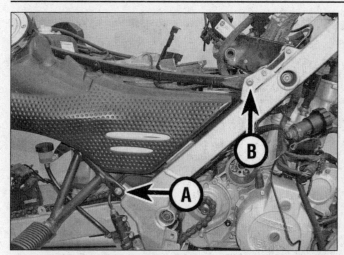

11.11a Unscrew the bolt (A) on each side and slacken the bolt (B) on each side . . .

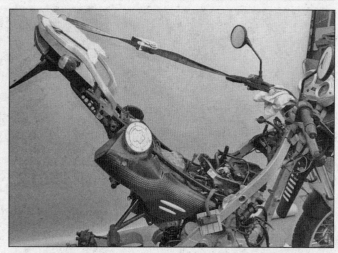

11.11b . . . then raise and secure the rear sub-frame

11.12 Displace the adjuster from the bracket, then remove the bracket from the frame

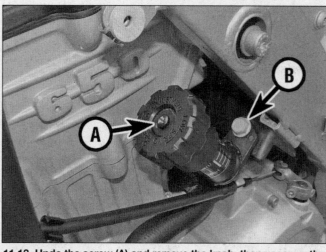

11.13 Undo the screw (A) and remove the knob, then unscrew the bolt (B)

11 Prepare a means of tying the rear sub-frame up or supporting it underneath. Unscrew the bottom bolts securing the sub-frame and slacken the top bolts **(see illustration)**. Raise the rear sub-frame enough to expose the shock absorber top bolt, but take care not to contact the seat mounts at the front. Secure the sub-frame in the raised position **(see illustration)**.

12 On GS and Dakar models unhook the cable-tie from the remote pre-load adjuster bracket. Unscrew the bolt securing the remote pre-load adjuster and displace it **(see illustration)**. Undo the adjuster bracket bolts and remove the bracket. Feed the adjuster through to the shock. On Dakar models release the remote reservoir from its clips.

13 On CS models with the adjustable shock remove the knob from the remote pre-load adjuster, noting there is a ball and spring between them that could ping away if you are not careful **(see illustration)**. Unscrew the bolt securing the adjuster and displace it. Feed it through to the shock.

14 Unscrew the bolt securing the bottom of

the shock absorber to the linkage arm, noting the washer on GS and Dakar models **(see illustration 12.5)**.

15 Unscrew the nut and on GS and Dakar models remove the washer on the bolt securing the top of the shock absorber, then withdraw the bolt and manoeuvre the shock out, bringing the remote pre-load adjuster and on Dakar models the reservoir with it **(see**

11.15a Unscrew the nut, then withdraw the bolt . . .

illustrations). Note that BMW specify that a new nut and bolt of the original type must be used on installation.

Inspection

16 Inspect the shock absorber for obvious physical damage and oil leakage, and the coil spring for looseness, cracks or signs of fatigue.

11.15b . . . and remove the shock absorber

11.17 Check the bush (arrowed) for wear

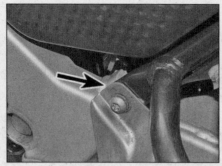

11.19 The frame locates inside the heat shield (arrowed)

12 Rear suspension linkage

Removal

1 Support the motorcycle so that no weight is transmitted through any part of the rear suspension – tie the front brake lever to the handlebar to ensure the bike can't roll forward. Position a support under the rear wheel or swingarm so that it does not drop when the shock absorber is detached, but also making sure that the weight of the machine is off the rear suspension so that the shock is not compressed.
2 Make a note of which side the bolts go in from, and so on which end the nuts are fitted. Also note the fitment of any washers with the nuts and bolts, keeping parts together.
3 Unscrew the nut and withdraw the bolt securing the linkage rods to the linkage arm (see illustration). On GS and Dakar models note the bearing covers between the rods and arm (see illustration).
4 Unscrew the nut(s) and withdraw the bolt(s) securing the linkage rods to the swingarm and remove the rods, noting which way round they fit (see illustration).
5 Unscrew the nut and withdraw the bolt securing the shock absorber to the linkage arm (see illustration).
6 Unscrew the nut and withdraw bolt securing the linkage arm to the frame and remove the arm, noting which way round it fits (see illustrations).

17 Check the bush in the top of the shock absorber and the mounting lugs on the bottom for wear or damage (see illustration). The bush is not available separately.
18 No other parts (except nuts and bolts, and the knob on the remote pre-load adjuster) are available for the shock absorber – if it is worn or damaged, it must be replaced with a new one.

Installation

19 Installation is the reverse of removal, noting the following:
● Apply multi-purpose grease to all pivot points.
● Fit both top and bottom mounting bolts before tightening either of them.
● On GS, Dakar and CS models use a new nut and bolt on the shock absorber top mount

and tighten the nut first to the torque setting specified at the beginning of the Chapter, and then through the specified angle – insert the bolt using an extension bar (see illustration 11.6c).
● On GS, Dakar and CS models when lowering the rear sub-frame make sure the rear brake hose is routed between the front of the rear mudguard and the frame, and on GS and Dakar models also make sure the left-hand side of the frame and the bottom locates on the inside of the exhaust shield (see illustration).
● On GS, Dakar and CS models clean the threads of the rear sub-frame bottom bolts and apply Loctite 2701 or equivalent. Tighten the sub-frame bolts to the specified torque setting.
● Tighten all nuts/bolts to the torque settings specified at the beginning of the Chapter.

12.3a Unscrew the nut . . .

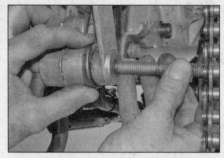

12.3b . . . then withdraw the bolt and swing the rods back, on GS and Dakar retrieving the bearing covers

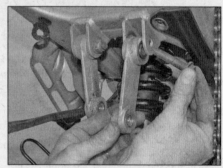

12.4 Unscrew the nut(s), withdraw the bolt(s), and remove the rods – GS shown

12.5 Unscrew the nut, withdraw the bolt and swing the arm down

12.6a Unscrew the nut . . .

12.6b . . . withdraw the bolt, and remove the arm

12.7a Withdraw the spacers . . .

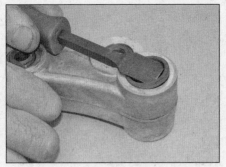

12.7b . . . then remove the seals

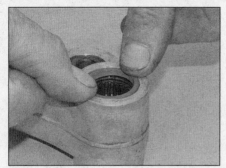

12.13 Press the new seals into place

Inspection

7 When removing the spacers and grease seals lay them out in relation to their location – different sizes are used and so each must be returned to its original place. Note that some of the bearings in the linkage components have uncaged rollers which could drop out when the spacers are removed (depending on how well they are greased). Withdraw the spacers from the linkage arm and from the linkage rods on Funduro, ST, GS and Dakar models or their mount on the swingarm on CS models (see illustration). Lever out the grease seals – new seals must be fitted but keep the old ones with their spacer(s) as a guide for installation of the new seals (see illustration).

8 Thoroughly clean all components, removing all traces of dirt, corrosion and grease. Take care not to lose any of the uncaged rollers.

9 Inspect all components closely, looking for obvious signs of wear such as heavy scoring, or for damage such as cracks or distortion. Slip each spacer back into its bearing(s) and check that there is not an excessive amount of freeplay between the two components. Replace worn or damaged components with new ones as required.

10 Check the condition of the bearings in the linkage arm, the linkage rods on Funduro, ST, GS and Dakar models, and in the swingarm on CS models. Refer to *Tools and Workshop Tips* (Section 5) in the Reference section for more information on bearings.

11 Worn bearings must be driven or drawn out of their bores, but note that removal will destroy them; new bearings should be obtained before work commences. Before removing the bearings measure the set depth (i.e. how much space is left for the grease seal) of each one using a Vernier caliper. The new bearings should be pressed or drawn into their bores (not driven in) to the correct set depth. In the absence of a press, a suitable drawbolt tool can be made up as described in *Tools and Workshop Tips* in the Reference section. Alternatively take the components to a BMW dealer who will be equipped with a set of purpose-made tools for the job. Heating the bearing housings to 80 to 100°C will ease removal and installation. When fitting the new bearings make sure the marked end faces out, with the correct gap (as measured before

removal) between each end and the rim of the bore for the seal.

12 Lubricate the needle bearings, spacers and seals with EP2 grease – use the grease to hold the uncaged rollers in place, and make sure all are fitted.

13 Press the new seals into place in all the mounts, making sure each is in its correct place as noted on removal (see illustration).

14 Fit the spacers into the bearing(s), making sure none of the uncaged rollers get dislodged (see illustration 12.7a).

Installation

15 Installation is the reverse of removal, noting the following:

● Make sure you have cleaned and re-greased the bearings as described in Steps 7 to 14 above.

● Make sure the bolts are inserted from the correct side as noted on removal. Install all nuts and bolts before tightening any of them.

● Counter-hold the bolts and tighten the nuts to the torque settings specified at the beginning of the Chapter.

13 Rear shock adjustment

Funduro and ST models

1 The shock absorber is adjustable for spring pre-load and rebound damping.

2 Spring pre-load is adjusted by turning the knob on the remote adjuster (see illustration).

13.2 Spring pre-load adjuster (arrowed)

Turn the knob clockwise to increase pre-load and anti-clockwise to reduce it. The standard setting for a solo rider with no luggage is 10 notches clockwise from the lowest (fully anti-clockwise) setting. The settings, including the standard (STD) position, are marked on the adjuster body, and also on a label on the frame.

3 Rebound damping adjustment is made by turning the adjuster screw on the bottom of the shock absorber on the left-hand side. Turn the screw clockwise to harden damping and anti-clockwise to soften it. The standard setting is 3/4 to 1 turn anti-clockwise from the hardest (fully clockwise) setting.

GS and Dakar models

4 The shock absorber is adjustable for spring pre-load and rebound damping.

5 Spring pre-load is adjusted by turning the knob on the remote adjuster (see illustration 11.12). Turn the knob clockwise to increase pre-load and anti-clockwise to reduce it. The standard setting for a solo rider with no luggage is 5 clicks clockwise on GS models and 20 clicks clockwise on Dakar models from the lowest (fully anti-clockwise) setting. The settings, including the standard (STD) position, are marked on the adjuster body.

6 Rebound damping adjustment is made by turning the adjuster screw on the bottom of the shock absorber (see illustration). Turn the screw clockwise to harden damping and anti-clockwise to soften it. The standard setting is 3/4 to 1 turn anti-clockwise from the hardest (fully clockwise) setting.

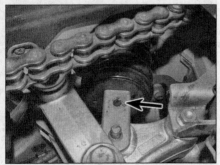

13.6 Rebound damping adjuster (arrowed)

14.2 Slip the belt off the pulley

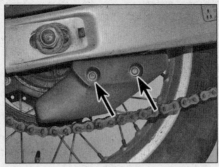

14.3a Sprocket guard bolts (arrowed) –
Funduro and ST

14.3b Belt guard nuts (arrowed) –
CS

14.6 Unscrew the nut and remove the
washer

14.7a Withdraw the pivot bolt . . .

CS models

7 On models fitted with the optional touring or 'comfort' shock absorber, it is adjustable for spring pre-load and rebound damping.

8 Spring pre-load is adjusted by turning the knob on the remote adjuster **(see illustration 11.13)**. Turn the knob clockwise to increase pre-load and anti-clockwise to reduce it. The settings, including the standard (STD) position for a solo rider with no luggage, are marked on the adjuster body.

9 Rebound damping adjustment is made by turning the adjuster screw on the bottom of the shock absorber **(see illustration 13.6)**. Turn the screw clockwise to harden damping

and anti-clockwise to soften it. The standard setting is 3/4 to 1 turn anti-clockwise from the hardest (fully clockwise) setting.

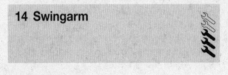

14 Swingarm

Removal

1 Remove the rear wheel (see Chapter 7).

2 On CS models, refer to Chapter 1 and create some slack in the drive belt, then slip it off the pulley **(see illustration)**. Displace the rear brake caliper (see Chapter 7). If required (for

example if a new swingarm is being installed) remove the rear drive axle assembly from the swingarm (see Chapter 7).

3 If required on Funduro and ST models remove the sprocket guard and on CS models remove the belt guard **(see illustrations)** – this can be done after removing the swingarm if preferred.

4 Release the brake hose and on ABS models the wheel sensor and/or its wiring from the swingarm as required according to model.

5 Unscrew the nut(s) and withdraw the bolt(s) securing the linkage rods to the swingarm **(see illustration 12.4)**.

6 Where fitted remove the swingarm pivot caps from the frame. Unscrew the nut on the end of the pivot bolt **(see illustration)**.

7 Withdraw the pivot bolt and manoeuvre the swingarm out of the frame **(see illustrations)**.

8 Remove the bearing cover from the outside of each pivot **(see illustration)**. Remove the chain slider from the front of the swingarm if necessary. If it is badly worn or damaged, it should be replaced with a new one. Clean, inspect and re-grease all pivot components (Steps 9 to 17).

Inspection

9 Thoroughly clean the swingarm, removing all traces of dirt, corrosion and grease.

10 Inspect the swingarm closely, looking for

14.7b . . . and remove the swingarm

14.8 Remove the bearing cover from each side

obvious signs of wear such as heavy scoring, and cracks or distortion due to accident damage. Any damaged or worn component must be replaced.

11 Check the swingarm pivot bolt is straight by rolling it on a flat surface such as a piece of plate glass (first wipe off all old grease and remove any corrosion using wire wool). Replace the pivot bolt with a new one if it is bent.

12 Withdraw the sleeve from the inner side of each pivot **(see illustration)**. On all except on CS models, remove the grease seal from each side (though the inner ones could have come away with the pivot) **(see illustration)**. New seals must be used on installation.

13 Clean all old grease off the sleeves and out of the bearings. Check the condition of the two needle bearings in each pivot **(see illustration)**. Slip each sleeve back into its bearings and check for freeplay between them. Refer to *Tools and Workshop Tips* (Section 5) in the Reference section for more information on bearings.

14 Worn bearings must be driven or drawn out of their bores, but note that removal will destroy them; new bearings should be obtained before work commences. Before removing each bearing measure its set depth using a Vernier caliper. The new bearings should be pressed or drawn into their bores (not driven in) to the correct set depth. In the absence of a press, a suitable drawbolt tool can be made up as described in *Tools and Workshop Tips* in the Reference section. Alternatively take the components to a BMW dealer who will be equipped with a set of purpose-made tools for the job. Heating the bearing housings to 80 to 100°C will ease removal and installation. When fitting the new bearings make sure the marked or sealed end faces out, with the correct gap (as measured before removal) between each end and the rim of the bore.

15 Lubricate the needle bearings and sleeves with EP2 grease.

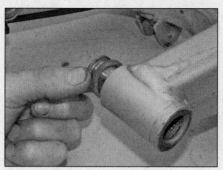

14.12a Withdraw the sleeves . . .

14.12b . . . then remove the seals

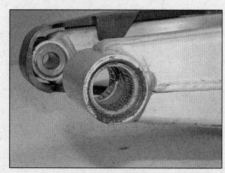

14.13 Each pivot contains two needle bearings

16 On all except CS models, press the seals into place **(see illustration)**.

17 Insert the bearing sleeves, holding the outer seals in place to prevent them being displaced by the sleeve **(see illustration 14.12a)**.

Installation

18 If removed, fit the chain slider. Fit the bearing covers **(see illustration 14.8)**.

19 Offer up the swingarm, making sure the drive chain or belt is correctly looped around the front **(see illustration 14.7b)**. Slide the pivot bolt through **(see illustration 14.7a)**.

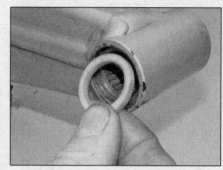

14.16 Press the new seals into place

20 Fit the washer and nut onto the pivot bolt and tighten it to the torque setting specified at the beginning of the Chapter, counter-holding the pivot bolt head **(see illustration 14.6)**. Where fitted, press the pivot caps into the frame.

21 Make sure the swingarm moves up and down freely.

22 Install the remaining components in a reverse of the removal procedure (Steps 5 to 1).

23 Check and adjust the drive chain or belt slack (see Chapter 1). Check the operation of the rear suspension and brake before taking the machine on the road.

Chapter 7
Brakes, wheels and tyres, final drive

Contents

Degrees of difficulty

Easy, suitable for novice with little experience		**Fairly easy,** suitable for beginner with some experience		**Fairly difficult,** suitable for competent DIY mechanic		**Difficult,** suitable for experienced DIY mechanic		**Very difficult,** suitable for expert DIY or professional	

Specifications

Front brake

Brake fluid type	DOT 4
Caliper type	Brembo twin piston sliding
Caliper piston diameter	30/32 mm
Disc diameter	300 mm
Disc thickness	
Standard	5.0 mm
Service limit	4.5 mm
Disc maximum runout	
Funduro, ST, GS and Dakar models	0.25 mm
CS models	0.14 mm
Master cylinder piston diameter	13 mm

Rear brake

Brake fluid type	DOT 4
Caliper type	Brembo single piston sliding
Caliper piston diameter	34 mm
Disc diameter	240 mm
Disc thickness	
Standard	5.0 mm
Service limit	4.5 mm
Disc maximum runout	
Funduro, ST, GS and Dakar models	0.25 mm
CS models	0.14 mm
Master cylinder piston diameter	
Funduro, ST, GS and Dakar models	11 mm
CS models	13 mm

ABS system

Sensor air gap	
Front	0.1 to 1.3 mm, max. 1.5 mm
Rear	
Funduro, ST, GS and Dakar models	0.1 to 1.3 mm, max. 1.5 mm.
CS models	0.7 mm max.

Wheels

Wheel size
  Funduro model
    Front . . . . 2.15 x 19 MT
    Rear . . . . 3.00 x 17 MT
  ST model
    Front . . . . 2.15 x 18 MT
    Rear . . . . 3.00 x 17 MT
  GS model
    Front . . . . 2.50 x 19 MT
    Rear . . . . 3.00 x 17 MT
  Dakar model
    Front . . . . 1.60 x 21 MT
    Rear . . . . 3.00 x 17 MT
  CS model
    Front . . . . 3.00 x 17 MT
    Rear . . . . 4.50 x 17 MT
Maximum wheel runout (front and rear)
  Funduro and ST models
    Axial (side-to-side) . . . . 0.25 mm
    Radial (out-of-round) . . . . 0.25 mm
  GS and Dakar models
    Axial (side-to-side) . . . . 2.0 mm
    Radial (out-of-round) . . . . 2.0 mm
  CS (2002 and 2003) models
    Axial (side-to-side) . . . . 0.3 mm
    Radial (out-of-round) . . . . 0.3 mm
  CS (2004-on) models
    Axial (side-to-side) . . . . 1.3 mm
    Radial (out-of-round) . . . . 1.3 mm

Tyres

Tyre pressures . . . . see *Pre-ride checks*
Tyre sizes*
  Funduro model
    Front . . . . 100/90-19 57S tubed
    Rear . . . . 130/80-17 65S tubed
  ST model
    Front . . . . 100/90-18 57S tubed
    Rear . . . . 130/80-17 65S tubed
  GS model
    Front . . . . 100/90-19 57S tubed
    Rear . . . . 130/80-17 65S tubed
  Dakar model
    Front . . . . 90/90-21 54S tubed
    Rear . . . . 130/80-17 65S tubed
  CS model
    Front . . . . 110/70-ZR17 tubeless
    Rear . . . . 160/60-ZR17 tubeless
*Refer to the owners handbook or the tyre information label on the swingarm for approved tyre brands.

Final drive

Funduro, ST, GS and Dakar models
  Drive chain slack and lubricant . . . . see Chapter 1
  Drive chain type . . . . O-ring 5/8 x 1/4
  Length
    Funduro and ST models . . . . 110 links
    GS and Dakar models . . . . 112 links
  Sprocket sizes (No. of teeth)
    Front (engine) sprocket 16
    Rear (wheel) sprocket 47
CS models
  Drive belt slack . . . . see Chapter 1
  Drive belt type . . . . Poly Chain GT, 11M-1892-26
  Length . . . . 172 teeth
  Pulley sizes (No. of teeth)
    Front (engine) pulley 28
    Rear (wheel) pulley 82

Torque settings

Brake hose banjo bolts	
Funduro and ST models	7 Nm
GS, Dakar and CS models	18 Nm
Brake pipe gland nuts	18 Nm
Drive belt eccentric adjuster clamp screws (CS models)	
Initial torque	10 Nm
Final torque	21 Nm
Front axle	
Funduro and ST models	80 Nm
GS and Dakar models	45 Nm
CS model	30 Nm
Front axle clamp nuts or bolt(s)	
Funduro and ST models	12 Nm
GS and Dakar models	21 Nm
CS model	23 Nm
Front brake caliper mounting bolts	
Funduro and ST models	50 Nm
GS, Dakar and CS models	41 Nm
Front brake disc bolts	
Funduro and ST models	12 Nm
GS and Dakar models	9 Nm
CS model	10 Nm
Front brake master cylinder clamp bolts	
Funduro and ST models	12 Nm
GS, Dakar and CS model	9 Nm
Front pulley nut – CS model	
2002 and 2003 models	180 Nm
2004-on models	220 Nm
Front sprocket nut	
Funduro and ST (1997-on) models	100 Nm
GS and Dakar models	140 Nm
Rear axle nut (Funduro, ST, GS and Dakar models)	100 Nm
Rear brake caliper bolts (CS model)	21 Nm
Rear brake disc bolts	
Funduro and ST models	12 Nm
GS and Dakar models	9 Nm
CS model	11 Nm
Rear master cylinder mounting bolts	
Funduro and ST models	12 Nm
GS, Dakar and CS models	10 Nm
Rear pulley bolts (CS model)	28 Nm
Rear pulley coupling nut (CS model)	160 Nm
Rear sprocket bolts/nuts	
Funduro and ST models	25 Nm
GS and Dakar models	21 Nm
Rear wheel nut (CS model)	160 Nm

1 General information

All models have hydraulically operated disc brakes, with a single disc at the front and rear. On all models the front brake has a twin piston sliding caliper, and the rear has a single piston sliding caliper.

An anti-lock braking system (ABS) available as an optional extra on GS, Dakar and CS models prevents the wheels from locking up under hard braking. On GS and Dakar the system can be turned off using a switch on the handlebar. The system is managed by a complex system of electronics and hydraulics. Such is the nature of the system and the fact that very little information is available from the manufacturer, no attempt is being made to cover it fully in this manual. A functional and operational description of the system is given later in this Chapter.

Drive to the rear wheel is by chain and sprockets on Funduro, ST, GS and Dakar models, and by belt and pulleys on CS models. The rear wheel hub incorporates a rubber 'cush-drive'.

Funduro, ST, GS and Dakar models are fitted with spoked wheels designed for tubed tyres only. CS models are fitted with cast alloy wheels designed for tubeless tyres only.

Note 1: *If a caliper or master cylinder is being overhauled (usually due to a sticking piston or fluid leaks) read through the entire procedure first, and make sure that you have obtained the rebuild kit and some new DOT 4 brake fluid. Rebuild kits are not always available.*

Check first with a BMW dealer, parts supplier or Brembo stockist exactly which parts are available for the caliper or master cylinder. Note that there are restrictions in place which allow caliper seals to be fitted by authorised BMW dealers, yet the seals are not available for sale over the counter.

Note 2: *On ABS models also note that any work done on the brake system that involves bleeding the system afterwards requires the use of special equipment only available to BMW dealers. Owners should not attempt to bleed the system themselves. Because of this all overhaul work on the calipers, master cylinders and brake hoses and pipes should be undertaken by a dealer, unless it is easy for the bike to be transported (NOT ridden) to a dealer following any such work.*

Caution: Disc brake components rarely

2.1 Undo the screws (arrowed) and remove the cover

2.2 Remove the clip . . .

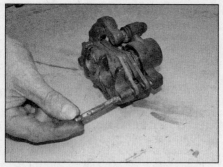

2.3a . . . then withdraw the pin

2.3b . . . and remove the pads

2.4 Unscrew the bolts (arrowed) and slide the caliper off the disc

require disassembly. Do not disassemble components unless absolutely necessary. If an hydraulic brake hose is loosened or disconnected, the union sealing washers must be replaced with new ones and the system must be bled upon reassembly. Do not use solvents on internal brake components. Solvents will cause the seals to swell and distort. Use only clean DOT 4 brake fluid. Use care when working with brake fluid as it can injure your eyes and it will damage painted surfaces and plastic parts.

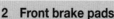
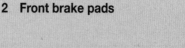

2 Front brake pads

⚠️ *Warning: The dust created by the brake system may contain asbestos, which is harmful to your*

health. Never blow it out with compressed air and don't inhale any of it. An approved filtering mask should be worn when working on the brakes.

Note: *Do not operate the brake lever while the pads are out of the caliper.*

1 On Funduro and ST models remove the caliper cover **(see illustration)**.

2 Remove the retaining clip from the pad pin **(see illustration)**.

3 Drive the pad pin out using a suitable punch **(see illustration)**. Remove the brake pads **(see illustration)**.

4 Unscrew the caliper mounting bolts and slide the caliper off the disc **(see illustration)**.

5 Inspect the surface of each pad for contamination and check that the friction material has not worn beyond its service limit (see Chapter 1, Section 11). If any pad is worn down to, or beyond, the service limit wear indicator, is fouled with oil or grease, or

is heavily scored or damaged, fit a set of new pads. **Note:** *It is not possible to degrease the friction material; if the pads are contaminated in any way they must be replaced with new ones.*

6 If the pads are in good condition clean them carefully, using a fine wire brush which is completely free of oil and grease to remove all traces of road dirt and corrosion. Using a pointed instrument, dig out any embedded particles of foreign matter. If available, spray with a dedicated brake cleaner and/or compressed air to remove any dust.

7 Check the condition of the brake disc (see Section 4).

8 Remove all traces of corrosion from the pad pin and check it for corrosion, wear and damage.

9 Slide the caliper off its bracket **(see illustration)**. Note the pad spring in the top of the caliper and the pad guide on the caliper bracket and remove them if required for cleaning or replacement, noting how they fit **(see illustrations)**. Clean off all traces of corrosion and hardened grease from the slider pins and from their rubber boots **(see illustration 3.15)**. Check the slider pin boots for cracks and splits and replace them with new ones if necessary (*refer to the* **Note** *in Section 1 regarding the availability of parts*), making sure they locate correctly.

10 Clean around the exposed section of each piston to remove any dirt or debris that could cause the seals to be damaged. If new pads are being fitted, now push the pistons all the way back into the caliper to create room for

2.9a Slide the caliper and bracket apart

2.9b Note the spring (arrowed) . . .

2.9c . . . and the guide (arrowed)

2.10 Push each piston back into the caliper

2.15 Slide the caliper onto the disc

them; if the old pads are still serviceable push the pistons in a little way. To push the pistons back use finger pressure or a piece of wood as leverage **(see illustration)**, or place the old pads back in the caliper and use a metal bar or a screwdriver inserted between them (but take care not to damage the friction surface if the pads are being reused), or use grips and a piece of wood, with rag or card to protect the caliper body. Alternatively you can use a proper piston-pushing tool. Depending on the fluid level in the reservoir it may be necessary to remove the cap and diaphragm and siphon out some fluid (see *Pre-ride checks*). If the pistons are difficult to push back, remove the bleed valve cap, then attach a length of clear hose to the bleed valve and place the open end in a suitable container, then open the valve and try again (see Section 12). Take great care not to draw any air into the system. If in doubt, bleed the brake afterwards.

11 If a piston appears seized, first block or hold the other piston using wood or cable-ties, then apply the brake lever and check whether the piston in question moves at all. If it moves out but can't be pushed back in, it is likely there is some hidden corrosion stopping it. If it doesn't move at all, or to fully clean and inspect the pistons, overhaul the caliper (see Section 3).

12 If removed fit the pad spring into the caliper and the guide onto the bracket **(see illustrations 2.9b and c)**. Apply some silicone grease to the slider pins and inside the boots. Slide the caliper onto the bracket **(see illustration 2.9a)**, making sure the boots locate correctly to provide a seal.

13 When fitting the pads into the caliper make sure the friction material on each pad faces the other.

14 Locate the pads in the caliper and press them against the spring to align the holes, then insert the pad pin, driving it fully home using a suitable punch if necessary, and secure it with the retaining clip **(see illustrations 2.3b and a and 2.2)**. If necessary the pin can be driven in after the caliper has been secured to the fork, but leave it in now to hold the pads in place.

15 Slide the caliper onto the disc making sure the pads locate correctly on each side **(see illustration)**. Fit the caliper mounting bolts and tighten them to the torque setting specified at the beginning of the Chapter. If not already done, drive the pad pin in and fit the retaining clip.

16 Operate the brake lever until the pads contact the disc. Check the level of fluid in the hydraulic reservoir and top-up if necessary (see *Pre-ride checks*).

17 Check the operation of the front brake before riding the motorcycle.

3 Front brake caliper

⚠️ *Warning: If a caliper is in need of overhaul all old brake fluid should be flushed from the system. Also, the dust created by the brake system may contain asbestos, which is harmful to your health. Never blow it out with compressed air and do not inhale any of it. An approved filtering mask should be worn when working on the brakes. Overhaul of the brake caliper must be done in a spotlessly clean work area to avoid contamination and possible failure of the brake hydraulic system components. Do not, under any circumstances, use petroleum-based solvents to clean brake parts. Use clean DOT 4 brake fluid, dedicated brake cleaner or denatured alcohol only, as described. To prevent damage from spilled brake fluid, always cover paintwork when working on the braking system.*

Note: *Refer to Section 1 regarding the availability of parts, and the bleeding of the brake system on ABS models.*

Removal

1 On Funduro and ST remove the caliper cover **(see illustration 2.1)**.

2 If the caliper is being completely removed or overhauled, unscrew the brake hose banjo bolt and detach the hose, noting how it aligns with the caliper **(see illustration)**. Wrap clingfilm around or fit the cut-off finger of a latex glove over the banjo union and secure the hose in an upright position to minimise fluid loss **(see illustration)**. Also wrap some rag or tissue around the caliper to catch the fluid inside. Discard the sealing washers, as new ones must be fitted on reassembly.

3 If the caliper is being overhauled, remove the brake pads (see Section 2).

4 If the caliper is just being displaced, unscrew the caliper mounting bolts and slide the caliper off the disc **(see illustrations 2.4 and 2.15)**. Secure the caliper with a cable-tie to avoid straining the brake hose. **Note:** *Do*

3.2a Unscrew the banjo bolt (arrowed) and detach the hose

3.2b Seal the end of the hose as described

3.6a Apply compressed air to the fluid passage . . .

3.6b . . . until the pistons are displaced . . .

3.8 . . . then remove the pistons

not operate the brake lever while either caliper is off the disc.

Overhaul

5 Clean the exterior of the caliper with denatured alcohol or brake system cleaner. Have some clean rag ready to catch any spilled brake fluid.

6 If not already done slide the caliper off its bracket, then remove the pad spring from the caliper **(see illustrations 2.9a and b)**. Place some rag, a piece of wood or an old brake pad between the pistons and the caliper body to stop the pistons leaving the bores entirely. Apply compressed air gradually and progressively, starting with a fairly low pressure, to the fluid inlet on the caliper and allow the pistons to ease out of their bores **(see illustrations)**. Make sure the pistons are displaced evenly, using a small piece of

wood to block one while the other moves if necessary.

7 If a piston is seized in its bore due to corrosion, the caliper should be replaced with a new one. Do not try to remove a piston by levering it out or by using pliers or other grips.

8 Remove the block and withdraw each piston from the caliper - mark each piston and its bore to ensure they can be matched on reassembly **(see illustration)**.

9 Remove the dust seals and the piston seals from the piston bores using a soft wooden or plastic tool to avoid scratching the bores **(see illustration)**. Discard the seals as new ones must be fitted on reassembly.

10 Clean the pistons and bores with clean DOT 4 brake fluid. If compressed air is available, blow it through the fluid galleries in the caliper to ensure they are clear (make sure it is filtered and unlubricated).

Caution: Do not, under any circumstances, use a petroleum-based solvent to clean brake parts.

11 Inspect the caliper bores and pistons for signs of corrosion, nicks and burrs and loss of plating. If surface defects are present, the caliper assembly must be replaced with a new one.

12 Lubricate the new piston seals with the special grease from the sachet if included with the rebuild kit, or with clean brake fluid, and fit them into their grooves in the caliper bores **(see illustration)**. Note that there are two sizes of bore in each caliper and care must therefore be taken to ensure that the correct size seals are fitted to the correct bores – the same applies when fitting the new dust seals and pistons.

13 Lubricate the new dust seals and fit them into their grooves in the caliper bores **(see illustration)**.

14 Lubricate the pistons and fit them, closed-end first, into the caliper bores, taking care not to displace the seals **(see illustration 2.10)**. Using your thumbs, push the pistons all the way in, making sure they enter the bore squarely.

15 Clean off all traces of corrosion and hardened grease from the slider pins and the rubber boots **(see illustration)**. Check the boots for cracks and splits and replace them with new ones if necessary *(refer to the* **Note** *in Section 1 regarding the availability of parts)*, making sure they locate correctly. Fit the pad spring into the caliper, and make sure the guide is on the bracket **(see illustrations 2.9b and c)**. Slide the caliper onto the bracket, making sure the boots locate correctly to provide a seal **(see illustration 2.9a)**.

Installation

16 If removed, install the brake pads (see Section 2).

17 Slide the caliper onto the disc, making sure the pads fit on each side **(see illustration 2.15)**.

18 Fit the caliper mounting bolts and tighten them to the torque setting specified at the beginning of the Chapter.

19 If removed, connect the brake hose to the caliper using new sealing washers **(see illustration)**. Align the hose correctly. Tighten the banjo bolt to the specified torque setting for your model.

3.9 Remove the seals and discard them

3.12 Lubricate the new piston seals and fit them into their grooves . . .

3.13 . . . followed by the new dust seals

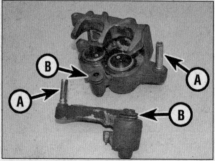

3.15 Clean the pins (A) and the boots (B)

3.19 Always use new sealing washers (arrowed)

20 Top up the hydraulic reservoir with DOT 4 brake fluid (see *Pre-ride checks*) and bleed the system as described in Section 12. Check that there are no fluid leaks and test the operation of the brake before riding the motorcycle.

4 Front brake disc

Inspection

1 Inspect the surface of the disc for score marks and other damage. Light scratches are normal after use and won't affect brake operation, but deep grooves and heavy score marks will reduce braking efficiency and accelerate pad wear. If a disc is badly grooved it must be replaced with a new one.

2 The disc must not be machined or allowed to wear down to a thickness less than the service limit listed in this Chapter's Specifications. The minimum thickness is also stamped on the disc. Check the thickness of the disc with a micrometer and replace it with a new one if necessary.

3 To check if the disc is warped, position the bike on an auxiliary stand with the front wheel raised off the ground. Mount a dial gauge to the fork leg, with the gauge plunger touching the surface of the disc about 10 mm from the outer edge **(see illustration)**. Rotate the wheel and watch the gauge needle, comparing the reading with the limit listed in the Specifications at the beginning of this Chapter. If the runout is greater than the service limit, check the wheel bearings for play (see Chapter 1). If the bearings are worn, install new ones (see Section 17) and repeat this check. If the disc runout is still excessive, a new pair of discs will have to be fitted.

Removal

4 Remove the wheel (see Section 15).
Caution: Don't lay the wheel down and allow it to rest on the disc – the disc could become warped. Set the wheel on wood blocks so the wheel rim supports the weight of the wheel.
5 If you are not replacing the disc with a new one, mark the relationship of the disc to the wheel, so it can be installed in the same position as originally fitted. Unscrew the disc retaining bolts, loosening them evenly and a little at a time in a criss-cross pattern to avoid distorting the disc – note that the bolts are coated with a threadlock and some heat may be required to loosen them up. Remove the disc, and on ABS equipped models the sensor rotor fitted on the outside of the disc **(see illustration)**. Where fitted note the washers with the bolts and the separators between the inner face of the disc and the hub.

Installation

6 Before installing the disc, make sure there is no dirt or corrosion where the disc seats on the hub. If the disc does not sit flat when it is bolted down, it will appear to be warped when checked or when the front brake is used. On ABS models do the same where the sensor rotor seats on the disc.
7 Where fitted place the separators onto the hub. Fit the disc on the wheel with its marked side facing out, aligning the previously applied matchmarks (if you're reinstalling the original disc), and making sure the arrow points in the direction of normal rotation. On ABS models fit the sensor rotor onto the disc with marked side facing out, again aligning the holes.
8 Clean the threads of the disc mounting bolts, then apply a suitable non-permanent thread locking compound – Loctite 270 is specified for Funduro and ST models, Loctite 243 for GS and Dakar models, and Loctite 2701 for CS models. Install the bolts, with their washers where fitted, and tighten them evenly and a little at a time in a criss-cross pattern to the torque setting specified at the beginning of this Chapter. Clean the disc using acetone or brake system cleaner. If a new disc has been installed, remove any protective coating from its working surfaces and fit new brake pads.
9 Install the front wheel (see Section 15).
10 Operate the brake lever several times to bring the pads into contact with the disc. Check the operation of the brake before riding the motorcycle.

5 Front brake master cylinder

⚠️ *Warning: If the brake master cylinder is in need of overhaul all old brake fluid should be flushed from the system. Overhaul of the brake master cylinder must be done in a spotlessly clean work area to avoid contamination and possible failure of the brake hydraulic system components. Do not, under any circumstances, use petroleum-based solvents to clean brake parts. Use clean DOT 4 brake fluid, dedicated brake cleaner or denatured alcohol only, as described. To prevent damage from spilled brake fluid, always cover paintwork when working on the braking system.*

Note: *Refer to Section 1 regarding the availability of parts, and the bleeding of the brake system on ABS models.*

4.3 Checking disc runout with a dial gauge

4.5 The disc is secured by six bolts – on models with ABS note how they also secure the sensor rotor (arrowed)

5.2 Undo the switch mounting screw (arrowed)

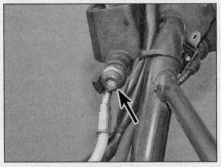

5.5 Brake hose banjo bolt (arrowed)

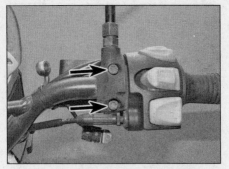

5.7 Unscrew the bolts (arrowed) and remove the master cylinder and its clamp

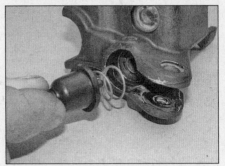

5.9a Remove the pushrod, boot and spring from the end of the master cylinder piston . . .

5.9b . . . then depress the piston and remove the circlip . . .

5.9c . . . and draw out the piston and spring

Removal

1 Remove the right-hand mirror (see Chapter 8).

2 Undo the screw securing the brake light switch to the bottom of the master cylinder and displace the switch **(see illustration)**.

3 If the master cylinder is just being displaced from the handlebar, make sure the fluid reservoir cover is secure. Unscrew the master cylinder clamp bolts, then wrap the master cylinder and reservoir assembly in some rag and position it clear of the handlebar **(see illustration 5.7)**. Make sure no strain is placed on the hydraulic hose. Keep the reservoir upright to prevent air entering the system.

4 If the master cylinder is being overhauled, remove the brake lever (see Chapter 6).

5 Unscrew the brake hose banjo bolt and detach the hose, noting its alignment with the master cylinder **(see illustration)**. Wrap clingfilm around the banjo union and secure

the hose in an upright position to minimise fluid loss, and wrap some rag or tissue around the master cylinder to catch the fluid inside. Discard the sealing washers as new ones must be fitted on reassembly.

6 Slacken and lightly retighten the reservoir cover screws.

7 Unscrew the master cylinder clamp bolts and lift the master cylinder and reservoir away from the handlebar **(see illustration)**.

8 Remove the reservoir cover and the diaphragm. Drain the brake fluid from the master cylinder and reservoir into a suitable container. Wipe any remaining fluid out of the reservoir with a clean rag.

Overhaul

9 Dislodge the rubber boot from the master cylinder, bringing the pushrod and spring with it – do not worry if the boot gets damaged on removal (its inner rim is a close fit and may

need to be levered out) as a new one comes with the rebuild kit **(see illustration)**. Depress the piston and use circlip pliers to remove the circlip, then slide out the piston assembly and spring, noting how they fit **(see illustrations)**. If they are difficult to remove, apply low pressure compressed air to the brake fluid outlet. Lay the parts out in the proper order to prevent confusion during reassembly.

10 Clean the master cylinder with clean brake fluid. If compressed air is available, blow it through the fluid galleries to ensure they are clear (make sure the air is filtered and unlubricated).

Caution: Do not, under any circumstances, use a petroleum-based solvent to clean brake parts.

11 Check the master cylinder bore for corrosion, scratches, nicks and score marks. If damage or wear is evident, the master cylinder must be replaced with a new one. If the master cylinder is in poor condition, then the caliper should be checked as well.

12 The dust boot, pushrod and its spring, and the cup should all be included in a master cylinder rebuild kit, along with some assembly grease (check with your dealer) **(see illustration)**. Use all of the new parts, regardless of the apparent condition of the old ones.

13 Fit the washer onto the inner end of the piston, then fit the new cup with its wider end away from the washer **(see illustrations)**. Fit the spring onto the end of the piston **(see illustration)**. Make sure the seal is on the outer end of the piston. Lubricate the piston, cup and seal with the grease **(see illustration)**.

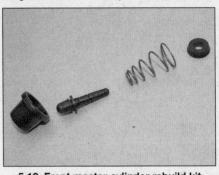

5.12 Front master cylinder rebuild kit components

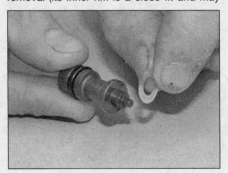

5.13a Fit the washer . . .

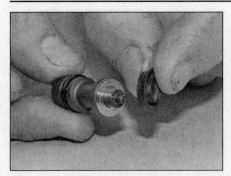

5.13b . . . the cup . . .

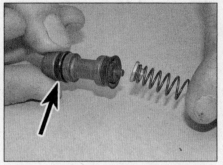

5.13c . . . and the spring onto the piston. Make sure the seal (arrow) is fitted . . .

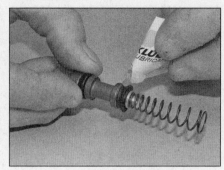

5.13d . . . then lubricate the piston, cup and seal

14 Fit the spring and piston assembly into the master cylinder, making sure the lips on the cup and seal do not turn inside out **(see illustration 5.9c)**. Push the piston all the way in, compressing the spring, and fit the new circlip **(see illustration 5.9b)**. Smear the inner end of the pushrod with silicone grease. Fit the narrow end of the spring onto the inner end of the pushrod, then fit the boot onto the outer end so its narrow outer end lips locate in the groove **(see illustration)**. Locate the inner end of the pushrod in the end of the piston **(see illustration 5.9a)**, then press the wider rim of the boot into the master cylinder until it clips into place using a deep 13 mm socket **(see illustration)**.
15 Inspect the fluid reservoir diaphragm and fit a new one if it is damaged or deteriorated.

Installation

16 Attach the master cylinder to the handlebar, aligning the clamp joint with the punch mark **(see illustrations)**. Tighten the upper bolt to the torque setting specified at the beginning of this Chapter, followed by the lower bolt.
17 Connect the brake hose to the master cylinder, using new sealing washers on each side of the banjo fitting **(see illustration)**. Align the hose as noted on removal **(see illustration 5.5)**. Tighten the banjo bolt to the torque setting specified at the beginning of this Chapter.
18 Install the brake lever (see Chapter 6), and the mirror (see Chapter 8).

19 Fit the brake light switch onto the bottom of the master cylinder **(see illustration 5.2)**.
20 Fill the fluid reservoir with new DOT 4 brake fluid (see *Pre-ride checks*). Refer to Section 12 and bleed the air from the system.
21 Check the operation of the brake before riding the motorcycle.

6 Rear brake pads

⚠ *Warning: The dust created by the brake system may contain asbestos, which is harmful to your health. Never blow it out with compressed air and don't inhale any of it. An approved filtering mask should be worn when working on the brakes.*
1 Push the caliper against the disc to force

the piston back in - this creates room for the new pads. Depending on the fluid level in the reservoir it may be necessary to remove the cap and diaphragm and siphon out some fluid (see *Pre-ride checks*). If the piston is difficult to push back, remove the bleed valve cap, then attach a length of clear hose to the bleed valve and place the open end in a suitable container, then open the valve and try again (see Section 12). Take great care not to draw any air into the system. If in doubt, bleed the brake afterwards.
2 Remove the retaining clip from the pad pin **(see illustration)**. Drive the pad pin out using a suitable punch **(see illustration)**. Remove the brake pads **(see illustration)**.
3 Inspect the surface of each pad for contamination and check that the friction material has not worn beyond its service limit (see Chapter 1, Section 11). If any pad

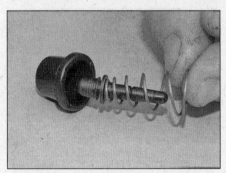

5.14a Fit the spring and boot onto the pushrod

5.14b Press the rim of the boot in using a deep 13 mm socket

5.16a Align the mating surfaces of the clamp with the punch mark (arrowed) . . .

5.16b . . . then fit the master cylinder assembly and tighten the bolts

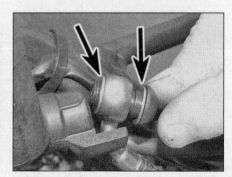

5.17 Always use new sealing washers (arrowed)

6.2a Remove the clip . . .

6.2b . . then drive the pin out . . .

6.2c . . . and remove the pads

is worn down to, or beyond, the service limit wear indicator, is fouled with oil or grease, or is heavily scored or damaged, fit a set of new pads. **Note:** *It is not possible to degrease the friction material; if the pads are contaminated in any way they must be replaced with new ones.*
4 If the pads are in good condition clean them carefully, using a fine wire brush which is completely free of oil and grease to remove all traces of road dirt and corrosion. Using a pointed instrument, dig out any embedded particles of foreign matter. If available, spray with a dedicated brake cleaner and/or compressed air to remove any dust.
5 Check the condition of the brake disc (see Section 8).
6 Remove all traces of corrosion from the pad pin and check it for corrosion, wear and damage.
7 Every so often you should displace the caliper and slide it off its bracket, then clean and re-grease the slider pins to ensure the

caliper functions properly – on the model photographed the caliper had seized on its slider pins. See Section 7 for the procedure.
8 If the piston appears seized, apply the brake pedal and check whether the piston moves at all. If it moves out but can't be pushed back in, it is likely there is some hidden corrosion stopping it. If it doesn't move at all, or to fully clean and inspect the piston, overhaul the caliper (see Section 7).
9 When fitting the pads into the caliper make sure the friction material on each pad faces the other.
10 Locate the pads in the caliper and press them against the spring to align the holes, then insert the pad pin, driving it fully home using a suitable punch **(see illustrations)**. Secure the pin with the retaining clip **(see illustration 6.2a)**.
11 Operate the brake pedal until the pads contact the disc. Check the level of fluid in the hydraulic reservoir and top-up if necessary (see *Pre-ride checks*).

12 Check the operation of the rear brake before riding the motorcycle.

7 Rear brake caliper

6.10a Fit the inner pad . . .

6.10b . . . then insert the pin part-way to hold it . . .

⚠ *Warning: If a caliper is in need of overhaul all old brake fluid should be flushed from the system. Also, the dust created by the brake system may contain asbestos, which is harmful to your health. Never blow it out with compressed air and do not inhale any of it. An approved filtering mask should be worn when working on the brakes. Overhaul must be done in a spotlessly clean work area to avoid contamination and possible failure of the brake hydraulic system components. Do not, under any circumstances, use petroleum-based solvents to clean brake parts. Use clean DOT 4 brake fluid, dedicated brake cleaner or denatured alcohol only, as described. To prevent damage from spilled brake fluid, always cover paintwork when working on the braking system.*
Note: *Refer to Section 1 regarding the availability of parts, and the bleeding of the brake system on ABS models.*

Removal

1 If the caliper is being completely removed or overhauled, unscrew the brake hose banjo bolt and detach the hose, noting its alignment with the caliper **(see illustration)**. Wrap clingfilm around the banjo union and secure the hose in an upright position to minimise

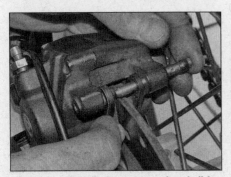

6.10c . . . then fit the outer pad and slide the pin through

6.10d Drive the pin fully in

7.1 Brake hose banjo bolt (arrowed)

7.4 Displace the caliper assembly, noting how it locates

7.5 Unscrew the bolts (arrowed) and slide the caliper off the disc

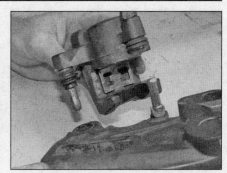
7.6a Slide the caliper and bracket apart

7.6b Note the spring (arrowed) . . .

7.6c . . . and the guide (arrowed)

fluid loss **(see illustration 3.2b)**. Also wrap some rag or tissue around the caliper to catch the fluid inside. Discard the sealing washers as new ones must be fitted on reassembly.

2 If required remove the brake pads (see Section 6).

3 Remove the rear wheel (see Section 16).

4 On Funduro, ST, GS and Dakar models displace the caliper from the swingarm **(see illustration)**.

5 On CS models unscrew the bolts and detach the caliper from the swingarm **(see illustration)**.

Overhaul

6 Slide the caliper off the bracket **(see illustration)**. If required remove the pad spring from the caliper and the guide from the bracket, noting how they fit **(see illustrations)**. Clean the exterior of the caliper with denatured alcohol or brake system cleaner. Have some clean rag ready to catch any spilled brake fluid.

7 Stuff some stout rag or place a piece of wood between the piston and the caliper body – it should be just thick enough to stop the piston leaving the bore entirely **(see illustration)**. Apply compressed air gradually and progressively, starting with a fairly low pressure, to the fluid inlet on the caliper and allow the piston to ease out of the bore **(see illustration)**.

8 If the piston is stuck in its bore due to corrosion the caliper should be replaced with a new one. Do not try to remove the piston by levering it out or by using pliers or other grips.

9 Remove the dust seal and the piston seal from the piston bore using a soft wooden or plastic tool to avoid scratching the bores **(see illustration)**. Discard the seals as new ones must be fitted on reassembly.

10 Clean the piston and bore with clean brake fluid. If compressed air is available, blow it through the fluid passages in the caliper to ensure they are clear (make sure it is filtered and unlubricated).

Caution: Do not, under any circumstances, use a petroleum-based solvent to clean brake parts.

11 Inspect the caliper bore and piston for signs of corrosion, nicks and burrs and loss of plating. If surface defects are present, the

caliper assembly must be replaced with a new one.

12 Lubricate the new piston seal with the special grease from the sachet if included with the rebuild kit, or with clean brake fluid, and

fit it into its groove in the caliper bore **(see illustration)**.

13 Lubricate the new dust seal and fit it into its groove in the caliper bore **(see illustration)**.

14 Lubricate the piston and fit it, closed-end

7.7a Using compressed air . . .

7.7b . . . to force the piston out

7.9 Remove the seals and discard them

7.12 Lubricate the new piston seal then fit it into its groove

7.13 . . . followed by the new dust seal

7.14a Lubricate the piston . . .

7.14b . . . then fit past the seals . . .

7.14c . . . and push it all the way in

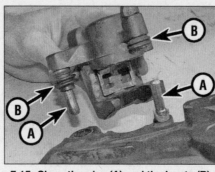

7.15 Clean the pins (A) and the boots (B)

7.21 Always use new sealing washers

first, into the caliper bore, taking care not to displace the seals **(see illustration)**. Using your thumbs, push the piston all the way in, making sure it enters the bore squarely **(see illustrations)**.

15 Clean off all traces of corrosion and hardened grease from the slider pins and the rubber boots **(see illustration)**. Check the boots for cracks and splits and replace them with new ones if necessary, making sure they locate correctly.

16 Fit the pad spring into the caliper, and the guide onto the bracket, if removed **(see illustrations 7.6b and c)**. Slide the caliper onto the bracket, making sure the boots locate correctly to provide a seal **(see illustration 7.6a)**.

Installation

17 On CS models fit the caliper onto the swingarm and tighten the bolts to the torque

setting specified at the beginning of the Chapter **(see illustration 7.5)**. Note that BMW state that the forward facing caliper bolt be renewed every time it is disturbed – the screw threads are micro-encapsulated with a locking agent.

18 On Funduro, ST, GS and Dakar models locate the caliper on the swingarm **(see illustration 7.4)**.

19 Install the rear wheel (see Section 16).

20 If removed install the brake pads (see Section 6).

21 If detached, connect the brake hose to the caliper, using new sealing washers on each side of the fitting **(see illustration)**. Make sure the hose is correctly aligned and tighten the banjo bolt to the torque setting specified at the beginning of the Chapter.

22 Top up the hydraulic reservoir with DOT 4 brake fluid (see *Pre-ride checks*) and bleed the system as described in Section 12.

23 Check that there are no fluid leaks and test the operation of the brake before riding the motorcycle.

8 Rear brake disc

Inspection

1 Refer to Section 4 of this Chapter, noting that the dial gauge should be attached to the swingarm.

Removal

2 Remove the wheel (see Section 16). On CS models remove the rear drive axle and eccentric adjuster from the swingarm (see Section 22).

Caution: On Funduro, ST, GS and Dakar models don't lay the wheel down and allow it to rest on the disc or sprocket – they could become warped. Set the wheel on wood blocks so the wheel rim supports the weight of the wheel.

3 If you are not replacing the disc with a new one, mark the relationship of the disc to the hub, so it can be installed in the same position as originally fitted. Unscrew the disc retaining bolts, loosening them evenly and a little at a time in a criss-cross pattern to avoid distorting the disc – note that the bolts are coated with a threadlock and some heat may be required to loosen them up. Remove the disc **(see illustrations)**.

8.3a Rear brake disc bolts –
Funduro, ST, GS and Dakar

8.3b Rear brake disc bolts –
CS

9.1a Unscrew the bolts and remove the footrest assembly

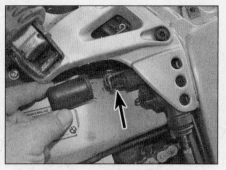

9.1b Disconnect the wiring connector (arrowed)

9.1c Release the retainer (arrowed) and detach the pushrod from the pedal

Installation

4 Before installing the disc, make sure there is no dirt or corrosion where the disc seats on the hub. If the disc does not sit flat when it is bolted down, it will appear to be warped when checked or when the rear brake is used.

5 Fit the disc on the hub with its marked side facing out, aligning the previously applied matchmarks (if you're reinstalling the original disc), and making sure the arrow points in the direction of normal rotation.

6 Clean the threads of the disc mounting bolts, then apply a suitable non-permanent thread locking compound – Loctite 270 is specified for Funduro and ST models, Loctite 243 for GS and Dakar models, and Loctite 2701 for CS models. Install the bolts and tighten them evenly and a little at a time in a criss-cross pattern to the torque setting specified at the beginning of this Chapter. Clean the disc using acetone or brake system cleaner. If a new disc has been installed, remove any protective coating from its working surfaces and fit new brake pads.

7 On CS models install the rear drive axle and eccentric adjuster (see Section 22). On all models install the rear wheel (see Section 16).

8 Operate the brake pedal several times to bring the pads into contact with the disc. Check the operation of the brake before riding the motorcycle.

9 Rear brake master cylinder

> ⚠ **Warning:** *If the brake master cylinder is in need of overhaul all old brake fluid should be flushed from the system. Overhaul must be done in a spotlessly clean work area to avoid contamination and possible failure of the brake hydraulic system components. Do not, under any circumstances, use petroleum-based solvents to clean brake parts. Use clean DOT 4 brake fluid, dedicated brake cleaner or denatured alcohol only, as described. To prevent damage from spilled brake fluid, always cover paintwork when working on the braking system.*

9.2a Release the clip . . .

9.2b . . . and withdraw the pin

Note: *Refer to Section 1 regarding the availability of parts, and the bleeding of the brake system on ABS models.*

Removal

1 On Funduro and ST models remove the right-hand side cover (see Chapter 8). Unscrew the passenger footrest bracket bolts and remove the footrest assembly **(see illustration)**. Pull the cover off the brake light switch and disconnect the wiring connector **(see illustration)**. Release the pushrod retainer and detach the pushrod from the brake pedal **(see illustration)**.

2 On GS, Dakar and CS models release and remove the clip pin securing the pushrod to the brake pedal **(see illustrations)**.

3 Prepare a container to drain the reservoir into. Unscrew the reservoir bolt, then undo the cap, remove the diaphragm and drain

the reservoir **(see illustration)**. Wipe any remaining fluid out with a clean rag.

4 On Funduro and ST models undo the brake light switch and detach the hose union, noting its alignment with the master cylinder. Wrap clingfilm around the banjo union and secure the hose in an upright position to minimise fluid loss **(see illustration 3.2b)**. Discard the sealing washers as new ones must be fitted on reassembly.

5 On GS, Dakar and CS models counter-hold the top of the master cylinder using a spanner on the flats then undo the brake pipe gland nut **(see illustration)**. Wrap clingfilm around the pipe end to minimise fluid loss **(see illustration 3.2b)**.

6 Undo the bolts securing the master cylinder and remove it, on GS, Dakar and CS models detaching the brake pipe as you do, and noting the heel guard where fitted **(see illustrations)**.

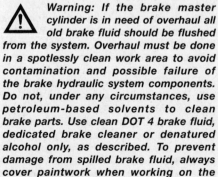

9.3 Unscrew the bolt (arrowed) and drain the reservoir

9.5 Hold the master cylinder with one spanner and undo the pipe nut with another

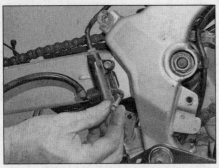

9.6a Unscrew the bolts . . .

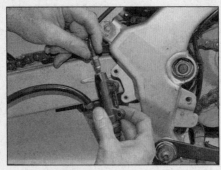

9.6b . . . and remove the master cylinder

9.6c Note the heel guard (arrowed) on the CS

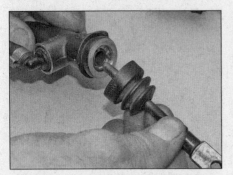

9.7a Remove the pushrod and boot from the end of the master cylinder piston . . .

9.7b . . . then depress the piston and remove the circlip to free the piston and spring assembly

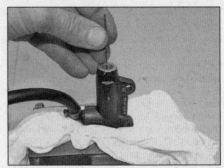

9.7c If necessary poke the piston out of the bottom using a rod inserted from the top . . .

Overhaul

7 Free the rubber dust boot from the base of the master cylinder and remove it along with the pushrod **(see illustration)**. Push the piston in and, using circlip pliers, remove the circlip from its groove in the master cylinder

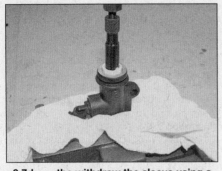

9.7d . . . the withdraw the sleeve using a puller . . .

9.7e . . . and retrieve the O-ring

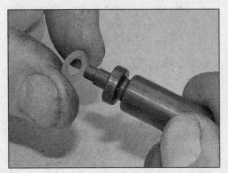

9.11a Fit the washer . . .

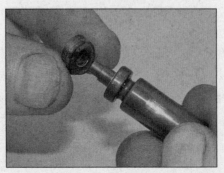

9.11b . . . the cup . . .

and slide out the piston assembly and spring, noting how they all fit **(see illustration)**. Lay the parts out in order as you remove them to prevent confusion during reassembly. On the model photographed the piston was very tight in the white sleeve, and the sleeve was even tighter in the cylinder (all components should slide out easily under spring pressure). It was necessary to drive the piston out using a thin rod inserted through the fluid inlet bore at the top, then to use an internal puller to get the sleeve out, and finally dig the O-ring out **(see illustrations)**.

8 Clean the master cylinder with clean brake fluid. If compressed air is available, blow it through the fluid galleries to ensure they are clear (make sure the air is filtered and unlubricated).

Caution: Do not, under any circumstances, use a petroleum-based solvent to clean brake parts.

9 Check the master cylinder bore for corrosion, scratches, nicks and score marks. If damage or wear is evident, the master cylinder must be replaced with a new one.

10 The cup and O-ring must be replaced with new ones and come in the rebuild kit, along with some assembly grease – use the new parts, regardless of the apparent condition of the old ones. The pushrod and rubber boot are also available if required.

11 Fit the washer onto the inner end of the piston, then fit the new cup with its wider end away from the washer **(see illustrations)**. Fit the spring onto the end of the piston **(see**

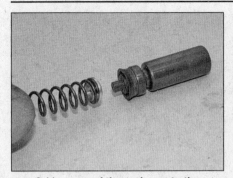
9.11c ... and the spring onto the piston ...

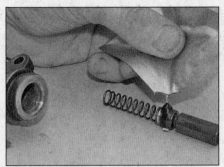
9.11d ... then lubricate the piston and cup

9.12a Slide the assembly into the master cylinder

illustration). Lubricate the piston and cup with the grease (see illustration).
12 Fit the spring and piston assembly into the master cylinder, making sure the lips on the cup do not turn inside out (see illustration). Fit the O-ring around the top of the piston (see illustration). Fit the white sleeve over the piston and push it all the way in until it seats (the circlip groove will be exposed) (see illustration) – it will push the O-ring down with it. Push the piston in below the level of the sleeve, then locate the circlip in the groove (see illustration 9.7b).
13 Fit the rubber boot onto the pushrod, locating its narrower end in the groove (see illustration). Smear some silicone grease onto the rounded end of the pushrod and locate it against the end of the piston, fitting the rubber boot onto the bottom of the cylinder (see illustration 9.7a).

Installation

14 Locate the master cylinder, with the heel guard where fitted, on GS, Dakar and CS models locating the brake pipe as you do, and tighten the bolts to the torque setting specified at the beginning of this Chapter (see illustrations 9.6c, b and a).

9.12b Fit the O-ring around the piston ...

9.12c ... then fit the sleeve ...

15 On Funduro and ST models connect the brake hose to the master cylinder, using new sealing washers on each side of the fitting, and making sure it is correctly aligned. Reconnect the wiring connector and fit the cover (see illustration 9.1b). Attach the pushrod to the brake pedal and secure it with the retainer (see illustration 9.1c). Fit the footrest assembly and tighten the bolts to the specified torque – see Chapter 6 Specifi-cations (see illustration 9.1a).
16 On GS, Dakar and CS models counter-hold the master cylinder and tighten the gland nut, to the torque setting specified at the beginning

of this Chapter if the correct tools are available (see illustration 9.5). Attach the pushrod to the brake pedal then insert and secure the clip pin (see illustrations 9.2b and a)
17 Fit the reservoir and tighten the bolt (see illustration 9.3). Check that the hose is secure at each end.
18 Fill the fluid reservoir with new DOT 4 brake fluid (see Pre-ride checks). Refer to Section 12 and bleed the air from the system.
19 On Funduro and ST install the right-hand side cover (see Chapter 8).
20 Check the operation of the brake carefully before riding the motorcycle.

9.12d ... and push it in

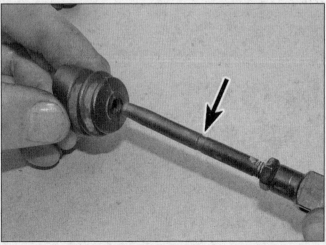
9.13 Locate the lip in the groove (arrowed)

10.1a ABS control unit (arrowed) – GS and Dakar

10.1b ABS control unit (arrowed) – CS

10 Anti-lock brake system – ABS

⚠️ **Warning: The ABS system works by comparing the relative speed of the wheels, and is programmed using the wheel and tyre sizes specified and fitted as standard. If non-specified wheels or tyres are fitted the control unit may become confused and the system will not function correctly.**

1 The anti-lock braking system (ABS) prevents the wheels from locking up under hard braking or on uneven road surfaces. A sensor on each wheel transmits information about the speed of wheel rotation, and if the control module senses that a wheel is about to lock, it releases brake pressure momentarily to that wheel, preventing a skid **(see illustrations)**. When the system is active a pulsing can be felt through the lever or pedal as the fluid pressure is released and reapplied as required.

2 The ABS system is self-checking, and is automatically switched on with the ignition, although on GS and Dakar models you can switch it off using the rocker switch in the centre of the handlebar (see Step 5). ABS will not function at speeds of less than 3.5 mph

(6 kph), or 7 mph (12 kph) if the brake lever or pedal has been applied prior to that speed being reached, with the ignition off, if a fault is indicated (ABS warning light remains on after start-up or comes on during use), or if the battery is flat. Note that the system turns itself off if the bike is ridden on one wheel for more than 10 seconds!

3 When the ignition switch is turned on, the ABS indicator light on the instrument panel comes on, then goes off when setting off. If the indicator light stays on, or comes on while riding, then there is probably a fault in the system, and it switches itself off. Stop the motorcycle and switch the ignition off. Switch it on again, start the engine and ride the bike - if the light goes off then the system is OK, but if the light remains on or comes on again, take the machine to a BMW dealer for testing.

4 Note that under certain conditions, the indicator light could come on and a fault code could be registered, even though there is no actual problem with the system. This is when the effects of the conditions themselves simulate an actual fault. This can occur if the machine is ridden continuously on very bumpy roads, or if the rider does a wheelie, or if the air pressure on one tyre is extremely low, or if the machine is placed on the centrestand or an auxiliary stand with the engine running

and the rear wheel is turning when the front is not. If this happens stop the bike and turn the engine off, then restart and ride the bike – the light may not come on again when the system realises everything is OK, but if it does the fault code must be retrieved and then erased before the indicator light will go out.

5 On GS and Dakar models it is possible, and preferable when riding off-road, to switch the ABS off. To do this make sure the bike is stationary (never switch it off while moving) and the engine is running. Press and hold the ABS switch in the centre of the handlebar for 3 seconds **(see illustration)**. The indicator light will start to flash. Release the button – the ABS is now deactivated. The indicator light will flash intermittently all the time the system is deactivated. To reactivate it switch the ignition off, then turn it on again – the system is reset to normal.

6 If the indicator light does not come on when the ignition is switched on, check the fuses and the bulb in the instrument panel (see Chapter 9), and the modulator wiring connectors. If the bulbs and connections are good, take the machine to a BMW dealer for testing.

7 The only maintenance required is firstly to make sure there is no dirt or debris on each wheel speed sensor tip or between the poles on the sensor rotor **(see illustration)**.

10.5 ABS switch (arrowed)

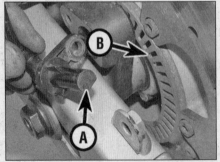

10.7a Make sure the rotor tip (A) and the gaps between the sensor poles (B) are clean

10.7b Use a feeler blade to check the air gap

Secondly check the air gap between the sensor tip and one of the poles on the rotor, though once set, this is unlikely to change. Check the gap by inserting a feeler gauge between the sensor and the tip of one of the poles **(see illustration)**. If the gap is not as specified at the beginning of the Chapter, remove the mounting bolts and adjust the air gap by inserting a replacement shim of the required thickness to bring the gap within specifications. Check the gap in different places by rotating the wheel.

8 Fault diagnosis and any other work on the system, including bleeding it and changing the brake fluid, must be undertaken by a BMW dealer.

11 Brake hoses, pipes and fittings

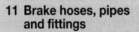

Inspection

1 Brake hose condition should be checked regularly and the hoses replaced with new ones at the specified interval (see Chapter 1). Twist and flex the hoses while looking for cracks, bulges and seeping hydraulic fluid. Check extra carefully around the areas where the hoses connect with the banjo fittings, as these are common areas for hose failure.

2 On GS, Dakar and CS models without ABS check the brake pipe to the rear master cylinder and the pipe joint with the hose to the rear caliper. On models with ABS also check the brake pipes, the pipe joints and the ABS modulator for signs of fluid leakage and for any dents or cracks in the pipes **(see illustrations 10.1a and b)**.

3 Inspect the banjo fittings connected to the brake hoses and the pipe joints on ABS models. If the fittings are rusted, scratched or cracked, fit new ones.

Removal and installation

Note: *Refer to Section 1 regarding the bleeding of the brake system on ABS models.*

4 The brake hoses have banjo fittings on each end. Cover the surrounding area with plenty of rags and unscrew the banjo bolt at each end of the hose, noting the alignment of the fitting with the master cylinder or brake caliper **(see illustrations 3.2a, 5.5, 7.1, and 9.4)**. Free the hose from any clips or guides and remove it, noting its routing. Discard the sealing washers.

Note: *Do not operate the brake lever or pedal while a brake hose is disconnected.*

5 Position the new hose, making sure it isn't twisted or otherwise strained, and ensure that it is correctly routed through any clips or guides and is clear of all moving components.

6 Check that the fittings align correctly, then install the banjo bolts, using new sealing washers on both sides of the fittings **(see illustration 3.19, 5.17, 7.21)**. Tighten the banjo bolts to the torque setting specified at the beginning of this Chapter.

7 The joints between the hoses and pipes, and where the pipes connect to the ABS modulator and to the rear master cylinder on GS, Dakar and CS models are held by nuts **(see illustrations 9.5 and 10.1a and b)**. There are no sealing washers. Unscrew the nuts to separates the hoses from the pipes and to detach the pipes from the master cylinder and hydraulic unit. When refitting them tighten the nuts to the specified torque setting if the correct tools are available.

8 Flush the old brake fluid from the system, refill with new DOT 4 brake fluid (see *Pre-ride checks*) and bleed the air from the system (see Section 12).

9 Check the operation of the brakes before riding the motorcycle.

12 Brake system bleeding and fluid change

Note: *Refer to Section 1 at the beginning of this Chapter regarding the bleeding of the brake system on ABS models.*

Note: *If bleeding the system using the conventional method (or one-man kit) described does not work sufficiently well, it is advisable to obtain a vacuum-type brake bleeding tool **(see illustration 12.17)**.*

Bleeding

1 Bleeding the brakes is simply the process of removing air from the brake fluid reservoir, the hose and the brake caliper. Bleeding is necessary whenever a brake system hydraulic connection is loosened, after a component or hose is replaced with a new one, or when the master cylinder or caliper is overhauled. Leaks in the system may also allow air to enter, but leaking brake fluid will reveal their presence and warn you of the need for repair.

2 To bleed the brakes, you will need some new DOT 4 brake fluid, a length of clear vinyl or plastic hose, a small container partially filled with clean brake fluid, some rags, a spanner to fit the brake caliper bleed valve, and help from an assistant **(see illustration)**.

3 Cover painted components to prevent damage in the event that brake fluid is spilled.

4 Refer to 'Pre-ride checks' and remove the reservoir cover or cap and diaphragm, and

12.2 Set-up for bleeding the brakes

slowly pump the brake lever (front brake) or pedal (rear brake) a few times, until no air bubbles can be seen floating up from the holes in the bottom of the reservoir. This bleeds the air from the master cylinder end of the line. Temporarily refit the reservoir cap or cover.

5 Pull the dust cap off the bleed valve **(see illustrations)**. Attach one end of the clear vinyl or plastic hose to the bleed valve and submerge the other end in the clean brake fluid in the container **(see illustration 12.2)**. If you're using a one-man type brake bleeder, there is no need for fluid in the container.

Note: *To avoid damaging the bleed valve during the procedure, loosen it and then tighten it temporarily with a ring spanner before attaching the hose. With the hose attached, the valve can then be opened and closed either with an open-ended spanner, or by leaving the ring spanner located on the valve and fitting the hose above it.*

6 Check the fluid level in the reservoir. Do not allow the fluid level to drop below the lower mark during the procedure.

7 Carefully pump the brake lever or pedal three or four times, then hold it in (front) or down (rear) and open the bleed valve. When the valve is opened, brake fluid will flow out of the caliper into the clear tubing, and the lever will move toward the handlebar, or the pedal will move down. If there is air in the system there will be air bubbles in the brake fluid coming out of the caliper.

8 Tighten the bleed valve, then release the brake lever or pedal gradually. Top-up the reservoir and repeat the process until no air bubbles are visible in the brake fluid leaving

12.5a Front brake caliper bleed valve (arrowed)

12.5b Rear brake caliper bleed valve (arrowed)

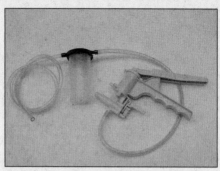

12.17 A vacuum-operated bleeding tool

the caliper, and the lever or pedal is firm when applied. On completion, disconnect the hose, check the bleed valve is tight (though do not overtighten) and fit the dust cap.

If it is not possible to produce a firm feel to the lever or pedal, the fluid may be aerated. Let the brake fluid in the system stabilise for a few hours and then repeat the procedure when the tiny bubbles in the system have settled out.

9 Top-up the reservoir, then install the diaphragm and cap (see *Pre-ride checks*). Wipe up any spilled brake fluid. Check the entire system for fluid leaks.
10 Check the operation of the brakes before riding the motorcycle.

Fluid change

11 Changing the brake fluid is a similar

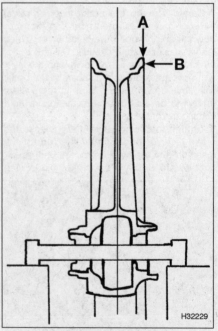

13.2 Check the wheel for radial (out-of-round) runout (A) and axial (side-to-side) runout (B)

process to bleeding the brakes and requires the same materials plus a suitable tool for siphoning the fluid out of the reservoir. Also ensure that the container is large enough to take all the old fluid when it is flushed out of the system.
12 Follow Steps 2, 3 and 5, then remove the reservoir cap, diaphragm plate and diaphragm and siphon the old fluid out of the reservoir. Fill the reservoir with new brake fluid, then carefully pump the brake lever or pedal three or four times and hold it in (front) or down (rear) while opening the caliper bleed valve. When the valve is opened, brake fluid will flow out of the caliper into the clear tubing, and the lever will move toward the handlebar, or the pedal will move down.
13 Tighten the bleed valve, then release the brake lever or pedal gradually. Keep the reservoir topped-up with new fluid to above the LOWER level at all times or air may enter the system and greatly increase the length of the task. Repeat the process until new fluid can be seen emerging from the caliper bleed valve.

Old brake fluid is invariably much darker in colour than new fluid, making it easy to see when all old fluid has been expelled from the system.

14 Disconnect the hose, then make sure the bleed valve is tightened to the specified torque setting and install the dust cap.
15 Top-up the reservoir, then install the diaphragm, diaphragm plate, and cap (see *Pre-ride checks*). Wipe up any spilled brake fluid. Check the entire system for fluid leaks.
16 Check the operation of the brakes before riding the motorcycle.

Draining the system for overhaul

17 Draining the brake fluid is again a similar process to bleeding the brakes. The quickest and easiest way is to use a commercially available vacuum-type brake bleeding tool **(see illustration)** – follow the manufacturer's instructions. Otherwise follow the procedure described above for changing the fluid, but quite simply do not put any new fluid into the reservoir – the system fills itself with air instead.

13 Wheel inspection and repair

1 In order to carry out a proper inspection of the wheels, it is necessary to support the bike upright so that the wheel being inspected is raised off the ground. Position the motorcycle on its centrestand, or on an auxiliary stand where only a sidestand is fitted. Clean the wheels thoroughly to remove mud and dirt that may interfere with the inspection procedure or mask defects. Make a general check of the

wheels (see Chapter 1) and tyres (see *Pre-ride checks*).
2 Attach a dial gauge to the fork or the swingarm and position its tip against the side of the wheel rim. Spin the wheel slowly and check the axial (side-to-side) runout of the rim **(see illustration)**.
3 In order to accurately check radial (out of round) runout with the dial gauge, remove the wheel from the machine, and the tyre from the wheel. With the axle clamped in a vice and the dial gauge positioned on the top of the rim, the wheel can be rotated to check the runout.
4 An easier, though slightly less accurate, method is to attach a stiff wire pointer to the fork or the swingarm and position the end a fraction of an inch from the wheel rim where the wheel and tyre join. If the wheel is true, the distance from the pointer to the rim will be constant as the wheel is rotated.
5 If wheel runout is excessive, on models with spoked wheels first make sure the spokes are properly tensioned (see Chapter 1). On all models check the wheel bearings. If all is good it may be that a new wheel is needed, but it is worth checking with a specialist first.
6 On CS models with cast wheels, inspect the wheels for cracks, flat spots on the rim and other damage. Look very closely for dents in the area where the tyre bead contacts the rim. Dents in this area may prevent complete sealing of the tyre against the rim, which leads to deflation of the tyre over a period of time. If damage is evident the wheel will have to be replaced with a new one. Never attempt to repair a damaged cast alloy wheel.
7 On Funduro, ST, GS and Dakar models with spoked wheels, regularly check the spokes as described in Chapter 1. Wheel rebuilding or spoke replacement must be left to a BMW dealer or wheel building specialist. A great deal of skill and some special equipment is required, and given the potential for poor handling and machine instability that could result from a poorly-built wheel, it is essential that owners do not attempt repairs themselves, unless suitably equipped and experienced.

14 Wheel alignment check

1 Misalignment of the wheels due to a bent frame or forks can cause strange and possibly serious handling problems. If the frame or forks are at fault, repair by a frame specialist or renewal are the only options.
2 To check wheel alignment you will need an assistant, a length of string or a perfectly straight piece of wood and a ruler. A plumb bob or spirit level for checking that the wheels are vertical will also be required.
3 In order to make a proper check of the wheels it is necessary to support the bike in an upright position, on its centestand or on auxiliary stand if only a sidestand is fitted. First ensure that the chain adjuster markings coincide on each side

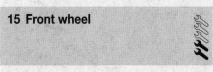

14.5 Wheel alignment check using string

of the swingarm (see Chapter 1, Section 1) on chain drive models. Next, measure the width of both tyres at their widest points. Subtract the smaller measurement from the larger measurement, then divide the difference by two. The result is the amount of offset that should exist between the front and rear tyres on both sides of the machine.

4 If a string is used, have your assistant hold one end of it about halfway between the floor and the rear axle, with the string touching the back edge of the rear tyre sidewall.

5 Run the other end of the string forward and pull it tight so that it is roughly parallel to the floor **(see illustration)**. Slowly bring the string into contact with the front edge of the rear tyre sidewall, then turn the front wheel until it is parallel with the string. Measure the distance from the front tyre sidewall to the string.

6 Repeat the procedure on the other side of the motorcycle. The distance from the front tyre sidewall to the string should be equal on both sides.

7 As previously mentioned, a perfectly straight length of wood or metal bar may be substituted for the string **(see illustration)**.

8 If the distance between the string and tyre is greater on one side, or if the rear wheel appears to be out of alignment, have your machine checked by a BMW dealer or frame specialist.

9 If the front-to-back alignment is correct, the wheels still may be out of alignment vertically.

10 Using a plumb bob or spirit level, check the rear wheel to make sure it is vertical. To do this, hold the string of the plumb bob against

the tyre upper sidewall and allow the weight to settle just off the floor. If the string touches both the upper and lower tyre sidewalls and is perfectly straight, the wheel is vertical. If it is not, adjust the stand until it is.

11 Once the rear wheel is vertical, check the front wheel in the same manner. If both wheels are not perfectly vertical, the frame and/or major suspension components are bent.

15 Front wheel

Removal

1 Position the motorcycle on its centrestand or an auxiliary stand so that the front wheel is off the ground. Always make sure the motorcycle is properly supported.

2 Displace the front brake caliper (see Section 3). Support the caliper with a cable-tie or a bungee cord so that no strain is placed on the hydraulic hose. There is no need to disconnect the hose from the caliper. **Note:** *Do not operate the front brake lever with the caliper removed.*

3 On ABS equipped models unscrew the wheel sensor bolt and displace the sensor from the fork, noting any shim fitted with it **(see illustration)** – there is no need to disconnect the wiring, just tie the sensor out of the way.

4 On Funduro and ST models slacken the axle clamp nuts on the bottom of the right-hand fork **(see illustration)** – remove the front

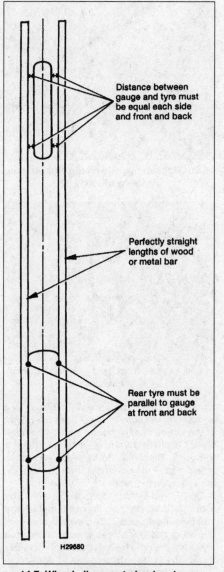

Distance between gauge and tyre must be equal each side and front and back

Perfectly straight lengths of wood or metal bar

Rear tyre must be parallel to gauge at front and back

14.7 Wheel alignment check using a straight edge

15.3 Unscrew the bolt (arrowed) and displace the sensor

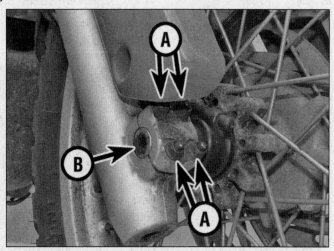

15.4 Slacken the axle clamp nuts (A), then unscrew the axle (B)

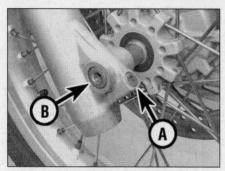

15.5a Slacken the axle clamp bolt (A), then unscrew the axle (B)

15.5b Withdraw the axle and remove the wheel

15.5c Remove the spacer from the left-hand side . . .

15.5d . . . and from the right-hand side of the wheel

15.6a Unscrew the axle bolt (A), then slacken the clamp bolt (B) on each side

15.6b Slide a screwdriver through the holes in the end of the axle to use as a handle to ease removal

mudguard to improve access if required (see Chapter 8). Unscrew the axle. Take the weight of the wheel, then withdraw the axle from the right. Carefully lower the wheel and draw it forwards. Displace the speedometer drive housing from the right-hand side and remove the spacer from the left.

5 On GS and Dakar models slacken the axle clamp bolt on the bottom of the right-hand fork (see illustration). Unscrew the axle. Take the weight of the wheel, then withdraw the axle from the right (see illustration). Carefully lower the wheel and draw it forwards. Remove the spacer from each side of the wheel, noting which fits where (see illustration).

6 On CS models unscrew the axle bolt (see illustration). Slacken the axle clamp bolt on the bottom of each fork. Take the weight of

the wheel, then withdraw the axle from the left (see illustration). Carefully lower the wheel and draw it forwards. Remove the spacer from each side of the wheel.

7 Clean all old grease off the speedometer drive housing (Funduro and ST models), spacer(s), axle and seals.

Caution: Do not allow the wheel to rest on the disc – it could become warped. If you lay the wheel flat set it on wood blocks.

8 Check the axle is straight by rolling it on a flat surface such as a piece of plate glass (first remove any corrosion using wire wool). If the equipment is available, place the axle in V-blocks and measure the runout using a dial gauge. If the axle is bent replace it with a new one.

9 Check the condition of the grease seals and wheel bearings (see Section 17).

Installation

10 Apply a smear of grease to the inside and outside of the wheel spacer(s), and on Funduro and ST models to the inside of the speedometer drive housing. Fit the spacers into each side of the wheel where possible, or as you fit the wheel, depending on type.

11 Manoeuvre the wheel into position between the forks with the disc on the left - if a new tyre has been fitted check that its directional arrow is pointing in the normal direction of rotation (see illustration). Apply a thin coat of grease to the axle.

12 On Funduro and ST models fit the speedometer drive housing onto the right-hand side of the wheel, making sure the drive tabs engage, and fit the spacer into the left side of the wheel. Lift the wheel into place, making sure the drive housing and spacer are correctly positioned (see illustration). Slide the axle in from the right-hand side and thread it into the left-hand fork. Tighten the axle to the torque setting specified at the beginning of the Chapter. Lower the front wheel to the ground, then install the brake caliper (see Section 3). Apply the front brake a few times to bring the pads back into contact with the disc, then with the brake applied pump the front forks a few times to settle all components in position. Now tighten the axle clamp nuts, top first, then bottom, to the specified torque – if the clamp was removed make sure it is fitted with the UP mark at the top (see illustration 15.4).

13 On GS and Dakar models fit the spacer into each side of the wheel (see illustrations 15.5d and c). Lift the wheel into place, making sure

15.11 Make sure the directional arrows on the wheel and tyre point in the same direction

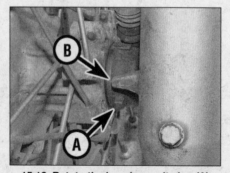

15.12 Rotate the housing so its lug (A) butts against the underside of the lug (B) on the fork

the spacers remain in position. Slide the axle in from the right-hand side and thread it in the fork **(see illustration 15.5b)**. Tighten the axle to the torque setting specified at the beginning of the Chapter **(see illustration)**. Lower the front wheel to the ground, then install the brake caliper (see Section 3). Apply the front brake a few times to bring the pads back into contact with the disc, then with the brake applied pump the front forks a few times to settle all components in position. Now tighten the axle clamp bolt on the bottom of the right-hand fork to the specified torque **(see illustration 15.5a)**.

14 On CS models fit the spacer into each side of the wheel. Lift the wheel into place, making sure the spacers remain in position. Slide the axle in from the left-hand side. Fit the axle bolt and tighten it to the torque setting specified at the beginning of the Chapter **(see illustration 15.6a)**. Lower the front wheel to the ground, then install the brake caliper (see Section 3). Apply the front brake a few times to bring the pads back into contact with the disc, then with the brake applied pump the front forks a few times to settle all components in position. Now tighten the axle clamp bolt on the bottom of each fork to the specified torque.

15 On models equipped with ABS, fit the sensor, along with any shim fitted with it, and tighten the bolt **(see illustration)**. Check the sensor air gap (see Section 10, Step 7).

16 Check for correct operation of the front brake before riding the motorcycle.

16 Rear wheel

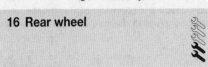

Funduro, ST, GS and Dakar models

Removal

1 Position the motorcycle on the centrestand or an auxiliary stand so that the rear wheel is off the ground. Always make sure the motorcycle is properly supported. Create some slack in the chain (see Chapter 1).

2 Unscrew the rear wheel cover/chain guard bolts and remove the cover/guard **(see illustration)**.

3 On GS and Dakar models with ABS unscrew the wheel sensor bolt and displace the sensor from the caliper bracket, noting any shim fitted with it **(see illustration)** – there is no need to disconnect the wiring, just tie the sensor out of the way.

4 Unscrew the axle nut and remove the washer **(see illustration)**.

5 Take the weight of the wheel, then withdraw the axle, and lower the wheel to the ground, making sure the caliper stays on the swingarm **(see illustration)**. If the axle is difficult to withdraw, drive it through, making sure you don't damage the threads. Note the washer with it.

6 Disengage the chain from the sprocket and remove the wheel from the swingarm **(see illustration)**.

15.13 **Tighten the axle to the specified torque**

16.2 **Remove the wheel/chain guard from the swingarm**

Caution: Do not lay the wheel down and allow it to rest on the disc or the sprocket. Set the wheel on wood blocks so the disc or the sprocket doesn't support the weight

16.4 **Unscrew the axle nut and remove the washer**

16.6 **. . . then disengage the chain and draw the wheel out the back**

15.15 **Fit the sensor and tighten the bolt**

16.3 **Unscrew the bolt and displace the sensor**

of the wheel. Do not operate the brake pedal with the wheel removed.

7 Remove the spacer from the left-hand side of the wheel **(see illustration)**. If required remove

16.5 **Withdraw the axle and lower the wheel . . .**

16.7a **Remove the spacer from the left-hand side of the wheel**

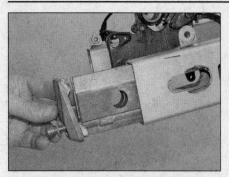

16.7b Remove the chain adjusters if required

the chain adjuster assembly from each side of the swingarm **(see illustration)**. Clean all old grease off the spacers, axle and seals.

8 Check the axle is straight by rolling it on a flat surface such as a piece of plate glass (first remove any corrosion with wire wool). If the equipment is available, place the axle in V-blocks and check the runout using a dial gauge. If the axle is bent replace it with a new one.

9 Check the condition of the grease seals and wheel bearings (see Section 17).

Installation

10 Apply a smear of grease to the inside of the wheel spacers, and also to the outside where they fit into the wheel. Apply a thin coat of grease to the axle. Fit the left-hand spacer with the narrow end fitting into the seal **(see illustration 16.7a)**.

16.11 Make sure the adjuster components are correctly aligned

11 Make sure the caliper bracket is correctly located on the swingarm. If removed, make sure the chain adjusters are correctly assembled with the nut locked in the cut-out **(see illustration)**. Slide the adjusters into the swingarm **(see illustration 16.7b)**.

12 Manoeuvre the wheel into position between the ends of the swingarm with the brake disc on the left-hand side – if a new tyre has been fitted check that its directional arrow is pointing in the normal direction of rotation. Engage the drive chain with the sprocket **(see illustration 16.6)**.

13 Lift the wheel into position and slide the axle with its washer in from the left **(see illustration 16.5)**, making sure the spacers and caliper remain correctly located. Fit the washer and axle nut but leave it loose **(see illustration 16.4)**.

14 Check and adjust the drive chain slack

(see Chapter 1). On completion tighten the axle nut to the torque setting specified at the beginning of the Chapter.

15 On GS and Dakar models with ABS fit the sensor, along with any shim fitted with it, and tighten the bolt **(see illustration 16.3)**. Check the sensor air gap (see Section 10, Step 7).

16 Operate the brake pedal several times to bring the pads into contact with the disc. Check the operation of the rear brake carefully before riding the bike. Install the rear wheel cover/chain guard **(see illustration 16.2)**.

CS models

Removal

17 Position the motorcycle on its centrestand or an auxiliary stand so that the rear wheel is off the ground. Always make sure the motorcycle is properly supported.

18 Remove the silencer (see Chapter 4B).

19 Remove the wheel nut cover **(see illustration)**. Remove the retaining ring, noting how it locates **(see illustration)**. Apply the rear brake and unscrew the axle nut – a 56 mm socket is required, and there should be one supplied with the bike and located under the seat **(see illustration)**. Remove the spring washer, the plain washer and the conical ring, noting which way round they all fit **(see illustrations)**.

20 Draw the wheel off the axle and lower it to the ground **(see illustration)**.

21 Check the condition of the grease seals and bearings in the rear hub assembly (see Section 17).

16.19a Remove the cover . . .

16.19b . . . and the retaining ring

16.19c Unscrew the nut using the socket provided

16.19d Remove the nut, the spring washer, the plain washer . . .

16.19e . . . and the conical ring . . .

16.20 . . . then remove the wheel

16.23 The drive pins on the disc carrier locate in the holes in the wheel

17.2 Lever out the bearing seal(s)

Installation

22 Clean the threads on the axle and the wheel nut. Smear some Optimoly TA grease onto the threads.

23 Lift the wheel onto the axle, locating the drive pins into the holes **(see illustration)**. Fit the conical ring, the plain washer and the spring washer, with the marked side facing out **(see illustrations 16.19e and d)**. Fit the wheel nut and tighten it to the torque setting specified at the beginning of the Chapter. Now tighten it further as required until the holes for the retaining ring end in the nut and axle align, then fit the ring **(see illustration 16.19b)**. Fit the wheel nut cover **(see illustration 16.19a)**.

24 Install the silencer (see Chapter 4B).

25 Operate the brake pedal several times to bring the pads into contact with the disc. Check the operation of the rear brake carefully before riding the bike.

17 Wheel bearings

Caution: Don't lay the wheel down and allow it to rest on the brake disc (front) or the disc/sprocket (rear) – they could become warped. Set the wheel on wood blocks so the wheel rim supports the weight of the wheel.

Note: *Always renew the wheel bearings in sets, never individually. Avoid using a high pressure cleaner on the wheel bearing area.*

Front wheel bearings

1 Remove the wheel (see Section 15).

2 On Funduro and ST models lever out the seal from the right-hand side of the hub using a flat-bladed screwdriver or a seal hook, then remove the speedometer drive plate, noting how the tabs locate. On GS and Dakar models lever out the seal from the right-hand side of the hub using a flat-bladed screwdriver or a seal hook **(see illustration)**. On CS models lever out the bearing seal from each side of the hub using a flat-bladed screwdriver or a seal hook. Take care not to damage the hub. Discard the seal(s) as new ones must be fitted on reassembly.

3 Inspect the bearings – check that the inner race turns smoothly and that the outer race is a tight fit in the hub (see *Tools and Workshop Tips* in the Reference Section). **Note:** *Do not remove the bearings unless they are going to be replaced with new ones.*

4 If the bearings are worn, remove the left-hand bearing using an internal expanding puller with slide-hammer attachment, which can be obtained commercially (see *Tools and Workshop Tips*) **(see illustrations)**. If necessary heat the bearing housing to ease removal. Remove the spacer which fits between the bearings.

17.4a Locate the curved bottom edge of the puller in the gap between the bearing and the spacer (arrowed) then expand the ends to lock it in place . . .

17.4b . . . then use the slide hammer to jar the bearing out

17.7 Using a socket to drive the bearing in

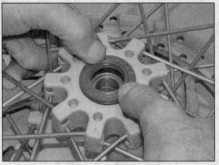

17.9 Press the seal into place setting it flush with the rim

17.11 Lift the sprocket coupling off the wheel

5 Either turn the wheel over and remove the remaining bearing using the same procedure, or leave the wheel as it is and drive the bearing out from the top using a suitable drift.

6 Thoroughly clean the hub area of the wheel and inspect the bearing seats for scoring and wear. If the seats are damaged, consult a BMW dealer or wheel specialist before reassembling the wheel.

7 Drive the new left-hand bearing, marked side facing out, into the hub until it seats using a bearing driver or suitable socket (see *Tools and Workshop Tips*) **(see illustration)**. Ensure that the driver or socket bears only on the outer race. Ensure the bearing is fitted squarely and all the way onto its seat. If necessary heat the bearing housing to ease installation.

8 Turn the wheel over and support it on the left-hand bearing so there is no possibility of driving it out when driving the right-hand bearing in. Install the bearing spacer and drive the new right-hand bearing in, again until it seats – there

should be at most only the smallest amount of axial play in the bearing spacer.

9 On Funduro and ST models smear the speedometer drive plate with grease and fit it into the right-hand side, locating the tabs in the cut-outs. Apply a smear of grease to the new seal, then press it **(see illustration)**. On GS and Dakar models apply a smear of grease to the new seal, then press it into the right-hand side. On CS models apply a smear of grease to the new seals, then press them into each side. Level the seal(s) with the rim of the hub with a small block of wood if necessary **(see illustration 17.19b)**.

10 Clean the brake disc using acetone or brake system cleaner, then install the wheel (see Section 15).

Rear wheel bearings

Funduro, ST, GS and Dakar models

11 Remove the wheel (see Section 16). Lift the sprocket coupling out of the hub (see

illustration). On Funduro and ST models remove the spacer from the inner side.

12 Lever out the bearing seal from the left-hand side of the hub using a flat-bladed screwdriver or a seal hook **(see illustration)**. Take care not to damage the hub. Discard the seal as a new one should be fitted on reassembly.

13 Inspect the bearings in both sides of the hub – check that the inner race turns smoothly and that the outer race is a tight fit in the hub (see *Tools and Workshop Tips* in the *Reference* section). **Note:** *Do not remove the bearings unless they are going to be replaced with new ones.*

14 If the bearings are worn, remove the circlip securing the left-hand bearing **(see illustration)**. Remove the left-hand bearing using an internal expanding puller with slide-hammer attachment, which can be obtained commercially (see *Tools and Workshop Tips*) **(see illustrations 17.4a and b)**. If necessary heat the bearing housing to ease removal. Remove the spacer which fits between the bearings.

15 Either turn the wheel over and remove the remaining bearing using the same procedure, or leave the wheel as it is and drive the bearing out from the top using a suitable drift.

16 Thoroughly clean the hub area of the wheel and inspect the bearing seats for scoring and wear. If the seats are damaged, consult a BMW dealer or wheel specialist before reassembling the wheel.

17 Drive the new left-hand bearing, marked side facing out, into the hub until it seats using a bearing driver or suitable socket (see *Tools and Workshop Tips*) **(see illustration 17.7)**. Ensure that the driver or socket bears only on the outer race. Ensure the bearing is fitted squarely and all the way onto its seat. If necessary heat the bearing housing to ease installation.

18 Turn the wheel over and support it on the left-hand bearing so there is no possibility of driving it out when driving the right-hand bearing in. Install the bearing spacer and drive the new right-hand bearing in, again until it seats – there should be at most only the smallest amount of axial play in the bearing spacer.

19 Fit the circlip into its grove in the left-hand side. Apply a smear of grease to the new seal, then press it into the left-hand side of the hub **(see illustration)**. Level the seal with the rim of the hub with a small block of wood **(see illustration)**.

17.12 Lever out the bearing seal

17.14 Remove the circlip (arrowed)

17.19a Press the seal into place . . .

17.19b . . . you can set it flush using a piece of wood

20 Check the sprocket coupling/rubber dampers (see Section 21).

21 On Funduro and ST models fit the spacer into the sprocket coupling. Fit the sprocket coupling into the wheel **(see illustration 17.11)**. Clean the brake disc using acetone or brake system cleaner, then install the wheel (see Section 16).

CS models

22 Remove the rear drive axle and eccentric adjuster from the swingarm, then draw the adjuster off the axle (see Section 22).

23 Remove the circlip from the left-hand side of the adjuster. Lever out the outer bearing seal using a flat-bladed screwdriver or a seal hook. Take care not to damage the hub. Discard the seal as a new one should be fitted on reassembly.

24 Inspect the bearings in both sides of the adjuster. There is a needle bearing in the left-hand side – check that the rollers turn freely and smoothly and there is no damage to the cage. There is a caged ball bearing in the right-hand side – check that the inner race turns smoothly and that the outer race is a tight fit in the hub (see *Tools and Workshop Tips* in the *Reference* section). **Note:** *Do not remove the bearings unless they are going to be replaced with new ones.*

25 To remove the needle bearing, support the coupling on blocks of wood, needle bearing side down, and heat the bearing housing to approximately 40°C. Using oven gloves, lift the pulley coupling and tap it down onto the wooden blocks – the bearing should drop out. Lever out the inner bearing seal using a flat-bladed screwdriver or a seal hook.

26 To remove the caged ball bearing, remove the circlip. Support the coupling on blocks of wood, bearing side down, and heat the bearing housing to approximately 40°C. Using oven gloves, lift the pulley coupling and tap it down onto the wooden blocks – the bearing should drop out.

27 Thoroughly clean the adjuster and inspect the bearing seats for scoring and wear. If the seats are damaged, consult a BMW dealer or wheel specialist.

28 Heat the bearing housing again then drive the new caged ball bearing, marked side facing out, into the right-hand side of the adjuster until it seats using a bearing driver or suitable socket (see *Tools and Workshop Tips*). Ensure that the driver or socket bears only on the outer race. Ensure the bearing is fitted squarely and all the way onto its seat. Fit the circlip into its groove.

29 Drive the new inner grease seal into the left-hand side of the adjuster until it seats using a using a bearing driver or suitable socket (see *Tools and Workshop Tips*). Heat the bearing housing again then drive the new needle bearing, marked side facing out, into the left-hand side of the adjuster until it seats using a bearing driver or suitable socket (see *Tools and Workshop Tips*). Fit the outer grease seal, then fit the circlip into its groove.

30 Fit the eccentric adjuster onto the drive axle, then fit the assembly back into the swingarm (see Section 22). Clean the brake disc using acetone or brake system cleaner.

Sprocket or pulley coupling bearing(s)

Funduro and ST models

31 Remove the rear wheel (see Section 16). Lift the sprocket coupling out of the hub, and remove the spacer from the inner side **(see illustration 17.11)**. Pull the outer spacer out using a puller, or drive it out from the inside.

32 Lever out the bearing seal on the outside of the coupling using a flat-bladed screwdriver or a seal hook. Take care not to damage the rim of the coupling. Discard the seal as a new one should be fitted on reassembly.

33 Inspect the bearing – check that the inner races turn smoothly and that the outer race is a tight fit in the coupling (see *Tools and Workshop Tips (Section 5)* in the Reference Section). **Note:** *Do not remove the bearing unless it is going to be replaced with a new one.*

34 If the bearing is worn, remove the circlip. Support the coupling on blocks of wood, sprocket side down, and drive the bearing out from the inside using a bearing driver or socket.

35 Thoroughly clean the bearing seat and inspect it for scoring and wear. If the seat is damaged, consult a BMW dealer or wheel specialist before reassembling the wheel.

36 Drive the bearing, with its marked side facing out, into the coupling from the outside

until it seats using a bearing driver or suitable socket (see *Tools and Workshop Tips*). Ensure that the driver or socket bears only on the outer race. Ensure the bearing is fitted squarely and all the way into the seat. Fit the circlip into its groove.

37 Apply a smear of grease to the new seal, then press it into the coupling. Level the seal with the rim of the coupling using a small block of wood. Drive the outer spacer into the bearing from the outside.

38 Check the sprocket coupling/rubber dampers (see Section 21).

39 Fit the inner spacer then fit the sprocket coupling into the wheel. Install the wheel (see Section 16).

GS and Dakar models

40 Remove the rear wheel (see Section 16). Lift the sprocket coupling out of the hub **(see illustration 17.11)**.

41 Drive the inner spacer out of the outer spacer using a suitable socket, then remove the outer spacer **(see illustrations)**. Lever out the bearing seal on the outside of the coupling using a flat-bladed screwdriver or a seal hook **(see illustration)**. Take care not to damage the rim of the coupling. Discard the seal as a new one should be fitted on reassembly.

42 Inspect the bearings – check that the inner races turn smoothly and that the outer race is a tight fit in the coupling (see *Tools and Workshop Tips (Section 5)* in the Reference Section). **Note:** *Do not remove the bearings unless they are going to be replaced with a new one.*

43 If the bearings are worn, support the

17.41a Drive the inner spacer out of the outer spacer . . .

17.41b . . . and remove it . . .

17.41c . . . then remove the outer spacer . . .

17.41d . . . and lever out the seal

17.43a Push the spacer aside to reveal the inner race (arrowed) . . .

17.43b . . . then locate the drift on it as shown and drive the bearing out

17.43c Drive the outer bearing out using a socket

17.45 Using a socket to drive the bearing in

17.46a Fit the inner spacer into the inner bearing . . .

coupling on blocks of wood. Move the centre spacer (between the two bearings) aside then drive the inner bearing out from the outside using a suitable drift located on the inner race, and moving it round so the bearing is driven out squarely **(see illustrations)**. Remove the circlip and the spacer, then drive the outer bearing out from the outside using a socket on the inner race **(see illustration)**. If necessary heat the bearing housing to ease removal.

44 Thoroughly clean the bearing seat and inspect it for scoring and wear. If the seat is damaged, consult a BMW dealer or wheel specialist before reassembling the wheel.

45 Drive the outer bearing, with its marked side facing out, into the coupling from the inside until it seats using a bearing driver or suitable socket (see *Tools and Workshop Tips*) **(see illustration)**. Ensure that the driver or socket bears only on the outer race. Ensure the bearing is fitted squarely and all the way into the seat. Fit the spacer and the circlip, then drive the inner bearing in, again using a driver or socket on its outer race.

46 Drive the inner spacer in from the inside using a suitable socket until seated **(see illustrations)**. Apply a smear of grease to the new seal, then press it into the coupling **(see illustration)**. Level the seal with the rim of the coupling using a small block of wood.

17.46b . . . and drive it all the way through until it seats

17.46c Fit the new seal

17.46d Fit the outer spacer onto the inner spacer . . .

17.46e . . . then use sockets as shown to support the inner spacer while driving the outer spacer onto it

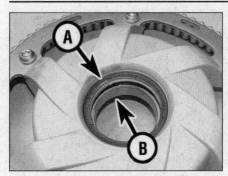

17.51 Seal (A) and bearing (B)

Support the inner spacer on a socket, then drive the outer spacer onto the inner spacer until seated **(see illustrations)**.

47 Check the sprocket coupling/rubber dampers (see Section 21).

48 Fit the sprocket coupling into the wheel **(see illustration 17.11)**. Install the wheel (see Section 16).

CS models

49 Remove the pulley coupling, then remove the back-plate and rubber dampers (see Section 21).

50 Inspect the bearing – check that the inner races turn smoothly and that the outer race

is a tight fit in the coupling (see *Tools and Workshop Tips (Section 5)* in the Reference Section). **Note:** *Do not remove the bearing unless it is going to be replaced with a new one.*

51 If the bearing is worn, lever out the bearing seal on the outside of the coupling using a flat-bladed screwdriver or a seal hook **(see illustration)**. Take care not to damage the rim of the coupling. Discard the seal as a new one should be fitted on reassembly.

52 Remove the circlip. Heat the bearing housing to approximately 80°C. Using oven gloves, lift the pulley coupling and tap the outer face down onto two wooden blocks so the bearing drops out between them.

53 Thoroughly clean the bearing seat and inspect it for scoring and wear. If the seat is damaged, consult a BMW dealer or wheel specialist before reassembling the wheel.

54 Drive the bearing, with its marked side facing out, into the coupling from the outside until it seats using a bearing driver or suitable socket (see *Tools and Workshop Tips*). Ensure that the driver or socket bears only on the outer race. Ensure the bearing is fitted squarely and all the way into the seat. Fit the circlip into its groove.

55 Apply a smear of grease to the new seal, then press it into the coupling **(see illus-**

tration **17.51)**. Level the seal with the rim of the coupling using a small block of wood.

56 Check the pulley coupling/rubber dampers (see Section 21).

57 Install the rubber dampers and back-plate, then install the pulley coupling (see Section 21).

18 Tyres

General information

1 The wheels fitted on Funduro, ST, GS and Dakar models are designed to take tubed tyres. On CS the wheels are designed to take tubeless tyres only. Tyre sizes are given in the Specifications at the beginning of this chapter.

2 Refer to the *Pre-ride checks* listed at the beginning of this manual for tyre maintenance.

Fitting new tyres

3 When selecting new tyres, refer to the tyre information in the Owner's Handbook. Ensure that front and rear tyre types are compatible, the correct size and correct speed rating; if necessary seek advice from a BMW dealer or tyre fitting specialist **(see illustration)**.

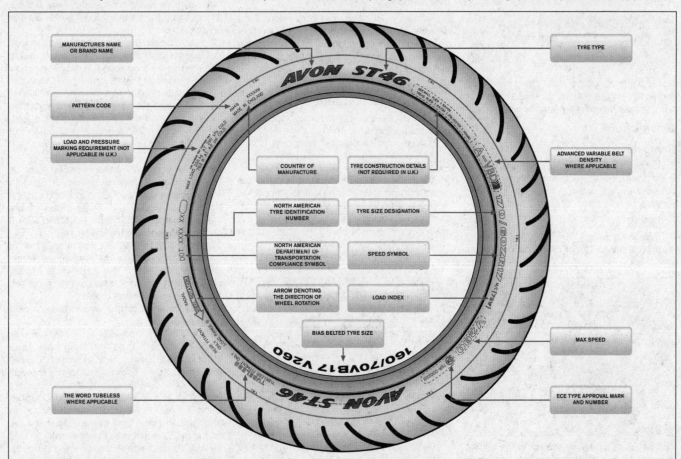

18.3 Common tyre sidewall markings

19.7 Unscrew the bolts (arrowed) and remove the cover – GS and Dakar shown

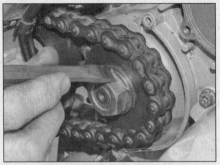

19.12 Bend back the tab(s) then unscrew the nut and remove the washer

19.14 Disengage the chain and draw the sprocket off the shaft

4 It is recommended that tyres are fitted by a motorcycle tyre specialist rather than attempted in the home workshop. This is particularly relevant in the case of tubeless tyres because the force required to break the seal between the wheel rim and tyre bead is substantial, and is usually beyond the capabilities of an individual working with normal tyre levers. Additionally, the specialist will be able to balance the wheels after tyre fitting.

5 Note that punctured tubeless tyres can in some cases be repaired. Seek the advice of a BMW dealer or a motorcycle tyre fitting specialist concerning tyre repairs.

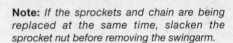

19 Drive chain and sprockets – Funduro, ST, GS and Dakar

Note: *If the sprockets and chain are being replaced at the same time, slacken the sprocket nut before removing the swingarm.*

Drive chain

Removal

1 Remove the front sprocket cover (see below).
2 Remove the swingarm (see Chapter 6).
3 Slip the chain off the front sprocket and remove it.

Cleaning

4 Refer to Chapter 1, Section 1, for details of routine cleaning with the chain installed on the sprockets.

5 If the chain is extremely dirty remove it from the motorcycle and soak it in paraffin (kerosene) or a dedicated chain cleaner for approximately five or six minutes, then clean it using a soft brush.
Caution: Don't use gasoline (petrol), solvent or other cleaning fluids which might damage its internal sealing properties. Don't use high-pressure water. Remove the chain, wipe it off, then blow dry it with compressed air immediately. The entire process shouldn't take longer than ten minutes – if it does, the O-rings in the chain rollers could be damaged.

Installation

6 Installation is the reverse of removal. Fit a new chain roller if the existing one is worn or damaged. On completion adjust and lubricate the chain following the procedures described in Chapter 1.

Front sprocket cover removal and installation

7 Unscrew the bolts and remove the cover (see illustrations).
8 Installation is the reverse of removal.

Sprocket check

9 Check the wear pattern on both sprockets (see Chapter 1, Section 1). If the sprocket teeth are worn excessively, replace the chain and both sprockets as a set. Whenever the sprockets are inspected, the drive chain should be inspected also (see Chapter 1). Always renew the chain and sprockets as

a set – worn sprockets can ruin a new drive chain and vice versa.

Sprocket removal and installation

Front sprocket

10 Remove the front sprocket cover (see Step 7).
11 On models up to 1997 remove the circlip securing the sprocket. Discard it and fit a new one on installation.
12 On 1997-on models bend back the locking tab on the washer using a suitable tool (see illustration). Have an assistant apply the rear brake, then unscrew the sprocket nut and remove the washer. If necessary heat the nut to loosen up the threadlock. Fit a new washer on installation.
13 Fully slacken the drive chain as described in Chapter 1. If the rear sprocket is being removed as well, remove the rear wheel now to give full slack (see Section 15). Otherwise disengage the chain from the rear sprocket.
14 Slip the chain off the sprocket and slide the sprocket off the shaft (see illustration). On Funduro and ST check the condition of the O-ring and replace it with a new one if necessary.
15 Smear some molybdenum grease (such as Optimoly TA) onto the shaft splines. On Funduro and ST make sure the O-ring is fitted. Engage the new sprocket with the chain, making sure the side marked EXT is facing out, and slide it on the shaft (see illustration 19.14).
16 If the rear wheel was removed, change the rear sprocket now then install the wheel (see Section 16). If the chain was merely disengaged, fit it back onto the rear sprocket. Take up the slack in the chain.
17 On models up to 1997 secure the sprocket using a new circlip.
18 On 1997-on models fit a new lockwasher with its raised tabs pointing out (see illustration). Clean the threads of the nut and shaft. Apply Loctite 243 to the threads of the nut and tighten it to the torque setting specified at the beginning of the Chapter, using the rear brake to prevent the sprocket turning. Bend up one of the tabs against a flat on the nut to lock it (see illustration).
19 Fit the sprocket cover (see above). Adjust and lubricate the chain following the procedures described in Chapter 1.

19.18a Slide a new washer onto the end of the splines and fit the nut with its recessed side innermost

19.18b Bend the tab(s) up against the nut

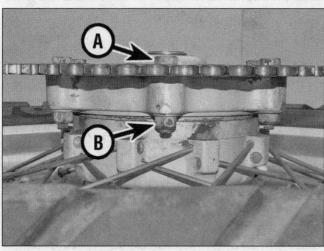

19.21 Counter-hold the bolt head (A) and unscrew the nut (B)

20.9 Front pulley nut (arrowed)

Rear sprocket

20 Remove the rear wheel (see Section 16).

21 Counter-hold the bolts then unscrew the nuts and remove the washers securing the sprocket to the hub assembly **(see illustration)**. Remove the sprocket, noting which way round it fits. Check the condition of the bolts and nuts and replace them all if any are damaged.

22 Fit the sprocket onto the hub with the stamped mark (denoting No. of teeth) facing out. Fit the bolts, washers and nuts and tighten them evenly and in a criss-cross sequence to the torque setting specified at the beginning of the Chapter.

23 Install the rear wheel (see Section 16).

20 Drive belt and pulleys - CS

Drive belt

Removal

1 Remove the front pulley cover (see below).

2 Remove the swingarm (see Chapter 6).

3 Slip the belt off the front pulley and remove it.

Installation

4 Installation is the reverse of removal. On completion adjust the belt tension following the procedure described in Chapter 1.

Front pulley cover removal and installation

5 Unscrew the bolts and remove the cover **(see illustration 19.7)**.

6 Installation is the reverse of removal.

Pulley check

7 Check the teeth on the belt and pulleys for wear and damage, and check the belt for any splits, cracks or exposed wires

Pulley removal and installation

Front pulley

Note: *On 2004-on models BMW specify that a puller (BMW part No. 271521 or equivalent) is needed to draw the pulley off, and that a threaded sleeve and press-on sleeve (part Nos. 271531 and 271532) are required to install the pulley – have the task performed by a BMW dealer if necessary to prevent potential damage to the shaft and pulley splines.*

8 Remove the front pulley cover (see Step 5).

9 On 2002 and 2003 models bend back the locking tab on the washer using a suitable tool. Put the bike into gear and have an assistant apply the rear brake, then unscrew the pulley nut and remove the washer **(see illustration)**. On 2002 and 2003 models Fit a new washer on installation. On 2004-on models BMW specify to use a new nut as it comes pre-treated with a special threadlock.

10 Fully slacken the drive belt as described in Chapter 1.

11 Slide or pull the pulley off the shaft and slip the belt off the pulley. On 2002 and 2003 models remove the two segments of the spit thrust washer.

12 Smear some molybdenum grease (such as Optimoly TA) onto the shaft splines.

13 On 2002 and 2003 models clean the threads

20.16 Unscrew the nut to allow some downward movement in the guard

of the nut and shaft. Fit the two segments of the thrust washer, using a dab of grease to hold them in place. Engage the pulley with the belt, making sure the side marked OUT is facing out, and slide it on the shaft **(see illustration 20.9)**. Fit a new lockwasher. Take up the slack in the belt to prevent it slipping over the pulley teeth. Apply Loctite 638 to the threads of the nut and tighten it to the torque setting specified at the beginning of the Chapter, using the rear brake to prevent the pulley turning. Bend up one side of the washer against a flat on the nut to lock it.

14 On 2004-on models clean the threads of the shaft. Screw the threaded sleeve (see **Note**) onto the shaft. Engage the pulley with the belt, making sure the side marked OUT is facing out, and slide it over the sleeve and onto the shaft, aligning the splines **(see illustration 20.9)**. Using the press-on sleeve fitted over the threaded sleeve, press the pulley onto the shaft until it seats. Remove the sleeves. Take up the slack in the belt to prevent it slipping over the pulley teeth. Fit the new nut and tighten it to the torque setting specified at the beginning of the Chapter, using the rear brake to prevent the pulley turning. Note that the threadlock on the nut should be allowed 6 hours to cure before using the bike.

15 Fit the sprocket cover (see above). Adjust the belt tension as described in Chapter 1.

Rear pulley

16 Unscrew the rear nut securing the belt guard, then draw the guard down **(see illustration)**. Create some slack in the drivebelt (see Chapter 1).

17 Lock the rear wheel by applying the rear brake then unscrew the pulley bolts **(see illustration)**. Remove the pulley from the carrier and slip it out of the belt.

18 Make sure the contact surfaces between the pulley and the carrier are clean. Clean the threads of the pulley bolts.

19 Fit the pulley onto the carrier. Fit the bolts and tighten them evenly and in a criss-cross

20.17 Rear pulley bolts (arrowed)

21.3 Check the rubber dampers as described

sequence to the torque setting specified at the beginning of the Chapter, using the rear brake to lock the wheel.
20 Remount the belt guard. Adjust the belt tension as described in Chapter 1.

21 Rear sprocket/pulley coupling/rubber dampers

Funduro, ST, GS and Dakar

1 Remove the rear wheel (see Section 16). Check for play between the sprocket coupling

and the wheel hub by turning the sprocket. Any play indicates worn rubber damper segments.
Caution: Do not lay the wheel down on the disc as it could become warped. Lay the wheel on wooden blocks so that the disc is off the ground.
2 Lift the sprocket coupling away from the wheel leaving the rubber dampers in position (see illustration 17.11). On Funduro and ST note the spacer inside the coupling and remove it if it is loose. Check the coupling for cracks or any obvious signs of damage.
3 Lift the rubber damper segments from the

wheel and check them for cracks, hardening and general deterioration (see illustration). Replace them with a new set if necessary.
4 Checking and replacement procedures for the sprocket coupling bearings are in Section 17.
5 Installation is the reverse of removal. On Funduro and ST make sure the spacer is correctly installed in the coupling.
6 Install the rear wheel (see Section 16).

CS

7 Unscrew the rear nut securing the belt guard, then draw the guard down (see illustration 20.16). Create some slack in the drive belt (see Chapter 1). Slip the belt off the rear pulley (see illustration).
8 Remove the retaining ring, noting how it locates (see illustration). Apply the rear brake and unscrew the coupling nut – a 46 mm bi-hex socket is required (see illustration). Draw the pulley coupling off the drive shaft (see illustration). Remove the spacer (see illustration).
9 Check for play between the back-plate and the coupling. Any play indicates worn rubber damper segments. Support the coupling on blocks and drive the back plate out of the bearing using a suitable socket

21.7 Slip the belt off the pulley

21.8a Remove the retaining ring . . .

21.8b . . . then unscrew the nut

21.8c Draw the coupling off the shaft . . .

21.8d . . . and remove the spacer

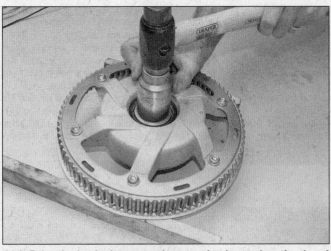

21.9 Drive the back plate out using a socket located on the rim of the splined shaft housing

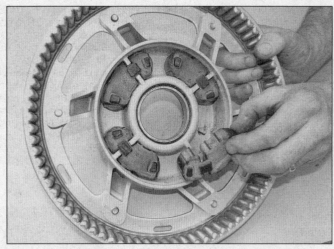

21.10 Check the rubber dampers as described

21.12a Fit the back plate . . .

21.12b . . . and tap it into the bearing

21.13 Fit the nut and tighten it to the specified torque

(see illustration). Check the coupling and back-plate for cracks or any obvious signs of damage.
10 Remove the rubber damper segments from the coupling and check them for cracks, hardening and general deterioration (see illustration). Replace them with a new set if necessary.
11 Clean the threads on the axle and the nut and the splines on the axle and back-plate. Smear some Optimoly TA grease onto the splines of the shaft and the back-plate.
12 Fit the damper segments into the coupling. Fit the back-plate and tap it into the bearing (see illustrations).

13 Fit the spacer (see illustration 21.8d). Slide the assembly onto the drive shaft (see illustration 21.8c). Fit the coupling nut and tighten it to the torque setting specified at the beginning of the Chapter, using the rear brake to lock the wheel (see illustration). Now tighten it further as required until the holes for the retaining ring end in the nut and axle align, then fit the ring (see illustration 21.8a).
14 Slip the belt onto the rear pulley (see illustration 21.7). Adjust the belt tension as described in Chapter 1. Remount the belt guard (see illustration 20.16).

22 Rear drive axle and eccentric adjuster - CS

1 Remove the rear wheel (see Section 16). Remove the pulley coupling (see Section 21).
2 Displace the rear brake caliper (see Section 7).
3 Displace the wheel speed sensor from the eccentric adjuster housing (see illustration). Unscrew and remove the eccentric adjustment screw (see illustration).
4 Grasp the input shaft/brake disc and draw it out, bring the eccentric adjuster with it (see illustration).

22.3a Undo the screw and displace the sensor

22.3b Remove the adjustment screw

22.4 Draw the shaft and adjuster assembly out of the swingarm

5 If you are separating the eccentric adjuster from the shaft, remove the brake disc (see Section 8).

6 The adjuster must be pulled off the shaft using a puller (BMW part Nos. 331552, 331307, 00750 and 331551, or equivalent).

7 Check the rear wheel bearings in the adjuster (see Section 17) and replace them with new ones if necessary.

8 Press the adjuster onto the shaft, making sure the end with the needle bearing faces the disc carrier, using BMW special tools (part Nos. 315691, 234782, 315611, 315696 and 315692) or suitable equivalent set-up, until it seats.

9 Install the brake disc (see Section 8).

10 Fit the adjuster all the way into the swing-arm from the left **(see illustration 22.4)**, setting it so the bore for the eccentric adjustment screw is aligned with the hole for it in the swingarm, then tighten the clamp bolts evenly and a little at a time first to the initial torque setting specified at the beginning of the Chapter, then to the final torque – this is just to set it square, do not worry about its position at this moment as this will be adjusted when tightening the belt after all components are installed.

11 Install the wheel speed sensor **(see illustration 22.3a)**. Thread the adjustment screw a couple of turns in but not it contacts the adjuster **(see illustration 22.3b)**.

12 Install the rear brake caliper (see Section 7).

13 Install the pulley coupling (see Section 21). Install the rear wheel (see Section 16). Clean the brake disc using acetone or brake system cleaner.

Chapter 8
Bodywork

Contents

Degrees of difficulty

Easy, suitable for novice with little experience	**Fairly easy,** suitable for beginner with some experience	**Fairly difficult,** suitable for competent DIY mechanic	**Difficult,** suitable for experienced DIY mechanic	**Very difficult,** suitable for expert DIY or professional

1 General information

This Chapter covers the procedures necessary to remove and install the bodywork. Since many service and repair operations on these motorcycles require the removal of the body panels, the procedures are grouped here and referred to from other Chapters.

In the case of damage to the bodywork, it is usually necessary to remove the broken component and replace it with a new (or used) one. The material that the body panels are composed of doesn't lend itself to conventional repair techniques. Note that there are however some companies that specialize in 'plastic welding' and there are a number of bodywork repair kits now available for motorcycles.

When attempting to remove any body panel, first study it closely, noting any fasteners and associated fittings, to be sure of returning everything to its correct place on installation. In some cases the aid of an assistant will be required when removing panels, to help avoid the risk of damage to paintwork. Once the evident fasteners have been removed, try to withdraw the panel as described but DO NOT FORCE IT – if it will not release, check that all fasteners have been removed and try again.

When installing a body panel, first study it closely, noting any fasteners and associated fittings removed with it, to be sure of returning everything to its correct place. Check that all fasteners are in good condition, including the trim clips and damping/rubber mounts; replace any faulty fasteners with new ones before the panel is reassembled. Check also that all mounting brackets are straight and repair them or replace them with new ones if necessary before attempting to install the panel.

Tighten the fasteners securely, but be careful not to overtighten any of them or the panel may break (not always immediately) due to the uneven stress.

2 Funduro and ST models

Seat

1 Insert the ignition key into the seat lock on the right-hand side and turn it to unlock the seat **(see illustration)**. Lift the rear of the seat then remove it, noting how it locates.
2 Installation is the reverse of removal. Make sure the seat locates correctly. Push down on the rear of the seat to engage the latch.

Side covers

3 Remove the seat.
4 Undo the two screws **(see illustration)**.

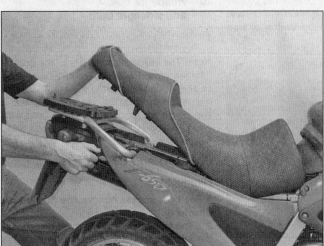
2.1 Removing the seat

2.4 Undo the screws (arrowed) . . .

2.5 . . . then release the peg from the grommet

2.7a Undo the screw (arrowed) at the bottom . . .

2.7b . . . and the screw at the top

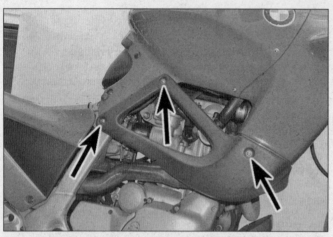

2.10 Engine trim panel screws (arrowed) – Funduro

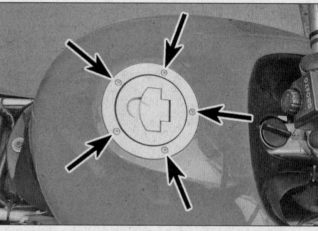

2.13 Undo the screws (arrowed) and remove the ring

5 Carefully pull the top front corner of the cover away from the frame to release the peg from the grommet **(see illustration)**.
6 Installation is the reverse of removal. Make sure the peg locates correctly.

Front mudguard

7 On Funduro models undo the two screws on each side securing the mudguard to the forks **(see illustrations)**. Draw the mudguard forwards. If required free the brake hose and speedometer cable from the brace, then unscrew the bolts securing the brace to each

fork and remove it.
8 On ST model undo the two screws securing the mudguard to the brace, noting how they secure the brake hose and speedometer cable guides. Draw the mudguard forwards. If required unscrew the bolts securing the brace to each fork and remove it.
9 Installation is the reverse of removal. Do not forget to secure the brake hose and speedometer cable.

Engine trim panels

10 Undo the screws (three on Funduro

and four on ST) and remove the panel **(see illustration)**.
11 Installation is the reverse of removal.

Fuel tank cover

12 Remove the seat.
13 Undo the filler cap ring screws and remove the ring **(see illustration)**.
14 Remove the engine trim panels.
15 Undo the screws securing the cover to the fairing and frame on each side **(see illustration)**.
16 Carefully draw the cover back and off the tank **(see illustration)**.

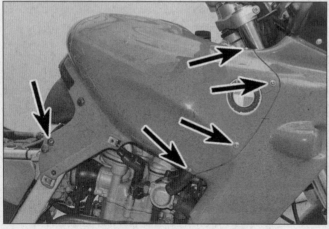

2.15 Undo the screws (arrowed) . . .

2.16 . . . and remove the top cover

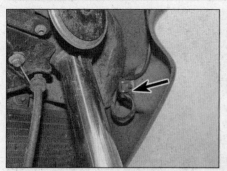

2.23 Release the wiring from the guides (arrowed)

2.24 Undo the screws (arrowed) on each side

2.25a Pull the sidelight out . . .

2.25b . . . then disconnect the headlight wiring connector . . .

2.25c . . . and the turn signal wiring connectors . . .

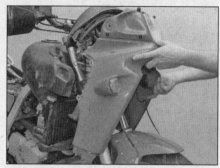

2.25d . . . and remove the fairing

17 Installation is the reverse of removal.

Windshield

18 Undo the four screws and remove the windshield.
19 Installation is the reverse of removal.

Fairing

20 Remove the windshield.
21 Remove the engine trim panels.
22 Undo the four screws securing the fairing to the fuel tank cover on each side (see illustration 2.15).
23 Release the turn signal wiring from the guides on each turn signal – this gives extra slack in the wiring (see illustration).
24 Undo the screws securing the fairing on each side (see illustration).
25 Carefully draw the fairing forwards, then pull the sidelight out of the headlight and disconnect the headlight and turn signal wiring connectors (see illustrations).
26 Installation is the reverse of removal.

Mirrors

27 Pull the boot up off the base of the mirror (see illustration).
28 Using a spanner on the base hex unscrew the complete mirror from the clutch lever bracket or brake master cylinder bracket, according to side.
29 Installation is the reverse of removal – thread the mirror into the bracket and tighten it, then adjust the mirror angle if required by counter-holding the base hex and slackening the adjuster nut above it, and turning the mirror stem. Tighten the adjuster when the mirror is correctly positioned.

Sump guard

30 Unscrew the bolts and remove the guard (see illustration).
31 Installation is the reverse of removal.

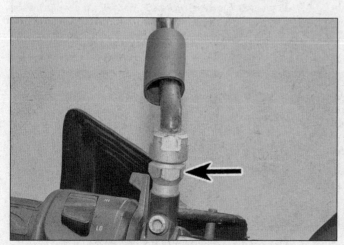

2.27 Pull the boot up to expose the hex (arrowed)

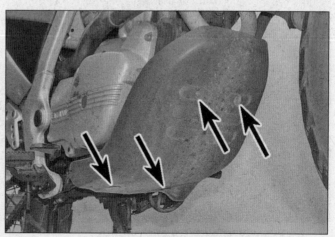

2.30 Sump guard bolts (arrowed)

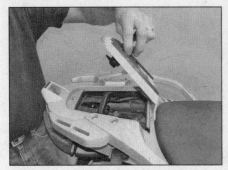

3.1a Unlock and remove the cover . . .

3.1b . . . then release and remove the seat

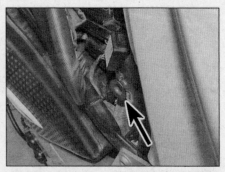

3.2 Make sure the seat locates correctly over the retainer (arrowed)

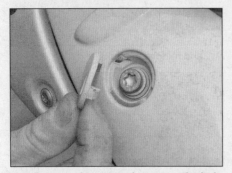

3.4 Remove the cap and unscrew the bolt

3.5a Undo the screws (arrowed) . . .

3.5b . . . and remove the cover

3 GS and Dakar models

Seat

1 Unlock and remove the storage compartment cover using the ignition key **(see illustration)**. Pull the seat release handle back, then lift the rear of the seat then remove it, noting how it locates **(see illustration)**.
2 Installation is the reverse of removal. Make sure the seat locates correctly at the front **(see illustration)**. Push down on the rear of the seat to engage the latch. Refit the storage compartment cover.

Rear side covers

3 Remove the seat.
4 Remove the bolt blanking cap, then unscrew the bolt **(see illustration)**.
5 Undo the two screws and carefully remove the cover, noting how it locates **(see illustrations)**.
6 Installation is the reverse of removal.

Front mudguard

7 To remove the upper mudguard unscrew the four bolts on the underside and manoeuvre the mudguard out **(see illustrations)**. If required undo the screws securing the top and bottom sections together and separate them.
8 To remove the lower mudguard first unscrew the nut securing the hose guide on the left-hand side and remove the guide **(see illustration)**. Unscrew the bolts securing the brace to the forks and draw the mudguard forwards **(see illustration)**. If required undo

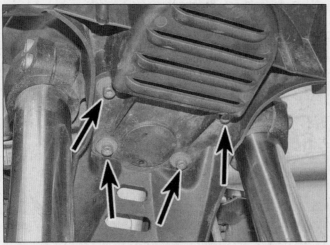

3.7a Unscrew the bolts (arrowed) . . .

3.7b . . . and remove the mudguard

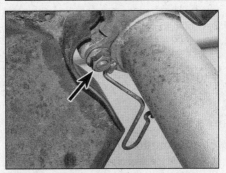

3.8a Unscrew the nut (arrowed) and remove the guide

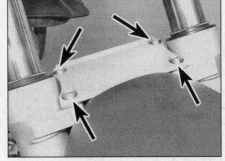

3.8b Unscrew the bolts (arrowed) and remove the mudguard

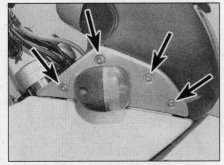

3.11a Undo the screws (arrowed) . . .

the screws securing the mudguard to the brace and separate them.

9 Installation is the reverse of removal.

Front side covers

10 Remove the seat.

11 Undo the turn signal panel screws and displace the panel, then disconnect the turn signal wiring connector **(see illustrations)**.

12 When removing the left-hand cover unscrew and remove the oil filler cap – replace the cap after the panel has been removed.

13 Undo the screw at the front, turning the handlebars so the mudguard is clear **(see illustration)**. Undo the two screws on the top and at the back **(see illustration)**. Carefully pull the bottom of the cover away to release the peg from the grommet and remove the cover, noting how it engages with the top cover **(see illustration)**.

14 Installation is the reverse of removal.

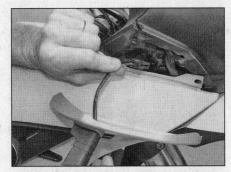

3.11b . . . then displace the panel and disconnect the wiring connector

Top cover

15 Remove the front side covers.

16 Undo the two screws and remove the cover **(see illustrations)**.

17 Installation is the reverse of removal – the

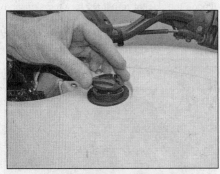

3.12 Remove the oil filler cap

two screws also secure the top of the electrical cover, so make sure this is properly in place.

Windshield

18 Undo the four screws and remove the windshield **(see illustration)** – note that

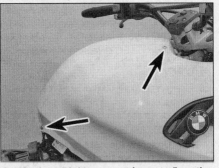

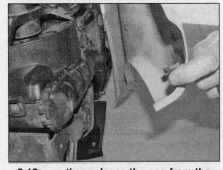

3.13a Undo the screw (arrowed) at the front . . .

3.13b . . . and the screws (arrowed) on the top and at the back . . .

3.13c . . . then release the peg from the grommet and remove the cover

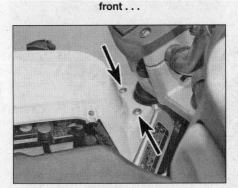

3.16a Undo the screws (arrowed) . . .

3.16b . . . and remove the top cover

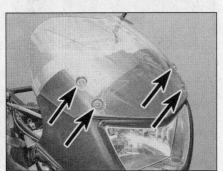

3.18 Undo the screws (arrowed) and remove the windshield

3.22 Undo the screws (arrowed) and remove the panel

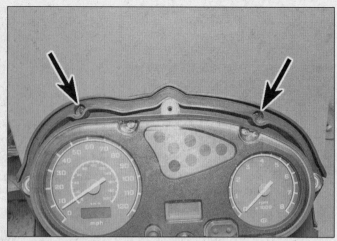

3.23 Undo the screws (arrowed) and displace the fairing . . .

3.24a . . . then disconnect the wiring connector . . .

3.24b . . . remove the boot . . .

3.24c . . . and pull the sidelight out

on some Dakar models, depending on the windshield fitted, there may be a spacer between it and the fairing.

19 Installation is the reverse of removal.

Fairing

20 Remove the windshield.
21 Remove the front side covers.
22 Undo the instrument trim panel screws and remove the panel **(see illustration)**.
23 Undo the screws securing the fairing **(see illustration)**.

24 Carefully draw the fairing forwards, bringing the headlight with it, then disconnect the headlight wiring connector, remove the rubber boot, and pull the sidelight out of the headlight **(see illustrations)**.
25 Installation is the reverse of removal.

Mirrors

26 Using a spanner on the base hex unscrew the complete mirror from the clutch lever bracket or brake master cylinder bracket, according to side **(see illustration)**.

27 Installation is the reverse of removal – thread the mirror into the bracket and tighten it, then adjust the mirror angle if required by counter-holding the base hex and slackening the adjuster nut above it, and turning the mirror stem. Tighten the adjuster when the mirror is correctly positioned.

Sump guard

28 Unscrew the bolts and remove the guard **(see illustration)**.
29 Installation is the reverse of removal.

3.26 Use the base hex to unscrew the mirror

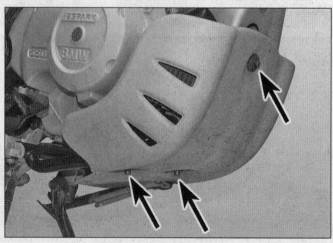

3.28 Sump bolts (arrowed)

4.1 Unlock and remove the seat

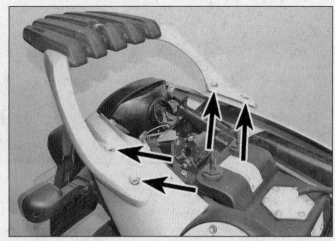

4.4a Unscrew the bolts (arrowed) and remove the rack . . .

4 CS models

Seat

1 Insert the ignition key into the seat lock on the right-hand side and turn it to unlock the seat (see illustration). Lift the rear of the seat then remove it, noting how it locates.
2 Installation is the reverse of removal. Make sure the seat locates correctly. Push down on the rear of the seat to engage the latch.

Rear side covers

3 Remove the seat.
4 Unscrew the luggage rack bolts and remove the rack, noting the washers (see illustrations).
5 Slacken the screw at the back, to the side of the seat lock (see illustration).
6 Undo the two screws and carefully remove the cover, noting how it locates (see illustrations).
7 Installation is the reverse of removal. Make sure the slot in the rear tab locates correctly around the screw at the back.

Front mudguard

8 To remove the front section undo the two screws on each side and draw the mudguard out to the front (see illustration).
9 To remove the rear section first remove the front wheel (see Chapter 7). Undo the screws and draw the rear section out to the rear.
10 Installation is the reverse of removal.

Top cover

11 Release the catch, unlocking it if necessary, and remove the top cover (see illustration).
12 Installation is the reverse of removal.

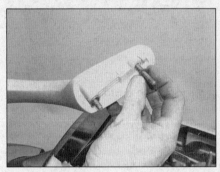

4.4b . . . noting the washers

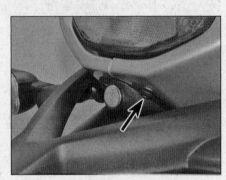

4.5 Slacken the screw (arrowed) . . .

4.6a . . . then undo the screws (arrowed) . . .

4.6b . . . and remove the cover

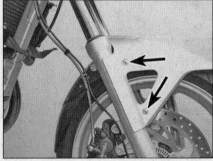

4.8 Undo the screws (arrowed) to release the front section

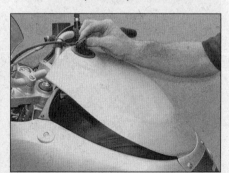

4.11 Release the catch and remove the cover

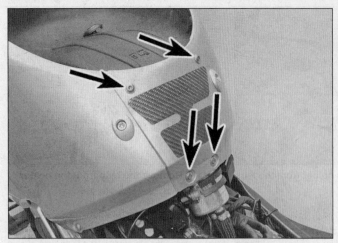

4.14 Undo the screws (arrowed) and remove the panel

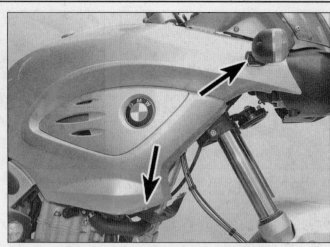

4.15a Undo the turn signal bolt and the bottom screw (arrowed)

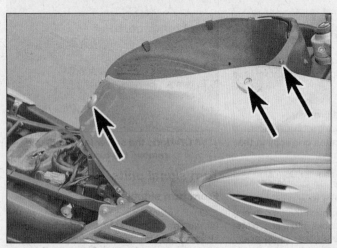

4.15b Undo the screw and the bolts . . .

4.15c . . . then displace the cover . . .

Front side covers

13 Remove the seat, and the top cover if fitted.

14 Remove the rear panel (see illustration).

15 Unscrew the front turn signal bolt and the screw securing the bottom of the cover (see illustration). Undo the screw joining the side cover to the front panel and the bolts on the top and at the back, and if fitted remove the hand rails (see illustration). Carefully displace the cover, noting how it locates, and disconnect the turn signal wiring connector when accessible (see illustrations).

16 Installation is the reverse of removal.

Frame covers

17 Remove the front side covers. Undo the screws and remove the cover from each side of the frame (see illustration).

18 Installation is the reverse of removal.

Windshield

19 Undo the four screws and remove the windshield (see illustration).

20 If required undo the two screws securing

4.15d . . . and disconnect the wiring connector

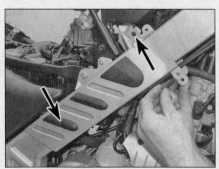

4.17 Undo the screws (arrowed) and remove the cover

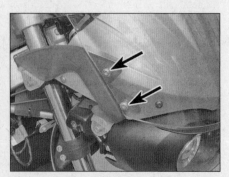

4.19 Undo the screws (arrowed) on each side and remove the windshield

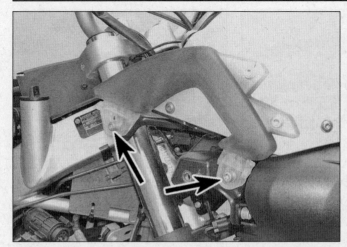

4.20 Undo the screws (arrowed) and remove the windshield holder

4.24a Undo the screws (arrowed) on each side . . .

each windshield holder and remove them **(see illustration)**.

21 Installation is the reverse of removal.

Fairing

22 Remove the windshield and the windshield holders.

23 Remove the front side covers.

24 Undo the screws securing the fairing and remove it **(see illustrations)**.

25 Installation is the reverse of removal.

Mirrors

26 Using a spanner on the base hex unscrew the complete mirror from the clutch lever bracket or brake master cylinder bracket, according to side **(see illustration 3.26)**.

27 Installation is the reverse of removal – thread the mirror into the bracket and tighten it, then adjust the mirror angle if required by counter-holding the base hex and slackening the adjuster nut above it, and turning the mirror stem. Tighten the adjuster when the mirror is correctly positioned.

4.24b . . . and remove the fairing

Chapter 9
Electrical system

Contents

Degrees of difficulty

Easy, suitable for novice with little experience	**Fairly easy,** suitable for beginner with some experience	**Fairly difficult,** suitable for competent DIY mechanic	**Difficult,** suitable for experienced DIY mechanic	**Very difficult,** suitable for expert DIY or professional

Specifications

Battery

Capacity	12 V, 12 Ah
Voltage	
Fully-charged	13.0 to 13.2 V, min 12.8 V
Discharged	below 12.3 V
Charging rate	
Normal	1.2 A for 5 to 10 hrs
Quick	4.0 A for 1 hr

Charging system

Current leakage	2 mA (max)
Max. power output	400W/14V
Max current output	29 A @ 7500rpm

Fuses

Ratings	see *Wiring Diagrams*

Bulbs

Funduro and ST models
Headlight 12V, 60/55W H4
Sidelight 12V, 4W
Brake/ tail light 12V, 21/5W
Turn signals. 12V, 10W
Instrument and warning lights
   High beam light. 12V, 2W
   All other lights. 12V, 3W

GS and Dakar models
Headlight 12V, 60/55W H4
Sidelight 12V, 5W
Brake/ tail light 12V, 21/5W
Turn signals. 12V, 10W
Instrument and warning lights 12V, 1.2W

CS models
Headlight . . . . 12V, 55W H1 and H3
Sidelight 12V, 5W
Brake/ tail light 12V, 21/5W
licence plate light 12V, 6W
Turn signals. 12V, 10W
Instrument and warning lights 12V 1.2W

Torque settings

Alternator cover bolts. . . . . 11 Nm
Alternator rotor nut. . . . . 180 Nm
Alternator stator bolts. . . . . 10 Nm
Fork clamp bolts (top yoke)
   Funduro and ST models. . . . . 25 Nm
   GS and Dakar models . . . . 23 Nm
   CS models . . . . 23 Nm
Ignition switch one-way bolts. . . . . 20 Nm
Oil pressure switch. . . . . 12 Nm
Oil return pipe banjo bolt (CS models). . . . . 42 Nm
Starter motor mounting bolts. . . . . 10 Nm
Steering head bearing adjuster (CS models)
   Initial setting . . . . 25 Nm
   Final setting . . . . 60° anti-clockwise
Steering stem clamp bolt (CS models). . . . . 23 Nm
Steering stem nut
   Funduro and ST models. . . . . 100 Nm
   GS and Dakar models . . . . 65 Nm

1 General information

All models have a 12 volt electrical system charged by a three-phase alternator with a separate regulator/rectifier.

The regulator maintains the charging system output within the specified range to prevent overcharging, and the rectifier converts the ac (alternating current) output of the alternator to dc (direct current) to power the lights and other components and to charge the battery. The alternator rotor is mounted on the right-hand end of the crankshaft.

The starter motor is mounted on the top of the crankcase in front of the cylinder. The starting system includes the motor, the battery, the relay and the various wires and switches. The clutch, neutral and sidestand switches are part of a starter interlock safety system.

Note: *Keep in mind that electrical parts, once purchased, often cannot be returned. To avoid unnecessary expense, make very sure the faulty component has been positively identified before buying a replacement part.*

2 Electrical system fault finding

1 A typical electrical circuit consists of an electrical component, the switches, relays, etc, related to that component and the wiring and connectors that link the component to the battery and the frame.

2 Before tackling any troublesome electrical circuit, first study the wiring diagram thoroughly to get a complete picture of what makes up that individual circuit. Trouble spots, for instance, can often be narrowed down by noting if other components related to that circuit are operating properly or not. If several components or circuits fail at one time, chances are the fault lies either in the fuse or in the common earth (ground) connection, as several circuits are often routed through the same fuse and earth (ground) connections.

3 Electrical problems often stem from simple causes, such as loose or corroded connections or a blown fuse. Prior to any electrical fault finding, always visually check the condition of the fuse, wires and connections in the problem circuit. Intermittent failures can be especially frustrating, since you can't always duplicate the failure when it's convenient to test. In such situations, a good practice is to clean all connections in the affected circuit, whether or not they appear to be good – where possible use a dedicated electrical cleaning spray along with sandpaper, wire wool or other abrasive material to remove corrosion, and a dedicated electrical protection spray to prevent further problems. All of the connections and wires should also be wiggled to check for looseness which can cause intermittent failure.

4 If you don't have a multimeter it is highly advisable to obtain one – they are not

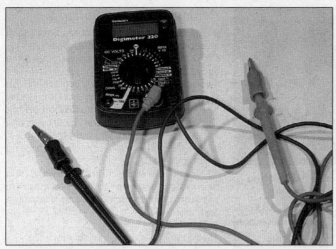

2.4a A digital multimeter can be used for all electrical tests

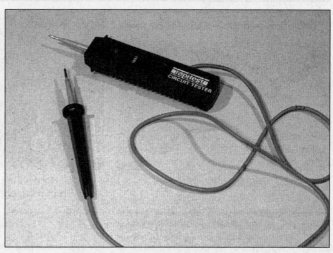

2.4b A battery-powered continuity tester

expensive and will enable a full range of electrical tests to be made. Go for a modern digital one with LCD display as they are easier to use. A continuity tester and/or test light are useful for certain electrical checks as an alternative, though are limited in their usefulness compared to a multimeter **(see illustrations)**.

Continuity checks

5 The term continuity describes the uninterrupted flow of electricity through an electrical circuit. Continuity can be checked with a multimeter set either to its continuity function (a beep is emitted when continuity is found), or to the resistance (ohms / Ω) function, or with a dedicated continuity tester. Both instruments are powered by an internal battery, therefore the checks are made with the ignition OFF. As a safety precaution, always disconnect the battery negative (-) lead before making continuity checks, particularly if ignition switch checks are being made.

6 If using a multimeter, select the continuity function if it has one, or the resistance (ohms) function. Touch the meter probes together and check that a beep is emitted or the meter reads zero, which indicates continuity. If there is no continuity there will be no beep or the meter will show infinite resistance. After using the meter, always switch it OFF to conserve its battery.
7 A continuity tester can be used in the same way – its light should come on or it should beep to indicate continuity in the switch ON position, but should be off or silent in the OFF position.
8 Note that the polarity of the test probes doesn't matter for continuity checks, although care should be taken to follow specific test procedures if a diode or solid-state component is being checked.

Switch continuity checks

9 If a switch is at fault, trace its wiring to the wiring connectors. Separate the connectors and inspect them for security and condition. A build-up of dirt or corrosion here will most

likely be the cause of the problem – clean up and apply a water dispersant such as WD40, or alternatively use a dedicated contact cleaner and protection spray.
10 If using a multimeter, select the continuity function if it has one, or the resistance (ohms) function, and connect its probes to the terminals in the connector **(see illustration)**. Simple ON/OFF type switches, such as brake light switches, only have two wires whereas combination switches, like the handlebar switches, have many wires. Study the wiring diagram to ensure that you are connecting to the correct pair of wires. Continuity should be indicated with the switch ON and no continuity with it OFF.

Wiring continuity checks

11 Many electrical faults are caused by damaged wiring, often due to incorrect routing or chaffing on frame components. Loose, wet or corroded wire connectors can also be the cause of electrical problems.
12 A continuity check can be made on a single length of wire by disconnecting it

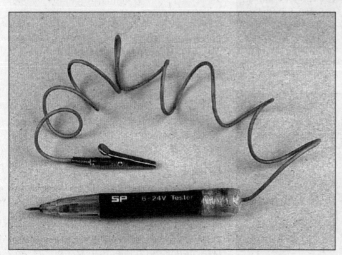

2.4c A simple test light is useful for voltage tests

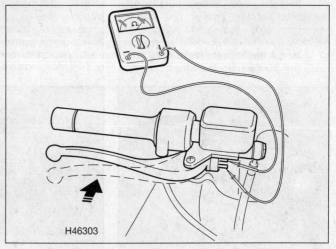

H46303

2.10 Continuity should be indicated across the switch terminals when lever is operated

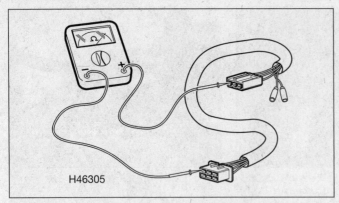

H46305

2.12 Wiring continuity check. Connect the meter probes across each end of the same wire

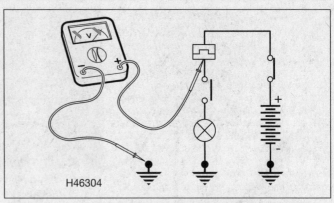

H46304

2.15 Voltage check. Connect the meter positive probe to the component and the negative probe to earth

at each end and connecting the meter or continuity tester probes to each end of the wire **(see illustration)**. Continuity (low or no resistance – 0 ohms) should be indicated if the wire is good. If no continuity (high resistance) is shown, suspect a broken wire.

13 To check for continuity to earth in any earth wire connect one probe of your meter or tester to the earth wire terminal in the connector and the other to the frame, engine, or battery earth (-) terminal. Continuity (low or no resistance – 0 ohms) should be indicated if the wire is good. If no continuity (high resistance) is shown, suspect a broken wire or corroded or loose earth point (see below).

Voltage checks

14 A voltage check can determine whether power is reaching a component. Use a multimeter set to the dc voltage scale, or a test light. The test light is the cheaper component, but the meter has the advantage of being able to give a voltage reading.

15 Connect the meter or test light in parallel, i.e. across the load **(see illustration)**.

16 First identify the relevant wiring circuit by referring to the wiring diagram at the end of this manual. If other electrical components share the same power supply (i.e. are fed from the same fuse), take note whether they are working correctly – this is useful information in deciding where to start checking the circuit.

17 If using a meter, check first that the meter leads are plugged into the correct terminals

on the meter (red to positive (+), black to negative (-). Set the meter to the dc volts function, where necessary at a range suitable for the battery voltage – 0 to 20 vdc. Connect the meter red probe (+) to the power supply wire and the black probe to a good metal earth (ground) on the motorcycle's frame or directly to the battery negative terminal. Battery voltage should be shown on the meter with the ignition switch, and if necessary any other relevant switch, ON.

18 If using a test light, connect its positive (+) probe to the power supply terminal and its negative (-) probe to a good earth (ground) on the motorcycle's frame. With the switch, and if necessary any other relevant switch, ON, the test light should illuminate.

19 If no voltage is indicated, work back towards the fuse continuing to check for voltage. When you reach a point where there is voltage, you know the problem lies between that point and your last check point.

Earth (ground) checks

20 Earth connections are made either directly to the engine or frame (such as neutral switch, oil pressure switch etc. which only have a positive feed) or by a separate wire into the earth circuit of the wiring harness. Alternatively a short earth wire is sometimes run from the component directly to the motorcycle's frame.

21 Corrosion is a common cause of a poor earth connection, as is a loose earth terminal fastener.

22 If total or multiple component failure is experienced, check the security of the main earth lead from the negative (-) terminal of the battery, the earth lead bolted to the engine, and the main earth point(s) on the frame. If corroded, dismantle the connection and clean all surfaces back to bare metal. Remake the connection and prevent further corrosion from forming by smearing battery terminal grease over the connection.

23 To check the earth of a component, use an insulated jumper wire to temporarily bypass its earth connection **(see illustration)** – connect one end of the jumper wire to the earth terminal or metal body of the component and the other end to the motorcycle's frame. If the circuit works with the jumper wire installed, the earth circuit is faulty.

24 To check an earth wire first check for corroded or loose connections, then check the wiring for continuity (Step 13) between each connector in the circuit in turn, and then to its earth point, to locate the break.

| 3 | Battery removal, installation, inspection and maintenance |

Caution: Be extremely careful when handling or working around the battery. The electrolyte is very caustic and an explosive gas (hydrogen) is given off when the battery is charging. Always disconnect the battery negative (-) lead first, and reconnect it last.

Removal and installation

1 Make sure the ignition is switched OFF. Remove the seat (see Chapter 8).

2 On Funduro and ST models remove the left-hand side cover (see Chapter 8). Unscrew the negative (–) terminal bolt and disconnect the lead from the battery. Unscrew the positive (+) terminal bolt and disconnect the lead. Detach the breather/overflow hose **(see illustration)**. Undo the battery holder screw **(see illustration)**. Remove the holder and remove the battery **(see illustration)**.

3 On GS and Dakar models remove the front

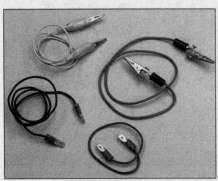

2.23 A selection of insulated jumper wires

3.2a Detach the hose . . .

3.2b . . . then remove the holder . . .

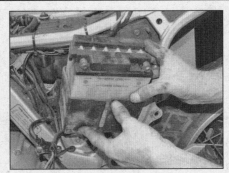

3.2c . . . and lift the battery out

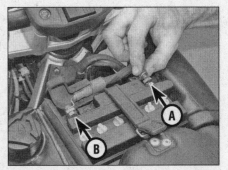

3.3a Disconnect the negative lead (A) first, then disconnect the positive lead (B)

3.3b Detach the hose (arrowed) . . .

3.3c . . . then release the strap . . .

Inspection and maintenance

6 The battery fitted to all models covered in this manual requires regular checking of the electrolyte level, and topping up when necessary – refer to Chapter 1 for details. In addition, the following checks should also be performed.

7 Check the battery terminals and leads are tight and free of corrosion. If corrosion is evident, clean the terminals as described in Step 5, then protect them from further corrosion (see *Haynes Hint*).

8 Keep the battery case clean to prevent current leakage, which can discharge the battery over a period of time (especially when it sits unused). Wash the outside of the case with a solution of baking soda and water. Rinse the battery thoroughly, then dry it.

9 Look for cracks in the case and replace the battery with a new one if any are found. If acid has been spilled on the frame or battery box, neutralise it with a baking soda and water solution, dry it thoroughly, then touch up any damaged paint.

10 If the motorcycle sits unused for long periods of time, disconnect the cables from the battery terminals, negative (–) terminal first. Refer to Section 4 and charge the battery once every month to six weeks.

11 Check the condition of the battery by measuring the voltage present at the battery

side covers and the top cover (see Chapter 8). Unscrew the negative (–) terminal bolt first and disconnect the lead from the battery **(see illustration)**. Lift up the red insulating cover then unscrew the positive (+) terminal bolt and disconnect the lead. Detach the breather/overflow hose **(see illustration)**. Release the battery strap and lift the battery out of its holder **(see illustrations)**.

4 On CS models remove the left-hand front side cover (see Chapter 8). Unscrew the negative (–) terminal bolt first and disconnect the lead from the battery **(see illustration)**. Lift up the red insulating cover then unscrew the positive (+) terminal bolt and disconnect

the lead. Detach the breather/overflow hose. Release the battery strap and lift the battery out of its holder.

5 On installation, clean the battery terminals and lead ends with a wire brush, fine sandpaper or steel wool. Reconnect the leads, connecting the positive (+) terminal first.

> **HAYNES HiNT** *Battery corrosion can be kept to a minimum by applying a layer of battery terminal grease or petroleum jelly (Vaseline) to the terminals after the leads have been connected. DO NOT use a mineral based grease.*

3.3d . . . and lift the battery out

3.4 Battery location on CS models

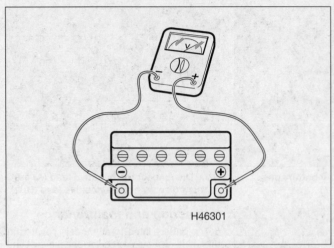

3.11 Measuring battery terminal voltage

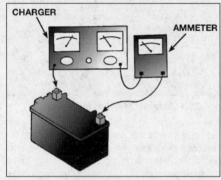

4.1 Battery connected to a charger

terminals. Connect the voltmeter positive (+) probe to the battery positive (+) terminal, and the negative (–) probe to the battery negative (–) terminal (see illustration). When fully-charged there should be around 13.0 to 13.2 volts present. If the voltage falls below 12.3 volts remove the battery (see above), and recharge it as described below in Section 4.

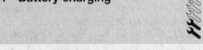

4 Battery charging

Caution: Be extremely careful when handling or working around the battery. The electrolyte is very caustic and an explosive gas (hydrogen) is given off when the battery is charging.

1 Remove the battery (see Section 3). Connect the charger to the battery, making sure that the positive (+) lead on the charger is connected to the positive (+) terminal on the battery, and the negative (–) lead is connected to the negative (–) terminal (see illustration).

2 BMW recommend that the battery is charged at the normal rate specified at the beginning of the Chapter. Exceeding this figure can cause the battery to overheat, buckling the plates and rendering it useless. If a basic charger without current control is used check

that after a possible initial peak, the charge rate falls to a safe level (see illustration). If the battery becomes hot during charging stop. Further charging will cause damage. **Note:** *In emergencies the battery can be charged at the quick rate specified. However, this is not recommended and the normal charging rate is by far the safer method of charging the battery.*

3 If the recharged battery discharges rapidly if left disconnected it is likely that an internal short caused by physical damage or sulphation has occurred. A new battery will be required. A sound item will tend to lose its charge at about 1% per day.

4 Install the battery (see Section 3).

5 If the motorcycle sits unused for long periods of time, charge the battery once every month to six weeks and leave it disconnected. An old battery that has become heavily discharged may require charging for longer than the 10 hours specified.

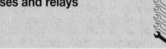

5 Fuses and relays

Fuses

Access

1 The electrical system components and

4.2 If the charger doesn't have an ammeter built in, connect one in series as shown. DO NOT connect the ammeter between the battery terminals or it will be ruined

wiring are protected from overload by fuses, which have different ratings for different circuits. If all circuits fail simultaneously it is likely the main fuse has blown (but check the battery and its terminals as well).

2 Remove the seat (see Chapter 8).

3 The fuses are housed together, inside a box on GS, Dakar and CS models – to access the fuses unclip the box lid (see illustrations). The identity of each fuse and its rating is marked on the inside of the lid and will correspond with the wiring diagrams at the end of this Chapter.

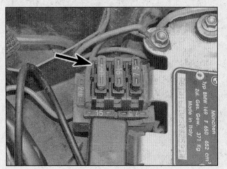

5.3a Fuse holder – Funduro and ST

5.3b Fusebox – GS and Dakar . . .

5.3c . . . unclip the lid to access the fuses

5.3d Fusebox – CS . . .

5.3e . . . unclip the lid to access the fuses

Check and replacement

4 The fuses can be removed and checked visually. If you can't pull the fuse out with your fingertips, use a pair of suitable pliers. A blown fuse is easily identified by a break in the element **(see illustration)**. Each fuse is clearly marked with its rating and must only be replaced by a fuse of the correct rating.

5 A spare fuse of each rating is supplied.

6 If a spare fuse is used, always replace it with a new one so that a spare of each rating is carried on the bike at all times.

 Warning: Never put in a fuse of a higher rating or bridge the terminals with any other substitute, however temporary it may be. Serious damage may be done to the circuit, or a fire may start.

7 If the new fuse blows immediately check the wiring circuit very carefully for evidence of a short-circuit. Look for bare wires and chafed, melted or burned insulation.

8 Occasionally a fuse will blow or cause an open-circuit for no obvious reason. Corrosion of the fuse ends and fusebox terminals may occur and cause poor fuse contact. If this happens, remove the corrosion with a wire brush or emery paper, and/or use a dedicated electrical contact cleaner, then spray the fuse end and terminals with a protection spray.

Relays

9 The electrical system incorporates various relays, and a relay/diode unit for the starter interlock circuit – refer to the *Wiring diagrams* at the end of the Chapter for more details. The starter relay is covered in Section 21. BMW provide no test details for the relays covered in this Section, so in the event of a problem in a circuit containing a relay, after checking for a blown fuse, loose or broken terminals, connectors and broken wires remove the relay and check the terminals and socket for corrosion, cleaning them as required. Refit the relay and check the function of the circuit. If the problem still exists substitute the relay with another one and see if the problem is solved.

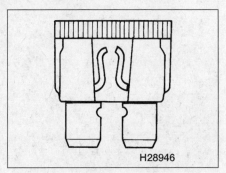

5.4 A blown fuse can be identified by a break in its element

10 On Funduro and ST models remove the seat for the turn signal relay and the fairing for the starter interlock circuit relay and diode unit (see Chapter 8) **(see illustrations)**.

11 On GS and Dakar models remove the top cover (see Chapter 8). Displace the starter relay from its mount **(see illustration)**. Undo

5.10a Turn signal relay (arrowed)

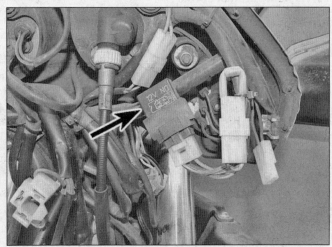

5.10b Starter interlock circuit relay and diode unit (arrowed)

5.11a Displace the starter relay . . .

5.11b . . . then undo the screw and displace the cover . . .

5.11c . . . the turn signal relay is clipped to it . . .

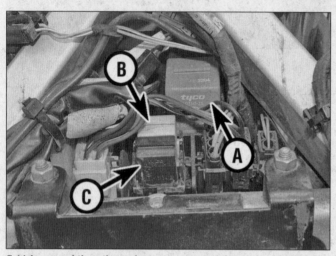

5.11d . . . and the other relays are connected to the sockets in the tray - starter interlock circuit relay and diode unit (A); BMS (fuel injection) relay (B); relief relay (C)

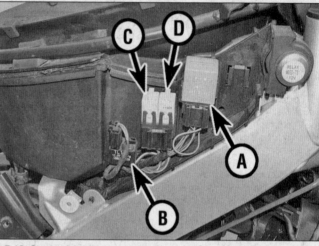

5.12 Starter interlock circuit relay and diode unit (A); turn signal relay (B); BMS (fuel injection) relay (C); relief relay (D)

the bolt securing the electrical cover and remove the cover – the turn signal relay is clipped to its underside, and the other relays are in the electrical tray (see illustrations).

12 On CS models remove the right-hand front side cover (see Chapter 8) (see illustration).

6 Lighting system check

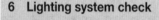

1 If a light fails first check the bulb (see relevant Section), and the bulb terminals in the holder. When checking for a blown filament in a bulb, it is advisable to back up a visual check with a continuity test of the filament as it is not always apparent that a bulb has blown. When testing for continuity, remember that on single terminal bulbs it is the metal body of the bulb that is the earth (ground).

2 If there is a problem with some or all the lights rather than just one check the battery and the fuse(s), and the ignition switch, and where appropriate the light switch or turn signal switch.

3 If the problem persists refer to Section 2 and to the wiring diagrams at the end of the Chapter and check all the wiring, connectors and terminals in the circuit(s) for loose or broken connections and poor contacts.

4 If the brake light fails to work also check the brake light switches (see Section 12).

5 If the turn signals fail to work also check the turn signal relay (see Section 5).

7 Headlight bulb and sidelight bulb

Note: *The headlight bulbs are of the quartz-halogen type. Do not touch the bulb glass as skin acids will shorten the bulb's service life. If the bulb is accidentally touched, it should be wiped carefully when cold with a rag soaked in methylated spirit and dried before fitting.*

Funduro and ST models

Headlight

1 For best access remove the fairing (see Chapter 8).

2 If the fairing was not removed disconnect the wiring connector, reaching up from the underside (see illustration).

3 Remove the rubber cover (see illustration).

7.2 Disconnect the wiring connector . . .

7.3 . . . then remove the dust cover . . .

7.4a ... release the clip ...

7.4b ... and remove the bulb

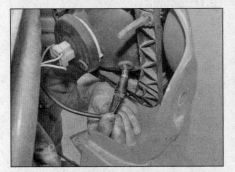

7.8 Pull the sidelight out of the headlight

4 Release the bulb retaining clip, noting how it fits, then remove the bulb (see illustrations).
5 Fit the bulb into the headlight, making sure it locates correctly, and secure it in position with the retaining clip.
6 Fit the rubber cover.
7 Connect the wiring connector (install the fairing if removed). Check the operation of the headlight.

Sidelight

8 Release the bulbholder from the right-hand side of the headlight, accessing it from the underside (see illustration). Carefully remove the bulb from the holder by pushing it in and turning it anti clockwise.
9 Fit the new bulb into the bulbholder then fit the holder into the headlight.

7.12a Disconnect the wiring connector ...

10 Check the operation of the sidelight.

 HAYNES HiNT *Always use a paper towel or dry cloth when handling a new bulb to prevent injury if the bulb should break and to increase bulb life.*

GS and Dakar models

Headlight

11 For best access remove the fairing (see Chapter 8).
12 If the fairing was not removed disconnect the wiring connector, turning the handlebar as required to improve access (see illustration). Remove the rubber cover (see illustration).

7.12b ... then remove the dust cover ...

13 Turn the bulb retaining ring anti-clockwise and remove it, noting how it fits, then remove the bulb (see illustrations).
14 Fit the bulb into the headlight, making sure it locates correctly, and secure it in position with the retaining ring, turning it clockwise to lock it.
15 If the fairing was not removed fit the rubber cover and connect the wiring connector.
16 Install the fairing if removed (see Chapter 8). Check the operation of the headlight.

Sidelight

17 Release the bulbholder from the right-hand side of the headlight, accessing it from the underside (see illustration). Carefully remove the bulb from the holder – if the bulb and holder have metal bodies push the bulb

7.13a ... release the ring ...

7.13b ... and remove the bulb

7.17a Pull the sidelight out of the headlight ...

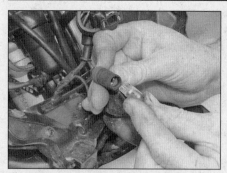

7.17b ... and remove the bulb

7.20 Remove the rubber cover from the back of each headlight to access the bulbs

7.25 Pull the sidelight (arrowed) out of the headlight

in and turn it anti-clockwise to release it, and if not just pull the bulb straight out **(see illustration)**.

18 Fit the new bulb into the bulbholder then fit the holder into the headlight.

19 Check the operation of the sidelight.

CS models

Headlight

20 Remove the rubber cover **(see illustration)**.

21 Either disconnect the wiring connector from the bulb, or disconnect it at the bullet connector, according to which bulb is being removed.

22 Release the bulb retaining clips and remove the bulb.

23 Fit the bulb into the headlight, making sure it locates correctly, and secure it in position with the retaining clips.

24 Connect the wiring connector and fit the rubber cover. Check the operation of the headlight.

Sidelight

25 Release the bulbholder from the headlight, accessing it from the underside **(see illustration)**. Carefully pull the bulb from the holder.

26 Fit the new bulb into the bulbholder then fit the holder into the headlight.

27 Check the operation of the sidelight.

8 Headlight

Removal and installation

1 Remove the fairing (see Chapter 8).

2 On Funduro and ST models undo the screws securing the headlight assembly to the fairing and lift it out **(see illustration)**. If required release the headlight unit from its frame.

3 On GS and Dakar models carefully release the headlight unit from the fairing by pressing out the three holders, which are a push fit **(see illustration)**.

4 On CS models undo the two screws securing the headlight shroud, then release the two clips on the top followed by the two on the bottom and remove the shroud **(see illustrations)**. Remove the rubber covers from the bulb-holders, and disconnect the bulb wiring connectors **(see illustration 7.20)**. Pull the sidelight bulbholder out **(see illustration 7.25)**.

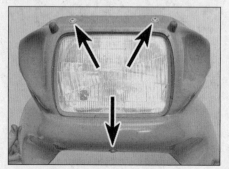

8.2 Undo the screws (arrowed) and remove the headlight

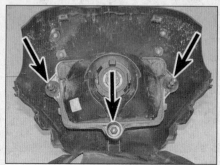

8.3 Release the holders (arrowed) from the fairing

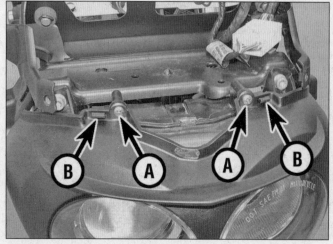

8.4a Undo the screws (A) then release the top clips (B) ...

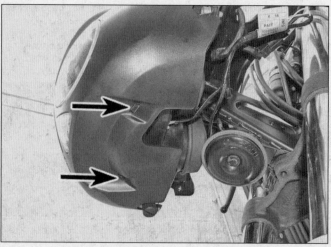

8.4b ... and the bottom clips (arrowed) ...

8.4c ... and remove the shroud

8.4d Unscrew the bolts (arrowed) on each side and remove the headlight

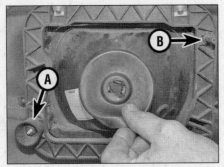

8.8 Vertical alignment adjuster (A); horizontal alignment adjuster (B) – Funduro and ST

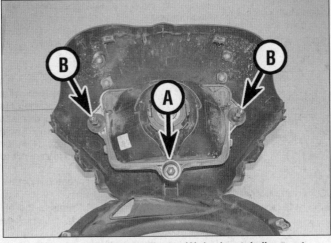

8.9 Vertical alignment adjuster (A); horizontal alignment adjuster (B) – GS and Dakar

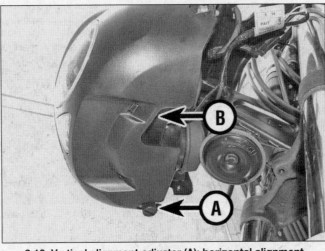

8.10 Vertical alignment adjuster (A); horizontal alignment adjuster (B) – CS

Release the cable-tie. Undo the four bolts securing the headlight and remove it **(see illustration)**.

5 If required remove the bulb(s) (see Section 7).

6 Installation is the reverse of removal. Make sure all the wiring is correctly routed, connected and secured. Check the operation of the headlight and sidelight. Check the headlight aim.

Headlight aim

Note: *An improperly adjusted headlight may cause problems for oncoming traffic or provide poor, unsafe illumination of the road ahead. Before adjusting the headlight aim, be sure to consult with local traffic laws and regulations – for UK models refer to MOT Test Checks in the Reference section.*

7 The headlight beam can adjusted both horizontally and vertically. Before making any adjustment, check that the tyre pressures are correct and the rear suspension is adjusted as required. Make any adjustments to the headlight aim with the machine on level ground, with the fuel tank half full and with an assistant sitting on the seat. If the bike is usually ridden with a passenger on the back, have a second assistant to do this.

8 On Funduro and ST models vertical adjustment is made by turning the adjuster knob on the bottom left of the headlight **(see illustration)**. Horizontal adjustment is made by turning the adjuster screw on the top right of the headlight.

9 On GS and Dakar models vertical adjustment is made by turning the adjuster knob on the bottom of the headlight in the middle **(see illustration)**. Horizontal adjustment is made by turning the adjuster screws on the side of the headlight.

10 On CS models vertical adjustment is made by turning the adjuster knob on the underside of the headlight on the right-hand end **(see illustration)**. Horizontal adjustment is made by turning the adjuster screw on the underside of the headlight just to the left of centre.

9 Brake/tail light bulb and licence plate bulb

Brake/tail light bulb

1 Undo the lens housing screws and remove the housing **(see illustration)**.

2 Push the bulb into the holder and twist it anti-clockwise to remove it **(see illustration)**.

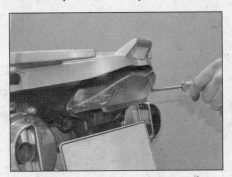

9.1 Undo the screws and remove the housing ...

9.2 ... then remove the bulb

9.5 Undo the screws and remove the housing

Check the socket terminals for corrosion and clean them if necessary.

3 Line up the pins of the new bulb with the slots in the socket, then push the bulb in and turn it clockwise until it locks into place. **Note:** *It is a good idea to use a paper towel or dry cloth when handling the new bulb to prevent injury if the bulb should break and to increase bulb life.*

4 Fit the lens housing and tighten the screws.

Licence plate light bulb (CS models)

5 Undo the housing screws and remove the housing **(see illustration)**.

6 Remove the rubber cover, then push the bulb into the holder and twist it anti-clockwise to remove it. Check the socket terminals for corrosion and clean them if necessary.

7 Line up the pins of the new bulb with the slots in the socket, then push the bulb in and turn it clockwise until it locks into place. Fit the rubber cap. **Note:** *It is a good idea to use*

a paper towel or dry cloth when handling the new bulb to prevent injury if the bulb should break and to increase bulb life.

8 Fit the housing and tighten the screws.

10 Tail light

Funduro and ST models

1 Remove the seat (see Chapter 8).

2 Disconnect the tail light wiring connector **(see illustration)**. Note the routing of the wiring and feed it through the tail light.

3 Undo the three nuts and remove the tail light, noting the washers and collars **(see illustrations)**.

4 Installation is the reverse of removal. Check the operation of the tail and brake lights.

GS and Dakar models

5 Remove the seat (see Chapter 8). Free the tail light wiring from its cable-ties to provide some slack. Unscrew the bolts securing the number plate/tail light holder and displace it, using a cable-tie or similar to hang it from the luggage rack **(see illustration)**. Note the captive nuts for the bolts and take care not to lose them.

6 Disconnect the wiring connectors from the tail light.

7 Undo the three nuts and remove the tail light, noting the washers and collars **(see illustration)**.

8 Installation is the reverse of removal. Check the operation of the tail and brake lights.

CS models

9 Remove the rear side covers (see Chapter 8). Disconnect the wiring connectors from the tail light, noting which fits where **(see illustration)**.

10 Release the retaining clip.

11 Undo the two bolts and remove the tail light, noting how it locates around the grommet **(see illustration)**.

12 Installation is the reverse of removal. Check the operation of the tail and brake lights.

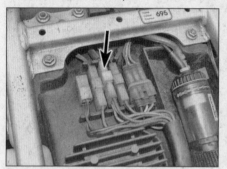

10.2 Disconnect the wiring connector (arrowed) . . .

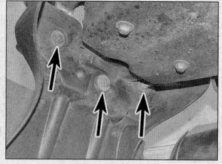

10.3 . . . then unscrew the nuts (arrowed)

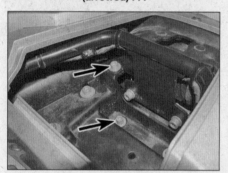

10.5 Unscrew the bolts (arrowed) on each side to free the holder

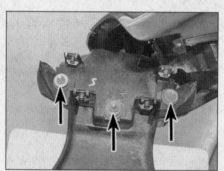

10.7 Unscrew the nuts (arrowed) and remove the tail light

10.9 Disconnect the wiring connectors (A), then release the clip (B)

10.11 Unscrew the bolts (arrowed) and remove the tail light

11.2 Undo the screw (arrowed) and remove the lens

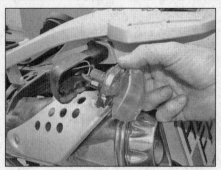

11.3 Release the bulb holder from the lens

11.4 Remove the bulb from the holder

11 Turn signals

Circuit check

1 Most turn signal problems are the result of a burned out bulb or corroded socket. This is especially true when the turn signals function properly in one direction, but fail to flash in the other direction. If this is the case, first check the bulbs, the sockets and the wiring connectors. If all the turn signals fail to work, first check the fuse, and then the relay (see Section 5). If they are good, the problem lies in the wiring or connectors (refer to Sections 6 and 2 and also to the wiring diagrams at the end of this Chapter), or the switch (refer to Section 16).

Bulb replacement

2 Undo the screw securing the lens and detach it from the housing, noting how it fits **(see illustration)**.
3 Detach the bulbholder from the lens **(see illustration)**.
4 Push the bulb into the holder and turn it anti-clockwise to remove it **(see**

11.6 Make sure it locates correctly in the housing

illustration).

Check the socket terminals for corrosion and clean them if necessary.
5 Line up the pins of the new bulb with the slots in the socket, then push the bulb in and turn it clockwise until it locks into place. **Note:** *It is a good idea to use a paper towel or dry cloth when handling the new bulb to prevent injury if the bulb should break and to increase bulb life.*
6 Fit bulbholder into the lens and the lens onto the housing, making sure they locate correctly, and secure them with the screw **(see illustration)**. Do not overtighten the screw as it is easy to strip the threads or crack the lens.

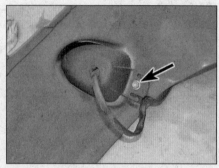

11.7 Undo the screw (arrowed) and remove the turn signal

Turn signal units

Front turn signals

7 On Funduro and ST models remove the fairing (see Chapter 8). Undo the screw securing the turn signal and detach it from the fairing, noting how it fits **(see illustration)**.
8 On GS and Dakar models undo the turn signal panel screws and displace the panel, then disconnect the turn signal wiring connector **(see illustrations)**. Undo the screw securing the lens and detach it and the bulbholder from the housing. Disconnect the wiring from the bulbholder. Unscrew the nut securing the stem to the panel **(see**

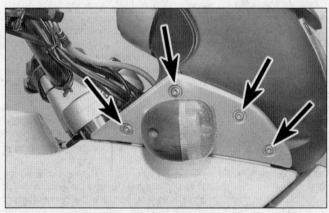

11.8a Undo the screws (arrowed) and remove the panel . . .

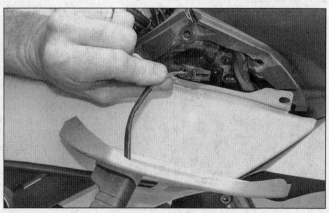

11.8b . . . then disconnect the wiring connector

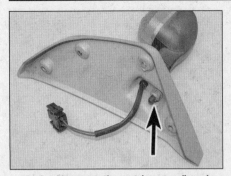

11.8c Unscrew the nut (arrowed) and remove the turn signal

11.11a Disconnect the wiring connectors (arrowed)

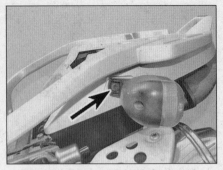

11.11b Unscrew the bolt (arrowed)

12.2 Front brake switch (arrowed)

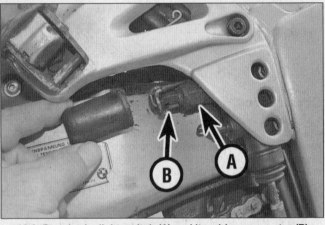

12.3 Rear brake light switch (A) and its wiring connector (B)

illustration). If required draw the wiring through to the inside of the panel.

9 On CS models remove the front side cover (see Chapter 8). Undo the screw securing the lens and detach it and the bulbholder from the housing. Disconnect the wiring from the bulbholder. Remove the stem from the panel. If required draw the wiring through to the inside of the panel.

10 Installation is the reverse of removal. Check the operation of the turn signals.

Rear turn signals

11 Undo the screw securing the lens and detach it and the bulbholder from the housing **(see illustration 11.2)**. Disconnect the wiring from the bulbholder. Unscrew the bolt securing the stem **(see illustrations)**. If required draw the wiring through to the inside of the panel.

12.4 Rear brake light switch (arrowed) - GS

12 Installation is the reverse of removal. Check the operation of the turn signals.

12 Brake light switches

1 Before checking the switches, check the brake light circuit (see Section 6).

2 The front brake light switch is mounted on the underside of the brake master cylinder **(see illustration)**. On Funduro and ST models remove the fairing (see Chapter 8). On GS and Dakar models remove the top cover (see Chapter 8), then displace the starter relay from its mount, undo the bolt securing the electrical cover and remove the cover **(see illustrations 5.11a and b)**. On CS models remove the air filter housing (see Chapter 4B). Trace the wiring from the switch and disconnect it at the connector. Using a continuity tester, connect the probes to the terminals in the loom side of the connector **(see illustration 2.10)**. With the brake lever at rest, there should be no continuity. With the brake lever applied, there should be continuity. If the switch does not behave as described, and the wiring and connector terminals are good, replace it with a new one – note the routing of the wiring and free it from any ties.

3 On Funduro and ST models the rear brake light switch is mounted on the back

of the master cylinder – pull the boot back and disconnect the wiring connector **(see illustration)**. Using a continuity tester, connect the probes to the terminals on the switch. With the brake pedal at rest, there should be no continuity. With the brake pedal applied, there should be continuity. If the switch does not behave as described, replace it with a new one – fit a new sealing washer with the switch, and bleed the rear brake system afterwards (see Chapter 7).

4 On GS, Dakar and CS models the rear brake light switch is mounted on the inside of the frame above the brake pedal **(see illustration)**. On GS and Dakar models remove the right-hand front side cover and on CS models remove the seat (see Chapter 8) to access the wiring connector, then trace the wiring from the switch and disconnect it at the connector. Using a continuity tester, connect the probes to the terminals in the switch side of the connector. With the brake pedal at rest, there should be no continuity. With the brake pedal applied, there should be continuity. If the switch does not behave as described, and the wiring and connector terminals are good, replace it with a new one – note the routing of the wiring and free it from any ties.

5 If the switch is good, check the wiring between the connector and the ignition switch via the fuse, and between the connector and the brake light bulb wiring connector (see *Wiring Diagrams* at the end of this Chapter).

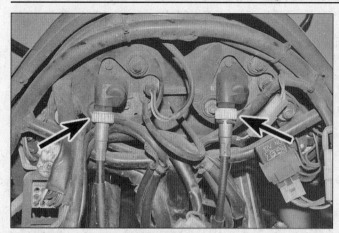

13.2a Unscrew the rings (arrowed) and detach the cables

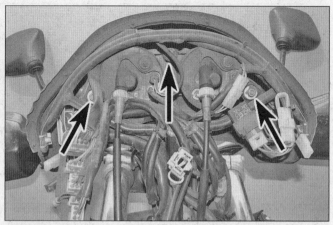

13.2b Unscrew the nuts (arrowed) and remove the instrument cluster

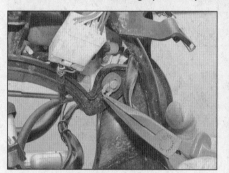

13.3a Release the three clips

13.3b Disconnect the warning light wiring connector . . .

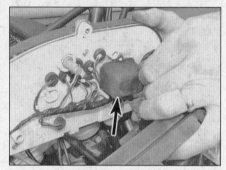

13.3c . . . then displace the cluster and pull the rubber boot back . . .

13 Instrument cluster

Removal and installation

1 Remove the fairing (see Chapter 8).
2 On Funduro and ST models detach the speedometer and tachometer cables **(see illustration)**. Carefully pull all the instrument and warning light bulbholders out of the casing. Disconnect the wiring at the connectors and from the instrument itself, as required. Unscrew the nuts and lift the instrument cluster off **(see illustration)**.
3 On GS and Dakar models disconnect the warning light wiring connector **(see illustration)**. Remove the clips and displace the instrument cluster. Pull the rubber boot off the instrument wiring connector, then release the catch and disconnect it from the instrument cluster **(see illustrations)**.
4 On CS models disconnect the warning light wiring connector **(see illustration)**. Pull the rubber boot off the instrument wiring connector, then release the catch and disconnect it from the instrument cluster. Remove the clips and displace the instrument cluster.

Disassembly

5 On Funduro and ST models each instrument is available separately. If you are removing the speedometer unscrew the trip reset knob retaining ring, then push the knob through the facia. Unscrew the nut(s) securing the instrument being removed and draw it out the front of the facia. Note the O-ring around

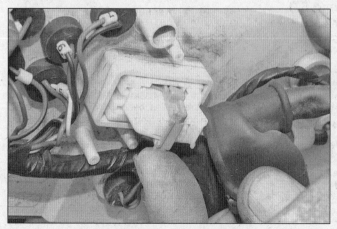

13.3d . . . and disconnect the instrument wiring connector

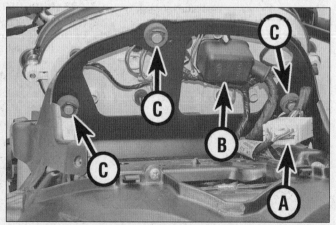

13.4 Warning light wiring connector (A), instrument wiring connector (B), clips (C)

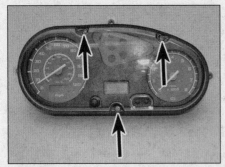

13.6a Undo the screws (arrowed) . . .

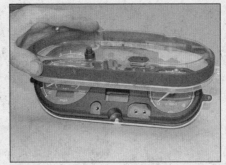

13.6b . . . and remove the outer cover . . .

13.6c . . . and the inner cover

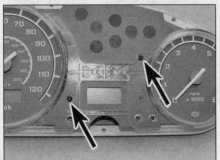

13.6d Undo the screws (arrowed) and remove the panel

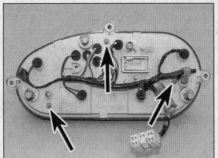
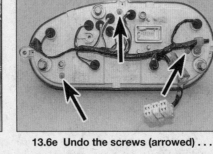
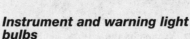
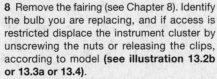

13.6e Undo the screws (arrowed) . . .

13.6f . . . then release the tabs . . .

each instrument and replace it with a new one if it is damaged, deformed or deteriorated. If required undo the drive gear housing screws and remove the housing from the back of the speedometer and/or tachometer. If required undo the warning light housing screws and remove the housing – all its components, including the individual light lenses, are available separately.

6 On GS, Dakar and CS models undo the screws on the front and remove the outer and inner covers **(see illustrations)**. Undo the two small screws on the front and remove the panel **(see illustration)**. Undo the three screws on the back, then release the tabs on the wiring socket while gently pulling the instrument board away from the housing so the tabs do not reseat after release **(see illustrations)**. Lift the instrument board out of the housing.

7 Reassemble the instruments in the reverse order.

Instrument and warning light bulbs

8 Remove the fairing (see Chapter 8). Identify the bulb you are replacing, and if access is restricted displace the instrument cluster by unscrewing the nuts or releasing the clips, according to model **(see illustration 13.2b or 13.3a or 13.4)**.
9 Carefully pull the relevant bulbholder out of the casing.
10 Remove the bulb and replace it with a new one, then fit the bulbholder back into the casing **(see illustration)**.
11 Check the operation of the bulb, then install the fairing.

Speedometer and tachometer cables (Funduro and ST)

12 Remove the fairing (see Chapter 8).
13 Detach the relevant cable from its instrument **(see illustration 13.2a)**.

14 If removing the speedometer cable detach it from the drive housing on the front wheel.
15 If removing the tachometer cable detach it from the engine.
16 Withdraw the cable, noting its routing.
17 Installation is the reverse of removal.

> **HAYNES HINT** *Before removing the cable from the bike, tape the lower end of the new cable to the upper end of the old cable. Slowly pull the lower end of the old cable out, guiding the new cable down into position. Using this method will ensure the cable is routed correctly.*

14 Oil pressure switch

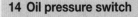

Check

1 The oil pressure switch is screwed into the crankcase behind the cylinder. The oil pressure warning display should come on when the ignition switch is turned ON and go out a few seconds after the engine is started. If the oil pressure warning light does not go out or comes on whilst the engine is running, stop the engine immediately and carry out an oil level check, and if the level is correct, an oil pressure check (see Chapter 2, Section 3).
2 If the oil pressure warning light does not come on when the ignition is turned ON, first check the bulb (see Section 13). If that is good

13.6g . . . and remove the instrument board

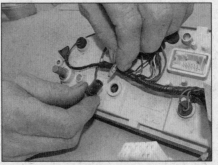

13.10 Pull the bulbholder out of the casing and remove the bulb

lift the rubber boot and disconnect the wiring connector from the switch **(see illustration)**. With the ignition switched ON, earth (ground) the wire on the crankcase and check that the warning light comes on. If it does, the switch is defective and must be replaced with a new one.

3 If the light still does not come on, check for voltage at the wiring connector. If there is no voltage present, check the wire between the switch and the instrument cluster for continuity (see the *Wiring Diagrams* at the end of this Chapter).

4 If the warning light does not go out when the engine is started or comes on whilst the engine is running, yet the oil pressure is satisfactory, detach the wire from the oil pressure switch (see above). With the wire detached and the ignition switched ON the light should be out. If it is illuminated, the wire between the switch and instrument cluster is earthed (grounded) at some point. If the wiring is good, the switch must be assumed faulty and replaced with a new one.

Removal

5 The oil pressure switch is screwed into the crankcase behind the cylinder.

6 Lift the rubber boot and disconnect the wiring connector from the switch **(see illustration 14.2)**.

7 Unscrew and remove the switch. Discard the sealing washer as a new one should be used.

Installation

8 Clean the switch threads and apply a thread lock (Loctite 243 or equivalent). Install the switch using a new sealing washer and tighten it to the torque setting specified at the beginning of the Chapter. Attach the wiring connector and fit the rubber boot **(see illustration 14.2)**.

9 Run the engine and check that the switch operates correctly without oil leakage.

15 Ignition switch
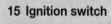

⚠ *Warning: To prevent the risk of short circuits, disconnect the battery negative (–) lead before making any ignition switch checks.*

Check

1 On Funduro and ST models remove the fairing (see Chapter 8).

2 On GS and Dakar models remove the top cover (see Chapter 8). Displace the starter relay from its mount **(see illustration 5.11a)**. Undo the bolt securing the electrical cover and remove the cover **(see illustration 5.11b)**.

3 On CS models remove the air filter housing (see Chapter 4B).

4 Trace the wiring from the ignition switch and disconnect it at the connector.

5 Using an ohmmeter or a continuity tester, check the continuity of the connector terminal pairs (see the *Wiring Diagrams* at the end of this Chapter). Continuity should exist between the terminals connected by a solid line on the diagram when the switch is in the indicated position.

6 If the switch fails any of the tests, replace it with a new one.

Removal

Note: *For security reasons the ignition switch is retained by shear-head bolts or one-way bolts (depending on model), which means they cannot be unscrewed using conventional tools. New bolts should be obtained before starting work.*

7 On Funduro and ST models remove the fairing (see Chapter 8).

8 On GS and Dakar models remove the top cover (see Chapter 8). Displace the starter relay from its mount **(see illustration 5.11a)**. Undo the bolt securing the electrical cover and remove the cover **(see illustration 5.11b)**.

9 On CS models remove the air filter housing (see Chapter 4B).

10 Trace the wiring from the ignition switch and disconnect it at the connector. Feed the wiring back to the switch, freeing it from any clips and ties and noting its routing.

11 Refer to Chapter 6, Section 9 and remove the top yoke – there is no need to remove the forks. On CS models make sure the front wheel is on the ground and the weight of the bike is on it.

12 Secure the yoke in a soft-jawed vice with plenty of rag to protect it, then tap the bolt heads around using a suitable chisel or punch until loose. Unscrew the bolts and withdraw the switch from the top yoke.

Installation

13 Tighten the new ignition switch bolts, preferably using shear-head bolts rather than the one-way bolts so you don't need a special tool, and tightening them until their heads shear off. If using one-way bolts tighten them to the torque setting specified at the beginning of the Chapter using BMW tool part No.510531. Make sure the wiring connector is correctly routed and securely connected.

14 On Funduro, ST, GS and Dakar models fit the top yoke onto the steering stem. Fit the steering stem nut and tighten it to the torque setting specified at the beginning of the Chapter. Tighten the fork clamp bolts to the specified torque.

15 On CS models fit the top yoke onto the steering stem. Thread the adjuster in and tighten it to the initial setting specified at the beginning of the Chapter. Turn the steering from lock-to-lock twice to settle the bearings, then position it at full left lock. Now slacken the adjuster by 60° (1/6th of a turn), using either a degree disc, or by making two marks, one on the adjuster and one 60° (1/6th of a turn) anti-clockwise from it on the top yoke, then bringing them into alignment. Tighten

14.2 Pull back the rubber boot and disconnect the wiring connector from the switch (arrowed)

the steering stem clamp bolt and the fork clamp bolts in the top yoke to the specified torque. Check the bearing adjustment again as described in Chapter 1 and re-adjust if necessary. Fit the plug into the adjuster.

16 Reconnect the wiring connector, making sure the wiring is correctly routed. Install all remaining components.

16 Handlebar switches

Check

1 Generally speaking, the switches are reliable and trouble-free. Most troubles, when they do occur, are caused by dirty or corroded contacts, but wear and breakage of internal parts is a possibility that should not be overlooked.

2 The switches can be checked for continuity using a multimeter or continuity tester.

3 On Funduro and ST models remove the fairing (see Chapter 8).

4 On GS and Dakar models remove the top cover (see Chapter 8). Displace the starter relay from its mount **(see illustration 5.11a)**. Undo the bolt securing the electrical cover and remove the cover **(see illustration 5.11b)**.

5 On CS models remove the air filter housing (see Chapter 4B).

6 Trace the wiring from the switch and disconnect it at the connector.

7 Check for continuity between the terminals of the switch connector with the switch in the various positions (i.e. switch off – no continuity, switch on – continuity) – see the *Wiring Diagrams* at the end of this Chapter. Continuity should exist between the terminals connected by a solid line on the diagram when the switch is in the indicated position.

8 If the continuity check indicates a problem exists, displace the switch housing and spray the switch contacts with electrical contact cleaner (there is no need to remove the switch completely) **(see illustration)**. If they are accessible, the contacts can be scraped clean and polished with crocus cloth. If switch components are damaged or broken, it will be obvious when the switch is disassembled.

16.8 Spray and clean the switch contacts

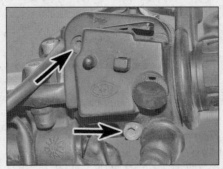

16.13a Handlebar switch housing screws (arrowed) – Funduro and ST, right-hand switches

16.13b Handlebar switch housing screws (arrowed) – Funduro and ST, left-hand switches

16.13c Handlebar switch housing screws (arrowed) – GS, Dakar and CS, right-hand switches

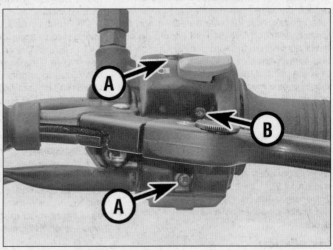

16.13d Handlebar switch housing screws (A) and pass switch retaining screw (B) – GS, Dakar and CS, left-hand switches

Removal and installation

9 On Funduro and ST models remove the fairing (see Chapter 8).

10 On GS and Dakar models remove the top cover (see Chapter 8). Displace the starter relay from its mount **(see illustration 5.11a)**. Undo the bolt securing the electrical cover and remove the cover **(see illustration 5.11b)**.

11 On CS models remove the air filter housing (see Chapter 4B).

12 Trace the wiring from the relevant switch and disconnect it at the connector(s). Feed the wiring back to the switch, freeing it from any clips and ties and noting its routing.

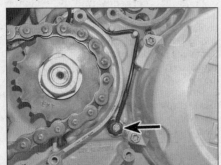

17.3 Undo the screw and detach the wiring – note how the wiring is routed

13 Unscrew the handlebar switch screws and free the switch from the handlebar **(see illustrations)**.

14 Installation is the reverse of removal.

17 Neutral switch

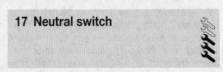

Check

1 The switch is located in the right-hand side of the engine behind the front sprocket or pulley cover. The switch is part of the starter

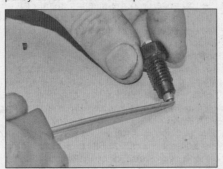

17.5 Make sure the plunger moves in and out smoothly and freely

interlock circuit which prevents or stops the engine running if the transmission is in gear whilst the sidestand is down, and prevents the engine from starting if the transmission is in gear unless the sidestand is up, and unless the clutch is pulled in. If the neutral light does not work first check the bulb (see Section 13).

2 Remove the front sprocket or pulley cover, according to model (see Chapter 7).

3 Undo the small screw in the centre of the switch and detach the wiring connector from the switch **(see illustration)**. Make sure the transmission is in neutral.

4 With the connector disconnected and the ignition switch ON, the neutral light should be out. If not, the wire between the connector and instrument cluster must be earthed (grounded) at some point. Ground the connector against the engine – the light should come on. If it does the wiring is good.

5 Check for continuity between the switch terminal and the crankcase. With the transmission in neutral, there should be continuity. With the transmission in gear, there should be no continuity. If the tests prove otherwise, then remove the switch (see below) and check whether the plunger is bent or damaged, or just stuck **(see illustration)**. Replace the switch with a new one if necessary.

6 If the continuity tests prove the switch is

good, check for voltage at the wire terminal with the ignition ON. If there's no voltage present, check the wire between the switch and the instrument cluster (see the *Wiring Diagrams* at the end of this Chapter).

7 If necessary also check the other components and the wiring and connectors between them in the starter circuit, namely the sidestand switch (Section 18), clutch switch (Section 19), and the starter circuit relay/diode unit (Section 5) – see the *Wiring Diagrams* at the end of this Chapter.

Removal and installation

8 The switch is located in the right-hand side of the engine behind the front sprocket or pulley cover. Remove the front sprocket or pulley cover, according to model (see Chapter 7).

9 Undo the screw and detach the wiring connector from the switch **(see illustration 17.3)**. Make sure the transmission is in neutral.

10 Clean the area around the switch, then unscrew it from the crankcase **(see illustration)**.

11 Clean the switch threads and apply a thread lock (Loctite 243 or equivalent), then thread the switch into the crankcase and tighten it.

12 Connect the wiring connector and check the operation of the neutral light **(see illustration 17.3)**. Install the front sprocket or pulley cover, according to model (see Chapter 7).

18 Sidestand switch

Check

1 The sidestand switch is mounted on the stand pivot. The switch is part of the starter interlock safety circuit which prevents or stops the engine running if the transmission is in gear whilst the sidestand is down, and prevents the engine from starting if the transmission is in gear unless the sidestand is up, and unless the clutch is pulled in.

2 Trace the wiring back from the switch and disconnect it at the wiring connector **(see illustration)** – remove the connector cover from the engine where required.

3 Check the operation of the switch using an ohmmeter or continuity test light. Connect the meter between the terminals on the switch side of the connector. With the sidestand up there should be continuity (zero resistance) between the terminals, and with the stand down there should be no continuity (infinite resistance).

4 If the switch does not perform as expected, it is faulty and must be replaced with a new one.

5 If the switch is good, check the other components and the wiring and connectors between them in the starter circuit, namely the neutral switch (Section 17), clutch switch (Section 19), and the starter circuit relay/diode

17.10 Unscrew and remove the switch

unit (Section 5) – see the *Wiring Diagrams* at the end of this Chapter.

Removal and installation

6 The sidestand switch is mounted on the stand bracket. Trace the wiring back from the switch and disconnect at the wiring connector – remove the connector cover from the engine where required **(see illustration 18.2)**. On GS and Dakar models turn the connector holder 1/4 turn anti-clockwise to release it from the frame. Feed the wiring back to the switch, freeing it from any clips and ties and noting its routing.

7 Release the switch retainer then remove the washer and the switch, noting how it fits **(see illustrations)**.

8 Fit and secure the new switch, making sure it locates correctly.

9 Feed the wiring to its connector, making sure it is correctly routed and secured by any clips.

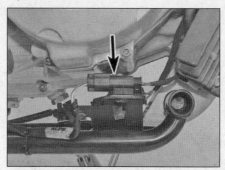

18.2 Sidestand switch wiring connector (arrowed) – GS and Dakar

18.7b . . . and the washer . . .

10 Reconnect the wiring connector and check the operation of the sidestand switch.

19 Clutch switch

Check

1 The clutch switch is in the clutch lever bracket **(see illustration 19.9)**. The switch is part of the starter interlock circuit which prevents or stops the engine running if the transmission is in gear whilst the sidestand is down, and prevents the engine from starting if the transmission is in gear unless the sidestand is up and the clutch lever is pulled in. The switch isn't adjustable.

2 On Funduro and ST models remove the fairing (see Chapter 8).

3 On GS and Dakar models remove the top cover (see Chapter 8). Displace the starter relay from its mount **(see illustration 5.11a)**. Undo the bolt securing the electrical cover and remove the cover **(see illustration 5.11b)**.

4 On CS models remove the air filter housing (see Chapter 4B).

5 Trace the wiring from the switch and disconnect it at the connector.

6 Connect the probes of an ohmmeter or a continuity tester to the two switch terminals. With the clutch lever pulled in, continuity should be indicated. With the clutch lever out, no continuity (infinite resistance) should be indicated.

7 If the switch is good, check the wiring

18.7a Remove the retainer . . .

18.7c . . . then lift the switch off the post

19.9 Clutch switch (arrowed)

20.2a Horn wiring connectors (A) and mounting bolt (B) – Funduro

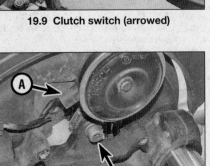

20.2b Horn wiring connector (A) and mounting bolt (B) – GS and Dakar

20.2c Horn wiring connector (arrowed) - CS

and connectors in the switch circuit (refer to Section 2 and the *Wiring Diagrams* at the end of this Chapter).

8 If the switch and wiring are good, check the other components and the wiring and

connectors between them in the starter circuit, namely the neutral switch (Section 17), sidestand switch (Section 18), and the starter circuit relay/diode unit (Section 5) – see the *Wiring Diagrams* at the end of this Chapter.

21.4a Starter relay (arrowed) – Funduro and ST

21.4b Starter relay – GS and Dakar

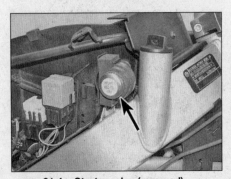

21.4c Starter relay (arrowed) – CS

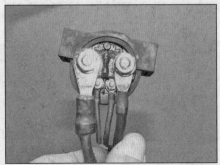

21.4d Displace the relay to access the terminals

Removal and installation

9 The clutch switch is mounted in the clutch lever bracket **(see illustration)**.

10 On Funduro and ST models remove the fairing (see Chapter 8).

11 On GS and Dakar models remove the top cover (see Chapter 8). Displace the starter relay from its mount **(see illustration 5.11a)**. Undo the bolt securing the electrical cover and remove the cover **(see illustration 5.11b)**.

12 On CS models remove the air filter housing (see Chapter 4B).

13 Trace the wiring from the switch and disconnect it at the connector. Feed it back to the switch, noting its routing and releasing it from any ties.

14 Unscrew the switch.

15 Installation is the reverse of removal.

20 Horn

Check

1 First check the fuse (see Section 5).

2 The horn is on the bottom yoke – on GS and Dakar models remove the upper section of the front mudguard (see Chapter 8). Disconnect the wiring connector(s) **(see illustrations)**. Check it for loose wires. Using two jumper wires, apply voltage from a fully-charged 12V battery directly to the terminals on the horn. If the horn doesn't sound, replace it with a new one.

3 If the horn works when connected directly to a battery check the horn circuit wiring and connectors (see Section 2 and the *Wiring Diagrams* at the end of this Chapter). If all the wiring and connectors are good, check the button contacts in the switch housing (see Section 16).

Replacement

4 The horn is on the bottom yoke – on GS and Dakar models remove the upper section of the front mudguard (see Chapter 8).

5 Disconnect the wiring connector(s) **(see illustration 20.2a, b or c)**. Unscrew the bracket bolt and remove the horn.

6 Fit the horn and tighten the bolt. Connect the wiring. Check that it works.

21 Starter motor relay

Check

1 On Funduro and ST models remove the left-hand side cover (see Chapter 8).

2 On GS and Dakar models remove the top cover (see Chapter 8).

3 On CS models remove the right-hand front side cover (see Chapter 8).

4 Displace the relay from its mount **(see illustrations)**. Lift the rubber terminal cover where fitted, then unscrew the nut securing the starter motor lead **(see illustration)**; position the lead away from the relay terminal. With the ignition switch ON, the engine kill switch in the RUN position, and the transmission in neutral, press the starter switch. The relay should be heard to click.

5 If the relay doesn't click, switch off the ignition and remove the relay as described below; test it as follows.

6 Set a multimeter to the ohms x 1 scale and connect it across the relay's starter motor and battery lead terminals. There should be no continuity. Using a fully-charged 12 volt battery and two insulated jumper wires, connect the battery to the small terminals on the relay. At this point the relay should be heard to click and the multimeter read 0 ohms (continuity). If this is the case the relay is good. If the relay does not click when battery voltage is applied and indicates no continuity (infinite resistance) across its terminals, it is faulty and must be replaced with a new one.

7 If the relay is good, check the heavy gauge cables from the battery to the relay, and from the relay to the starter motor, particularly that their terminals are tight and corrosion-free.

8 Next check the wiring and connectors in the circuit to the relay (refer to Section 2 and the *Wiring Diagrams* at the end of this Chapter).

Replacement

9 On Funduro and ST models remove the left-hand side cover (see Chapter 8).

10 On GS and Dakar models remove the top cover (see Chapter 8).

11 On CS models remove the front side covers (see Chapter 8).

12 Disconnect the battery terminals, remembering to disconnect the negative (–) terminal first (see Section 3).

13 Displace the relay from its mount **(see illustration 21.4a, b or c)**. Make a note of which lead fits where. Lift the rubber terminal covers where fitted, then unscrew the nuts securing the battery and starter motor leads and detach the leads **(see illustration 21.4d)**.

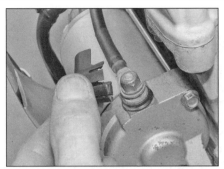

22.2 Remove the terminal cover then undo the nut and detach the lead

Unscrew the nuts securing the small gauge wiring and detach it. Remove the relay from its rubber sleeve.

14 Installation is the reverse of removal. Make sure the terminal nuts are securely tightened. Connect the negative (–) lead last when reconnecting the battery.

22 Starter motor removal and installation

Removal

1 The starter motor is mounted on the front of the engine. Disconnect the battery negative lead (see Section 3). On Funduro and ST models remove the left-hand engine trim panel (see Chapter 8).

2 Remove the terminal cover on the starter motor **(see illustration)**. Undo the nut securing the starter lead to the motor and detach the lead.

3 Unscrew the two bolts securing the starter motor to the crankcase **(see illustration)**. Slide the starter motor out and remove it **(see illustration)** – if it is tight apply gentle leverage with a screwdriver.

4 Remove the O-ring on the end of the starter motor and discard it as a new one must be used.

22.3a Unscrew the two bolts (arrowed) . . .

Installation

5 Fit a new O-ring onto the end of the starter motor, making sure it is seated in its groove **(see illustration)**. Apply a smear of engine oil to the O-ring. Make sure the bottom of the mounting lugs on the motor and tops of the mounts on the engine are clean.

6 Manoeuvre the motor into position and slide it into the crankcase **(see illustration 22.3b)**. Ensure that the starter motor teeth mesh correctly with those of the starter idle/reduction gear. Install the mounting bolts and tighten them to the torque setting specified at the beginning of the Chapter **(see illustration 22.3a)**.

7 Connect the starter lead to the motor and secure it with the nut **(see illustration 22.2)**. Fit the cover over the terminal.

8 Connect the battery negative (–) lead (see Section 3).

23 Starter motor overhaul

Check

1 Remove the starter motor (see Section 22). Cover the body in some rag and clamp the motor in a soft-jawed vice – do not overtighten it.

2 Using a fully-charged 12 volt battery and

22.3b . . . and remove the starter motor

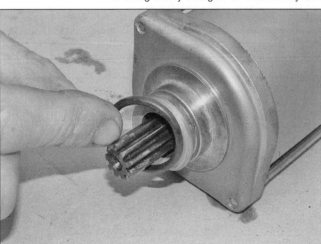

22.5 Fit a new O-ring and lubricate it

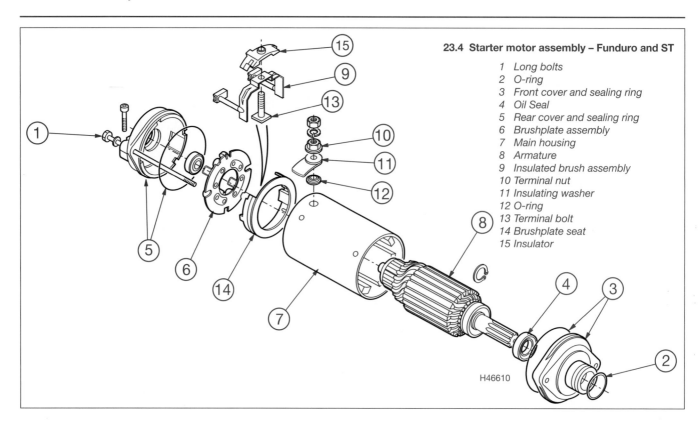

23.4 Starter motor assembly – Funduro and ST

1 Long bolts
2 O-ring
3 Front cover and sealing ring
4 Oil Seal
5 Rear cover and sealing ring
6 Brushplate assembly
7 Main housing
8 Armature
9 Insulated brush assembly
10 Terminal nut
11 Insulating washer
12 O-ring
13 Terminal bolt
14 Brushplate seat
15 Insulator

H46610

two insulated jumper wires, connect the positive (+) terminal of the battery to the protruding terminal on the starter motor, and the negative (–) terminal to one of the motor's mounting lugs. At this point the starter motor should spin. If this is the case the motor is proved good, though it is worth disassembling it and checking it if you suspect it of not working properly under load.

Disassembly

Funduro and ST models

3 Remove the starter motor (see Section 22).
4 Note the alignment marks between the main housing and the front and rear covers, or make your own if they aren't clear (see illustration).
5 Unscrew the two long bolts and withdraw them from the starter motor.
6 Remove the front cover from the motor.

Check the sealing ring and replace it with a new one if it is damaged, deformed or deteriorated.
7 Remove the rear cover from the motor. Check the sealing ring and replace it with a new one if it is damaged, deformed or deteriorated.
8 Withdraw the armature from the main housing, noting that you will have to pull it out against the attraction of the magnets.
9 Slide the brushes with the insulated wires out of their housings. Remove the brushplate assembly from the main housing, noting how it locates.
10 Unscrew the terminal nut and remove the insulating washer and the O-ring, noting how they fit. Withdraw the terminal bolt, then remove the insulated brush assembly from the brushplate seat, noting how it fits. Remove the insulator and the brushplate seat. Check the

condition of the terminal bolt O-ring and renew it if it is damaged, deformed or deteriorated.

GS, Dakar and CS models

11 Remove the starter motor (see Section 22).
12 Note the alignment mark between the main housing and the rear cover, or make your own if it isn't clear (see illustration).
13 Unscrew the two long bolts, then remove the front cover (see illustrations). Check the sealing ring and replace it with a new one if it is damaged, deformed or deteriorated.
14 Remove the rear cover (see illustration) – the brushplate assembly comes with it. Remove the shims from the end of the armature or from the rear cover (see illustration 23.33b). Unscrew the nut on the terminal bolt then remove the outer insulator (see illustrations 23.36c). Remove the brushplate and terminal bolt from the rear

23.12 Note the alignment of the indent (arrowed) with the rear cover

23.13a Unscrew and remove the two bolts . . .

23.13b . . . then remove the front cover and sealing ring (arrowed)

23.14a Remove the rear cover and brushplate assembly, noting the sealing ring (arrowed)

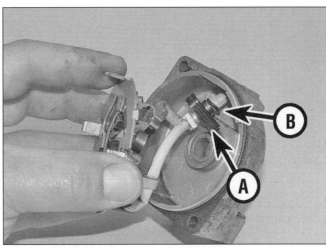

23.14b Remove the brushplate, noting the insulator (A) and O-ring (B) on the terminal bolt

cover **(see illustration)**. Remove the O-ring and inner insulator from the bolt.

15 Draw the armature out of the main housing – resistance will be felt due to the attraction of the magnets **(see illustration)**.

Inspection

Note: *On Funduro and ST models all parts are available for the starter motor. On GS, Dakar and CS models the only parts available are a replacement brush set and the housing sealing rings – if anything else is damaged or worn a new starter motor must be fitted.*

16 The parts of the starter motor that are most likely to require attention are the brushes

– when new they are about 12 mm long, but wear down. If they are worn to about 6 mm, are cracked, chipped, or otherwise damaged fit a new set **(see illustration)**.

17 Inspect the commutator bars on the armature for scoring, scratches and discoloration **(see illustration)**. Also make sure the insulating mica between the bars is 0.5 mm below each bar – if not cut some of the insulating mica away using a commutator saw **(see illustration)**. The commutator can be cleaned and polished with crocus cloth, but do not use sandpaper or emery paper. After cleaning, wipe away any residue with a

cloth soaked in electrical system cleaner or denatured alcohol.

18 Using an ohmmeter or a continuity test light, check for continuity between the commutator bars **(see illustration)**. Continuity should exist between each bar and all of the others. Also, check for continuity between the commutator bars and the armature shaft **(see illustration)**. There should be no continuity (infinite resistance) between the commutator and the shaft. If the checks indicate otherwise, the armature is defective.

19 Check the front end of the armature shaft for worn, cracked, chipped and broken teeth.

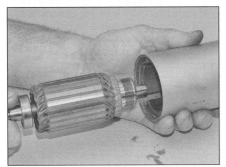

23.15 Draw the armature out of the housing

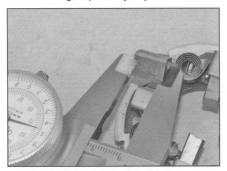

23.16 Measure the length of each brush

23.17a Check the commutator bars . . .

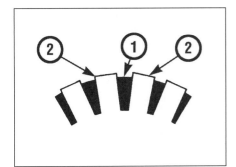

23.17b . . . and the depth of the mica (1) between the bars (2)

23.18a There should be continuity between the bars . . .

23.18b . . . and no continuity between the bars and the shaft

23.20a Check the seal in the front cover . . .

20 Inspect the front and rear covers for signs of cracks or wear. Check the oil seal in the front cover, the bearing on the armature shaft, and the bush in the rear cover for wear and damage **(see illustrations)** – on GS, Dakar and CS models although these parts are not available from BMW, after-market seals and bearings are readily available from good suppliers, you just need to remove the old ones and note the size markings.

21 Inspect the magnets in the main housing and the housing itself for cracks.

22 Inspect the O-rings and sealing rings for signs of damage, deformation and deterioration and replace them with new ones if necessary.

Reassembly

Funduro and ST models

23 Fit the brushplate seat and insulator into the main housing **(see illustration 23.4)**.

23.32a Position each brush and spring end as shown

23.32c . . . aligning the tabs with the indent (arrowed)

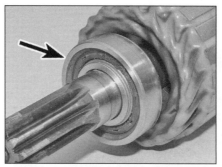

23.20b . . . the bearing (arrowed) on the shaft . . .

Fit the insulated brush assembly, locating the arms into the brushplate seat. Insert the terminal bolt, then fit the O-ring, insulating washer and nut onto the bolt and tighten the nut. Use a new O-ring if necessary.

24 Place each brush spring end onto the top of its brush housing – this allows the brushes to be slid right in so they do not foul the commutator bars when the armature is installed. Fit the brushplate assembly onto the main housing, locating the insulated brush wires in the cut-outs and making sure the tab on the plate locates in the cut-out in the housing.

25 Fit each insulated brush into its housing and slide them fully in.

26 Insert the armature into the main housing, noting that it will be forcibly drawn in by the attraction of the magnets. Locate each brush spring end onto its brush. Check that each brush is securely pressed against

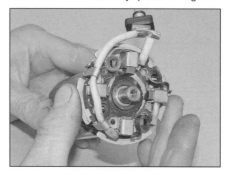

23.32b Slide the brushplate onto the commutator . . .

23.32d Move each spring end onto the back of its brush

23.20c . . . and the bush (arrowed) in the rear cover

the commutator and is free to move in its housing.

27 Make sure the rear cover sealing ring is in place. Fit the rear cover onto the housing, aligning the marks noted or made earlier, and locating the tab on the housing in the slot in the cover.

28 Make sure the front cover sealing ring is in place. Apply a smear of grease to the lips of the front cover oil seal. Fit the cover, aligning the marks made on removal.

29 Check the alignment marks made on removal are correctly aligned, then install the long bolts and tighten them.

30 Install the starter motor (see Section 22).

GS, Dakar and CS models

31 Carefully fit the armature into main housing, noting that it will be forcibly drawn in by the magnets **(see illustration 23.15)**.

32 Push each brush fully into its housing and lift the spring end onto the top of the brush to hold it in place – this is so the brushes do not foul the commutator bars when the armature is installed **(see illustration)**. Fit the brushplate assembly over the commutator and onto the main housing, aligning the tabs on each side of the indent in the housing **(see illustrations)**. Locate each brush spring end in the indent in the end of its brush **(see illustration)**. Check that each brush is securely pressed against the commutator and is free to move in its housing.

33 Fit the inner insulator piece onto the terminal bolt **(see illustration)**. Fit the shims onto the end of the armature **(see illustration)**.

34 Make sure the rear cover sealing ring is in place and apply a smear of grease to the

23.33a Fit the insulator piece to the bolt with its recessed side fitting over the bolt base

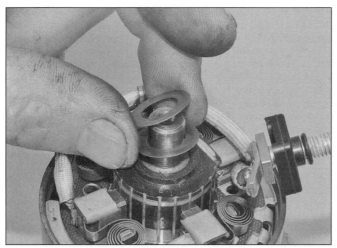

23.33b Fit the shim(s) onto the shaft

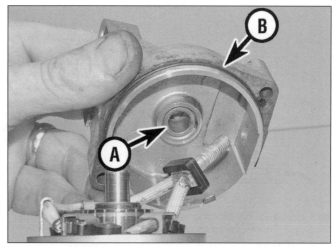

23.34 Grease the bush (A), make sure the sealing ring (B) is in place, then fit the rear cover

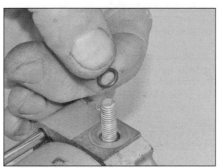

23.36a Fit the O-ring onto the bolt . . .

23.36b . . . so it sits around the base as shown . . .

23.36c . . . then fit the outer insulator (arrowed) and the nut

bush **(see illustration)**. Fit the rear cover onto the housing, locating the terminal bolt through the hole and aligning the indent in the housing with the hole.

35 Apply a smear of grease to the front cover oil seal lip **(see illustration 23.20a)**. Make sure the sealing ring is in place. Slide the front cover onto the housing, aligning the bolt holes with those in the rear cover **(see illustration 23.13b)**. Fit the long bolts and tighten them **(see illustration 23.13a)**.

36 Carefully feed the small O-ring down the terminal bolt so it sits around its base between it and the rear cover **(see illustrations)**. Fit the outer insulator then fit and tighten the nut **(see illustration)**.

37 Install the starter motor (see Section 22).

24 Charging system testing

1 If the performance of the charging system is suspect, the system as a whole should be checked first, followed by testing of the individual components. **Note:** *Before beginning the checks, make sure the battery is fully charged and that all system connections are clean and tight.*

2 Checking the output of the charging system

and the performance of the various components within the charging system requires the use of a multimeter (with voltage, current, resistance checking facilities). If a multimeter is not available, the job of checking the charging system should be left to a BMW dealer.

3 When making the checks, follow the procedures carefully to prevent incorrect connections or short circuits resulting in irreparable damage to electrical system components.

Leakage test

Caution: Always connect an ammeter in series, never in parallel with the battery, otherwise it will be damaged. Do not turn the ignition ON or operate the starter motor when the ammeter is connected – a sudden surge in current will blow the meter's fuse.

4 Ensure the ignition is OFF, then disconnect the battery negative (-) lead (see Section 3).

5 Set the multimeter to the Amps function and connect its negative (-) probe to the battery negative (-) terminal, and positive (+) probe to the disconnected negative (-) lead **(see illustration)**. Always set the meter to a high amps range initially and then bring it down to the mA (milli Amps) range; if there is a high current flow in the circuit it may blow the meter's fuse.

6 Battery current leakage should not exceed

the maximum limit (see Specifications). If a higher leakage rate is shown there is a short circuit in the wiring, although if an after-market immobiliser or alarm is fitted, its current draw should be taken into account. Disconnect the meter and reconnect the battery negative (-) lead.

7 If leakage is indicated, refer to *Wiring Diagrams* at the end of this Chapter to systematically disconnect individual electrical components and repeat the test until the source is identified.

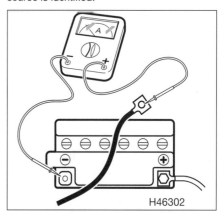

H46302

24.5 Checking the charging system leakage rate - connect the meter as shown

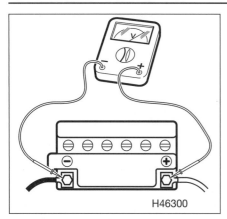

24.9 Checking the charging rate - connect the meter as shown

Output test

8 Refer to Section 3 for access to the battery terminals. Start the engine and warm it up.

9 To check the regulated (DC) voltage output, allow the engine to idle. Connect a multimeter set to the 0 – 20 volts DC scale across the terminals of the battery with the positive (+) meter probe to the battery positive (+) terminal and the negative (-) meter probe to battery negative (-) terminal (see Section 3) (see illustration).

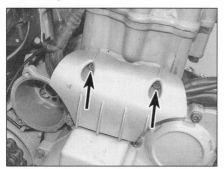

25.1a Unscrew the bolts (arrowed) and remove the cover . . .

10 Slowly increase the engine speed and note the reading obtained – it should rise from 13 to 15V. If the regulated voltage output is outside the specification, check the alternator and the regulator (see Sections 25 and 26).

 HAYNES HiNT *Clues to a faulty regulator are constantly blowing bulbs, with brightness varying considerably with engine speed, and battery overheating.*

25 Alternator

Check

1 Remove the wiring connector cover (see illustrations).

2 Trace the wiring from the alternator and disconnect it at the connector. Check the connector terminals for corrosion and security.

3 Using a multimeter set to the ohms x 1 (ohmmeter) scale check for a resistance between each of the wires on the alternator side of the connector, taking a total of three

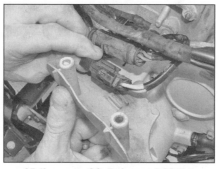

25.1b . . . on GS, Dakar and CS the alternator connector clips to the inside of it

readings, then check for continuity between each terminal and ground (earth). If the stator coil windings are in good condition the three readings should be the same (BMW do not give a figure, but if the reading should not be very high), and there should be no continuity (infinite resistance) between any of the terminals and ground (earth). If not, the alternator stator coil assembly is at fault and should be replaced with a new one. **Note:** *Before condemning the stator coils, check the fault is not due to damaged wiring between the connector and the coils.*

Removal

4 Remove the front sprocket/pulley cover (see illustration).

5 On Funduro, ST, GS and Dakar models place the bike on its sidestand to minimise oil loss. Remove the sump guard (see Chapter 8).

6 On GS and Dakar models displace the regulator/rectifier (see Section 26).

7 If required detach the breather hose from the alternator cover.

8 On CS models drain the engine oil (see Chapter 1). Unscrew the oil return pipe banjo bolt on the underside of the engine (see illustration). Discard the sealing washers – new ones must be used.

9 Remove the wiring connector cover (see illustrations 25.1a and b). Trace the wiring from the alternator and ignition timing sensor and disconnect them at the connectors.

10 Working in a criss-cross pattern, evenly slacken the alternator cover bolts (see illustration). Draw the cover off the engine, noting that it will be restrained by the force of the rotor magnets, and be prepared to catch any residual oil. Discard the gasket – a new one must be used. Note the thrust washer on the end of the starter idle gear shaft – if it is not there it will be stuck to the cover (see illustration 25.23).

11 On Funduro and ST models unscrew the ignition timing sensor bolts and move it aside to avoid the possibility of damage.

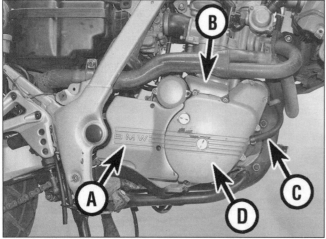

25.4 Front sprocket cover (A), wiring cover (B), breather hose (C), alternator cover (D) – Funduro and ST

25.8 Unscrew the oil pipe banjo bolt (arrowed)

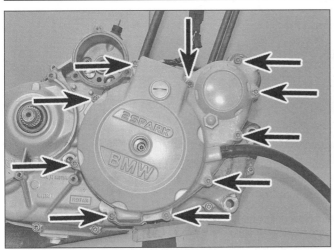

25.10 Alternator cover bolts (arrowed) – GS, Dakar and CS

25.12 Counter-hold the rotor and unscrew the nut

12 To remove the rotor nut it is necessary to stop the rotor from turning – refer to Chapter 2, Section 8, Step 5 and fit the crankshaft holding tool. Alternatively you can hold the crankshaft using a hex bit and socket bar, and use a ring spanner on the nut, but note that you cannot do this to tighten the nut on installation as a torque wrench must be used **(see illustration)**. The nut is very tight. Slacken the nut, but leave

25.13a Thread the puller onto the rotor . . .

it threaded on the end of the shaft – it will then retain the rotor and prevent it jumping off when the puller is used to free it from its taper.
13 To remove the rotor from the shaft it is necessary to use a rotor puller (BMW part No. 125510 or equivalent). Thread the body of the rotor puller onto the hub of the rotor, then turn the bolt in its centre until the rotor is displaced from the shaft **(see illustrations)**. Remove the puller, then thread the nut off and remove the washer and the rotor **(see illustration 25.22a)**. Remove the Woodruff key from its slot **(see illustration 25.19)**. Remove the starter driven gear from the back of the rotor if they came away together, rotating it clockwise to free it from the starter clutch, or slide the starter driven gear off the end of the crankshaft **(see illustration 25.20)**.
14 If required remove the starter clutch from the rotor (see Chapter 2).
15 To remove the stator from the cover, unscrew its bolts, and the bolt securing the wiring clamp, then remove the assembly, noting how the rubber wiring grommet fits **(see illustration)**.

Installation

16 Clean all traces of old gasket and sealant from the cover and crankcase mating surfaces. Clean the threads of the stator and clamp bolts. Fit the stator into the cover, aligning the rubber wiring grommet with the groove **(see illustration 25.15)**. Apply a thread locking compound (Loctite 243 or equivalent) to the stator and wiring clamp bolts and tighten them to the torque setting specified at the beginning of the Chapter. Apply a suitable sealant to the wiring grommet, then press it into the cut-out in the cover.
17 If removed fit the starter clutch onto the rotor (see Chapter 2).
18 Clean the tapered end of the crankshaft and the corresponding mating surface on the inside of the rotor thoroughly with a suitable solvent and a clean cloth.
19 Fit the Woodruff key into its slot in the crankshaft **(see illustration)**.
20 Smear some molybdenum grease onto the inner flat section of the crankshaft (not the tapered section) and to the outer face of the

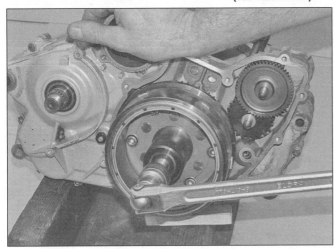

25.13b . . . then hold the rotor and turn the puller bolt

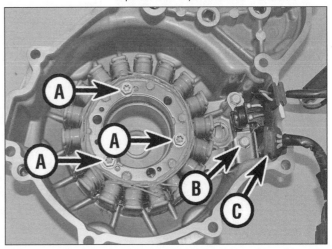

25.15 Unscrew the stator bolts (A) and the wiring clamp bolt (B) and free the grommet (C) – GS/Dakar/CS layout

25.19 Fit the key into its slot (arrow)

25.20 Fit the starter driven gear

25.21 Slide the rotor onto the shaft

starter driven gear where it seats on the clutch housing, and smear clean engine oil onto the outside of the starter driven gear hub where it contacts the sprags. Fit the starter driven gear into the clutch, rotating it clockwise as you do to spread the sprags and allow the hub to enter **(see illustration)**.

21 Make sure that no metal objects have attached themselves to the magnet on the inside of the rotor. Slide the rotor onto the shaft, locating its slot over the Woodruff key, and engaging the teeth of the starter driven gear with those of the idle gear **(see illustration)**.

22 Install the rotor nut with its washer and tighten it to the torque setting specified at the beginning of the Chapter, using the method employed on removal to prevent the rotor from turning **(see illustrations)**.

23 Make sure the thrust washer is on the end

of the starter idle gear shaft **(see illustration)**.
24 Apply a smear of suitable sealant all round the wiring grommets and locate them in their cut-outs **(see illustration)**. Fit a new gasket **(see illustration)**. Install the alternator cover, noting that the rotor magnets will forcibly draw the cover/stator on, making sure it locates onto the dowels **(see illustration)**. Tighten the cover bolts evenly in a criss-cross sequence to the specified torque setting.
25 Reconnect the wiring at the connectors. Fit the wiring connector cover. Remove the crankshaft locking tool and refit the blanking bolt.
26 Install all remaining components in reverse sequence as required according to model (Steps 8 to 4). On CS models fit the oil pipe banjo bolt using new sealing washers and tighten the bolt to the specified torque. Refer to Chapter 1 and refill the engine oil.

26 Regulator/rectifier

Check

1 Disconnect the regulator/rectifier wiring connectors (see below) and check the connector terminals for corrosion and security. BMW provide no test details for the regulator/ rectifier. If after testing the charging system as described in Section 24 it is suspected of being faulty substitute it with a new one and retest the system.

Removal and installation

2 On Funduro and ST models remove the seat (see Chapter 8). Disconnect the regulator/ rectifier wiring connectors **(see illustration)**.

25.22a Fit the nut with its washer . . .

25.22b . . . and tighten it as described

25.23 Make sure the thrust washer (arrowed) is in place

25.24a Apply sealant . . .

25.24b . . . then fit the new gasket onto the dowels . . .

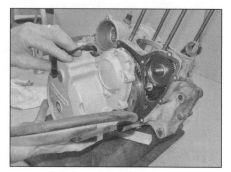

25.24c . . . and fit the cover

Unscrew the bolts securing the regulator/rectifier and remove it **(see illustration)**.

3 On GS and Dakar models remove the sump guard (see Chapter 8), and the wiring cover **(see illustrations 25.1a and b)**. Disconnect the regulator/rectifier wiring connectors **(see illustration)**. Unscrew the bolts securing the regulator/rectifier and remove it **(see illustration)**.

4 On CS models remove the wiring cover **(see illustrations 25.1a and b)**. Disconnect the regulator/rectifier wiring connectors **(see illustration 26.3a)**. The regulator/rectifier sits inside the front section of the frame – for best access refer to Chapter 2, Section 4, referring to the relevant Steps, and remove it. Unscrew the bolts securing the regulator/rectifier and remove it.

5 Installation is the reverse of removal.

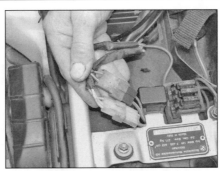

26.2a Disconnect the wiring connectors . . .

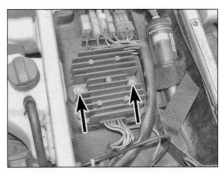

26.2b . . . then unscrew the bolts (arrowed)

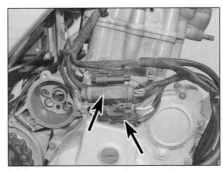

26.3a Disconnect the wiring connectors (arrowed) . . .

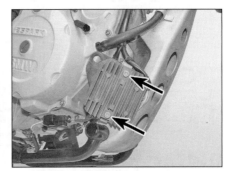

26.3b . . . then unscrew the bolts (arrowed)

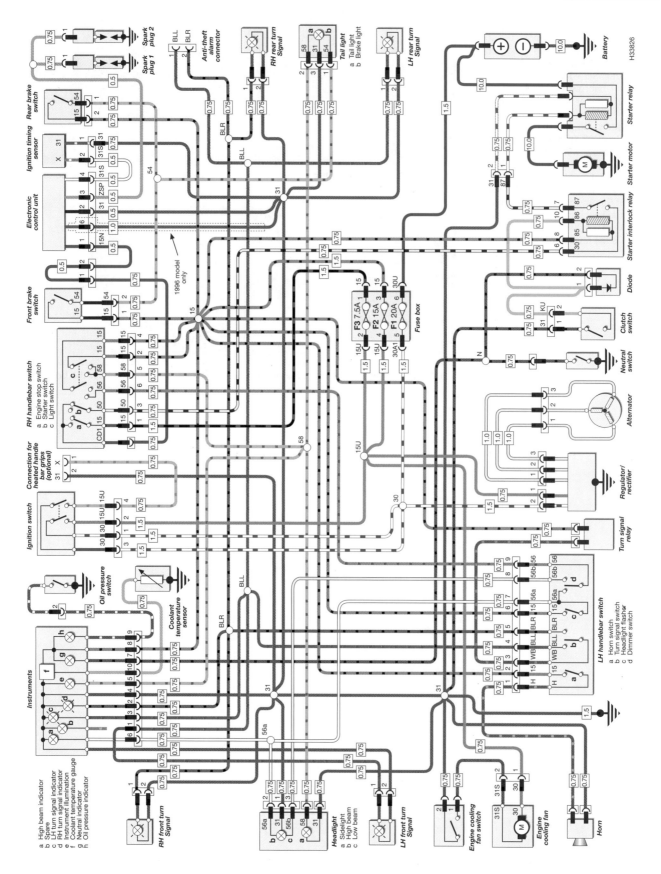

F650 Funduro 1994-96

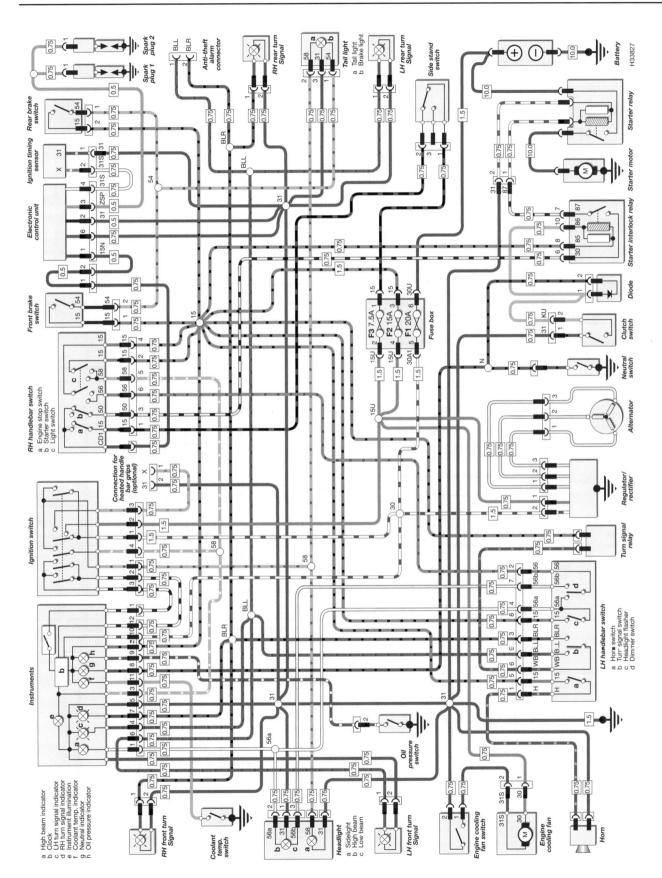

F650 Funduro 1997–01 and F650 ST

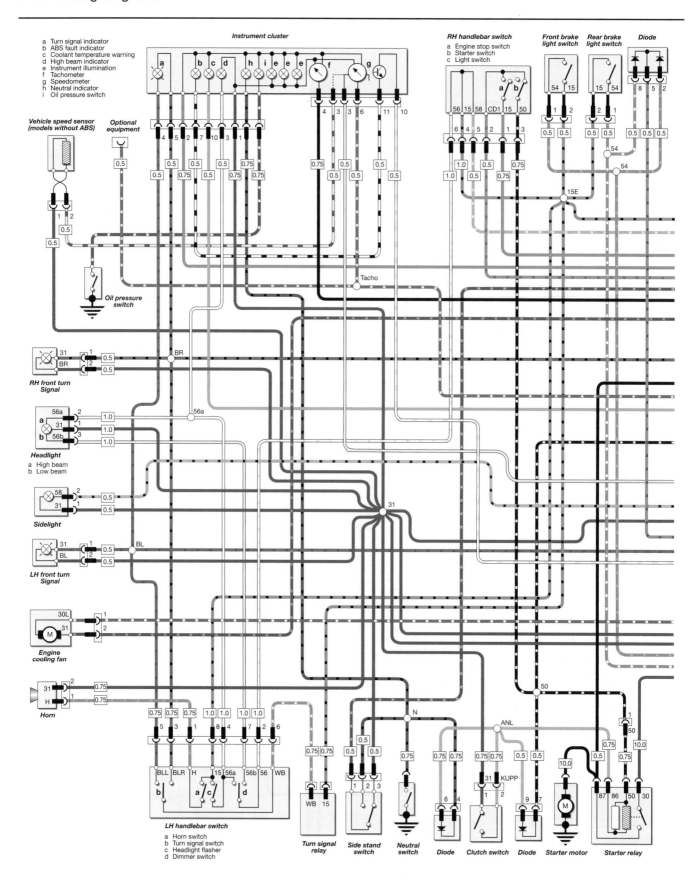

a Turn signal indicator
b ABS fault indicator
c Coolant temperature warning
d High beam indicator
e Instrument illumination
f Tachometer
g Speedometer
h Neutral indicator
i Oil pressure switch

Instrument cluster

RH handlebar switch
a Engine stop switch
b Starter switch
c Light switch

Front brake light switch   Rear brake light switch   Diode

Vehicle speed sensor
(models without ABS)

Optional equipment

Oil pressure switch

RH front turn Signal

Headlight
a High beam
b Low beam

Sidelight

LH front turn Signal

Engine cooling fan

Horn

Tacho

LH handlebar switch
a Horn switch
b Turn signal switch
c Headlight flasher
d Dimmer switch

Turn signal relay

Side stand switch

Neutral switch

Diode

Clutch switch

Diode

Starter motor

Starter relay

F650 GS 2000 to 2003 and F650 GS Dakar 2001 to 2003

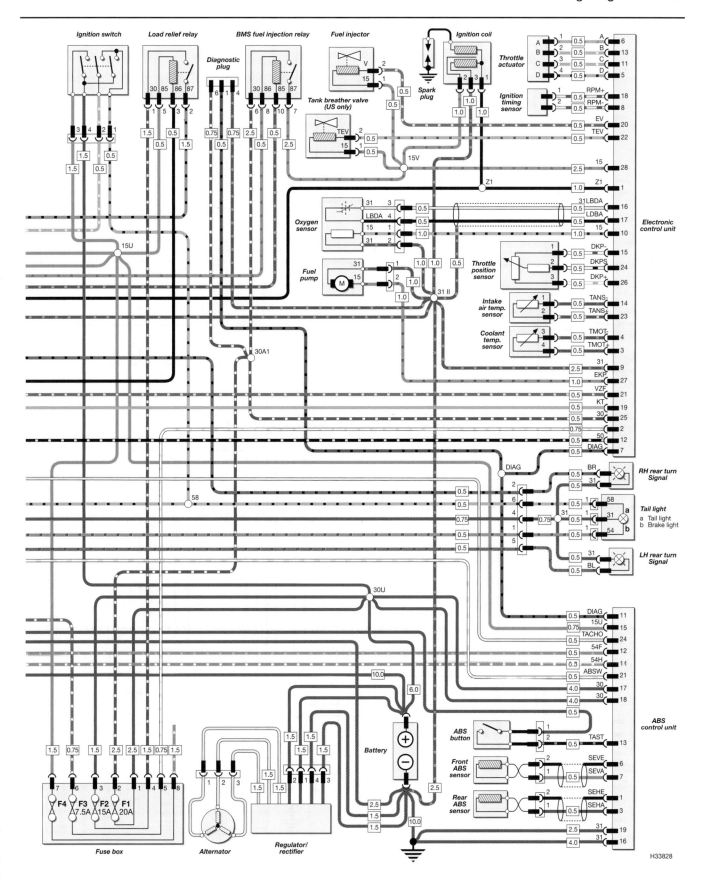

F650 GS 2000 to 2003 and F650 GS Dakar 2001 to 2003

H33828

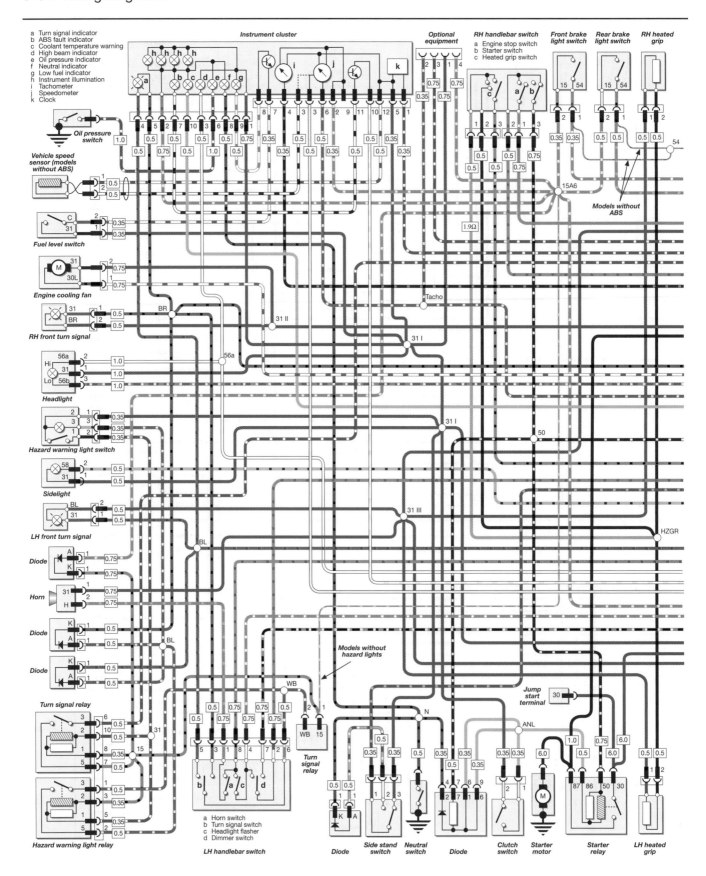

F650 GS and F650 GS Dakar 2004 to 2007

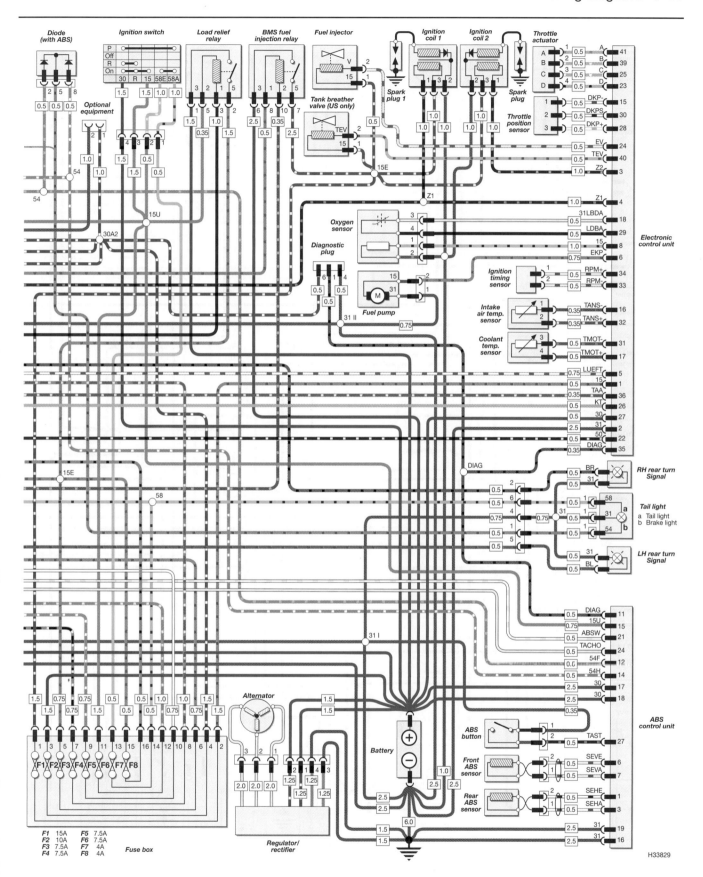

F650 GS and F650 GS Dakar 2004 to 2007

H33829

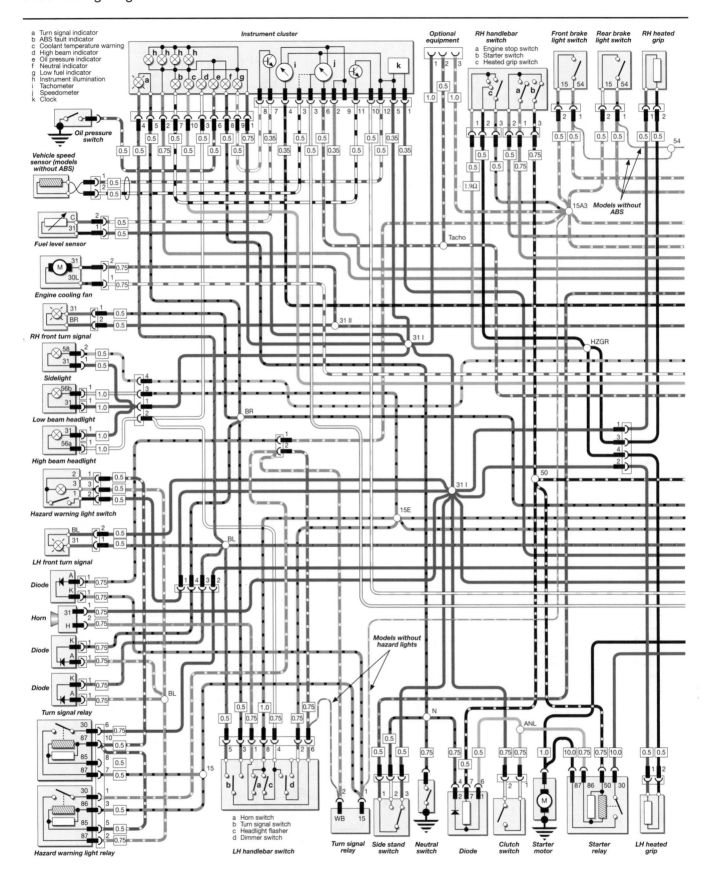

a Turn signal indicator
b ABS fault indicator
c Coolant temperature warning
d High beam indicator
e Oil pressure indicator
f Neutral indicator
g Low fuel indicator
h Instrument illumination
i Tachometer
j Speedometer
k Clock

F650 CS 2002 to 2003

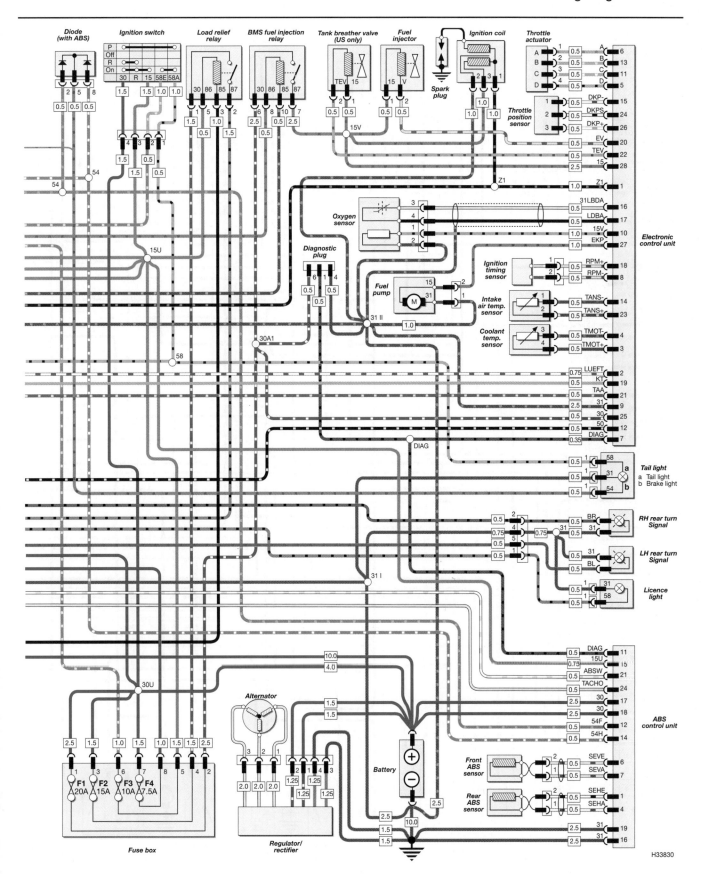

F650 CS 2002 to 2003

H33830

a Turn signal indicator
b ABS fault indicator
c Coolant temperature warning
d High beam indicator
e Oil pressure indicator
f Neutral indicator
g Low fuel indicator
h Instrument illumination
i Tachometer
j Speedometer
k Clock

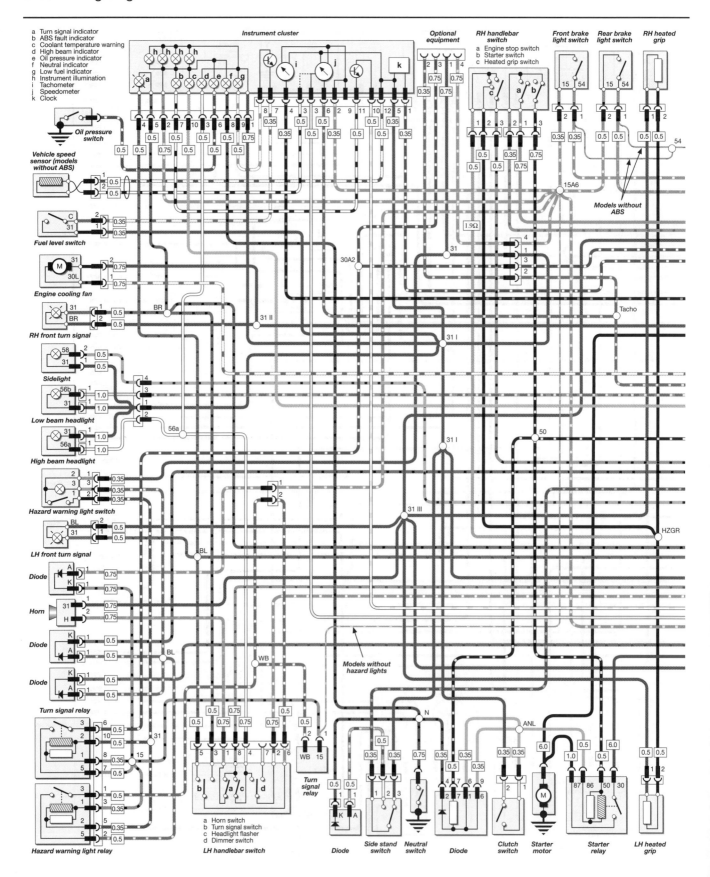

a Horn switch
b Turn signal switch
c Headlight flasher
d Dimmer switch

F650 CS 2004 and 2005

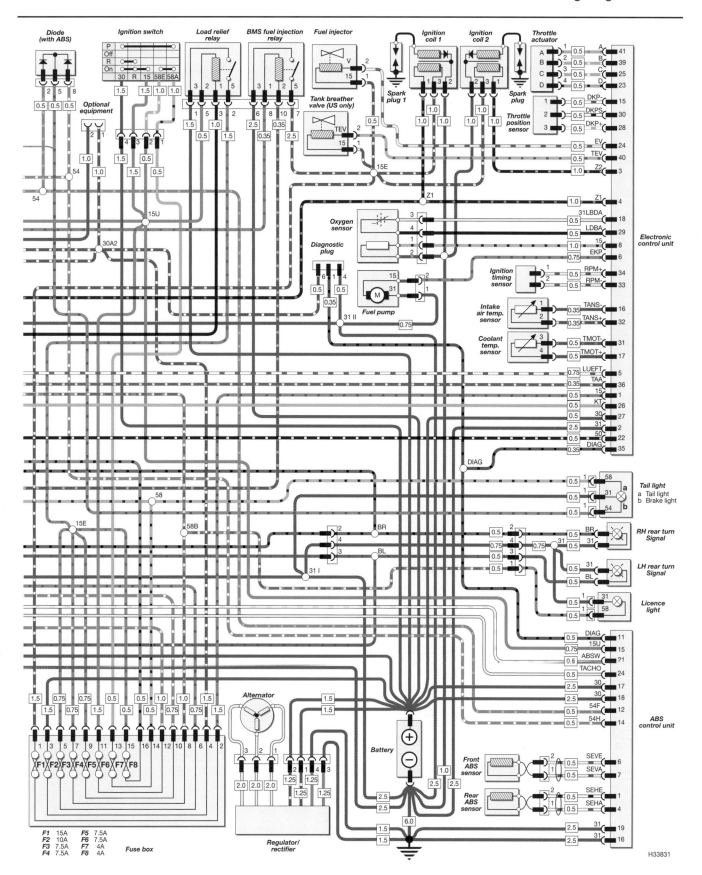

F650 CS 2004 and 2005

H33831

Notes

Reference

Tools and Workshop Tips

- ● Building up a tool kit and equipping your workshop ● Using tools ● Understanding bearing, seal, fastener and chain sizes and markings ● Repair techniques

Security

- ● Locks and chains ● U-locks ● Disc locks ● Alarms and immobilisers ● Security marking systems ● Tips on how to prevent bike theft

Lubricants and fluids

REF•23

- ● Engine oils ● Transmission (gear) oils ● Coolant/anti-freeze ● Fork oils and suspension fluids ● Brake/clutch fluids ● Spray lubes, degreasers and solvents

Conversion Factors **REF•26**

$$34 \text{ Nm} \times 0.738$$
$$= 25 \text{ lbf ft}$$

- ● Formulae for conversion of the metric (SI) units used throughout the manual into Imperial measures

MOT Test Checks

- ● A guide to the UK MOT test ● Which items are tested ● How to prepare your motorcycle for the test and perform a pre-test check

Storage

- ● How to prepare your motorcycle for going into storage and protect essential systems ● How to get the motorcycle back on the road

Fault Finding **REF•35**

- ● Common faults and their likely causes ● How to check engine cylinder compression ● How to make electrical tests and use test meters

Technical Terms Explained **REF•47**

- ● Component names, technical terms and common abbreviations explained

Index **REF•52**

Buying tools

A toolkit is a fundamental requirement for servicing and repairing a motorcycle. Although there will be an initial expense in building up enough tools for servicing, this will soon be offset by the savings made by doing the job yourself. As experience and confidence grow, additional tools can be added to enable the repair and overhaul of the motorcycle. Many of the specialist tools are expensive and not often used so it may be preferable to hire them, or for a group of friends or motorcycle club to join in the purchase.

As a rule, it is better to buy more expensive, good quality tools. Cheaper tools are likely to wear out faster and need to be renewed more often, nullifying the original saving.

> ⚠ **Warning: To avoid the risk of a poor quality tool breaking in use, causing injury or damage to the component being worked on, always aim to purchase tools which meet the relevant national safety standards.**

The following lists of tools do not represent the manufacturer's service tools, but serve as a guide to help the owner decide which tools are needed for this level of work. In addition, items such as an electric drill, hacksaw, files, soldering iron and a workbench equipped with a vice, may be needed. Although not classed as tools, a selection of bolts, screws, nuts, washers and pieces of tubing always come in useful.

For more information about tools, refer to the Haynes *Motorcycle Workshop Practice Techbook* (Bk. No. 3470).

Manufacturer's service tools

Inevitably certain tasks require the use of a service tool. Where possible an alternative tool or method of approach is recommended, but sometimes there is no option if personal injury or damage to the component is to be avoided. Where required, service tools are referred to in the relevant procedure.

Service tools can usually only be purchased from a motorcycle dealer and are identified by a part number. Some of the commonly-used tools, such as rotor pullers, are available in aftermarket form from mail-order motorcycle tool and accessory suppliers.

Maintenance and minor repair tools

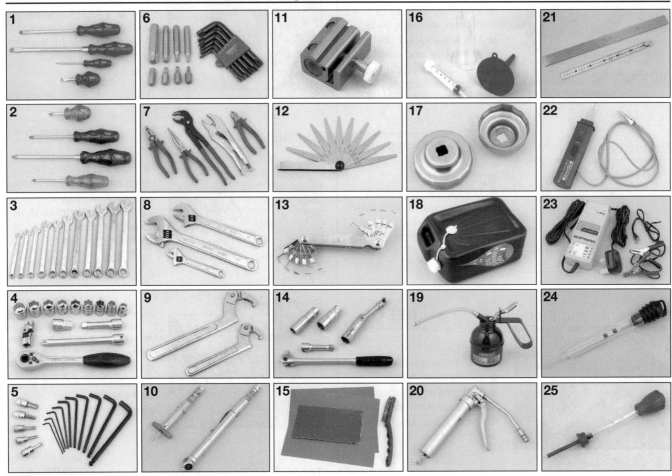

1 Set of flat-bladed screwdrivers
2 Set of Phillips head screwdrivers
3 Combination open-end and ring spanners
4 Socket set (3/8 inch or 1/2 inch drive)
5 Set of Allen keys or bits
6 Set of Torx keys or bits
7 Pliers, cutters and self-locking grips (Mole grips)
8 Adjustable spanners
9 C-spanners
10 Tread depth gauge and tyre pressure gauge
11 Cable oiler clamp
12 Feeler gauges
13 Spark plug gap measuring tool
14 Spark plug spanner or deep plug sockets
15 Wire brush and emery paper
16 Calibrated syringe, measuring vessel and funnel
17 Oil filter adapters
18 Oil drainer can or tray
19 Pump type oil can
20 Grease gun
21 Straight-edge and steel rule
22 Continuity tester
23 Battery charger
24 Hydrometer (for battery specific gravity check)
25 Anti-freeze tester (for liquid-cooled engines)

Repair and overhaul tools

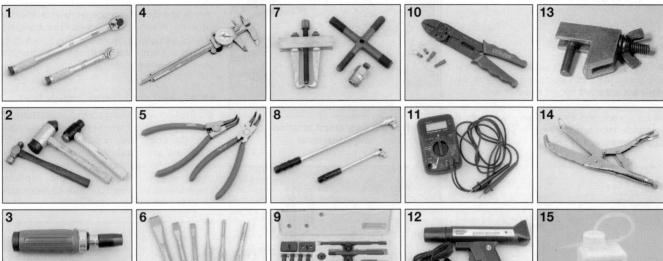

1 Torque wrench
   (small and mid-ranges)
2 Conventional, plastic or
   soft-faced hammers
3 Impact driver set

4 Vernier gauge
5 Circlip pliers (internal and
   external, or combination)
6 Set of cold chisels
   and punches

7 Selection of pullers
8 Breaker bars
9 Chain breaking/
   riveting tool set

10 Wire stripper and
   crimper tool
11 Multimeter (measures
   amps, volts and ohms)
12 Stroboscope (for
   dynamic timing checks)

13 Hose clamp
   (wingnut type shown)
14 Clutch holding tool
15 One-man brake/clutch
   bleeder kit

Specialist tools

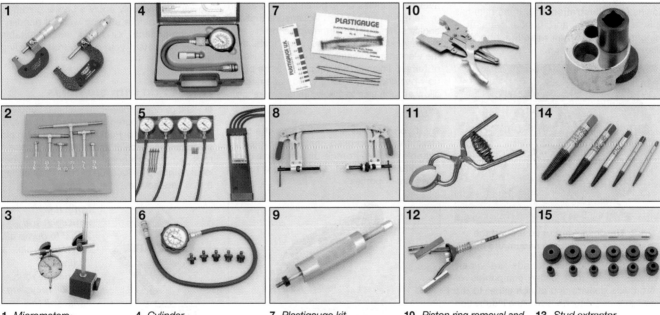

1 Micrometers
   (external type)
2 Telescoping gauges
3 Dial gauge

4 Cylinder
   compression gauge
5 Vacuum gauges (left) or
   manometer (right)
6 Oil pressure gauge

7 Plastigauge kit
8 Valve spring compressor
   (4-stroke engines)
9 Piston pin drawbolt tool

10 Piston ring removal and
   installation tool
11 Piston ring clamp
12 Cylinder bore hone
   (stone type shown)

13 Stud extractor
14 Screw extractor set
15 Bearing driver set

1 Workshop equipment and facilities

The workbench

● Work is made much easier by raising the bike up on a ramp - components are much more accessible if raised to waist level. The hydraulic or pneumatic types seen in the dealer's workshop are a sound investment if you undertake a lot of repairs or overhauls **(see illustration 1.1)**.

1.1 Hydraulic motorcycle ramp

● If raised off ground level, the bike must be supported on the ramp to avoid it falling. Most ramps incorporate a front wheel locating clamp which can be adjusted to suit different diameter wheels. When tightening the clamp, take care not to mark the wheel rim or damage the tyre - use wood blocks on each side to prevent this.

● Secure the bike to the ramp using tie-downs **(see illustration 1.2)**. If the bike has only a sidestand, and hence leans at a dangerous angle when raised, support the bike on an auxiliary stand.

1.2 Tie-downs are used around the passenger footrests to secure the bike

● Auxiliary (paddock) stands are widely available from mail order companies or motorcycle dealers and attach either to the wheel axle or swingarm pivot **(see illustration 1.3)**. If the motorcycle has a centrestand, you can support it under the crankcase to prevent it toppling whilst either wheel is removed **(see illustration 1.4)**.

1.3 This auxiliary stand attaches to the swingarm pivot

1.4 Always use a block of wood between the engine and jack head when supporting the engine in this way

Fumes and fire

● Refer to the Safety first! page at the beginning of the manual for full details. Make sure your workshop is equipped with a fire extinguisher suitable for fuel-related fires (Class B fire - flammable liquids) - it is not sufficient to have a water-filled extinguisher.

● Always ensure adequate ventilation is available. Unless an exhaust gas extraction system is available for use, ensure that the engine is run outside of the workshop.

● If working on the fuel system, make sure the workshop is ventilated to avoid a build-up of fumes. This applies equally to fume build-up when charging a battery. Do not smoke or allow anyone else to smoke in the workshop.

Fluids

● If you need to drain fuel from the tank, store it in an approved container marked as suitable for the storage of petrol (gasoline) **(see illustration 1.5)**. Do not store fuel in glass jars or bottles.

1.5 Use an approved can only for storing petrol (gasoline)

● Use proprietary engine degreasers or solvents which have a high flash-point, such as paraffin (kerosene), for cleaning off oil, grease and dirt - never use petrol (gasoline) for cleaning. Wear rubber gloves when handling solvent and engine degreaser. The fumes from certain solvents can be dangerous - always work in a well-ventilated area.

Dust, eye and hand protection

● Protect your lungs from inhalation of dust particles by wearing a filtering mask over the nose and mouth. Many frictional materials still contain asbestos which is dangerous to your health. Protect your eyes from spouts of liquid and sprung components by wearing a pair of protective goggles **(see illustration 1.6)**.

1.6 A fire extinguisher, goggles, mask and protective gloves should be at hand in the workshop

● Protect your hands from contact with solvents, fuel and oils by wearing rubber gloves. Alternatively apply a barrier cream to your hands before starting work. If handling hot components or fluids, wear suitable gloves to protect your hands from scalding and burns.

What to do with old fluids

● Old cleaning solvent, fuel, coolant and oils should not be poured down domestic drains or onto the ground. Package the fluid up in old oil containers, label it accordingly, and take it to a garage or disposal facility. Contact your local authority for location of such sites or ring the oil care hotline.

OIL CARE

FOLLOW THE CODE

O I L   B A N K   L I N E
0800 66 33 66
www.oilbankline.org.uk

Note: It is antisocial and illegal to dump oil down the drain. To find the location of your local oil recycling bank, call this number free.

In the USA, note that any oil supplier must accept used oil for recycling.

2 Fasteners -
screws, bolts and nuts

Fastener types and applications

Bolts and screws

● Fastener head types are either of hexagonal, Torx or splined design, with internal and external versions of each type **(see illustrations 2.1 and 2.2)**; splined head fasteners are not in common use on motorcycles. The conventional slotted or Phillips head design is used for certain screws. Bolt or screw length is always measured from the underside of the head to the end of the item **(see illustration 2.11)**.

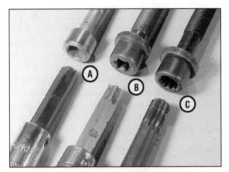

2.1 Internal hexagon/Allen (A), Torx (B) and splined (C) fasteners, with corresponding bits

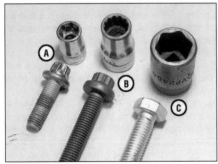

2.2 External Torx (A), splined (B) and hexagon (O) fasteners, with corresponding sockets

● Certain fasteners on the motorcycle have a tensile marking on their heads, the higher the marking the stronger the fastener. High tensile fasteners generally carry a 10 or higher marking. Never replace a high tensile fastener with one of a lower tensile strength.

Washers (see illustration 2.3)

● Plain washers are used between a fastener head and a component to prevent damage to the component or to spread the load when torque is applied. Plain washers can also be used as spacers or shims in certain assemblies. Copper or aluminium plain washers are often used as sealing washers on drain plugs.

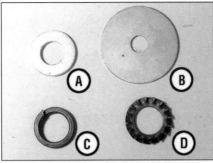

2.3 Plain washer (A), penny washer (B), spring washer (C) and serrated washer (D)

● The split-ring spring washer works by applying axial tension between the fastener head and component. If flattened, it is fatigued and must be renewed. If a plain (flat) washer is used on the fastener, position the spring washer between the fastener and the plain washer.
● Serrated star type washers dig into the fastener and component faces, preventing loosening. They are often used on electrical earth (ground) connections to the frame.
● Cone type washers (sometimes called Belleville) are conical and when tightened apply axial tension between the fastener head and component. They must be installed with the dished side against the component and often carry an OUTSIDE marking on their outer face. If flattened, they are fatigued and must be renewed.
● Tab washers are used to lock plain nuts or bolts on a shaft. A portion of the tab washer is bent up hard against one flat of the nut or bolt to prevent it loosening. Due to the tab washer being deformed in use, a new tab washer should be used every time it is disturbed.
● Wave washers are used to take up endfloat on a shaft. They provide light springing and prevent excessive side-to-side play of a component. Can be found on rocker arm shafts.

Nuts and split pins

● Conventional plain nuts are usually six-sided **(see illustration 2.4)**. They are sized by thread diameter and pitch. High tensile nuts carry a number on one end to denote their tensile strength.

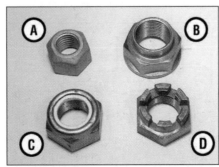

2.4 Plain nut (A), shouldered locknut (B), nylon insert nut (C) and castellated nut (D)

● Self-locking nuts either have a nylon insert, or two spring metal tabs, or a shoulder which is staked into a groove in the shaft - their advantage over conventional plain nuts is a resistance to loosening due to vibration. The nylon insert type can be used a number of times, but must be renewed when the friction of the nylon insert is reduced, ie when the nut spins freely on the shaft. The spring tab type can be reused unless the tabs are damaged. The shouldered type must be renewed every time it is disturbed.
● Split pins (cotter pins) are used to lock a castellated nut to a shaft or to prevent slackening of a plain nut. Common applications are wheel axles and brake torque arms. Because the split pin arms are deformed to lock around the nut a new split pin must always be used on installation - always fit the correct size split pin which will fit snugly in the shaft hole. Make sure the split pin arms are correctly located around the nut **(see illustrations 2.5 and 2.6)**.

2.5 Bend split pin (cotter pin) arms as shown (arrows) to secure a castellated nut

2.6 Bend split pin (cotter pin) arms as shown to secure a plain nut

> *Caution: If the castellated nut slots do not align with the shaft hole after tightening to the torque setting, tighten the nut until the next slot aligns with the hole - never slacken the nut to align its slot.*

● R-pins (shaped like the letter R), or slip pins as they are sometimes called, are sprung and can be reused if they are otherwise in good condition. Always install R-pins with their closed end facing forwards **(see illustration 2.7)**.

2.7 Correct fitting of R-pin. Arrow indicates forward direction

Circlips (see illustration 2.8)

● Circlips (sometimes called snap-rings) are used to retain components on a shaft or in a housing and have corresponding external or internal ears to permit removal. Parallel-sided (machined) circlips can be installed either way round in their groove, whereas stamped circlips (which have a chamfered edge on one face) must be installed with the chamfer facing away from the direction of thrust load **(see illustration 2.9)**.

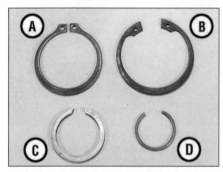

2.8 External stamped circlip (A), internal stamped circlip (B), machined circlip (C) and wire circlip (D)

● Always use circlip pliers to remove and install circlips; expand or compress them just enough to remove them. After installation, rotate the circlip in its groove to ensure it is securely seated. If installing a circlip on a splined shaft, always align its opening with a shaft channel to ensure the circlip ends are well supported and unlikely to catch **(see illustration 2.10)**.

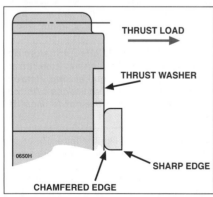

2.9 Correct fitting of a stamped circlip

THRUST LOAD

THRUST WASHER

SHARP EDGE

CHAMFERED EDGE

0650H

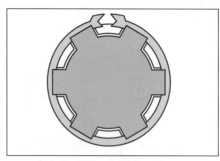

2.10 Align circlip opening with shaft channel

● Circlips can wear due to the thrust of components and become loose in their grooves, with the subsequent danger of becoming dislodged in operation. For this reason, renewal is advised every time a circlip is disturbed.
● Wire circlips are commonly used as piston pin retaining clips. If a removal tang is provided, long-nosed pliers can be used to dislodge them, otherwise careful use of a small flat-bladed screwdriver is necessary. Wire circlips should be renewed every time they are disturbed.

Thread diameter and pitch

● Diameter of a male thread (screw, bolt or stud) is the outside diameter of the threaded portion **(see illustration 2.11)**. Most motorcycle manufacturers use the ISO (International Standards Organisation) metric system expressed in millimetres, eg M6 refers to a 6 mm diameter thread. Sizing is the same for nuts, except that the thread diameter is measured across the valleys of the nut.
● Pitch is the distance between the peaks of the thread **(see illustration 2.11)**. It is expressed in millimetres, thus a common bolt size may be expressed as 6.0 x 1.0 mm (6 mm thread diameter and 1 mm pitch). Generally pitch increases in proportion to thread diameter, although there are always exceptions.
● Thread diameter and pitch are related for conventional fastener applications and the accompanying table can be used as a guide. Additionally, the AF (Across Flats), spanner or socket size dimension of the bolt or nut **(see illustration 2.11)** is linked to thread and pitch specification. Thread pitch can be measured with a thread gauge **(see illustration 2.12)**.

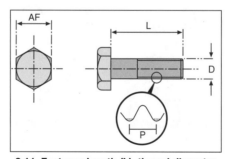

2.11 Fastener length (L), thread diameter (D), thread pitch (P) and head size (AF)

AF

L

D

P

2.12 Using a thread gauge to measure pitch

AF size	Thread diameter x pitch (mm)
8 mm	M5 x 0.8
8 mm	M6 x 1.0
10 mm	M6 x 1.0
12 mm	M8 x 1.25
14 mm	M10 x 1.25
17 mm	M12 x 1.25

● The threads of most fasteners are of the right-hand type, ie they are turned clockwise to tighten and anti-clockwise to loosen. The reverse situation applies to left-hand thread fasteners, which are turned anti-clockwise to tighten and clockwise to loosen. Left-hand threads are used where rotation of a component might loosen a conventional right-hand thread fastener.

Seized fasteners

● Corrosion of external fasteners due to water or reaction between two dissimilar metals can occur over a period of time. It will build up sooner in wet conditions or in countries where salt is used on the roads during the winter. If a fastener is severely corroded it is likely that normal methods of removal will fail and result in its head being ruined. When you attempt removal, the fastener thread should be heard to crack free and unscrew easily - if it doesn't, stop there before damaging something.
● A smart tap on the head of the fastener will often succeed in breaking free corrosion which has occurred in the threads **(see illustration 2.13)**.
● An aerosol penetrating fluid (such as WD-40) applied the night beforehand may work its way down into the thread and ease removal. Depending on the location, you may be able to make up a Plasticine well around the fastener head and fill it with penetrating fluid.

2.13 A sharp tap on the head of a fastener will often break free a corroded thread

● If you are working on an engine internal component, corrosion will most likely not be a problem due to the well lubricated environment. However, components can be very tight and an impact driver is a useful tool in freeing them **(see illustration 2.14)**.

2.14 Using an impact driver to free a fastener

● Where corrosion has occurred between dissimilar metals (eg steel and aluminium alloy), the application of heat to the fastener head will create a disproportionate expansion rate between the two metals and break the seizure caused by the corrosion. Whether heat can be applied depends on the location of the fastener - any surrounding components likely to be damaged must first be removed **(see illustration 2.15)**. Heat can be applied using a paint stripper heat gun or clothes iron, or by immersing the component in boiling water - wear protective gloves to prevent scalding or burns to the hands.

2.15 Using heat to free a seized fastener

● As a last resort, it is possible to use a hammer and cold chisel to work the fastener head unscrewed **(see illustration 2.16)**. This will damage the fastener, but more importantly extreme care must be taken not to damage the surrounding component.

Caution: Remember that the component being secured is generally of more value than the bolt, nut or screw - when the fastener is freed, do not unscrew it with force, instead work the fastener back and forth when resistance is felt to prevent thread damage.

2.16 Using a hammer and chisel to free a seized fastener

Broken fasteners and damaged heads

● If the shank of a broken bolt or screw is accessible you can grip it with self-locking grips. The knurled wheel type stud extractor tool or self-gripping stud puller tool is particularly useful for removing the long studs which screw into the cylinder mouth surface of the crankcase or bolts and screws from which the head has broken off **(see illustration 2.17)**. Studs can also be removed by locking two nuts together on the threaded end of the stud and using a spanner on the lower nut **(see illustration 2.18)**.

2.17 Using a stud extractor tool to remove a broken crankcase stud

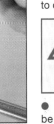

2.18 Two nuts can be locked together to unscrew a stud from a component

● A bolt or screw which has broken off below or level with the casing must be extracted using a screw extractor set. Centre punch the fastener to centralise the drill bit, then drill a hole in the fastener **(see illustration 2.19)**. Select a drill bit which is approximately half to three-quarters the

2.19 When using a screw extractor, first drill a hole in the fastener . . .

diameter of the fastener and drill to a depth which will accommodate the extractor. Use the largest size extractor possible, but avoid leaving too small a wall thickness otherwise the extractor will merely force the fastener walls outwards wedging it in the casing thread.
● If a spiral type extractor is used, thread it anti-clockwise into the fastener. As it is screwed in, it will grip the fastener and unscrew it from the casing **(see illustration 2.20)**.

2.20 . . . then thread the extractor anti-clockwise into the fastener

● If a taper type extractor is used, tap it into the fastener so that it is firmly wedged in place. Unscrew the extractor (anti-clockwise) to draw the fastener out.

⚠️ *Warning: Stud extractors are very hard and may break off in the fastener if care is not taken - ask an engineer about spark erosion if this happens.*

● Alternatively, the broken bolt/screw can be drilled out and the hole retapped for an oversize bolt/screw or a diamond-section thread insert. It is essential that the drilling is carried out squarely and to the correct depth, otherwise the casing may be ruined - if in doubt, entrust the work to an engineer.
● Bolts and nuts with rounded corners cause the correct size spanner or socket to slip when force is applied. Of the types of spanner/socket available always use a six-point type rather than an eight or twelve-point type - better grip

2.21 Comparison of surface drive ring spanner (left) with 12-point type (right)

is obtained. Surface drive spanners grip the middle of the hex flats, rather than the corners, and are thus good in cases of damaged heads **(see illustration 2.21).**

● Slotted-head or Phillips-head screws are often damaged by the use of the wrong size screwdriver. Allen-head and Torx-head screws are much less likely to sustain damage. If enough of the screw head is exposed you can use a hacksaw to cut a slot in its head and then use a conventional flat-bladed screwdriver to remove it. Alternatively use a hammer and cold chisel to tap the head of the fastener around to slacken it. Always replace damaged fasteners with new ones, preferably Torx or Allen-head type.

A dab of valve grinding compound between the screw head and screw-driver tip will often give a good grip.

Thread repair

● Threads (particularly those in aluminium alloy components) can be damaged by overtightening, being assembled with dirt in the threads, or from a component working loose and vibrating. Eventually the thread will fail completely, and it will be impossible to tighten the fastener.

● If a thread is damaged or clogged with old locking compound it can be renovated with a thread repair tool (thread chaser) **(see illustrations 2.22 and 2.23);** special thread

2.22 A thread repair tool being used to correct an internal thread

2.23 A thread repair tool being used to correct an external thread

chasers are available for spark plug hole threads. The tool will not cut a new thread, but clean and true the original thread. Make sure that you use the correct diameter and pitch tool. Similarly, external threads can be cleaned up with a die or a thread restorer file **(see illustration 2.24).**

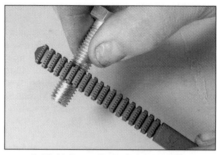

2.24 Using a thread restorer file

● It is possible to drill out the old thread and retap the component to the next thread size. This will work where there is enough surrounding material and a new bolt or screw can be obtained. Sometimes, however, this is not possible - such as where the bolt/screw passes through another component which must also be suitably modified, also in cases where a spark plug or oil drain plug cannot be obtained in a larger diameter thread size.

● The diamond-section thread insert (often known by its popular trade name of Heli-Coil) is a simple and effective method of renewing the thread and retaining the original size. A kit can be purchased which contains the tap, insert and installing tool **(see illustration 2.25).** Drill out the damaged thread with the size drill specified **(see illustration 2.26).** Carefully retap the thread **(see illustration 2.27).** Install the

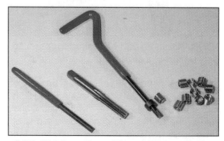

2.25 Obtain a thread insert kit to suit the thread diameter and pitch required

2.26 To install a thread insert, first drill out the original thread . . .

2.27 . . . tap a new thread . . .

2.28 . . . fit insert on the installing tool . . .

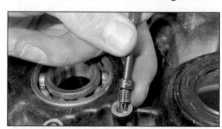

2.29 . . . and thread into the component . . .

2.30 . . . break off the tang when complete

insert on the installing tool and thread it slowly into place using a light downward pressure **(see illustrations 2.28 and 2.29).** When positioned between a 1/4 and 1/2 turn below the surface withdraw the installing tool and use the break-off tool to press down on the tang, breaking it off **(see illustration 2.30).**

● There are epoxy thread repair kits on the market which can rebuild stripped internal threads, although this repair should not be used on high load-bearing components.

Thread locking and sealing compounds

● Locking compounds are used in locations where the fastener is prone to loosening due to vibration or on important safety-related items which might cause loss of control of the motorcycle if they fail. It is also used where important fasteners cannot be secured by other means such as lockwashers or split pins.

● Before applying locking compound, make sure that the threads (internal and external) are clean and dry with all old compound removed. Select a compound to suit the component being secured - a non-permanent general locking and sealing type is suitable for most applications, but a high strength type is needed for permanent fixing of studs in castings. Apply a drop or two of the compound to the first few threads of the fastener, then thread it into place and tighten to the specified torque. Do not apply excessive thread locking compound otherwise the thread may be damaged on subsequent removal.

● Certain fasteners are impregnated with a dry film type coating of locking compound on their threads. Always renew this type of fastener if disturbed.

● Anti-seize compounds, such as copper-based greases, can be applied to protect threads from seizure due to extreme heat and corrosion. A common instance is spark plug threads and exhaust system fasteners.

---

3 Measuring tools and gauges

Feeler gauges

● Feeler gauges (or blades) are used for measuring small gaps and clearances (see illustration 3.1). They can also be used to measure endfloat (sideplay) of a component on a shaft where access is not possible with a dial gauge.

● Feeler gauge sets should be treated with care and not bent or damaged. They are etched with their size on one face. Keep them clean and very lightly oiled to prevent corrosion build-up.

3.1 Feeler gauges are used for measuring small gaps and clearances - thickness is marked on one face of gauge

● When measuring a clearance, select a gauge which is a light sliding fit between the two components. You may need to use two gauges together to measure the clearance accurately.

Micrometers

● A micrometer is a precision tool capable of measuring to 0.01 or 0.001 of a millimetre. It should always be stored in its case and not in the general toolbox. It must be kept clean and never dropped, otherwise its frame or measuring anvils could be distorted resulting in inaccurate readings.

● External micrometers are used for measuring outside diameters of components and have many more applications than internal micrometers. Micrometers are available in different size ranges, eg 0 to 25 mm, 25 to 50 mm, and upwards in 25 mm steps; some large micrometers have interchangeable anvils to allow a range of measurements to be taken. Generally the largest precision measurement you are likely to take on a motorcycle is the piston diameter.

● Internal micrometers (or bore micrometers) are used for measuring inside diameters, such as valve guides and cylinder bores. Telescoping gauges and small hole gauges are used in conjunction with an external micrometer, whereas the more expensive internal micrometers have their own measuring device.

External micrometer

Note: *The conventional analogue type instrument is described. Although much easier to read, digital micrometers are considerably more expensive.*

● Always check the calibration of the micrometer before use. With the anvils closed (0 to 25 mm type) or set over a test gauge (for

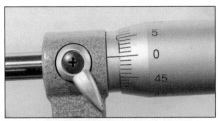

3.2 Check micrometer calibration before use

the larger types) the scale should read zero (see illustration 3.2); make sure that the anvils (and test piece) are clean first. Any discrepancy can be adjusted by referring to the instructions supplied with the tool. Remember that the micrometer is a precision measuring tool - don't force the anvils closed, use the ratchet (4) on the end of the micrometer to close it. In this way, a measured force is always applied.

● To use, first make sure that the item being measured is clean. Place the anvil of the micrometer (1) against the item and use the thimble (2) to bring the spindle (3) lightly into contact with the other side of the item (see illustration 3.3). Don't tighten the thimble down because this will damage the micrometer - instead use the ratchet (4) on the end of the micrometer. The ratchet mechanism applies a measured force preventing damage to the instrument.

● The micrometer is read by referring to the linear scale on the sleeve and the annular scale on the thimble. Read off the sleeve first to obtain the base measurement, then add the fine measurement from the thimble to obtain the overall reading. The linear scale on the sleeve represents the measuring range of the micrometer (eg 0 to 25 mm). The annular scale

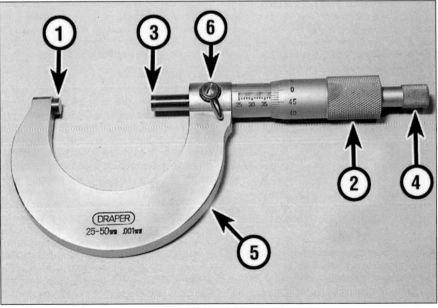

3.3 Micrometer component parts

1 Anvil	3 Spindle	5 Frame
2 Thimble	4 Ratchet	6 Locking lever

on the thimble will be in graduations of 0.01 mm (or as marked on the frame) - one full revolution of the thimble will move 0.5 mm on the linear scale. Take the reading where the datum line on the sleeve intersects the thimble's scale. Always position the eye directly above the scale otherwise an inaccurate reading will result.

In the example shown the item measures 2.95 mm (see illustration 3.4):

Linear scale	2.00 mm
Linear scale	0.50 mm
Annular scale	0.45 mm
Total figure	**2.95 mm**

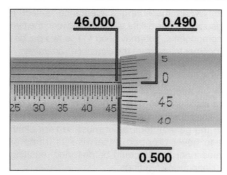

3.5 Micrometer reading of 46.99 mm on linear and annular scales . . .

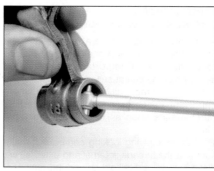

3.7 Expand the telescoping gauge in the bore, lock its position . . .

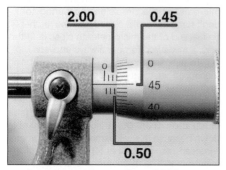

3.4 Micrometer reading of 2.95 mm

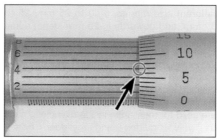

3.6 . . . and 0.004 mm on vernier scale

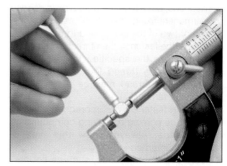

3.8 . . . then measure the gauge with a micrometer

Most micrometers have a locking lever (6) on the frame to hold the setting in place, allowing the item to be removed from the micrometer.

● Some micrometers have a vernier scale on their sleeve, providing an even finer measurement to be taken, in 0.001 increments of a millimetre. Take the sleeve and thimble measurement as described above, then check which graduation on the vernier scale aligns with that of the annular scale on the thimble Note: *The eye must be perpendicular to the scale when taking the vernier reading - if necessary rotate the body of the micrometer to ensure this.* Multiply the vernier scale figure by 0.001 and add it to the base and fine measurement figures.

In the example shown the item measures 46.994 mm (see illustrations 3.5 and 3.6):

Linear scale (base)	46.000 mm
Linear scale (base)	00.500 mm
Annular scale (fine)	00.490 mm
Vernier scale	00.004 mm
Total figure	**46.994 mm**

Internal micrometer

● Internal micrometers are available for measuring bore diameters, but are expensive and unlikely to be available for home use. It is suggested that a set of telescoping gauges and small hole gauges, both of which must be used with an external micrometer, will suffice for taking internal measurements on a motorcycle.

● Telescoping gauges can be used to measure internal diameters of components. Select a gauge with the correct size range, make sure its ends are clean and insert it into the bore. Expand the gauge, then lock its position and withdraw it from the bore (see illustration 3.7). Measure across the gauge ends with a micrometer (see illustration 3.8).

● Very small diameter bores (such as valve guides) are measured with a small hole gauge. Once adjusted to a slip-fit inside the component, its position is locked and the gauge withdrawn for measurement with a micrometer (see illustrations 3.9 and 3.10).

Vernier caliper

Note: *The conventional linear and dial gauge type instruments are described. Digital types are easier to read, but are far more expensive.*

● The vernier caliper does not provide the precision of a micrometer, but is versatile in being able to measure internal and external diameters. Some types also incorporate a depth gauge. It is ideal for measuring clutch plate friction material and spring free lengths.

● To use the conventional linear scale vernier, slacken off the vernier clamp screws (1) and set its jaws over (2), or inside (3), the item to be measured (see illustration 3.11). Slide the jaw into contact, using the thumb-wheel (4) for fine movement of the sliding scale (5) then tighten the clamp screws (1). Read off the main scale (6) where the zero on the sliding scale (5) intersects it, taking the whole number to the left of the zero; this provides the base measurement. View along the sliding scale and select the division which

3.9 Expand the small hole gauge in the bore, lock its position . . .

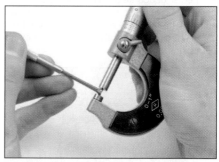

3.10 . . . then measure the gauge with a micrometer

lines up exactly with any of the divisions on the main scale, noting that the divisions usually represents 0.02 of a millimetre. Add this fine measurement to the base measurement to obtain the total reading.

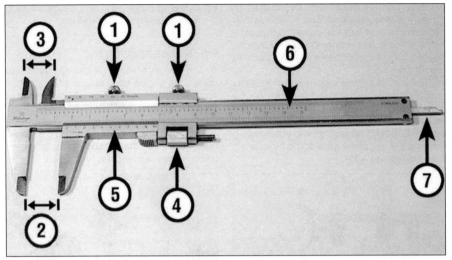

3.11 Vernier component parts (linear gauge)

1 Clamp screws	3 Internal jaws	5 Sliding scale	7 Depth gauge
2 External jaws	4 Thumbwheel	6 Main scale	

In the example shown the item measures 55.92 mm **(see illustration 3.12)**:

Base measurement	55.00 mm
Fine measurement	00.92 mm
Total figure	**55.92 mm**

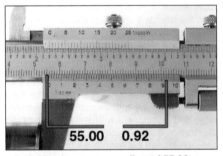

3.12 Vernier gauge reading of 55.92 mm

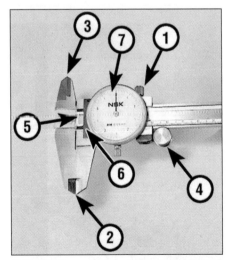

3.13 Vernier component parts (dial gauge)

1 Clamp screw	5 Main scale
2 External jaws	6 Sliding scale
3 Internal jaws	7 Dial gauge
4 Thumbwheel	

● Some vernier calipers are equipped with a dial gauge for fine measurement. Before use, check that the jaws are clean, then close them fully and check that the dial gauge reads zero. If necessary adjust the gauge ring accordingly. Slacken the vernier clamp screw (1) and set its jaws over (2), or inside (3), the item to be measured **(see illustration 3.13)**. Slide the jaws into contact, using the thumbwheel (4) for fine movement. Read off the main scale (5) where the edge of the sliding scale (6) intersects it, taking the whole number to the left of the zero; this provides the base measurement. Read off the needle position on the dial gauge (7) scale to provide the fine measurement; each division represents 0.05 of a millimetre. Add this fine measurement to the base measurement to obtain the total reading.

In the example shown the item measures 55.95 mm **(see illustration 3.14)**:

Base measurement	55.00 mm
Fine measurement	00.95 mm
Total figure	**55.95 mm**

3.14 Vernier gauge reading of 55.95 mm

Plastigauge

● Plastigauge is a plastic material which can be compressed between two surfaces to measure the oil clearance between them. The width of the compressed Plastigauge is measured against a calibrated scale to determine the clearance.

● Common uses of Plastigauge are for measuring the clearance between crankshaft journal and main bearing inserts, between crankshaft journal and big-end bearing inserts, and between camshaft and bearing surfaces. The following example describes big-end oil clearance measurement.

● Handle the Plastigauge material carefully to prevent distortion. Using a sharp knife, cut a length which corresponds with the width of the bearing being measured and place it carefully across the journal so that it is parallel with the shaft **(see illustration 3.15)**. Carefully install both bearing shells and the connecting rod. Without rotating the rod on the journal tighten its bolts or nuts (as applicable) to the specified torque. The connecting rod and bearings are then disassembled and the crushed Plastigauge examined.

3.15 Plastigauge placed across shaft journal

● Using the scale provided in the Plastigauge kit, measure the width of the material to determine the oil clearance **(see illustration 3.16)**. Always remove all traces of Plastigauge after use using your fingernails.

Caution: Arriving at the correct clearance demands that the assembly is torqued correctly, according to the settings and sequence (where applicable) provided by the motorcycle manufacturer.

**3.16 Measuring the width
of the crushed Plastigauge**

Dial gauge or DTI (Dial Test Indicator)

● A dial gauge can be used to accurately measure small amounts of movement. Typical uses are measuring shaft runout or shaft endfloat (sideplay) and setting piston position for ignition timing on two-strokes. A dial gauge set usually comes with a range of different probes and adapters and mounting equipment.

● The gauge needle must point to zero when at rest. Rotate the ring around its periphery to zero the gauge.

● Check that the gauge is capable of reading the extent of movement in the work. Most gauges have a small dial set in the face which records whole millimetres of movement as well as the fine scale around the face periphery which is calibrated in 0.01 mm divisions. Read off the small dial first to obtain the base measurement, then add the measurement from the fine scale to obtain the total reading.

In the example shown the gauge reads 1.48 mm **(see illustration 3.17)**:

Base measurement	1.00 mm
Fine measurement	0.48 mm
Total figure	**1.48 mm**

3.17 Dial gauge reading of 1.48 mm

● If measuring shaft runout, the shaft must be supported in vee-blocks and the gauge mounted on a stand perpendicular to the shaft. Rest the tip of the gauge against the centre of the shaft and rotate the shaft slowly whilst watching the gauge reading **(see illustration 3.18)**. Take several measurements along the length of the shaft and record the

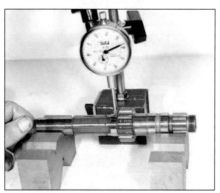

3.18 Using a dial gauge to measure shaft runout

maximum gauge reading as the amount of runout in the shaft. **Note:** *The reading obtained will be total runout at that point - some manufacturers specify that the runout figure is halved to compare with their specified runout limit.*

● Endfloat (sideplay) measurement requires that the gauge is mounted securely to the surrounding component with its probe touching the end of the shaft. Using hand pressure, push and pull on the shaft noting the maximum endfloat recorded on the gauge **(see illustration 3.19)**.

3.19 Using a dial gauge to measure shaft endfloat

● A dial gauge with suitable adapters can be used to determine piston position BTDC on two-stroke engines for the purposes of ignition timing. The gauge, adapter and suitable length probe are installed in the place of the spark plug and the gauge zeroed at TDC. If the piston position is specified as 1.14 mm BTDC, rotate the engine back to 2.00 mm BTDC, then slowly forwards to 1.14 mm BTDC.

Cylinder compression gauges

● A compression gauge is used for measuring cylinder compression. Either the rubber-cone type or the threaded adapter type can be used. The latter is preferred to ensure a perfect seal against the cylinder head. A 0 to 300 psi (0 to 20 Bar) type gauge (for petrol/gasoline engines) will be suitable for motorcycles.

● The spark plug is removed and the gauge either held hard against the cylinder head (cone type) or the gauge adapter screwed into the cylinder head (threaded type) **(see illustration 3.20)**. Cylinder compression is measured with the engine turning over, but not running - carry out the compression test as described in

3.20 Using a rubber-cone type cylinder compression gauge

Fault Finding Equipment. The gauge will hold the reading until manually released.

Oil pressure gauge

● An oil pressure gauge is used for measuring engine oil pressure. Most gauges come with a set of adapters to fit the thread of the take-off point **(see illustration 3.21)**. If the take-off point specified by the motorcycle manufacturer is an external oil pipe union, make sure that the specified replacement union is used to prevent oil starvation.

3.21 Oil pressure gauge and take-off point adapter (arrow)

● Oil pressure is measured with the engine running (at a specific rpm) and often the manufacturer will specify pressure limits for a cold and hot engine.

Straight-edge and surface plate

● If checking the gasket face of a component for warpage, place a steel rule or precision straight-edge across the gasket face and measure any gap between the straight-edge and component with feeler gauges **(see illustration 3.22)**. Check diagonally across the component and between mounting holes **(see illustration 3.23)**.

3.22 Use a straight-edge and feeler gauges to check for warpage

3.23 Check for warpage in these directions

● Checking individual components for warpage, such as clutch plain (metal) plates, requires a perfectly flat plate or piece or plate glass and feeler gauges.

4 Torque and leverage

What is torque?

● Torque describes the twisting force about a shaft. The amount of torque applied is determined by the distance from the centre of the shaft to the end of the lever and the amount of force being applied to the end of the lever; distance multiplied by force equals torque.

● The manufacturer applies a measured torque to a bolt or nut to ensure that it will not slacken in use and to hold two components securely together without movement in the joint. The actual torque setting depends on the thread size, bolt or nut material and the composition of the components being held.

● Too little torque may cause the fastener to loosen due to vibration, whereas too much torque will distort the joint faces of the component or cause the fastener to shear off. Always stick to the specified torque setting.

Using a torque wrench

● Check the calibration of the torque wrench and make sure it has a suitable range for the job. Torque wrenches are available in Nm (Newton-metres), kgf m (kilograms-force metre), lbf ft (pounds-feet), lbf in (inch-pounds). Do not confuse lbf ft with lbf in.

● Adjust the tool to the desired torque on the scale (see illustration 4.1). If your torque wrench is not calibrated in the units specified, carefully convert the figure (see Conversion Factors). A manufacturer sometimes gives a torque setting as a range (8 to 10 Nm) rather than a single figure - in this case set the tool midway between the two settings. The same torque may be expressed as 9 Nm ± 1 Nm. Some torque wrenches have a method of locking the setting so that it isn't inadvertently altered during use.

4.1 Set the torque wrench index mark to the setting required, in this case 12 Nm

● Install the bolts/nuts in their correct location and secure them lightly. Their threads must be clean and free of any old locking compound. Unless specified the threads and flange should be dry - oiled threads are necessary in certain circumstances and the manufacturer will take this into account in the specified torque figure. Similarly, the manufacturer may also specify the application of thread-locking compound.

● Tighten the fasteners in the specified sequence until the torque wrench clicks, indicating that the torque setting has been reached. Apply the torque again to double-check the setting. Where different thread diameter fasteners secure the component, as a rule tighten the larger diameter ones first.

● When the torque wrench has been finished with, release the lock (where applicable) and fully back off its setting to zero - do not leave the torque wrench tensioned. Also, do not use a torque wrench for slackening a fastener.

Angle-tightening

● Manufacturers often specify a figure in degrees for final tightening of a fastener. This usually follows tightening to a specific torque setting.

● A degree disc can be set and attached to the socket (see illustration 4.2) or a protractor can be used to mark the angle of movement on the bolt/nut head and the surrounding casting (see illustration 4.3).

4.2 Angle tightening can be accomplished with a torque-angle gauge . . .

4.3 . . . or by marking the angle on the surrounding component

Loosening sequences

● Where more than one bolt/nut secures a component, loosen each fastener evenly a little at a time. In this way, not all the stress of the joint is held by one fastener and the components are not likely to distort.

● If a tightening sequence is provided, work in the REVERSE of this, but if not, work from the outside in, in a criss-cross sequence (see illustration 4.4).

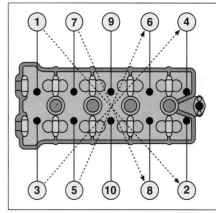

4.4 When slackening, work from the outside inwards

Tightening sequences

● If a component is held by more than one fastener it is important that the retaining bolts/nuts are tightened evenly to prevent uneven stress build-up and distortion of sealing faces. This is especially important on high-compression joints such as the cylinder head.

● A sequence is usually provided by the manufacturer, either in a diagram or actually marked in the casting. If not, always start in the centre and work outwards in a criss-cross pattern (see illustration 4.5). Start off by securing all bolts/nuts finger-tight, then set the torque wrench and tighten each fastener by a small amount in sequence until the final torque is reached. By following this practice,

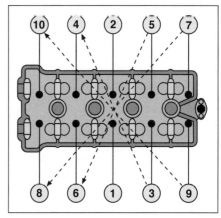

4.5 When tightening, work from the inside outwards

the joint will be held evenly and will not be distorted. Important joints, such as the cylinder head and big-end fasteners often have two- or three-stage torque settings.

Applying leverage

● Use tools at the correct angle. Position a socket wrench or spanner on the bolt/nut so that you pull it towards you when loosening. If this can't be done, push the spanner without curling your fingers around it **(see illustration 4.6)** - the spanner may slip or the fastener loosen suddenly, resulting in your fingers being crushed against a component.

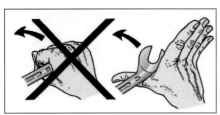

4.6 If you can't pull on the spanner to loosen a fastener, push with your hand open

● Additional leverage is gained by extending the length of the lever. The best way to do this is to use a breaker bar instead of the regular length tool, or to slip a length of tubing over the end of the spanner or socket wrench.
● If additional leverage will not work, the fastener head is either damaged or firmly corroded in place (see *Fasteners*).

5 Bearings

Bearing removal and installation

Drivers and sockets

● Before removing a bearing, always inspect the casing to see which way it must be driven out - some casings will have retaining plates or a cast step. Also check for any identifying markings on the bearing and if installed to a certain depth, measure this at this stage. Some roller bearings are sealed on one side - take note of the original fitted position.
● Bearings can be driven out of a casing using a bearing driver tool (with the correct size head) or a socket of the correct diameter. Select the driver head or socket so that it contacts the outer race of the bearing, not the balls/rollers or inner race. Always support the casing around the bearing housing with wood blocks, otherwise there is a risk of fracture. The bearing is driven out with a few blows on the driver or socket from a heavy mallet. Unless access is severely restricted (as with wheel bearings), a pin-punch is not recommended unless it is moved around the bearing to keep it square in its housing.

● The same equipment can be used to install bearings. Make sure the bearing housing is supported on wood blocks and line up the bearing in its housing. Fit the bearing as noted on removal - generally they are installed with their marked side facing outwards. Tap the bearing squarely into its housing using a driver or socket which bears only on the bearing's outer race - contact with the bearing balls/rollers or inner race will destroy it **(see illustrations 5.1 and 5.2)**.
● Check that the bearing inner race and balls/rollers rotate freely.

5.1 Using a bearing driver against the bearing's outer race

5.2 Using a large socket against the bearing's outer race

Pullers and slide-hammers

● Where a bearing is pressed on a shaft a puller will be required to extract it **(see illustration 5.3)**. Make sure that the puller clamp or legs fit securely behind the bearing and are unlikely to slip out. If pulling a bearing

5.3 This bearing puller clamps behind the bearing and pressure is applied to the shaft end to draw the bearing off

off a gear shaft for example, you may have to locate the puller behind a gear pinion if there is no access to the race and draw the gear pinion off the shaft as well **(see illustration 5.4)**.

> *Caution: Ensure that the puller's centre bolt locates securely against the end of the shaft and will not slip when pressure is applied. Also ensure that puller does not damage the shaft end.*

5.4 Where no access is available to the rear of the bearing, it is sometimes possible to draw off the adjacent component

● Operate the puller so that its centre bolt exerts pressure on the shaft end and draws the bearing off the shaft.
● When installing the bearing on the shaft, tap only on the bearing's inner race - contact with the balls/rollers or outer race with destroy the bearing. Use a socket or length of tubing as a drift which fits over the shaft end **(see illustration 5.5)**.

5.5 When installing a bearing on a shaft use a piece of tubing which bears only on the bearing's inner race

● Where a bearing locates in a blind hole in a casing, it cannot be driven or pulled out as described above. A slide-hammer with knife-edged bearing puller attachment will be required. The puller attachment passes through the bearing and when tightened expands to fit firmly behind the bearing **(see illustration 5.6)**. By operating the slide-hammer part of the tool the bearing is jarred out of its housing **(see illustration 5.7)**.
● It is possible, if the bearing is of reasonable weight, for it to drop out of its housing if the casing is heated as described opposite. If this

5.6 Expand the bearing puller so that it locks behind the bearing . . .

5.7 . . . attach the slide hammer to the bearing puller

method is attempted, first prepare a work surface which will enable the casing to be tapped face down to help dislodge the bearing - a wood surface is ideal since it will not damage the casing's gasket surface. Wearing protective gloves, tap the heated casing several times against the work surface to dislodge the bearing under its own weight **(see illustration 5.8).**

5.8 Tapping a casing face down on wood blocks can often dislodge a bearing

● Bearings can be installed in blind holes using the driver or socket method described above.

Drawbolts

● Where a bearing or bush is set in the eye of a component, such as a suspension linkage arm or connecting rod small-end, removal by drift may damage the component. Furthermore, a rubber bushing in a shock absorber eye cannot successfully be driven out of position. If access is available to a engineering press, the task is straightforward. If not, a drawbolt can be fabricated to extract the bearing or bush.

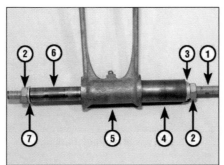

5.9 Drawbolt component parts assembled on a suspension arm

1 *Bolt or length of threaded bar*
2 *Nuts*
3 *Washer (external diameter greater than tubing internal diameter)*
4 *Tubing (internal diameter sufficient to accommodate bearing)*
5 *Suspension arm with bearing*
6 *Tubing (external diameter slightly smaller than bearing)*
7 *Washer (external diameter slightly smaller than bearing)*

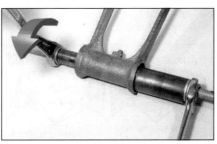

5.10 Drawing the bearing out of the suspension arm

● To extract the bearing/bush you will need a long bolt with nut (or piece of threaded bar with two nuts), a piece of tubing which has an internal diameter larger than the bearing/bush, another piece of tubing which has an external diameter slightly smaller than the bearing/bush, and a selection of washers **(see illustrations 5.9 and 5.10).** Note that the pieces of tubing must be of the same length, or longer, than the bearing/bush.
● The same kit (without the pieces of tubing) can be used to draw the new bearing/bush back into place **(see illustration 5.11).**

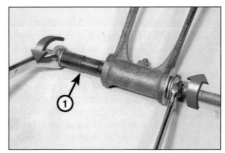

5.11 Installing a new bearing (1) in the suspension arm

Temperature change

● If the bearing's outer race is a tight fit in the casing, the aluminium casing can be heated to release its grip on the bearing. Aluminium will expand at a greater rate than the steel bearing outer race. There are several ways to do this, but avoid any localised extreme heat (such as a blow torch) - aluminium alloy has a low melting point.
● Approved methods of heating a casing are using a domestic oven (heated to 100°C) or immersing the casing in boiling water **(see illustration 5.12).** Low temperature range localised heat sources such as a paint stripper heat gun or clothes iron can also be used **(see illustration 5.13).** Alternatively, soak a rag in boiling water, wring it out and wrap it around the bearing housing.

> ⚠ **Warning: All of these methods require care in use to prevent scalding and burns to the hands. Wear protective gloves when handling hot components.**

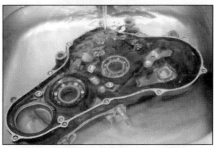

5.12 A casing can be immersed in a sink of boiling water to aid bearing removal

5.13 Using a localised heat source to aid bearing removal

● If heating the whole casing note that plastic components, such as the neutral switch, may suffer - remove them beforehand.
● After heating, remove the bearing as described above. You may find that the expansion is sufficient for the bearing to fall out of the casing under its own weight or with a light tap on the driver or socket.
● If necessary, the casing can be heated to aid bearing installation, and this is sometimes the recommended procedure if the motorcycle manufacturer has designed the housing and bearing fit with this intention.

● Installation of bearings can be eased by placing them in a freezer the night before installation. The steel bearing will contract slightly, allowing easy insertion in its housing. This is often useful when installing steering head outer races in the frame.

Bearing types and markings

● Plain shell bearings, ball bearings, needle roller bearings and tapered roller bearings will all be found on motorcycles (see illustrations 5.14 and 5.15). The ball and roller types are usually caged between an inner and outer race, but uncaged variations may be found.

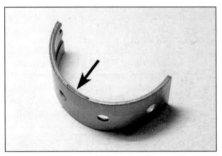

5.14 Shell bearings are either plain or grooved. They are usually identified by colour code (arrow)

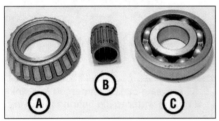

5.15 Tapered roller bearing (A), needle roller bearing (B) and ball journal bearing (C)

● Shell bearings (often called inserts) are usually found at the crankshaft main and connecting rod big-end where they are good at coping with high loads. They are made of a phosphor-bronze material and are impregnated with self-lubricating properties.

● Ball bearings and needle roller bearings consist of a steel inner and outer race with the balls or rollers between the races. They require constant lubrication by oil or grease and are good at coping with axial loads. Taper roller bearings consist of rollers set in a tapered cage set on the inner race; the outer race is separate. They are good at coping with axial loads and prevent movement along the shaft - a typical application is in the steering head.

● Bearing manufacturers produce bearings to ISO size standards and stamp one face of the bearing to indicate its internal and external diameter, load capacity and type (see illustration 5.16).

● Metal bushes are usually of phosphor-bronze material. Rubber bushes are used in suspension mounting eyes. Fibre bushes have also been used in suspension pivots.

5.16 Typical bearing marking

Bearing fault finding

● If a bearing outer race has spun in its housing, the housing material will be damaged. You can use a bearing locking compound to bond the outer race in place if damage is not too severe.

● Shell bearings will fail due to damage of their working surface, as a result of lack of lubrication, corrosion or abrasive particles in the oil (see illustration 5.17). Small particles of dirt in the oil may embed in the bearing material whereas larger particles will score the bearing and shaft journal. If a number of short journeys are made, insufficient heat will be generated to drive off condensation which has built up on the bearings.

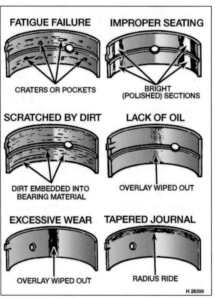

5.17 Typical bearing failures

● Ball and roller bearings will fail due to lack of lubrication or damage to the balls or rollers. Tapered-roller bearings can be damaged by overloading them. Unless the bearing is sealed on both sides, wash it in paraffin (kerosene) to remove all old grease then allow it to dry. Make a visual inspection looking to dented balls or rollers, damaged cages and worn or pitted races (see illustration 5.18).

● A ball bearing can be checked for wear by listening to it when spun. Apply a film of light oil to the bearing and hold it close to the ear - hold the outer race with one hand and spin the inner

5.18 Example of ball journal bearing with damaged balls and cages

5.19 Hold outer race and listen to inner race when spun

race with the other hand (see illustration 5.19). The bearing should be almost silent when spun; if it grates or rattles it is worn.

6 Oil seals

Oil seal removal and installation

● Oil seals should be renewed every time a component is dismantled. This is because the seal lips will become set to the sealing surface and will not necessarily reseal.

● Oil seals can be prised out of position using a large flat-bladed screwdriver (see illustration 6.1). In the case of crankcase seals, check first that the seal is not lipped on the inside, preventing its removal with the crankcases joined.

6.1 Prise out oil seals with a large flat-bladed screwdriver

● New seals are usually installed with their marked face (containing the seal reference code) outwards and the spring side towards the fluid being retained. In certain cases, such as a two-stroke engine crankshaft seal, a double lipped seal may be used due to there being fluid or gas on each side of the joint.

● Use a bearing driver or socket which bears only on the outer hard edge of the seal to install it in the casing - tapping on the inner edge will damage the sealing lip.

Oil seal types and markings

● Oil seals are usually of the single-lipped type. Double-lipped seals are found where a liquid or gas is on both sides of the joint.

● Oil seals can harden and lose their sealing ability if the motorcycle has been in storage for a long period - renewal is the only solution.

● Oil seal manufacturers also conform to the ISO markings for seal size - these are moulded into the outer face of the seal **(see illustration 6.2)**.

6.2 These oil seal markings indicate inside diameter, outside diameter and seal thickness

7 Gaskets and sealants

Types of gasket and sealant

● Gaskets are used to seal the mating surfaces between components and keep lubricants, fluids, vacuum or pressure contained within the assembly. Aluminium gaskets are sometimes found at the cylinder joints, but most gaskets are paper-based. If the mating surfaces of the components being joined are undamaged the gasket can be installed dry, although a dab of sealant or grease will be useful to hold it in place during assembly.

● RTV (Room Temperature Vulcanising) silicone rubber sealants cure when exposed to moisture in the atmosphere. These sealants are good at filling pits or irregular gasket faces, but will tend to be forced out of the joint under very high torque. They can be used to replace a paper gasket, but first make sure that the width of the paper gasket is not essential to the shimming of internal components. RTV sealants should not be used on components containing petrol (gasoline).

● Non-hardening, semi-hardening and hard setting liquid gasket compounds can be used with a gasket or between a metal-to-metal joint. Select the sealant to suit the application: universal non-hardening sealant can be used on virtually all joints; semi-hardening on joint faces which are rough or damaged; hard setting sealant on joints which require a permanent bond and are subjected to high temperature and pressure. **Note:** *Check first if the paper gasket has a bead of sealant*

impregnated in its surface before applying additional sealant.

● When choosing a sealant, make sure it is suitable for the application, particularly if being applied in a high-temperature area or in the vicinity of fuel. Certain manufacturers produce sealants in either clear, silver or black colours to match the finish of the engine. This has a particular application on motorcycles where much of the engine is exposed.

● Do not over-apply sealant. That which is squeezed out on the outside of the joint can be wiped off, whereas an excess of sealant on the inside can break off and clog oilways.

Breaking a sealed joint

● Age, heat, pressure and the use of hard setting sealant can cause two components to stick together so tightly that they are difficult to separate using finger pressure alone. Do not resort to using levers unless there is a pry point provided for this purpose **(see illustration 7.1)** or else the gasket surfaces will be damaged.

● Use a soft-faced hammer **(see illustration 7.2)** or a wood block and conventional hammer to strike the component near the mating surface. Avoid hammering against cast extremities since they may break off. If this method fails, try using a wood wedge between the two components.

> **Caution: If the joint will not separate, double-check that you have removed all the fasteners.**

7.1 If a pry point is provided, apply gently pressure with a flat-bladed screwdriver

7.2 Tap around the joint with a soft-faced mallet if necessary - don't strike cooling fins

Removal of old gasket and sealant

● Paper gaskets will most likely come away complete, leaving only a few traces stuck on

Most components have one or two hollow locating dowels between the two gasket faces. If a dowel cannot be removed, do not resort to gripping it with pliers - it will almost certainly be distorted. Install a close-fitting socket or Phillips screwdriver into the dowel and then grip the outer edge of the dowel to free it.

the sealing faces of the components. It is imperative that all traces are removed to ensure correct sealing of the new gasket.

● Very carefully scrape all traces of gasket away making sure that the sealing surfaces are not gouged or scored by the scraper **(see illustrations 7.3, 7.4 and 7.5)**. Stubborn deposits can be removed by spraying with an aerosol gasket remover. Final preparation of

7.3 Paper gaskets can be scraped off with a gasket scraper tool . . .

7.4 . . . a knife blade . . .

7.5 . . . or a household scraper

7.6 Fine abrasive paper is wrapped around a flat file to clean up the gasket face

7.7 A kitchen scourer can be used on stubborn deposits

the gasket surface can be made with very fine abrasive paper or a plastic kitchen scourer (see illustrations 7.6 and 7.7).

● Old sealant can be scraped or peeled off components, depending on the type originally used. Note that gasket removal compounds are available to avoid scraping the components clean; make sure the gasket remover suits the type of sealant used.

8 Chains

Breaking and joining final drive chains

● Drive chains for all but small bikes are continuous and do not have a clip-type connecting link. The chain must be broken using a chain breaker tool and the new chain securely riveted together using a new soft rivet-type link. Never use a clip-type connecting link instead of a rivet-type link, except in an emergency. Various chain breaking and riveting tools are available, either as separate tools or combined as illustrated in the accompanying photographs - read the instructions supplied with the tool carefully.

⚠ **Warning: The need to rivet the new link pins correctly cannot be overstressed - loss of control of the motorcycle is very likely to result if the chain breaks in use.**

● Rotate the chain and look for the soft link. The soft link pins look like they have been

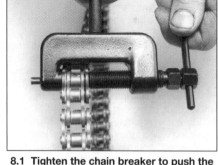

8.1 Tighten the chain breaker to push the pin out of the link . . .

8.2 . . . withdraw the pin, remove the tool . . .

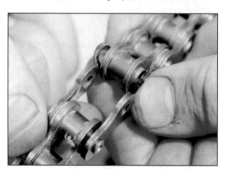

8.3 . . . and separate the chain link

deeply centre-punched instead of peened over like all the other pins (see illustration 8.9) and its sideplate may be a different colour. Position the soft link midway between the sprockets and assemble the chain breaker tool over one of the soft link pins (see illustration 8.1). Operate the tool to push the pin out through the chain (see illustration 8.2). On an O-ring chain, remove the O-rings (see illustration 8.3). Carry out the same procedure on the other soft link pin.

Caution: Certain soft link pins (particularly on the larger chains) may require their ends to be filed or ground off before they can be pressed out using the tool.

● Check that you have the correct size and strength (standard or heavy duty) new soft link - do not reuse the old link. Look for the size marking on the chain sideplates (see illustration 8.10).

● Position the chain ends so that they are engaged over the rear sprocket. On an O-ring

8.4 Insert the new soft link, with O-rings, through the chain ends . . .

8.5 . . . install the O-rings over the pin ends . . .

8.6 . . . followed by the sideplate

chain, install a new O-ring over each pin of the link and insert the link through the two chain ends (see illustration 8.4). Install a new O-ring over the end of each pin, followed by the sideplate (with the chain manufacturer's marking facing outwards) (see illustrations 8.5 and 8.6). On an unsealed chain, insert the link through the two chain ends, then install the sideplate with the chain manufacturer's marking facing outwards.

● Note that it may not be possible to install the sideplate using finger pressure alone. If using a joining tool, assemble it so that the plates of the tool clamp the link and press the sideplate over the pins (see illustration 8.7). Otherwise, use two small sockets placed over

8.7 Push the sideplate into position using a clamp

8.8 Assemble the chain riveting tool over one pin at a time and tighten it fully

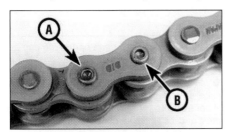

8.9 Pin end correctly riveted (A), pin end unriveted (B)

the rivet ends and two pieces of the wood between a G-clamp. Operate the clamp to press the sideplate over the pins.

● Assemble the joining tool over one pin (following the maker's instructions) and tighten the tool down to spread the pin end securely **(see illustrations 8.8 and 8.9)**. Do the same on the other pin.

> **Warning: Check that the pin ends are secure and that there is no danger of the sideplate coming loose. If the pin ends are cracked the soft link must be renewed.**

Final drive chain sizing

● Chains are sized using a three digit number, followed by a suffix to denote the chain type **(see illustration 8.10)**. Chain type is either standard or heavy duty (thicker sideplates), and also unsealed or O-ring/X-ring type.

● The first digit of the number relates to the pitch of the chain, ie the distance from the centre of one pin to the centre of the next pin **(see illustration 8.11)**. Pitch is expressed in eighths of an inch, as follows:

8.10 Typical chain size and type marking

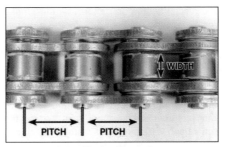

8.11 Chain dimensions

Sizes commencing with a 4 (eg 428) have a pitch of 1/2 inch (12.7 mm)
Sizes commencing with a 5 (eg 520) have a pitch of 5/8 inch (15.9 mm)
Sizes commencing with a 6 (eg 630) have a pitch of 3/4 inch (19.1 mm)

● The second and third digits of the chain size relate to the width of the rollers, again in imperial units, eg the 525 shown has 5/16 inch (7.94 mm) rollers **(see illustration 8.11)**.

9 Hoses

Clamping to prevent flow

● Small-bore flexible hoses can be clamped to prevent fluid flow whilst a component is worked on. Whichever method is used, ensure that the hose material is not permanently distorted or damaged by the clamp.

a) A brake hose clamp available from auto accessory shops **(see illustration 9.1)**.
b) A wingnut type hose clamp **(see illustration 9.2)**.

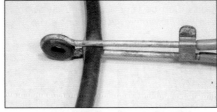

9.1 Hoses can be clamped with an automotive brake hose clamp . . .

9.2 . . . a wingnut type hose clamp . . .

c) Two sockets placed each side of the hose and held with straight-jawed self-locking grips **(see illustration 9.3)**.
d) Thick card each side of the hose held between straight-jawed self-locking grips **(see illustration 9.4)**.

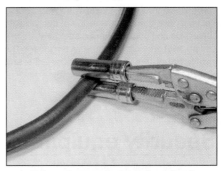

9.3 . . . two sockets and a pair of self-locking grips . . .

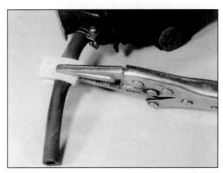

9.4 . . . or thick card and self-locking grips

Freeing and fitting hoses

● Always make sure the hose clamp is moved well clear of the hose end. Grip the hose with your hand and rotate it whilst pulling it off the union. If the hose has hardened due to age and will not move, slit it with a sharp knife and peel its ends off the union **(see illustration 9.5)**.

● Resist the temptation to use grease or soap on the unions to aid installation; although it helps the hose slip over the union it will equally aid the escape of fluid from the joint. It is preferable to soften the hose ends in hot water and wet the inside surface of the hose with water or a fluid which will evaporate.

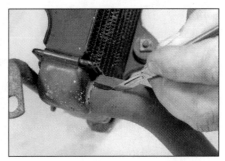

9.5 Cutting a coolant hose free with a sharp knife

Introduction

In less time than it takes to read this introduction, a thief could steal your motorcycle. Returning only to find your bike has gone is one of the worst feelings in the world. Even if the motorcycle is insured against theft, once you've got over the initial shock, you will have the inconvenience of dealing with the police and your insurance company.

The motorcycle is an easy target for the professional thief and the joyrider alike and the official figures on motorcycle theft make for depressing reading; on average a motorcycle is stolen every 16 minutes in the UK!

Motorcycle thefts fall into two categories, those stolen 'to order' and those taken by opportunists. The thief stealing to order will be on the look out for a specific make and model and will go to extraordinary lengths to obtain that motorcycle. The opportunist thief on the other hand will look for easy targets which can be stolen with the minimum of effort and risk.

Whilst it is never going to be possible to make your machine 100% secure, it is estimated that around half of all stolen motorcycles are taken by opportunist thieves. Remember that the opportunist thief is always on the look out for the easy option: if there are two similar motorcycles parked side-by-side, they will target the one with the lowest level of security. By taking a few precautions, you can reduce the chances of your motorcycle being stolen.

Security equipment

There are many specialised motorcycle security devices available and the following text summarises their applications and their good and bad points.

Once you have decided on the type of security equipment which best suits your needs, we recommended that you read one of the many equipment tests regularly carried

Ensure the lock and chain you buy is of good quality and long enough to shackle your bike to a solid object

out by the motorcycle press. These tests compare the products from all the major manufacturers and give impartial ratings on their effectiveness, value-for-money and ease of use.

No one item of security equipment can provide complete protection. It is highly recommended that two or more of the items described below are combined to increase the security of your motorcycle (a lock and chain plus an alarm system is just about ideal). The more security measures fitted to the bike, the less likely it is to be stolen.

Lock and chain

Pros: *Very flexible to use; can be used to secure the motorcycle to almost any immovable object. On some locks and chains, the lock can be used on its own as a disc lock (see below).*

Cons: *Can be very heavy and awkward to carry on the motorcycle, although some types*

will be supplied with a carry bag which can be strapped to the pillion seat.

● Heavy-duty chains and locks are an excellent security measure **(see illustration 1)**. Whenever the motorcycle is parked, use the lock and chain to secure the machine to a solid, immovable object such as a post or railings. This will prevent the machine from being ridden away or being lifted into the back of a van.

● When fitting the chain, always ensure the chain is routed around the motorcycle frame or swingarm **(see illustrations 2 and 3)**. Never merely pass the chain around one of the wheel rims; a thief may unbolt the wheel and lift the rest of the machine into a van, leaving you with just the wheel! Try to avoid having excess chain free, thus making it difficult to use cutting tools, and keep the chain and lock off the ground to prevent thieves attacking it with a cold chisel. Position the lock so that its lock barrel is facing downwards; this will make it harder for the thief to attack the lock mechanism.

Pass the chain through the bike's frame, rather than just through a wheel . . .

. . . and loop it around a solid object

U-locks

Pros: *Highly effective deterrent which can be used to secure the bike to a post or railings. Most U-locks come with a carrier which allows the lock to be easily carried on the bike.*

Cons: *Not as flexible to use as a lock and chain.*

● These are solid locks which are similar in use to a lock and chain. U-locks are lighter than a lock and chain but not so flexible to use. The length and shape of the lock shackle limit the objects to which the bike can be secured **(see illustration 4)**.

Disc locks

Pros: *Small, light and very easy to carry; most can be stored underneath the seat.*

Cons: *Does not prevent the motorcycle being lifted into a van. Can be very embarrassing if you*

U-locks can be used to secure the bike to a solid object – ensure you purchase one which is long enough

forget to remove the lock before attempting to ride off!

● Disc locks are designed to be attached to the front brake disc. The lock passes through one of the holes in the disc and prevents the wheel rotating by jamming against the fork/brake caliper **(see illustration 5)**. Some are equipped with an alarm siren which sounds if the disc lock is moved; this not only acts as a theft deterrent but also as a handy reminder if you try to move the bike with the lock still fitted.

● Combining the disc lock with a length of cable which can be looped around a post or railings provides an additional measure of security **(see illustration 6)**.

Alarms and immobilisers

Pros: *Once installed it is completely hassle-free to use. If the system is 'Thatcham' or 'Sold Secure-approved', insurance companies may give you a discount.*

Cons: *Can be expensive to buy and complex to install. No system will prevent the motorcycle from being lifted into a van and taken away.*

● Electronic alarms and immobilisers are available to suit a variety of budgets. There are three different types of system available: pure alarms, pure immobilisers, and the more expensive systems which are combined alarm/immobilisers **(see illustration 7)**.
● An alarm system is designed to emit an audible warning if the motorcycle is being tampered with.
● An immobiliser prevents the motorcycle being started and ridden away by disabling its electrical systems.
● When purchasing an alarm/immobiliser system, check the cost of installing the system unless you are able to do it yourself. If the motorcycle is not used regularly, another consideration is the current drain of the system. All alarm/immobiliser systems are powered by the motorcycle's battery; purchasing a system with a very low current drain could prevent the battery losing its charge whilst the motorcycle is not being used.

A typical disc lock attached through one of the holes in the disc

A disc lock combined with a security cable provides additional protection

A typical alarm/immobiliser system

Indelible markings can be applied to most areas of the bike – always apply the manufacturer's sticker to warn off thieves

Chemically-etched code numbers can be applied to main body panels . . .

. . . again, always ensure that the kit manufacturer's sticker is applied in a prominent position

Security marking kits

Pros: *Very cheap and effective deterrent. Many insurance companies will give you a discount on your insurance premium if a recognised security marking kit is used on your motorcycle.*

Cons: *Does not prevent the motorcycle being stolen by joyriders.*

● There are many different types of security marking kits available. The idea is to mark as many parts of the motorcycle as possible with a unique security number (see illustrations 8, 9 and 10). A form will be included with the kit to register your personal details and those of the motorcycle with the kit manufacturer. This register is made available to the police to help them trace the rightful owner of any motorcycle or components which they recover should all other forms of identification have been removed. Always apply the warning stickers provided with the kit to deter thieves.

Ground anchors, wheel clamps and security posts

Pros: *An excellent form of security which will deter all but the most determined of thieves.*

Cons: *Awkward to install and can be expensive.*

● Whilst the motorcycle is at home, it is a good idea to attach it securely to the floor or a solid wall, even if it is kept in a securely locked garage. Various types of ground anchors, security posts and wheel clamps are available for this purpose (see illustration 11). These security devices are either bolted to a solid concrete or brick structure or can be cemented into the ground.

Permanent ground anchors provide an excellent level of security when the bike is at home

Security at home

A high percentage of motorcycle thefts are from the owner's home. Here are some things to consider whenever your motorcycle is at home:
✔ Where possible, always keep the motorcycle in a securely locked garage. Never rely solely on the standard lock on the garage door, these are usual hopelessly inadequate. Fit an additional locking mechanism to the door and consider having the garage alarmed. A security light, activated by a movement sensor, is also a good investment.

✔ Always secure the motorcycle to the ground or a wall, even if it is inside a securely locked garage.
✔ Do not regularly leave the motorcycle outside your home, try to keep it out of sight wherever possible. If a garage is not available, fit a motorcycle cover over the bike to disguise its true identity.
✔ It is not uncommon for thieves to follow a motorcyclist home to find out where the bike is kept. They will then return at a later date. Be aware of this whenever you are returning

home on your motorcycle. If you suspect you are being followed, do not return home, instead ride to a garage or shop and stop as a precaution.
✔ When selling a motorcycle, do not provide your home address or the location where the bike is normally kept. Arrange to meet the buyer at a location away from your home. Thieves have been known to pose as potential buyers to find out where motorcycles are kept and then return later to steal them.

Security away from the home

As well as fitting security equipment to your motorcycle here are a few general rules to follow whenever you park your motorcycle.
✔ Park in a busy, public place.
✔ Use car parks which incorporate security features, such as CCTV.

✔ At night, park in a well-lit area, preferably directly underneath a street light.
✔ Engage the steering lock.
✔ Secure the motorcycle to a solid, immovable object such as a post or railings with an additional lock. If this is not possible,

secure the bike to a friend's motorcycle. Some public parking places provide security loops for motorcycles.
✔ Never leave your helmet or luggage attached to the motorcycle. Take them with you at all times.

Lubricants and fluids

A wide range of lubricants, fluids and cleaning agents is available for motor-cycles. This is a guide as to what is available, its applications and properties.

Four-stroke engine oil

● Engine oil is without doubt the most important component of any four-stroke engine. Modern motorcycle engines place a lot of demands on their oil and choosing the right type is essential. Using an unsuitable oil will lead to an increased rate of engine wear and could result in serious engine damage. Before purchasing oil, always check the recommended oil specification given by the manufacturer. The manufacturer will state a recommended 'type or classification' and also a specific 'viscosity' range for engine oil.

● The oil 'type or classification' is identified by its API (American Petroleum Institute) rating. The API rating will be in the form of two letters, e.g. SG. The S identifies the oil as being suitable for use in a petrol (gasoline) engine (S stands for spark ignition) and the second letter, ranging from A to J, identifies the oil's performance rating. The later this letter, the higher the specification of the oil; for example API SG oil exceeds the requirements of API SF oil. **Note:** *On some oils there may also be a second rating consisting of another two letters, the first letter being C, e.g. API SF/CD. This rating indicates the oil is also suitable for use in a diesel engines (the C stands for compression ignition) and is thus of no relevance for motorcycle use.*

● The 'viscosity' of the oil is identified by its SAE (Society of Automotive Engineers) rating. All modern engines require multigrade oils and the SAE rating will consist of two numbers, the first followed by a W, e.g. 10W/40. The first number indicates the viscosity rating of the oil at low temperatures (W stands for winter – tested at –20°C) and the second number represents the viscosity of the oil at high temperatures (tested at 100°C). The lower the number, the thinner the oil. For example an oil with an SAE 10W/40 rating will give better cold starting and running than an SAE 15W/40 oil.

● As well as ensuring the 'type' and 'viscosity' of the oil match the recommendations, another consideration to make when buying engine oil is whether to purchase a standard mineral-based oil, a semi-synthetic oil (also known as a synthetic blend or synthetic-based oil) or a fully-synthetic oil. Although all oils will have a similar rating and viscosity, their cost will vary considerably; mineral-based oils are the cheapest, the fully-synthetic oils the most expensive with the semi-synthetic oils falling somewhere in-between. This decision is very much up to the owner, but it should be noted that modern synthetic oils have far better lubricating and cleaning qualities than traditional mineral-based oils and tend to retain these properties for far longer. Bearing in mind the operating conditions inside a modern, high-revving motorcycle engine it is highly recommended that a fully synthetic oil is used. The extra expense at each service could save you money in the long term by preventing premature engine wear.

● As a final note always ensure that the oil is specifically designed for use in motorcycle engines. Engine oils designed primarily for use in car engines sometimes contain additives or friction modifiers which could cause clutch slip on a motorcycle fitted with a wet-clutch.

Two-stroke engine oil

● Modern two-stroke engines, with their high power outputs, place high demands on their oil. If engine seizure is to be avoided it is essential that a high-quality oil is used. Two-stroke oils differ hugely from four-stroke oils. The oil lubricates only the crankshaft and piston(s) (the transmission has its own lubricating oil) and is used on a total-loss basis where it is burnt completely during the combustion process.

● The Japanese have recently introduced a classification system for two-stroke oils, the JASO rating. This rating is in the form of two letters, either FA, FB or FC – FA is the lowest classification and FC the highest. Ensure the oil being used meets or exceeds the recommended rating specified by the manufacturer.

● As well as ensuring the oil rating matches the recommendation, another consideration to make when buying engine oil is whether to purchase a standard mineral-based oil, a semi-synthetic oil (also known as a synthetic blend or synthetic-based oil) or a fully-synthetic oil. The cost of each type of oil varies considerably; mineral-based oils are the cheapest, the fully-synthetic oils the most expensive with the semi-synthetic oils falling somewhere in-between. This decision is very much up to the owner, but it should be noted that modern synthetic oils have far better lubricating properties and burn cleaner than traditional mineral-based oils. It is therefore recommended that a fully synthetic oil is used. The extra expense could save you money in the long term by preventing premature engine wear, engine performance will be improved, carbon deposits and exhaust smoke will be reduced.

● Always ensure that the oil is specifically designed for use in an injector system. Many high quality two-stroke oils are designed for competition use and need to be pre-mixed with fuel. These oils are of a much higher viscosity and are not designed to flow through the injector pumps used on road-going two-stroke motorcycles.

Transmission (gear) oil

● On a two-stroke engine, the transmission and clutch are lubricated by their own separate oil bath which must be changed in accordance with the Maintenance Schedule.
● Although the engine and transmission units of most four-strokes use a common lubrication supply, there are some exceptions where the engine and gearbox have separate oil reservoirs and a dry clutch is used.
● Motorcycle manufacturers will either recommend a monograde transmission oil or a four-stroke multigrade engine oil to lubricate the transmission.
● Transmission oils, or gear oils as they are often called, are designed specifically for use in transmission systems. The viscosity of these oils is represented by an SAE number, but the scale of measurement applied is different to that used to grade engine oils. As a rough guide a SAE90 gear oil will be of the same viscosity as an SAE50 engine oil.

Shaft drive oil

● On models equipped with shaft final drive, the shaft drive gears are will have their own oil supply. The manufacturer will state a recommended 'type or classification' and also a specific 'viscosity' range in the same manner as for four-stroke engine oil.
● Gear oil classification is given by the number which follows the API GL (GL standing for gear lubricant) rating, the higher the number, the higher the specification of the oil, e.g. API GL5 oil is a higher specification than API GL4 oil. Ensure the oil meets or

exceeds the classification specified and is of the correct viscosity. The viscosity of gear oils is also represented by an SAE number but the scale of measurement used is different to that used to grade engine oils. As a rough guide an SAE90 gear oil will be of the same viscosity as an SAE50 engine oil.
● If the use of an EP (Extreme Pressure) gear oil is specified, ensure the oil purchased is suitable.

Fork oil and suspension fluid

● Conventional telescopic front forks are hydraulic and require fork oil to work. To ensure the forks function correctly, the fork oil must be changed in accordance with the Maintenance Schedule.
● Fork oil is available in a variety of viscosities, identified by their SAE rating; fork oil ratings vary from light (SAE 5) to heavy (SAE 30). When purchasing fork oil, ensure the viscosity rating matches that specified by the manufacturer.
● Some lubricant manufacturers also produce a range of high-quality suspension fluids which are very similar to fork oil but are designed mainly for competition use. These fluids may have a different viscosity rating system which is not to be confused with the SAE rating of normal fork oil. Refer to the manufacturer's instructions if in any doubt.

Brake and clutch fluid

● All disc brake systems and some clutch systems are hydraulically operated. To ensure correct operation, the hydraulic fluid must be changed in accordance with the Maintenance Schedule.
● Brake and clutch fluid is classified by its DOT rating with most motorcycle manufacturers specifying DOT 3 or 4 fluid. Both fluid types are glycol-based and can be mixed together without adverse effect; DOT 4 fluid exceeds the requirements of DOT 3

fluid. Although it is safe to use DOT 4 fluid in a system designed for use with DOT 3 fluid, never use DOT 3 fluid in a system which specifies the use of DOT 4 as this will adversely affect the system's performance. The type required for the system will be marked on the fluid reservoir cap.
● Some manufacturers also produce a DOT 5 hydraulic fluid. DOT 5 hydraulic fluid is silicone-based and is not compatible with the glycol-based DOT 3 and 4 fluids. Never mix DOT 5 fluid with DOT 3 or 4 fluid as this will seriously affect the performance of the hydraulic system.

Coolant/antifreeze

● When purchasing coolant/antifreeze, always ensure it is suitable for use in an aluminium engine and contains corrosion inhibitors to prevent possible blockages of the internal coolant passages of the system. As a general rule, most coolants are designed to be used neat and should not be diluted whereas antifreeze can be mixed with distilled water to  provide a coolant solution of the required strength. Refer to the manufacturer's instructions on the bottle.
● Ensure the coolant is changed in accordance with the Maintenance Schedule.

Chain lube

● Chain lube is an aerosol-type spray lubricant specifically designed for use on motorcycle final drive chains. Chain lube has two functions, to minimise friction between the final drive chain and sprockets and to prevent corrosion of the chain. Regular use of a good-quality chain lube will extend the life of the drive chain and sprockets and thus maximise the power being transmitted from the transmission to the rear wheel.
● When using chain lube, always allow some time for the solvents in the lube to evaporate before riding the motorcycle. This will minimise the amount of lube which will

'fling' off from the chain when the motorcycle is used. If the motorcycle is equipped with an 'O-ring' chain, ensure the chain lube is labelled as being suitable for use on 'O-ring' chains.

Degreasers and solvents

● There are many different types of solvents and degreasers available to remove the grime and grease which accumulate around the motorcycle during normal use. Degreasers and solvents are usually available as an aerosol-type spray or as a liquid which you apply with a brush. Always closely follow the manufacturer's instructions and wear eye protection during use. Be aware that many solvents are flammable and may give off noxious fumes; take adequate precautions when using them (see Safety First!).

● For general cleaning, use one of the many solvents or degreasers available from most motorcycle accessory shops. These solvents are usually applied then left for a certain time before being washed off with water.

Brake cleaner is a solvent specifically designed to remove all traces of oil, grease and dust from braking system components. Brake cleaner is designed to evaporate quickly and leaves behind no residue.

Carburettor cleaner is an aerosol-type solvent specifically designed to clear carburettor blockages and break down the hard deposits and gum often found inside carburettors during overhaul.

Contact cleaner is an aerosol-type solvent designed for cleaning electrical components. The cleaner will remove all traces of oil and dirt from components such as switch contacts or fouled spark plugs and then dry, leaving behind no residue.

Gasket remover is an aerosol-type solvent designed for removing stubborn gaskets from engine components during overhaul. Gasket remover will minimise the amount of scraping required to remove the gasket and therefore reduce the risk of damage to the mating surface.

Spray lubricants

● Aerosol-based spray lubricants are widely available and are excellent for lubricating lever pivots and exposed cables and switches. Try to use a lubricant which is of the dry-film type as the fluid evaporates, leaving behind a dry-film of lubricant. Lubricants which leave behind an oily residue will attract dust and dirt which will increase the rate of wear of the cable/lever.

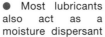

● Most lubricants also act as a moisture dispersant and a penetrating fluid. This means they can also be used to 'dry out' electrical components such as wiring connectors or switches as well as helping to free seized fasteners.

Greases

● Grease is used to lubricate many of the pivot-points. A good-quality multi-purpose grease is suitable for most applications but some manufacturers will specify the use of specialist greases for use on components such as swingarm and suspension linkage bushes. These specialist greases can be purchased from most motorcycle (or car) accessory shops; commonly specified types include molybdenum disulphide grease, lithium-based grease, graphite-based grease, silicone-based grease and high-temperature copper-based grease.

Gasket sealing compounds

● Gasket sealing compounds can be used in conjunction with gaskets, to improve their sealing capabilities, or on their own to seal metal-to-metal joints. Depending on their type, sealing compounds either set hard or stay relatively soft and pliable.

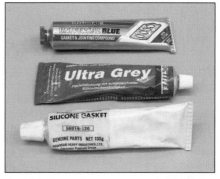

● When purchasing a gasket sealing compound, ensure that it is designed specifically for use on an internal combustion engine. General multi-purpose sealants available from DIY stores may appear visibly similar but they are not designed to withstand the extreme heat or contact with fuel and oil encountered when used on an engine (see 'Tools and Workshop Tips' for further information).

Thread locking compound

● Thread locking compounds are used to secure certain threaded fasteners in position to prevent them from loosening due to vibration. Thread locking compounds can be purchased from most motorcycle (and car) accessory shops. Ensure the threads of the both components are completely clean and dry before sparingly applying the locking compound (see 'Tools and Workshop Tips' for further information).

Fuel additives

● Fuel additives which protect and clean the fuel system components are widely available. These additives are designed to remove all traces of deposits that build up on the carburettors/injectors and prevent wear, helping the fuel system to operate more efficiently. If a fuel additive is being used, check that it is suitable for use with your motorcycle, especially if your motorcycle is equipped with a catalytic converter.

● Octane boosters are also available. These additives are designed to improve the performance of highly-tuned engines being run on normal pump-fuel and are of no real use on standard motorcycles.

Conversion Factors

Length (distance)

Inches (in)	x 25.4	= Millimetres (mm)	x 0.0394	= Inches (in)
Feet (ft)	x 0.305	= Metres (m)	x 3.281	= Feet (ft)
Miles	x 1.609	= Kilometres (km)	x 0.621	= Miles

Volume (capacity)

Cubic inches (cu in; in³)	x 16.387	= Cubic centimetres (cc; cm³)	x 0.061	= Cubic inches (cu in; in³)
Imperial pints (Imp pt)	x 0.568	= Litres (l)	x 1.76	= Imperial pints (Imp pt)
Imperial quarts (Imp qt)	x 1.137	= Litres (l)	x 0.88	= Imperial quarts (Imp qt)
Imperial quarts (Imp qt)	x 1.201	= US quarts (US qt)	x 0.833	= Imperial quarts (Imp qt)
US quarts (US qt)	x 0.946	= Litres (l)	x 1.057	= US quarts (US qt)
Imperial gallons (Imp gal)	x 4.546	= Litres (l)	x 0.22	= Imperial gallons (Imp gal)
Imperial gallons (Imp gal)	x 1.201	= US gallons (US gal)	x 0.833	= Imperial gallons (Imp gal)
US gallons (US gal)	x 3.785	= Litres (l)	x 0.264	= US gallons (US gal)

Mass (weight)

Ounces (oz)	x 28.35	= Grams (g)	x 0.035	= Ounces (oz)
Pounds (lb)	x 0.454	= Kilograms (kg)	x 2.205	= Pounds (lb)

Force

Ounces-force (ozf; oz)	x 0.278	= Newtons (N)	x 3.6	= Ounces-force (ozf; oz)
Pounds-force (lbf; lb)	x 4.448	= Newtons (N)	x 0.225	= Pounds-force (lbf; lb)
Newtons (N)	x 0.1	= Kilograms-force (kgf; kg)	x 9.81	= Newtons (N)

Pressure

Pounds-force per square inch (psi; lbf/in²; lb/in²)	x 0.070	= Kilograms-force per square centimetre (kgf/cm²; kg/cm²)	x 14.223	= Pounds-force per square inch (psi; lbf/in²; lb/in²)
Pounds-force per square inch (psi; lbf/in²; lb/in²)	x 0.068	= Atmospheres (atm)	x 14.696	= Pounds-force per square inch (psi; lbf/in²; lb/in²)
Pounds-force per square inch (psi; lbf/in²; lb/in²)	x 0.069	= Bars	x 14.5	= Pounds-force per square inch (psi; lbf/in²; lb/in²)
Pounds-force per square inch (psi; lbf/in²; lb/in²)	x 6.895	= Kilopascals (kPa)	x 0.145	= Pounds-force per square inch (psi; lbf/in²; lb/in²)
Kilopascals (kPa)	x 0.01	= Kilograms-force per square centimetre (kgf/cm²; kg/cm²)	x 98.1	= Kilopascals (kPa)
Millibar (mbar)	x 100	= Pascals (Pa)	x 0.01	= Millibar (mbar)
Millibar (mbar)	x 0.0145	= Pounds-force per square inch (psi; lbf/in²; lb/in²)	x 68.947	= Millibar (mbar)
Millibar (mbar)	x 0.75	= Millimetres of mercury (mmHg)	x 1.333	= Millibar (mbar)
Millibar (mbar)	x 0.401	= Inches of water (inH₂O)	x 2.491	= Millibar (mbar)
Millimetres of mercury (mmHg)	x 0.535	= Inches of water (inH₂O)	x 1.868	= Millimetres of mercury (mmHg)
Inches of water (inH₂O)	x 0.036	= Pounds-force per square inch (psi; lbf/in²; lb/in²)	x 27.68	= Inches of water (inH₂O)

Torque (moment of force)

Pounds-force inches (lbf in; lb in)	x 1.152	= Kilograms-force centimetre (kgf cm; kg cm)	x 0.868	= Pounds-force inches (lbf in; lb in)
Pounds-force inches (lbf in; lb in)	x 0.113	= Newton metres (Nm)	x 8.85	= Pounds-force inches (lbf in; lb in)
Pounds-force inches (lbf in; lb in)	x 0.083	= Pounds-force feet (lbf ft; lb ft)	x 12	= Pounds-force inches (lbf in; lb in)
Pounds-force feet (lbf ft; lb ft)	x 0.138	= Kilograms-force metres (kgf m; kg m)	x 7.233	= Pounds-force feet (lbf ft; lb ft)
Pounds-force feet (lbf ft; lb ft)	x 1.356	= Newton metres (Nm)	x 0.738	= Pounds-force feet (lbf ft; lb ft)
Newton metres (Nm)	x 0.102	= Kilograms-force metres (kgf m; kg m)	x 9.804	= Newton metres (Nm)

Power

Horsepower (hp)	x 745.7	= Watts (W)	x 0.0013	= Horsepower (hp)

Velocity (speed)

Miles per hour (miles/hr; mph)	x 1.609	= Kilometres per hour (km/hr; kph)	x 0.621	= Miles per hour (miles/hr; mph)

Fuel consumption*

Miles per gallon (mpg)	x 0.354	= Kilometres per litre (km/l)	x 2.825	= Miles per gallon (mpg)

Temperature

Degrees Fahrenheit = (°C x 1.8) + 32   Degrees Celsius (Degrees Centigrade; °C) = (°F - 32) x 0.56

It is common practice to convert from miles per gallon (mpg) to litres/100 kilometres (l/100km), where mpg x l/100 km = 282

About the MOT Test

In the UK, all vehicles more than three years old are subject to an annual test to ensure that they meet minimum safety requirements. A current test certificate must be issued before a machine can be used on public roads, and is required before a road fund licence can be issued. Riding without a current test certificate will also invalidate your insurance.

For most owners, the MOT test is an annual cause for anxiety, and this is largely due to owners not being sure what needs to be checked prior to submitting the motorcycle for testing. The simple answer is that a fully roadworthy motorcycle will have no difficulty in passing the test.

This is a guide to getting your motorcycle through the MOT test. Obviously it will not be possible to examine the motorcycle to the same standard as the professional MOT tester, particularly in view of the equipment required for some of the checks. However, working through the following procedures will enable you to identify any problem areas before submitting the motorcycle for the test.

It has only been possible to summarise the test requirements here, based on the regulations in force at the time of printing. Test standards are becoming increasingly stringent, although there are some exemptions for older vehicles. More information about the MOT test can be obtained from the TSO publications, *How Safe is your Motorcycle* and *The MOT Inspection Manual for Motorcycle Testing*.

Many of the checks require that one of the wheels is raised off the ground. If the motorcycle doesn't have a centre stand, note that an auxiliary stand will be required. Additionally, the help of an assistant may prove useful.

Certain exceptions apply to machines under 50 cc, machines without a lighting system, and Classic bikes - if in doubt about any of the requirements listed below seek confirmation from an MOT tester prior to submitting the motorcycle for the test.

Check that the frame number is clearly visible.

Electrical System

Lights, turn signals, horn and reflector

✔ With the ignition on, check the operation of the following electrical components. **Note:** *The electrical components on certain small-capacity machines are powered by the generator, requiring that the engine is run for this check.*

a) *Headlight and tail light. Check that both illuminate in the low and high beam switch positions.*

b) *Position lights. Check that the front position (or sidelight) and tail light illuminate in this switch position.*

c) *Turn signals. Check that all flash at the correct rate, and that the warning light(s) function correctly. Check that the turn signal switch works correctly.*

d) *Hazard warning system (where fitted). Check that all four turn signals flash in this switch position.*

e) *Brake stop light. Check that the light comes on when the front and rear brakes are independently applied. Models first used on or after 1st April 1986 must have a brake light switch on each brake.*

f) *Horn. Check that the sound is continuous and of reasonable volume.*

✔ Check that there is a red reflector on the rear of the machine, either mounted separately or as part of the tail light lens.

✔ Check the condition of the headlight, tail light and turn signal lenses.

Headlight beam height

✔ The MOT tester will perform a headlight beam height check using specialised beam setting equipment **(see illustration 1)**. This equipment will not be available to the home mechanic, but if you suspect that the headlight is incorrectly set or may have been maladjusted in the past, you can perform a rough test as follows.

✔ Position the bike in a straight line facing a brick wall. The bike must be off its stand, upright and with a rider seated. Measure the height from the ground to the centre of the headlight and mark a horizontal line on the wall at this height. Position the motorcycle 3.8 metres from the wall and draw a vertical

Headlight beam height checking equipment

line up the wall central to the centreline of the motorcycle. Switch to dipped beam and check that the beam pattern falls slightly lower than the horizontal line and to the left of the vertical line **(see illustration 2)**.

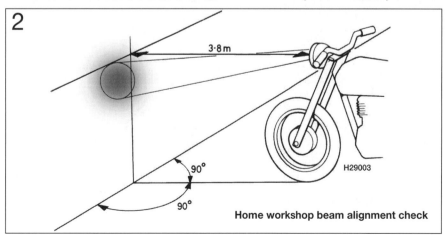

Home workshop beam alignment check

Exhaust System and Final Drive

Exhaust

✔ Check that the exhaust mountings are secure and that the system does not foul any of the rear suspension components.
✔ Start the motorcycle. When the revs are increased, check that the exhaust is neither holed nor leaking from any of its joints. On a linked system, check that the collector box is not leaking due to corrosion.

✔ Note that the exhaust decibel level ("loudness" of the exhaust) is assessed at the discretion of the tester. If the motorcycle was first used on or after 1st January 1985 the silencer must carry the BSAU 193 stamp, or a marking relating to its make and model, or be of OE (original equipment) manufacture. If the silencer is marked NOT FOR ROAD USE, RACING USE ONLY or similar, it will fail the MOT.

Final drive

✔ On chain or belt drive machines, check that the chain/belt is in good condition and does not have excessive slack. Also check that the sprocket is securely mounted on the rear wheel hub. Check that the chain/belt guard is in place.
✔ On shaft drive bikes, check for oil leaking from the drive unit and fouling the rear tyre.

Steering and Suspension

Steering

✔ With the front wheel raised off the ground, rotate the steering from lock to lock. The handlebar or switches must not contact the fuel tank or be close enough to trap the rider's hand. Problems can be caused by damaged lock stops on the lower yoke and frame, or by the fitting of non-standard handlebars.
✔ When performing the lock to lock check, also ensure that the steering moves freely without drag or notchiness. Steering movement can be impaired by poorly routed cables, or by overtight head bearings or worn bearings. The tester will perform a check of the steering head bearing lower race by mounting the front wheel on a surface plate, then performing a lock to

lock check with the weight of the machine on the lower bearing (see illustration 3).
✔ Grasp the fork sliders (lower legs) and attempt to push and pull on the forks (see

Front wheel mounted on a surface plate for steering head bearing lower race check

illustration 4). Any play in the steering head bearings will be felt. Note that in extreme cases, wear of the front fork bushes can be misinterpreted for head bearing play.
✔ Check that the handlebars are securely mounted.
✔ Check that the handlebar grip rubbers are secure. They should by bonded to the bar left end and to the throttle cable pulley on the right end.

Front suspension

✔ With the motorcycle off the stand, hold the front brake on and pump the front forks up and down (see illustration 5). Check that they are adequately damped.

Checking the steering head bearings for freeplay

Hold the front brake on and pump the front forks up and down to check operation

Inspect the area around the fork dust seal for oil
leakage (arrow)

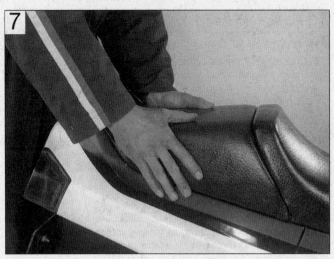

Bounce the rear of the motorcycle to check rear
suspension operation

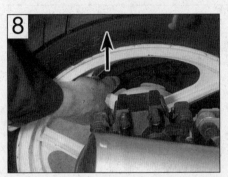

Checking for rear suspension linkage play

✔ Inspect the area above and around the
front fork oil seals **(see illustration 6)**. There
should be no sign of oil on the fork tube
(stanchion) nor leaking down the slider (lower

leg). On models so equipped, check that there
is no oil leaking from the anti-dive units.
✔ On models with swingarm front
suspension, check that there is no freeplay in
the linkage when moved from side to side.

Rear suspension

✔ With the motorcycle off the stand and an
assistant supporting the motorcycle by its
handlebars, bounce the rear suspension **(see
illustration 7)**. Check that the suspension
components do not foul on any of the cycle
parts and check that the shock absorber(s)
provide adequate damping.
✔ Visually inspect the shock absorber(s) and

check that there is no sign of oil leakage from
its damper. This is somewhat restricted on
certain single shock models due to the
location of the shock absorber.
✔ With the rear wheel raised off the
ground, grasp the wheel at the highest point
and attempt to pull it up **(see illustration 8)**.
Any play in the swingarm pivot or suspension
linkage bearings will be felt as movement.
Note: *Do not confuse play with actual
suspension movement.* Failure to lubricate
suspension linkage bearings can lead to
bearing failure **(see illustration 9)**.
✔ With the rear wheel raised off the ground,
grasp the swingarm ends and attempt to
move the swingarm from side to side and
forwards and backwards - any play indicates
wear of the swingarm pivot bearings **(see
illustration 10)**.

Worn suspension linkage pivots (arrows) are usually the cause of
play in the rear suspension

Grasp the swingarm at the ends to check for play in its pivot
bearings

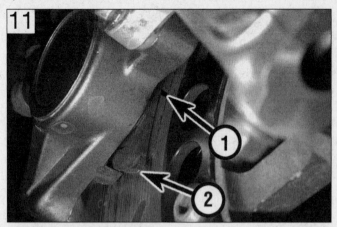

Brake pad wear can usually be viewed without removing the caliper. Most pads have wear indicator grooves (1) and some also have indicator tangs (2)

On drum brakes, check the angle of the operating lever with the brake fully applied. Most drum brakes have a wear indicator pointer and scale.

Brakes, Wheels and Tyres

Brakes

✔ With the wheel raised off the ground, apply the brake then free it off, and check that the wheel is about to revolve freely without brake drag.

✔ On disc brakes, examine the disc itself. Check that it is securely mounted and not cracked.

✔ On disc brakes, view the pad material through the caliper mouth and check that the pads are not worn down beyond the limit (see illustration 11).

✔ On drum brakes, check that when the brake is applied the angle between the operating lever and cable or rod is not too great (see illustration 12). Check also that the operating lever doesn't foul any other components.

✔ On disc brakes, examine the flexible hoses from top to bottom. Have an assistant hold the brake on so that the fluid in the hose is under pressure, and check that there is no sign of fluid leakage, bulges or cracking. If there are any metal brake pipes or unions, check that these are free from corrosion and damage. Where a brake-linked anti-dive system is fitted, check the hoses to the anti-dive in a similar manner.

✔ Check that the rear brake torque arm is secure and that its fasteners are secured by self-locking nuts or castellated nuts with split-pins or R-pins (see illustration 13).

✔ On models with ABS, check that the self-check warning light in the instrument panel works.

✔ The MOT tester will perform a test of the motorcycle's braking efficiency based on a calculation of rider and motorcycle weight. Although this cannot be carried out at home, you can at least ensure that the braking systems are properly maintained. For hydraulic disc brakes, check the fluid level, lever/pedal feel (bleed of air if its spongy) and pad material. For drum brakes, check adjustment, cable or rod operation and shoe lining thickness.

Wheels and tyres

✔ Check the wheel condition. Cast wheels should be free from cracks and if of the built-up design, all fasteners should be secure. Spoked wheels should be checked for broken, corroded, loose or bent spokes.

✔ With the wheel raised off the ground, spin the wheel and visually check that the tyre and wheel run true. Check that the tyre does not foul the suspension or mudguards.

✔ With the wheel raised off the ground, grasp the wheel and attempt to move it about the axle (spindle) (see illustration 14). Any play felt here indicates wheel bearing failure.

Brake torque arm must be properly secured at both ends

Check for wheel bearing play by trying to move the wheel about the axle (spindle)

Checking the tyre tread depth

Tyre direction of rotation arrow can be found on tyre sidewall

Castellated type wheel axle (spindle) nut must be secured by a split pin or R-pin

Two straightedges are used to check wheel alignment

✔ Check the tyre tread depth, tread condition and sidewall condition **(see illustration 15)**.
✔ Check the tyre type. Front and rear tyre types must be compatible and be suitable for road use. Tyres marked NOT FOR ROAD USE, COMPETITION USE ONLY or similar, will fail the MOT.

✔ If the tyre sidewall carries a direction of rotation arrow, this must be pointing in the direction of normal wheel rotation **(see illustration 16)**.
✔ Check that the wheel axle (spindle) nuts (where applicable) are properly secured. A self-locking nut or castellated nut with a split-pin or R-pin can be used **(see illustration 17)**.
✔ Wheel alignment is checked with the motorcycle off the stand and a rider seated. With the front wheel pointing straight ahead, two perfectly straight lengths of metal or wood and placed against the sidewalls of both tyres **(see illustration 18)**. The gap each side of the front tyre must be equidistant on both sides. Incorrect wheel alignment may be due to a cocked rear wheel (often as the result of poor chain adjustment) or in extreme cases, a bent frame.

General checks and condition

✔ Check the security of all major fasteners, bodypanels, seat, fairings (where fitted) and mudguards.

✔ Check that the rider and pillion footrests, handlebar levers and brake pedal are securely mounted.

✔ Check for corrosion on the frame or any load-bearing components. If severe, this may affect the structure, particularly under stress.

Sidecars

A motorcycle fitted with a sidecar requires additional checks relating to the stability of the machine and security of attachment and swivel joints, plus specific wheel alignment (toe-in) requirements. Additionally, tyre and lighting requirements differ from conventional motorcycle use. Owners are advised to check MOT test requirements with an official test centre.

Preparing for storage

Before you start

If repairs or an overhaul is needed, see that this is carried out now rather than left until you want to ride the bike again.

Give the bike a good wash and scrub all dirt from its underside. Make sure the bike dries completely before preparing for storage.

Engine

● Remove the spark plug(s) and lubricate the cylinder bores with approximately a teaspoon of motor oil using a spout-type oil can **(see illustration 1)**. Reinstall the spark plug(s). Crank the engine over a couple of times to coat the piston rings and bores with oil. If the bike has a kickstart, use this to turn the engine over. If not, flick the kill switch to the OFF position and crank the engine over on the starter **(see illustration 2)**. If the nature on the ignition system prevents the starter operating with the kill switch in the OFF position,

remove the spark plugs and fit them back in their caps; ensure that the plugs are earthed (grounded) against the cylinder head when the starter is operated **(see illustration 3)**.

⚠️ *Warning: It is important that the plugs are earthed (grounded) away from the spark plug holes otherwise there is a risk of atomised fuel from the cylinders igniting.*

HAYNES HINT *On a single cylinder four-stroke engine, you can seal the combustion chamber completely by positioning the piston at TDC on the compression stroke.*

● Drain the carburettor(s) otherwise there is a risk of jets becoming blocked by gum deposits from the fuel **(see illustration 4)**.

● If the bike is going into long-term storage, consider adding a fuel stabiliser to the fuel in the tank. If the tank is drained completely, corrosion of its internal surfaces may occur if left unprotected for a long period. The tank can be treated with a rust preventative especially for this purpose. Alternatively, remove the tank and pour half a litre of motor oil into it, install the filler cap and shake the tank to coat its internals with oil before draining off the excess. The same effect can also be achieved by spraying WD40 or a similar water-dispersant around the inside of the tank via its flexible nozzle.

● Make sure the cooling system contains the correct mix of antifreeze. Antifreeze also contains important corrosion inhibitors.

● The air intakes and exhaust can be sealed off by covering or plugging the openings. Ensure that you do not seal in any condensation; run the engine until it is hot,

Squirt a drop of motor oil into each cylinder

Flick the kill switch to OFF . . .

. . . and ensure that the metal bodies of the plugs (arrows) are earthed against the cylinder head

Connect a hose to the carburettor float chamber drain stub (arrow) and unscrew the drain screw

5

Exhausts can be sealed off with a plastic bag

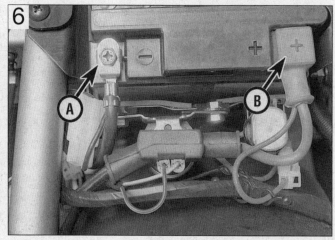

6

Disconnect the negative lead (A) first, followed by the positive lead (B)

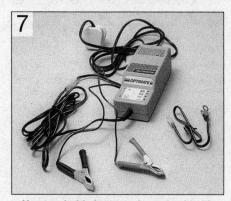

7

Use a suitable battery charger - this kit also assess battery condition

then switch off and allow to cool. Tape a piece of thick plastic over the silencer end(s) **(see illustration 5)**. Note that some advocate pouring a tablespoon of motor oil into the silencer(s) before sealing them off.

Battery

● Remove it from the bike - in extreme cases of cold the battery may freeze and crack its case **(see illustration 6)**.

● Check the electrolyte level and top up if necessary (conventional refillable batteries). Clean the terminals.
● Store the battery off the motorcycle and away from any sources of fire. Position a wooden block under the battery if it is to sit on the ground.
● Give the battery a trickle charge for a few hours every month **(see illustration 7)**.

Tyres

● Place the bike on its centrestand or an auxiliary stand which will support the motorcycle in an upright position. Position wood blocks under the tyres to keep them off the ground and to provide insulation from damp. If the bike is being put into long-term storage, ideally both tyres should be off the ground; not only will this protect the tyres, but will also ensure that no load is placed on the steering head or wheel bearings.
● Deflate each tyre by 5 to 10 psi, no more or the beads may unseat from the rim, making subsequent inflation difficult on tubeless tyres.

Pivots and controls

● Lubricate all lever, pedal, stand and footrest pivot points. If grease nipples are fitted to the rear suspension components, apply lubricant to the pivots.
● Lubricate all control cables.

Cycle components

● Apply a wax protectant to all painted and plastic components. Wipe off any excess, but don't polish to a shine. Where fitted, clean the screen with soap and water.
● Coat metal parts with Vaseline (petroleum jelly). When applying this to the fork tubes, do not compress the forks otherwise the seals will rot from contact with the Vaseline.
● Apply a vinyl cleaner to the seat.

Storage conditions

● Aim to store the bike in a shed or garage which does not leak and is free from damp.
● Drape an old blanket or bedspread over the bike to protect it from dust and direct contact with sunlight (which will fade paint). This also hides the bike from prying eyes. Beware of tight-fitting plastic covers which may allow condensation to form and settle on the bike.

Getting back on the road

Engine and transmission

● Change the oil and replace the oil filter. If this was done prior to storage, check that the oil hasn't emulsified - a thick whitish substance which occurs through condensation.
● Remove the spark plugs. Using a spout-type oil can, squirt a few drops of oil into the cylinder(s). This will provide initial lubrication as the piston rings and bores comes back into contact. Service the spark plugs, or fit new ones, and install them in the engine.

● Check that the clutch isn't stuck on. The plates can stick together if left standing for some time, preventing clutch operation. Engage a gear and try rocking the bike back and forth with the clutch lever held against the handlebar. If this doesn't work on cable-operated clutches, hold the clutch lever back against the handlebar with a strong elastic band or cable tie for a couple of hours **(see illustration 8)**.
● If the air intakes or silencer end(s) were blocked off, remove the bung or cover used.
● If the fuel tank was coated with a rust

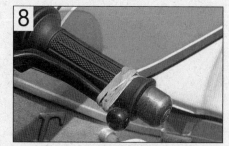

8

Hold clutch lever back against the handlebar with elastic bands or a cable tie

preventative, oil or a stabiliser added to the fuel, drain and flush the tank and dispose of the fuel sensibly. If no action was taken with the fuel tank prior to storage, it is advised that the old fuel is disposed of since it will go off over a period of time. Refill the fuel tank with fresh fuel.

Frame and running gear

● Oil all pivot points and cables.
● Check the tyre pressures. They will definitely need inflating if pressures were reduced for storage.
● Lubricate the final drive chain (where applicable).
● Remove any protective coating applied to the fork tubes (stanchions) since this may well destroy the fork seals. If the fork tubes weren't protected and have picked up rust spots, remove them with very fine abrasive paper and refinish with metal polish.
● Check that both brakes operate correctly. Apply each brake hard and check that it's not possible to move the motorcycle forwards, then check that the brake frees off again once released. Brake caliper pistons can stick due to corrosion around the piston head, or on the sliding caliper types, due to corrosion of the slider pins. If the brake doesn't free after repeated operation, take the caliper off for examination. Similarly drum brakes can stick

due to a seized operating cam, cable or rod linkage.
● If the motorcycle has been in long-term storage, renew the brake fluid and clutch fluid (where applicable).
● Depending on where the bike has been stored, the wiring, cables and hoses may have been nibbled by rodents. Make a visual check and investigate disturbed wiring loom tape.

Battery

● If the battery has been previously removal and given top up charges it can simply be reconnected. Remember to connect the positive cable first and the negative cable last.
● On conventional refillable batteries, if the battery has not received any attention, remove it from the motorcycle and check its electrolyte level. Top up if necessary then charge the battery. If the battery fails to hold a charge and a visual checks show heavy white sulphation of the plates, the battery is probably defective and must be renewed. This is particularly likely if the battery is old. Confirm battery condition with a specific gravity check.
● On sealed (MF) batteries, if the battery has not received any attention, remove it from the motorcycle and charge it according to the information on the battery case - if the battery fails to hold a charge it must be renewed.

Starting procedure

● If a kickstart is fitted, turn the engine over a couple of times with the ignition OFF to distribute oil around the engine. If no kickstart is fitted, flick the engine kill switch OFF and the ignition ON and crank the engine over a couple of times to work oil around the upper cylinder components. If the nature of the ignition system is such that the starter won't work with the kill switch OFF, remove the spark plugs, fit them back into their caps and earth (ground) their bodies on the cylinder head. Reinstall the spark plugs afterwards.
● Switch the kill switch to RUN, operate the choke and start the engine. If the engine won't start don't continue cranking the engine - not only will this flatten the battery, but the starter motor will overheat. Switch the ignition off and try again later. If the engine refuses to start, go through the fault finding procedures in this manual. **Note:** *If the bike has been in storage for a long time, old fuel or a carburettor blockage may be the problem. Gum deposits in carburettors can block jets - if a carburettor cleaner doesn't prove successful the carburettors must be dismantled for cleaning.*
● Once the engine has started, check that the lights, turn signals and horn work properly.
● Treat the bike gently for the first ride and check all fluid levels on completion. Settle the bike back into the maintenance schedule.

This Section provides an easy reference-guide to the more common faults that are likely to afflict your machine. Obviously, the opportunities are almost limitless for faults to occur as a result of obscure failures, and to try and cover all eventualities would require a book. Indeed, a number have been written on the subject.

Successful troubleshooting is not a mysterious 'black art' but the application of a bit of knowledge combined with a systematic and logical approach to the problem. Approach any troubleshooting by first accurately identifying the symptom and then checking through the list of possible causes, starting with the simplest or most obvious and progressing in stages to the most complex.

Take nothing for granted, but above all apply liberal quantities of common sense.

The main symptom of a fault is given in the text as a major heading below which are listed the various systems or areas which may contain the fault. Details of each possible cause for a fault and the remedial action to be taken are given, in brief, in the paragraphs below each heading. Further information should be sought in the relevant Chapter.

1 Engine doesn't start or is difficult to start

- [ ] Starter motor doesn't rotate
- [ ] Starter motor rotates but engine does not turn over
- [ ] Starter works but engine won't turn over (seized)
- [ ] No fuel flow
- [ ] Engine flooded
- [ ] No spark or weak spark
- [ ] Compression low
- [ ] Stalls after starting
- [ ] Rough idle

2 Poor running at low speed

- [ ] Spark weak
- [ ] Fuel/air mixture incorrect
- [ ] Compression low
- [ ] Poor acceleration

3 Poor running or no power at high speed

- [ ] Firing incorrect
- [ ] Fuel/air mixture incorrect
- [ ] Compression low
- [ ] Knocking or pinking
- [ ] Miscellaneous causes

4 Overheating

- [ ] Engine overheats
- [ ] Firing incorrect
- [ ] Fuel/air mixture incorrect
- [ ] Compression too high
- [ ] Engine load excessive
- [ ] Lubrication inadequate
- [ ] Miscellaneous causes

5 Clutch problems

- [ ] Clutch slipping
- [ ] Clutch not disengaging completely

6 Gear changing problems

- [ ] Doesn't go into gear, or lever doesn't return
- [ ] Jumps out of gear
- [ ] Overselects

7 Abnormal engine noise

- [ ] Knocking or pinking
- [ ] Piston slap or rattling
- [ ] Valve noise
- [ ] Other noise

8 Abnormal driveline noise

- [ ] Clutch noise
- [ ] Transmission noise
- [ ] Final drive noise

9 Abnormal frame and suspension noise

- [ ] Front end noise
- [ ] Shock absorber noise
- [ ] Brake noise

10 Oil pressure warning light comes on

- [ ] Engine lubrication system
- [ ] Electrical system

11 Excessive exhaust smoke

- [ ] White smoke
- [ ] Black smoke
- [ ] Brown smoke

12 Poor handling or stability

- [ ] Handlebar hard to turn
- [ ] Handlebar shakes or vibrates excessively
- [ ] Handlebar pulls to one side
- [ ] Poor shock absorbing qualities

13 Braking problems

- [ ] Brakes are spongy, don't hold
- [ ] Brake lever or pedal pulsates
- [ ] Brakes drag

14 Electrical problems

- [ ] Battery dead or weak
- [ ] Battery overcharged

1 Engine doesn't start or is difficult to start

Starter motor doesn't rotate

- ☐ Engine kill switch OFF.
- ☐ Fuse blown (Chapter 9).
- ☐ Battery voltage low. Check and recharge battery (Chapter 9).
- ☐ Starter motor defective. Make sure the wiring to the starter is secure. Make sure the starter relay clicks when the start button is pushed. If the relay clicks, then the fault is in the wiring or motor.
- ☐ Starter relay faulty. Check it according to the procedure in Chapter 9.
- ☐ Starter switch not contacting. The contacts could be wet, corroded or dirty. Disassemble and clean the switch (Chapter 9).
- ☐ Wiring open or shorted. Check all wiring connections and harnesses to make sure that they are dry, tight and not corroded. Also check for broken or frayed wires that can cause a short to ground (earth) (see wiring diagram, Chapter 9).
- ☐ Ignition switch defective. Check the switch according to the procedure in Chapter 9. Replace the switch with a new one if it is defective.
- ☐ Engine kill switch defective. Check for wet, dirty or corroded contacts. Clean or replace the switch as necessary (Chapter 9).
- ☐ Faulty neutral, side stand or clutch switch, or starter interlock circuit relay/diode unit. Check the wiring to each switch and the switch itself according to the procedures in Chapter 9.

Starter motor rotates but engine does not turn over

- ☐ Starter clutch defective. Inspect and repair or replace (Chapter 2).
- ☐ Damaged idle/reduction or starter gears. Inspect and replace the damaged parts (Chapter 2).

Starter works but engine won't turn over (seized)

- ☐ Seized engine caused by one or more internally damaged components. Failure due to wear, abuse or lack of lubrication. Damage can include seized valves, followers, camshafts, pistons, crankshaft, connecting rod bearings, or transmission gears or bearings. Refer to Chapter 2 for engine disassembly.

No fuel flow

- ☐ No fuel in tank.
- ☐ Fuel tank breather hose obstructed.
- ☐ Fuel tap filter (carburettor models) clogged. Remove the tap and clean it and the filter (Chapter 4A).
- ☐ Fuel line clogged. Pull the fuel line loose and carefully blow through it.

- ☐ Float needle valve clogged (carburettor models). Either a very bad batch of fuel with an unusual additive has been used, or some other foreign material has entered the tank. Many times after a machine has been stored for many months without running, the fuel turns to a varnish-like liquid and forms deposits on the inlet needle valves and jets. The carburettors should be removed and overhauled if draining the float chambers doesn't solve the problem.
- ☐ Fuel pump faulty (fuel injection models). Check the fuel pump (Chapter 4B).

Engine flooded

- ☐ Float height too high (carburettor models). Check as described in Chapter 4A.
- ☐ Float needle valve worn or stuck open (carburettor models). A piece of dirt, rust or other debris can cause the valve to seat improperly, causing excess fuel to be admitted to the float chamber. In this case, the float chamber should be cleaned and the needle valve and seat inspected. If the needle and seat are worn, then the leaking will persist and the parts should be replaced with new ones (Chapter 4A).
- ☐ Starting technique incorrect. Under normal circumstances (i.e., if all the carburettor functions are sound) the machine should start with little or no throttle. When the engine is cold, the choke should be operated and the engine started without opening the throttle. When the engine is at operating temperature, only a very slight amount of throttle should be necessary. If the engine is flooded, turn the fuel tap OFF and hold the throttle open while cranking the engine. This will allow additional air to reach the cylinders. Remember to turn the fuel tap back ON after the engine starts.

No spark or weak spark

- ☐ Ignition switch OFF.
- ☐ Engine kill switch turned to the OFF position.
- ☐ Battery voltage low. Check and recharge the battery as necessary (Chapter 9).
- ☐ Spark plug(s) dirty, defective or worn out. Locate reason for fouled plugs using spark plug condition chart and follow the plug maintenance procedures (Chapter 1).
- ☐ Spark plug cap(s) or lead(s) faulty (where fitted). Check condition. Replace either or both components if cracks or deterioration are evident (Chapter 5).
- ☐ Spark plug cap(s) or direct coil(s) (according to model) not making good contact. Make sure that the plug cap(s) or coil(s) fit snugly over the plug top(s).

1 Engine doesn't start or is difficult to start (continued)

☐ Electronic control unit defective. Check the unit, referring to Chapter 5 for details.

☐ Ignition timing sensor defective. Check the sensor, referring to Chapter 5 for details.

☐ Ignition coil(s) defective. Check the coil(s), referring to Chapter 5.

☐ Ignition or kill switch shorted. This is usually caused by water, corrosion, damage or excessive wear. The switches can be disassembled and cleaned with electrical contact cleaner. If cleaning does not help, replace the switches (Chapter 9).

☐ Wiring shorted or broken between:
   a)   Ignition switch and engine kill switch (or blown fuse)
   b)   Electronic control unit and engine kill switch
   c)   Electronic control unit and ignition coil(s)
   d)   Ignition coil(s) and spark plug(s)
   e)   Electronic control unit and timing sensor

☐ Make sure that all wiring connections are clean, dry and tight. Look for chafed and broken wires (Chapters 5 and 9).

Compression low

☐ Spark plug(s) loose. Remove the plug(s) and inspect the threads. Reinstall and tighten to the specified torque (Chapter 1).

☐ Cylinder head not sufficiently tightened down. If the cylinder head is suspected of being loose, then there's a chance that the gasket or head is damaged if the problem has persisted for any length of time. The head nuts and bolts should be tightened to the proper torque in the correct sequence (Chapter 2).

☐ Incorrect valve clearance. This means that the valve is not closing completely and compression pressure is leaking past the valve. Check and adjust the valve clearances (Chapter 1).

☐ Cylinder and/or piston worn. Excessive wear will cause compression pressure to leak past the rings. This is usually accompanied by worn rings as well. A top-end overhaul is necessary (Chapter 2).

☐ Piston rings worn, weak, broken, or sticking. Broken or sticking piston rings usually indicate a lubrication or carburetion problem that causes excess carbon deposits or seizures to form on the pistons and rings. Top-end overhaul is necessary (Chapter 2).

☐ Piston ring-to-groove clearance excessive. This is caused by excessive wear of the piston ring lands. Piston replacement is necessary (Chapter 2).

☐ Cylinder head gasket damaged. If a head is allowed to become loose, or if excessive carbon build-up on the piston crown and combustion chamber causes extremely high compression, the head gasket may leak. Retorquing the head is not always sufficient to restore the seal, so gasket replacement is necessary (Chapter 2).

☐ Cylinder head warped. This is caused by overheating or improperly tightened head nuts. Machine shop resurfacing or head replacement is necessary (Chapter 2).

☐ Valve spring broken or weak. Caused by component failure or wear; the springs must be replaced (Chapter 2).

☐ Valve not seating properly. This is caused by a bent valve (from over-revving or improper valve adjustment), burned valve or seat (improper fuel/air mix) or an accumulation of carbon deposits on the seat (from fuelling or lubrication problems). The valves must be cleaned and/or replaced and the seats serviced if possible (Chapter 2).

Stalls after starting

☐ Improper choke action (carburettor models). Make sure the choke linkage shaft is getting a full stroke and staying in the out position (Chapter 4).

☐ Ignition malfunction. See Chapter 5.

☐ Carburettor or fuel injection malfunction. See Chapter 4A or 4B according to model.

☐ Fuel contaminated. The fuel can be contaminated with either dirt or water, or can change chemically if the machine is allowed to sit for several months or more. Drain the tank and on carburettor models the float chambers (Chapter 4A or 4B). Also check that the fuel flows freely and is not being restricted.

☐ Intake air leak. Check for loose carburettor or throttle body-to-intake manifold connections, or loose carburettor tops (Chapter 4A or 4B).

☐ Engine idle speed incorrect. On Carburettor models turn idle adjusting screw until the engine idles at the specified rpm (Chapter 1).

Rough idle

☐ Ignition malfunction. See Chapter 5.

☐ Idle speed incorrect. See Chapter 1.

☐ Carburettor or fuel injection malfunction. See Chapter 4A or 4B according to model.

☐ Fuel contaminated. The fuel can be contaminated with either dirt or water, or can change chemically if the machine is allowed to sit for several months or more. Drain the tank and on carburettor models the float chambers (Chapter 4A or 4B).

☐ Intake air leak. Check for loose carburettor-to-intake manifold connections or loose carburettor tops (Chapter 4A or 4B).

☐ Air filter clogged. Replace the air filter element (Chapter 1).

2 Poor running at low speeds

Spark weak

☐ Battery voltage low. Check and recharge battery (Chapter 9).
☐ Spark plug(s) fouled, defective or worn out. Refer to Chapter 1 for spark plug maintenance.
☐ Spark plug cap(s) or lead(s) faulty (where fitted). Check condition. Replace either or both components if cracks or deterioration are evident (Chapter 5).
☐ Spark plug cap(s) or direct coil(s) (according to model) not making good contact. Make sure that the plug cap(s) or coil(s) fit snugly over the plug top(s).
☐ Incorrect spark plugs. Wrong type, heat range or cap configuration. Check and install correct plugs listed in Chapter 1.
☐ Electronic control unit defective. See Chapter 5.
☐ Ignition timing sensor defective. See Chapter 5.
☐ Ignition coils defective. See Chapter 5.

Fuel/air mixture incorrect (carburettor models)

☐ Pilot screws out of adjustment (Chapter 4).
☐ Pilot jet or air passage clogged. Remove and overhaul the carburettors (Chapter 4A).
☐ Air bleed holes clogged. Remove carburettor and blow out all passages (Chapter 4A).
☐ Air filter clogged, poorly sealed or missing (Chapter 1).
☐ Air filter housing poorly sealed. Look for cracks, holes or loose clamps and replace or repair defective parts.
☐ Fuel level too high or too low. Check the float height (Chapter 4A).
☐ Fuel tank breather hose obstructed.
☐ Carburettor intake manifolds loose. Check for cracks, breaks, tears or loose clamps. Replace the rubber intake manifold joints if split or perished.

Compression low

☐ Spark plug(s) loose. Remove the plug(s) and inspect the threads. Reinstall and tighten to the specified torque (Chapter 1).
☐ Cylinder head not sufficiently tightened down. If the cylinder head is suspected of being loose, then there's a chance that the gasket or head is damaged if the problem has persisted for any length of time. The head nuts and bolts should be tightened to the proper torque in the correct sequence (Chapter 2).
☐ Incorrect valve clearance. This means that the valve is not closing completely and compression pressure is leaking past the valve. Check and adjust the valve clearances (Chapter 1).
☐ Cylinder and/or piston worn. Excessive wear will cause compression pressure to leak past the rings. This is usually accompanied by worn rings as well. A top-end overhaul is necessary (Chapter 2).
☐ Piston rings worn, weak, broken, or sticking. Broken or sticking piston rings usually indicate a lubrication or carburetion problem that causes excess carbon deposits or seizures to form on the pistons and rings. Top-end overhaul is necessary (Chapter 2).
☐ Piston ring-to-groove clearance excessive. This is caused by excessive wear of the piston ring lands. Piston replacement is necessary (Chapter 2).
☐ Cylinder head gasket damaged. If a head is allowed to become loose, or if excessive carbon build-up on the piston crown and combustion chamber causes extremely high compression, the head gasket may leak. Retorquing the head is not always sufficient to restore the seal, so gasket replacement is necessary (Chapter 2).
☐ Cylinder head warped. This is caused by overheating or improperly tightened head nuts. Machine shop resurfacing or head replacement is necessary (Chapter 2).
☐ Valve spring broken or weak. Caused by component failure or wear; the springs must be replaced (Chapter 2).
☐ Valve not seating properly. This is caused by a bent valve (from over-revving or improper valve adjustment), burned valve or seat (improper fuel/air mix) or an accumulation of carbon deposits on the seat (from fuelling or lubrication problems). The valves must be cleaned and/or replaced and the seats serviced if possible (Chapter 2).

Poor acceleration

☐ Carburettors leaking or dirty. Overhaul the carburettors (Chapter 4A).
☐ Timing not advancing. The ignition timing sensor or the electronic control unit may be defective. If so, they must be replaced with new ones, as they can't be repaired.
☐ Engine oil viscosity too high. Using a heavier oil than that recommended in *Pre-ride checks* can damage the oil pump or lubrication system and cause drag on the engine.
☐ Brakes dragging. Usually caused by debris which has entered the brake piston seals, or from a warped disc or bent axle. Repair as necessary (Chapter 7).

3 Poor running or no power at high speed

Firing incorrect

- ☐ Air filter restricted. Clean or replace filter (Chapter 1).
- ☐ Spark plug(s) fouled, defective or worn out. See Chapter 1 for spark plug maintenance.
- ☐ Spark plug cap(s) or lead(s) faulty (where fitted). Check condition. Replace either or both components if cracks or deterioration are evident (Chapter 5).
- ☐ Spark plug cap(s) or direct coil(s) (according to model) not making good contact. Make sure that the plug cap(s) or coil(s) fit snugly over the plug top(s).
- ☐ Incorrect spark plugs. Wrong type, heat range or cap configuration. Check and install correct plugs listed in Chapter 1.
- ☐ Electronic control unit defective. See Chapter 5.
- ☐ Ignition coils defective. See Chapter 5.

Fuel/air mixture incorrect (carburettor models)

- ☐ Main jet clogged. Dirt, water or other contaminants can clog the main jets. Clean the fuel tap filter, the in-line filter, the float chamber area, and the jets and carburettor orifices (Chapter 4A).
- ☐ Main jet wrong size. The standard jetting is for sea level atmospheric pressure and oxygen content.
- ☐ Throttle shaft-to-carburettor body clearance excessive. Refer to Chapter 4A for inspection and part replacement procedures.
- ☐ Air bleed holes clogged. Remove and overhaul carburettors (Chapter 4A).
- ☐ Air filter clogged, poorly sealed, or missing (Chapter 1).
- ☐ Air filter housing poorly sealed. Look for cracks, holes or loose clamps, and replace or repair defective parts.
- ☐ Fuel level too high or too low. Check the float height (Chapter 4A).
- ☐ Fuel tank breather hose obstructed.
- ☐ Carburettor intake manifolds loose. Check for cracks, breaks, tears or loose clamps. Replace the rubber intake manifolds if they are split or perished (Chapter 4A).

Compression low

- ☐ Spark plug(s) loose. Remove the plug(s) and inspect the threads. Reinstall and tighten to the specified torque (Chapter 1).
- ☐ Cylinder head not sufficiently tightened down. If the cylinder head is suspected of being loose, then there's a chance that the gasket or head is damaged if the problem has persisted for any length of time. The head nuts and bolts should be tightened to the proper torque in the correct sequence (Chapter 2).
- ☐ Incorrect valve clearance. This means that the valve is not closing completely and compression pressure is leaking past the valve. Check and adjust the valve clearances (Chapter 1).
- ☐ Cylinder and/or piston worn. Excessive wear will cause compression pressure to leak past the rings. This is usually accompanied by worn rings as well. A top-end overhaul is necessary (Chapter 2).
- ☐ Piston rings worn, weak, broken, or sticking. Broken or sticking piston rings usually indicate a lubrication or carburetion problem that causes excess carbon deposits or seizures to form on the pistons and rings. Top-end overhaul is necessary (Chapter 2).

- ☐ Piston ring-to-groove clearance excessive. This is caused by excessive wear of the piston ring lands. Piston replacement is necessary (Chapter 2).
- ☐ Cylinder head gasket damaged. If a head is allowed to become loose, or if excessive carbon build-up on the piston crown and combustion chamber causes extremely high compression, the head gasket may leak. Retorquing the head is not always sufficient to restore the seal, so gasket replacement is necessary (Chapter 2).
- ☐ Cylinder head warped. This is caused by overheating or improperly tightened head nuts. Machine shop resurfacing or head replacement is necessary (Chapter 2).
- ☐ Valve spring broken or weak. Caused by component failure or wear; the springs must be replaced (Chapter 2).
- ☐ Valve not seating properly. This is caused by a bent valve (from over-revving or improper valve adjustment), burned valve or seat (improper fuel/air mix) or an accumulation of carbon deposits on the seat (from fuelling or lubrication problems). The valves must be cleaned and/or replaced and the seats serviced if possible (Chapter 2).

Knocking or pinking

- ☐ Carbon build-up in combustion chamber. Use of a fuel additive that will dissolve the adhesive bonding the carbon particles to the crown and chamber is the easiest way to remove the build-up. Otherwise, the cylinder head will have to be removed and decarbonised (Chapter 2).
- ☐ Incorrect or poor quality fuel. Old or improper grades of fuel can cause detonation. This causes the piston to rattle, thus the knocking or pinking sound. Drain old fuel and always use the recommended fuel grade.
- ☐ Spark plug heat range incorrect. Uncontrolled detonation indicates the plug heat range is too hot. The plug in effect becomes a glow plug, raising cylinder temperatures. Install the proper heat range plug (Chapter 1).
- ☐ Improper air/fuel mixture. This will cause the cylinders to run hot, which leads to detonation. Clogged jets or injector or an air leak can cause this imbalance. See Chapter 4A or B.

Miscellaneous causes

- ☐ Throttle valve doesn't open fully. Adjust the throttle grip freeplay (Chapter 1). Check carburettor or throttle body (see Chapter 4A or B)
- ☐ Clutch slipping. May be caused by loose or worn clutch components. Refer to Chapter 2 for clutch overhaul procedures.
- ☐ Timing not advancing.
- ☐ Engine oil viscosity too high. Using a heavier oil than the one recommended in Pre-ride checks can damage the oil pump or lubrication system and cause drag on the engine.
- ☐ Brakes dragging. Usually caused by debris which has entered the brake piston seals, or from a warped disc or bent axle. Repair as necessary.

4 Overheating

Engine overheats

☐ Coolant level low. Check and add coolant (see *Pre-ride checks*).
☐ Leak in cooling system. Check cooling system hoses and radiator for leaks and other damage. Repair or replace parts as necessary (Chapter 3).
☐ Thermostat sticking open or closed. Check and replace as described in Chapter 3.
☐ Faulty radiator cap. Remove the cap and have it pressure tested.
☐ Coolant passages clogged. Have the entire system drained and flushed, then refill with fresh coolant.
☐ Water pump defective. Remove the pump and check the components (Chapter 3).
☐ Clogged radiator fins. Clean them by blowing compressed air through the fins from the rear of the radiator.
☐ Cooling fan or fan switch fault (Chapter 3).

Firing incorrect

☐ Spark plug(s) fouled, defective or worn out. See Chapter 1 for spark plug maintenance.
☐ Incorrect spark plug(s).
☐ Electronic control unit defective. See Chapter 5.
☐ Faulty ignition coil(s) (Chapter 5).

Fuel/air mixture incorrect (carburettor models)

☐ Main jet clogged. Dirt, water and other contaminants can clog the main jets. Clean the fuel tap filter, the fuel pump in-line filter, the float chamber area and the jets and carburettor orifices (Chapter 4A).
☐ Main jet wrong size. The standard jetting is for sea level atmospheric pressure and oxygen content.
☐ Air filter clogged, poorly sealed or missing (Chapter 1).
☐ Air filter housing poorly sealed. Look for cracks, holes or loose clamps and replace or repair.
☐ Fuel level too low. Check float height (Chapter 4A).
☐ Fuel tank breather hose obstructed.
☐ Carburettor intake manifolds loose. Check for cracks, breaks, tears or loose clamps. Replace the rubber intake manifold joints if split or perished.

Compression too high

☐ Carbon build-up in combustion chamber. Use of a fuel additive that will dissolve the adhesive bonding the carbon particles to the piston crown and chamber is the easiest way to remove the build-up. Otherwise, the cylinder head will have to be removed and decarbonised (Chapter 2).
☐ Improperly machined head surface or installation of incorrect gasket during engine assembly.

Engine load excessive

☐ Clutch slipping. Can be caused by damaged, loose or worn clutch components. Refer to Chapter 2 for overhaul procedures.
☐ Engine oil level too high. The addition of too much oil will cause pressurisation of the crankcase and inefficient engine operation. Check Specifications and drain to proper level (Chapter 1 and *Pre-ride checks*).
☐ Engine oil viscosity too high. Using a heavier oil than the one recommended in *Pre-ride checks* can damage the oil pump or lubrication system as well as cause drag on the engine.
☐ Brakes dragging. Usually caused by debris which has entered the brake piston seals, or from a warped disc or bent axle. Repair as necessary.

Lubrication inadequate

☐ Engine oil level too low. Friction caused by intermittent lack of lubrication or from oil that is overworked can cause overheating. The oil provides a definite cooling function in the engine. Check the oil level (see *Pre-ride checks*).
☐ Poor quality engine oil or incorrect viscosity or type. Oil is rated not only according to viscosity but also according to type. Some oils are not rated high enough for use in this engine.

Miscellaneous causes

☐ Modification to the exhaust system. Most aftermarket exhaust systems cause the engine to run leaner, which make them run hotter. When installing an after market exhaust system, have the bike checked on a dyno, or follow the manufacturer' instructions regarding rejetting the carburettors or remapping the ECU according to model.

5 Clutch problems

Clutch slipping

- ☐ Insufficient clutch cable freeplay. Check and adjust (Chapter 1).
- ☐ Friction plates worn or warped. Overhaul the clutch assembly (Chapter 2).
- ☐ Plain plates warped (Chapter 2).
- ☐ Clutch springs broken or weak. Old or heat-damaged (from slipping clutch) springs should be replaced with new ones (Chapter 2).
- ☐ Clutch release mechanism defective. Replace any defective parts (Chapter 2).
- ☐ Clutch centre or housing unevenly worn. This causes improper engagement of the plates. Replace the damaged or worn parts (Chapter 2).

Clutch not disengaging completely

- ☐ Excessive clutch cable freeplay. Check and adjust (Chapter 1).
- ☐ Clutch plates warped or damaged. This will cause clutch drag, which in turn will cause the machine to creep. Overhaul the clutch assembly (Chapter 2).

- ☐ Clutch spring tension uneven. Usually caused by a sagged or broken spring. Check and replace the springs as a set (Chapter 2).
- ☐ Engine oil deteriorated. Old, thin, worn out oil will not provide proper lubrication for the plates, causing the clutch to drag. Replace the oil and filter (Chapter 1 and *Pre-ride checks*).
- ☐ Engine oil viscosity too high. Using a heavier oil than recommended can cause the plates to stick together, putting a drag on the engine. Change to the correct weight oil (see *Pre-ride checks*).
- ☐ Clutch housing guide seized on input shaft. Lack of lubrication, severe wear or damage can cause the guide to seize on the shaft. Overhaul of the clutch, and perhaps transmission, may be necessary to repair the damage (Chapter 2).
- ☐ Clutch release mechanism defective. Overhaul the clutch cover components (Chapter 2).
- ☐ Loose clutch centre nut. Causes housing and centre misalignment putting a drag on the engine. Engagement adjustment continually varies. Overhaul the clutch assembly (Chapter 2).

6 Gear changing problems

Doesn't go into gear or lever doesn't return

- ☐ Clutch not disengaging. See above.
- ☐ Selector fork(s) bent or seized. Often caused by dropping the machine or from lack of lubrication. Overhaul the transmission (Chapter 2).
- ☐ Gear(s) stuck on shaft. Most often caused by a lack of lubrication or excessive wear in transmission bearings and bushings. Overhaul the transmission (Chapter 2).
- ☐ Selector drum binding. Caused by lubrication failure or excessive wear. Replace the drum and bearing (Chapter 2).
- ☐ Gearchange lever return spring weak or broken (Chapter 2).
- ☐ Gearchange lever broken. Splines stripped out of lever or shaft, caused by allowing the lever to get loose or from dropping the machine. Replace necessary parts (Chapter 2).
- ☐ Gearchange mechanism stopper arm broken or worn. Full engagement and rotary movement of selector drum results. Replace the arm (Chapter 2).
- ☐ Stopper arm spring broken. Allows arm to float, causing sporadic gearchange operation. Replace the spring (Chapter 2).

Jumps out of gear

- ☐ Selector fork(s) worn. Overhaul the transmission (Chapter 2).
- ☐ Gear groove(s) worn. Overhaul the transmission (Chapter 2).
- ☐ Gear dogs or dog slots worn or damaged. The gears should be inspected and replaced. No attempt should be made to service the worn parts.

Overselects

- ☐ Stopper arm spring weak or broken (Chapter 2).
- ☐ Gearchange shaft return spring post broken or distorted (Chapter 2).

7 Abnormal engine noise

Knocking or pinking

- ☐ Carbon build-up in combustion chamber. Use of a fuel additive that will dissolve the adhesive bonding the carbon particles to the piston crown and chamber is the easiest way to remove the build-up. Otherwise, the cylinder head will have to be removed and decarbonised (Chapter 2).
- ☐ Incorrect or poor quality fuel. Old or improper fuel can cause detonation. This causes the pistons to rattle, thus the knocking or pinking sound. Drain the old fuel and always use the recommended grade fuel (Chapter 4A or 4B).
- ☐ Spark plug heat range incorrect. Uncontrolled detonation indicates that the plug heat range is too hot. The plug in effect becomes a glow plug, raising cylinder temperatures. Install the proper heat range plug(s) (Chapter 1).
- ☐ Improper fuel/air mixture (carburettor models). This will cause the cylinders to run hot and lead to detonation. Clogged jets or an air leak can cause this imbalance. See Chapter 4A.

Piston slap or rattling

- ☐ Cylinder-to-piston clearance excessive. Caused by improper assembly. Inspect and overhaul top-end parts (Chapter 2).
- ☐ Connecting rod bent. Caused by over-revving, trying to start a badly flooded engine or from ingesting a foreign object into the combustion chamber. Replace the damaged parts (Chapter 2).
- ☐ Piston pin or piston pin bore worn or seized from wear or lack of lubrication. Replace damaged parts (Chapter 2).
- ☐ Piston ring(s) worn, broken or sticking. Overhaul the top-end (Chapter 2).
- ☐ Piston seizure damage. Usually from lack of lubrication or overheating. Replace the pistons and bore the cylinders, as necessary (Chapter 2).
- ☐ Connecting rod upper or lower end clearance excessive. Caused by excessive wear or lack of lubrication. Replace worn parts.

Valve noise

- ☐ Incorrect valve clearances. Adjust the clearances by referring to Chapter 1.
- ☐ Valve spring broken or weak. Check and replace weak valve springs (Chapter 2).
- ☐ Camshaft or cylinder head worn or damaged. Lack of lubrication at high rpm is usually the cause of damage. Insufficient oil or failure to change the oil at the recommended intervals are the chief causes. Since there are no replaceable bearings in the head, the head itself will have to be replaced if there is excessive wear or damage (Chapter 2).

Other noise

- ☐ Cylinder head gasket leaking.
- ☐ Exhaust pipe leaking at cylinder head connection. Caused by improper fit of pipe(s) or loose exhaust flange. All exhaust fasteners should be tightened evenly and carefully. Failure to do this will lead to a leak.
- ☐ Crankshaft runout excessive. Caused by a bent crankshaft (from over-revving) or damage from an upper cylinder component failure. Can also be attributed to dropping the machine on either of the crankshaft ends.
- ☐ Engine mounting bolts loose. Tighten all engine mounting bolts (Chapter 2).
- ☐ Crankshaft bearings worn (Chapter 2).
- ☐ Camchain defective. Replace according to the procedure in Chapter 2.

8 Abnormal driveline noise

Clutch noise
- [ ] Clutch outer drum/friction plate clearance excessive (Chapter 2).
- [ ] Loose or damaged clutch pressure plate and/or bolts (Chapter 2).

Transmission noise
- [ ] Bearings worn. Also includes the possibility that the shafts are worn. Overhaul the transmission (Chapter 2).
- [ ] Gears worn or chipped (Chapter 2).
- [ ] Metal chips jammed in gear teeth. Probably pieces from a broken clutch, gear or selector mechanism that were picked up by the gears. This will cause early bearing failure (Chapter 2).

- [ ] Engine oil level too low. Causes a howl from transmission. Also affects engine power and clutch operation (see Pre-ride checks).

Final drive noise
- [ ] Chain or belt not adjusted properly (Chapter 1).
- [ ] Front or rear sprocket or pulley loose. Tighten fasteners (Chapter 7).
- [ ] Sprockets or pulleys worn. Renew (Chapter 7).
- [ ] Rear sprocket or pulley warped. Renew (Chapter 7).
- [ ] Rubber dampers in rear wheel hub worn. Check and renew (Chapter 7).

9 Abnormal frame and suspension noise

Front end noise
- [ ] Low fluid level or improper viscosity oil in forks. This can sound like spurting and is usually accompanied by irregular fork action (Chapter 6).
- [ ] Spring weak or broken. Makes a clicking or scraping sound. Fork oil, when drained, will have a lot of metal particles in it (Chapter 6).
- [ ] Steering head bearings loose or damaged. Clicks when braking. Check and adjust or replace as necessary (Chapters 1 and 6).
- [ ] Fork yokes loose. Make sure all clamp pinch bolts are tightened to the specified torque (Chapter 6).
- [ ] Fork tube bent. Good possibility if machine has been dropped. Replace tube with a new one (Chapter 6).
- [ ] Front axle bolt or axle clamp bolts loose. Tighten them to the specified torque (Chapter 7).
- [ ] Loose or worn wheel bearings. Check and replace as needed (Chapter 7).

Shock absorber noise
- [ ] Fluid level incorrect. Indicates a leak caused by defective seal. Shock will be covered with oil. Replace shock or seek advice on repair (Chapter 6).
- [ ] Defective shock absorber with internal damage. This is in the body of the shock and can't be remedied. The shock must be replaced with a new one (Chapter 6).

- [ ] Bent or damaged shock body. Replace the shock with a new one (Chapter 6).
- [ ] Loose or worn suspension linkage components. Check and replace as necessary (Chapter 6).

Brake noise
- [ ] Squeal caused by pad shim not installed or positioned correctly (where fitted) (Chapter 7).
- [ ] Squeal caused by dust on brake pads. Usually found in combination with glazed pads. Clean using brake cleaning solvent (Chapter 7).
- [ ] Contamination of brake pads. Oil, brake fluid or dirt causing brake to chatter or squeal. Clean or replace pads (Chapter 7).
- [ ] Pads glazed. Caused by excessive heat from prolonged use or from contamination. Do not use sandpaper, emery cloth, carborundum cloth or any other abrasive to roughen the pad surfaces as abrasives will stay in the pad material and damage the disc. A very fine flat file can be used, but pad replacement is suggested as a cure (Chapter 7).
- [ ] Disc warped. Can cause a chattering, clicking or intermittent squeal. Usually accompanied by a pulsating lever and uneven braking. Replace the disc (Chapter 7).
- [ ] Loose or worn wheel bearings. Check and replace as needed (Chapter 7).
- [ ] Faulty ABS system, if fitted (Chapter 7).

10 Oil pressure warning light comes on

Engine lubrication system

☐ Engine oil pump(s) defective, blocked oil strainer gauze or failed relief valve. Carry out an oil pressure check (Chapter 2).

☐ Engine oil level low. Inspect for leak or other problem causing low oil level and add recommended oil (see *Pre-ride checks*).

☐ Engine oil viscosity too low. Very old, thin oil or an improper weight of oil used in the engine. Change to correct oil (see *Pre-ride checks*).

☐ Camshaft or journals worn. Excessive wear causing drop in oil pressure. Replace cam and/or cylinder head. Abnormal wear could be caused by oil starvation at high rpm from low oil level or improper weight or type of oil.

☐ Crankshaft and/or bearings worn. Same problems as above. Check and replace crankshaft and/or bearings (Chapter 2).

Electrical system

☐ Oil pressure switch defective. Check the switch according to the procedure in Chapter 9. Replace it if it is defective.

☐ Oil pressure warning light circuit defective. Check for pinched, shorted, disconnected or damaged wiring (Chapter 9).

11 Excessive exhaust smoke

White smoke

☐ Piston oil ring worn. The ring may be broken or damaged, causing oil from the crankcase to be pulled past the piston into the combustion chamber. Replace the rings with new ones (Chapter 2).

☐ Cylinder worn, cracked, or scored. Caused by overheating or oil starvation (Chapter 2)

☐ Valve oil seal damaged or worn. Replace oil seals with new ones (Chapter 2).

☐ Valve guide worn. Perform a complete valve job (Chapter 2).

☐ Engine oil level too high, which causes the oil to be forced past the rings. Drain oil to the proper level (see *Pre-ride checks*).

☐ Head gasket broken between oil return and cylinder. Causes oil to be pulled into the combustion chamber. Replace the head gasket and check the head for warpage (Chapter 2).

☐ Abnormal crankcase pressurisation, which forces oil past the rings. Clogged breather is usually the cause.

Black smoke

☐ Air filter clogged. Clean or replace the element (Chapter 1).

☐ Main jet too large or loose (carburettor models). Compare the jet size to the Specifications (Chapter 4A).

☐ Choke cable or linkage shaft stuck (carburettor models), causing fuel to be pulled through choke circuit (Chapter 4A).

☐ Fuel level too high (carburettor models). Check and adjust the float height(s) as necessary (Chapter 4A).

☐ Float needle valve held off needle seat (carburettor models). Clean the float chambers and fuel line and replace the needles and seats if necessary (Chapter 4A).

Brown smoke

☐ Main jet too small or clogged (carburettor models). Lean condition caused by wrong size main jet or by a restricted orifice. Clean float chambers and jets and compare jet size to Specifications (Chapter 4A).

☐ Fuel flow insufficient (carburettor models). Float needle valve stuck closed due to chemical reaction with old fuel. Float height incorrect. Restricted fuel line. Blocked tap or strainer. Clean line and float chamber and adjust floats if necessary (Chapter 4A).

☐ Fuel flow insufficient (fuel injection models). Faulty injector, faulty fuel pump or blocked strainer or filter (Chapter 4B).

☐ Intake manifold clamp loose (Chapter 4A or B).

☐ Air filter poorly sealed or not installed (Chapter 1).

12 Poor handling or stability

Handlebar hard to turn

☐ Steering head bearing adjuster nut too tight. Check adjustment as described in Chapter 1.
☐ Bearings damaged. Roughness can be felt as the bars are turned from side-to-side. Replace bearings and races (Chapter 6).
☐ Races dented or worn. Denting results from wear in only one position (e.g., straight ahead), from a collision or hitting a pothole or from dropping the machine. Replace races and bearings (Chapter 6).
☐ Steering stem lubrication inadequate. Causes are grease getting hard from age or being washed out by high pressure car washes. Disassemble steering head and repack bearings (Chapter 6).
☐ Steering stem bent. Caused by a collision, hitting a pothole or by dropping the machine. Replace damaged part. Don't try to straighten the steering stem (Chapter 6).
☐ Front tyre air pressure too low (see *Pre-ride checks*).

Handlebar shakes or vibrates excessively

☐ Tyres worn or out of balance (Chapter 7).
☐ Swingarm bearings worn. Replace worn bearings (Chapter 6).
☐ Wheel rim(s) warped or damaged. Inspect wheels for runout (Chapter 7).
☐ Wheel bearings worn. Worn front or rear wheel bearings can cause poor tracking. Worn front bearings will cause wobble (Chapter 7).
☐ Handlebar clamp bolts loose (Chapter 6).
☐ Fork yoke bolts loose. Tighten them to the specified torque (Chapter 6).
☐ Engine mounting bolts loose. Will cause excessive vibration with increased engine rpm (Chapter 2).

Handlebar pulls to one side

☐ Frame bent. Definitely suspect this if the machine has been dropped. May or may not be accompanied by cracking near the bend. Replace the frame (Chapter 6).
☐ Wheels out of alignment. Caused by improper location of axle spacers or from bent steering stem or frame (Chapter 6).
☐ Swingarm bent or twisted. Caused by age (metal fatigue) or impact damage. Replace the arm (Chapter 6).
☐ Steering stem bent. Caused by impact damage or by dropping the motorcycle. Replace the steering stem (Chapter 6).
☐ Fork tube bent. Disassemble the forks and replace the damaged parts (Chapter 6).
☐ Fork oil level uneven. Check and add or drain as necessary (Chapter 6).

Poor shock absorbing qualities

Too hard:
 a) Fork oil level excessive (Chapter 6).
 b) Fork oil viscosity too high. Use a lighter oil (see the Specifications in Chapter 6).
 c) Fork tube bent. Causes a harsh, sticking feeling (Chapter 6).
 d) Shock shaft or body bent or damaged (Chapter 6).
 e) Fork internal damage (Chapter 6).
 f) Shock internal damage.
 g) Tyre pressure too high (Pre-ride checks).
Too soft:
 a) Fork or shock oil insufficient and/or leaking (Chapter 6).
 b) Fork oil level too low (Chapter 6).
 c) Fork oil viscosity too light (Chapter 6).
 d) Fork springs weak or broken (Chapter 6).
 e) Shock internal damage or leakage (Chapter 6).

13 Braking problems

Brakes are spongy, don't hold

☐ Air in brake line. Caused by inattention to master cylinder fluid level or by leakage. Locate problem and bleed brakes (Chapter 7).
☐ Pad or disc worn (Chapters 1 and 7).
☐ Brake fluid leak. See paragraph 1.
☐ Contaminated pads. Caused by contamination with oil, grease, brake fluid, etc. Clean or replace pads. Clean disc thoroughly with brake cleaner (Chapter 7).
☐ Brake fluid deteriorated. Fluid is old or contaminated. Drain system, replenish with new fluid and bleed the system (Chapter 7).
☐ Master cylinder internal parts worn or damaged causing fluid to bypass (Chapter 7).
☐ Master cylinder bore scratched by foreign material or broken spring. Repair or replace master cylinder (Chapter 7).
☐ Disc warped. Replace disc (Chapter 7).
☐ Faulty ABS system, if fitted (Chapter 7).

Brake lever or pedal pulsates

☐ Disc warped. Replace disc (Chapter 7).
☐ Axle bent. Replace axle (Chapter 7).

☐ Brake caliper bolts loose (Chapter 7).
☐ Brake caliper slider pins damaged or sticking, causing caliper to bind. Lubricate the slider pins or replace them if they are corroded or bent (Chapter 7).
☐ Wheel warped or otherwise damaged (Chapter 7).
☐ Wheel bearings damaged or worn (Chapter 7).
☐ Faulty ABS system, if fitted (Chapter 7).

Brakes drag

☐ Master cylinder piston seized. Caused by wear or damage to piston or cylinder bore (Chapter 7).
☐ Lever balky or stuck. Check pivot and lubricate (Chapter 7).
☐ Brake caliper binds on bracket. Caused by inadequate lubrication or damage to caliper slider pins (Chapter 7).
☐ Brake caliper piston seized in bore. Caused by wear or ingestion of dirt past deteriorated seal (Chapter 7).
☐ Brake pad damaged. Pad material separated from backing plate. Usually caused by faulty manufacturing process or from contact with chemicals. Replace pads (Chapter 7).
☐ Pads improperly installed (Chapter 7).
☐ Faulty ABS system, if fitted (Chapter 7).

14 Electrical problems

Battery dead or weak

☐ Battery faulty. Caused by sulphated plates which are shorted through sedimentation. Also, broken battery terminal making only occasional contact (Chapter 9).

☐ Battery cables making poor contact (Chapter 9).

☐ Load excessive. Caused by addition of high wattage lights or other electrical accessories.

☐ Ignition switch defective. Switch either grounds (earths) internally or fails to shut off system. Replace the switch (Chapter 9).

☐ Regulator/rectifier defective (Chapter 9).

☐ Alternator stator coil open or shorted (Chapter 9).

☐ Wiring faulty. Wiring grounded (earthed) or connections loose in ignition, charging or lighting circuits (Chapter 9).

Battery overcharged

☐ Regulator/rectifier defective. Overcharging is noticed when battery gets excessively warm (Chapter 9).

☐ Battery defective. Replace battery with a new one (Chapter 9).

☐ Battery amperage too low, wrong type or size. Install manufacturer's specified amp-hour battery to handle charging load (Chapter 9).

A

ABS (Anti-lock braking system) A system, usually electronically controlled, that senses incipient wheel lockup during braking and relieves hydraulic pressure at wheel which is about to skid.

Aftermarket Components suitable for the motorcycle, but not produced by the motorcycle manufacturer.

Allen key A hexagonal wrench which fits into a recessed hexagonal hole.

Alternating current (ac) Current produced by an alternator. Requires converting to direct current by a rectifier for charging purposes.

Alternator Converts mechanical energy from the engine into electrical energy to charge the battery and power the electrical system.

Ampere (amp) A unit of measurement for the flow of electrical current. Current = Volts ÷ Ohms.

Ampere-hour (Ah) Measure of battery capacity.

Angle-tightening A torque expressed in degrees. Often follows a conventional tightening torque for cylinder head or main bearing fasteners **(see illustration)**.

Angle-tightening cylinder head bolts

Antifreeze A substance (usually ethylene glycol) mixed with water, and added to the cooling system, to prevent freezing of the coolant in winter. Antifreeze also contains chemicals to inhibit corrosion and the formation of rust and other deposits that would tend to clog the radiator and coolant passages and reduce cooling efficiency.

Anti-dive System attached to the fork lower leg (slider) to prevent fork dive when braking hard.

Anti-seize compound A coating that reduces the risk of seizing on fasteners that are subjected to high temperatures, such as exhaust clamp bolts and nuts.

API American Petroleum Institute. A quality standard for 4-stroke motor oils.

Asbestos A natural fibrous mineral with great heat resistance, commonly used in the composition of brake friction materials. Asbestos is a health hazard and the dust created by brake systems should never be inhaled or ingested.

ATF Automatic Transmission Fluid. Often used in front forks.

ATU Automatic Timing Unit. Mechanical device for advancing the ignition timing on early engines.

ATV All Terrain Vehicle. Often called a Quad.

Axial play Side-to-side movement.

Axle A shaft on which a wheel revolves. Also known as a spindle.

B

Backlash The amount of movement between meshed components when one component is held still. Usually applies to gear teeth.

Ball bearing A bearing consisting of a hardened inner and outer race with hardened steel balls between the two races.

Bearings Used between two working surfaces to prevent wear of the components and a build-up of heat. Four types of bearing are commonly used on motorcycles: plain shell bearings, ball bearings, tapered roller bearings and needle roller bearings.

Bevel gears Used to turn the drive through 90°. Typical applications are shaft final drive and camshaft drive **(see illustration)**.

Bevel gears are used to turn the drive through 90°

BHP Brake Horsepower. The British measurement for engine power output. Power output is now usually expressed in kilowatts (kW).

Bias-belted tyre Similar construction to radial tyre, but with outer belt running at an angle to the wheel rim.

Big-end bearing The bearing in the end of the connecting rod that's attached to the crankshaft.

Bleeding The process of removing air from an hydraulic system via a bleed nipple or bleed screw.

Bottom-end A description of an engine's crankcase components and all components contained there-in.

BTDC Before Top Dead Centre in terms of piston position. Ignition timing is often expressed in terms of degrees or millimetres BTDC.

Bush A cylindrical metal or rubber component used between two moving parts.

Burr Rough edge left on a component after machining or as a result of excessive wear.

C

Cam chain The chain which takes drive from the crankshaft to the camshaft(s).

Canister The main component in an evaporative emission control system (California market only); contains activated charcoal granules to trap vapours from the fuel system rather than allowing them to vent to the atmosphere.

Castellated Resembling the parapets along the top of a castle wall. For example, a castellated wheel axle or spindle nut.

Catalytic converter A device in the exhaust system of some machines which converts certain pollutants in the exhaust gases into less harmful substances.

Charging system Description of the components which charge the battery, ie the alternator, rectifier and regulator.

Circlip A ring-shaped clip used to prevent endwise movement of cylindrical parts and shafts. An internal circlip is installed in a groove in a housing; an external circlip fits into a groove on the outside of a cylindrical piece such as a shaft. Also known as a snap-ring.

Clearance The amount of space between two parts. For example, between a piston and a cylinder, between a bearing and a journal, etc.

Coil spring A spiral of elastic steel found in various sizes throughout a vehicle, for example as a springing medium in the suspension and in the valve train.

Compression Reduction in volume, and increase in pressure and temperature, of a gas, caused by squeezing it into a smaller space.

Compression damping Controls the speed the suspension compresses when hitting a bump.

Compression ratio The relationship between cylinder volume when the piston is at top dead centre and cylinder volume when the piston is at bottom dead centre.

Continuity The uninterrupted path in the flow of electricity. Little or no measurable resistance.

Continuity tester Self-powered bleeper or test light which indicates continuity.

Cp Candlepower. Bulb rating commonly found on US motorcycles.

Crossply tyre Tyre plies arranged in a criss-cross pattern. Usually four or six plies used, hence 4PR or 6PR in tyre size codes.

Cush drive Rubber damper segments fitted between the rear wheel and final drive sprocket to absorb transmission shocks **(see illustration)**.

Cush drive rubbers dampen out transmission shocks

D

Degree disc Calibrated disc for measuring piston position. Expressed in degrees.

Dial gauge Clock-type gauge with adapters for measuring runout and piston position. Expressed in mm or inches.

Diaphragm The rubber membrane in a master cylinder or carburettor which seals the upper chamber.

Diaphragm spring A single sprung plate often used in clutches.

Direct current (dc) Current produced by a dc generator.

Decarbonisation The process of removing carbon deposits - typically from the combustion chamber, valves and exhaust port/system.

Detonation Destructive and damaging explosion of fuel/air mixture in combustion chamber instead of controlled burning.

Diode An electrical valve which only allows current to flow in one direction. Commonly used in rectifiers and starter interlock systems.

Disc valve (or rotary valve) A induction system used on some two-stroke engines.

Double-overhead camshaft (DOHC) An engine that uses two overhead camshafts, one for the intake valves and one for the exhaust valves.

Drivebelt A toothed belt used to transmit drive to the rear wheel on some motorcycles. A drivebelt has also been used to drive the camshafts. Drivebelts are usually made of Kevlar.

Driveshaft Any shaft used to transmit motion. Commonly used when referring to the final driveshaft on shaft drive motorcycles.

E

Earth return The return path of an electrical circuit, utilising the motorcycle's frame.

ECU (Electronic Control Unit) A computer which controls (for instance) an ignition system, or an anti-lock braking system.

EGO Exhaust Gas Oxygen sensor. Sometimes called a Lambda sensor.

Electrolyte The fluid in a lead-acid battery.

EMS (Engine Management System) A computer controlled system which manages the fuel injection and the ignition systems in an integrated fashion.

Endfloat The amount of lengthways movement between two parts. As applied to a crankshaft, the distance that the crankshaft can move side-to-side in the crankcase.

Endless chain A chain having no joining link. Common use for cam chains and final drive chains.

EP (Extreme Pressure) Oil type used in locations where high loads are applied, such as between gear teeth.

Evaporative emission control system Describes a charcoal filled canister which stores fuel vapours from the tank rather than allowing them to vent to the atmosphere. Usually only fitted to California models and referred to as an EVAP system.

Expansion chamber Section of two-stroke engine exhaust system so designed to improve engine efficiency and boost power.

F

Feeler blade or gauge A thin strip or blade of hardened steel, ground to an exact thickness, used to check or measure clearances between parts.

Final drive Description of the drive from the transmission to the rear wheel. Usually by chain or shaft, but sometimes by belt.

Firing order The order in which the engine cylinders fire, or deliver their power strokes, beginning with the number one cylinder.

Flooding Term used to describe a high fuel level in the carburettor float chambers, leading to fuel overflow. Also refers to excess fuel in the combustion chamber due to incorrect starting technique.

Free length The no-load state of a component when measured. Clutch, valve and fork spring lengths are measured at rest, without any preload.

Freeplay The amount of travel before any action takes place. The looseness in a linkage, or an assembly of parts, between the initial application of force and actual movement. For example, the distance the rear brake pedal moves before the rear brake is actuated.

Fuel injection The fuel/air mixture is metered electronically and directed into the engine intake ports (indirect injection) or into the cylinders (direct injection). Sensors supply information on engine speed and conditions.

Fuel/air mixture The charge of fuel and air going into the engine. See **Stoichiometric ratio**.

Fuse An electrical device which protects a circuit against accidental overload. The typical fuse contains a soft piece of metal which is calibrated to melt at a predetermined current flow (expressed as amps) and break the circuit.

G

Gap The distance the spark must travel in jumping from the centre electrode to the side electrode in a spark plug. Also refers to the distance between the ignition rotor and the pickup coil in an electronic ignition system.

Gasket Any thin, soft material - usually cork, cardboard, asbestos or soft metal - installed between two metal surfaces to ensure a good seal. For instance, the cylinder head gasket seals the joint between the block and the cylinder head.

Gauge An instrument panel display used to monitor engine conditions. A gauge with a movable pointer on a dial or a fixed scale is an analogue gauge. A gauge with a numerical readout is called a digital gauge.

Gear ratios The drive ratio of a pair of gears in a gearbox, calculated on their number of teeth.

Glaze-busting see **Honing**

Grinding Process for renovating the valve face and valve seat contact area in the cylinder head.

Gudgeon pin The shaft which connects the connecting rod small-end with the piston. Often called a piston pin or wrist pin.

H

Helical gears Gear teeth are slightly curved and produce less gear noise that straight-cut gears. Often used for primary drives.

Installing a Helicoil thread insert in a cylinder head

Helicoil A thread insert repair system. Commonly used as a repair for stripped spark plug threads **(see illustration)**.

Honing A process used to break down the glaze on a cylinder bore (also called glaze-busting). Can also be carried out to roughen a rebored cylinder to aid ring bedding-in.

HT (High Tension) Description of the electrical circuit from the secondary winding of the ignition coil to the spark plug.

Hydraulic A liquid filled system used to transmit pressure from one component to another. Common uses on motorcycles are brakes and clutches.

Hydrometer An instrument for measuring the specific gravity of a lead-acid battery.

Hygroscopic Water absorbing. In motorcycle applications, braking efficiency will be reduced if DOT 3 or 4 hydraulic fluid absorbs water from the air - care must be taken to keep new brake fluid in tightly sealed containers.

I

lbf ft Pounds-force feet. An imperial unit of torque. Sometimes written as ft-lbs.

lbf in Pound-force inch. An imperial unit of torque, applied to components where a very low torque is required. Sometimes written as in-lbs.

IC Abbreviation for Integrated Circuit.

Ignition advance Means of increasing the timing of the spark at higher engine speeds. Done by mechanical means (ATU) on early engines or electronically by the ignition control unit on later engines.

Ignition timing The moment at which the spark plug fires, expressed in the number of crankshaft degrees before the piston reaches the top of its stroke, or in the number of millimetres before the piston reaches the top of its stroke.

Infinity (∞) Description of an open-circuit electrical state, where no continuity exists.

Inverted forks (upside down forks) The sliders or lower legs are held in the yokes and the fork tubes or stanchions are connected to the wheel axle (spindle). Less unsprung weight and stiffer construction than conventional forks.

J

JASO Quality standard for 2-stroke oils.

Joule The unit of electrical energy.

Journal The bearing surface of a shaft.

K

Kickstart Mechanical means of turning the engine over for starting purposes. Only usually fitted to mopeds, small capacity motorcycles and off-road motorcycles.

Kill switch Handebar-mounted switch for emergency ignition cut-out. Cuts the ignition circuit on all models, and additionally prevent starter motor operation on others.

km Symbol for kilometre.

kmh Abbreviation for kilometres per hour.

L

Lambda (λ) sensor A sensor fitted in the exhaust system to measure the exhaust gas oxygen content (excess air factor).

Lapping see **Grinding**.
LCD Abbreviation for Liquid Crystal Display.
LED Abbreviation for Light Emitting Diode.
Liner A steel cylinder liner inserted in a aluminium alloy cylinder block.
Locknut A nut used to lock an adjustment nut, or other threaded component, in place.
Lockstops The lugs on the lower triple clamp (yoke) which abut those on the frame, preventing handlebar-to-fuel tank contact.
Lockwasher A form of washer designed to prevent an attaching nut from working loose.
LT Low Tension Description of the electrical circuit from the power supply to the primary winding of the ignition coil.

M

Main bearings The bearings between the crankshaft and crankcase.
Maintenance-free (MF) battery A sealed battery which cannot be topped up.
Manometer Mercury-filled calibrated tubes used to measure intake tract vacuum. Used to synchronise carburettors on multi-cylinder engines.
Micrometer A precision measuring instrument that measures component outside diameters **(see illustration)**.

Tappet shims are measured with a micrometer

MON (Motor Octane Number) A measure of a fuel's resistance to knock.
Monograde oil An oil with a single viscosity, eg SAE80W.
Monoshock A single suspension unit linking the swingarm or suspension linkage to the frame.
mph Abbreviation for miles per hour.
Multigrade oil Having a wide viscosity range (eg 10W40). The W stands for Winter, thus the viscosity ranges from SAE10 when cold to SAE40 when hot.
Multimeter An electrical test instrument with the capability to measure voltage, current and resistance. Some meters also incorporate a continuity tester and buzzer.

N

Needle roller bearing Inner race of caged needle rollers and hardened outer race. Examples of uncaged needle rollers can be found on some engines. Commonly used in rear suspension applications and in two-stroke engines.
Nm Newton metres.
NOx Oxides of Nitrogen. A common toxic pollutant emitted by petrol engines at higher temperatures.

O

Octane The measure of a fuel's resistance to knock.
OE (Original Equipment) Relates to components fitted to a motorcycle as standard or replacement parts supplied by the motorcycle manufacturer.
Ohm The unit of electrical resistance. Ohms = Volts ÷ Current.
Ohmmeter An instrument for measuring electrical resistance.
Oil cooler System for diverting engine oil outside of the engine to a radiator for cooling purposes.
Oil injection A system of two-stroke engine lubrication where oil is pump-fed to the engine in accordance with throttle position.
Open-circuit An electrical condition where there is a break in the flow of electricity - no continuity (high resistance).
O-ring A type of sealing ring made of a special rubber-like material; in use, the O-ring is compressed into a groove to provide the sealing action.
Oversize (OS) Term used for piston and ring size options fitted to a rebored cylinder.
Overhead cam (sohc) engine An engine with single camshaft located on top of the cylinder head.
Overhead valve (ohv) engine An engine with the valves located in the cylinder head, but with the camshaft located in the engine block or crankcase.
Oxygen sensor A device installed in the exhaust system which senses the oxygen content in the exhaust and converts this information into an electric current. Also called a Lambda sensor.

P

Plastigauge A thin strip of plastic thread, available in different sizes, used for measuring clearances. For example, a strip of Plastigauge is laid across a bearing journal. The parts are assembled and dismantled; the width of the crushed strip indicates the clearance between journal and bearing.
Polarity Either negative or positive earth (ground), determined by which battery lead is connected to the frame (earth return). Modern motorcycles are usually negative earth.
Pre-ignition A situation where the fuel/air mixture ignites before the spark plug fires. Often due to a hot spot in the combustion chamber caused by carbon build-up. Engine has a tendency to 'run-on'.
Pre-load (suspension) The amount a spring is compressed when in the unloaded state. Preload can be applied by gas, spacer or mechanical adjuster.
Premix The method of engine lubrication on older two-stroke engines. Engine oil is mixed with the petrol in the fuel tank in a specific ratio. The fuel/oil mix is sometimes referred to as "petroil".
Primary drive Description of the drive from the crankshaft to the clutch. Usually by gear or chain.
PS Pfedestärke - a German interpretation of BHP.
PSI Pounds-force per square inch. Imperial measurement of tyre pressure and cylinder pressure measurement.
PTFE Polytetrafluroethylene. A low friction substance.

Pulse secondary air injection system A process of promoting the burning of excess fuel present in the exhaust gases by routing fresh air into the exhaust ports.

Q

Quartz halogen bulb Tungsten filament surrounded by a halogen gas. Typically used for the headlight **(see illustration)**.

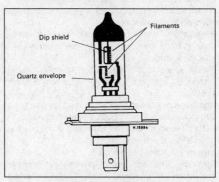

Quartz halogen headlight bulb construction

R

Rack-and-pinion A pinion gear on the end of a shaft that mates with a rack (think of a geared wheel opened up and laid flat). Sometimes used in clutch operating systems.
Radial play Up and down movement about a shaft.
Radial ply tyres Tyre plies run across the tyre (from bead to bead) and around the circumference of the tyre. Less resistant to tread distortion than other tyre types.
Radiator A liquid-to-air heat transfer device designed to reduce the temperature of the coolant in a liquid cooled engine.
Rake A feature of steering geometry - the angle of the steering head in relation to the vertical **(see illustration)**.

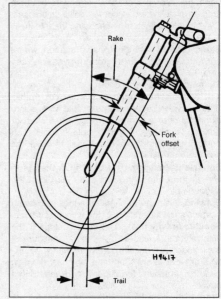

Steering geometry

Rebore Providing a new working surface to the cylinder bore by boring out the old surface. Necessitates the use of oversize piston and rings.

Rebound damping A means of controlling the oscillation of a suspension unit spring after it has been compressed. Resists the spring's natural tendency to bounce back after being compressed.

Rectifier Device for converting the ac output of an alternator into dc for battery charging.

Reed valve An induction system commonly used on two-stroke engines.

Regulator Device for maintaining the charging voltage from the generator or alternator within a specified range.

Relay A electrical device used to switch heavy current on and off by using a low current auxiliary circuit.

Resistance Measured in ohms. An electrical component's ability to pass electrical current.

RON (Research Octane Number) A measure of a fuel's resistance to knock.

rpm revolutions per minute.

Runout The amount of wobble (in-and-out movement) of a wheel or shaft as it's rotated. The amount a shaft rotates `out-of-true'. The out-of-round condition of a rotating part.

S

SAE (Society of Automotive Engineers) A standard for the viscosity of a fluid.

Sealant A liquid or paste used to prevent leakage at a joint. Sometimes used in conjunction with a gasket.

Service limit Term for the point where a component is no longer useable and must be renewed.

Shaft drive A method of transmitting drive from the transmission to the rear wheel.

Shell bearings Plain bearings consisting of two shell halves. Most often used as big-end and main bearings in a four-stroke engine. Often called bearing inserts.

Shim Thin spacer, commonly used to adjust the clearance or relative positions between two parts. For example, shims inserted into or under tappets or followers to control valve clearances. Clearance is adjusted by changing the thickness of the shim.

Short-circuit An electrical condition where current shorts to earth (ground) bypassing the circuit components.

Skimming Process to correct warpage or repair a damaged surface, eg on brake discs or drums.

Slide-hammer A special puller that screws into or hooks onto a component such as a shaft or bearing; a heavy sliding handle on the shaft bottoms against the end of the shaft to knock the component free.

Small-end bearing The bearing in the upper end of the connecting rod at its joint with the gudgeon pin.

Spalling Damage to camshaft lobes or bearing journals shown as pitting of the working surface.

Specific gravity (SG) The state of charge of the electrolyte in a lead-acid battery. A measure of the electrolyte's density compared with water.

Straight-cut gears Common type gear used on gearbox shafts and for oil pump and water pump drives.

Stanchion The inner sliding part of the front forks, held by the yokes. Often called a fork tube.

Stoichiometric ratio The optimum chemical air/fuel ratio for a petrol engine, said to be 14.7 parts of air to 1 part of fuel.

Sulphuric acid The liquid (electrolyte) used in a lead-acid battery. Poisonous and extremely corrosive.

Surface grinding (lapping) Process to correct a warped gasket face, commonly used on cylinder heads.

T

Tapered-roller bearing Tapered inner race of caged needle rollers and separate tapered outer race. Examples of taper roller bearings can be found on steering heads.

Tappet A cylindrical component which transmits motion from the cam to the valve stem, either directly or via a pushrod and rocker arm. Also called a cam follower.

TCS Traction Control System. An electronically-controlled system which senses wheel spin and reduces engine speed accordingly.

TDC Top Dead Centre denotes that the piston is at its highest point in the cylinder.

Thread-locking compound Solution applied to fastener threads to prevent slackening. Select type to suit application.

Thrust washer A washer positioned between two moving components on a shaft. For example, between gear pinions on gearshaft.

Timing chain See **Cam Chain.**

Timing light Stroboscopic lamp for carrying out ignition timing checks with the engine running.

Top-end A description of an engine's cylinder block, head and valve gear components.

Torque Turning or twisting force about a shaft.

Torque setting A prescribed tightness specified by the motorcycle manufacturer to ensure that the bolt or nut is secured correctly. Undertightening can result in the bolt or nut coming loose or a surface not being sealed. Overtightening can result in stripped threads, distortion or damage to the component being retained.

Torx key A six-point wrench.

Tracer A stripe of a second colour applied to a wire insulator to distinguish that wire from another one with the same colour insulator. For example, Br/W is often used to denote a brown insulator with a white tracer.

Trail A feature of steering geometry. Distance from the steering head axis to the tyre's central contact point.

Triple clamps The cast components which extend from the steering head and support the fork stanchions or tubes. Often called fork yokes.

Turbocharger A centrifugal device, driven by exhaust gases, that pressurises the intake air. Normally used to increase the power output from a given engine displacement.

TWI Abbreviation for Tyre Wear Indicator. Indicates the location of the tread depth indicator bars on tyres.

U

Universal joint or U-joint (UJ) A double-pivoted connection for transmitting power from a driving to a driven shaft through an angle. Typically found in shaft drive assemblies.

Unsprung weight Anything not supported by the bike's suspension (ie the wheel, tyres, brakes, final drive and bottom (moving) part of the suspension).

V

Vacuum gauges Clock-type gauges for measuring intake tract vacuum. Used for carburettor synchronisation on multi-cylinder engines.

Valve A device through which the flow of liquid, gas or vacuum may be stopped, started or regulated by a moveable part that opens, shuts or partially obstructs one or more ports or passageways. The intake and exhaust valves in the cylinder head are of the poppet type.

Valve clearance The clearance between the valve tip (the end of the valve stem) and the rocker arm or tappet/follower. The valve clearance is measured when the valve is closed. The correct clearance is important - if too small the valve won't close fully and will burn out, whereas if too large noisy operation will result.

Valve lift The amount a valve is lifted off its seat by the camshaft lobe.

Valve timing The exact setting for the opening and closing of the valves in relation to piston position.

Vernier caliper A precision measuring instrument that measures inside and outside dimensions. Not quite as accurate as a micrometer, but more convenient.

VIN Vehicle Identification Number. Term for the bike's engine and frame numbers.

Viscosity The thickness of a liquid or its resistance to flow.

Volt A unit for expressing electrical "pressure" in a circuit. Volts = current x ohms.

W

Water pump A mechanically-driven device for moving coolant around the engine.

Watt A unit for expressing electrical power. Watts = volts x current.

Wear limit see **Service limit**

Wet liner A liquid-cooled engine design where the pistons run in liners which are directly surrounded by coolant **(see illustration).**

Wet liner arrangement

Wheelbase Distance from the centre of the front wheel to the centre of the rear wheel.

Wiring harness or loom Describes the electrical wires running the length of the motorcycle and enclosed in tape or plastic sheathing. Wiring coming off the main harness is usually referred to as a sub harness.

Woodruff key A key of semi-circular or square section used to locate a gear to a shaft. Often used to locate the alternator rotor on the crankshaft.

Wrist pin Another name for gudgeon or piston pin.

Note: *References throughout this index are in the form* **"Chapter number"** • **"Page number"**. *So, for example, 2•15 refers to page 15 of Chapter 2.*

Note: *References throughout this index are in the form* "**Chapter number**" • "**Page number**". *So, for example, 2•15 refers to page 15 of Chapter 2.*

Note: *References throughout this index are in the form* "**Chapter number**" • "**Page number**". *So, for example, 2•15 refers to page 15 of Chapter 2.*

*Note: References throughout this index are in the form "**Chapter number**" • "**Page number**". So, for example, 2•15 refers to page 15 of Chapter 2.*